JOSEPH ANTON

JOSEPH ANTON

SALMAN RUSHDIE

A Memoir

RANDOM HOUSE

NEW YORK

Published in the United States by Random House,
an imprint of The Random House Publishing Group, a division of
Random House, Inc., New York.

RANDOM HOUSE and colophon are registered trademarks
of Random House, Inc.

*Grateful acknowledgment is made to the following for permission to reprint
previously published material:*

GROVE/ATLANTIC, INC., FABER AND FABER LIMITED, AND JUDY DAISH ASSOCIATES
LIMITED: "Len Hutton" by Harold Pinter from *Various Voices* by Harold Pinter
(Grove/Atlantic, Inc.) and *Collected Poems and Prose* (Faber and Faber Limited),
copyright © 1998 by Harold Pinter. Electronic book rights are administered by
Judy Daish Associates Limited. Reprinted by permission of Grove/Atlantic, Inc.,
Faber and Faber Limited, and Judy Daish Associates Limited.

JOHN LE CARRÉ: Letters from John le Carré printed in *The Guardian.*
Copyright © 1997 by John le Carré. Reprinted by permission.

NEW DIRECTIONS PUBLISHING CORPORATION: "The Ivy Crown" by
William Carlos Williams from *The Collected Poems: Volume II, 1939–1962,*
copyright © 1953 by William Carlos Williams. Reprinted by permission
of New Directions Publishing Corporation.

ISBN 978-0-8129-9278-6
eISBN 978-0-679-64388-3

Printed in the United States of America on acid-free paper

www.atrandom.com

2 4 6 8 9 7 5 3 1

FIRST EDITION

To my children
Zafar and Milan
and their mothers
Clarissa and Elizabeth
and to everyone
who helped

And by that destiny to perform an act
Whereof what's past is prologue, what to come
In yours and my discharge.

—WILLIAM SHAKESPEARE,
The Tempest

Contents

Prologue
The First Blackbird
1

I
A Faustian Contract in Reverse
17

II
"Manuscripts Don't Burn"
93

III
Year Zero
137

IV
The Trap of Wanting to Be Loved
221

V
"Been Down So Long It Looks Like Up to Me"
279

VI
Why It's Impossible to Photograph the Pampas
335

VII

A Truckload of Dung

413

VIII

Mr. Morning and Mr. Afternoon

479

IX

His Millenarian Illusion

563

X

At the Halcyon Hotel

611

Acknowledgments

635

Prologue

The First Blackbird

AFTERWARDS, WHEN THE WORLD WAS EXPLODING AROUND HIM AND THE lethal blackbirds were massing on the climbing frame in the school playground, he felt annoyed with himself for forgetting the name of the BBC reporter, a woman, who had told him that his old life was over and a new, darker existence was about to begin. She had called him at home on his private line without explaining how she got the number. "How does it feel," she asked him, "to know that you have just been sentenced to death by the Ayatollah Khomeini?" It was a sunny Tuesday in London but the question shut out the light. This is what he said, without really knowing what he was saying: "It doesn't feel good." This is what he thought: *I'm a dead man.* He wondered how many days he had left to live and thought the answer was probably a single-digit number. He put down the telephone and ran down the stairs from his workroom at the top of the narrow Islington row house where he lived. The living room windows had wooden shutters and, absurdly, he closed and barred them. Then he locked the front door.

It was Valentine's Day but he hadn't been getting on with his wife, the American novelist Marianne Wiggins. Six days earlier she had told him she was unhappy in the marriage, that she "didn't feel good around him anymore," even though they had been married for little more than a year, and he, too, already knew it had been a mistake. Now she was staring at him as he moved nervously around the house, drawing curtains, checking window bolts, his body galvanized by the news as if an electric current were passing through it, and he had to explain to her what was happening. She reacted well, beginning to discuss what they should do next. She used the word "we." That was courageous.

A car arrived at the house, sent by CBS television. He had an appointment at the American network's studios in Bowater House, Knightsbridge, to appear live, by satellite link, on its morning show. "I should go," he said. "It's live television. I can't just not show up."

Later that morning the memorial service for his friend Bruce Chatwin was to be held at the Orthodox church on Moscow Road in Bayswater. Less than two years earlier he had celebrated his fortieth birthday at Homer End, Bruce's house in Oxfordshire. Now Bruce was dead of AIDS, and death had arrived at his own door as well. "What about the memorial," his wife asked. He didn't have an answer for her. He unlocked the front door, went outside, got into the car and was driven away, and although he did not know it then, so that the moment of leaving his home did not feel unusually freighted with meaning, he would not go back to that house, his home for five years, until three years later, by which time it was no longer his.

The children in the classroom in Bodega Bay, California, sing a sad nonsense song. She combed her hair but once a year, ristle-te, rostle-te, mo, mo, mo. Outside the school a cold wind is blowing. A single blackbird flies down from the sky and settles on the climbing frame in the playground. The children's song is a roundelay. It begins but it doesn't end. It just goes round and round. With every stroke she shed a tear, ristle-te, rostle-te, hey-bombosity, knickety-knackety, retroquo-quality, willoby-wallaby, mo, mo, mo. *There are four blackbirds on the climbing frame, and then a fifth arrives. Inside the school the children are singing. Now there are hundreds of blackbirds on the climbing frame and thousands more birds fill the sky, like a plague of Egypt. A song has begun, to which there is no end.*

When the first blackbird comes down to roost on the climbing frame it seems individual, particular, specific. It is not necessary to deduce a general theory, a wider scheme of things, from its presence. Later, after the plague begins, it's easy for people to see the first blackbird as a harbinger. But when it lands on the climbing frame it's just one bird.

In the years to come he will dream about this scene, understanding that his story is a sort of prologue: the tale of the moment when the first blackbird lands. When it begins it's just about him; it's individual, particular, specific. Nobody feels inclined to draw any conclusions from it. It will be a dozen years and more before the story grows until it fills the sky, like the Archangel Gabriel standing upon the horizon, like a pair of planes flying into tall buildings, like the plague of murderous birds in Alfred Hitchcock's great film.

At the CBS offices he was the big news story of the day. People in the newsroom and on various monitors were already using the word that would soon be hung around his neck like a millstone. They used the word as if it were a synonym for "death sentence" and he wanted to argue, pedantically, that that was not what the word meant. But from this day forward it would mean that for most people in the world. And for him.

Fatwa.

"I inform the proud Muslim people of the world that the author of the 'Satanic Verses' book, which is against Islam, the Prophet and the Qur'an, and all those involved in its publication who were aware of its content, are sentenced to death. I ask all the Muslims to execute them wherever they find them." Somebody gave him a printout of the text as he was escorted toward the studio for his interview. Again, his old self wanted to argue, this time with the word "sentence." This was not a sentence handed down by any court he recognized, or which had any jurisdiction over him. It was the edict of a cruel and dying old man. But he also knew that his old self's habits were of no use anymore. He was a new self now. He was the person in the eye of the storm, no longer the *Salman* his friends knew but the *Rushdie* who was the author of *Satanic Verses,* a title subtly distorted by the omission of the initial *The. The Satanic Verses* was a novel. *Satanic Verses* were verses that were satanic, and he was their satanic author, "Satan Rushdy," the horned creature on the placards carried by demonstrators down the streets of a faraway city, the hanged man with protruding red tongue in the crude cartoons they bore. *Hang Satan Rushdy.* How easy it was to erase a man's past and to construct a new version of him, an overwhelming version, against which it seemed impossible to fight.

King Charles I had denied the legitimacy of the sentence handed down against him. That hadn't stopped Oliver Cromwell from having him beheaded.

He was no king. He was the author of a book.

He looked at the journalists looking at him and he wondered if this was how people looked at men being taken to the gallows or the electric chair or the guillotine. One foreign correspondent came up to be friendly. He asked this man what he should think about what Khomeini had said. How seriously should he take it? Was it just a rhetorical flourish or something genuinely dangerous?

"Oh, don't worry too much," the journalist said. "Khomeini sentences the president of the United States to death every Friday afternoon."

On air, when he was asked how he responded to the threat, he said, "I wish I'd written a more critical book." He was proud, then and always, that he had said this. It was the truth. He did not feel his book was especially critical of Islam, but, as he said on American television that morning, a religion whose leaders behaved in this way could probably do with a little criticism.

When the interview was over they told him his wife had called. He phoned the house. "Don't come back here," she said. "There are two hundred journalists on the sidewalk waiting for you."

"I'll go to the agency," he said. "Pack a bag and meet me there."

His literary agency, Wylie, Aitken & Stone, had its offices in a white-stuccoed house on Fernshaw Road in Chelsea. There were no journalists camped outside—evidently the world's press hadn't thought he was likely to visit his agent on such a day—and when he walked in every phone in the building was ringing and every call was about him. Gillon Aitken, his British agent, gave him an astonished look. He was on the phone with the British-Indian member of Parliament for Leicester East, Keith Vaz. He covered the mouthpiece and whispered, "Do you want to talk to this fellow?"

Vaz said, in that phone conversation, that what had happened was "appalling, absolutely appalling," and promised his "full support." A few weeks later he was one of the main speakers at a demonstration against *The Satanic Verses* attended by over three thousand Muslims, and described that event as "one of the great days in the history of Islam and Great Britain."

He found that he couldn't think ahead, that he had no idea what the shape of his life ought now to be, or how to make plans. He could focus only on the immediate, and the immediate was the memorial service for Bruce Chatwin. "My dear," Gillon said, "do you think you ought to go?" He made his decision. Bruce had been his close friend. "Fuck it," he said, "let's go."

Marianne arrived, a faintly deranged look glinting in her eye, upset about having been mobbed by photographers when she left the house at 41 St. Peter's Street. The next day that look would be on the front pages of every newspaper in the land. One of the papers gave the look a name, in letters two inches high: THE FACE OF FEAR. She didn't say much. Neither of them did. They got into their car, a black Saab, and he drove it across the park to Bayswater. Gillon Aitken, his worried expression and long, languid body folded into the backseat, came along for the ride.

His mother and his youngest sister lived in Karachi. What would happen to them? His middle sister, long estranged from the family, lived in Berkeley, California. Would she be safe there? His oldest sister, Sameen, his "Irish twin," was in a north London suburb with her family, in Wembley, not far from the great stadium. What should be done to protect them? His son, Zafar, just nine years and eight months old, was with his mother, Clarissa, in their house at 60 Burma Road, off Green Lanes, near Clissold Park. At that moment Zafar's tenth birthday felt far, far away. "Dad," Zafar had asked, "why don't you write books I can read?" It made him think of a line in "St. Judy's Comet," a song by Paul Simon written as a lullaby for his young son. *If I can't sing my boy to sleep, well, it makes your famous daddy look so dumb.* "Good question," he had replied. "Just let me finish this book I'm working on now, and then I'll write a book for you. Deal?" "Deal." So he had finished the book and it had been published and now, perhaps, he would not have time to write another. *You should never break a promise made to a child,* he thought, and then his whirling mind added the idiotic rider, *but is the death of the author a reasonable excuse?*

His mind was running on murder.

Five years ago he had been traveling with Bruce Chatwin in Australia's "red center," making a note of the graffito in Alice Springs that read SURREN-DER, WHITE MAN, YOUR TOWN IS SURROUNDED, *and hauling himself painfully up Ayers Rock while Bruce, who was proud of having recently made it all the way up to Everest base camp, skipped ahead as if he were running up the gentlest of slopes, and listening to the locals' tales about the so-called "dingo baby" case, and staying in a fleapit called the Inland Motel where, the previous year, a thirty-six-year-old long-distance truck driver called Douglas Crabbe had been refused a drink because he was already too drunk, had become abusive to the bar staff, and, after he was thrown out, had driven his truck at full speed into the bar, killing five people.*

Crabbe was giving evidence in a courtroom in Alice Springs and they went along to listen. The driver was conservatively dressed, with downcast eyes, and spoke in a low, even voice. He insisted he was not the sort of person who could have done such a thing, and, when asked why he was so sure of that, replied that he had been driving trucks for many years, and "looking after them as if they were my own" (here there was a beat of silence, and the unspoken word in that silence might have been "children"), and for him to half destroy a truck was completely against his character. The members of the jury stiffened visibly when they heard that, and it was obvious that his cause was lost. "But of course," Bruce murmured, "he's absolutely telling the truth."

The mind of one murderer valued trucks more highly than human beings. Five years later there might be people on their way to execute a writer for his blasphemous words, and faith, or a particular interpretation of faith, was the truck they loved more than human life. This was not his first blasphemy, he reminded himself. His climb up Ayers Rock with Bruce would now also be forbidden. The Rock, returned to Aboriginal ownership and given back its ancient name of Uluru, was sacred territory, and climbers were no longer permitted.

It was on the flight home from that Australian journey in 1984 that he had begun to understand how to write The Satanic Verses.

The service at the Greek Orthodox Cathedral of Saint Sophia of the Archdiocese of Thyateria and Great Britain, built and lavishly decorated 110 years earlier to resemble a grand cathedral of old Byzantium, was all sonorous, mysterious Greek. Its rituals were ornately Byzantine. Blah blah blah Bruce Chatwin, intoned the priests, blah blah Chatwin blah blah. They stood up, they sat down, they knelt, they stood and then sat again. The air was full of the stink of holy smoke. He remembered his father taking him, as a child in Bombay, to pray on the day of Eid-ul-Fitr. There at the Idgah, the praying field, it was all Arabic, and a good deal of up-down forehead bumping, and standing up with your palms held in front of you like a book, and much mumbling of unknown words in a language he didn't speak. "Just do what I do," his father said. They were not a religious family and hardly ever went to such ceremonies. He never learned the prayers or their meanings. This occasional prayer by imitation and mumbled rote was all he knew. Consequently, the meaningless ceremony in the church on Moscow Road felt familiar. Marianne and he were seated next to Martin Amis and his wife, Antonia Phillips. "We're worried about you," Martin said, embracing him. "*I'm* worried about me," he replied. Blah Chatwin blah Bruce blah. The novelist Paul Theroux was sitting in the pew behind him. "I suppose we'll be here for you next week, Salman," he said.

There had been a couple of photographers on the sidewalk outside when he arrived. Writers didn't usually draw a crowd of paparazzi. As the service progressed, however, journalists began to enter the church. One incomprehensible religion was playing host to a news story generated by another religion's incomprehensibly violent assault. *One of the worst aspects of what happened,* he wrote later, *was that the incomprehensible became comprehensible, the unimaginable became imaginable.*

The service ended and the journalists pushed their way toward him. Gillon, Marianne and Martin tried to run interference. One persistent gray fellow (gray suit, gray hair, gray face, gray voice) got through the crowd, shoved a tape recorder toward him and asked the obvious questions. "I'm sorry," he replied. "I'm here for my friend's memorial service. It's not appropriate to do interviews." "You don't understand," the gray fellow said, sounding puzzled. "I'm from *The Daily Telegraph.* They've sent me down *specially.*"

"Gillon, I need your help," he said.

Gillon leaned down toward the reporter from his immense height and said, firmly, and in his grandest accent, *"Fuck off."*

"You can't talk to me like that," said the man from the *Telegraph.* "I've been to public school."

After that there was no more comedy. When he got out onto Moscow Road there were journalists swarming like drones in pursuit of their queen, photographers climbing on one another's backs to form tottering hillocks bursting with flashlight. He stood there blinking and directionless, momentarily at a loss to know what to do.

There didn't seem to be any escape. There was no possibility of walking to the car, which was parked a hundred yards down the road, without being followed by cameras and microphones and men who had been to various kinds of school, and who had been sent down specially. He was rescued by his friend Alan Yentob of the BBC, the filmmaker and senior executive whom he had first met eight years earlier, when Alan was making an *Arena* documentary about a young writer who had just published a well-received novel called *Midnight's Children*. Alan had a twin brother but people often said, "Salman's the one who looks like your twin." They both disagreed with this view but it persisted. And today might not be the best day for Alan to be mistaken for his not-twin.

Alan's BBC car pulled up in front of the church. "Get in," he said, and then they were driving away from the shouting journalists. They circled around Notting Hill for a while until the crowd outside the church dispersed and then went back to where the Saab was parked.

He got into his car with Marianne and suddenly they were alone and the silence weighed heavily on them both. They didn't turn on the car radio, knowing the news would be full of hatred. "Where shall we go?" he asked, even though they both knew the answer. Marianne had recently rented a small basement apartment in the southwest corner of Lonsdale Square in Islington, not far from the house on St. Peter's Street, ostensibly to use as a work space but actually because of the growing strain between them. Very few people knew of this apartment's existence. It would give them space and time to take stock and make decisions. They drove to Islington in silence. There didn't seem to be anything to say.

Marianne was a fine writer and a beautiful woman, but he had been discovering things he didn't like.

When she had moved into his house she left a message on the answering machine of his friend Bill Buford, the editor of *Granta* magazine, to tell him that her number had changed. "You may recognize the new number," the message went on, and then, after what Bill thought of as an alarming pause, *"I've got him."* He had asked her to marry him in the highly emotional state that followed his father's death in November 1987 and things between them had not remained good for very long. His closest friends, Bill Buford, Gillon Aitken and his American colleague Andrew Wylie, the Guyanese actress and writer Pauline Melville, and his sister Sameen, who had always been closer to him than anyone else, had all begun to confess that they didn't like her, which was what friends did when people were breaking up, of course, and so, he thought, some of that had to be discounted. But he himself had caught her in a few lies and that had shaken him. What did she think of him? She often seemed angry and had a way of looking at the air over his shoulder when she spoke to him, as if she were addressing a ghost. He had always been drawn to her intelligence and wit and that was still there, and the physical attraction as well, the falling waves of her auburn hair, her wide, full-lipped American smile. But she had become mysterious to him and sometimes he thought he had married a stranger. A woman in a mask.

It was midafternoon and on this day their private difficulties felt irrelevant. On this day there were crowds marching down the streets of Tehran carrying posters of his face with the eyes poked out, making him look like one of the corpses in *The Birds,* with their blackened, bloodied, bird-pecked eye sockets. That was the subject today: his un-funny Valentine from those bearded men, those shrouded women, and the lethal old man dying in his room, making his last bid for some sort of dark, murderous glory. After he came to power the imam murdered many of those who brought him there and everyone else he disliked. Unionists, feminists, socialists, Communists, homosexuals, whores, and his own former lieutenants as well. There was a portrait of an imam like him in *The Satanic Verses,* an imam grown monstrous, his gigantic mouth eating his own revolution. The real imam had taken his country into a useless war with its neighbor, and a generation of young people had died, hundreds of thousands of his country's young, before the old man called a halt. He said that accepting peace with Iraq was like eating poison, but he had eaten it. After that the dead cried out against the imam and his revolution became unpopular. He needed a way to rally the faithful and he found it in the form of a book and its author. The book was the devil's work and the author was the devil and that gave him the enemy he needed. This author in this basement flat in Islington huddling with the wife from whom he was half es-tranged. This was the necessary devil of the dying imam.

Now that the school day was over he had to see Zafar. He called Pauline Melville and asked her to keep Marianne company while he made his visit. She had been his neighbor in Highbury Hill in the early 1980s, a bright-eyed, flamboyantly gesticulating, warmhearted, mixed-race actress full of stories, about Guyana, where one of her Melville ancestors had met Evelyn Waugh and shown him around and was probably, she thought, the model for Mr. Todd, the crazy old coot who captured Tony Last in the rain forest and forced him to read Dickens aloud forever in *A Handful of Dust;* and about rescuing her husband, Angus, from the Foreign Legion by standing at the gates of the fort and yelling until they let him out; and about playing Adrian Edmondson's mum in the hit TV comedy series *The Young Ones.* She did stand-up comedy and had invented a male character who "became so dangerous and frightening that I had to stop playing him," she said. She wrote down several of her Guyana stories and showed them to him. They were very, very good, and when they were published in her first book, *Shape-Shifter,* were widely praised. She was tough, shrewd and loyal, and he trusted her completely. She came over at once without any discussion even though it was her birthday, and in spite of her reservations about Marianne. He felt relieved to be leaving Marianne behind in the Lonsdale Square basement and driving by himself to Burma Road. The beautiful sunny day, whose astonishing wintry radiance had been like a rebuke to the unbeautiful news, was over. London in February was dark as the children made their way home. When he got to Clarissa and Zafar's house the police were already there. "There you are," said a police officer. "We've been wondering where you'd gone."

"What's going on, Dad?" His son had a look on his face that should never visit the face of a nine-year-old boy. "I've been telling him," Clarissa brightly said, "that you'll be properly looked after until this blows over, and it's going to be just fine." Then she hugged him as she had not hugged him in five years, since their marriage ended. She was the first woman he had ever loved. He met her on December 26, 1969, five days before the end of the sixties, when he was twenty-two and she was twenty-one. Clarissa Mary Luard. She had long legs and green eyes and that day she wore a hippie sheepskin coat and a headband around her tightly curled russet hair, and there flowed from her a radiance that lightened every heart. She had friends in the world of pop music who called her *Happily* (though, also happily, that name perished with the fey decade that spawned it) and had a mother who drank too much, and a father who came home shell-shocked from the war, in which he had been a Pathfinder pilot, and who leaped off the top of a building when she was fifteen years old. She had a beagle called Bauble who pissed on her bed.

There was much about her that was locked away beneath the brightness; she didn't like people to see the shadows in her and when melancholy struck she would go into her room and shut the door. Maybe she felt her father's sadness in her then and feared it might propel her off a building as it had him, so she sealed herself off until it passed. She bore the name of Samuel Richardson's tragic heroine and had been educated, in part, at Harlow Tech. Clarissa from Harlow, strange echo of Clarissa Harlowe, another suicide in her ambit, this one fictional; another echo to be feared and blotted out by the dazzle of her smile. Her mother, Lavinia Luard, also bore an embarrassing nickname, *Lavvy-Loo,* and stirred family tragedy into a glass of gin and dissolved it there so that she could play the merry widow with men who took advantage of her. At first there had been a married ex-Guards officer called Colonel Ken Sweeting, who came down from the Isle of Man to romance her, but he never left his wife, never intended to. Later, when she emigrated to the village of Mijas in Andalusia, there was a string of European wastrels ready to live off her and spend too much of her money. Lavinia had been strongly opposed to her daughter's determination first to live with and then marry a strange long-haired Indian writer of whose family background she was uncertain, and who didn't seem to have much money. She was friendly with the Leworthy family of Westerham in Kent and the plan was for the Leworthys' accountant son Richard, a pale, bony fellow with Warholesque white-blond hair, to marry her beautiful daughter. Clarissa and Richard dated but she also began to see the long-haired Indian writer in secret, and it took her two years to decide between them, but one night in January 1972 when he threw a housewarming party at his newly rented flat in Cambridge Gardens, Ladbroke Grove, she arrived with her mind made up, and after that they were inseparable. It was always women who did the choosing, and men's place was to be grateful if they were lucky enough to be the chosen ones.

All their years of desire, love, marriage, parenthood, infidelity (mostly his), divorce, and friendship were in the hug she gave him that night. The event had flooded over the pain between them and washed it away, and beneath the pain was something old and deep that had not been destroyed. And also of course they were the parents of this beautiful boy and as parents they had always been united and in agreement. Zafar had been born in June 1979 just as *Midnight's Children* was getting close to being finished. "Keep your legs crossed," he told her, "I'm writing as fast as I can." One afternoon there was a false alarm and he had thought, *The child is going to be born at midnight,* but that didn't happen, he was born on Sunday, June 17, at 2:15 P.M. He put that in the dedication of his novel. *For Zafar Rushdie who, contrary to all expectations, was born in the afternoon.* And who was now nine and a half years old and asking, anxiously, *What's going on.*

"We need to know," the police officer was saying, "what your immediate plans might be." He thought before replying. "I'll probably go home," he finally said, and the stiffening postures of the men in uniform confirmed his suspicions. "No, sir, I wouldn't recommend that." Then he told them, as he had known all along he would, about the Lonsdale Square basement where Marianne was waiting. "It's not generally known as a place you frequent, sir?" No, officer, it is not. "That's good. When you do get back, sir, don't go out again tonight, if that's all right. There are meetings taking place, and you will be advised of their outcome tomorrow, as early as possible. Until then you should stay indoors."

He talked to his son, holding him close, deciding at that moment that he would tell the boy as much as possible, giving what was happening the most positive coloring he could; that the way to help Zafar deal with the event was to make him feel on the inside of it, to give him a parental version he could trust and hold on to while he was being bombarded with other versions, in the school playground, or on television. The school was being terrific, Clarissa said, holding off photographers and a TV crew who wanted to film the threatened man's son, and the boys too had been great. Without discussion they had closed ranks around Zafar and allowed him to have a normal, or an almost normal, day at school. Almost all the parents had been supportive, and the one or two who had demanded that Zafar be withdrawn from school, because his continued presence there might endanger their children, had been scolded by the headmaster and had beaten a shamefaced retreat. It was heartening to see courage, solidarity and principle at work on that day, the best of human values setting themselves against violence and bigotry—the human race's dark side—in the very hour when the rising tide of darkness seemed so difficult to resist. What had been unthinkable until that day was becoming thinkable. But in Hampstead, at the Hall School, the resistance had already begun.

"Will I see you tomorrow, Dad?" He shook his head. "But I'll call you," he said. "I'll call you every evening at seven. If you're not going to be here," he told Clarissa, "please leave me a message on the answering machine at home and say when I should call instead." This was early 1989. The terms *PC, laptop, cellphone, mobile phone, Internet, Wi-Fi, SMS, email,* were either unknown or very new. He did not own a computer or a mobile phone. But he did own a house, even if he could not spend the night there, and in the house there was an answering machine, and he could call in and *interrogate* it, a new use of an old word, and get, no, *retrieve,* his messages. "Seven o'clock," he repeated. "Every night, okay?" Zafar nodded gravely. "Okay, Dad."

He drove home alone and the news on the radio was all bad. Two days earlier there had been a "Rushdie riot" outside the U.S. Cultural Center in Islamabad, Pakistan. (It was not clear why the United States was being held responsible for *The Satanic Verses.*) The police had fired on the crowd and there were five dead and sixty injured. The demonstrators carried signs saying RUSHDIE, YOU ARE DEAD. Now the danger had been greatly multiplied by the Iranian edict. The Ayatollah Khomeini was not just a powerful cleric. He was a head of state ordering the murder of the citizen of another state, over whom he had no jurisdiction; and he had assassins at his service and they had been used before against "enemies" of the Iranian Revolution, including enemies living outside Iran. There was another new word he had to learn. Here it was on the radio: *extraterritoriality.* Also known as *state-sponsored terrorism.* Voltaire had once said that it was a good idea for a writer to live near an international frontier so that, if he angered powerful men, he could skip across the border and be safe. Voltaire himself left France for England after he gave offense to an aristocrat, the Chevalier de Rohan, and remained in exile for seven years. But to live in a different country from one's persecutors was no longer to be safe. Now there was *extra-territorial action*. In other words, they came after you.

Night in Lonsdale Square was cold, dark and clear. There were two policemen in the square. When he got out of his car they pretended not to notice. They were on short patrol, watching the street near the flat for one hundred yards in each direction, and he could hear their footsteps even when he was indoors. He realized, in that footstep-haunted silence, that he no longer understood his life, or what it might become, and he thought for the second time that day that there might not be very much more of life to understand. Pauline went home and Marianne went to bed early. It was a day to forget. It was a day to re-member. He got into bed beside his wife and she turned toward him and they embraced, rigidly, like the unhappily married couple they were. Then, separately, each lying with their own thoughts, they failed to sleep.

Footsteps. Winter. A black wing fluttering on a climbing frame. *I inform the proud Muslim people of the world, ristle-te, rostle-te, mo, mo, mo. To execute them wherever they may find them. Ristle-te, rostle-te, hey bombos-ity, knickety-knackety, retroquo-quality, willoby-wallaby, mo, mo, mo.*

I

A Faustian Contract
in Reverse

WHEN HE WAS A SMALL BOY HIS FATHER AT BEDTIME TOLD HIM THE GREAT wonder tales of the East, told them and re-told them and re-made them and re-invented them in his own way—the stories of Schehe-razade from the *Thousand and One Nights,* stories told against death to prove the ability of stories to civilize and overcome even the most murderous of tyrants; and the animal fables of the *Panchatantra;* and the marvels that poured like a waterfall from the *Kathasaritsagara,* the "Ocean of the Streams of Story," the immense story-lake created in Kashmir where his ancestors had been born; and the tales of mighty heroes collected in the *Hamzanama* and the *Adventures of Hatim Tai* (this was also a movie, whose many embellishments of the original tales were added to and augmented in the bedtime re-tellings). To grow up steeped in these tellings was to learn two unforgettable lessons: first, that stories were not true (there were no "real" genies in bottles or fly-ing carpets or wonderful lamps), but by being untrue they could make him feel and know truths that the truth could not tell him, and second, that they all belonged to him, just as they belonged to his father, Anis, and to everyone else, they were all his, as they were his father's, bright stories and dark stories, sacred stories and profane, his to alter and renew and discard and pick up again as and when he pleased, his to laugh at and rejoice in and live in and with and by, to give the stories life by loving them and to be given life by them in return. Man was the storytelling animal, the only creature on earth that told itself stories to understand what kind of creature it was. The story was his birthright, and nobody could take it away.

His mother, Negin, had stories for him too. Negin Rushdie had been born Zohra Butt. When she married Anis she changed not just her surname but her given name as well, reinventing herself for him, leaving behind the Zohra he didn't want to think about, who had once been deeply in love with another man. Whether she was Zohra or Negin in her heart of hearts her son never knew, for she never spoke to him about the man she left behind, choosing, instead, to spill every-one's secrets except her own. She was a gossip of world class, and sit-ting on her bed pressing her feet the way she liked him to, he, her eldest child and only son, drank in the delicious and sometimes sala-cious local news she carried in her head, the gigantic branching inter-woven forests of whispering family trees she bore within her, hung with the juicy forbidden fruit of scandal. And these secrets too, he came to feel, belonged to him, for once a secret had been told it no longer belonged to her who told it but to him who received it. If you did not want a secret to get out there was only one rule: *Tell it to nobody.* This rule, too, would be useful to him in later life. In that later life, when he had become a writer, his mother said to him, "I'm going to stop telling you these things, because you put them in your books and then I get into trouble." Which was true, and perhaps she would have been well advised to stop, but gossip was her addiction, and she could not, any more than her husband, his father, could give up drink.

Windsor Villa, Warden Road, Bombay-26. It was a house on a hill and it overlooked the sea and the city flowing between the hill and the sea; and yes, his father was rich, though he spent his life losing all that money and died broke, unable to pay off his debts, with a stash of rupee notes in the top left drawer of his desk that was all the cash he had left in the world. Anis Ahmed Rushdie ("B.A. Cantab., Bar-at-Law" it proudly said on the brass nameplate screwed into the wall by the front door of Windsor Villa) inherited a fortune from the textile mag-nate father whose only son he was, spent it, lost it, and then died, which could be the story of a happy life, but was not. His children knew certain things about him: that in the mornings he was cheerful until he shaved, and then, after the Philishave had done its work, he grew irritable and they were careful to keep out of his way; that when he took them to the beach on the weekend he would be lively and funny on the way there but angry on the way home; that when he played golf with their mother at the Willingdon Club she had to be careful to lose, though she was a stronger player than he, because it was not worth her while to win; and that when he was drunk he grimaced hideously at them, pulling his features into bizarre and terrifying positions, which frightened them horribly, and which no outsider ever saw, so that nobody understood what they meant when they said that their father "made faces." But when they were little there were the stories and then sleep, and if they heard raised voices in another room, if they heard their mother crying, there was nothing they could do about it. They pulled their sheets over their heads and dreamed.

Anis took his thirteen-year-old son to England in January 1961 and for a week or so, before he began his education at Rugby School, they shared a room in the Cumberland Hotel near the Marble Arch in London. By day they went shopping for the school's prescribed items, tweed jackets, gray flannel trousers, Van Heusen shirts with detached semistiff collars that necessitated the use of collar studs that pressed into the boy's neck and made it hard to breathe. They drank chocolate milk shakes at the Lyons Corner House on Coventry Street and they went to the Odeon Marble Arch to watch *The Pure Hell of St. Trinian's* and he wished there were going to be girls at his boarding school. In the evening his father bought grilled chicken from the Kardomah takeout on Edgware Road and made him smuggle it into the hotel room inside his new double-breasted blue serge mackintosh. At night Anis got drunk and in the small hours would shake his horrified son awake to shout at him in language so filthy that it didn't seem possible to the boy that his father could even know such words. Then they went to Rugby and bought a red armchair and said their goodbyes. Anis took a photograph of his son outside his boarding house in his blue-and-white-striped house cap and his chicken-scented mackintosh, and if you looked at the sadness in the boy's eyes you would think he was sad to be going to school so far from home. But in fact the son couldn't wait for the father to leave so that he could start trying to forget the nights of foul language and unprovoked, red-eyed rage. He wanted to put the sadness in the past and begin his future, and after that it was perhaps inevitable that he would make his life as far away from his father as he could, that he would put oceans between them and keep them there. When he graduated from Cambridge University and told his father he wanted to be a writer a pained yelp burst uncontrollably out of Anis's mouth. "What," he cried, "am I going to tell my friends?"

But nineteen years later, on his son's fortieth birthday, Anis Rushdie sent him a letter written in his own hand that became the most precious communication that writer had ever received or would receive. This was just five months before Anis's death at seventy-seven of rapidly advancing multiple myeloma—cancer of the bone marrow. In that letter Anis showed how carefully and deeply he had read and understood his son's books, how eagerly he looked forward to reading more of them, and how profoundly he felt the fatherly love he had spent half a lifetime failing to express. He lived long enough to be happy at the success of *Midnight's Children* and *Shame,* but by the time the book that owed the greatest debt to him was published he was no longer there to read it. Perhaps that was a good thing, because he also missed the furor that followed; although one of the few things of which his son was utterly certain was that in the battle over *The Satanic Verses* he would have had his father's unqualified, unyielding support. Without his father's ideas and example to inspire him, in fact, that novel would never have been written. *They fuck you up, your mum and dad?* No, that wasn't it at all. Well, they did do that, perhaps, but they also allowed you to become the person, and the writer, that you had it in you to be.

The first gift he received from his father, a gift like a message in a time capsule, which he didn't understand until he was an adult, was the family name. "Rushdie" was Anis's invention; *his* father's name had been quite a mouthful, Khwaja Muhammad Din Khaliqi Dehlavi, a fine Old Delhi name that sat well on that old-school gentleman glaring fiercely out of his only surviving photograph, that successful industrialist and part-time essayist who lived in a crumbling *haveli* in the famous old *muhallah* or neighborhood of Ballimaran, a warren of small winding lanes off Chandni Chowk that had been the home of the great Farsi and Urdu poet Ghalib. Muhammad Din Khaliqi died young, leaving his son a fortune (which he would squander) and a name that was too heavy to carry around in the modern world. Anis renamed himself "Rushdie" because of his admiration for Ibn Rushd, "Averroës" to the West, the twelfth-century Spanish-Arab philosopher of Córdoba who rose to become the *qadi* or judge of Seville, the translator of and acclaimed commentator upon the works of Aristotle. His son bore the name for two decades before he understood that his father, a true scholar of Islam who was also entirely lacking in religious belief, had chosen it because he respected Ibn Rushd for being at the forefront of the rationalist argument against Islamic literalism in his time; and twenty more years elapsed before the battle over *The Satanic Verses* provided a twentieth-century echo of that eight-hundred-year-old argument.

"At least," he told himself when the storm broke over his head, "I'm going into this battle bearing the right name." From beyond the grave his father had given him the flag under which he was ready to fight, the flag of Ibn Rushd, which stood for intellect, argument, analysis and progress, for the freedom of philosophy and learning from the shackles of theology, for human reason and against blind faith, submission, acceptance and stagnation. Nobody ever wanted to go to war, but if a war came your way, it might as well be the right war, about the most important things in the world, and you might as well, if you were going to fight it, be called "Rushdie," and stand where your father had placed you, in the tradition of the grand Aristotelian, Averroës, Abul Walid Muhammad ibn Ahmad ibn Rushd.

They had the same voice, his father and he. When he answered the telephone at home Anis's friends would begin to talk to him as if he were his father and he would have to stop them before they said anything embarrassing. They looked like each other, and when, during the smoother passages of their bumpy journey as father and son, they sat on a veranda in a warm evening with the scent of bougainvillea in their nostrils and argued passionately about the world, they both knew that although they disagreed on many topics they had the same cast of mind. And what they shared above all else was unbelief.

Anis was a godless man—still a shocking statement to make in the United States, though an unexceptional one in Europe, and an incomprehensible idea in much of the rest of the world, where the thought of *not believing* is hard even to formulate. But that was what he was, a godless man who knew and thought a great deal about God. The birth of Islam fascinated him because it was the only one of the great world religions to be born within recorded history, whose prophet was not a legend described and glorified by "evangelists" writing a hundred years or more after the real man lived and died, or a dish recooked for easy global consumption by the brilliant proselytizer Saint Paul, but rather a man whose life was largely on the record, whose social and economic circumstances were well known, a man living in a time of profound social change, an orphan who grew up to become a successful merchant with mystical tendencies, and who saw, one day on Mount Hira near Mecca, the Archangel Gabriel standing upon the horizon and filling the sky and instructing him to "recite" and thus, slowly, to create the book known as the Recitation: *al-Qur'an*.

This passed from the father to the son: the belief that the story of the birth of Islam was fascinating because it was an event *inside history*, and that, as such, it was obviously influenced by the events and pressures and ideas of the time of its creation; that to historicize the story, to try to understand how a great idea was shaped by those forces, was the only possible approach to the subject; and that one could accept Muhammad as a genuine mystic—just as one could accept Joan of Arc's voices as having genuinely been heard by her, or the revelations of Saint John the Divine as being that troubled soul's "real" experiences—without needing also to accept that, had one been standing next to the Prophet of Islam on Mount Hira that day, one would also have seen the Archangel. Revelation was to be understood as an interior, subjective event, not an objective reality, and a revealed text was to be scrutinized like any other text, using all the tools of the critic, literary, historical, psychological, linguistic, and sociological. In short, the text was to be regarded as a human artifact and thus, like all such artifacts, prey to human fallibility and imperfection. The American critic Randall Jarrell famously defined the novel as "a long piece of writing that has something wrong with it." Anis Rushdie thought he knew what was wrong with the Qur'an; it had become, in places, jumbled up.

According to tradition, when Muhammad came down from the mountain he began to recite—he himself was perhaps illiterate—and whichever of his close companions was nearest would write down what he said on whatever came to hand (parchment, stone, leather, leaves, and sometimes, it's said, even bones). These passages were stored in a chest in his home until after his death, when the Companions gathered to determine the correct sequence of the revelation; and that determination had given us the now canonical text of the Qur'an. For that text to be "perfect" required the reader to believe (a) that the Archangel, in conveying the Word of God, did so without slipups—which may be an acceptable proposition, since Archangels are presumed to be immune from errata; (b) that the Prophet, or, as he called himself, the Messenger, remembered the Archangel's words with perfect accuracy; (c) that the Companions' hasty transcriptions, written down over the course of the twenty-three-year-long revelation, were likewise error-free; and finally (d) that when they got together to arrange the text into its final form, their collective memory of the correct sequence was also perfect.

Anis Rushdie was disinclined to contest propositions (a), (b) and (c). Proposition (d), however, was harder for him to swallow, because as anyone who read the Qur'an could easily see, several *suras,* or chapters, contained radical discontinuities, changing subject without warning, and the abandoned subject sometimes cropped up unannounced in a later *sura* that had been, up to that point, about something else entirely. It was Anis's long-nurtured desire to unscramble these discontinuities and so arrive at a text that was clearer and easier to read. It should be said that this was not a secret or furtive plan; he would discuss it openly with friends over dinner. There was no sense that the undertaking might create risks for the revisionist scholar, no *frisson* of danger. Perhaps the times were different, and such ideas could be entertained without fear of reprisals; or else the company was trustworthy; or maybe Anis was an innocent fool. But this was the atmosphere of open inquiry in which he raised his children. Nothing was off-limits. There were no taboos. Everything, even holy writ, could be investigated and, just possibly, improved.

He never did it. When he died no text was found among his papers. His last years were dominated by alcohol and business failures and he had little time or inclination for the hard grind of deep Qur'anic scholarship. Maybe it had always been a pipe dream, or empty, whiskey-fueled big talk. But it left its mark on his son. This was Anis's second great gift to his children: that of an apparently fearless skepticism, accompanied by an almost total freedom from religion. There was a certain amount of tokenism, however. The "flesh of the swine" was not eaten in the Rushdie household, nor would you find on their dinner table the similarly proscribed "scavengers of the earth and the sea"; no Goan prawn curry on this dining table. There were those very occasional visits to the Idgah for the ritual up-and-down of the prayers. There was, once or twice a year, fasting during what Indian Muslims, Urdu—rather than Arabic—speaking, called Ramzán rather than Ramadan. And once, briefly, there was a *maulvi,* a religious scholar, hired by Negin to teach her heathen son and daughters the rudiments of faith. But when the heathen children revolted against the *maulvi,* a pint-sized Ho Chi Minh look-alike, teasing him so mercilessly that he complained bitterly to their parents about their disrespect for the great sanctities, Anis and Negin just laughed and took their children's side. The *maulvi* flounced off, never to return, muttering imprecations against the unbelievers as he went, and after that there were no further attempts at religious instruction. The heathen grew up heathenish and, in Windsor Villa at least, that was just fine.

When he turned away from his father, wearing the blue-and-white-striped cap of Bradley House and the serge mackintosh, and plunged into his English life, the sin of *foreignness* was the first thing that was made plain to him. Until that point he had not thought of himself as anyone's Other. After Rugby School he never forgot the lesson he learned there: that there would always be people who just didn't like you, to whom you seemed as alien as little green men or the Slime from Outer Space, and there was no point trying to change their minds. Alienation: It was a lesson he relearned in more dramatic circumstances later on.

At an English boarding school in the early 1960s, he quickly discovered, there were three bad mistakes you could make, but if you made only two of the three you could be forgiven. The mistakes were: to be foreign; to be clever; and to be bad at games. At Rugby the foreign, clever boys who had a good time were also elegant cricketers or, in the case of one of his contemporaries, the Pakistani Zia Mahmood, so good at cards that he grew up to become one of the world's finest bridge players. The boys who had no sporting ability had to be careful not to be too clever and, if possible, not too foreign, which was the worst of the three mistakes.

He made all three mistakes. He was foreign, clever, non-*sportif*. And as a result his years were, for the most part, unhappy, though he did well academically and left Rugby with the abiding feeling of having been wonderfully well taught—with that nourishing memory of great teachers that, if we are lucky, we can carry with us for the rest of our lives. There was P. G. Lewis, known, inevitably, as "Pig," who so inspired him with the love of French that he rose in the course of one term from the bottom to the top of the class, and there were his history teachers J. B. Hope-Simpson, a.k.a. "Hope Stimulus," and J. W. "Gut" Hele, thanks to whose skilled tutelage he was able to go on to win an exhibition, a minor scholarship, to read history at his father's old alma mater of King's College, Cambridge, where he would meet E. M. Forster and discover sex, though not at the same time. (Less valuably, perhaps, "Hope Stimulus" was also the person who introduced him to Tolkien's *The Lord of the Rings,* which entered his consciousness like a disease, an infection he never managed to shake off.) His old English teacher Geoffrey Helliwell would be seen on British television on the day after the *fatwa,* ruefully shaking his head and asking, in sweet, vague, daffy tones, "Who'd have thought such a nice, quiet boy could get into so much trouble?"

Nobody had forced him to go to boarding school in England. Negin had been against the idea of sending her only son away across oceans and continents. Anis had offered him the opportunity and encouraged him to take the Common Entrance exam, but, even after he came through that with some distinction and the place at Rugby was his, the final decision to go or stay was left entirely to him. In later life he would wonder at the choice made by this thirteen-year-old self, a boy rooted in his city, happy in his friends, having a good time at school (apart from a little local difficulty with the Marathi language), the apple of his parents' eye. Why did that boy decide to leave it all behind and travel halfway across the world into the unknown, far from everyone who loved him and everything he knew? Was it the fault, perhaps, of literature (for he was certainly a bookworm)? In which case the guilty parties might have been his beloved Jeeves and Bertie,

SALMAN RUSHDIE

or possibly the Earl of Emsworth and his mighty sow, the Empress of Blandings. Or might it have been the dubious attractions of the world of Agatha Christie that persuaded him, even if Christie's Miss Marple made her home in the most murderous village in England, the lethal St. Mary Mead? Then there was Arthur Ransome's *Swallows and Amazons* series telling of children messing about in boats in the Lake District, and, much, much worse, the terrible literary escapades of Billy Bunter, the "Owl of the Remove," the fat boy at Frank Richards's ridiculous Grayfriars School, where, among Bunter's classmates, there was at least one Indian, Hurree Jamset Ram Singh, the "dusky nabob of Bhanipur," who spoke a bizarre, grand, syntactically contorted English ("the contortfulness," as the dusky nabob might well have put it, "was terrific"). Was it, in other words, a *childish* decision, to venture forth into an imaginary England that only existed in books? Or was it, alternatively, an indication that beneath the surface of the "nice, quiet boy" there lurked a stranger being, a fellow with an unusually adventurous heart, possessed of enough gumption to take a leap in the dark exactly *because* it was a step into the unknown—a youth who intuited his future adult self's ability to survive, even to thrive, wherever in the world his wanderings might take him, and who was able, too easily, even a little ruthlessly, to follow the dream of "away," breaking away from the lure, which was also, of course, the tedium, of "home," leaving his sorrowing mother and sisters behind without too much regret? Perhaps a little of each. At any rate, he took the leap, and the forking paths of time bifurcated at his feet. He took the westward road and ceased to be who he might have been if he had stayed at home.

A pink stone set into the Doctor's Wall, named for the legendary headmaster Dr. Arnold and overlooking the storied playing fields of the Close, bore an inscription that purported to celebrate an act of revolutionary iconoclasm. "This is to commemorate the exploit of William Webb Ellis," it read, "who, with a fine disregard for the rules of football as played in his time, first picked up the ball and ran with it, thus originating the distinctive feature of the rugby game." But the Webb Ellis story was apocryphal, and the school was anything but iconoclastic. The sons of stockbrokers and solicitors were being educated here and "a fine disregard for the rules" was not on the curricu-

lum. Putting both your hands in your pockets was against the rules. So
was "running in the corridors." However, fagging—acting as an older
boy's unpaid servant—and beating were still permitted. Corporal punishment could be administered by the housemaster or even by the boy
named as Head of House. In his first term the Head of House was a
certain R.A.C. Williamson who kept his cane hanging in full view
over the door of his study. There were notches in it, one for each
thrashing Williamson had handed out.

He was never beaten. He was a "nice, quiet boy." He learned the
rules and observed them scrupulously. He learned the school slang, *dics*
for bedtime prayers in the dormitories (from the Latin *dicere,* to speak),
topos for the toilets (from the Greek word for "place"), and, rudely, *oiks*
for non–Rugby School inhabitants of the town, a place best known for
the manufacture of cement. Though the Three Mistakes were never
forgiven, he did his best to fit in. In the sixth form he won the Queen's
Medal for a history essay about Napoléon's foreign minister, the club-
footed, cynical, amoral libertine Talleyrand, whom he vigorously defended. He became secretary of the school's debating society and
spoke eloquently in favor of fagging, which was abolished not long
after his school days ended. He came from a conservative Indian family
and was in no sense a radical. But racism was something he quickly
understood. When he returned to his little study, he more than once
found an essay he had written torn to pieces, which were scattered on
the seat of his red armchair. Once somebody wrote the words WOGS
GO HOME on his wall. He gritted his teeth, swallowed the insults, and
did his work. He did not tell his parents what school had been like
until after he left it (and when he did tell them they were horrified that
he had kept so much pain to himself). His mother was suffering because of his absence, his father was paying a fortune for him to be
there, and it would not be right, he told himself, to complain. So in
his letters home he created his first fictions, about idyllic school days
of sunshine and cricket. In fact he was no good at cricket and Rugby
in winter was bitterly cold, doubly so for a boy from the tropics who
had never slept under heavy blankets and found it hard to go to sleep
when so weighed down. But if he cast them off, then he shivered. He
had to get used to this weight also, and he did. At night in the dormi-

tories, after lights-out, the metal-frame beds began to shake as the boys relieved their adolescent urges, and the banging of the beds against the heating pipes running around the walls filled the large dark rooms with the night music of inexpressible desire. In this matter, as in all else, he strove to be like the others, and join in. Again: He was not, by nature, rebellious. In those early days, he preferred the Rolling Stones to the Beatles, and, after one of his friendlier housemates, a serious, cherubic boy named Richard Shearer, made him sit down and listen to *The Freewheelin' Bob Dylan,* he became an enthusiastic Dylan worshipper; but he was, at heart, a conformist.

Still: Almost as soon as he came to Rugby he did rebel. The school insisted that all boys should enroll in the CCF, or Combined Cadet Force, and then climb into full military khaki on Wednesday afternoons to play war games in the mud. He was not the sort of boy who thought that might be fun—indeed, it struck him as a kind of torture—and in the first week of his school career he went to see his housemaster, Dr. George Dazeley, a mild-natured mad-scientist type with a glittering, mirthless smile, to explain to him that he did not wish to join. Dr. Dazeley stiffened, glittered, and pointed out, just a little icily, that boys did not have the right to opt out. The boy from Bombay, suddenly possessed by an unaccustomed stubbornness, drew himself up straight. "Sir," he said, "my parents' generation have only recently fought a war of liberation against the British Empire, and therefore I cannot possibly agree to join its armed forces." This unexpected burst of postcolonial passion stymied Dr. Dazeley, who limply gave in and said, "Oh, very well, then you'd better stay in your study and read instead." As the young conscientious objector left his office Dazeley pointed to a picture on the wall. "That is Major William Hodson," he said. "Hodson of Hodson's Horse. He was a Bradley boy." William Hodson was the British cavalry officer who, after the suppression of the Indian Uprising of 1857 (at Rugby it was called *the Indian Mutiny*), captured the last Mughal emperor, the poet Bahadur Shah Zafar, and murdered his three sons, stripping them naked, shooting them dead, taking their jewelry, and throwing their bodies down in the dirt at one of the gates of Delhi, which was thereafter known as the *Khooni Darvaza,* the gate of blood. That Hodson was a former Bradley House resident made the young Indian rebel even prouder of having refused to join the army in which the executioner of the Mughal princes had served. Dr. Dazeley added, vaguely, and perhaps incorrectly, that he believed Hodson had been one of the models for the character of Flashman, the school bully in Thomas Hughes's novel of Rugby, *Tom Brown's Schooldays*. There was a statue of Hughes on the lawn outside the school library, but here at Bradley House the presiding old-timer was the alleged real-life original version of the most famous bully in English literature. That seemed just about right.

The lessons one learns at school are not always the ones the school thinks it's teaching.

For the next four years he spent Wednesday afternoons reading yellow-jacketed science fiction novels borrowed from the town library, while eating egg salad sandwiches and potato chips, drinking Coca-Cola and listening to *Two-Way Family Favourites* on the transistor radio. He became an expert on the so-called golden age of science fiction, devouring such masterworks as Isaac Asimov's *I, Robot,* wherein the Three Laws of Robotics were enshrined, Philip K. Dick's *The Three Stigmata of Palmer Eldritch,* Zenna Henderson's *Pilgrimage* novels, the wild fantasies of L. Sprague de Camp, and, above all, Arthur C. Clarke's haunting short story "The Nine Billion Names of God," about the world quietly coming to an end once its secret purpose, the listing of all God's names, had been fulfilled by a bunch of Buddhist monks with a supercomputer. (Like his father, he was fascinated by God, even if religion held little appeal.) It might not have been the greatest revolution in history, this four-and-a-half-year fall toward the fantastic fueled by tuckshop snack foods, but every time he saw his schoolfellows come lurching in from their war games, exhausted, muddy and bruised, he was reminded that standing up for oneself could sometimes be well worth it.

In the matter of God: The last traces of belief were erased from his mind by his powerful dislike of the architecture of Rugby Chapel. Many years later, when by chance he passed through the town, he was shocked to find that Herbert Butterfield's neo-Gothic building was in fact extremely beautiful. As a schoolboy he thought it hideous, deciding, in that science-fiction-heavy time of his life, that it resembled nothing so much as a brick rocket ship ready for takeoff; and one day when he was staring at it through the window of a classroom in the New Big School during a Latin lesson, a question occurred. "What kind of God," he wondered, "would live in a house as ugly as that?" An instant later the answer presented itself: Obviously no self-respecting God would live there—in fact, obviously, there *was* no God, not even a God with bad taste in architecture. By the end of the Latin lesson he was a hard-line atheist, and to prove it, he marched determinedly into the school tuckshop during break and bought himself a ham sandwich. The flesh of the swine passed his lips for the first time that day, and the failure of the Almighty to strike him dead with a thunderbolt proved to him what he had long suspected: that there was nobody up there with thunderbolts to hurl.

Inside Rugby Chapel he joined the rest of the school, one term, in rehearsing and singing the "Hallelujah Chorus" as part of a performance of the full *Messiah* with professional soloists. He took part in compulsory matins and evensong—having attended the Cathedral School in Bombay, he had no leg to stand on if he wanted to make an argument that would excuse him from mumbling his way through Christian prayers—and he couldn't deny that he liked the hymns, whose music lifted his heart. Not all the hymns; he didn't, for example, need to *survey the wondrous cross / on which the prince of glory died;* but a lonely boy could not help but be touched when he was asked to sing *The night is dark and I am far from home / Lead Thou me on.* He liked singing "O Come, All Ye Faithful" in Latin, which somehow took the religious sting out of it: *venite, venite in Bethlehem.* He liked "Abide with Me" because it was sung by the whole 100,000-strong crowd at Wembley Stadium before the FA Cup Final, and what he thought of as the "geography hymn," "The Day Thou Gavest, Lord, Is Ended," made him sweetly homesick: *The sun that bids us rest is waking / our brethren 'neath the western* [here he would substitute *"eastern"*] *sky.* The language of unbelief was distinctly poorer than that of belief. But at least the music of unbelief was becoming fully the equal of the songs of the faithful, and as he moved through his teenage years and the golden age of rock music filled his ears with its pet sounds, its I-can't-get-no and hard rain and try-to-see-it-my-way and da doo ron

ron, even the hymns lost some of their power to move him. But there were still things in Rugby Chapel to touch a bookish unbeliever's heart: the memorials to Matthew Arnold and his ignorant armies clashing by night, and Rupert Brooke, killed by a mosquito bite while fighting just such an army, lying in some corner of a foreign field that was forever England; and, above all, the stone in memory of Lewis Carroll, with its Tenniel silhouettes dancing around the edges in black-and-white marble in a—why, a kind of—yes!—quadrille. "Would not, could not, would not, could not, would not join the dance," he sang softly to himself. "Would not, could not, would not, could not, could not join the dance." It was his private hymn to himself.

Before he left Rugby he did a terrible thing. All school leavers were allowed to hold a "study sale," which allowed them to pass on their old desks, lamps and other bric-a-brac to younger boys in return for small amounts of cash. He posted an auction sheet on the inside of his study door, stipulated modest starting prices for his redundant possessions, and waited. Most study sale items were heavily worn; he, however, had his red armchair, which had been new when his father bought it for him. An armchair with only one user was a high-quality, sought-after rarity in the study sales and the red chair attracted some serious bidding. In the end there were two energetic bidders: one of his fags, a certain P.A.F. Reed-Herbert, known as "Weed Herbert," a small, bespectacled little worm of a fellow who hero-worshipped him a little, and an older boy named John Tallon, whose home was on Bishop's Avenue, the millionaires' row of north London, and who could presumably afford to bid high.

When the bidding slowed down—the top bid was Reed-Herbert's offer of around five pounds—he had his terrible idea. He secretly asked John Tallon to post a seriously high bid, something like *eight pounds,* and promised him that he would not hold him to it if that ended up as the highest offer. Then, at *dics,* he told Weed Herbert solemnly that he knew for a fact that his wealthy rival, Tallon, was prepared to go even higher, perhaps even as high as twelve whole pounds. He saw Weed Herbert's face fall, noted his crushed expression, and went in for the kill. "Now, if you were to offer me, say, ten quid right away, I could close the auction and declare the chair sold." Weed Herbert looked nervous. "That's a lot of money, Rushdie," he said. "Think about it," said Rushdie magnanimously, "while you say your prayers."

When *dics* were over, Weed Herbert took the bait. The Machiavellian Rushdie smiled reassuringly. "Excellent decision, Reed-Herbert." He had cold-bloodedly persuaded the boy to bid against himself, doubling his own top bid. The red armchair had a new owner. Such was the power of prayer.

This happened in the spring of 1965. Nine and a half years later, during the British general election campaign of October 1974, he turned on his television set and saw the end of a speech by the candidate for the far-right, racist, fascist, vehemently anti-immigrant British National Front. The candidate's name was titled on the screen. *Anthony Reed-Herbert.* "Weed Herbert!" he cried aloud in horror. "My god, I've invented a Nazi!" It all instantly became plain. Weed Herbert, tricked into spending too much of his own money by a conniving, godless wog, had nursed his bitter rage through wormy childhood into wormier adulthood and had become a racist politician so that he could be revenged upon all wogs, with or without overpriced red armchairs to sell. (But was it the same Weed Herbert? Could there possibly have been two of them? No, he thought, it had to be little P.A.F., little no more.) In the 1977 election Weed Herbert received 6 percent of the vote in the Leicester East constituency, 2,967 votes in all. In August 1977 he ran again, in the Birmingham Ladywood by-election, and came in third, ahead of the Liberal candidate. Mercifully that was his last significant appearance on the national scene.

Mea culpa, thought the vendor of the red armchair. *Mea maxima culpa.* In the true story of his schooldays there would always be much loneliness and some sadness. But there would also be this stain on his character; this unrecorded, unexpiated crime.

On his second day at Cambridge he went to a gathering of freshmen in King's College Hall and gazed for the first time upon the great Brunelleschian dome of Noel Annan's head. Lord Annan, provost of King's, the sonorous cathedral of a man whose dome that was, stood before him in all his cold-eyed, plump-lipped glory. "You are here," Annan told the assembled freshmen, "for three reasons: Intellect! Intellect! Intellect!" One, two, three fingers stabbed the air as he counted off the three reasons. Later in his speech he surpassed even that aperçu. "The most important part of your education here will not take place in the lecture rooms or libraries or supervisions," he intoned. "It will happen when you sit in one another's rooms, late at night, fertilizing one another."

He had left home in the middle of a war, the pointless India-Pakistan conflict of September 1965. The eternal bone of contention, Kashmir, had triggered a five-week war in which almost seven thousand soldiers died, and at the end of which India had acquired an extra seven hundred square miles of Pakistani territory, while Pakistan had seized two hundred square miles of Indian land, and nothing, less than nothing, had been achieved. (In *Midnight's Children,* this would be the war in which most of Saleem's family is killed by falling bombs.) For some days he had stayed with distant relatives in London in a room without a window. It was impossible to get through to his family on the telephone, and telegrams from home, he was told, were taking three weeks to get through. He had no way of knowing how everyone was. All he could do was to catch the train to Cambridge, and hope. He arrived at King's College's Market Hostel in bad shape, exacerbated by his fear that the university years ahead would be a repeat of the largely wretched Rugby years. He had pleaded with his father not to send him to Cambridge, even though he had already won his place. He didn't want to go back to England, he said, to spend more years of his life among all those cold unfriendly fish. Couldn't he stay home and go to college among warmer-blooded creatures? But Anis, an old Kingsman himself, persuaded him to go. And then told him he had to change his subject of study. History was a useless thing to waste three years on. He had to tell the college he wanted to switch to economics. There was even a threat: If he didn't do that, Anis would not pay his fees.

Burdened by three fears—of unfriendly English youth, of economics, and of war—he found, on his first day "up" at King's, that he couldn't get out of bed. His body felt heavier than usual, as if gravity itself were trying to hold him back. More down than up, he ignored several knocks on the door of his somewhat Scandinavian-modern room. (It was the year of the Beatles' *Rubber Soul,* and he spent a good deal of it humming "Norwegian Wood.") But in the early evening a particularly insistent pounding forced him out of bed. At the door wearing a huge Old Etonian grin and Rupert Brooke's wavy blond hair was the tall, relentlessly friendly figure of "Jan Pilkington-Miksa— I'm half-Polish, you know," the welcoming angel at the gateway to the future, who brought him forth on a tide of loud bonhomie into his new life.

Jan Pilkington-Miksa, the very Platonic form of the English public schoolboy, looked exactly like all the creatures at Rugby who had made his life so unpleasant, but he was the sweetest natured of young men, and seemed to have been sent as a sign that things were going to be different this time around. And so they were; Cambridge largely healed the wounds that Rugby had inflicted, and showed him that there were other, more attractive Englands to inhabit, in which he could easily feel at home.

So much for the first burden. As for economics, he was rescued by a second welcoming angel, the director of studies, Dr. John Broadbent, an Eng. lit. don so magnificently groovy that he could easily have been (though he was not) one of the models for the supercool and ultra-permissive Dr. Howard Kirk, hero of Malcolm Bradbury's novel *The History Man.* Dr. Broadbent asked him, when he gloomily said that he was supposed to change subjects because his father insisted on it, "And what do *you* want to do?" Well, he didn't want to read economics, obviously; he had a history exhibition and he wanted to read history. "Leave it to me," Dr. Broadbent said, and wrote Anis Rushdie a gentle but fierce letter stating that in the opinion of the college Anis's son Salman was not qualified to read economics and that if he continued to insist upon doing so it would be better to remove him from the university to make room for someone else. Anis Rushdie never mentioned economics again.

The third burden, too, was soon lifted. The war in the subcontinent ended, and everyone he loved was safe. His university life began.

He did the usual things: made friends, lost his virginity, learned how to play the mysterious matchstick game featured in *L'année dernière à Marienbad,* played a melancholy game of croquet with E. M. Forster on the day Evelyn Waugh died, slowly understood the meaning of the word "Vietnam," became less conservative, and was elected to the Footlights, became a minor bulb in that dazzling group of illuminati—Clive James, Rob Buckman, Germaine Greer—and watched Germaine perform her Stripping Nun routine, bumping and grinding her way out of her sisterly habit to reveal a full frogman's outfit beneath, on the tiny club stage in Petty Cury on the floor below the office of the Chinese Red Guards where Chairman Mao's Little Red Book was on sale. He also inhaled, saw one friend die of bad acid in the room across the hall, saw another succumb to drug-induced brain damage, was introduced to Captain Beefheart and the Velvet Underground by a third friend who died soon after they graduated; enjoyed miniskirts and see-through blouses; wrote briefly for the student paper *Varsity* until it decided it didn't need his services; acted in Brecht, Ionesco and Ben Jonson; and crashed Trinity May Ball with the future art critic of the London *Times* to listen to Françoise Hardy sing the anthem of young loveless anguish, "Tous les garçons et les filles."

In later life he often spoke of the happiness of his Cambridge years, and agreed with himself to forget the hours of howling loneliness when he sat alone in a room and wept, even if King's Chapel was right outside his window blazing with beauty (this was in his final year, when he was living on the ground floor of S staircase in the college itself, in a room with a view, if ever there was one—chapel, lawn, river, punts—a cliché of gorgeousness). In that final year he had returned from the holidays in low spirits. That was at the end of the summer of 1967, the Summer of Love, when, if you were going to San Francisco, you had to be sure to wear some flowers in your hair. He, unfortunately, had been in London with nobody to love. By chance he had found himself at the very heart of "where," in the parlance of those days, "it was at," staying in a rented room above the coolest boutique of all, Granny Takes a Trip, at the World's End end of the King's Road. John Lennon's wife, Cynthia, wore the frocks.

Mick Jagger was rumored to wear the frocks. Here, too, there was an education to be had. He learned not to say "fab" or "groovy." At

Granny's, you said "beautiful" to express mild approval, and, when you wanted to call something beautiful, you said "really nice." He got used to nodding his head a lot, wisely. In the quest for cool, it helped that he was Indian. "India, man," people said. "Far out." "Yeah," he said, nodding. "Yeah." "The maharishi, man," people said. "Beautiful." "Ravi Shankar, man," he replied. At this point people usually ran out of Indians to talk about and everyone all just went on nodding, beatifically. "Right, right," everyone said. "Right."

He learned an even more profound lesson from the girl who ran the shop, an ethereal presence sitting in that fashionably darkened, patchouli-oil-scented space heavy with sitar music, in which, after a time, he became aware of a low purple glow, in which he could make out a few motionless shapes. These were probably clothes, probably for sale. He didn't like to ask. Granny's was frightening. But one day he plucked up his courage and went downstairs to introduce himself, *Hi, I'm living upstairs, I'm Salman.* The girl in the shop came close, so that he could see the contempt on her face. Then slowly, fashionably, she shrugged.

"Conversation's dead, man," she said.

Up and down the King's Road walked the most beautiful girls in the world, ridiculously underdressed, laughing, accompanied by pea-cocking men who were equally ridiculously overdressed, in high-collared frock coats and frilly shirts and flared crushed velvet trousers and fake-snakeskin boots, also laughing. He seemed to be the only one who didn't know what it was to be happy.

He returned to Cambridge feeling, at the ripe old age of twenty, that life was passing him by. (Others had the final-year blues, too. Even the invariably cheerful Jan Pilkington-Miksa was deeply depressed; though happily he did recover to declare that he had decided to be a film director, and intended to head for the south of France as soon as he was done with Cambridge, "because," he said airily, "they probably need film directors down there.") He took refuge in work, just as he had at Rugby. *The intellect of man is forced to choose / Perfection of the life or of the work,* Yeats said, and since the perfect life was plainly beyond him he had better look to the work instead.

That was the year he found out about the satanic verses. In Part

Two of the History Tripos he was expected to choose three "special subjects" from a wide selection on offer, and concentrate on those. He chose to work on Indian history during the period of the independence struggle against the British, from the 1857 uprising to Independence Day in August 1947; and the extraordinary first century or so of the history of the United States, 1776–1877, from the Declaration of Independence to the end of the post–Civil War period known as Reconstruction; and a third subject, offered, that year, for the first time, titled "Muhammad, the Rise of Islam and the Early Caliphate." In 1967 few history students at Cambridge were interested in the Prophet of Islam—so few, in fact, that the course's designated lecturer canceled his proposed lectures and declined to supervise the few students who had chosen the course. This was a way of saying that the subject was no longer available, and another choice should be made. All the other students did indeed abandon the Muhammad paper and go elsewhere. He, however, felt an old stubbornness rise in him. If the subject was offered, it could not be canceled as long as there was a single student who wished to study it; that was the rule. Well, he did want to study it. He was his father's son, godless, but fascinated by gods and prophets. He was also a product, at least in part, of the deep-rooted Muslim culture of South Asia, the inheritor of the artistic, literary and architectural riches of the Mughals and their predecessors. He was determined to study this subject. All he needed was a historian who was willing to supervise him.

Of the three great historians who were Fellows of King's at that time, Christopher Morris was the most published, with the most established reputation, historian of Tudor political thought, ecclesiastical history, and the Enlightenment, while John Saltmarsh was one of the grand eccentrics of the university with his wild white hair, mutton-chop side-whiskers, long-john underwear poking out at his trouser cuffs above his sockless, sandaled feet, the unrivaled expert in the history of the college and chapel, and, more broadly, in the local history of the region, often seen tramping the country lanes around Cambridge with a rucksack on his back. Both Morris and Saltmarsh were disciples of Sir John Clapham, the scholar who established economic history as a serious field of study, and both conceded that the third member of the King's history trinity, Arthur Hibbert, a medievalist, was the most brilliant of them all, a genius who, according to college legend, had answered the questions he knew least about in his own history finals exams, so that he could complete the answers in the time allotted. Hibbert, it was decided, was the most appropriate person to deal with the matter in hand; and he agreed to do so without a moment's fuss. "I'm not a specialist in this field," he said, modestly, "but I know a little about it, so if you will accept me as your supervisor, I am willing to supervise you."

This offer was gratefully accepted by the stubborn young undergraduate standing in his study sipping a glass of sherry. So came about a strange state of affairs. The special subject about Muhammad, the rise of Islam and the early caliphate had not been offered before; and in that academic year, 1967–68, only this one, obdurate student took it; and the following year, owing to lack of interest, it was not offered again. For that single student, the course was his father's vision made real. It studied the life of the Prophet and the birth of the religion as events inside history, analytically, judiciously, *properly*. It might have been designed especially for him.

At the beginning of their work together Arthur Hibbert gave him a piece of advice he never forgot. "You must never write history," Hibbert said, "until you can hear the people speak." He thought about that for years, and in the end it came to feel like a valuable guiding principle for fiction as well. If you didn't have a sense of how people spoke, you didn't know them well enough, and so you couldn't—you *shouldn't*—tell their story. The way people spoke, in short, clipped phrases, or long, flowing rambles, revealed so much about them: their place of origin, their social class, their temperament, whether calm or angry, warmhearted or cold-blooded, foulmouthed or clean-spoken, polite or rude; and beneath their temperament, their true nature, intellectual or earthy, plainspoken or devious, and, yes, good or bad. If that had been all he learned at Arthur's feet, it would have been enough. But he gained much more than that. He learned a world. And in that world one of the world's great religions was being born.

They were nomads who had just begun to settle down. Their cities were new. Mecca was only a few generations old. Yathrib, later re-named Medina, was a group of encampments around an oasis without so much as a serious city wall. They were still uneasy in their new ur-banized lives, and the changes made many of them unhappy.

A nomadic society was conservative, full of rules, valuing the well-being of the group more highly than individual liberty, but it was also inclusive. The nomadic world had been a matriarchy. Under the umbrella of its extended families even orphaned children could find protection, and a sense of identity and belonging. All that was chang-ing now. The city was a patriarchy and its preferred family unit was nuclear. The crowd of the disenfranchised grew larger and more restive every day. But Mecca was prosperous, and its ruling elders liked it that way. Inheritance now followed the male line. This, too, the governing families preferred.

At the gates to the city stood temples to three goddesses, Al-Lat, Al-Manat, and Al-Uzza. Winged goddesses, like exalted birds. Or an-gels. Each time the trading caravans from which the city gained its wealth left the city gates, or came back through them, they paused at one of the temples and made an offering. Or, to use modern language: paid a tax. The wealthiest families in Mecca controlled the temples and much of their wealth came from these "offerings." The winged god-desses were at the heart of the economy of the new city, of the urban civilization that was coming into being.

In the building known as the Cube or Kaaba in the center of town there were idols of hundreds of gods. One of these statues, by no means the most popular, represented a deity called al-Lah, meaning *the god,* just as al-Lat was *the goddess.* Al-Lah was unusual in that he didn't specialize, he wasn't a rain god or a wealth god or a war god or a love god, he was just, vaguely, an everything god. It may be that this failure to specialize explained his relative unpopularity. People making offer-ings to gods usually did so for specific reasons, the health of a child, the future of a business enterprise, a drought, a quarrel, a romance. They preferred gods who were experts in their field to this nonspecific all-rounder of a deity. However, al-Lah was about to become more popular than any pagan deity had ever been.

The man who would pluck al-Lah from near obscurity and become his Prophet, transforming him into the equal, or at least equivalent, of the Old Testament God *I Am* and the New Testament's Three-in-One, was Muhammad ibn Abdullah of the Banu Hashim family (which had fallen, in his childhood, upon hard times), an orphan living in his uncle's house. As a teenager he began to journey with that uncle, Abu Talib, on his trading journeys to Syria. On those journeys he almost certainly encountered his first Christians, adherents of the Nestorian sect, and heard their stories, many of which adapted Old and New Testament stories to fit in with local conditions. According to the Nestorians, for example, Jesus Christ was born in an oasis, under a palm tree. Later, in the Qur'an, the Archangel Gabriel revealed to Muhammad the *sura* known as "Maryam," Mary, in which Jesus is born under a palm tree, in an oasis.

Muhammad ibn Abdullah grew up with a reputation as a skilled merchant and honest man and at the age of twenty-five this brought him a marriage proposal from an older, wealthier woman, Khadijah, and in the next fifteen years he was successful in business and happy in his marriage. However, he was clearly a man with a need for solitude, and for many years he would spend weeks at a time living like a hermit in a cave on Mount Hira. When he was forty years old, the Angel Gabriel disturbed his solitude there and ordered him to recite. Naturally, he immediately believed he had lost his mind, and fled. He only returned to hear what the Angel had to say when his wife and close friends persuaded him that it might be worth a return trip up the mountain, just in case; that it was probably a good idea to check if God was really trying to get in touch.

It was easy to admire much of what followed as the merchant transformed himself into the Messenger of God; easy to sympathize with his persecution and eventual flight to Medina, and to respect his rapid evolution at the oasis community of Yathrib into respected lawgiver, able ruler and skilled military leader. It was also easy to see how the world into which the Qur'an was revealed, and the events in the life of the Messenger, directly influenced the revelation. When Muslim men were killed in battle, the Angel was prompt to encourage their brothers to marry their widows, in order that the bereaved women might not be lost to the faith by remarrying outside it. When the Prophet's beloved Aisha was rumored to have behaved inappropriately while lost in the desert with a certain Safwan ibn Marwan, the Angel of the Lord came down in some haste to point out that no, in God's opinion, the virtuous lady had not fooled around. And, more generally, it was evident that the ethos of the Qur'an, the value system it endorsed, was, in essence, the vanishing code of nomadic Arabs, the matriarchal, more caring society that did not leave orphans out in the cold; orphans like, for example, Muhammad himself, whose success as a merchant, he believed, entitled him to a place on the city's ruling body, and who had been denied such preferment because he didn't have a powerful family to fight for him.

Here was a fascinating paradox: that an essentially conservative theology, looking backward with affection toward a vanishing culture, became a revolutionary idea, because the people whom it attracted most strongly were those who had been marginalized by urbanization— the disaffected poor, the street mob. This, perhaps, was why Islam, the new idea, felt so threatening to the Meccan elite; why it was persecuted so viciously; and why its founder may—just may—have been offered an attractive deal, designed to buy him off.

The historical record was incomplete, but most of the major collections of *hadith* or traditions about the life of the Prophet—those compiled by Ibn Ishaq, Waqidi, Ibn Sa'd, Bukhari, and Tabari—told the story of an incident that afterward became known as the incident of the satanic verses. The Prophet came down from the mountain one day and recited the *sura* (number 53) called *an-Najm,* the Star. It contained these words: "Have you heard of al-Lat and al-Uzza, and al-Manat, the third, the other one? They are the exalted birds, and their intercession is greatly to be desired." At a later point—Was it days later? Or weeks, or months?—he returned to the mountain and came down, abashed, to state that he had been deceived on his previous visit; the Devil had appeared to him in the guise of the Archangel, and the verses he had been given were therefore not divine, but Satanic, and should be expunged from the Qur'an at once. The Angel had, on this occasion, brought new verses from God, which were to replace the Satanic verses in the great book: "Have you heard of al-Lat and al-Uzza, and al-Manat, the third, the other one? They are but names that your forefathers invented, and there is no truth in them. Shall God have daughters while you have sons? That would be an unjust division." And in this way the Recitation was purified of the Devil's work. But the questions remained: Why did Muhammad initially accept the first, "false" revelation as true? And what happened in Mecca in the period between the two revelations, Satanic and angelic?

This much was known: Muhammad wanted to be accepted by the people of Mecca. "He longed," Ibn Ishaq wrote, "for a way to attract them." And when the people heard that he had accepted the three winged goddesses, the news was popular. "They were delighted and greatly pleased at the way in which he spoke of their gods," Ibn Ishaq wrote, "saying, 'Muhammad has spoken of our gods in splendid fashion.' " And Bukhari reported, "The Prophet . . . prostrated while reciting *An-Najm,* and with him prostrated the Muslims, the pagans, the jinns, and all human beings."

Why, then, did the Prophet afterward recant? Western historians (the Scottish scholar of Islam W. Montgomery Watt, the French Marxist Maxime Rodinson) proposed a politically motivated reading of the episode. The temples of the three winged goddesses were economically important to the city's ruling elite, an elite from which Muhammad was excluded, unfairly, in his opinion. So perhaps the "deal" that was offered ran something like this: If Muhammad, or the Archangel Gabriel, or Allah could agree that the bird-goddesses could be worshipped by followers of Islam—not as the equals of Allah, obviously, but as secondary, lesser beings, like, for example, angels—and there already were angels in Islam, so what harm could there be in adding three more, who just happened already to be popular and lucrative figures in Mecca?—then the persecution of Muslims would cease, and Muhammad himself would be granted a seat on the city's ruling council. And it was perhaps to this temptation that the Prophet briefly succumbed.

Then what happened? Did the city's grandees renege on the deal, reckoning that by flirting with polytheism Muhammad had undone himself in the eyes of his followers? Did the followers refuse to accept the revelation about the goddesses? Did Muhammad himself regret having compromised his ideas by yielding to the siren call of accept-ability? It was not possible to say for sure. Imagination had to fill in the gaps in the record. But the Qur'an spoke of how all the prophets had been tested by temptation. "Never have We sent a single prophet or apostle before you with whose wishes Satan did not tamper," it said in Sura 22. And if the incident of the Satanic verses was the Temptation of Muhammad, it had to be said that he came out of it pretty well. He both confessed to having been tempted and also repudiated that temp-tation. Tabari quotes him thus: "I have fabricated things against God and have imputed to Him words which He has not spoken." After that the monotheism of Islam, having been tested in the cauldron, remained unwavering and strong, in spite of persecution, exile and war, and be-fore long the Prophet had the victory over his enemies and the new faith spread like a conquering fire across the world.

"Shall God have daughters while you have sons? That would be an unjust division."

The "true" verses, angelic or divine, were clear: It was the female-ness of the winged goddesses—the "exalted birds"—that rendered them inferior and fraudulent and proved they could not be the chil-dren of God, as the angels were. Sometimes the birth of a great idea revealed things about its future; the way in which newness enters the world prophesied how it would behave when it grew old. At the birth of this particular idea, femaleness was seen as a disqualification from exaltation.

Good story, he thought when he read about it. Even then he was dream-ing of being a writer, and he filed the good story away in the back of his mind for future consideration. Twenty years later he would find out exactly how good a story it was.

JE SUIS MARXISTE, TENDANCE GROUCHO, said the graffiti in Paris that revolutionary spring. A few weeks after the Paris *évènements* of May 1968, and a few nights before his graduation day, some anonymous wit, possibly a Marxist of the Grouchonian tendency, chose to redecorate his bourgeois, elitist college room, in his absence, by hurling a bucketful of gravy and onions all over the walls and furniture, to say nothing of his record player and clothes. With that ancient tradition of fairness and justice upon which the colleges of Cambridge prided themselves, King's instantly held him solely responsible for the mess, ignored all his representations to the contrary, and informed him that unless he paid for the damage, he would not be permitted to graduate. It was the first, but, alas, not the last occasion on which he would find himself falsely accused of muck spreading.

He paid up, and, in a defiant spirit, went to the ceremony wearing brown shoes. He was promptly plucked out of the parade of his properly black-shod contemporaries, and ordered to change. People in brown shoes were mysteriously deemed to be dressed improperly, and this again was a judgment against which there could be no appeal. Again he gave in, sprinted off to change his shoes, got back to the parade in the nick of time; and at length, when his turn came, he was required to hold a university officer by his little finger and to follow him slowly up to where the vice chancellor sat upon a mighty throne. He knelt at the old man's feet and held up his hands, palms together, in a gesture of supplication, and begged in Latin for the degree, for which, he could not help thinking, he had worked extremely hard for three years, supported by his family at considerable expense. He had been advised to hold his hands way up above his head, in case the elderly vice chancellor, leaning forward to clutch at them, should topple off his great chair and land on top of him.

Looking back at those incidents, he was always appalled by the memory of his passivity, hard though it was to see what else he could have done. He could have refused to pay for the gravy damage to his room, could have refused to change his shoes, could have refused to kneel to supplicate for his B.A. He had preferred to surrender and get the degree. The memory of that surrender made him more stubborn, less willing to compromise, to make an accommodation with injustice, no matter how persuasive the reasons. Injustice would always thereafter conjure up the memory of gravy. Injustice was a brown, lumpy, congealing fluid, and it smelled pungently, tearfully, of onions. Unfairness was the feeling of running back to one's room, flat out, at the last minute, to change one's outlawed brown shoes. It was the business of being forced to beg, on one's knees, in a dead language, for what was rightfully yours.

Many years later he told this story at a Bard College commencement ceremony. "This is the message I have derived from the parables of the Unknown Gravy Bomber, the Vetoed Footwear, and the Unsteady Vice Chancellor upon His Throne, and which I pass on to you today," he told the graduating class of 1996 on a sunny afternoon in Annandale-on-Hudson, New York. "First, if, as you go through life, people should some day accuse you of what one might call Aggravated Gravy Abuse—and they will, they will—and if in fact you are innocent of abusing gravy, do not take the rap. Second: Those who would reject you because you are wearing the wrong shoes are not worth being accepted by. And third: Kneel before no man. Stand up for your rights." The members of the class of '96 skipped up to get their degrees, some barefoot, some with flowers in their hair, cheering, fist punching, voguing, uninhibited. *That's the spirit,* he thought. It was as far from the formality of Cambridge as you could go, and much the better for it.

His parents didn't come to his graduation. His father said they couldn't afford the airfare. This was untrue.

There were novelists among his contemporaries—Martin Amis, Ian McEwan—whose careers took off almost as soon as they were out of the egg, so to speak, and they soared into the sky like exalted birds. His own early hopes were not fulfilled. He lived for a time in an attic on Acfold Road off the Wandsworth Bridge Road, in a house he shared with his sister Sameen and three friends from Cambridge. He pulled up the stepladder and closed the hatch and then he was alone in a triangular world of wood, pretending to write. He had no idea what he was doing. For a long time no book took shape. In these early days his confusion—which he afterward understood was a confusion in the self, a bewilderment about who and what he had become after being uprooted from Bombay—had a harmful effect on his personality. He was often sharp, often got into heated arguments about unimportant things. There was a claw of tension in him, and he had to work hard to hide his fear. Everything he tried went badly. To escape from the futility of the attic he joined fringe theater groups—"Sidewalk," "Zatch"—at the Oval House in Kennington. He put on a long black dress and a blond wig, and kept his mustache, to play a male agony aunt in a piece by a fellow Cambridge graduate, Dusty Hughes. He was a member of the cast of a British revival of *Viet Rock,* the anti-Vietnam agitprop show created in New York by the La MaMa group. These performances were less than seminal, and to make matters worse, he was broke. A year after graduating from Cambridge he was on the dole. "What am I going to tell my friends?" Anis Rushdie had cried when he announced his literary aspirations, and as he stood in the dole queue Anis's son began to see his father's point. In the house on Acfold Road there was much youthful misery. Sameen had an unsuccessful fling with one of his college friends, Stephen Brandon, and when it failed she left the house and went home. A young woman called Fiona Arden moved in and he found her one night half-conscious at the foot of the stairs, having swallowed a bottle of sleeping pills. She clutched his wrist and wouldn't let go, and he went with her in the ambulance to the hospital where they pumped her stomach empty and saved her life. He moved out of the attic after that and wandered from flat-share to flat-share in Chelsea and Earls Court. Forty years later he heard about Fiona again. She was a baroness in the House of Lords and had attained great eminence in the world of business. Youth was often wretched, the struggle to become themselves tore the young to shreds, but sometimes, after the struggle, better days began.

Not long after he left Acfold Road a troubled local boy set fire to the house.

Dusty Hughes got a job writing advertising copy at the J. Walter Thompson agency in Berkeley Square. Suddenly he had a comfortable salary, and was making shampoo commercials with beautiful blond models. "You should do this," Dusty told him. "It's easy." He took the J. Walter Thompson "copy test," done under exam conditions at the agency offices, wrote an ad for After Eight chocolates and a jingle promoting the use of seat belts in cars, to the tune of Chuck Berry's "No Particular Place to Go," and tried, as requested, to tell a visitor from

Mars in fewer than one hundred words what bread was, and how to make a piece of toast; and failed. In the opinion of the mighty JWT, he didn't have what it took to make it as a writer. In the end he got a job at a smaller, less distinguished agency called Sharp MacManus on Albemarle Street, and his working life began. On his first day he was asked to write an ad for a coupon-clipping magazine selling cigars packaged, for Christmas, inside red crackers. His mind was a blank. At last the kindly "creative director," Oliver Knox, who afterward became a well-praised novelist, leaned over his shoulder and murmured, "Five cracking ideas from *Players* to help Christmas go with a bang." *Oh,* he thought, feeling foolish, *so that's how.*

He shared an office at Sharps with a great dark-haired beauty, Fay Coventry, who was dating Tom Maschler, the publisher at Jonathan Cape. Every Monday she would tell him stories about their weekends with their amusing friends, "Arnold" (Wesker) and "Harold" (Pinter) and "John" (Fowles). How delightful these stories were; what fun they all had! Envy, resentment, longing and despair tumbled over one another in the young copywriter's heart. There it was, the world of literature, so close to him, so horribly far away. When Fay left to marry Maschler and, later, to become a respected restaurant critic, he felt almost relieved that the literary world, into which she had given him such tantalizing glimpses, had moved further away again.

He had left university in June 1968. *Midnight's Children* was published in April 1981. It took him almost thirteen years just to begin. During that time he wrote unbearable amounts of garbage. There was a novel, "The Book of the Peer," that might have been good if he had known how to write it. It was the story of a holy man, a *pir* or *peer,* in a country like Pakistan, who was used by three other men, a military leader, a political leader, and a capitalist, to lead a coup after which, they believed, he would be the figurehead while they wielded the power. But he proved more capable and ruthless than his backers and they realized they had unleashed a monster they could not control. This was many years before the Ayatollah Khomeini ate the revolution whose figurehead he was supposed to be. If the novel had been written plainly, as a political thriller, it might have served; instead the story was told in several different characters' "streams of consciousness," and was more or less incomprehensible. Nobody liked it. It came nowhere near publication. It was a stillbirth.

There was much worse to come. The BBC announced a competition to find a new television playwright and he entered a play featuring the two criminals crucified with Christ, talking to each other before the great man gets to Golgotha, in the manner of Beckett's tramps Didi and Gogo. The play was called (of course) "Crosstalk." It was deeply foolish. It did not win the competition. After that there was another novel-length text, "The Antagonist," so bad, in a sub-Pynchon kind of manner, that he never showed it to anyone. Advertising kept him going. He didn't dare to call himself a novelist. He was a copywriter who, like all copywriters, dreamed of being a "real" writer. He knew, however, that he was still unreal.

It was curious that so avowedly godless a person should keep trying to write about faith. Belief had left him but the subject remained, nagging at his imagination. The structures and metaphors of religion (Hinduism and Christianity as much as Islam) shaped his irreligious mind, and the concerns of these religions with the great questions of existence—Where do we come from? And now that we are here, how shall we live?—were also his, even if he came to conclusions that required no divine arbiter to underwrite and certainly no earthly priest class to sanction and interpret. His first published novel, *Grimus,* was published by Liz Calder at Victor Gollancz, before she moved to Cape. It was based on the *Mantiq ut-Tair,* or *Conference of the Birds,* a mystical narrative poem by the John Bunyan of Islam, the twelfth-century Sufi Muslim Farid ud-din Attar, born in Nishapur in present-day Iran four years after the death of that town's more celebrated local son, Omar Khayyam. In the poem—a sort of Muslim *Pilgrim's Progress*—a hoopoe led thirty birds on a journey through seven valleys of travail and revelation toward the circular mountain of Qâf, home of their god the Simurg. When they reached the mountaintop there was no god there and it was explained to them that the name "Simurg," if broken down into its syllables *si* and *murg,* means "thirty birds." Having overcome the travails of the quest they had become the god they sought.

"Grimus" was an anagram of "Simurg." In his science-fantasy retelling of Attar's tale an "American Indian" crudely named Flapping

Eagle searches for the mysterious Calf Island. The novel was met for the most part with dismissive notices, some of which bordered on the contemptuous, and its reception shook him profoundly. Fighting off despair, he quickly wrote a short—novella length—satirical fiction in which the career of the prime minister of India, Mrs. Indira Gandhi, was transposed into the world of the Bombay film industry. (Philip Roth's satire about Richard M. Nixon, *Our Gang,* was a distant model.) The book's vulgarity—at one point the Indira character, a powerful movie star, grows her dead father's penis—meant that it was rejected as swiftly as it had been written. This was the bottom of the barrel.

The sixth valley through which the thirty birds journeyed in Attar's poem was the place of bewilderment, in which they came to feel that they knew and understood nothing, and were plunged into hopelessness and grief. The seventh was the valley of death. The young advertising copywriter and novelist *manqué* felt, in the mid-1970s, like the thirty-first despairing bird.

Advertising itself, in spite of its reputation as the great enemy of promise, was good to him, on the whole. He was now working at a grander agency, Ogilvy & Mather, whose founder, David Ogilvy, was the author of the celebrated dictum "The consumer is not a moron; she is your wife." There were a few hiccups, such as the time an American airline refused to allow him to feature black stewardesses in their ads, even though the women in question actually were members of the airline's staff. "What would the union say if they knew?" he wondered, and the Airline Client replied, "Well, you're not going to tell them, are you?" And there was the time he refused to work on an ad for Campbell's Corned Beef because it was made in South Africa and the African National Congress had called for a boycott of such products. He could have been fired, but the Corned Beef Client did not insist upon it, and he was not. In the world of 1970s advertising the mavericks and oddballs never got sacked. The people who did were the dogged worker ants who were trying really hard to hang on to their jobs. If you acted like you didn't give a damn, came in late and took long boozy lunches, you got promotions and pay raises and the gods smiled down on your creative eccentricity, at least as long as you were, on the whole, delivering the goods.

And for much of the time he worked with people who appreciated and supported him, talented people, many of whom were using advertising as he was, as a stepping-stone to better things, or a source of easy money. He made a commercial for Scotch Magic Tape that starred John Cleese demonstrating the merits of a sticky tape that disappeared on contact ("And here you see it, not being seen; unlike this ordinary tape, which, as you can see, you can see"), and one for Clairol's gray-hair cover-up product Loving Care that was directed by Nicolas Roeg, the celebrated director of *Performance* and *Don't Look Now.* For almost six months, during the British three-day week of 1974, caused by the miners' strike and featuring daily power outages and much chaos in the Wardour Street world of recording and dubbing studios, he made three commercials a week for the *Daily Mirror,* and in spite of all the problems every single one aired on time. Filmmaking held no terrors for him after that. Advertising introduced him to America, too, sending him on a journey across the United States so that he could write tourism ads for the U.S. Travel Service under the slogan "The Great American Adventure," with photographs by the legendary Elliott Erwitt. Longhaired and mustachioed, he arrived at the San Francisco airport, where a large sign read A FEW MINUTES EXTRA IN CUSTOMS IS A SMALL PRICE TO PAY TO SAVE YOUR CHILDREN FROM THE MENACE OF DRUGS. A fabulously rednecked American gentleman was noting this sign with approval. Then, with a complete change of heart and no apparent awareness of any internal contradictions in his position, he turned to the longhaired, mustachioed visitor—who looked, it must be admitted, suspiciously as if he intended to head straight for Haight-Ashbury, the world capital of the "counterculture" of sex, drugs and rock 'n' roll—and said, "Buddy, I sure feel sorry for you, because even if you ain't got nothing, they'll find something." However, no drugs were planted, and the young advertising writer was allowed to enter the magic kingdom. And when he finally reached New York, he was encouraged, on his first night in the city, to put on that strangest of uniforms, a suit and tie, so that friends could take him to have a drink at the Windows on the World bar at the top of the World

Trade Center. This was his first and never-forgotten image of the city; those massive buildings that seemed to say *We are here forever.*

He himself felt painfully temporary. His private life with Clarissa was happy, and this had calmed the storm inside him a little, while another young man might have been pleased that his job was going well. But the troubles of the interior life, his repeated failures to be, or become, a decent, publishable writer of fiction, dominated his thoughts. He resolved to set aside the many criticisms others had made of his work and to make his own critique of it instead. He was already beginning to understand that what was wrong with his writing was that there was something wrong, something misconceived, about him. If he hadn't become the writer he thought he had it in him to be, it was because he didn't know who he was. And slowly, from his ignominious place at the bottom of the literary barrel, he began to understand who that person might be.

He was a migrant. He was one of those who had ended up in a place that was not the place where he began. Migration tore up all the traditional roots of the self. The rooted self flourished in a place it knew well, among people who knew it well, following customs and traditions with which it and its community were familiar, and speaking its own language among others who did the same. Of these four roots, place, community, culture and language, he had lost three. His beloved Bombay was no longer available to him; in their old age his parents had sold his childhood home without discussion and mysteriously de-camped to Karachi, Pakistan. They didn't enjoy living in Karachi; why would they? It was to Bombay what Duluth was to New York. Nor did their reasons for moving ring true. They felt, they said, increasingly alien in India as Muslims. They wanted, they said, to find good Mus-lim husbands for their daughters. It was bewildering. After a lifetime of happy irreligion they were using religious rationales. He didn't be-lieve them for a moment. He was convinced there must have been business problems, tax problems, or other real-world problems that had driven them to sell the home to which they were devoted and abandon the city they loved. Something was fishy here. There was a secret he was not being told. Sometimes he said this to them; they did not reply. He never solved the mystery. Both his parents died without admitting that any secret explanation existed. But they were no more godly in Karachi than they had been in Bombay, so the Muslim explanation continued to feel inadequate and wrong.

It was unsettling not to understand why the shape of life had changed. He often felt meaningless, even absurd. He was a Bombay boy who had made his life in London among the English, but often he felt cursed by a double unbelonging. The root of language, at least, remained, but he began to appreciate how deeply he felt the loss of the other roots, and how confused he felt about what he had become. In the age of migration the world's millions of migrated selves faced colossal problems, problems of homelessness, hunger, unemployment, disease, persecution, alienation, fear. He was one of the luckier ones, but one great problem remained: that of authenticity. The migrated self became, inevitably, heterogeneous instead of homogeneous, belonging to more than one place, multiple rather than singular, responding to more than one way of being, more than averagely mixed up. Was it possible to be—to become *good* at being—not rootless, but multiply rooted? Not to suffer from a loss of roots but to benefit from an excess of them? The different roots would have to be of equal or near-equal strength, and he worried that his Indian connection had weakened. He needed to make an act of reclamation of the Indian identity he had lost, or felt he was in danger of losing. The self was both its origins and its journey.

To know the meaning of his journey, he had to begin again at the beginning and learn as he went.

It was at this point in his meditations that he remembered "Saleem Sinai." This West London–based proto-Saleem had been a secondary character in his abandoned manuscript "The Antagonist," and had deliberately been created as an alter ego, "Saleem" in memory of his Bombay classmate Salim Merchant (and because of its closeness to "Salman"), and "Sinai" after the eleventh-century Muslim polymath Ibn Sina ("Avicenna"), just as "Rushdie" had been derived from Ibn Rushd. The Saleem of "The Antagonist" was an entirely forgettable fellow and deserved to drift up Ladbroke Grove into oblivion, but he had one characteristic that suddenly seemed valuable: He had been born at midnight, August 14–15, 1947, the "freedom-at-midnight" moment of India's independence from British rule. Maybe this Saleem, Bombay-Saleem, midnight-Saleem, needed his own book.

He himself had been born eight weeks to the day before the end of the empire. He remembered his father's joke, "Salman was born and eight weeks later the British ran away." Saleem's feat would be even more impressive. The British would run away at the exact moment of his birth.

He had been born in Dr. Shirodkar's Nursing Home—the celebrated gynecologist V. N. Shirodkar, creator of the famous "Shirodkar stitch" or cervical cerclage operation—and now, in his pages, he would bring the doctor back to life under a new name. Westfield Estate, overlooking Warden Road (now renamed Bhulabhai Desai Road), its villas bought from a departing Englishman and named after the royal palaces of Britain, Glamis Villa, Sandringham Villa, Balmoral, and his own home, Windsor Villa, would be reborn as Methwold's Estate, and "Windsor" would become "Buckingham." Cathedral School, founded "under the auspices of the Anglo-Scottish Education Society," would keep its own name, and the small and large incidents of childhood—the loss of a fingertip in a slammed door, the death of a classmate during school hours, Tony Brent singing "The Clouds Will Soon Roll By," Sunday morning jazz "jam sessions" in Colaba, the Nanavati affair, a cause célèbre in which a high-flying navy officer murdered his wife's lover and shot the wife as well, although not fatally—would also be here, transmuted into fiction. The gates of memory opened and the past surged back. He had a book to write.

For a moment it seemed that this might be a simple novel about childhood, but the implications of his protagonist's birth date quickly became clear. If his reimagined Saleem Sinai and the newborn nation were twins, then the book would have to tell the story of both twins. History rushed into his pages, immense and intimate, creative and destructive, and he understood that this dimension, too, had been lacking from his work. He was a historian by training and the great point of history, which was to understand how individual lives, communities, nations, and social classes were shaped by great forces, yet retained, at times, the ability to change the direction of those forces, must also be the point of his fiction. He began to feel very excited. He had found an intersection between the private and the public and would build his book on that crossroads. The political and the personal could no longer be kept apart. This was no longer the age of Jane Austen, who could write her entire oeuvre during the Napoleonic Wars without mentioning them, and for whom the major role of the British Army was to wear dress uniforms and look cute at parties. Nor would he write his book in cool Forsterian English. India was not cool. It was *hot*. It was hot and overcrowded and vulgar and loud and it needed a language to match that and he would try to find that language.

He realized he was taking on a gigantic, all-or-nothing project, and that the risk of failure was far greater than the possibility of success. He found himself thinking that that was just fine. If he was going to have one last try at achieving his dream, he didn't want it to be with a safe, conservative, middling little book. He would do the most artistically challenging thing he could think of, and this was it, this untitled novel, "Sinai," no, terrible title, would make people think it was about the Middle East conflict or the Ten Commandments, "Child of Midnight," but there would have to be more than one, wouldn't there, how many children would be born in the midnight hour, hundreds, maybe a thousand, or, yes, why not, one thousand and one, so "Children of Midnight"? No, boring title, sounded like pedophiles gathering at a Black Sabbath, but . . . *Midnight's Children*? Yes!

The advance for *Grimus* had been the princely sum of £750, and there had been two translation sales, to France and Israel, so that was about £825 in the bank, and he took a deep breath and suggested to Clarissa that he give up his good job at Ogilvys and that they go to India for as long as they could make the money last, traveling as cheaply as possible, just plunging into the inexhaustible Indian reality, so that he could drink deeply from that horn of plenty and then come home and write. "Yes," she said at once. He loved her for her adventurous spirit, the same spirit that had led her away from the maternally approved Mr. Leworthy of Westerham, Kent, and into his arms. Yes, they would go for broke. She had backed him this far and would not stop backing him now. They set off on their Indian odyssey, staying in flophouses, going on twenty-hour bus rides during which chickens vomited on their feet, arguing with local villagers at Khajuraho who thought the famous temple complex with its Tantric carvings was obscene and only for tourists, rediscovering Bombay and Delhi, staying with old family friends and at least one notably inhospitable uncle with a new and even more inhospitable Australian wife, a convert to Islam who couldn't wait to see the back of them and then, many years later, wrote him a letter asking for money. He discovered the widows' hostel in Benares and, in Amritsar, visited Jallianwala Bagh, the scene of General Dyer's notorious "massacre" of 1919; and returned, glutted with India, to write his book.

Five years later, he and Clarissa had married, their son, Zafar, had been born, the novel had been completed, and it had found publishers. An Indian woman stood up at a reading and said, "Thank you, Mr. Rushdie, because you have told my story," and he felt a lump rise in his throat. Another Indian woman, at another reading, said, "Mr. Rushdie, I have read your novel *Midnight's Children*. It's a very long novel, but never mind, I read it through. And my question for you is this: Fundamentally, what's your point?" A Goan journalist said, "You're lucky, you just finished your book first," and showed him a typed chapter of his own novel, about a boy born in Goa on that same midnight. *The New York Times Book Review* said the novel "sounded like a continent finding its voice," and many of the literary voices of South Asia, speaking in the myriad languages of the subcontinent, returned a resounding, "Oh, yeah?" And many things happened about which he had not even dared to dream, awards, bestsellerdom, and, on the whole, popularity. India took the book to its heart, claiming the author as its own just as he had hoped to reclaim the country, and that was a greater prize than anything awarded by juries. At the very bottom of the barrel he had found the open-sesame door that led to the bright air at the top. Once again, after the Khomeini *fatwa,* he would revisit the barrel's bottom, and, again, would find there the strength to go on, and to be more fully himself.

He had returned to copywriting part-time after the Indian trip,

persuading first Ogilvys and later another agency, Ayer Barker Hege-
mann, to employ him for two or three days a week, leaving him four
or five days a week free to write the book that grew into *Midnight's
Children*. After the book came out he decided the time had come to
give up this work once and for all, lucrative as it was. He had a small
son, and the money would be tight, but it was what he needed to do.
He asked Clarissa her opinion. "We'd have to prepare to be poor," he
told her. "Yes," she said without hesitation. "Of course that's what
you must do." The book's commercial success, which neither of them
had expected, when it came felt like a reward for their joint willingness
to leap away from security into the financial dark.

When he resigned his boss thought he was asking for more money.
"No," he said. "I'm just going to try to be a full-time writer." Oh, his
boss said, you want a *lot* more money. "No, really," he said. "This isn't
a negotiation. I'm just giving you my thirty days' notice. Thirty-one
days from now, I won't be coming in." Hmm, his boss replied. I don't
think we can give you as much money as *that*.

Thirty-one days later, in the summer of 1981, he became a full-
time writer, and the feeling of liberation as he left the agency for
the last time was heady and exhilarating. He shed advertising like an
unwanted skin, though he continued to take a sneaky pride in his
best-known slogan, "Naughty but nice" (created for the Fresh Cream
Cake Client), and in his "bubble words" campaign for Aero chocolate
(IRRESISTIBUBBLE, DELECTABUBBLE, ADORABUBBLE, the billboards cried,
and bus sides read TRANSPORTABUBBLE, trade advertising said PROFIT-
ABUBBLE, and storefront decals proclaimed AVAILABUBBLE HERE). Later
that year, when *Midnight's Children* was awarded the Booker Prize, the
first telegram he received—there were these communications called
"telegrams" in those days—was from his formerly puzzled boss. "Congratulations," it read. "One of us made it."

On the night of the Booker Prize he was walking with Clarissa toward
the Stationers' Hall and ran into the firebrand Lebanese-Australian
publisher Carmen Callil, creator of the feminist imprint Virago.
"Salman," cried Carmen, "darling, you're going to win!" He imme-

diately became convinced that she had jinxed him and that he would not win. The short list was formidable. Doris Lessing, Muriel Spark, Ian McEwan . . . he didn't stand a chance. And then there was D. M. Thomas and his novel *The White Hotel,* which many critics were calling a masterwork. (This was before accusations of excessive borrowing from Anatoly Kuznetsov's *Babi Yar* surfaced to sully the book's reputation in some people's eyes at least.) No, he told Clarissa: Forget about it.

Many years later one of the judges, the distinguished presenter of TV arts programs Joan Bakewell, told him of her fear that Malcolm Bradbury, the chairman of the jury, might try to steamroller his fellow judges into awarding the prize to *The White Hotel.* As a result she and two other judges, the critic Hermione Lee and Professor Sam Hynes of Princeton University, met privately before the final judging session to assure one another that they would hold firm and vote for *Midnight's Children.* In the end Bradbury and the fifth judge, Brian Aldiss, voted for *The White Hotel,* and *Midnight's Children* carried the day by the narrowest of margins: three votes to two.

D. M. Thomas was not at the prize-giving ceremony and his editor Victoria Petrie-Hay was so nervous that she might have to accept the award on his behalf that she was drinking a little too quickly. After the announcement he bumped into her again. By now she was pretty far gone and confessed her relief at not having to read Thomas's acceptance speech. She took the speech out of her handbag and waved the envelope around vaguely. "I don't know what to do with this now," she said. "Give it to me," he told her, mischievously. "I'll look after it." And she had drunk so much that she did as he suggested. For half an hour after that he had Thomas's victory speech in his pocket. Then conscience got the better of him and he sought out the sodden editor and returned the unopened envelope. "You should probably hold on to this," he said.

He showed his editor Liz Calder the handsome leather-bound presentation copy of *Midnight's Children* and opened it to the bookplate inside that read WINNER. She was so happy and excited that she poured a glass of champagne over it, to "baptize" it. The words smudged a little and he cried out in horror, "Look what you've done!" A couple of days later the Booker people sent him a new, pristine bookplate, but by then the baptized plate, bearing the smudge of victory, was the one he wanted. He never replaced it.

The good years began.

He had seven good years, more than many writers are granted, and for those years, during the bad times that followed, he was always grateful. Two years after *Midnight's Children* he published *Shame,* the second part of the diptych in which he examined the world of his origins, a work deliberately conceived to be the formal opposite of its precursor, dealing for the most part not with India but with Pakistan, shorter, more tightly plotted, written in the third person rather than the first, with a series of characters occupying the center of the stage one after the other instead of a single dominant narrator-antihero. Nor was this a book written with love; his feelings toward Pakistan were ferocious, satirical, personal. Pakistan was that place where the crooked few ruled the impotent many, where bent civilian politicians and un-scrupulous generals allied with one another, supplanted one another, and executed one another, echoing the Rome of the Caesars, where mad tyrants bedded their sisters and made their horses into senators and fiddled while their city burned. But, for the ordinary Roman— and so also for the ordinary Pakistani—the murderous, psychotic may-hem inside the palace changed nothing. The palace was still the palace. The ruling class continued to rule.

Pakistan was the great mistake of his parents, the blunder that had deprived him of his home. It was easy for him to see Pakistan itself as a historical blunder too, a country *insufficiently imagined,* conceived of the misguided notion that a religion could bind together peoples (Pun-jabi, Sindhi, Bengali, Baloch, Pathan) whom geography and history had long kept apart, born as a misshapen bird, "two Wings without a body, sundered by the land-mass of its greatest foe, joined by nothing but God," whose East Wing had subsequently fallen off. What was the sound of one Wing flapping? The answer to this version of the famous Zen *koan* was undoubtedly "Pakistan." So in *Shame,* his Pakistan-novel (the description was an oversimplification; there was plenty of Pakistan in *Midnight's Children,* and a fair bit of India in *Shame*), the comedy was blacker, the politics more bloodily comic, as if, he told himself, the calamities in the palaces of the Twelve Caesars, or in a Shakespearean tragedy, were being enacted by buffoons, people unworthy of high tragedy—as if *King Lear* were to be performed by circus clowns, becoming *simultaneously* tragic and farcical, a circus catastrophe. The book drove itself forward at a speed that was new to him; after spending five years on *Midnight's Children,* he had finished *Shame* in just over a year and a half. This novel, too, had a wonderful reception everywhere, or almost everywhere. In Pakistan itself it was unsurprisingly banned by Pakistan's dictator, Zia ul-Haq, the point of origin for the character of "Raza Hyder" in the novel. However, many copies of the book found their way into Pakistan, including, he was told by Pakistani friends, quite a few that were brought in through the diplomatic pouches of various embassies, whose staffs read the book avidly and then passed it on.

Some years later he learned that *Shame* had even been awarded a prize in Iran. It had been published in Farsi without his knowledge, in a state-sanctioned pirate edition, and then had been named the best novel translated into Farsi that year. He never received the award, nor was he sent any formal notification of it; but it meant—according to stories emerging from Iran—that when *The Satanic Verses* was published five years later, the few Iranian booksellers who sold English-language books assumed that it would be unproblematic to sell this new title, its author having already gained the mullocracy's approval with his previous work; and so copies were imported and put on sale at the time of the book's first publication in September 1988, and these copies remained on sale for six months, without arousing any opposition, until the *fatwa* of February 1989. He was never able to find out if this story was true, but he hoped it was, because it demonstrated what he believed: that the furor over his book was created from the top down, not from the bottom up.

But in the mideighties the *fatwa* was an unimaginable cloud hidden below the far horizon. Meanwhile, the success of his books had a beneficial effect on his character. He felt something relax deep within him, and became happier, sweeter natured, easier to be around. Strangely, however, older novelists gave him warnings in those balmy times of worse days to follow. He was taken to lunch by Angus Wilson at the Athenaeum Club not long after Wilson's seventieth birthday; and, listening to the author of *Anglo-Saxon Attitudes* and *The Old Men at the Zoo* speak wistfully of the days "when I used to be a fashionable writer" he understood that he was being told, gently, that the wind always changes; yesterday's hot young kid is tomorrow's melancholy, ignored senior citizen.

When he went to America for the publication of *Midnight's Children* he had his picture taken by the photographer Jill Krementz and met her husband, Kurt Vonnegut; and they invited him out to their house in Sagaponack, Long Island, for the weekend. "Are you serious about this writing business?" Vonnegut unexpectedly asked him as they sat drinking beers in the sunshine, and when he replied that he was, the author of *Slaughterhouse-Five* told him, "Then you should know that the day is going to come when you won't have a book to write, and you're still going to have to write a book."

On his way to Sagaponack he had read a bundle of reviews sent over by his American publishers, Knopf. There was an astonishingly generous notice by Anita Desai in *The Washington Post*. If she thought well of the book then he could be happy; perhaps he really had done something worthwhile. And there was a positive review in the *Chicago Tribune*, written by Nelson Algren. *The Man with the Golden Arm, A Walk on the Wild Side . . . that* Nelson Algren? The lover of Simone de Beauvoir, the friend of Hemingway? It was as if literature's golden past had reached out to anoint him. *Nelson Algren,* he thought in wonderment. *I thought he was dead.* He arrived in Sagaponack earlier than expected. The Vonneguts were on their way out of the house to go to the housewarming party of their friend and neighbor . . . Nelson Algren. It was an amazing coincidence. "Well," said Kurt, "if he reviewed your book I'm sure he'd like to meet you. I'll go call him and tell him you're coming over with us." He went indoors. A few moments later he came back from the telephone looking shaken and gray. "Nelson Algren just died," he said. Algren had prepared his party and then suffered a fatal heart attack. The first guests to arrive found the host dead on the living room rug. His review of *Midnight's Children* was the last thing he ever wrote.

Nelson Algren. I thought he was dead. Algren's death darkened Vonnegut's mood. His own thoughts were sober, too. The sudden, unforeseeable plunge toward the rug awaited us all.

The critical success of *Midnight's Children* in the United States took Knopf by surprise. He had come to New York at his own expense just to be there when his book was published, and no interviews had been arranged for him, and none were, not even after the excellent notices appeared. The print run was small, there was a small reprint, a small paperback sale, and that was that. However, he was fortunate enough to shake hands, at the entrance to the offices at 201 East 50th Street, with the legendary Alfred A. Knopf himself, an elderly, courteous gentleman in an expensive coat and a dark beret. And he also met his gangling, intense publisher, Robert Gottlieb, who was something of a legend himself. He was taken to Bob Gottlieb's office, which was decorated with fiftieth-birthday bunting and cards, and after they had spoken for a while, Gottlieb said, "Now that I know I like you, I can tell you that I thought I wasn't going to." This was shocking. "Why?" he said, fumbling for words. "Didn't you like my book? I mean, you published my book. . . ." Bob shook his head. "It wasn't because of your book," he said. "But I recently read a very great book by a very great writer and after it I thought I wouldn't be able to like anyone with a Muslim background." This was, if anything, an even more astonishing statement. "What was this very great book?" he asked Gottlieb, "and who is this very great writer?" "The book," said Bob Gottlieb, "is called *Among the Believers,* and the author is V. S. Naipaul." "That," he said to the editor-in-chief of Knopf, "is a book I definitely want to read."

Bob Gottlieb didn't appear to know how his words were being received, and, in fairness, he went on to be extremely hospitable toward the author he hadn't thought he would like, inviting him to eat at his town house in Turtle Bay, the tony Manhattan neighborhood whose other residents included Kurt Vonnegut, Stephen Sondheim and Katharine Hepburn. (The septuagenarian movie star had recently showed up on Gottlieb's doorstep after a snowstorm, carrying a shovel, and offered to clear the snow off the publisher's roof.) Gottlieb was also on the board of George Balanchine's New York City Ballet and invited his new young Indian novelist—who had once seen Balanchine's greatest love, Suzanne Farrell, dance in London with the Maurice Béjart ballet company after her quarrel with the great Russian choreographer—to watch a performance. "There is only one condition," Bob said. "You have to forget about Béjart and agree that Balanchine is God."

He offered literary hospitality, too. When Gottlieb left Knopf in 1987 to step into William Shawn's shoes as editor of *The New Yorker,* the doors of that august journal finally opened to allow the author of *Midnight's Children* to enter. Under Mr. Shawn's regime those doors had remained resolutely closed, and Salman was not one of those who mourned the end of the great editor's fifty-three-year reign. Bob Gottlieb published both his fiction and nonfiction, and was a brilliant, detailed and passionate editor of the long essay "Out of Kansas" (1992), a response to *The Wizard of Oz,* which, as Gottlieb rightly encouraged him to stress, was one of the sweetest of odes to friendship in the movies.

During the *fatwa* years he saw Gottlieb only once. Liz Calder and Carmen Callil gave a joint birthday party at the Groucho Club in Soho, and he was able to go for a while. When he said hello to Bob, the publisher said, with great intensity, "I'm always defending you, Salman. I always tell people, if you had known that your book was going to kill people, of course you wouldn't have written it." He counted very slowly to ten. It would not be right to hit this old man. It would be better to make an excuse and just walk away. He inclined his head in a meaningless gesture and turned on his heel. In the years that followed they did not speak. He owed a great deal to Bob Gottlieb but he couldn't get those final words out of his head, and he knew that, just as Gottlieb hadn't understood the impact of his words about Naipaul's book when they had met for the first time, he also didn't understand what was wrong with what he said at this, their last meeting. Bob believed he was being a friend.

In 1984 his marriage ended. They had been together for fourteen years and had grown apart without noticing it. Clarissa wanted a country life, and they had spent one summer looking at houses west of London, but in the end he realized that to move into the countryside would drive him insane. He was a city boy. He told her this and she acquiesced, but it was a difficulty between them. They had fallen in love when they were both very young and now that they were older their interests often failed to coincide. There were parts of his life in London that didn't greatly interest her. One such part was his antiracist work. He had been involved for a long time with a race relations group, the Camden Committee for Community Relations, or CCCR, and his voluntary work there, overseeing the community work team, had become important to him. It had shown him a city he had previously known little about, the immigrant London of deprivation and prejudice, what he would afterward call *a city visible but unseen.* The immigrant city was right there in plain sight, in Southall and Wembley and Brixton as well as Camden, but in those days its problems were largely ignored, except during brief explosions of racial violence. This was a chosen blindness: an unwillingness to accept the city, the world, as it really was. He gave a lot of his spare time to race relations work, and used his experiences with CCCR as the basis of a polemical broadcast titled "The New Empire Within Britain," an attempt to describe the growth of a new underclass of black and brown Britons, made for the *Opinions* slot on Channel Four, and it was obvious she didn't much care for the rhetoric he used in that talk, either.

But their biggest problem was a more intimate one. Ever since Zafar's birth they, and in particular Clarissa, had wanted more children, and the children had not come. Instead there was a series of early miscarriages. There had been one such miscarriage before Zafar's conception and birth and there were two more afterward. He discovered that the problem was genetic. He had inherited (probably from his father's side) a condition known as a *simple chromosome translocation.*

A chromosome was a stick of genetic information and all human cells contained twenty-two pairs of such sticks, as well as a twenty-third pair that determined gender. In rare cases a piece of genetic information broke off one chromosome and attached itself to another. There were then two faulty chromosomes, one with too little genetic information and another with too much. When a child was conceived, half the father's chromosomes, chosen at random, combined with half the mother's, to create a new set of pairs. If the father had a simple chromosome translocation and *both* his faulty chromosomes were selected, the child would be born normally, except that it would inherit the condition. If *neither* of the faulty chromosomes were selected, the pregnancy would also be normal and the child would not inherit the condition. But if only one of the two problem chromosomes were to be selected, then the fetus would not form, and the pregnancy would miscarry.

Trying to have a baby became a kind of biological roulette. Their luck had not been good, and the stress of all those miscarriages, all those dashed hopes, had worn them both down. Their physical relationship came to an end. Neither of them could bear the idea of yet another attempt followed by yet another failure. And perhaps it was humanly impossible for Clarissa not to blame him for the end of her dream of a family of children running around her and becoming the meaning of her life. It was impossible for him not to blame himself.

Any long relationship that no longer included sex was probably doomed. For thirteen of their fourteen years together he had been unquestioningly faithful to her but in the fourteenth year the bond of loyalty had broken, or been eroded, and there were brief infidelities during literary trips to Canada and Sweden and a longer infidelity in London, with an old Cambridge friend who played the violin. (Clarissa had been unfaithful to him only once, but that was long ago, in 1973, when he was still writing *Grimus,* and although she was briefly tempted to leave him for her lover she soon gave the other man up, and they both forgot the episode; or almost forgot. He never forgot his rival's name. It was, a little improbably, Aylmer Gribble.)

At the time he was idiotically certain that he had concealed his affairs so well that his wife knew nothing, suspected nothing. In retrospect he was amazed that he could have been so vain. Of course she knew.

He went by himself to Australia, to take part in the Adelaide Festival and, afterward, accompanied Bruce Chatwin into the Australian desert. They were in a bookstore in Alice Springs when he saw a paperback copy of Robyn Davidson's *Tracks,* an account of her solo trek across the Gibson Desert accompanied by camels she had caught and trained herself. His editor at Cape, Liz Calder, had praised the book and its intrepid author when it came out, and he had said, dismissively, "Why walk across the desert when you can go by Airbus?" But now he was seeing the places the book talked about and so he bought it and was impressed. "You should meet her when you go to Sydney," Bruce said. "Let's call her. I've got her phone number." "Of course you do," he replied. In Bruce's famous Moleskine notebooks were the phone numbers of everyone on earth who had ever amounted to anything. If you had asked him for the queen of England's unlisted personal line he would have found it in an instant.

Robyn, blond, blue-eyed, anguished, not at all his type, invited him to dinner in her tiny house in Annandale and the thunderbolt hit them both hard. When she went to get the roast chicken she found it was still cold. She had been so distracted that she had forgotten to turn the oven on. Their three-year affair began the next morning and was the polar opposite of his long, calm, mostly happy relationship with Clarissa. They were strongly attracted to each other but in every other way incompatible. They yelled at each other almost every day.

She took him out into the Australian outback and he, the city mouse, was awed by her ability to survive in the wilderness. They slept under the stars and were not murdered by scorpions or eaten by kangaroos or stomped flat by the giant Old Woman Dreamtime Ancestor, Dancing. It was an extraordinary gift to be given. They transported her camels from a "station" or ranch in the Australian northwest, near Shark Bay (where he swam with dolphins and saw a house built entirely out of shells), down to new accommodations on a friend's property to the south of Perth. He learned two new things about camels. The first thing was that camels are happily incestuous; the baby of this group was the result of an uncomplicated union between a male camel and his mother. (This incest camel was given his name, or an Australianized version of it. It became "Selman the Camel.") And the second thing was that when a camel is upset its shit changes from dry innocuous pellets to a liquid spray that blasts out a considerable distance behind the aggrieved dromedary. You should never stray behind a grumpy camel. These were both important lessons.

She moved to England but it proved impossible for them to live together and in their final year they broke up more than a dozen times. Two months after their last separation he awoke in the middle of the night in his new home, the house on St. Peter's Street, and there was someone in his bedroom. He leaped naked to his feet. She had used her key to get in—he had not changed the locks—and she insisted that they "had to talk." When he refused and tried to leave the room she grabbed him and, at one point, stamped hard with her heel on his foot. After that one of his toes lost all feeling. "If I were a woman and you were a man," he asked her, "what would you call this?" That got through to her and she left. When she published her first and only novel, *Ancestors,* it featured a highly unpleasant American character who became the sadistic lover of the main female character. In an interview she gave to *The Guardian* she was asked, "Was he based on Salman Rushdie?" and she replied, "Not as much as in the first draft."

There was a novel growing in him but its exact nature eluded him. He had fragments of narratives and characters, and an obstinate instinct that in spite of the enormous differences between these fragments, they all belonged in the same book. The precise shape and nature of the book remained obscure. It would be a big book, he knew that much, ranging widely over space and time. A book of journeys. That felt right. After he finished *Shame* the first part of his plan had been completed. He had dealt, as well as he knew how to deal, with the worlds from which he had come. Now he needed to connect those worlds to the very different world in which he had made his life. He was beginning to see that this, rather than India or Pakistan or politics or magic realism, would be his real subject, the one he would worry away at for the rest of his life, the great matter of *how the world joined up,* not only how the East flowed into the West and the West into the East, but how the past shaped the present while the present changed our understanding of the past, and how the imagined world, the location of dreams, art, invention and, yes, belief, leaked across the frontier that separated it from the everyday, "real" place in which human beings mistakenly believed they lived.

This was what had happened to the shrinking planet: People—communities, cultures—no longer lived in little boxes, sealed away from one another. Now all the little boxes opened up into all the other little boxes, a man's job in one country could be lost because of the machinations of a currency speculator from a faraway land whose name he didn't know and whose face he would never see, and, as the theorists of the new science of chaos told us, when a butterfly flapped its wings in Brazil it could cause a hurricane in Texas. The original opening sentence of *Midnight's Children* had been "Most of what matters in our lives takes place in our absence," and even though in the end he had buried it elsewhere in the text, thinking it too Tolstoyan an opening—if there was one thing *Midnight's Children* was not, it was not *Anna Karenina*—the idea continued to nag at him. How to tell the stories of such a world, a world in which character was no longer always destiny, in which your fate could be determined not by your own choices but by those of strangers, in which economics could be destiny, or a bomb?

He was on a plane home from Sydney, with his emotions running high after his first few overwhelming days with Robyn. He took out a little black notebook and, to control himself, made himself think about his half-formed book. This was what he had: a bunch of migrants, or, to use the British term, "immigrants," from India, Pakistan and Bangladesh, through whose personal journeys he could explore the joinings-up and also disjointednesses of *here* and *there, then* and *now,* reality and dreams. He had the beginnings of a character named Salahuddin Chamchawala, Anglicized to Saladin Chamcha, who had a difficult relationship with his father and had retreated into Englishness. He liked the name "Chamcha" for its echoes of Kafka's poor metamorphosed dung beetle, Gregor Samsa, and of Gogol's scavenger of dead souls, Chichikov. Also for the meaning of the name in Hindustani, literally "spoon," but colloquially "toady" or "sycophant." Chamcha would be a portrait of a deracinated man, fleeing from his father and country, from Indianness itself, toward an Englishness that wasn't really letting him in, an actor with many voices who did well as long as he remained unseen, on radio and doing TV voiceovers; whose face was, in spite of all his Anglophilia, still "the wrong colour for their colour TVs."

And opposite Chamcha . . . well, a fallen angel, perhaps.

In 1982 the actor Amitabh Bachchan, the biggest star of the Bombay cinema, had suffered a near-fatal injury to his spleen while doing his own movie stunts in Bangalore. In the months that followed, his hospitalization was daily front-page news. Crowds waited outside the hospital for news, and politicians rushed to his bedside. As he lay close to death the nation held its breath; when he rose again the effect was almost Christlike. There were actors in south India who had attained almost godlike status by portraying the gods in movies called "mythologicals." Bachchan had become semidivine even without the benefit of such a career. But what if a god–actor, afflicted by a terrible injury, had called out to his god in his hour of need and heard no reply? What if, as a result of that appalling divine silence, such a man were to begin to question, or even to lose, the faith that had sustained him? Might he, in such a crisis of the soul, begin to lose his mind? And might he in his dementia flee halfway across the world, forgetting that when you run away you can't leave yourself behind?

What would such a falling star be called? The name came to him at once, as if it had been floating thirty-five thousand feet above sea level all this time, waiting for him to capture it. *Gibreel.* The Angel Gabriel, "Gibreel Farishta." Gibreel and Chamcha: the angel who had been abandoned by God and the faux-Englishman who had been estranged from his father. Two lost souls in the roofless continuum of the unhoused. They would be his protagonists. This much he knew.

If Gibreel was an angel, was Chamcha a devil? Or might an angel become demonic and could a devil wear a halo too?

The journeys multiplied. Here was a fragment from somewhere else entirely. In February 1983 thirty-eight Shia Muslims, followers of a man named Sayyad Willayat Hussain Shah, were convinced by him that God would part the waters of the Arabian Sea at his request, so that they could make a pilgrimage across the ocean floor to the holy city of Karbala in Iraq. They followed him into the waters and many of them were drowned. The most extraordinary part of the incident was that some of those who survived claimed, in spite of all the evidence to the contrary, to have witnessed the miracle. He had been thinking about this story for over a year now. He didn't want to write about Pakistan, or Shias, so in his imagination the believers became Sunni, and Indian, and their leader became female. He remembered a giant banyan tree he had once seen in south India near Mysore, a tree so large that there were huts and wells inside it, and clouds of butterflies. A village began to take shape in his mind, Titlipur, Butterfly Town, and the mystic girl moved in a butterfly cloud. As Sunnis they wanted to go to Mecca, not Karbala, but the idea of the parting of the sea was still at the heart of this tale.

And other fragments crowded in, many of them about the "city visible but unseen," immigrant London in the Age of Thatcher. The actually-existing London neighborhoods of Southall in west London and Brick Lane to the east, where Asian immigrants lived, merged with Brixton, south of the river, to form the imaginary central London borough of Brickhall, in which a Muslim family of orthodox parents and rebellious teenage daughters ran the Shaandaar Café, its name a thinly disguised Urdu-ing of the real Brilliant Café in Southall. In this borough, interracial trouble was brewing, and perhaps, soon, the streets would burn.

And here, reinvented, was Clarissa, given the Richardsonian name of "Pamela Lovelace," and here, transformed from desert walker into mountaineer and from Christian into Jew, was an avatar of Robyn named Alleluia Cohen, or Cone. And here, for some reason, was Clarissa's grandmother, May Jewell, a grand old lady living by the beach in Pevensey Bay, Sussex. The Norman ships of 1066, she would tell anyone who listened, would have sailed through her living room; the coastline was a mile farther out to sea now than it had been nine centuries ago. Granny May had many tales to tell—and told them many times, always in the same, ritual phrases—of her Anglo-Argentine past on an *estancia* called Las Petacas in the company of a vague, philatelic husband, Charles "Don Carlos" Jewell, several hundred gauchos, *very fierce and proud,* and a herd of prime Argentine cattle.

When the British ruled a quarter of the world they went forth from their cold little northern island and became, on the great plains and beneath the immense skies of India and Africa, more glamorous, extroverted, operatic personalities—bigger characters—than there was room for back home. But then the age of empires ended and they had to diminish back into their smaller, colder, grayer island selves. Granny May in her little turret house, dreaming of the infinite pampas and the prize bulls who came like unicorns to lay their heads in her lap, seemed like such a figure, and all the more interesting, less clichéd, because her story had happened not in the territories of the British Empire, but in Argentina. He wrote down a name for her in his notebook. "Rosa Diamond."

He was flying over India now, still making notes. He remembered hearing an Indian politician on TV talking about the British prime minister and being unable to pronounce her name properly. "Mrs. Torture," he kept saying. "Mrs. Margaret Torture." This was unaccountably funny even though—perhaps *because*—Margaret Thatcher was obviously not a torturer. If this was to be a novel about Mrs. T.'s London, maybe there was room—*comic* room—for this variant of her name.

"The act of migration," he wrote, "puts into crisis everything about the migrating individual or group, everything about identity and selfhood and culture and belief. So if this is a novel about migration it must be that act of putting in question. It must perform the crisis it describes."

He wrote: "How does newness enter the world?"

And he wrote: "The Satanic verses."

Maybe there were three books here, or seven. Or none. He had actually tried to write the "Rosa Diamond" story once already, as a screenplay for Walter Donohue at the fledgling Channel Four, but after he had finished and delivered a first draft he asked Walter if he could withdraw it, because instinct told him he needed it for the novel, though he had no idea of how or where it would fit in. Maybe the "parting of the Arabian Sea" story was best treated as a separate book, and the Satanic verses material would be strongest by itself as well.

Why was he trying to force all his eggs into this one basket? Afterward he liked to think that the answer to these questions had come into his head when he was flying over Bombay. *These are scenes,* he found himself thinking as he flew over the city of his birth, *from the life of the Archangel Gabriel.* His conscious mind was, as usual, at odds with his unconscious, which kept throwing angels and miracles at his rationality and insisting that he find ways to incorporate them into his way of seeing. So, a book about angels and devils, but perhaps it would be difficult to know which was which. Angels could do terrible deeds in the service of allegedly holy principles, and it was possible to have much compassion for Lucifer, the rebel angel whose punishment for rising up against the stultifying absolutist harp music of God's will was, as Daniel Defoe put it, to be "confined to a vagabond, wandering, unsettled condition . . . without any certain abode . . . without any fixed place, or space, allowed him to rest the sole of his foot upon." This unhoused, exiled Satan was perhaps the heavenly patron of all exiles, all unhoused people, all those who were torn from their place and left floating, half-this, half-that, denied the rooted person's comforting, defining sense of having solid ground beneath their feet. So, scenes from the life of the Archangel and the Archdevil, in which his own sympathy lay more on the Devil's side, because, as Blake said of Milton, a true poet was of the Devil's party.

He didn't know the beginning of the novel until a year later. In June 1985 Air India Flight 182, the *Emperor Kanishka,* was blown up by Sikh terrorists fighting to carve an independent Sikh state, to be called Khalistan, out of the Indian Punjab. The plane fell into the Atlantic Ocean to the south of Ireland and among the 329 people who died (mostly Canadian Indians or Indian citizens) was his childhood friend Neelam Nath, on her way to Bombay with her children to see her parents G. V. Nath ("Uncle Nath") and Lila, his own parents' closest friends. Soon after he heard about this atrocity he wrote the scene in which Gibreel Farishta and Saladin Chamcha, traveling from Bombay to London, are in a plane that is blown up by Sikh terrorists. Gibreel and Saladin are luckier than Neelam was. They make a soft landing on the beach at Pevensey Bay, outside Rosa Diamond's house.

———

The book took more than four years to write. Afterward, when people tried to reduce it to an "insult," he wanted to reply, *I can insult people a lot faster than that.* But it did not strike his opponents as strange that a serious writer should spend a tenth of his life creating something as crude as an insult. That was because they refused to see him as a serious writer. In order to attack him and his work it was necessary to paint him as a bad person, an apostate traitor, an unscrupulous seeker of fame and wealth, an opportunist whose work was without merit, who "attacked Islam" for his own personal gain. This was what was meant by the much repeated phrase *He did it on purpose.*

Well, of course he had done it on purpose. How would one write a quarter of a million words by accident? The problem was, as Bill Clinton might have said, what one meant by "it." The strange truth was that, after two novels that engaged directly with the public history of the Indian subcontinent, he saw this new book as a much more personal, interior exploration, a first attempt to create a work out of his own experience of migration and metamorphosis: To him, it was the least political book of the three. And the material derived from the origin story of Islam was, he thought, essentially admiring of the Prophet of Islam and even respectful toward him. It treated him as he always said he wanted to be treated, as a man ("the Messenger"), not a divine figure (like the Christians' "Son of God"). It showed him as a man of his time, shaped by that time, and, as a leader, both subject to temptation and capable of overcoming it. "What kind of idea are you?" the novel asked the new religion, and suggested that an idea that refused to bend or compromise would in most cases be destroyed, but conceded that, in very rare instances, such ideas became the ones that changed the world. His Prophet flirted with compromise, then rejected it; and his unbending idea grew strong enough to bend history to its will.

When he was first accused of being offensive, he was genuinely perplexed. He thought he had made an artistic engagement with the phenomenon of revelation; an engagement from the point of view of an unbeliever, certainly, but a proper one nonetheless. How could that be thought offensive? The thin-skinned years of rage-defined identity politics that followed taught him, and everyone else, the answer to that question.

Anyway, his Prophet was not called Muhammad, lived in a city not called Mecca, and created a religion not (or not quite) called Islam. And he appeared only in the dream sequences of a man being driven insane by his loss of faith. These many distancing devices were, in their creator's opinion, indicators of the fictive nature of his project. To his opponents, they were transparent attempts at concealment. "He is hiding," they said, "behind his fiction." As if fiction were a veil, or an arras, and a man might be run through by a sword if, like Polonius, he foolishly hid behind such a flimsy shield.

While he was writing the novel he received an invitation from the American University in Cairo, asking him to come and talk to their students. They said they couldn't pay him much but they could, if he were interested, arrange for him to take a boat up the Nile for a few days in the company of one of their leading Egyptologists. To see the world of ancient Egypt was one of his great unfulfilled dreams and he wrote back quickly. "If I could just finish my novel and arrange to come after that, that would be best," he suggested. Then he finished the novel, and it was *The Satanic Verses,* and a trip to Egypt became impossible, and he had to accept that he might never see the Pyramids, or Memphis, or Luxor, or Thebes, or Abu Simbel. It was one of the many futures he would lose.

In January 1986 the writing was not going well. He was invited to attend what became a legendary gathering of writers, the 48th Congress of International PEN in New York, and he was grateful to escape his desk. The congress was quite a show. Norman Mailer was president of PEN American Center back then, and had used all his powers of persuasion and charm to raise the funds that brought more than fifty of the world's leading writers to Manhattan to debate, with almost one hundred of America's finest, the exalted theme of "The Writer's Imagination and the Imagination of the State," and to be wined and dined at, among other tony locations, Gracie Mansion and the Metropolitan Museum of Art's Temple of Dendur.

As one of the younger participants he was more than a little awestruck. Brodsky, Grass, Oz, Soyinka, Vargas Llosa, Bellow, Carver,

Doctorow, Morrison, Said, Styron, Updike, Vonnegut, Barthelme, and Mailer himself were some of the big names reading their work and arguing with one another at the Essex House and St. Moritz hotels on Central Park South. One afternoon he was asked by the photographer Tom Victor to sit in one of the park's horse-drawn carriages for a picture, and when he climbed in, there were Susan Sontag and Czesław Miłosz to keep him company. He was not usually a tongue-tied individual but he said very little during that ride.

The atmosphere was electric from the start. Much to the chagrin of PEN members, Mailer had invited Secretary of State George Shultz to speak at the opening ceremony, at the Public Library. This prompted howls of protest by the South African writers Nadine Gordimer, J. M. Coetzee and Sipho Sepamla, who accused Shultz of supporting apartheid. Other writers, including E. L. Doctorow, Grace Paley, Elizabeth Hardwick, and John Irving, protested that writers were being set up "as a forum for the Reagan administration," as Doctorow put it.

Cynthia Ozick circulated a petition attacking Bruno Kreisky, the Jewish ex-chancellor of Austria and a congress participant, because he had met with Arafat and Gadhafi. (Kreisky's defenders pointed out that during his chancellorship, Austria had taken in more refugee Russian Jews than any other country.) During a panel discussion Ozick rose from the floor to denounce Kreisky, who handled the situation with such grace that the trouble quickly passed.

Many women at the congress demanded, with much justification, to know why there were so few women on the panels. Sontag and Gordimer, both panelists, did not join the revolt. It was Susan who came up with the argument that "literature is not an equal opportunity employer." This remark did not improve the protesters' mood. Nor did his own observation that while there were, after all, several women on the various panels, he himself was the sole representative of South Asia, which was to say, of one-sixth of the human race.

In those days in New York literature felt important, and the arguments between the writers were widely reported and seemed still to matter outside the narrow confines of the world of books. John Updike delivered a quietist paean to the little blue mailboxes of America, those everyday symbols of the free exchange of ideas, to a considerably

bewildered audience of world writers. Donald Barthelme was drunk
and Edward Said was friendly. At the party at the Temple of Dendur,
Rosario Murillo—the poet and companion of the Sandinista president
of Nicaragua, Daniel Ortega—stood next to the Egyptian shrine surrounded by a phalanx of astonishingly beautiful, dangerous-looking
Sandinista men in sunglasses. She invited the young Indian writer (and
member of the British Nicaragua Solidarity Campaign) to come and
see the *contra* war for himself.

In one of the sessions he was dragged into the heavyweight prize
fight between Saul Bellow and Günter Grass. He was sitting next to
the German novelist, whom he greatly admired, and after Bellow—
also one of his favorite writers—made a speech containing a familiar
Bellovian riff about how the success of American materialism had
damaged the spiritual life of Americans, Grass rose to point out that
many people routinely fell through the holes in the American dream,
and offered to show Bellow some real American poverty in, for example, the South Bronx. Bellow, irritated, spoke sharply in return.
When Grass returned to his seat, he was trembling with anger.

"Say something," the author of *The Tin Drum* ordered the representative of one-sixth of the human race.

"Who, me?"

"Yes. Say something."

So he went to the microphone and asked Bellow why it was that
so many American writers had avoided—or, actually, more provoca-
tively, "abdicated"—the task of taking on the subject of America's
immense power in the world. Bellow bridled. "We don't have tasks,"
he said, majestically. "We have inspirations."

Yes, literature still felt important in 1986. In those last years of the
cold war, it was important to hear Eastern European writers like Danilo
Kiš and Czesław Miłosz, György Konrád and Ryszard Kapuściński setting their visions against the visionless Soviet regime. Omar Cabezas,
Nicaragua's deputy interior minister at the time, who had just published a memoir of his life as a Sandinista guerrilla, and Mahmoud
Darwish, the Palestinian poet, were there to articulate views not often
heard on American platforms; and American writers such as Robert
Stone and Kurt Vonnegut did indeed offer their critiques of American

power, while the Bellows and Updikes looked inward into the American soul. In the end it was the gravity of the event, not the levity, that was memorable. Yes, in 1986 it still felt natural for writers to claim to be, as Shelley said, "the unacknowledged legislators of the world," to believe in the literary art as the proper counterweight to power, and to see literature as a lofty, transnational, transcultural force that could, in Bellow's great formulation, "open the universe a little more." Twenty years later, in a dumbed-down and frightened world, it would be harder to make such exalted claims for mere wordsmiths. Harder, but no less necessary, perhaps.

Back in London he remembered the invitation to Nicaragua. Maybe, he thought, it would do him good to get away from his small literary difficulties and go and report on people with real problems. He flew to Managua in July. When he returned several weeks later he had been so affected by what he saw that he could not stop thinking or talking about it and became a Nicaragua bore. The only way forward was to write his feelings down. He sat at his desk in a sort of frenzy and wrote a ninety-page text in three weeks. That was neither one thing nor another, too short to be a book, too long to be an article. In the end, revised and expanded, it did grow into a short book, *The Jaguar Smile*. The day he finished it, he dedicated it to Robyn Davidson (they were still just about together then) and gave it to her to read. When she saw the dedication she said, "I suppose this means I won't get the novel," and the conversation spiraled downward from there.

His agent Deborah Rogers didn't much care for *The Jaguar Smile*, but it was rush-published by Sonny Mehta at Picador UK and, soon afterward, by Elisabeth Sifton at Viking USA. On his U.S. book tour a radio talk-show host in San Francisco, displeased by the book's opposition to the American economic blockade of Nicaragua and the Reagan administration's support of the *contra* forces fighting to topple the Sandinista government, asked him, "Mr. Rushdie, to what extent are you a Communist stooge?" His surprised laughter—this was on live radio—annoyed his host more than any answer he might have given.

His favorite moments came when he was being interviewed by

Bianca Jagger, herself a Nicaraguan, for *Interview* magazine. Whenever he mentioned a prominent Nicaraguan, whether left- or right-wing, Bianca would reply, vaguely, neutrally, "Oh, yes, I used to date him once." This was the truth about Nicaragua. It was a small country with a very small elite class. The warring combatants had all gone to school together, were all members of that elite and knew one another's families, or even, in the case of the divided Chamorro dynasty, came from the same family; and they had all dated one another. Bianca's (unwritten) version of events would be more interesting—certainly more intimate—than his own.

Once *The Jaguar Smile* had been published he returned to his troublesome novel, and discovered that the problems had largely disappeared. Unusually for him, he had not written the book in narrative sequence. The interpolated passages—the story of the village that walked into the sea, the account of an imam who first led and then ate a revolution, and the subsequently contentious dream sequences set in a city of sand named Jahilia (a name taken from the Arabic term for the period of "ignorance" that preceded the coming of Islam)—had been written first, and for a long time he hadn't understood exactly how he should stitch them into the book's main, framing narrative, the story of Saladin and Gibreel. But the break had done him good, and he began to write.

Forty had weight. At forty a man came into his manhood and felt substantial, grounded, strong. On his thirtieth birthday he had thought himself a failure, and had been wretchedly unhappy. On his fortieth, on a golden June afternoon at Bruce Chatwin's home, in a sylvan setting near Oxford, he was surrounded by literary friends—Angela Carter; Nuruddin Farah; Bill Buford, the editor of *Granta;* his own editor Liz Calder of Jonathan Cape (still an independent publishing company then, before it was gobbled up by Random House); and Bruce himself—and he was happy. Life seemed to have worked out as he had dreamed it might, and he was working on what felt like his most formally and intellectually ambitious book, whose obstacles had finally been overcome. The future was bright.

It would soon be the fortieth anniversary of India's independence—"Saleem's fortieth birthday"—and he was persuaded by his
friend Jane Wellesley, a television producer, another guest at his birthday party, to write and present a feature-length "state of the nation"
documentary for Channel Four. His idea was to avoid public and political figures entirely, or almost entirely, and make a portrait of India at
forty, a consideration of the "idea of India," through the eyes and in
the voices of forty-year-old Indians; not quite midnight's children, but
children of the year of freedom, at least. He embarked on his longest
Indian journey since he and Clarissa had crisscrossed the country more
than a decade earlier. This second journey was just as gluttonous. The
Indian horn of plenty poured its excess of stories into him once again.
Give me excess of it, he thought, *that I may surfeit, and so die.*

On one of the first days of the shoot the project was almost de-
railed by a moment of cultural insensitivity. They were filming in the
home of a Delhi tailor, in one of the poorer parts of the city. It was a
very hot day and after a couple of hours the crew took a break. Crates
of ice-cold fizzy drinks were brought from the back of a production
van and distributed to everyone *except the tailor and his family.* He asked
the director, Geoff Dunlop, for a private word and they went up to the
flat roof of the tailor's home and he told Geoff that if the situation
wasn't rectified at once he would walk off the film, and if anything like
it ever happened again that would be the end of it for sure. Then it
occurred to him to ask what sort of location fee was being paid. Geoff
named a sum of rupees that converted to a very low sterling amount.
"That isn't what you'd pay in England," he said. "You should give
them your normal location fee." "But," Geoff said, "in India that
would be a fortune." "That isn't your business," he replied. "You have
to treat people here with the same respect you'd show back home."
For a few beats there was a standoff between them. Then Geoff said,
"Okay," and they went back downstairs. The tailor and his family were
offered cold Cokes. The rest of the shoot went smoothly.

In Kerala he watched a famous oral storyteller work his magic. The
interesting thing about this performance was that it broke all the rules.
"Begin at the beginning," the King of Hearts had instructed the flus-
tered White Rabbit in *Alice's Adventures in Wonderland,* "and go on

until you come to the end; then stop." This was how stories were meant to be told, according to whichever king of hearts had made up the rules, but this was not what happened in that open-air Keralan theater. The storyteller stirred stories into one another, digressed frequently from the main narrative, told jokes, sang songs, connected his political story to the ancient tales, made personal asides, and generally misbehaved. And yet the audience did not get up and walk out in disgust. It did not hiss or boo or throw vegetables or benches at the performer. Instead, it roared with laughter, wept in despair, and remained on the edge of its seat until he was done. Did it do so in spite of the storyteller's complicated story-juggling act, or *because of it*? Might it be that this pyrotechnic way of telling might in fact be *more* engrossing than the King of Hearts' preferred version—that the oral story, the most ancient of narrative forms, had survived because of its adoption of complexity and playfulness and its rejection of start-to-finish linearity? If so, then here in this warm Keralan night all his own thoughts about writing were being amply confirmed.

If you gave ordinary people a voice, and enough time to use it, an everyday poetry flowed movingly from them. A Muslim woman sleeping in a *jhopadpatti,* a Bombay sidewalk shack, spoke of her suspicions about her children's willingness to care for her in later life. "When I am old, when I must walk with a stick, then we'll see what they will do." He asked her what it meant to her to be an Indian and she answered that she had lived all her life in India and "when I die and am put in my grave, then I will go into India." A sweetly smiling Communist lady in Kerala worked hard in the rice fields all day and then came home to her much older husband, who sat on their veranda rolling *beedis* for money. "Since I got married," she said, still smiling, and well within her husband's earshot, "I have never had one day of joy."

There was some black comedy. The only politician he interviewed was Chaggan Bhujbal, the first mayor of Bombay to be a member of the Shiv Sena, the thuggish Marathi-nationalist and Hindu communalist party headed by a former political cartoonist, Bal Thackeray. Chaggan Bhujbal was a walking political cartoon. He allowed the TV crew to accompany him to the annual Ganpati celebrations and film how that festival in honor of elephant-headed Ganesh, which was once a day of celebration for members of all religious backgrounds, had been reduced to a fist-pumping, neo-Nazi assertion of Hindu power. "You can call us fascist," he said. "We *are* fascist. And you can call us racist. We *are* racist." On his desk, in his office, was a telephone in the shape of a green plastic frog. The brilliant cameraman, Mike Fox, unobtrusively filmed it. But when they saw the rushes they decided to leave the frog out. It was impossible not to feel a little rush of love for a man who spoke vehemently to a green frog. They did not want the film's viewers to feel that affection, and so the frog was left on the cutting-room floor. But nothing is ever lost. The frog, and the name *Mainduck* (frog), would eventually make their way into *The Moor's Last Sigh.*

The great mosque of Old Delhi, the Juma Masjid, was flying black flags to mark the killings of Muslims in the town of Meerut. He wanted to film at the mosque and old Imam Bukhari, a firebrand and an ultra-conservative, agreed to meet him because "Salman Rushdie" was a Muslim name. He met the imam in his "garden," a heavily cordoned-off area of earth and stone and not a single blade of grass. The imam, gap-toothed, ample, fierce, his beard tinged with henna, sat in an armchair with his legs spread wide and an enormous number of crumpled currency notes in his lap. Aides stood all around, guarding him. Next to him there was an empty chair with a woven cane seat. As he spoke he smoothed and rolled the rupee notes one by one until they looked like the *beedis* another old man had been rolling on a veranda in Kerala. When he was satisfied with his work on a banknote he stuck it into one of the holes in the cane seat bottom, which quickly filled up with these rupee-*beedis,* the largest notes nearest the imam, the lower denominations farthest away. "Yes," he said. "You can film." After the Khomeini *fatwa* this same Imam Bukhari denounced the author of *The Satanic Verses* from the pulpit of the Juma Masjid without knowing that they had once had a more or less cordial encounter. But he made a mistake. He failed to remember the author's name correctly and denounced "Salman Khurshid" instead. Salman Khurshid was a prominent Muslim politician. This was embarrassing, both for the imam and for the "wrong Salman."

In Kashmir he spent several days with a group of traveling players who performed *bhand pather* or, literally, "clown stories," of Kashmiri history and legend, one of the last such troupes, driven to near penury by the harshness and violence of the political situation in Kashmir, but also by movies and TV. They were eloquent about their lives and ferocious in their criticisms of the authoritarian Indian military and security forces; but whenever the camera was turned on they lied. Too afraid of the consequences to be honest on the record, they said, "Oh, we love the Indian Army." Because he could not get their story on film he had to cut them out of the final version of the documentary, but he never forgot their unfilmed stories, never forgot the woodland glade full of tumbling and tightrope-walking children where a next generation of "clowns" was being trained, clowns who might no longer have an audience to perform to, who might even, when they were grown, relinquish the fake swords of actors and pick up the real guns of the Islamic jihad. Many years later they became the heart of his "Kashmir novel" *Shalimar the Clown.*

Most eloquent of all his witnesses was R., a Sikh woman living in a Delhi tenement whose husband and children had been murdered before her eyes by the mobs, incited and perhaps even directed by Congress Party leaders, who had "taken revenge" against the entire Sikh community for the assassination of Indira Gandhi on October 31, 1984, by two Sikh bodyguards, Beant Singh and Satwant Singh, who were loyal to the separatist Khalistan movement and killed her to avenge the attack on the Sikh holy of holies, the Golden Temple, where the leader of the movement, Sant Jarnail Singh Bhindran-wale, had holed up with many of his gunmen. Three years later the widow, R., had the grace and strength to say, "I don't want revenge, or violence, or Khalistan. I just want justice. That is all I want."

To his amazement the Indian authorities had refused him permission to film her, or any material related to the Sikh killings. But he managed to get her testimony on audiotape and in the finished film her photograph was one of many such widows used in a photo montage that was if anything even more powerful than her moving image would have been. The Indian High Commission in London reacted by trying to force Channel Four to cancel the screening of the documentary. But the screening went ahead as scheduled. It was astonishing that—as an aspect of the cover-up of the ruling party's involvement in the atrocities, during which many thousands of Sikhs died—the Indian government had tried to suppress the testimony, not of a terrorist, but of a victim of terrorism; and laudable that the television network had had the courage and principle to reject their appeal.

To leave India was to feel replete: full of ideas, arguments, images, sounds, smells, faces, stories, sensuality, intensity, and love. He did not know it then, but this was the beginning of a long exile. After India became the first country in the world to ban *The Satanic Verses* it would also refuse to give him a travel visa. (UK citizens needed visas to visit India.) He would not be allowed to come back, to *come home,* for twelve and a half years.

He heard about his father's cancer while they were editing the film, which was now called *The Riddle of Midnight.* His brother-in-law Safwan, married to his youngest sister, Nabeelah (known in the family as "Guljum," *sweetheart*), called from Karachi to say that Anis had multiple myeloma, cancer of the bone marrow. He was receiving treatment, but there wasn't much that could be done. There was one drug, Melphalan, that could give him some months, maybe even a couple of years, if he responded to it well. It wasn't clear yet how he was responding, so it was hard to say how long he had. "What should I do?" he wondered. "Maybe Sameen and I should come one after the other, because then Amma would always have one of us there at least." (Sameen had returned to live in London, working in community relations.) There was a pause and then Safwan gravely said, "Salman *bhai,* just come. Just get on a plane and come." He spoke to Jane Wellesley and Geoff Dunlop and they both agreed at once. "Just go." Two days later he arrived in Pakistan, and was there in time for the last six days of his father's life.

They were loving days, a kind of return to innocence. He had agreed with himself to un-know all the bad things, the overheard parental quarrels of his childhood, the drunken abuse to which he had been subjected in the Cumberland Hotel in London in January 1961, and the day he punched his father on the jaw. He had been twenty years old and suddenly Anis's alcoholic rages were too much to take, especially because on this occasion his mother had been the target. He hit his father and then thought, *Oh, god, now he's going to hit me back.* Anis was short but very strong, with butcher's forearms, and a blow from him would have been devastating. But Anis did not hit his son— he just walked silently away, feeling ashamed. None of that mattered now. Anis in the Aga Khan hospital in Karachi was no longer strong. His face was drawn and his body emaciated. He looked gentle, and ready. "I told them from the beginning it was a cancer," he said. "I asked them, where has all the blood gone?" Long ago, when he read *Midnight's Children,* Anis had been incensed by the character of "Ahmed Sinai," also a father with a drinking problem. He had refused to speak to his son and had threatened to divorce his wife for "putting the boy up to it." He had calmed down when the book became a success and his friends called to congratulate him. He told Salman, "When you have a baby on your lap, sometimes it wets you, but you forgive it." After which the son felt insulted by the father, and the strain between them remained. All that was gone now. Anis held his son's hand and whispered to him, "I was angry because every word you wrote was true."

In the next days they re-created their love until it was there, theirs again, as if it had never been lost. In Proust's great novel-sequence the aim is to recapture the past not through the distorting prism of memory but *as it was.* This was what they were able to do with love. *L'amour retrouvé.* Tenderly, one afternoon, he picked up an electric shaver and shaved his father's face.

Anis was weak, and after a few days he wanted to go home. The house in Karachi was the opposite of Windsor Villa in Bombay, a modern split-level building rather than an old villa. There were frogs croaking in the empty swimming pool, sitting in the small puddle of green stagnant water in the deep end and singing through the night. Once when Anis was healthy he had been driven mad by the racket and had run downstairs from his bedroom in the middle of the night and swatted many of the frogs with a rubber swimming flipper. He knocked out several of them but did not kill them. By the morning they had all regained consciousness and had hopped away, out of sight. Clearly frogs were made of rubber too.

Now Anis could not go upstairs to his bedroom. A bed was made for him in his study on the ground floor and he lay there surrounded by books. It turned out he was flat broke. In the top left-hand desk drawer there were blocks of five-hundred-rupee notes, and that was all the money he had left. His bank accounts were in the red. There were some small debts against the house. He had reached the end of the line.

Over dinner Safwan, Guljum's husband and a successful electronic engineer, told a strange story. He claimed to have personally smuggled into Pakistan the world's fastest computer, the so-called FPS or Floating Point System, which boasted something called VAX "accessing equipment." This computer could make seventy-six million calculations a second. The human brain could make just eighteen. "Even top ordinary computers," he said, "can only make one million calculations." Then he explained that the FPS was essential for the building of the Islamic nuclear bomb. Even in the United States there were only about twenty such computers. "If it was known that we have one sitting in our Lahore warehouse," he said, smiling happily, "all international aid to Pakistan would be canceled."

This was Pakistan. When he visited Pakistan he lived in the bubble of his family, and a few friends who were really Sameen's old friends, not his. Outside the bubble was a country from which he had always felt profoundly alien. Every so often news like Safwan's, from outside the bubble, would make him want to catch the first plane out and never return. Such news was invariably delivered by sweet-natured, smiling people, and in the contradiction between their nature and their deeds lay the schizophrenia that was tearing the country apart.

In the end Safwan and Guljum separated and that beautiful girl began a long slide toward immense, shocking obesity, mental problems, and drug abuse. One day, in her midforties, she would be found dead in her bed, the youngest child of four and the first to depart. Because he was banned from the country he was unable to attend her funeral, just as he had been unable to bury his mother. When Negin Rushdie died a Pakistani newspaper ran an article saying that all those who had been at her funeral should beg forgiveness of God because she was the mother of the apostate author. These were additional reasons for disliking Pakistan.

Anis's moment came in the middle of the night on November 11, 1987, less than two days after his return home from hospital. Salman had to take him to the toilet and clean him after the black diarrhea leaked out of him. Then he vomited immensely into a bucket and they put him in the car and Sameen drove like the wind to the Aga Khan hospital. Afterward he thought they should have kept him at home and let him slip quietly away, but at the time they all deluded themselves that the hospital could save his life, so that they could keep him for a while longer. It would have been better to spare him the useless violence of the electricity in his last moments. But he was not spared, and it did not work, and then he was gone, and Negin, in spite of her long difficult marriage, sank to the ground and wailed, "He swore he would never leave me and now he has gone and what will I do?"

He put his arm around his mother. He would look after her now.

The Aga Khan hospital, the best facility in Karachi, was free to all Ismailis but extremely expensive for non-Ismailis, which was fair enough, he thought. They would not release his father's body until the bill was paid. Fortunately he had an American Express card in his pocket and used it to buy his father back from the hospital where he had died. When they brought him home, the impression of his body was still visible in his bedsheets and his old slippers sat on the floor. The men came, family and friends, because this was a hot country and the burial would take place in a few hours. He should have been the one making the arrangements but he was helpless in this alien land and didn't know who to call and so Sameen's friends found the graveyard and arranged for a bier and even—this was compulsory—summoned a mullah from the local mosque, a modern building that looked like a poured-concrete version of Buckminster Fuller's geodesic dome.

They washed Anis—it was the first time he had ever seen his father's naked body—and the shroud tailor sewed him into his winding sheet. The cemetery was nearby and when the bier arrived, fragrant with flowers and sandalwood shavings, the grave yawned ready. The grave digger stood at the foot end while he climbed down at the head end and they lowered Anis into the hole. To stand in his father's grave and place his hand under the dead man's shrouded head, to lay that head upon its last resting place, was a thing of immense power. He felt sad that his father, a man of great culture and learning, born in Ghalib's Old Delhi *muhallah* of Ballimaran and afterward for decades a happy Bombayite, should have come to so poor an end in a place that had not proved to be good for him and had never felt like his. Anis Ahmed Rushdie was a disappointed man but at least he had ended his days knowing that he was loved. As he climbed out of the grave he tore the nail on the big toe of his left foot and had to go to the local Jinnah hospital for a tetanus shot.

In the years that followed Anis visited his son's dreams perhaps once a month. In those dreams he was invariably affectionate, witty, wise, understanding and supportive: the best of fathers. It struck him that their relationship after Anis's death was a big improvement on the way things had been when his father was still alive.

Saladin Chamcha in *The Satanic Verses* had a difficult relationship with his father, Changez Chamchawala, as well. In the original plan for the novel Changez died, too, but his son didn't get back to Bombay in time to see him before the end, and as a result was left carrying the burden of the unresolved conflict between them. But the happiness and deep feeling of those six days with his own father was the most important thing he brought back to London from Karachi. He made a big decision: He would allow Saladin and Changez to have the experience he had had with Anis. His father had only just died but he would write about his death. He was worried about the morality of doing this. Was it wrong, ghoulish, vampiric? He didn't know the answer. He told himself that if, in the doing of it, he felt that it was a sleazy thing to do, then he would destroy those pages and return to the original plan.

He used much that was true, even the details of the medication he had had to give Anis in those last days. "Apart from the daily Melphalan tablet, [Changez] had been prescribed a whole battery of drugs in an attempt to combat the cancer's pernicious side-effects: anaemia, the strain on the heart, and so on. Isosorbide dinitrate, two tablets, four times a day; Furosemide, one tablet, three times; Prednisolone, six tablets, twice daily." And so on. Agarol, Spironolactone, Allopurinol. An army of wonder drugs marched from reality into fiction.

He wrote about shaving his father's face—about Saladin shaving Changez's face—and about the dying man's uncomplaining courage in the face of death. *"First one falls in love with one's father all over again, and then one learns to look up to him, too."* He wrote about the black diarrhea and the vomiting and the voltage and the bedsheets and the slippers and the washing of the body and the burial. And he wrote this: *"He is teaching me how to die,* Salahuddin thought. *He does not avert his eyes, but looks death right in the face.* At no point in his dying did Changez Chamchawala speak the name of God."

That was how Anis Ahmed Rushdie died as well.

As he wrote this ending, it did not feel exploitative. It felt respectful. When it was complete, he knew it would remain in the book.

The day he left London to be with his father, Marianne found a scrap of paper in one of his trouser pockets. On it, in his handwriting, was Robyn's name and a line from a Beatles song, *excites me like no other lover.* He didn't recall writing it, or know how long the paper had been in his pocket—he hadn't seen Robyn in well over a year, and the note had probably been sitting in the pocket for longer than that—but it made Marianne jealous, and their parting was harsh. They had planned to celebrate her fortieth birthday in Paris. That would not happen now, because of Anis's illness.

He was still full of the emotion engendered by Anis's death when— in a long-distance telephone call—he asked Marianne to marry him. She accepted his proposal. On January 23, 1988, they were married at Finsbury Town Hall, had a wedding lunch with friends at Frederick's restaurant in Islington, and then spent the night at the Ritz. He only learned years afterward that his sister Sameen and his closest friends had been full of foreboding about the match but had not known how to tell him not to do it.

Four days later he wrote in his diary: "How easy it is to destroy a man! Your invented foe: how easily you can crush him; how fast he crumbles! Evil: ease is its seduction." Afterward he could not remember why he had written this. No doubt it was a thought for some aspect of his work in progress, though it did not make it into the finished book. But a year later it felt like—well, like a prophecy.

He also wrote this: "If I ever finish *The Satanic Verses,* in spite of emotional upheavals, divorce, house move, Nicaragua book, India film, et al., I will, I feel, have completed my 'first business,' that of naming the parts of myself. Then there will be nothing left to write about; except, of course, the whole of human life."

At 4:10 P.M. on Tuesday, February 16, 1988, he wrote in his diary in capital letters, "I REACHED THE END." On Wednesday, February 17, he made minor revisions and "declared the book finished." On Thursday he made photocopies and delivered the book to his agents. That weekend Sameen and Pauline began to read *The Satanic Verses.* Sameen finished reading it by Monday and was for the most part delighted by it. But the description of Changez's death left her feeling very disturbed. "I kept wanting to say, 'I was there, too. He didn't say that to you, he said it to me. You didn't do that for him, I did it.' But you have left me out of the story, and now everyone will always think that this is the way it was." He had no defenses against her accusations. "It's okay," she told him. "I've said my piece now. I'll get over it."

When a book leaves its author's desk it changes. Even before anyone has read it, before eyes other than its creator's have looked upon a single phrase, it is irretrievably altered. It has become *a book that can be read,* that no longer belongs to its maker. It has acquired, in a sense, free will. It will make its journey through the world and there is no longer anything the author can do about it. Even he, as he looks at its sentences, reads them differently now that they can be read by others. They look like different sentences. The book has gone out into the world and the world has remade it.

The Satanic Verses had left home. Its metamorphosis, its transformation by its engagement with the world beyond the author's desk, would be unusually extreme.

Throughout the writing of the book he had kept a note to himself pinned to the wall above his desk. "To write a book is to make a Faustian contract in reverse," it said. "To gain immortality, or at least posterity, you lose, or at least ruin, your actual daily life."

II

"Manuscripts Don't Burn"

"Tell me, why does Margarita call you the master?" enquired Woland.

The man laughed and said:

"An understandable weakness of hers. She has too high an opinion of a novel that I've written."

"Which novel?"

"A novel about Pontius Pilate." . . .

"About what? About whom?" said Woland, ceasing to laugh. "But that's extraordinary! In this day and age? Couldn't you have chosen another subject? Let me have a look." Woland stretched out his hand palm uppermost.

"Unfortunately I cannot show it to you," replied the master, "because I burned it in my stove."

"I'm sorry but I don't believe you," said Woland. "You can't have done. Manuscripts don't burn." He turned to Behemoth and said: "Come on, Behemoth, give me the novel."

The cat jumped down from its chair and where he had been sitting was a pile of manuscripts. With a bow the cat handed the top copy to Woland. Margarita shuddered and cried out, moved to tears: "There's the manuscript! There it is!"

—The Devil, Woland, gives the master back his destroyed novel in Mikhail Bulgakov's *The Master and Margarita*

IN THE SMALL HOURS OF FEBRUARY 15, 1989, HE LAY UNQUIET IN BED beside his sleeping wife. In the morning he would be visited by a senior officer from "A" Squad of the Special Branch of the Metropolitan Police, which was in charge of all personal protection in the United

Kingdom (except for the protection of the royal family, which was the job of the Royal Protection Squad). The Special Branch had originally been the Special Irish Branch, created, in 1883, to combat the Irish Republican Brotherhood, and until recently the main threats against which it protected individuals—the prime minister, the defense secretary, the foreign secretary, the Northern Ireland secretary, and various outspoken members of Parliament—came from the Brotherhood's descendants, the Provisional IRA. But terrorism had diversified and its opponents had to take on new enemies. Jewish community leaders required protection from time to time after receiving credible Islamist threats. And now there was this novelist, too, lying insomniac in the dark in Lonsdale Square. A mullah with a long arm was reaching out across the world to squeeze the life out of him. That was a police matter.

The man from the Branch would be accompanied by an intelligence officer and they would tell him what security decisions had been made concerning the threat. *Threat* was a technical term, and it was not the same as *risk*. The *threat level* was general, but *risk levels* were specific. The level of threat against an individual might be high—and it was for the intelligence services to determine this—but the level of risk attached to a particular action by that individual might be much lower, for example if nobody knew what he was planning to do, or when. Risk assessment was the job of the police protection team. These were concepts he would have to master, because threat and risk assessments would, from now on, shape his daily life. In the meanwhile he was thinking about the island of Mauritius.

Ten days after he delivered *The Satanic Verses,* Marianne finished her new novel, *John Dollar,* a novel involving cannibalism among characters marooned on a desert island that she insisted—unwisely, to his mind—on calling "a feminist *Lord of the Flies.*" On the night of the 1988 Booker Prize dinner, when *The Satanic Verses* finished runner-up to Peter Carey's *Oscar and Lucinda,* she even described it in these words to William Golding himself. This was most definitely unwise. Two days after she delivered her book they flew, along with Marianne's daughter Lara Porzak, a junior at Dartmouth and a budding photographer, to Mauritius on vacation. It was not a desert island, fortunately, so there was no "long pork" on the menu. It was his first ever experience of an "island paradise" holiday, and he was ready for a little lazy hedonism; the novel had drained him more completely than anything he had written before. While they were on the beach, Andrew Wylie in New York and Gillon Aitken in London sent out copies of *The Satanic Verses* and the wheels of the publishing business began to turn. He swam in water so warm that when you walked into it there was no alteration in temperature, and watched tropical sunsets, and drank drinks with fruit and umbrellas in them, and dined on the delicious local fish called *sacréchien,* and thought about Sonny Mehta at Knopf, Peter Mayer at Viking, and editors at Doubleday, Collins and elsewhere reading his big, strange book. He had brought a sack of books to read or re-read to take his mind off the forthcoming auction. He was considerably anxious to know its outcome, but during those idyllic days lapped by the Indian Ocean it was impossible to believe that anything might go wrong.

He should have paid attention to the birds. The dead flightless birds who had been unable to soar away from their predators, who tore them apart. Mauritius was the world capital, the extermination camp and mass graveyard, of extinct flightless birds.

"L'île Maurice," unusually for an island of its size, until the seventeenth century had no human population at all. However, forty-five species of bird had lived there, many of them unable to leave the ground, including the red rail, the solitaire, and the dodo. Then came the Dutch, who stayed there only from 1638 to 1710, but by the time they left all the dodoes were dead, slaughtered, for the most part, by the settlers' dogs. In all, twenty-four of the island's forty-five bird species were driven into extinction, as well as the previously plentiful tortoises and other creatures. There was a skeleton of a dodo in the museum in Port Louis. Its flesh had been revolting to human beings, but the dogs had been less picky. The dogs saw a helpless creature and ripped it to bits. They were trained hunting dogs, after all. They were unfamiliar with mercy.

The Dutch, and the French colonists who followed them, both imported African slaves to cultivate sugarcane. These slaves were not treated kindly. Punishments included amputations and executions. The

British conquered Mauritius in 1810 and in 1835 slavery was abolished. Almost all the slaves immediately fled the island on which they had been so cruelly used. To replace them the British shipped in a new population of indentured laborers from India. Most of the Indians living in Mauritius in 1988 had never seen India, but many still spoke an Indian dialect, Bhojpuri, which in a century and a half had undergone some local creolization but was still recognizable, and they were still Hindus and Muslims. To meet an Indian from India, an Indian who had walked real Indian streets and eaten real Indian pomfret instead of Mauritian *sacréchien,* who had been warmed by the Indian sun and drenched by the monsoon rains and who had gone swimming off the Indian coast in the actual Arabian Sea, was a kind of miracle. He was a visitor from an antique and mythic land, and they opened their homes to him. One of Mauritius's leading Hindi-language poets, who had in fact recently been to India for the first time in his life to attend a poetry congress, told him that his reading had mystified Indian audiences, because he read to convey meaning, in the manner that was "normal" to him, instead of declaiming his lines rhythmically, in the habitual fashion of Indian Hindi poets. It was a small cultural shift in "normality," a minor side effect of the migration of his indentured forebears, but it had had a profound impact on the distinguished poet, showing him that for all his mastery of India's largest language, he could not truly belong. The émigré Indian author to whom this story was told understood that belonging was a big, uneasy subject for them both. They had to answer questions that immobile one-place one-language one-culture writers did not, and they had to satisfy themselves that their answers were true. Who were they, and to what and whom did they belong? Or was the idea of belonging itself a trap, a cage from which they had been lucky enough to escape? He had concluded that the questions needed to be rephrased. The questions he knew how to answer were not about place or roots, but about love. *Who do you love? What can you leave behind, and what do you need to hold on to? Where does your heart feel full?*

Once, at the Cheltenham Literature Festival, at a dinner for the many Indian writers invited that year, he was told, apropos of nothing, by the Indian novelist Githa Hariharan, "Of course, your position in Indian literature is highly problematic." He was shocked and slightly hurt. "Really?" he replied, sounding foolish. "Oh, yes," she said emphatically. *"Highly."*

On the beach outside their hotel he met a small, slightly built man in a natty straw hat, selling tourist trinkets with unusual fervor. "Hello, sir, buy something, sir," the man said, smiling a huge smile, and adding, "My name is Body Building." It was as though Mickey Mouse had introduced himself as "Arnold Schwarzenegger." He shook his head. "No, it isn't," he said, and then switched into Hindi. "You must have an Indian name." The effect of the language was dramatic. "You are proper Indian, sir?" Body Building asked, also in Hindi. "From India proper?" In three days' time it would be Holi, the spring festival of colors, when all over India—and, apparently, in Mauritius too—people "played Holi," that is, drenched one another with colored water and threw colored powders at one another. "You must play Holi at my house," Body Building insisted, and the delighted laughter of the Holi players offered some release of the growing tension between himself and his companions. It was a good day in the five-week-old marriage that was already showing signs of strain. There were electric sparks crackling between Marianne and Lara, and himself and Lara, and himself and Marianne. The warm Indian Ocean could not wash that fact away, nor could the bright colors of Holi conceal it. "I'm in your shadow," Marianne said to him, and he saw the resentment on her face. Andrew Wylie and Gillon Aitken were her agents too. He had introduced her and they had taken her on. But now *The Satanic Verses* was being sold and her novel had to wait in line.

When they got back from the festivities, soaking wet and colored pink and green, there was a message from Andrew waiting for him. He called New York from the hotel bar. Celebratory sunset colors exploded across the sky. The bids were in. They were high, almost shockingly high, to his mind, more than ten times higher than his previous highest advance. But the big money came at a price. Two good friendships had been seriously damaged.

Liz Calder, his first and only editor and his close friend for fifteen years, had resigned from Jonathan Cape earlier that year to become one of the founders of the new Bloomsbury publishing house. Because of their friendship there was an assumption that he would follow her. At that time Andrew Wylie represented him only in the United States; his British agent was still the highly respected Deborah Rogers, also a close friend of Calder's. Deborah quickly agreed with Liz that "the new Rushdie" would go to Bloomsbury for a modest fee, as the new publishing house couldn't afford high advances. It was the kind of sweetheart deal that was common in British publishing, and he didn't like it. Andrew Wylie told him that if he accepted a low figure in the United Kingdom it would ruin the book's prospects in the United States. After much hesitation he agreed to allow Andrew, and his British counterpart, Gillon Aitken, to represent him worldwide. The sweetheart deal was canceled, Liz and Deborah were both deeply hurt, and the auction followed. It occurred to him to point out to Liz that, in fact, *she* had been the one who had left *him* by leaving Cape and going to Bloomsbury, but she wasn't inclined to listen to such arguments. There wasn't much to say to Deb. She was no longer his agent. There was no way to sugar-coat that pill.

Friendship had always been of great importance to him. He had spent much of his life physically distant from his family and also emotionally distant from much of it. Friends were the family one chose. Goethe used the scientific term *elective affinities* to propose that the connections of love, marriage and friendship between human beings were similar to chemical reactions. People were drawn to one another chemically to form stable compounds—marriages—or, when exposed to other influences, they fell apart from one another; one part of the compound was displaced by a new element and, perhaps, a new compound was formed. He himself didn't much like the use of chemistry as metaphor. It felt too determinist and left too little room for the action of human will. *Elective* to him meant *chosen,* not by one's unconscious biochemical nature but by one's conscious self. His love of his chosen friends, and of those who had chosen him, had sustained and nourished him; and the wounds his actions had inflicted, even though they were justifiable in business terms, felt humanly wrong.

He had met Liz through Clarissa's closest friend, Rosanne Edge-Partington, in the early seventies. Clarissa's mother, Lavinia, had recently emigrated to the village of Mijas in the south of Spain, General Franco's favorite Andalusian beauty spot, a magnet for ultracon- servative expatriates from all over Europe, and, eventually, the model for the fictional but not dissimilar village of Benengeli in *The Moor's Last Sigh.* She sold her large house at 35 Lower Belgrave Street to the actors Michael Redgrave and Rachel Kempson, who later sold it— strangely enough—to the wife of the dictator of Nicaragua, Hope Somoza; but Lavinia kept the smaller maisonette, No. 37a, which had originally been attached to the main house, for her daughter to live in. Clarissa and he lived there for three and a half years until they bought the house at 19 Raveley Street in Kentish Town in north London, where he wrote *Midnight's Children,* dreaming of heat-hazy Indian ho- rizons while looking out at leaden English skies; and for most of those three and a half years Liz Calder was their lodger. Her then boyfriend Jason Spender was pursuing a doctorate at Manchester University while she worked in the publicity department at the publishers Victor Gollancz in London, and she was commuting between Manchester and London, spending three or four days a week in the office and the rest up north.

She was a gorgeous woman and one of the jobs she gave him was that when men drove her home from various book-world events, as men often did, he had to stay up and chat to them cheerfully until they went home. "Don't ever leave me alone with them," she ordered him, as if she were not perfectly able to handle whatever a man might try on her. One of these night visitors was the writer Roald Dahl, a long, unpleasant man with huge strangler's hands, who gave him hate-filled looks that made him determined not to budge an inch. Finally Dahl stormed off into the night, barely saying goodnight, even to Liz. An- other of her gentlemen callers was the *New Statesman* magazine's film critic John Coleman, supposedly a reformed alcoholic, who opened his briefcase, took out a couple of seriously alcoholic bottles and an- nounced, "These are for me." Coleman stayed so late that in the end he betrayed her trust and went to bed, with Liz looking daggers at him as he went. The next morning she revealed that Coleman had torn all his clothes off in the living room and cried, "Take me, I'm yours." She had gently made the eminent critic dress again and had shown him to the door.

Liz had married young, moved from New Zealand to Brazil with her husband, Richard, had a son and a daughter, worked as a model, left her husband and gone to London. Brazil remained a great love and once, when a "Brazilian ball" in London offered two plane tickets to Rio as first prize for the best carnival costume, she covered her naked body in white cold cream, struck a pose and was drawn around the ballroom on a little trolley by her new boyfriend, Louis Baum, the editor of the publishing trade's weekly bible *The Bookseller,* who was dressed in smock and beret as a sculptor, with a chisel in his hand. Naturally, she won.

She was promoted from the publicity department at Gollancz and became an editor just as he finished *Grimus.* She had been sleeping at night in the room he wrote in by day and, unknown to him, had been sneaking looks at the growing manuscript. When it was done she published it, and so his first novel as an author was also her first novel as a publisher. After Zafar was born they had all vacationed together in France along with Louis's little boy Simon. This was the connection he had broken, for money. What did that say about him?

The association with Deborah Rogers wasn't as old as his friendship with Liz, but it was close. She was a kindly, mothering, emotionally capacious and generous woman, whose relationship with her authors was as affectionate as it was businesslike. After the publication of *Midnight's Children,* long before its Booker award and international bestsellerdom, it was in her office that he had worked out that, if he were to be very careful, he might be able to live by his pen. Her encouragement gave him the strength to go home and tell Clarissa to "prepare to be poor," and then Clarissa's faith had redoubled his confidence and allowed him to go into the ad agency and resign. He and Clarissa had spent happy times at Middle Pitts, the farm in Wales owned by Deb and her composer husband, Michael Berkeley. This rift, too, left behind a guilty ache. But when the storm broke over his head both Deborah and Liz at once set aside their grievances and behaved toward him with spectacular loyalty and generosity. It was the love and loyalty of his friends that enabled him to survive those years, and, yes, their forgiveness, too.

And Liz came to feel that she had dodged a bullet. If she had published *The Satanic Verses,* the ensuing crisis, with its bomb threats, death threats, security expenses, building evacuations and fear would very probably have sunk her new publishing venture right away, and Bloomsbury would never have survived to discover an obscure, unpublished children's author called Jo Rowling.

There was one more thing. In the battle of *The Satanic Verses,* no writer could have wished for more courageous, unflinching, determined allies than Andrew Wylie and Gillon Aitken. When he appointed them he did not know they would be going to war together, and nor could they have known what lay ahead. But when the war came he was glad they were standing with him.

The highest offer for the English-language rights to publish *The Satanic Verses* was not made by Viking Penguin. Another offer was a full $100,000 higher, but Andrew and Gillon both advised him strongly against accepting it. He was not accustomed to figures of this size, much less with turning them down, and he asked Andrew, "Could you just explain again why I should not agree to receive an extra one hundred thousand dollars?" Andrew was adamant. "They would be the wrong publishers for you." Later, after the storm broke, an interview with Mr. Rupert Murdoch was printed in *The New Yorker,* in which he stated emphatically, "I think you should not give offense to people's religious beliefs. For instance, I hope that our people would never have published the Salman Rushdie book." It was possible that Rupert Murdoch didn't know that some of "his people" had been so enthusiastic about the novel that they had outbid the opposition by a considerable distance, but it seemed probable, in the light of this *New Yorker* profile, that had Murdoch found himself in the position of being the publisher of *The Satanic Verses* he would have withdrawn the book the moment the trouble began. Andrew Wylie's advice had been unusually prescient. Murdoch was indeed the wrong publisher for the book.

There was no such thing as "ordinary life." He had always liked the idea of the surrealists that our ability to experience the world as extraordinary was dulled by habituation. We grew used to the way things were, to the dailiness of life, and a sort of dust or film obscured our vision, and the true, miraculous nature of life on earth eluded us. It was the task of the artist to wipe away that blinding layer and renew our capacity for wonderment. That felt right to him; but the problem was not only one of habituation. People also suffered from a form of chosen blindness. People pretended that there was such a thing as *ordinary,* such a thing as *normal,* and that was the public fantasy, far more escapist than the most escapist fiction, inside which they cocooned themselves. People retreated behind their front doors into the hidden zone of their private, family worlds and when outsiders asked how things were they answered, Oh, everything's going along just fine, not much to report, situation normal. But everyone secretly knew that behind that door things were rarely humdrum. More typically, all hell was breaking loose, as people dealt with their angry fathers, drunken mothers, resentful siblings, mad aunts, lecherous uncles and crumbling grandparents. The family was not the firm foundation upon which society rested, but stood at the dark chaotic heart of everything that ailed us. It was not normal, but surreal; not humdrum, but filled with event; not ordinary, but bizarre. He remembered with what excitement he had listened, at the age of twenty, to the Reith Lectures delivered on BBC Radio by Edmund Leach, the great anthropologist and interpreter of Claude Lévi-Strauss who, a year earlier, had succeeded Noel Annan as provost of King's. "Far from being the basis of the good society," Leach had said, "the family, with its narrow privacy and tawdry secrets, is the source of all our discontents." *Yes!* he thought. *Yes! That is a thing I also know.* The families in the novels he later wrote would be explosive, operatic, arm-waving, exclamatory, wild. People who did not like his books would sometimes criticize these fictional families for being unrealistic—not "ordinary" enough. However, readers who did like his books said to him, "Those families are exactly like my family."

English-language publication rights to *The Satanic Verses* were sold to Viking Penguin on March 15, 1988. It was published in London on September 26. Those were the last six months of his "ordinary life," after which the patinas of habituation and self-deception were roughly torn away and what became visible was not the surreal beauty of the world, but its beastly monstrosity. It would be his task, in the years that followed, to rediscover, as Beauty did, the beauty in the Beast.

When Marianne moved into the house on St. Peter's Street she looked for a local physician. He offered to introduce her to his own GP. "No," she said, "I want a woman doctor." But, he said, his GP *was* a woman. "Still," she said, "I need to find someone who understands the treatment I had." She was, she said, a survivor of colonic cancer, which she had beaten by undergoing an avant-garde form of treatment in Canada. (It was legal there but not in the United States, she told him.) "So I'm asking around on the cancer network." After a couple of days she said she had found the doctor she wanted.

In the spring of 1988 he and Marianne were thinking about the future. At one point they briefly thought they might buy a new house in New York and keep only an apartment in London, but Zafar was not quite nine years old so they soon gave up that idea. They looked at houses in Hampstead, on Kemplay Road, and then on Willow Road on the edge of the Heath, and they even made an offer for the Willow Road house that was accepted. But he backed out of the deal, saying he didn't really want the disruption of a house move. The truth was darker: He didn't want to buy a house *with Marianne,* because he wasn't sure their relationship would last.

She began to complain, that spring, of feeling ill again. After a violent quarrel about his continuing "obsession" with Robyn, which was in reality her obsession, she spoke of feeling a shadow within her, a deep ache in her blood. She needed to see the doctor. She feared the onset of cervical cancer. He felt the bitter irony of such a crisis arising at the very moment when they had both finished books, and had much to look forward to; of the possibility of a horrifying loss rising up to dwarf their joy. "You're always talking about what you have lost," she told him. "But it's obvious how many things you have gained."

Then she learned that her application for a Guggenheim had not been successful, and her mood deflated. She heard from the doctor; the news was inconclusive but not great. But within a couple of weeks, as abruptly as the possibility of cancer had been introduced, it was dismissed. The gathering clouds disappeared. She was healthy. The future existed again.

Why did he feel that there was something wrong with this narrative? He couldn't put his finger on it. Perhaps the trust between them was already too badly eroded. She could not forgive the piece of paper she had found in his pocket. His decision not to buy the Willow Road house had dealt another blow to her faith in their marriage. And he, too, had some difficult questions in his head.

Clarissa's father had jumped off a building. Robyn Davidson's mother had hanged herself. Now he learned that Marianne's father had committed suicide also. What did it mean that all the important women in his life were the children of suicides? He couldn't, or didn't want to, answer the question. Soon after he met Elizabeth West, who would become his third wife and the mother of his second son, he felt obliged to ask about her parents. It was a relief to learn that there was no suicide in Elizabeth's background. But her mother had died when she was very young, and her father, a much older parent, had been unable to look after her, and she had been raised by other relatives. The parent-shaped hole was there again.

He was trying to kick-start his imagination because the eternal question, *What next?*, was already nagging at him. He read Graham Greene's *The Confidential Agent* and was impressed by the simplicity of Greene's effects. A man does not look like his passport photograph, and that's enough for Greene to conjure up an uncertain, even sinister world. He read *Little Dorrit* and loved, as always, Dickens's gift for animating the inanimate: the city of Marseille staring at the sky, at strangers, at one and all, a stare so fierce that blinds and shutters had to be closed against it. He read *Herzog* for the umpteenth time and this time around the book's attitude to women really grated. Why did so many of Bellow's male characters fantasize that they would be more sexually successful if they were more violent? From Moses Herzog to Kenneth Trachten-berg in *More Die of Heartbreak,* the same fantasy. *Mr. B., your slip is showing,* he noted. He read *The Key* by Junichiro Tanizaki and enjoyed its tale of secret journals and sexual high jinks in old Japan. Marianne said it was an evil book. He thought it was a book about the manipula-tive nature of erotic desire. The soul had many dark corners and books sometimes illuminated them. But what did he, an atheist, mean when he used the word "soul"? Was it just poetry? Or was there something noncorporeal in us, something more than flesh, blood and bone, the thing that Koestler called the ghost in the machine? He toyed with the notion that we might have a mortal soul instead of an immortal one; a spirit housed in the body that died when the body died. A spirit that might be what we meant when we spoke of *das Ich,* the I.

Reading was living, too. He read William Kennedy, *Billy Phelan's Greatest Game,* and admiringly wrote down "the end of behavior was not action but comprehension on which to base action." He read Hawking's *A Brief History of Time* and it made his head hurt but even though he understood only a fraction of it he knew enough to argue with the great man's contention that we were nearing the point at which everything would be known. The completion of knowledge: Only a scientist could be crazy enough or grand enough to imagine that that was possible.

Zia ul-Haq died in a plane crash: no loss.

A book, which he initially thought might be a play, maybe some reinvention of *Othello,* began to bud in him, though when he wrote it several years later it had grown in ways he did not then understand. He thought it might be called *The Moor's Last Sigh.* Meanwhile, in a dream, an Indian woman he knew appeared to him, having read *The Satanic Verses,* and warned him that there would be "a bill to pay" for it. The London parts of the novel meant nothing to her, and the story about the parting of the Arabian Sea "just shows me your interest in cinema." The dream enacted a fear he had: that people would react only to those parts of the novel with which they felt they had some personal—positive or negative—connection, and ignore the rest of it. He was beginning, as always after completing a book and before pub-lication, to doubt what he had done. At times he thought it a little gawky, a "loose, baggy monster," to use Henry James's phrase. At other times he thought he had managed to control and shape it into something fine. He worried about several sequences: the "Rosa Diamond" passage with its Argentinian backstory, and the devilish metamorphosis of his character Chamcha in a police van and a hospital. He had real doubts about the workings of the main narrative, and the transformation scenes in particular. Then suddenly his doubts evaporated. The book was done, and he was proud of it.

He flew to Lisbon for a few days in May. For a couple of years in the late 1980s the Wheatland Foundation—a collaborative venture between the British publisher George Weidenfeld and the American Ann Getty, who was "bankrolled," as *The New York Times* put it, by her husband, Gordon Getty—hosted a series of lavish literary conferences around the world, a program that came to a halt when the Getty-Weidenfeld relationship collapsed in 1989 under the pressure of losses reported in *The New York Times* as being "at least $15 million." Some of those millions were no doubt lost at the conference staged at the Queluz Palace in May 1988 and attended by the most extraordinary gathering of writers he had seen since the 1986 PEN Congress in New York. Sontag, Walcott, Tabucchi, Enzensberger and so on. He went with Martin Amis and Ian McEwan and after their "British" panel discussion the Italians grumbled that they had spoken too much about politics, whereas literature was about "sentences," and Lord Weidenfeld grumbled that they had been critical of Margaret Thatcher, to whom they owed so much. While he was on stage the extraordinary Montenegran writer Danilo Kiš, who turned out to be a skilled caricaturist, drew a picture of him on a conference notepad and presented it to him at the end of the session. At the New York PEN Congress, Danilo, a writer of brilliance and wit, had defended the idea that the state could have an imagination. "In fact," he said, "the state also has a sense of humor, and I will give you an example of a joke by the state." He was living in Paris and one day received a letter from a friend in Yugoslavia. When he opened it he found an official stamp on the first page. It read THIS LETTER HAS NOT BEEN CENSORED. Kiš looked like Tom

Baker as Doctor Who and spoke no English. Serbo-Croat not really being an option either, they became friends in French. By the time of the Lisbon conference Kiš was in the grip of illness—he died of lung cancer in 1989—and his vocal cords were badly affected, making it hard for him to speak at all. The caricature was offered in lieu of conversation and became a treasured possession.

The little argument about the utterances of the "British panel" were no more than an *amuse-bouche*. The main event was the sharp confrontation that took place between the Russian writers and those from the area they insisted should be known as "central Europe"— Kiš himself, the Hungarians György Konrád and Péter Esterházy, the Canadian Czech émigré Josef Škvorecky, and the great Polish poets Adam Zagajewski and Czesław Miłosz. These were the days of *glasnost,* and it was the first time the Soviets had let the "real" writers out—not the Writers' Union stooges, but the likes of Tatyana Tolstaya. The major writers of the Russian emigration, led by Joseph Brodsky, were there too, and so the event offered a kind of reunification of Russian literature, which was a moving thing to witness (Brodsky refused to speak in English, wishing, he said, to be a Russian among Russians). However, when the central European writers, ignoring the Italian view that literature was about sentences, launched into passionate denunciations of Russian hegemony, the Russians reacted badly. Several of them claimed that they had never heard of a separate central European culture. Tolstaya added that if writers were worried about the Red Army they could always retreat into their imaginations, as she did, and there they would be totally free. This didn't go down well. Brodsky averred, in an almost comically cultural-imperialist formulation, that Russia was in the process of solving its own problems, and once it had done so all the central Europeans' problems would also be solved. (This was the same Brodsky who, after the *fatwa,* would join the he-knew-what-he-was-doing, he-did-it-on-purpose party.) Czesław Miłosz rose from the floor to take issue with Brodsky in stentorian terms, and the seventy-odd writers in the room were treated to the spectacle of the two giants, both Nobel laureates (and old friends), angrily clashing in terms that left all who heard it in no doubt that a great change was brewing in the East. It was like watching a preview of Communism's fall, the dialectic of history brought to life, expressed and enacted by the greatest intellectuals of the region in the presence of their international colleagues: a moment never to be forgotten by those lucky enough to be there.

If history progressed dialectically, as Hegel proposed, then the fall of Communism and the rise of revolutionary Islam demonstrated that dialectical materialism, Karl Marx's reworking of Hegel and Fichte that identified the dialectic as one of class struggle, was flawed at the root. The thinking of the central European intellectuals at Queluz Palace, and also the very different philosophy of the radical Islam whose power was growing so rapidly, both scorned the Marxian idea that *economics was primary,* that economic conflict, expressed in the struggle of the classes, offered the best explanation of how things worked. In this new world, in the dialectics of the world beyond the Communism-capitalism confrontation, it would be made clear that culture could be primary too. The culture of central Europe was asserting itself against Russianness to unmake the Soviet Union. And ideology, as Ayatollah Khomeini and his cohorts were insisting, could certainly be primary. The wars of ideology and culture were moving to the center of the stage. And his novel, unfortunately for him, would become a battlefield.

He was asked to go on the radio show *Desert Island Discs,* a bigger honor, in Britain, than any mere literary prize. One of the eight musical choices he took with him to his imaginary desert island was an Urdu *ghazal* written by Faiz Ahmed Faiz, a close family friend who had been the first great writer he ever knew, both a public poet whose verses about the partition of India and Pakistan were the finest anyone ever wrote, and a somewhat jaundiced creator of much-admired poems of love. He had learned from Faiz that the writer's task was to be both public and private, an arbiter both of society and of the human heart. Another of his choices was, perhaps, the music playing beneath the text of his new novel: "Sympathy for the Devil," by the Rolling Stones.

Bruce Chatwin was mortally ill, and he visited him several times. The illness was affecting the balance of Bruce's mind. He had been refusing to say the words *AIDS* or *HIV,* but now he deliriously claimed to have found the cure. He said he was calling his wealthy friends "like the Aga Khan" to raise money for research, and wanted his literary friends to contribute too. The "experts" at the Radcliffe Hospital in Oxford were "very excited" and sure he was "onto something." Bruce was also sure that he had become extremely rich himself. His books had sold "an immense number of copies." One day he telephoned to say that he had bought a Chagall oil painting. This was not his only extravagant "purchase." His wife, Elizabeth, was obliged quietly to return his acquisitions and to explain that Bruce was not himself. In the end his father had to go to court to take charge of his son's finances, and that caused a melancholy rift in the family. Bruce had a book coming out too, his last novel, *Utz.* One day he called up to say, "If we're both listed for the Booker we should just announce that we intend to share it. If I win, I'll share it with you, and you should say the same thing." Until then, Bruce had always scorned the Booker Prize.

He was asked to review *Dear Mili,* a Grimm tale illustrated by Maurice Sendak, for *The New York Times,* and though he took care to express his admiration for much of Sendak's oeuvre he could not avoid saying that these illustrations seemed to be repetitive of what the great illustrator had done before. After that Sendak told interviewers that it was the most hurtful review he had ever received and he "hated" its author. (He wrote two other book reviews, for the British *Observer,* in which he found the book under consideration less wonderful than the author's earlier work, and the authors of *The Russia House* and *Hocus Pocus,* John le Carré and Kurt Vonnegut, both friendly acquaintances until then, declared themselves his foes, too. This was what book reviewing did. If you loved a book, the author thought your praise no more than his rightful due, and if you didn't like it, you made enemies. He decided to stop doing it. It was a mug's game.)

On the day he received the bound proofs of *The Satanic Verses* he was visited at home on St. Peter's Street by a journalist he thought of as a friend, Madhu Jain of *India Today*. When she saw the thick, dark blue cover with the large red title she grew extremely excited, and pleaded to be given a copy so that she could read it while vacationing in England with her husband. And once she had read it she demanded that she be allowed to interview him and that *India Today* be allowed to publish an extract. Again, he agreed. For many years afterward he thought of this publication as the match that lit the fire. And certainly the magazine highlighted what came to be seen as the book's "controversial" aspects, using the headline AN UNEQUIVOCAL ATTACK ON RELIGIOUS FUNDAMENTALISM, which was the first of innumerable inaccurate descriptions of the book's contents, and, in another headline, ascribing a quote to him—MY THEME IS FANATICISM—that further misrepresented the work. The last sentence of the article, "*The Satanic Verses* is bound to trigger an avalanche of protests . . ." was an open invitation for those protests to begin. The article was read by the Indian parliamentarian and Islamic conservative Syed Shahabuddin, who responded by writing an "open letter" titled "You Did This with Satanic Forethought, Mr. Rushdie," and it had begun. The most powerful way to attack a book is to demonize its author, to turn him into a creature of base motives and evil intentions. The "Satan Rushdy" who would afterward be paraded down the world's streets by angry demonstrators, hanged in effigy with a red tongue hanging out and wearing a crude tuxedo, was being created; born in India, as the real Rushdie had been. Here was the first proposition of the assault: that anyone who wrote a book with the word "satanic" in the title must be satanic, too. Like many false propositions that flourished in the incipient Age of Information (or disinformation), it became true by repetition. Tell a lie about a man once and many people will not believe you. Tell it a million times and it is the man himself who will no longer be believed.

With the passage of time came forgiveness. Rereading the *India Today* piece many years later, in a calmer time, he could concede that the piece was fairer than the magazine's headline writer had made it look, more balanced than its last sentence. Those who wished to be offended would have been offended anyway. Those who were looking to be inflamed would have found the necessary spark. Perhaps the magazine's most damaging act was to break the traditional publishing embargo and print its piece nine days before the book's publication, at a time when not a single copy had arrived in India. This allowed Mr. Shahabuddin and his ally, another opposition MP named Khurshid Alam Khan, free rein. They could say whatever they pleased about the book, but it could not be read and therefore could not be defended. One man who had read an advance copy, the journalist Khushwant Singh, called for a ban in *The Illustrated Weekly of India* as a measure to prevent trouble. He thus became the first member of the small group of world writers who joined the censorship lobby. Khushwant Singh further claimed that he had been asked for his advice by Viking Penguin and had warned the author and publishers of the consequences of publication. The author was unaware of any such warning. If it was ever given, it was never received.

Disappointingly, the attack on his character was not confined to Muslim critics. In Britain's newborn *Independent* newspaper the writer Mark Lawson quoted an anonymous Cambridge contemporary who called him "pompous" and who, as a "grammar school lad," felt "alienated from him by his education." So the wretched years at Rugby were to be held against him by the nameless. Another "close friend," also anonymous, could "see" why he might appear "surly and arrogant." And there was more: He was "schizophrenic," he was "completely bonkers," he *corrected people's mispronunciations of his name!*, and—worst of all—he once got into a taxi that Mr. Lawson had ordered and left the journalist stranded. This was small, and small-minded, stuff, and there was a good deal more of it elsewhere, in other newspapers. "Close friends often confess that he is not actually likeable," Bryan Appleyard wrote in *The Sunday Times*. "Rushdie is massively egotistical." (What sorts of "close friends" talked about their friends like this? Only the anonymous ones unearthed by profile writers.) In "ordinary life" all of it would have been hurtful but none of it would have mattered much. But in the great conflict that followed the notion that he was not a very nice man was to prove very damaging indeed.

———

Lord Byron intensely disliked the work of the eighteenth-century poet laureate Robert Southey and venomously attacked it in print. Southey replied that Byron was part of a "Satanic school" of writing, and his poetry was nothing but "Satanic verses."

The British edition of *The Satanic Verses* was published on Monday, September 26, 1988, and in retrospect he felt a deep nostalgia for that moment when trouble still felt far away. For a brief moment that fall, the publication of *The Satanic Verses* was a literary event, discussed in the language of books. Was it any good? Was it, as Victoria Glendinning suggested in the London *Times,* "better than *Midnight's Children,* because it is more contained, but only in the sense that the Niagara Falls are contained," or, as Angela Carter said in *The Guardian,* "an epic into which holes have been punched to let in visions . . . [a] populous, loquacious, sometimes hilarious, extraordinary contemporary novel"? Or was it, as Claire Tomalin wrote in *The Independent,* a "wheel that did not turn," or a novel that went "plunging down, on melting wings," in Hermione Lee's even harsher opinion in the *Observer,* "towards unreadability"? How large was the membership of the apocryphal "Page 15 Club" of readers who could not get past that point in the book?

Soon enough the language of literature would be drowned beneath the cacophony of other discourses, political, religious, sociological, postcolonial, and the subject of quality, of serious artistic intent, would come to seem almost frivolous. The book about migration and transformation that he had written was vanishing and being replaced by one that scarcely existed, in which *Rushdie refers to the Prophet and his Companions as "scums and bums"* (he didn't, but he did allow those characters who persecuted the followers of his fictional Prophet to use abusive language), *Rushdie calls the wives of the Prophet whores* (he hadn't, though whores in a brothel in his imaginary Jahilia take on the names of the Prophet's wives to arouse their clients; the wives themselves are clearly described as living chastely in the harem),

Rushdie uses the word "fuck" too many times (well, okay, he did use it a fair bit). This imaginary novel was the one against which the rage of Islam would be directed, and after that few people wished to talk about the real book, except, often, to concur with Hermione Lee's negative assessment.

When friends asked what they could do to help he often pleaded, "Defend the text." The attack was very specific, yet the defense was often a general one, resting on the mighty principle of freedom of speech. He hoped for, he often felt he needed, a more particular defense, like the quality defense made in the cases of other assaulted books, *Lady Chatterley's Lover, Ulysses, Lolita;* because this was a violent assault not on the novel in general or on free speech per se, but on a particular accumulation of words (literature being, as the Italians had reminded him at Queluz Palace, made up of sentences), and on the intentions and integrity and ability of the writer who had put those words together. *He did it for money. He did it for fame. The Jews made him do it. Nobody would have bought his unreadable book if he hadn't vilified Islam.* That was the nature of the attack, and so, for many years, *The Satanic Verses* was denied the ordinary life of a novel. It became something smaller and uglier: an insult. There was something surreally comical about this metamorphosis of a novel about angelic and satanic metamorphoses into a devil-version of itself, and he could think of a few black jokes to make about it. (Soon enough there would be jokes about him. *Have you heard about Rushdie's new novel? It's called "Buddha, You Big Fat Bastard."*) But for him to be humorous would be out of place in this new world, a comic remark would sound a jarring note, lightheartedness was utterly inappropriate. As his book became simply an insult, so he became the Insulter; not only in Muslim eyes, but in the opinion of the public at large. Polls taken after the "Rushdie Affair" began showed that a large majority of the British public felt he should apologize for his "offensive" book. This would not be an easy argument to win.

But for those few weeks in the fall of 1988 the book was still "only a novel," and he was still himself. Viking UK gave a launch party for their autumn list and at it he met Robertson Davies and Elmore Leonard. He huddled in a corner with the two grand old men as Elmore

Leonard told the story of how, after the devastation of his wife's death, he had been wondering how he would ever find another life partner when he looked out of the window of his home in Bloomfield Township, just outside Detroit, and saw a woman standing there. Her name was Christine and she was a master gardener and she came to Bloomfield regularly to take care of Leonard's garden. They got married within the year. "I didn't know where I would find a wife," he said, "and then I found her right outside my window, watering my plants."

There was the usual round of readings and signings around Britain. He traveled to Toronto to speak at the International Festival of Authors at Harbourfront. *The Satanic Verses* was short-listed for the Booker Prize alongside novels by Peter Carey, Bruce Chatwin, Marina Warner, David Lodge and Penelope Fitzgerald. (He avoided calling Bruce to reopen the subject of sharing the award.) The only cloud on the horizon was Syed Shahabuddin, the Indian MP, demanding that action be taken in India against his "blasphemous" book, which he declared that he had not read, saying, "I do not have to wade through a filthy drain to know what filth is," which was a good point, about drains. It was briefly possible to ignore that cloud and enjoy publication (though, to tell the absolute truth, the publication of a book always made a large part of him want to hide behind the furniture). Then on Thursday, October 6, 1988, the cloud covered the sun. His friend Salman Haidar, whose family and his had been close for generations, and who was deputy high commissioner of India in London, had the tough job of calling him to tell him formally on behalf of his government that *The Satanic Verses* had been banned in India.

In spite of India's much-trumpeted secularism, Indian governments from the mid-seventies onward—ever since the time of Indira and Sanjay Gandhi—had often given in to pressure from religious interest groups, especially those claiming to control large blocs of votes. By 1988, Rajiv Gandhi's weak government, with elections due in November, cravenly surrendered to threats from two opposition Muslim MPs who were in no position to "deliver" the Muslim electorate's votes to the Congress Party. The book was not examined by any properly authorized body, nor was there any semblance of judicial process. The ban came, improbably enough, from the Finance Ministry, under

Section 11 of the Customs Act, which prevented the book from being imported. Weirdly, the Finance Ministry stated that the ban "did not detract from the literary and artistic merit" of his work. *Thanks a lot,* he thought.

Strangely—innocently, naïvely, even ignorantly—he hadn't expected it. In the years that followed, attacks on artistic freedom would multiply in India, and not even the most eminent would be spared: The painter Maqbool Fida Husain, the novelist Rohinton Mistry, the filmmaker Deepa Mehta would all be targeted, among many others. But in 1988 it was possible to believe in India as a free country in which artistic expression was respected and defended. He had believed it. Book banning was something that happened all too frequently across the border in Pakistan. It wasn't the Indian way. Jawaharlal Nehru had written in 1929, "It is a dangerous power in the hands of a government; the right to determine what shall be read and what shall not. . . . In India, the power is likely to be misused." The young Nehru was writing, at that time, against the censorship of books by India's British overlords. It was sad to think that his words could be used, almost sixty years later, as a critique of India itself.

To be free one had to make the presumption of freedom. And a further presumption: that one's work would be treated as having been created with integrity. He had always written presuming that he had the right to write as he chose, and presuming that it would at the very least be treated as serious work; and knowing, too, that countries whose writers could not make such presumptions inevitably slid toward, or had already arrived at, authoritarianism and tyranny. Banned writers in unfree parts of the world were not merely proscribed; they were also vilified. In India, however, the presumption of intellectual freedom and respect had been ever-present except during the dictatorial years of "emergency rule" imposed by Indira Gandhi between 1974 and 1977 after her conviction for electoral malpractice. He had been proud of that openness and had boasted of it to people in the West. India was surrounded by unfree societies—Pakistan, China, Burma—but remained an open democracy; flawed, certainly, perhaps even deeply flawed, but free.

Ever since *Midnight's Children* had been so enthusiastically received, the Indian response to his work had been a source of great pride to him, and so the embargo on the importation of *The Satanic Verses* was a painful blow. Out of that pain he published an open letter to Prime Minister Rajiv Gandhi, Nehru's grandson, a letter some commentators found excessively aggressive. He complained of the official statements that the book had been banned as a preemptive measure. "Certain passages had been identified as susceptible to distortion and misuse, presumably by unscrupulous religious fanatics and such. The banning order had been issued to prevent this misuse. Apparently, my book is not deemed blasphemous or objectionable in itself, but is being proscribed for, so to speak, its own good! . . . It is as though, having identified an innocent person as a likely target for assault by muggers or rapists, you were to put that person in jail for protection. This is no way, Mr. Gandhi, for a free society to behave." This was also not how novelists were supposed to behave: scolding a prime minister. This was . . . arrogant. This was cheek. The Indian press was calling the ban "a Philistine decision," and an example of "thought control," but he was supposed to watch what he said.

He had not done so. "What sort of India do you wish to govern? Is it to be an open or a repressive society? Your action in the matter of *The Satanic Verses* will be an important indicator for many people around the world." No doubt unwisely, he had accused Rajiv Gandhi of carrying on a family vendetta. "Perhaps you feel that by banning my fourth novel you are taking long overdue revenge for the treatment of your mother in my second, but can you be sure that Indira Gandhi's reputation will endure better and longer than *Midnight's Children?*" Well, okay, that was arrogant. Angry and injured also, but the arrogance was undeniably there. Very well. So it was. He was defending a thing he revered above most things, the art of literature, against a piece of blatant political opportunism. Maybe a little intellectual arrogance was called for. It was not a practical defense, of course; not one calculated to change his adversary's mind. It was an attempt to take the cultural high ground, and it concluded with a rhetorical appeal to that posterity whose judgment could not be known by either Rajiv Gandhi or himself. "You own the present, Mr. Prime Minister; but the centuries belong to art."

The letter was widely published on Sunday, October 9, 1988. The next day the first death threat was received at the offices of Viking Penguin. The day after that a scheduled reading in Cambridge was canceled by the venue because it, too, had received threats. The cloud thickened.

The 1988 Booker Prize jury's decision was swiftly made. The chairman of the judges, Michael Foot, MP, the former Labour Party leader and devotee of Hazlitt and Swift, was a passionate advocate of *The Satanic Verses*. The other four judges were adamantly convinced of the superior merits of Peter Carey's excellent novel *Oscar and Lucinda*. A vote was taken after a short discussion and that was that. Three years earlier Carey's wonderful comic-picaresque *Illywhacker* and Doris Lessing's excellent IRA novel *The Good Terrorist* had deadlocked the judges and in the end, in a compromise decision, the prize had gone to Keri Hulme's Maori epic *The Bone People*. He had had dinner with Peter Carey the night after that result and had told him that his book should have won. Carey talked about the novel he had begun to write. One of his reasons for being in England was to do some research. There was a particular beach in Devon he wanted to visit. He had offered to drive Peter down to the West Country, and they had spent a fine day traveling through England to the "Hennacombe" in which the child Oscar Hopkins and his fierce father, Theophilus, would live in his novel, just as their real-life models, the writer Edmund Gosse and his father, Philip (like Theophilus, a naturalist, a widower and a member of the Plymouth Brethren), had done in the middle of the nineteenth century. They found the beach four hundred steps down from the top of the cliff. They collected a few shells and many distinctive pink and gray pebbles. They ate a heavy pub lunch of warm beer and meat in dark gravy. All day they spoke of love. He was still with Robyn in those days, and she was Australian, like Carey, of course; and Peter had recently married the Sydney theater director Alison Summers, and was full of passion and joy. By the time they got back to London they had become friends. He broke up with Robyn soon afterward and Peter eventually separated acrimoniously from Alison, but that love could die did not mean it had not lived. After the Booker result was announced he went quickly across the Guildhall to embrace Peter and congratulate him, and to murmur wryly in his ear that the moral of the story was that Writer A should never help Writer B to do his research, because then Writer B would use that research to beat Writer A to the Booker.

It would have been nice to win, but he was happy for Peter and, in truth, more concerned about the growing public argument over his book. A win for *The Satanic Verses* would have been helpful; it would have moved the "quality defense" back to center stage. But there were bigger issues to worry about. When he got home, around 11 P.M., he found a message on his answering machine asking him to call a Muslim cleric in South Africa urgently, even if it was very late. He had been invited to Johannesburg by the antiapartheid newspaper the *Weekly Mail* to deliver the keynote address at a conference about apartheid and censorship—an invitation made with the agreement of the "broad democratic movement" in South Africa, in other words, with the implicit backing of the African National Congress—and was scheduled to leave London in four days' time. "I must speak to you before you fly," the message said. He was in a strange mood, brought on by a combination of marital difficulties and the events of the evening (this was the night when Marianne told William Golding that she had written a feminist *Lord of the Flies*), and in the end he decided to make the call. He sat in a darkened living room and listened to a voice from another world tell him he must not come to speak at the *Weekly Mail's* conference. The voice described itself as a liberal, modern person, whose concern was twofold: for his safety, and for the well-being of the antiapartheid movement. If he were to visit Johannesburg in the present climate the Muslim reaction would be large and hostile. That would be dangerous both at the personal and political levels. A quarrel within the antiapartheid coalition would be catastrophic and would only serve the interests of the white supremacist regime. He should avoid becoming the catalyst for such a quarrel, and stay away.

The next morning he called Nadine Gordimer who, as the patron of the Congress of South African Writers (COSAW), was the other sponsor of his invitation to speak. This tiny, indomitable woman was an old friend, and one of the people he most respected and admired. She was extremely agitated and distressed. South African Muslims, usually vociferous in their opposition to the restrictions of apartheid, were threatening a holy war against the blasphemous author and his book. They would kill him and bomb his meetings and attack those who had invited him. The police seemed unable or unwilling to guarantee the safety of those who were being threatened. There was a danger of a rift in COSAW, with its Muslim members threatening to resign en masse, and the loss of funding that would result from such a rupture would be disastrous for that organization. The staff of the *Weekly Mail* was predominantly Jewish and there was a lot of unpleasant anti-Semitism in the Muslim vitriol. Nadine Gordimer had tried to meet with Muslim leaders to solve the problem, and many highly respected figures in the antiapartheid movement had appealed to the Muslim extremists to back down, but they had not. The prominent Muslim intellectual professor Fatima Meer had stated, "In the final analysis it is the Third World that Rushdie attacks." In spite of a lifetime of anticolonialism he was being transformed into an oppressor, who had made a "malicious attack on his ethnic past." Faced with this crisis, the ANC had remarkably said nothing at all. There were many voices raised against the Muslim assault, including those of J. M. Coetzee, Athol Fugard and André Brink, but the Islamists grew more vociferously threatening by the day. Gordimer was plainly shaken and, as a friend, protective. "I can't bring you into this kind of danger," she said.

That week, the South African government also banned *The Satanic Verses.* The banning order disparaged the novel as a "work thinly disguised as a piece of literature," criticized its "foul language," and said that it was "disgusting not only to Muslims but to any reader who holds clear values of decency and culture." Interestingly, the same language could be found in the letter to "Brothers in Islam"—evidently "Sisters in Islam" were not worth addressing—issued by the UK Action Committee on Islamic Affairs just a few days earlier, on October 28. In that document, the description "thinly disguised as a piece of literature" was also to be found, as well as many of the accusations of abusiveness, filth, and so on. The white racists of South Africa were

apparently taking dictation from Mr. Mughram al-Ghamdi, the signatory of the UK Action Committee letter.

After many phone conversations, with Nadine and Anton Harber,
the coeditor of the *Weekly Mail,* he was told that COSAW, for all its
political radicalism, was recommending to the newspaper that his invitation be withdrawn. He was saddened to hear that this had precipitated a public quarrel between South Africa's two greatest writers.
J. M. Coetzee opposed the withdrawal of the invitation, saying that
the decision to come or not come should be Rushdie's alone. Nadine
Gordimer, immensely regretful, said that the issue of safety was paramount. They were both right, but he did not want his fellow writers
to be quarreling over him. He accepted the decision to withdraw the
invitation. On the same day, Tony Lacey, his editorial director at Viking, called him to tell him in confidence that *The Satanic Verses* had
won the Whitbread Prize for Best Novel. Its "thin disguise as a piece
of literature" had obviously worked.

The first piece of hate mail arrived at his London home. The *Evening Standard* reported on a global Islamic threat to "end Penguin."
The famous lawyer David Napley demanded that he be tried under the
Public Order Act. Meanwhile, he and Clarissa took Zafar to watch the
Guy Fawkes Night fireworks on Highbury Fields. Marianne turned
forty-one, and at lunchtime he went to the Whitbread prize-giving
ceremony to receive his award. In the afternoon she quarreled with
him. She was hidden in his shadow, she said, and she hated it. That
night, still irritable with each other, they went to see Harold Pinter's
play *Mountain Language* at the National Theatre. He came away feeling
that like the people in the play he, too, was being forbidden to use his
language. His language was improper, even criminal. He should be
tried in court, hounded out of society, even killed. This was all legitimate because of his language. It was the language of literature that was
the crime.

A year had passed since his father died. He was glad Anis was not
around to see what was happening to his son. He called his mother.
Negin supported him staunchly, *these terrible people,* but, strangely, she
defended their God. "Don't blame Allah for what these people say."
He argued with her. What sort of god could be excused the actions of

his followers? Didn't it, in a way, infantilize the deity to say he was powerless against the faithful? She was adamant. "It's not Allah's fault." She said she would pray for him. He was shocked. This was not the kind of family they had been. His father had been dead for just a year and suddenly his mother was praying? "Don't pray for me," he said. "Don't you get it? That's not our team." She laughed, humoring him, but didn't understand what he was saying.

A solution of sorts was found for the South African problem. He agreed to speak to the *Weekly Mail* conference by telephone link from London. His voice went to South Africa, his ideas were heard in a Johannesburg hall he couldn't see, but he stayed at home. It wasn't satisfying, but it felt better than nothing.

The grand sheikh of al-Azhar, Gad el-Haq Ali Gad el-Haq: The name sounded almost impossibly antiquated to him, an *Arabian Nights* name belonging to the age of flying carpets and wonderful lamps. This grand sheikh, one of the grand eminences of Islamic theology, a hard-line conservative priest based at the al-Azhar University in Cairo, on November 22, 1988, delivered himself of an utterance against the blasphemous book. He decried the way in which "lies and figments of the imagination" were passed off as facts. He called on British Muslims to bring legal actions against the author. He wanted action from the forty-six-member Organization of the Islamic Conference. *The Satanic Verses* was not the only book he was upset by. He also renewed his objections to the great Egyptian writer and Nobel laureate Naguib Mahfouz's novel *Children of Gebelawi*—also accused of blasphemy because its contemporary narrative was an allegory of the lives of prophets from Abraham to Muhammad. "A novel cannot just be permitted into circulation because its author won the Nobel Prize for Literature," he declared. "That award does not justify the propagation of misguided ideas."

Nor was Gad el-Haq Ali Gad el-Haq the only Egyptian sheikh to be offended by these books and their authors. The so-called "Blind Sheikh," Omar Abdel-Rahman, afterward jailed for his involvement in the first attack on the World Trade Center in New York, announced that if Mahfouz had been properly punished for *Children of Gebelawi,* then Rushdie would not have dared to publish *The Satanic Verses.* In 1994 one of his followers, understanding this statement to be a *fatwa,* stabbed Naguib Mahfouz in the neck. The elderly novelist survived, fortunately. After the Khomeini *fatwa* Mahfouz had initially come to the defense of *The Satanic Verses,* denouncing Khomeini's act as "intellectual terrorism," but subsequently he slid toward the opposite camp, declaring that "Rushdie did not have the right to insult anything, especially a prophet or anything considered holy."

Quasi-mythological names were coming after him now, grand sheikhs and blind ones, the seminarians of Darul Uloom in India, the Wahhabi mullahs of Saudi Arabia (where the book had also been banned), and, in the near future, the turbaned Iranian theologians of Qom. He had never given much thought to these august personages, but they were certainly thinking about him. Rapidly, ruthlessly, the world of religion was setting the terms of the debate. The secular world, less organized, less united, and, essentially, less concerned, lagged far behind; and much vital ground was given up without a struggle.

As the demonstrations of the faithful grew in number, size and clamor, the South African writer Paul Trewhela, in a bold essay that defended him and his novel from a position on the left, and in uncompromisingly secularist terms, described the Islamic campaign as a "bursting forth of mass popular irrationalism," a formulation that implied an interesting question, a tough one for the left to deal with: How should one react when the masses were being irrational? Could "the people" ever be, quite simply, wrong? Trewhela argued that it was "the novel's secularizing tendency that was at issue . . . its intention (says Rushdie) to 'discuss Muhammad as if he were human,'" and he compared this project to that of the Young Hegelians in Germany in the 1830s and '40s, and their critique of Christianity, their belief that—in Marx's words—"man makes religion, religion does not make man." Trewhela defended *The Satanic Verses* as belonging to the antireligious literary tradition of Boccaccio, Chaucer, Rabelais, Aretino and Balzac, and argued for a robust secularist response to the religious attack. "The book will not be silenced," he wrote. "We are at the birth, painful, bloody and difficult, of a new period of revolutionary enlightenment."

There were many on the left—Germaine Greer, John Berger, John le Carré—for whom the idea that the masses could be wrong was unpalatable. And while liberal opinion dithered and equivocated, the movement of mass popular irrationalism grew daily in its irrationality, and in its popularity, too.

He was a signatory to Charter 88, whose name (which some conservative commentators found "vainglorious") was a *homage* to the great charter of liberties, Charter 77, published by Czech dissident intellectuals eleven years earlier. Charter 88 was a call for British constitutional reform, and was launched at a House of Commons press conference at the end of November. The only frontline British politician who showed up at the meeting was the future Labour foreign secretary Robin Cook. This was the period of high Thatcherism, and the Labour leader, Neil Kinnock, had privately dismissed Charter 88 as a bunch of "wankers, whingers and whiners." There were no votes in constitutional reform in those days, before the great devolution debates changed British politics so dramatically. Cook was there because of his commitment to Scottish devolution.

Eleven years later, the friendly acquaintanceship forged that day would indirectly lead to the resolution of the international crisis surrounding *The Satanic Verses*. It would be Robin Cook who, as foreign secretary in the Blair government, committed himself to solving the problem; who, with his deputy Derek Fatchett, MP, fought for, and gained, the breakthrough.

The year ended badly. There was a demonstration against *The Satanic Verses* in Bradford, the Yorkshire city with Britain's largest Muslim population, on December 2. On December 3, Clarissa received her first threatening phone call. On December 4, her fortieth birthday, there was another one. A voice said, "We'll get you tonight, Salman Rushdie, at 60 Burma Road." That was her home address. She called the police and they stayed at her house overnight.

Nothing happened. The tension ratcheted up another notch.

On December 28 there was another bomb scare at the offices of

Viking Penguin. Andrew Wylie called him to tell him. "Fear is beginning to be a factor," Andrew said.

Then it was 1989, the year the world changed.

On the day they burned his book he took his American wife to see
Stonehenge. He had heard about the proposed stunt in Bradford and
something in him rebelled violently. He didn't want to wait around all
day to see what happened and then field the inevitable press inquiries,
as if he had nothing better to do than be the servant of the day's ugliness. Under a leaden sky they headed for the ancient stones. Geoffrey
of Monmouth said it was Merlin who built Stonehenge. Geoffrey was
an unreliable source, of course, but this was a more appealing Stonehenge than the ancient burial ground the archaeologists said it was, or
the altar of a Druid cult. Driving fast, he was not in the mood for
Druids. Religious cults, large and small, belonged in history's dustbin
and he wished somebody would put them there along with the rest of
the juvenilia of mankind, the flat earth, for example, or the moon
made of cheese.

Marianne was at her brightest. There were days when an almost
frightening brightness blazed from her face, her habitual intensity
turned up too high. She was from Lancaster, Pennsylvania, but there
was nothing Amish about her. She had a flamboyant personal style.
They had been invited to a royal garden party at Buckingham Palace
and she had worn a shiny black slip instead of a dress, accompanied by
a smart bolero jacket and a little pillbox hat. In spite of strong encouragement from her daughter she refused to wear a bra. He walked round
the gardens of the palace with his braless wife in her undergarment.
The royals, dressed in primary colors, stood surrounded by hordes of
guests, like racehorses, each in his or her personal paddock. The crowds
around the queen and the Charles-Diana combo were by far the largest. Princess Margaret's fan club was almost embarrassingly small. "I
wonder," Marianne said, "what the queen has in her handbag." That
was a funny question and they spent a few happy moments inventing
the contents. Mace, perhaps. Or tampons. Obviously not money.
Nothing with her face on it.

When Marianne got going she was fun to be with. There was no denying her smartness, her wit. She took notes wherever she went and her handwriting was as flamboyant as she. He was sometimes alarmed by the speed at which she transformed experience into fiction. There was almost no pause for reflection. Stories poured from her, yesterday's incidents becoming today's sentences. And when the brightness blazed from her face she could look fabulously attractive, or nuts, or both. She told him that all the women in her fiction who had names beginning with the letter *M* were versions of herself. In the novel she published before *John Dollar*, a novel he had liked called *Separate Checks*, the main character bore the last name of McQueen: Ellery McQueen, after the thriller writer. The writer Ellery Queen had actually been two Brooklyn writers, cousins, named Frederic Dannay and Manfred Bennington Lee, except that those were aliases, too, and their real names were Daniel Nathan and Emanuel Lepofsky. Marianne's character was an alias whose name was a play on the pen name of a divided-self pair of writers who used that alias to disguise names that were themselves aliases for other names. Ellery McQueen in *Separate Checks* was an inmate in a private psychiatric hospital. The balance of her mind was disturbed.

In Bradford a crowd was gathering outside the police station in the Tyrls, a square also overlooked by the Italianate city hall and the courthouse. There was a pool with a fountain and an area designated as a "speaker's corner" for people to sound off about whatever they liked. The Muslim demonstrators were uninterested in soapbox oratory, however. The Tyrls was a more modest location than Berlin's Opera Square had been on May 10, 1933, and in Bradford only one book was at issue, not twenty-five thousand or more; very few of the people gathered there would have known much about the events presided over more than fifty-five years earlier by Joseph Goebbels, who cried, "No to decadence and moral corruption! Yes to decency and morality in family and state! I consign to the flames the writings of Heinrich Mann, Ernst Gläser, Erich Kästner." The work of Bertolt Brecht, Karl Marx, Thomas Mann and even Ernest Hemingway were also burned that day. No, the demonstrators knew nothing about that bonfire, or the Nazis' desire to "purge" and "purify" German culture of "degenerate" ideas. Perhaps they were also unfamiliar with the term "auto-da-fé," or with the activities of the Catholic Inquisition, but even if they lacked a sense of history they were still part of it. They too had come to destroy a heretical text with fire.

He walked among the stones of what he wanted to think of as Merlin's henge and for an hour the present slipped away. He may even have taken his wife by the hand. On the way home there was Runnymede, the water meadow by the Thames in which King John's nobles obliged him to sign the Magna Carta. This was the place in which the British had begun to gain their liberty from tyrant rulers 774 years ago. The British memorial to John F. Kennedy stood here also and the fallen president's words, etched in stone, had much to say to him that day. *Let every Nation know, whether it wishes us well or ill, that we shall pay any price, bear any burden, meet any hardship, support any friend or oppose any foe, in order to assure the survival and success of liberty.*

He turned on the car radio and the Bradford burning was at the top of the news. Then they were home, and the present engulfed him. He saw on television what he had spent the day trying to avoid. There were perhaps a thousand people in the demonstration, and all of them were male. Their faces were angry, or, to be precise, their faces were performing anger for the cameras. He could see in their eyes the excitement they felt at the presence of the world's press. It was the excitement of celebrity, of what Saul Bellow had called "event glamour." To be bathed in flashlight was glorious, almost erotic. This was their moment on the red carpet of history. They were carrying placards reading RUSHDIE STINKS and RUSHDIE EAT YOUR WORDS. They were ready for their close-up.

A copy of the novel had been nailed to a piece of wood and then set on fire: crucified and then immolated. It was an image he couldn't forget: the happily angry faces, rejoicing in their anger, believing their identity was born of their rage. And in the foreground a smug man in a trilby with a little Poirot mustache. This was a Bradford councilor, Mohammad Ajeeb—the word *"ajeeb,"* oddly, was Urdu for "odd"— who had told the crowd, "Islam is peace."

He looked at his book burning and thought of course of Heine. (But to the smug and angry men and boys in Bradford, Heinrich Heine meant nothing. *Dort, wo man Bücher verbrennt, verbrennt man am Ende auch Menschen*.) Where they burn books they will in the end burn people too. The line from *Almansor,* prophetically written over a century before the Nazi bonfires, and later engraved in the ground at the Berlin Opernplatz, the site of that old Nazi book burning: Would it one day also be inscribed on the sidewalk of the Tyrls to commemorate this much smaller, but still shameful deed? No, he thought. Probably not. Even though the book burned in *Almansor* was the Qur'an, and the book burners were members of the Inquisition.

Heine was a Jew who converted to Lutheranism. An apostate, you could say, if that was the sort of language you cared to use. He too was being accused of apostasy, among many other offenses: blasphemy, insult, offense. *The Jews made him do it,* they said. *His publisher was a Jew and paid him to do it. His wife, a Jew, put him up to it.* This was bleakly comic. Marianne was not a Jew; and the way things were between them most of the time she couldn't have persuaded him to wait for the signal before crossing a busy road. But on this day, January 14, 1989, they had sunk their differences and held hands.

He had been sent a T-shirt as a gift from an unknown admirer. BLASPHEMY IS A VICTIMLESS CRIME. But now the victory of the Enlightenment was looking temporary, reversible. Old language had been renewed, defeated ideas were on the march. In Yorkshire they had burned his book.

Now he was angry, too.

"How fragile civilization is," he wrote in the *Observer,* "how easily, how merrily a book burns! Inside my novel, its characters seek to become fully human by facing up to the great facts of love, death and (with or without God) the life of the soul. Outside it, the forces of inhumanity are on the march. 'Battle lines are being drawn up in India today,' one of my characters remarks. 'Secular versus religious, the light versus the dark. Better you choose which side you are on.' Now that the battle has spread to Britain, I can only hope it will not be lost by default. It is time for us to choose."

Not everyone saw it that way. There were many equivocations, particularly from members of Parliament with significant numbers of Muslim constituents. One of Bradford's MPs, Max Madden, along with Jack Straw, both of them parliamentarians with a strong history of defending freedom of speech, placed themselves meekly on the Muslim side of the fence along with other pugnacious Labour Party eminences, such as Roy Hattersley and Brian Sedgemore. Defending the play *Perdition,* Straw had written in September 1988, "Its idea is . . . offensive to me . . . but democracy is about according rights of free expression to those with whom one profoundly disagrees." On this occasion, though, Straw decided to support those calling for an extension of the blasphemy law to cover all religions (the United Kingdom's law of blasphemous libel protected only the established Church of England), and to outlaw material that "outraged religious feeling." (The blasphemy law was abolished altogether in 2008, in spite of Mr. Straw.) Max Madden was "sad" that "Rushdie has heightened protests about *The Satanic Verses* by refusing to give Muslims any right of reply (I suggested a brief insert [in the novel] allowing Muslims to explain why they find his book offensive.)" His fellow Bradford MP, Bob Cryer, robustly opposed the Muslim demonstrators, and did not lose his seat.

He was accused by Max Madden of being "coy" about confronting his opponents. He took the train to Birmingham to appear on the BBC TV lunchtime program *Daytime Live* to debate with one of the Muslim leaders, Hesham el-Essawy, an oleaginous Harley Street dentist who positioned himself as a moderate seeking only to soothe the inflamed situation. While they were on the air a demonstration gathered outside the BBC offices and could be seen through the plate glass windows behind him, shouting menacingly. The inflamed situation was neither mollified nor soothed.

The day after the Bradford book burning, Britain's biggest chain of booksellers, W. H. Smith, took the book off its shelves in all 430 of its stores. Its managing director, Malcolm Field, said, "In no way do we wish to be regarded as censors. It is our wish to provide the public with what they want."

The gulf between the private "Salman" he believed himself to be and the public "Rushdie" he barely recognized was growing by the day. One of them, Salman or Rushdie, he himself was unsure which, was dismayed by the numbers of Labour parliamentarians who were jumping on the Muslim bandwagon—after all, he had been a Labour supporter all his life—and noted gloomily that "the true conservatives of Britain are now in the Labour Party, while the radicals are all in blue."

It was difficult not to admire the efficiency of his adversaries. Faxes and telexes flew from country to country, single-page documents with bullet points were circulated through mosques and other religious organizations, and pretty soon everyone was singing from the same song sheet. Modern information technology was being used in the service of retrograde ideas: The modern was being turned against itself by the medieval, in the service of a worldview that disliked modernity itself—rational, reasonable, innovative, secular, skeptical, challenging, creative modernity, the antithesis of mystical, static, intolerant, stultifying faith. The rising tide of Islamic radicalism was described by its own ideologues as a "revolt against history." History, the forward progress of peoples through time, was itself the enemy, more than any mere infidels or blasphemers. But the new, which was history's supposedly despised creation, could be employed to revive the power of the old.

Allies came forward as well as opponents. He had lunch with Aziz al-Azmeh, the Syrian professor of Islamic studies at Exeter University, who would write, in the following years, some of the most trenchant criticisms of the attack on *The Satanic Verses,* as well as some of the most scholarly defenses of the novel from within the Islamic tradition. He met Gita Sahgal, a writer and activist for women's rights and human rights whose mother was the distinguished Indian novelist Nayantara Sahgal, and whose great-uncle was Jawaharlal Nehru himself. Gita was one of the founders of Women Against Fundamentalism, a group that tried, with some courage, to argue against the Muslim demonstrators. On January 28, 1989, perhaps eight thousand Muslims marched through the streets of London to gather in Hyde Park. Gita and her colleagues set up a counterdemonstration to challenge the marchers, and they were physically assaulted and even knocked to the ground. This did not diminish their resolve.

On January 18, Bruce Chatwin died in Nice at the home of his friend Shirley Conran.

The novel was about to be published in the United States—the finished U.S. edition arrived at his home, looking beautiful—and there were threats of "murder and mayhem" from American Muslims. There were rumors that there was a $50,000 contract out on his life. Arguments raged on in the press but for the moment most of the editorial commentary was on his side. "I am fighting the battle of my life," he wrote in his journal, "and in the last week I have begun to feel I'm winning. But the fear of violence remains." When he read this entry later he marveled at its optimism. Even at this close proximity to the hammer blow from Iran he had not been able to foresee the future. He would not have made much of a prophet.

He had begun to lead two lives: the public life of the controversy, and what remained of his old private life. January 23, 1989, was his and Marianne's first wedding anniversary. She took him to the opera to see *Madama Butterfly*. She had booked excellent seats in the front row of the grand tier and as the lights went down Princess Diana came in and sat down next to him. He wondered what she thought of the opera's story, about a woman promised love by a man who left her and eventually returned, having married another woman, to break her heart.

At the Whitbread Book of the Year awards the next day, his novel, winner of the Best Novel category, was up against four other category winners, including A. N. Wilson's biography of Tolstoy and a first novel by a former staff nurse in a psychiatric hospital, Paul Sayer's *The Comforts of Madness*. He ran into Sayer in the men's toilets. The young man was feeling physically ill with nerves and he tried to comfort him. An hour later Sayer won the award. When news of the jury's deliberations leaked out it was plain that two of the judges, the Tory cabinet minister Douglas Hurd, the home secretary, and the conservative journalist Max Hastings, had scuppered *The Satanic Verses* for reasons that were not wholly literary. The noise of the demonstrations had, so to speak, reached the jury chamber, and made its point.

He had his first quarrel with Peter Mayer and Peter Carson at Viking Penguin, because they were unwilling to contest the Indian ban on his novel in the courts.

He was invited to lunch by Graham Greene, who was interested to meet London-based writers of non-British origin. He went to the Reform Club for lunch along with Michael Ondaatje, Ben Okri, Hanan al-Shaykh, Wally Mongane Serote and a few others, including Marianne. When he arrived, Greene's long form was folded into a deep armchair, but the great man sprang to his feet and cried, "Rushdie! Come and sit here and tell me how you managed to make so much trouble! I never made nearly as much trouble as that!" This was oddly comforting. He understood how heavy his heart had grown and how much he needed such a moment of lightness and support. He sat beside the great man and told him as much as he could and Greene listened with great attention, and then, without offering any judgment at all, clapped his hands and cried, "Right. Lunch." At lunch he ate almost nothing but drank liberal quantities of wine. "I only eat," he said, "because it allows me to drink a little more." After lunch a photograph was taken on the steps of the club, Greene beaming in the center of the picture in a short brown coat, looking like Gulliver in Lilliput.

Several weeks later he showed this photograph to one of the Special Branch officers on his protection team. "This is Graham Greene," he said, "the great British novelist." "Oh, yeah," said the policeman reflectively. "He used to be one of ours."

The book was getting excellent reviews in the United States but on February 8 he received a mixed one from his wife, who told him she was leaving him; however, she still wanted him to come to the publication dinner for her novel *John Dollar*. Four days later the strange interregnum between publication and calamity came to an end.

Two thousand protesters was a small crowd in Pakistan. Even the most modestly potent politico could put many more thousands on the streets just by clapping his hands. That only two thousand "fundamentalists" could be found to storm the U.S. Information Center in the heart of Islamabad was, in a way, a good sign. It meant the protests hadn't really caught fire. Prime Minister Benazir Bhutto was out of the country at the time, on a state visit to China, and it was speculated that destabilizing her administration had been the demonstrators' real aim. Religious extremists had long suspected her of being guilty of the crime of secularism, and they wanted to put her on the spot. Not for the last time, *The Satanic Verses* was being used as a football in a political game that had little or nothing to do with it.

Objects were thrown at the security forces, bricks and stones, and there were screams of *American dogs* and *Hang Salman Rushdie,* the usual stuff. None of this fully explained the police response, which was to open fire and still fail to prevent some demonstrators from storming the building. The moment the first bullet hit its human target the story changed. The police used rifles, semiautomatic weapons and pump-action shotguns, and the confrontation lasted for three hours, and in spite of all that weaponry the demonstrators reached the roof of the building and the U.S. flag was burned and so were effigies of "the United States" and himself. On another day he might have asked himself where the factory was that supplied the thousands of American flags that were burned each year around the world. On this day everything else that happened was dwarfed by a single fact.

Five people were shot dead.

Rushdie you are dead, the demonstrators shouted, and for the first time he thought they might be right. Violence begat violence. The next day there was another riot in Kashmir—his beloved Kashmir, his family's original home—and another man was killed.

Blood will have blood, he thought.

Here was a mortally ill old man lying in a darkened room. Here was his son telling him about Muslims shot dead in India and Pakistan. There is a book that caused this, the son told the old man, a book that is against Islam. A few hours later the son arrived at the offices of Iranian television with a document in his hand. A *fatwa* or edict was usually a formal document, signed and witnessed and given under seal, but this was just a piece of paper bearing a typewritten text. Nobody ever saw the formal document, if one existed, but the son of the mortally ill old man said this was his father's edict and nobody was disposed to argue with him. The piece of paper was handed to the station news-reader and he began to read.

It was Valentine's Day.

III

Year Zero

III
——————
Year Zero

The Special Branch officer was Wilson and the intelligence officer was Wilton and they both answered to the name of Will. Will Wilson and Will Wilton: It was like a music-hall joke except that there was nothing funny about anything that day. He was told that as the threat against him was considered to be extremely serious—it was at "level two," which meant he was considered to be in more danger than anyone in the country except, perhaps, the queen—and as he was being menaced by a foreign power, he was entitled to the protection of the British state. Protection was formally offered and accepted. It was explained to him that he would be allocated two protection officers, two drivers and two cars. The second car was in case the first one broke down. He was to understand that because of the unique nature of the assignment and the imponderable risks involved all the officers protecting him were volunteers. Nobody on this job was here against his will. He was introduced to his first "prot" team: Stanley Doll and Ben Winters. Stanley was one of the best tennis players in the police force. Benny was one of the few black officers in the Branch and wore a chic tan leather jacket. They were both strikingly handsome and packing heat. The Branch were the stars of the Metropolitan Police, the double-o elite. He had never before met anyone who actually was licensed to kill, and Stan and Benny were presently licensed to do so *on his behalf.*

They wore their weapons at waist level, clipped to the backs of their trouser belts. American detectives used holsters under their jackets but, as Stan and Benny demonstrated, this was less desirable, because if you had to draw your weapon from that holster it had to move through an arc of maybe as much as ninety degrees before it was pointing at its target. The risk of firing slightly too soon or too late and hitting the wrong person was considerable. If you drew from the hip your weapon came up in line with the target and your level of accuracy increased. But there was a different sort of risk. If you squeezed the trigger too early you shot yourself in the behind.

Regarding the matter in hand, Benny and Stan were reassuring. "It can't be allowed," Stan said. "Threatening a British citizen. It's not on. It'll get sorted. You just need to lie low for a couple of days and let the politicians sort it out." "You can't go home, obviously," Benny said. "That wouldn't be too kosher. Is there anywhere you'd like to go for a few days?" "Pick somewhere nice," said Stan, "and we'll just whiz you off there for a stretch until you're in the clear." He wanted to believe in their optimism. Maybe the Cotswolds, he said. Maybe somewhere in that picture-postcard region of rolling hills and houses of golden stone. There was a famous country inn in the Cotswold village of Broadway called the Lygon Arms. He had often wanted to go there for a weekend but had never made it. Would the Lygon Arms be a possibility? Stan and Benny looked at each other and something passed between them. "I don't see why not," Stan said. "We'll look into it."

For most of that day Marianne and he stayed in the basement apartment at 38 Lonsdale Square. Benny stayed with them while Stan looked into things. He wanted to see his son again before diving for cover, he said, and he'd like to see his sister, too, and even though they warned him that those might be locations the "bad guys" would expect him to visit, they agreed to "set it up." Once it was dark he was driven to Burma Road in an armored Jaguar. The armor plating was so thick that the headroom was much less than it should have been. Tall politicians like Douglas Hurd found these cars impossibly uncomfortable. The doors were so heavy that if they swung shut accidentally and hit you they could injure you quite seriously. If the car was parked on a tilt it was almost impossible to pull the door toward you. The fuel consumption of an armored Jaguar was around six miles to the gallon. It weighed as much as a small tank. He was given this information by his first Special Branch driver, Dennis "the Horse" Chevalier, a big, cheerful, jowly, thick-lipped man, "one of the older fellows," he said. "Do you know the technical term for us Special Branch drivers?" Dennis the Horse asked him. He did not know. "The term is OFDs," said Dennis. "That's us." And what did OFD stand for? Dennis laughed a big, throaty, slightly wheezing laugh. "Only Fucking Drivers," he said. He would grow accustomed to police humor. One of his other drivers was known throughout the Branch as the king of Spain, because he had once left his Jag unlocked while he went to the tobacconist's and had returned to find that it had been stolen. Hence the nickname, because the king of Spain's name was—you had to say it slowly—Juan Car-los.

The bad guys were not lying in wait for him at Burma Road. He told Zafar and Clarissa what the prot team had said. "It will be over in a few days." Zafar looked immensely relieved. On Clarissa's face were all the doubts he was trying to pretend he didn't feel. Zafar asked when they could see each other again and he didn't know the answer. Clarissa said they might go for the weekend to her friends the Hoffmans' home in Oxfordshire. He said, "Okay, maybe there, if I can make it." He hugged his son tightly and left.

(Neither Zafar nor Clarissa were offered police protection at any time. It was not thought, the police told him, that they were in danger. That failed to reassure him, and his fear for them both preyed on him every day. But Clarissa and he decided that it would be best if Zafar continued to lead as normal a life as possible. She made it her business to give him that normal life; which was more than brave.)

It occurred to him that he hadn't eaten all day. On the way to Wembley to see Sameen they stopped at a McDonald's drive-through and he discovered that the thick windows of the Jaguar didn't open. There were other armored cars, Mercedes and BMWs, that could be custom-made with opening windows, but they were more expensive and not British and so were not part of the police fleet. Stan, sitting in the front passenger seat, had to get out to order and then walk to the pickup point to collect the food. When they finished eating, the Jaguar would not start. They had to leave Dennis the Horse swearing blue murder at his broken-down vehicle and get into the backup car, a Range Rover known as the Beast, driven by another gentle, smiling giant called Mickey Crocker, another of the "older fellows." The Beast was very old too, and very heavy and a beast to steer. It would get stuck in mud and would sometimes be incapable of getting to the top of an icy hill road. This was mid-February, the coldest, iciest time of the year. "Sorry about this, mate," Mick Crocker said. "It's not the best vehicle in the garridge." He sat in the back of the Beast and hoped the men protecting him worked better than their cars.

Sameen, a qualified lawyer (though no longer practicing—she worked in adult education now), had always had a sharp political mind and had a lot to say about what was going on. The Iranian Revolution had been shaky ever since Khomeini had been forced, in his own words, to "eat poison" and accept the unsuccessful end of his Iraq war, which had left a generation of young Iranians dead or maimed. The *fatwa* was his way of regaining political momentum, reenergizing the faithful. It was her brother's bad luck to be the dying man's last stand. As for the British Muslim "leaders," who exactly did they lead? They were leaders without followers, mountebanks trying to make careers out of her brother's misfortune. For a generation the politics of ethnic minorities in Britain had been secular and socialist. This was the mosques' way of destroying that project and getting religion into the driving seat. British "Asians" had never splintered into Hindu, Muslim and Sikh factions before (though there had been splinterings of a different sort; during the Bangladesh war, a bitter British-Pakistani and British-Bangladeshi schism had developed). Somebody needed to answer these people who were driving a communalist, sectarian wedge through the community, she said, these mullahs and so-called leaders, to name them as the hypocrites and opportunists that they were. She was ready to be that person, and he knew that, as articulate and skilled in advocacy as she was, she would make a formidable representative.

But he asked her not to do it. Her daughter Maya was less than a year old. If she became his public spokesman the media would camp outside her house and there would be no escape from the glare of publicity; her private life, her daughter's young life, would become a thing of klieg lights and microphones. Also, it was impossible to know what danger it might draw toward her. He didn't want her to be at risk because of him. And there was another problem: If she were to be very publicly identified as his "voice," then, the prot team said, it would become much harder for him to be brought to her home to visit her. He understood that he needed to divide the people he knew into "private" and "public" camps. He needed her, he said, as a private supporter more than as a public champion. Reluctantly, she agreed.

One of the unforeseen consequences of this decision was that as the "affair" blazed on, he himself was obliged to be mostly invisible, because the police urged him not to speak out and further inflame the situation, advice he accepted for a time, until he refused to be silent any longer; and in his absence there was nobody who loved him speaking for him, not his wife, not his sister, not his closest friends—the ones he wanted to continue to be able to see. He became, in the media, a man whom nobody loved but many people hated. "Death, perhaps, is a bit too easy for him," said Mr. Iqbal Sacranie of the UK Action Committee on Islamic Affairs. "His mind must be tormented for the rest of his life unless he asks for forgiveness from Almighty Allah." In 2005, this same Sacranie was knighted at the recommendation of the Blair government for his services to community relations.

On the way to the Cotswolds the car stopped to fill up with gas. He needed to go to the toilet and opened the door and got out. Every single person in the gas station turned their heads in unison to stare at him. He was on the front page of every newspaper—Martin Amis said, memorably, that he had "vanished into the front page"—and had overnight become one of the most recognizable men in the country. The faces looked friendly—a man waved, another gave the thumbs-up sign—but it was alarming to be so intensely visible at exactly the moment that he was being asked to lie low. When he set foot on the village streets of Broadway the reaction was the same. A woman came up to him in the street and said, "Good luck." In the hotel the highly trained staff could not prevent themselves from gawping. He had become a freak show and he and Marianne were both relieved when they reached the privacy of their beautiful old-world room. He was given a "panic button" to press if he was worried about anything. He tested the panic button. It didn't work.

They were given a small private room to eat their meals in. The hotel had warned Stan and Benny of a possible difficulty. One of their other guests was a journalist from the *Daily Mirror,* who had taken a neighboring room for a few days with a lady who was not his wife. As it turned out this did not become a problem. The lady was clearly possessed of powerful charms, because the man from the *Mirror* did not emerge from their room for several days, and so, at that moment when the tabloid press had employed teams of snoops to find out where the author of *The Satanic Verses* had gone to ground, the tabloid journalist in the room next door to his own missed his scoop.

On his second day at the Lygon Arms, Stan and Benny came to see him with a piece of paper in their hands. President Ali Khamenei of Iran had hinted that if he apologized "this wretched man might yet be spared." "It's felt," Stan said, "that you should do something to lower the temperature." "Yeah," Benny assented, "that's the thinking. The right statement from you could be of assistance." Felt by whom, he wanted to know; whose thinking was this? "It's the general opinion," Stan said opaquely, "upstairs." Was it a police opinion or a government opinion? "They've taken the liberty of preparing a text," said Stan. "By all means read it through." "By all means make alterations if the style isn't pleasing," said Ben. "You're the writer." "I should say, in fairness," said Stan, "that the text has been approved."

The text he was handed was unacceptable: craven, self-abasing. To sign it would be a defeat. Could it really be that this was the deal he was being offered: that he would only receive government support and police protection if, abandoning his principles and the defense of his book, he fell to his knees and groveled? Stan and Ben looked extremely uncomfortable. "As I say," said Benny, "you're free to make alterations." "Then we'll see how they play," said Stan. And supposing he chose not to make a statement at all at this time? "It's thought to be a good idea," Stan said. "There are high-level negotiations taking place on your behalf. And then there are the Lebanon hostages to consider and Mr. Roger Cooper in jail in Tehran. Their situation is worse than yours. You're asked to do your bit." (In the 1980s the Lebanese Hezbollah group, wholly funded from Tehran, used a number of different pseudonyms to capture ninety-six foreign nationals from twenty-one countries, including several Americans and Britons. In addition Mr. Cooper, a British businessman, was seized and imprisoned in Iran.)

It was an impossible task: to write something that could be received as an olive branch without giving way on what was important. The statement he came up with was one he mostly loathed. "As author of *The Satanic Verses* I recognize that Muslims in many parts of the world are genuinely distressed by the publication of my novel. I profoundly regret the distress that publication has occasioned to the sincere followers of Islam. Living as we do in a world of many faiths this experience has served to remind us that we must all be conscious of the sensibilities of others." His private, self-justifying voice argued that he was apologizing for the distress—and after all he had never wanted to cause distress—but he was not apologizing for the book itself. And yes, we should be conscious of others' sensibilities, but that did not mean we should surrender to them. That was his combative, unstated subtext. But he knew that for the text to be effective it had to be read as a straightforward apology. That thought made him feel physically ill.

It was a useless gesture. It was rejected, then half-accepted, then rejected again, both by British Muslims and by the Iranian leadership. The strong position would have been to refuse to negotiate with intolerance. He had taken the weak position and was therefore treated as a weakling. The *Observer* defended him—"neither Britain nor the author has anything to apologize for"—but his feeling of wrongness, of having made a serious misstep, was soon confirmed. "Even if Salman Rushdie becomes the most pious man of all time, it is incumbent on every Muslim to employ everything he has got, his life and his wealth, to send him to hell," said the dying imam. It felt like the bottom of the barrel. It was not. The bottom of the barrel would be reached a few months later.

The protection officers said he should not spend more than two nights at the Lygon Arms. He was lucky the media hadn't found him yet, and in another day or so they surely would. This was when another harsh truth was explained: It was up to him to find places to stay. The police advice, which was more like an instruction, was that he could not return to his home, as it would be impossible (which was to say, very expensive) to protect him there. But "safe houses" would not be provided. If such places existed, he never saw them. The generality of people, trained by spy fiction, firmly believed in the existence of safe houses, and assumed that he was being protected in one such fortress at the public's expense. Criticisms of the money spent on his protection would grow more vociferous with the passing weeks: an indication of a shift in public opinion. But on his second day at the Lygon Arms he was told he had twenty-four hours to find himself somewhere else to go.

He made his daily phone call to Clarissa's house to speak to Zafar and she offered him a temporary solution. She was working then as a literary agent at the A. P. Watt agency, whose senior partner, Hilary Rubinstein, had a country cottage in the village of Thame in Oxfordshire, and had offered it for a night or two. It was the first of many acts of generosity by friends and acquaintances, without whose kindness he would have been rendered homeless. Hilary's cottage was relatively small and not very secluded, not an ideal location, but he needed it and was grateful. The arrival of the repaired Jaguar, the Beast, Stan the tennis player, Benny the sharp dresser, Dennis the Horse and big Mickey C., plus Marianne and the invisible man could not go unnoticed in a tiny village. He was certain that everyone knew exactly what was going on at the Rubinstein place. But nobody came nosing around. A proper English distance and reserve was maintained. It was even possible for him to be driven to see Zafar for a few hours at the Hoffmans' country house. He had no idea where to go next. He had been making phone calls to everyone he could think of, without success. Then he checked his voice mail and found a message from Deborah Rogers, the agent he had dismissed when he appointed Andrew Wylie. "Call me," the message said. "I think we may be able to help."

Deb and her husband, the composer Michael Berkeley, offered him their farm in Wales. "If you need it," she said simply, "it's yours." He was deeply moved. "Look," she said, "it's perfect, actually, because everyone thinks we've fallen out, and so nobody would ever imagine you'd be here." The next day his strange little circus descended on Middle Pitts, that homely farmhouse in the hilly Welsh border country. Low clouds and rain and the renewal of a broken friendship, all disputes swept away by the pressure of events and by long, loving embraces. "Stay as long as you need to," Deb said, but he knew he would not abuse her and Michael's hospitality. He needed to find a place of his own. Marianne agreed to contact local estate agents the next day and start looking at rental properties. They had to hope that her face would be less instantly recognizable than his.

As for him, he could not be seen at the farm or its safety would be "compromised." There was a farmer who looked after the sheep for Michael and Deb and at one point he came down off the hill to talk to Michael about something. An ordinary moment became a crisis when invisibility was deemed essential. "You'd better get out of sight," Michael told him and he had to duck down behind a kitchen counter. As he crouched there listening to Michael get rid of his man as quickly as possible he felt a sense of deep shame. To hide in this way was to be stripped of all self-respect. To be told to hide was a humiliation. Maybe, he thought, to live like this would be worse than death. In his novel *Shame* he had written about the workings of Muslim "honor culture," at the poles of whose moral axis were honor and shame, very different from the Christian narrative of guilt and redemption. He came from that culture even though he was not religious, and had been raised to care deeply about questions of pride. To skulk and hide was to lead a dishonorable life. He felt, very often in those years, profoundly ashamed. Both shamed and ashamed.

It was rare for a world news story to rest so squarely on the acts, motives, character, and alleged crimes of a single individual. The sheer weight of events was a crushing burden. He imagined the Great Pyramid of Giza turned upside down with the apex resting on his neck. The news roared in his ears. It seemed that everyone on earth had an opinion. Hesham al-Essawy, the "moderate" dentist from the BBC program, called him a product of sixties permissiveness, "which has now produced the AIDS crisis." Members of the Pakistani parliament recommended the immediate dispatch of assassins to the United Kingdom. In Iran the most powerful clerics, Khamenei and Rafsanjani, fell into line behind the imam. "A black arrow of retribution is flying towards the heart of that blasphemous bastard," Khamenei said during a visit to Yugoslavia. An Iranian ayatollah named Hassan Sanei offered $1 million in bounty money for the apostate's head. It was not clear if this ayatollah possessed $1 million, or how easy it would be to claim the reward, but these were not logical days. The television was full of bearded (and clean-shaven) men shouting about death. The British Council's library in Karachi—a drowsy, pleasant place he had often visited—was bombed.

Somehow, in these blaring, terrible days, his literary reputation survived the battering. Much of the British and American and Indian commentary continued to stress the quality of his art and of the book under attack, but there were signs that this, too, might change. He watched a terrible episode of the *Late Show* on BBC television in which Ian McEwan, Aziz al-Azmeh and the courageous Jordanian novelist Fadia Faqir, who had also received death threats for her work, attempted to defend him against one of the Bradford book burners and the ubiquitous dentist Essawy. The program was intemperate and dire language issued from his opponents' mouths, at once ignorant, bigoted and menacing. What made the episode especially terrible for him was that the prominent intellectual George Steiner—the very antithesis of an ignorant bigot—launched a powerful literary attack on his work. Soon after that other well-known British media figures, Auberon Waugh, Richard Ingrams, Bernard Levin, added their hostile comments. He was defended in other newspapers by Edward Said and Carlos Fuentes but he sensed the mood was beginning to shift. And his book tour to the United States was canceled, of course. There were gratifyingly positive notices in most of the American press but he would not be flying across the Atlantic anytime soon.

The publishing problems were multiplying. At the offices of Viking Penguin in London, and now in New York, many threatening telephone calls were received. Young women heard anonymous voices saying, "We know where you live. We know where your children go to school." There were many bomb scares though, fortunately, there was never a bomb at any of his publishers' offices, though Cody's bookstore in Berkeley, California, was hit by a pipe bomb. (Many years later he visited Cody's and was shown with great pride the damaged, burned-out area on the shelves where the bomb had been planted, and which Andy Ross and his staff had agreed to keep unrepaired, as the bookstore's badge of courage.) And in a cheap hotel in London, in Sussex Gardens near Paddington Station, a would-be bomber whose target may have been the Penguin offices—though it was also rumored that he was planning to attack the Israeli embassy—blew himself to bits, scoring what in Special Branch parlance was called an "own goal." After that there were dogs in the Penguin mailroom, trained to sniff out explosives.

Peter Mayer, the head of the company, commissioned a security report from Control Risks Information Services Limited of London, analyzing the "own goal" and the continuing threat to the company. Copies were sent to Andrew Wylie and Gillon Aitken. In this report the major players in the story were, presumably for security reasons, not referred to by name. Instead they were given the names of birds. The document was magnificently titled *Assessment of Strength and Potential of Dotterel Protest Against Godwit of Arctic Tern's Pigeon and Implications for Golden Plover.* It was perhaps not too difficult to work out that *Dotterel* meant Muslims, *Godwit* meant "the publisher" or "Viking Penguin," *Pigeon* was *The Satanic Verses* and *Golden Plover* was Penguin's parent company, the Pearson Group. The author of *Pigeon* was *Arctic Tern.*

Peter Mayer (who lacked his own ornithological identity, though in the newspapers he was often the King Penguin) forbade all "Pigeon-related personnel," on pain of instant dismissal, to speak to the press about Pigeon or Arctic Tern. The only public statements emanating from Godwit were to be made by their lawyer Martin Garbus or an official spokesman named Bob Gregory. Such statements as were made were cautiously defensive. All of this was understandable (except for the silly bird names, perhaps) but one consequence of this diktat by the King Penguin was that at the very moment at which the company's beleaguered author needed his publishers to speak up for him, his editors were gagged and silenced. That silence created a rift between publisher and author. For the moment, however, the cracks in the relationship were minor, because the company was behaving with great courage and high principle. Muslim voices were threatening Penguin with dire reprisals against its offices around the world, and threatening, too, a global ban on Penguin Books and on all the business activities of Pearson, a conglomerate with large interests across the Muslim world. In the face of these threats the Pearson leadership did not flinch.

Publication continued, and very large quantities of books were shipped and sold. When the book entered the *New York Times* bestseller list at number one, John Irving, who was used to being in that position but found himself stuck at number two, quipped that if that was what it took to get to the top spot, he was content to be runner-up. He himself well knew, as did Irving, that this was not a "real" number one bestseller; that scandal, not literary merit or popularity, was driving the sales. He also knew, and much appreciated, that many people bought a copy of *The Satanic Verses* to demonstrate their solidarity. John Irving had been his friend ever since Liz Calder had introduced them back in 1980. The joke was John's way of sending a friendly wave in his direction.

On the day the novel was published in America, February 22, 1989, there was a full-page advertisement in *The New York Times* paid for by the Association of American Publishers, the American Booksellers' Association and the American Library Association. "Free people write books," it said. "Free people publish books. Free people sell books. Free people buy books. Free people read books. In the spirit of America's commitment to free expression we inform the public that this book will be available to readers at bookshops and libraries throughout the country." PEN American Center, passionately led by his beloved friend Susan Sontag, held readings from the novel. Sontag, Don DeLillo, Norman Mailer, Claire Bloom and Larry McMurtry were among the readers. He was sent a tape of the event. It brought a lump to his throat. Long afterward he was told that some senior American writers had initially ducked for cover. Even Arthur Miller had made an excuse—that his Jewishness might be a counterproductive factor. But within days, whipped into line by Susan, almost all of them had found their better selves and stood up to be counted.

The fear that spread through the publishing industry was real because the threat was real. Publishers and translators were threatened by the *fatwa,* too. And yet the world of the book, in which free people made free choices, had to be defended. He thought often that the crisis was like an intense light shining down on everyone's choices and deeds, creating a world without shadows, a stark unequivocal place of right and wrong action, good and bad choices, yes and no, strength and weakness. In that harsh glare some publishers looked heroic while others looked spineless. Perhaps the most spineless of all was the head of a European publishing house, whom it would be unkind to name, who had bulletproof glass installed in the second-floor windows of his own office, but not in the first-floor windows through which his employees could be seen; and then brought a screwdriver to work so he could unscrew his company's nameplate from the front door of the office building. The German publishers, the distinguished house of Kiepenheuer und Witsch, summarily canceled his contract and tried to charge him for their security costs. (In the end the German edition was brought out by a large consortium of publishers and eminent individuals, which was the method also employed in Spain.) The French publisher Christian Bourgois was initially reluctant to bring out his edition and postponed publication a number of times, but was eventually persuaded to do so by the increasingly strident criticisms leveled at him in the French media. Andrew Wylie and Gillon Aitken were astonishing. They went country by country to coax, cajole, threaten and flatter publishers into doing their job. In many countries the book was only published because of their determined pressure on nervous editors.

In Italy, however, there were local heroes. His Italian publishers, Mondadori, published their edition a couple of days after the *fatwa*. Their proprietors—Silvio Berlusconi's holding company Fininvest, Carlo De Benedetti's CIR and the heirs of Arnoldo Mondadori—were wobblier than Viking Penguin's, and there were doubts expressed about the wisdom of publication, but the determination of the editorial director Giancarlo Bonacina and his staff won the day. The book was published as planned.

While all this and much more was happening the author of *The Satanic Verses* was crouching in shame behind a kitchen counter to avoid being seen by a sheep farmer.

Yes, as well as the screaming headlines there were the private crises, the knot in his stomach created by the constant need to find the next place to live, his fear for his family (his mother had arrived in London to stay with Sameen so that she could be nearer to him, but it would be some time before he could see her), and, of course, there was Marianne, whose daughter, Lara, in several impassioned phone calls, told her mother that "none of her friends could understand" why her mother was courting such danger. That was a fair point, a point anyone's daughter might have made. Marianne had found a house to rent and they could have it in a week. That had been a helpful deed, but he was privately certain that she would leave him if the crisis went on much longer. She was finding this new life very hard. Her book tour had been canceled, and if he had been in her position he would probably have left too. In the meanwhile she plunged into something like her normal work process, making copious notes about their location, copying bits of Welsh into her notebook, and beginning, almost at once, to write stories that weren't really fictions but dramatizations of what they were living through. One of these stories was called "Croeso i Gymru," which meant "Welcome to Wales," and began *We were on the lam in Wales,* a sentence that annoyed him because to be on the lam was to be running from the law. They were not criminals, he wanted to say, but did not. She wasn't in the mood for criticism. She was writing a story called "Learning Urdu."

The foreign secretary was on television telling lies about him. The British people, Sir Geoffrey Howe said, had no love for this book. It was extremely rude about Britain. It compared Britain, he said, to Hitler's Germany. The author of the unloved book found himself shouting at the television. "Where? On what page? Show me where I did that." The television did not reply. Sir Geoffrey's smug, bland, oddly docile features blinked back at him impassively. He recalled that the former Labour cabinet minister Denis Healey had once compared being attacked by Howe to being "savaged by a dead sheep" and for a quarter of a minute he considered suing the dead sheep for defamation. But that was stupid, of course. In the eyes of the world he himself was the great Defamer and as a result it was permissible to defame him back.

The dead sheep had company. The big unfriendly giant, Roald Dahl, was in the papers saying, "Rushdie is a dangerous opportunist." A couple of days earlier the archbishop of Canterbury, Robert Runcie, had said that he "understood the Muslims' feelings." Soon the pope would understand those feelings too, and the British chief rabbi, and the cardinal of New York. The God squad was lining up its troops. But

Nadine Gordimer wrote in his defense and on the day that he and Marianne left Deb and Michael's farm and moved into the rented house the so-called World Writers' Statement was published to support him, signed by thousands of writers. Britain and Iran had severed diplomatic relations. Bizarrely, it was Iran who had broken them off and not the Thatcher government. Apparently the British protection of the apostate renegade was more upsetting to the ayatollahs than the extraterritorial assault on a British citizen was to Britain. Or maybe the Iranians just got their retaliation in first.

The modest white-walled cottage with the pitched slate roof was called Tyn-y-Coed, the house in the woods, a common name for a house in those parts. It was near the village of Pentrefelin in Brecon, not far from the Black Mountains and the Brecon Beacons. There was a great deal of rain. When they arrived it was cold. The police officers tried to light the stove and after a good deal of clanking and swearing succeeded. He managed to find a small upstairs room where he could shut the door and pretend to work. The house felt bleak, as did the days. Margaret Thatcher was on television, understanding the insult to Islam and sympathizing with the insulted. He spoke to Gillon Aitken and Bill Buford and they both warned that there would be a backlash of public opinion against him for a while. He read the statements of support by the world's great writers published in *The New York Times Book Review* and took some comfort there. He spoke to Michael Foot on the phone and was uplifted by Foot's jerky, exclamatory declarations of absolute solidarity. He pictured Michael's long white hair flapping vehemently and his wife, Jill Craigie, by his side, serenely ferocious. "An outrage. All of it. Jill and I both say so. Yes, indeed."

There had been a change of protection team. Stan, Benny, Dennis and Mick had gone back to their families and he was now in the care of Dev Stonehouse, a "character" with a face suffused by the color of what looked like a drinking problem, full of scurrilous loose-tongued tales about other "principals" he had taken care of: the night the Irish politician Gerry Fitt drank sixteen gin and tonics, the intolerably high-handed behavior of the minister Tom King toward his prot team, "that chap might get a bullet put in his back one of these days," and, by contrast, the gentlemanly behavior of the firebrand Ulsterman Ian

Paisley, who remembered everyone's names, asked about their families, and prayed with his protection officers at the start of every day. In Dev's team were two more smiling, gentle-natured drivers, Alex and Phil, who turned a deaf ear to Dev "spouting his nonsense," and a second protection officer, Peter Huddle, who clearly loathed Detective-Sergeant Stonehouse. "He's like hemorrhoids," he said loudly in the kitchen, "a royal pain in the arse."

They took him for a walk in the Black Mountains—the landscape in which Bruce Chatwin had set his best book, *On the Black Hill*—and, out for once in the open air, with countryside and a skyline to look at instead of the interior walls of a house, he felt his spirits lift. This team liked to talk. "I can't buy my wife presents," mourned Alex, a lowland Scot. "She dislikes whatever I get her." Phil had been left to take care of the cars. "He'll be all right," said Alex. "OFDs like sitting in their vehicles." And apropos of nothing Dev announced that he had got laid the previous night. Alex and Peter's faces acquired expressions of distaste. Then suddenly he felt a sharp pain in his lower jaw. It was his lower wisdom teeth acting up. The pain faded after a while, but it was a warning. He might need to see a dentist.

They had told him they didn't like the idea of him going to London too often but they also understood that he needed to see his son. His friends made their homes available and he was driven in to meet Zafar there, at the Archway home of his old Cambridge friend Teresa Gleadowe and her husband, the gallerist Tony Stokes, at whose little Covent Garden gallery the launch party for *Midnight's Children* had been held in another lifetime, or at the Kentish Town home of Sue Moylan and Gurmukh Singh, who had met and fallen in love at his wedding to Clarissa and would never be apart again. They were an ideally suited odd couple: she the judge's daughter and classic English rose and he the tall, handsome Sikh from Singapore, a pioneer in the nascent science of computer software. (When Gurmukh decided to learn gardening he built a computer program that told him exactly what to do every day of the year. His garden, planted and maintained according to the program's instructions, thrived mightily.) Harold Pinter and Antonia Fraser opened their doors to him and so did many other friends. Bill Buford told him: "Your friends are going to close around you like an iron circle, and inside that ring you will be able to lead your life." That was exactly what they did. Their code of silence was unbreakable. Not one of them ever inadvertently let slip any details of his movements, not once. He wouldn't have survived six months without them. After much initial mistrust, the Special Branch came to rely on his friends, too—to appreciate that these were serious people who understood what needed to be done.

This was what had to happen for him to meet his boy. The team's "fifth man," who was based at Scotland Yard, would visit the "venue" in advance, assessing it for security, instructing the homeowners on what they had to do, lock those doors, draw those curtains. Then he would be driven to the venue, always by the most circuitous route, with many countersurveillance tricks being employed, a process known as "dry-cleaning"—making sure they weren't being followed. (Countersurveillance driving involved, in part, driving as weirdly as possible. On a motorway he was sometimes driven at wildly varying speeds, because, if anyone else did the same thing, it meant they had a tail. Sometimes Alex would get into an exit lane and drive very fast. Anyone following would not know if he was going to leave the motorway or not and would have to drive very fast behind them, thus revealing his presence.) Meanwhile another car would collect Zafar and bring him to the meeting place, also after being "dry-cleaned." It was a lot, but then he saw the joy in his child's eyes and that told him everything he needed to know.

He saw Zafar for an hour at the Stokes household. He spent another hour with his mother and Sameen at the Pinters' home in Campden Hill Square and in his mother's iron self-control he saw again the woman she had been in the days before and after his father's death. She hid her fear and worry behind a tight but loving smile, but her fists often clenched. Then, because it was too late to drive all the way back to Wales, he was taken to Ian McEwan's cottage in the village of Chedworth in Gloucestershire, and was able to spend a night in the company of good and loving friends—Alan Yentob and his partner, Philippa Walker, as well as Ian. In an interview with *The New Yorker*, Ian later said, "I'll never forget—the next morning we got up early. He had to move on. Terrible time for him. We stood at the kitchen counter making toast and coffee, listening to the eight o'clock BBC news. He was standing right by my side and he was the lead item on the news. Hezbollah had put its sagacity and weight behind the project to kill him." Ian's memory was slightly at fault. The threat on the news that day did not come from the Iranian-financed Hezbollah group in Lebanon but from Ahmad Jibril, leader of the Popular Front for the Liberation of Palestine–General Command.

Commander John Howley of the Special Branch—the high-flying police officer in charge of "A" Squad, who afterward rose to the rank of deputy assistant commissioner and became the head both of the Special Branch and the antiterrorism work of Scotland Yard—came to see him in Wales, accompanied by Bill Greenup, the officer whom Marianne, in her Welsh story, had renamed "Mr. Browndown." Mr. Greenup's attitude toward him was unfriendly. It was plainly his view that they were dealing with a troublemaker who had got more than he bargained for and now good police officers had to risk their necks to save his, to rescue him from the consequences of his own actions. And the troublemaker was a Labour voter too and had criticized the very government, the Thatcher administration, which was now obliged to sanction his protection. There were hints from Mr. Greenup that the Special Branch was thinking of handing over his protection to regular uniformed police, and he could take his chances. It looked now as though he would be at risk for a very considerable time and that was not what the Special Branch had foreseen, or wanted. This was the bad news that Commander Howley, a man of few words, had come all the way to Wales to give him. It was no longer a matter of lying low for a few days to let the politicians sort it out. There was no prospect of his being allowed (*allowed?*) to resume his normal life in the foreseeable future. He could not just decide to go home and take his chances. To do so would be to endanger his neighbors and to place an intolerable burden on police resources, because an entire street, or more than one street, would need to be sealed off and protected. He had to wait until there was a "major political shift." What did that mean, he asked: Until Khomeini died? Or: Never? Howley did not have an opinion. It was not possible for him to estimate how long.

He had been living with the threat of death for one month. There had been further rallies against *The Satanic Verses* in Paris, New York, Oslo, Kashmir, Bangladesh, Turkey, Germany, Thailand, the Netherlands, Sweden, Australia and West Yorkshire. The toll of injuries and deaths had continued to rise. The novel had by now also been banned in Syria, Lebanon, Kenya, Brunei, Thailand, Tanzania, Indonesia, and across the Arab world. A Muslim "leader" named Abdul Hussain Chowdhury asked the chief metropolitan magistrate in London to grant him a summons against Salman Rushdie and his publishers, alleging "blasphemous libel and seditious libel," but the injunction was not granted. Fifth Avenue in New York had to be sealed off because there was a bomb scare in a bookstore. In those days there were still bookstores up and down Fifth Avenue.

The united front of the literary world cracked, and it caused him real pain to see his own world fracturing under the pressure of these events. First the West Berlin Academy of Arts refused to allow a "pro-Rushdie" solidarity rally to take place on its premises because of security concerns. This led Germany's greatest writer, Günter Grass, and the philosopher Günther Anders, to resign from the academy in protest. Then, in Stockholm, the Swedish Academy, which awarded the Nobel Prize in Literature, decided not to issue a formal statement condemning the *fatwa*. The eminent novelist Kerstin Ekman resigned her seat at the table of eighteen academicians. Lars Gyllensten also withdrew from the academy's deliberations.

He felt awful. "Don't do it, Günter, Günther, Kerstin, Lars," he wanted to shout. "Don't do it on my account." He didn't want to split academies, to injure the world of books. That was the opposite of what he wanted. He was trying to defend the book against the burners of books. These small battles of the bookish seemed like tragedies at a time when literary freedom itself was so violently under attack.

On the Ides of March he was flung without warning into the lowest circle of Orwellian hell. *"You asked me once,"* said O'Brien, *"what was in Room 101. I told you that you knew the answer already. Everyone knows it. The thing that is in Room 101 is the worst thing in the world."* The worst thing in the world was different for every individual. For Winston

Smith in Orwell's *1984,* it was rats. For himself in a cold Welsh cottage it was an unanswered phone call.

He had established a daily routine with Clarissa. At seven o'clock every evening, without fail, he would call to say hello to Zafar. He was talking to his son as openly as he could about everything that was going on, trying to put an optimistic spin on it, to keep the monsters in his child's imagination at bay, but keeping him informed. He had quickly learned that as long as Zafar heard the news from him first, the boy was able to handle it. If by some mischance they failed to speak and Zafar heard something shocking from friends in the school playground, he became very upset. It was vital to communicate. Hence the daily call. He had agreed with Clarissa that if for some reason she couldn't be at home with Zafar at seven she should leave a message on the St. Peter's Street answering machine telling him when they would be back. He called the Burma Road house. There was no reply. He left a message on Clarissa's machine and then *interrogated* his own. She had not left a message. Oh, well, he thought, they're a little late. Fifteen minutes later he called again. Nobody picked up. He called his own machine again: nothing there. Ten minutes later he made a third call. Still nothing. By now he had begun to worry. It was almost 7:45 P.M. on a school night. Not normal for them to be out so late. He called twice more in the next ten minutes. No response. Now he began to panic.

The day's events faded away. The Islamic Conference Organization had called him an apostate but had avoided supporting the Iranian death order. Muslims were planning a march in Cardiff. Marianne was upset because her just-published novel *John Dollar* had sold exactly twenty-four copies in the preceding week. None of it mattered. He called Burma Road repeatedly, dialing and redialing like a madman, and his hands began to shake. He was sitting on the floor, wedged up against a wall, with the phone on his lap, dialing, redialing. The prot team had changed over again; Stan and Benny were back with two new drivers, a cheeky-chappie good sort called Keith, a.k.a. "Stumpy," and a red-haired Welshman named Alan Owen. Stan noticed his "principal's" agitated phone activity and came to ask if everything was all right.

He said no, it didn't seem to be. Clarissa and Zafar were by now an hour and a quarter late for their phone appointment with him and had left no word of explanation. Stan's face was serious. "Is this," he asked, "a break in routine? That's one of the things to be concerned about, any unexpected break." Yes, he said, it was a break in routine. "Okay," said Stan, "leave it with me. I'll make some inquiries." A few minutes later he came back to say he had spoken to "Metpol"—the London Metropolitan Police—and a car would be sent to the address to do a "drive-by." After that the minutes moved as slowly and coldly as glacial ice and when the report came it froze his heart. "The car drove by the premises just now," Steve told him, "and the report, I'm sorry to say, is that the front door is open and all the lights are on." He was unable to reply. "Obviously the officers did not attempt to go up to the house or enter," Steve said. "In the situation as it is they would not know what they might encounter."

He saw bodies sprawling on the stairs in the front hall. He saw the brightly lit rag-doll corpses of his son and his first wife drenched in blood. Life was over. He had run away and hidden like a terrified rabbit and his loved ones had paid the price. "Just to inform you on what we're doing," said Stan. "We will be going in there, but you'll have to give us approximately forty minutes. They need to assemble an army."

Maybe they were not both dead. Maybe his son was alive and taken hostage. "You understand," he said to Stan, "that if they have him and they want a ransom, they want me to exchange myself for him, then I'm going to do that, and you guys can't stop me doing it. I just want that to be clear."

Stan took a slow, dark pause, like a character in a Pinter play. Then he said, "That thing about exchanging hostages, that only happens in the movies. In real life, I'm sorry to tell you, if this is a hostile intervention, they are both probably dead already. The question you have to ask yourself is, do you want to die as well."

The police in the kitchen had fallen silent. Marianne sat facing him, staring at him, unable to offer comfort. He had no more to say. There was only the crazy dialing, every thirty seconds, the dialing and then the ring tone and then Clarissa's voice asking him to leave a message. That beautiful, long, green-eyed girl. The mother of his gentle, lively, loving son. There was no message worth leaving. *I'm sorry* didn't begin to cover it. He hung up and redialed and there was her voice again. And again.

After a very long time Stan came and said quietly, "Won't be long now. They're just about ready." He nodded and waited for reality to deal him what would be a fatal blow. He was not aware of weeping but his face was wet. He went on dialing Zafar's number. As if the telephone possessed occult powers, as if it was a Ouija board that could put him in touch with the dead.

Then unexpectedly there was a click. Somebody had picked up the receiver at the other end. "Hello?" he said, his voice unsteady. "Dad?" said Zafar's voice. "What's going on, Dad? There's a policeman at the door and he says there are fifteen more on the way." Relief cascaded over him and momentarily tied his tongue. "Dad? Are you there?" "Yes," he said, "I'm here. Is your mother all right? Where were you?" They had been at a school drama performance that had run very late. Clarissa came on to the phone and apologized. "I'm sorry, I should have left you a message, I just forgot. I'm sorry."

The usual aftershock biochemicals ran in his veins and he didn't know if he was happy or enraged. "But what about the door?" he asked. "Why was the front door open and all the lights left on?" It was Zafar on the other end again. "It wasn't, Dad," he said. "We just got back and opened the door and turned the lights on and then the policeman came."

"It would seem," said Detective-Sergeant Stan, "that there has been a regrettable error. The car we sent to have a look, looked at the wrong house."

The wrong house. A police mistake. Just a stupid mistake. Everything was all right. The monsters were back in the broom cupboard and under the floorboards. The world had not exploded. His son was alive. The door of Room 101 swung open. Unlike Winston Smith, he had escaped.

This had been the worst day of his life.

The message on his machine was from the novelist Margaret Drabble. "Do call if you can." And when he did call she made, in her brisk, efficient, no-nonsense way, an offer as impossibly generous in its way as Deborah Rogers's had been. She and her husband, Michael Holroyd, the biographer of Lytton Strachey, Augustus John and George Bernard Shaw, had been doing up a cottage in Porlock Weir on the Somerset coast. "It's done now," she said, "and we were just about to move in, and then I said to Michael, maybe Salman might like it. You could certainly have it for a month or so." The gift of a month, the chance of being able to stay in one place for that long, was precious beyond words. For one month he would be a person from Porlock. "Thank you," he said, inadequately.

Porlock Weir sat a little west of the village of Porlock itself, a tiny outcrop of the village that had grown up around the harbor. The cottage was a thatched beauty and quite substantial. A journalist from *The New York Times,* interviewing Drabble there a decade later, thought it "a kind of Bloomsburyian vision of whimsy and cultivation, with rooms painted different colors—mint green, rose, lilac and Tuscan yellow—and faded rugs, books and paintings everywhere you look." It felt grand to reenter a house of books. He and Marianne were two writers being gifted the home of two other writers and there was something extraordinarily comforting about that. There was enough room for the two protection officers to stay on the premises as well; the drivers rented rooms at a bed-and-breakfast place in the village and pretended to be friends on a walking tour of the region. There was a beautiful garden, and it was as secluded as any invisible man could wish for. He arrived there in the last week of March and, almost happily, settled in.

"The flame of the Enlightenment is waning," a journalist said to Günter Grass. *"But,"* he replied, *"there is no other source of light."* The public argument raged on. In private, just days after his arrival at Porlock Weir, he faced a very different crisis. Fire of a sort was also involved.

Marianne went to London for a couple of days (there were no restrictions on her movements) and saw a couple of mutual friends—Dale, an American woman working at Wylie, Aitken & Stone, and his old pal Pauline Melville. He called Pauline to see how things were and found her in a state of horrified shock. "Okay," she said, "this is so serious that I'm going to tell you what Marianne said, and both Dale and I heard it, and we're both so stunned that we are prepared to repeat her words to her face." Marianne had told them that he and she were fighting constantly and that she, Marianne, had, in Pauline's words, "beaten him up." She then said, astonishingly, that he had asked the Special Branch to "fly in Isabelle Adjani." He had never met or spoken to the French actress, but she had recently made a gesture of support, which he had greatly appreciated. At the César Awards in Paris—the "French Oscars"—she went up to receive the Best Actress César for her performance in the title role of *Camille Claudel,* and had read a short text at the end of which she revealed that it was a quotation from *"Les versets sataniques, de Salman Rushdie."* She had an Algerian father of Muslim origin, so this was not a small thing to do. He had written to thank her. The rest—Marianne's allegation— was pure fabrication, and there was worse to come. "He tortures me," she told Pauline, "by burning me with lighted cigarettes." When Pauline told him this he burst out laughing at the horror of it. "But," he cried, "I don't have any cigarettes—I don't even smoke!"

When Marianne returned to Porlock from London he confronted her in the beautiful living room with its pink wallpaper and large windows offering a view of the shining waters of the Bristol Channel. At first she flatly denied having said any of it. He called her bluff. "Let's phone Pauline and Dale and see what they say." At this she broke down and admitted that yes, she had said those things. He asked her specifically about the worst allegation, the cigarette torture story. "Why did you say such a thing," he demanded, "when you know it isn't true?" She looked him boldly in the eye. "It was a metaphor," she said, "of how unhappy I felt." That was, in its way, brilliant. Deranged, but brilliant. It deserved applause. He said, "Marianne, that is not a metaphor; it's a lie. If you can't tell the difference between the two you are in bad trouble." She had no more to say to him. She went to the room in which she worked and closed the door.

This was the choice he had to make: to stay with her, even though she was capable of such untruths, or to separate and face what he had to face alone.

He needed a name, the police told him. He needed to choose one "pretty pronto" and then talk to his bank manager and get the bank to issue checkbooks either bearing the pseudonym or no name at all, and to agree to accept checks signed with the false name, so that he could pay for things without being identified. But the new name was also for the benefit of his protectors. They needed to get used to it, to call him by it at all times, when they were with him and when they weren't, so they didn't accidentally let his real name slip when they were walking or running or going to the gym or the supermarket in his immediate neighborhood and blow his cover.

The "prot" had a name: Operation Malachite. He did not know why they had given the job the name of a green stone and neither did they. They were not writers and the reasons for names were not important to them. It was just a name. Now it was his turn to rename himself. His own name was worse than useless, it was a name that could not be spoken, like the name *Voldemort* in the then-unwritten Harry Potter books. He could not rent a house with it, or register to vote, because to vote you needed to provide a home address and that, of course, was impossible. To protect his democratic right of free expression he had to surrender his democratic right to choose his government. "It doesn't matter what the name is," Stan said, "but it would be useful to have one in place, sharpish."

To be asked to give up your name was not a small thing. "Probably better not to make it an Asian name," said Stan. "People put two and two together sometimes." So he was to give up his race as well. He would be an invisible man in a whiteface mask.

He had a fragment of a character in a notebook, called Mr. Mamouli. Mr. Mamouli was a benighted, even cursed, Everyman figure whose literary relatives were Zbigniew Herbert's Mr. Cogito and Italo Calvino's Mr. Palomar. His full name was Ajeeb Mamouli—Ajeeb, like the Bradford councilor, whose name meant "odd." Mamouli meant "ordinary." He was Mr. Odd Ordinary, Mr. Strange Normal, Mr. Peculiar Everyday: an oxymoron, a contradiction in terms. He had written a fragment in which Mr. Mamouli was obliged to carry a giant inverted pyramid on his head, with the tip resting on his bald head and grievously irritating his scalp.

Mr. Mamouli had come into being the first time he felt that his name had been stolen from him, or half his name, anyway, when *Rushdie* detached itself from *Salman* and went spiraling off into the headlines, into newsprint, into the video-heavy ether, becoming a slogan, a rallying cry, a term of abuse, or anything else that other people wanted it to be. He had lost control over his name then and so it felt better to slip into Mr. Mamouli's shoes. Mr. Ajeeb Mamouli was a novelist too, his very name a contradiction, as befitted a novelist's name. Mr. Mamouli thought of himself as an ordinary man but his life was decidedly odd. When he drew doodles of Mamouli's face they looked like the famous Common Man created by the cartoonist R. K. Laxman in *The Times of India:* innocent, bemused, bald, with tufts of graying hair spraying out over his ears.

There was a character in *The Satanic Verses* called Mimi Mamoulian, a plump actress obsessed by the acquisition of real estate. Mr. Mamouli was her relative, or perhaps her antithesis, an anti-Mimi whose problem was the opposite of hers: that he had no home he could call his own. This was also, he was well aware, the fate of the fallen Lucifer. So Mr. Ajeeb Mamouli was the name of the devil he had been turned into by others, the horned metamorphic being like his Saladin Chamcha, to whom his demonic transformation is explained thus: *"They have the power of description, and we succumb."*

They didn't like the name. Mamouli, Ajeeb: These words were a bit of a mouthful, too hard to remember, and far too "Asian." He was asked to think again. Mr. Mamouli receded, then faded, and eventually found a room in the dilapidated rooming house reserved for unused ideas, the Hotel California of the imagination, and was lost.

He thought of writers he loved and tried combinations of their names. Vladimir Joyce. Marcel Beckett. Franz Sterne. He made lists of such combinations and all of them sounded ridiculous. Then he found one that did not. He wrote down, side by side, the first names of Conrad and Chekhov, and there it was, his name for the next eleven years.

"Joseph Anton."

"Jolly good," said Stan. "You won't mind if we call you Joe."

In fact he did mind. He soon discovered he detested the abbreviation for reasons he did not fully understand—after all why was *Joe* so much worse than *Joseph*? He was neither one, and both should strike him as equally phony or equally suitable. But "Joe" grated on him almost from the beginning. Nevertheless, that monosyllable was what the protection officers found easiest to master, and remember, and avoid getting wrong in public places. So, as far as they were concerned, Joe it had to be.

"Joseph Anton." He was trying to get used to what he had invented. He had spent his life naming fictional characters. Now by naming himself he had turned himself into a sort of fictional character as well. "Conrad Chekhov" wouldn't have worked. But "Joseph Anton" was someone who might exist. Who now did exist.

Conrad, the translingual creator of wanderers, lost and not lost, of voyagers into the heart of darkness, of secret agents in a world of killers and bombs, and of at least one immortal coward, hiding from his shame; and Chekhov, the master of loneliness and melancholy, of the beauty of an old world destroyed, like the trees in the cherry orchard, by the brutality of the new; Chekhov, whose *Three Sisters* believed that real life was elsewhere and yearned eternally for a Moscow to which they could not return: These were his godfathers now. It was Conrad who gave him the motto to which he clung as if to a lifeline in the long years that would follow. In his now-unacceptably-titled *The Nigger of the* Narcissus, the title character, a sailor named James Wait, stricken down by tuberculosis on a long sea voyage, was asked by a fellow sailor why he came aboard, knowing, as he must have known, that he was unwell. "I must live until I die, mustn't I?" Wait replied. So must we all, he had thought when he read the book, but in his present circumstances the sentence's power felt like a command.

"Joseph Anton," he told himself, "you must live until you die."

It had never occurred to him before the attack to stop writing, to be something else, to become *not a writer*. To have become a writer—to discover that he was able to do the thing he had most wanted to do— had been one of his greatest joys. The reception of *The Satanic Verses* had, for the moment at least, robbed him of that joy, not because of fear but on account of a deep disappointment. If one spent five years of one's life struggling with a large and complex project, trying to wrestle it to the ground, to bring it under control, and give it all the shapely beauty his talent allowed—and if, when it came out, it was received in this distorted, ugly way, then maybe the effort wasn't worth it. If that was what he got for making his best effort, then he should perhaps try doing something else. He should be a bus conductor, a bellhop, a busker tap-dancing for change in a subway tunnel in winter. All those professions sounded nobler than his.

To stave off such thoughts he began to write book reviews. Before the *fatwa* his friend Blake Morrison, at the *Observer*'s book pages, had asked him to review Philip Roth's memoir *The Facts*. He wrote the piece and sent it off. It could not be mailed from anywhere nearby, and he had no fax machine, so a protection officer agreed to mail it in London when he went off duty. He added a covering note apologizing for the review's late delivery. When the newspaper ran his review they published a facsimile of his handwritten note *on page one*. He had become so unreal to so many people so quickly that this proof of his existence was treated as front-page news.

He asked Blake if he could continue reviewing for him and after that, every few weeks, he managed to deliver eight hundred words or so. They didn't come easily—*like pulling teeth,* he thought, the cliché feeling apt because his wisdom teeth were aching quite often now, and the protection team was looking for a "solution"—but they represented his first awkward steps back toward himself, away from *Rushdie* and back toward *Salman,* toward literature again and away from the bleak, defeated idea of becoming *not a writer.*

It was Zafar who finally brought him back to himself, Zafar whom he worked constantly to see—the police drove back and forth, "dry-cleaning" father and son, making these intermittent meetings possible—in London at Sue and Gurmukh's house on Patshull Road in Kentish Town, at the Pinters' in Campden Hill Square, at Liz Calder's place in Archway and once, wonderfully, for a weekend in Cornwall at the home of Clarissa's oldest friend, Rosanne, a farmhouse with goats and chickens and geese deep in a valley near Liskeard. They played soccer—he showed promise as a goalie, diving eagerly this way and that—and computer games. They put together model train sets and model cars. They did ordinary, everyday, father-and-son things and it felt like a miracle. Meanwhile Rosanne's little daughter Georgie persuaded the police to dress up in princess crowns and feather boas from her dressing-up box.

Marianne had not come for the weekend so he and Zafar shared a bedroom. And it was Zafar who reminded him of his promise: "Dad, what about my book?"

It was the only time in his working life that he knew almost the whole plot from the beginning. The story dropped into his head like a gift. He had told Zafar stories while the boy took his evening bath, bath-time stories instead of bedtime ones. There were little sandalwood animals and shikara boats from Kashmir floating in the bathwater and the sea of stories was born there, or perhaps reborn. The original sea was to be found in the title of an old Sanskrit book. In Kashmir in the eleventh century A.D., a Shaivite Brahman named Somadeva had assembled a gigantic compendium of tales called the *Kathasaritsagara*. *Katha* meant story, *sarit* was streams and *sagara* was the sea or ocean; thus, *Kathasaritsagara*, the story-stream sea, usually rendered in English as the Ocean of the Streams of Story. In Somadeva's huge book there wasn't actually a sea. But suppose there was such a sea, where all the stories ever invented flowed in intertwining streams? While Zafar was bathing, his dad would take a mug and dip it into his son's bathwater and pretend to sip, and to find a story to tell, a story-stream flowing through the bath of stories.

And now in Zafar's book he would visit the ocean itself. There would be a storyteller in the story, who lost the Gift of the Gab after his wife left him, and his son would travel to the source of all stories to find out how to renew his father's gift. The only part of his original vision that changed in the telling was the ending. At first he had thought this could be a "modern" book, in which the broken family stayed broken, and the boy got used to it, dealt with it, as children had to do in the real world, as his own son was doing. But the shape of the story demanded that what was broken at the beginning was made whole at the end. A happy ending had to be found and he agreed with himself that he was ready to find one. He had of late become extremely interested in happy endings.

Many years earlier, after reading the *Travels* of Ibn Battuta, he had written a short story called "The Princess Khamosh." Ibn Battuta was a fourteenth-century Moroccan scholar with itchy feet whose account of his quarter century of journeys throughout the Arab world and beyond, to India, Southeast Asia and China, made Marco Polo sound like a stay-at-home lazybones. "The Princess Khamosh" was an imaginary fragment of the *Travels,* a few lost pages from the manuscript of Battuta's book. In it the Moroccan traveler comes to a divided country in which two tribes are at war, the Guppees, a chatterbox people, and the Chupwalas, among whom a cult of silence has grown up, and who worship a stone deity called Bezaban, that is, *without a tongue.* When the Chupwalas capture the Guppee princess and threaten to sew her lips shut as an offering to their god, war breaks out between the lands of Gup and Chup.

He had been dissatisfied with the story when he wrote it; the missing-pages conceit didn't really come off, and he had put it away and forgotten it. Now he realized that this little tale about a war between language and silence could be given a meaning that was not only linguistic; that hidden inside it was a parable about freedom and tyranny whose potential he finally understood. The story had been ahead of him, so to speak, and now his life had caught up with it. By some miracle he remembered in which desk drawer he had put the folder containing the story, and asked Pauline to go into the St. Peter's Street house and get it for him. By this time there were no longer reporters watching the building, so she was able to go in quietly and bring the pages out. When he read them again he became excited. Reshaped, stripped of the redundant Battuta element, they would give his book its dramatic heart.

At first the book was called "Zafar and the Sea of Stories," but he soon felt the need to place a little fictive distance between the boy in the book and the one in the bath. Haroun was Zafar's middle name. The change felt like an improvement as soon as it was made. At first Zafar was disappointed. It was his book, he said, so it should be about him. But he, too, changed his mind. He understood that Haroun both was and was not him, and that was better.

They returned to Porlock Weir from the blessed weekend with Zafar in Cornwall and when they neared the front door they could hear noises inside the house. The police officers at once shielded him and drew their weapons and then one of them opened the door. There were clear signs that the house had been disturbed: scattered papers, a fallen vase. Then another noise: like the beating of frightened wings.

"It's a bird," he said, his voice made much too loud by his relief. "There's a bird in there." Tension drained from the team as well. Panic over. A bird had fallen down the chimney and was now perched on a curtain rod in the living room, terrified. A blackbird, he thought. *Ristle-te, rostle-te, mo, mo, mo.* A window was opened and the bird flew out to freedom. He began to tidy up the house and songs about birds filled his head. *Take these broken wings and learn to fly.* And the old Caribbean song about that bird "up high in banana tree." *You can fly away / in the sky away / you more lucky than me.*

The book did not immediately begin to flow, even though he had the story. The noise of the storm outside the windows of the cottage was too loud, and his wisdom teeth hurt, and the book's language proved hard to find. He made false starts—too childish, too grown-up—and the tone of voice he needed eluded him. It would be some months before he wrote the words that unlocked the mystery. "There was once, in the country of Alifbay, a sad city, the saddest of cities, a city so ruinously sad that it had forgotten its name. It stood by a mournful sea full of glumfish . . ." Joseph Heller had once told him that his books grew out of sentences. The sentences "I get the willies when I see closed doors" and "In the office in which I work there are five people of whom I am afraid" had been the genesis of his great novel *Something Happened,* and *Catch-22* too sprang from its opening sentences. He understood what Heller meant. There were sentences that one knew, when one wrote them, contained or made possible dozens or perhaps even hundreds of other sentences. *Midnight's Children* had revealed its secrets, after much struggle, only when he sat down one day and wrote *I was born in the city of Bombay . . . once upon a time.* And so it was with *Haroun.* The moment he had the sad city and the glumfish he knew how the book had to go. He may even have leaped to his feet and clapped his hands. But that moment was months in the future. For now there was only the struggle and the storm.

In Britain a gaggle of self-appointed "leaders" and "spokesmen" continued to clamber to fame by sticking knives in his back and then skipping up the ladder of blades. The most outspoken and dangerous of these was a silver-bearded garden gnome called Kalim Siddiqui, who emphatically defended and justified the *fatwa* on several television programs, and who, in a series of public meetings (including some attended by members of Parliament) called for a show of hands to demonstrate the unanimous desire in the community that the blasphemer and apostate should be killed. Every hand flew up into the air. Nobody was prosecuted. Siddiqui's Muslim Institute was a paltry thing but he was being given the red carpet treatment by the ayatollahs of Iran, visiting frequently and meeting all the most senior figures, demanding that they keep the pressure on. On a British TV show Siddiqui said what he thought Muslims were like. "We hit back," he said. "Sometimes we hit back first."

More bookstores were firebombed—Collet's and Dillons in London, Abbey's in Sydney, Australia. More libraries refused to stock the book, more chains refused to carry it, a dozen printers in France refused to print the French edition, and more threats were made against publishers, for example against his Norwegian publisher, William Nygaard of H. Aschehoug & Co., who had to be given a police guard. But most people working at the offices of his novel's publishers around the world received no protection. He could easily imagine the tension they felt at work and at home, for their families and themselves. Not enough attention was paid to the courage with which these "ordinary people," who revealed themselves every day to be extraordinary, continued to do their work, to defend the principles of freedom, to hold the front line.

Muslims began to be killed by other Muslims if they expressed non-bloodthirsty opinions. In Belgium the mullah who was said to be the "spiritual leader" of the country's Muslims, the Saudi national Abdullah Ahdal, and his Tunisian deputy Salim Bahri were killed for saying that, whatever Khomeini had said for Iranian consumption, in Europe there was freedom of expression.

"I am gagged and imprisoned," he wrote in his journal, "I can't even speak. I want to kick a football in a park with my son. Ordinary, banal life: my impossible dream." Friends who saw him in those days were shocked by his physical deterioration, his increase in weight, the way he had let his beard grow out into an ugly bulbous mass, his sunken stance. He looked like a beaten man.

———

In a very short time he had grown extremely fond of his protectors but Marianne found the invasion of her space harder to take and kept her distance. He appreciated the way they tried to be constantly upbeat and cheerful in his company to raise his spirits, and their efforts at self-effacement also. They knew it was hard for "principals" to have policemen in the kitchen, leaving their footprints in the butter. They tried very hard and without any rancor to give him as much space as they could. And most of them, he quickly understood, found the confinement of this particular prot harder, in some ways, than he did. These were men of action, their needs the opposite of a sedentary novelist trying to hold on to what remained of the inner life, the life of the mind. He could sit still and think in a room for hours and be content. They went stir-crazy if they had to stay indoors for any length of time. On the other hand they could go home after two weeks and have a break. Several of them said to him, with worried respect, "We couldn't do what you're doing," and that knowledge earned him their sympathy.

Many of them said that this was the wrong way to run a prot. Every other "principal" had a "dedicated team" that looked after that individual alone. He could not have a dedicated team because the undercover work was too much for the officers to bear on a full-time basis. So his team was patched together from other teams. It wasn't right, his protectors said. Everyone else they protected went about his or her normal and professional life and they took care of the protection while shifts of uniformed officers protected the principal's home. At night the Special Branch officers brought the principal home and then went home themselves while the uniformed officers remained on guard. "What we have to do on Malachite isn't proper protection," they told him. "We weren't trained to hide people. This isn't our job." But a normal protection was more expensive, because the shifts of uniformed officers cost a lot of money. And if the principal had more than one home then the cost increased. The higher-ups at the Yard weren't prepared to spend that sort of money on Operation Malachite. It was cheaper to hide the principal and pay the prot teams overtime to stay with him around the clock. There was a view among the senior officers, he was learning, that the Malachite principal didn't "deserve" the full protection services of the British police.

He quickly learned that there was a wide gulf between the officers in the field and the higher-ups at the Yard. Few of the higher-ups had earned the lads' respect. In the years that followed he very rarely had any difficulty with the members of the teams sent to look after him, and many of them became friends. The senior officers—it was entirely wrong, he was told, to call them "superior officers," because "they may be senior to us, but they're not superior"—were a different matter. There would be more than one censorious Mr. Greenup in the days ahead.

They broke the rules to help him. At a time when they had been forbidden to take him into any public spaces they took him to the movies, going in after the lights went down, taking him out before they went up again, no problem. At a time when the senior officers said he should not be brought to London, they brought him to his friends' houses so that he could meet his son. And they did what they could to assist his work as a father. They took him and Zafar to police sports grounds and formed impromptu rugby teams so that he could run with them and pass the ball. On bank holidays they sometimes took him and Zafar to amusement parks. One day at such a park Zafar saw a soft toy being offered as a prize at a shooting gallery and decided he wanted it. One of the protection officers, known to one and all as Fat Jack, heard him. "You fancy that, do you?" he said, and pursed his lips. "Mmm hmm." He went up to the booth and put down his money. The carny handed him the usual pistol with deformed gunsights and Fat Jack nodded gravely. "Mmm hmm," he said, inspecting the weapon, "all right then." He began to shoot. *Boom boom boom boom,* the targets fell one by one while the carny watched with gold-toothed mouth hanging wide. "Yes, that should do nicely," said Fat Jack, putting down the weapon and pointing at the soft toy. "We'll have that, thanks." Some months later Zafar was watching the happy scenes on television of Nelson Mandela arriving at Wembley Stadium to take a bow at the rock concert being staged there to celebrate his freedom. When Zafar saw Mandela coming down the tunnel from the changing rooms to the field he pointed and said, "Look, Dad, there's Fat Jack."

And there indeed was Fat Jack, right behind Mandela's left shoulder, pursing his lips and probably saying *Mmm hmm.*

He learned a lot from the lads about security—how to enter a room, for example, where to look, what to look for. "Cops and criminals," Dev Stonehouse told him. "You can always tell 'em. They stand in the doorway and scope out the scene before coming in, how many exits, who's standing where, all of that." He learned, too, that the police force was in the end just another department of the civil service. It was an office, and it had office politics. There was much jealousy and envy aimed at the Branch, and there were people who wanted to shut it down. There would be moments when they came to him for help, asking him to write letters in support of the work done by "A" Squad, and he was happy to be able to do a little in return for all they did for him. What made him happiest is that none of those men who were there because they were prepared to take a bullet for him ever had to do so.

There were not many women on "A" Squad, six or seven at most, and in all the years of the prot only two of them were ever part of his team: a tall handsome woman named Rachel Clooney, who ended up being one of Margaret Thatcher's dedicated team, and a small, compact, businesslike blond called Julie Remmick, who eventually had to leave the team because her shooting didn't come up to standard. Everyone on prot duty had to take regular tests of marksmanship in a police shooting gallery, shooting off balance, against moving targets, in poor visibility, and the acceptable score was somewhere over 90 percent. If they dropped below that score they had to surrender their weapon instantly and do a desk job instead. He was told they could arrange for him to be given shooting lessons. He would be taught by the best instructors and maybe it was a skill he should learn. He thought about it long and hard and said no, he wouldn't do that, thanks all the same. He knew that if he owned a gun and the bad guys were to attack it would be taken from him and turned against him. Better to live without it and hope the bad guys wouldn't get that close.

Sometimes they cooked for him but mostly they kept the domestic arrangements separate. They would do his supermarket shopping when they did their own. They each used the kitchen at different, agreed-upon times. In the evenings the policemen stayed in one room and watched TV, athletes obliged by circumstances to behave like couch potatoes. How miserable they must have been!

They were fit and handsome and girls liked them. Many of them became friendly with women they met through him in the world of publishing. There was a particular team, Rob and Ernie, who were reckoned to be major heartthrobs. Another officer had an affair with a friend's nanny, then dumped her and broke her heart. And lots of them had extramarital affairs, the job's secrecy offering the perfect camouflage. One of them, a golden-haired youth named Sammy, turned out to be a bigamist, with two wives whom he called by the same nicknames, and two lots of children who were also identically named. He was caught because the costs of bigamy were too great for a policeman's salary and he fell deeply into debt. These were interesting fellows.

Dev Stonehouse, it turned out, did have a drinking problem, and was eventually taken off the team after he became drunk and indiscreet in a pub, and sent to work in Siberia, otherwise known as Heathrow Airport. There were a couple of protection officers who wanted to play devil's advocate and, taking the Muslim side, argue the case for "respect," but their colleagues led them gently and thoughtfully away.

There was one high-handed officer who treated him more like a prisoner than a principal and he objected to that. And there was Siegfried, the British-German lad who was built like a tank and just once, when he asked to be taken for a walk in a park, squared up to him and said he was endangering the team. He saw Siegfried's hands turning into fists but he stood his ground and stared him down. Siegfried was led away and never returned. Fear made good men do bad things.

That was the sum total of problems he had with the protection teams. Many years later a disaffected driver, Ron Evans, fired from the police force for embezzlement, published lurid untruths in a British tabloid claiming, among other things, that the protection teams had disliked this particular principal so much that they would lock him in a closet and go off to the pub to drink. The moment the allegations were published he was contacted by several members of his old teams. These officers were disgusted by the lies, by the failure of the senior officers at the Yard to defend him, and perhaps most of all by the sacked driver's breach of the Branch's almost Sicilian code of *omertà,* silence. They took pride in the fact that nobody in the Branch leaked or gossiped or planted or fabricated stories in the media—unlike, as many of them said, those leaky fellows in the (separate) Royal Protection Squad—and that pride had taken a bad blow. Many of them told him they were prepared to testify in his defense. When the driver apologized in the High Court and admitted his lies, the old prot team celebrated, sending triumphant congratulatory emails to the man they were supposed to have loathed.

The driver was not the only liar. Perhaps the most unfair of the defamations leveled against him was that he was "ungrateful" for what was being done for him. This was a part of the "arrogant," "unpleasant" persona that was carefully constructed for him by much of the British tabloid press, to diminish him in the public eye and damage his ability to speak with credibility. The fact was that *of course he was grateful,* he was grateful every day for nine years, and he said so repeatedly to anyone who would listen. The men who guarded him and became his friends, and those of his friends who were "inside the circle," all knew the truth.

There was a documentary about Ronald Reagan on television and he sat with the team and watched John Hinckley, Jr., shoot the president. "Look at the security team," Stan told him. "Everyone is in the right place. Nobody is out of position. Everyone's reaction times are terrific. Nobody failed. Everyone did their job to the highest standards. And the president still got shot." The most dangerous zone, the zone that could never be sanitized 100 percent, was the space between the exit door of a building and the door of the car. "The Israeli," said Benny, meaning the ambassador, "he knows that all right. He puts his head down and runs." That was the zone in which Hinckley hit the president. But there was a more general truth here. The finest protection officers in the United States, all of them highly experienced and heavily armed, had performed to the very best of their abilities and yet the gunman got through. POTUS was down. There was no such thing as absolute security. There were only varying degrees of insecurity. He would have to learn to live with that.

He was offered Kevlar bulletproof vests to wear. He refused them. And when he walked from the door of a car to the door of a building or back again, he consciously slowed down. He would not scuttle. He would try to walk with his head held high.

"If you succumb to the security description of the world," he told himself, "then you will be its creature forever, its prisoner." The security worldview was based on the so-called worst-case analysis. But the worst-case analysis of crossing a road is that there was a chance you would be hit by a truck, and therefore you should not cross the road. But people crossed roads every day and were not hit by trucks. This was a thing he would have to remember. *There were only varying degrees of insecurity.* He had to go on crossing roads.

"History is a nightmare from which I am trying to awake," said Joyce's Dedalus, but what did little Stephen Hero know about nightmares? The most nightmarish thing that ever happened to him was getting drunk in Nighttown and going home with Poldy to build the New Bloomusalem and maybe be pimped out by the cuckold Bloom to service randy Molly. *This* was a nightmare—bloodthirsty priests shooting arrows of retribution and an effigy of himself in a demonstration with that arrow through his head—and he was already awake. In Pakistan one of his uncles, married to his mother's sister, put an ad in the paper essentially saying *Don't blame us, we never liked him anyway,* while his aunt told my mother, who was still in Wembley with Sameen, that Pakistanis didn't want her in the country. This wasn't true. It was probably the aunt and uncle who were embarrassed by their kin and didn't want her close. She went anyway and nobody attacked her. Sometimes in the bazaar people would ask if her son was all right and sympathized with her, *such a terrible thing.* So some civility remained in the midst of the bloodthirsty riots. Meanwhile he was in the care of police officers nicknamed Piggy and Stumpy and Fat Jack and Horse—he was getting used to the nicknames and the rotation of personnel—and trying to find a place to move to when he had to leave Porlock Weir (the Holroyds had generously allowed him to stay an extra six weeks, but time was almost up). Suitable houses were proving hard to find especially when he had to do all the looking by proxy. He didn't exist. Only Joseph Anton existed; and he could not be seen.

The world of books continued to send him messages. Bharati Mukherjee and Clark Blaise wrote from America to tell him that people were making I AM SALMAN RUSHDIE button badges and proudly wearing them as a sign of their solidarity. He wanted one of those badges. Maybe Joseph Anton could wear a badge in solidarity with the person he both was and was not. Gita Mehta told him by telephone, a little waspishly, that "*The Satanic Verses* is not your *Lear. Shame* is your *Lear.*" Blake Morrison said, "Many writers are feeling paralyzed by the affair. Writing feels like fiddling while Rome burns." Tariq Ali unkindly described him as being "a dead man on leave" and sent him the text of a play he had written with Howard Brenton that was to be staged at the Royal Court Theatre. *Iranian Nights.* It struck him as a shoddy, hurried, slapstick thing, which included the gibes at his work that were by now becoming conventional. "It was a book that no-one could read" was a sort of leitmotif. Among the subjects the play did not explore were: religion as political repression and as international terrorism; the need for blasphemy (the writers of the French Enlightenment had deliberately used blasphemy as a weapon, refusing to accept the power of the church to set limiting points on thought); religion as the enemy of the intellect. Those were the themes he might have treated if it had been his play, but it was not. He was only its subject, the author of the unreadable book.

When he was able to visit people he noticed that they were more excited by the security precautions—the dry-cleaning, the curtains being drawn, the exploration of their homes by handsome men with guns—than by his visit. Afterward his friends' most vivid memories of those days were invariably memories of the Special Branch. An improbable friendship was deepening between the London literary world and the British secret police. The protection officers liked his friends, who would make them welcome, make sure they were comfortable, and feed them. "You have no idea," he was told, "how we get treated elsewhere." Political grandees and their wives often treated these good men like the help.

Sometimes people were too excited. He was once invited to visit

Edward Said, who was staying in London at the Mayfair home of a Kuwaiti friend. When he arrived the Indian maid, wide-eyed, recognized him at once and became overwrought. She telephoned Said's host's household back in Kuwait and shouted incoherently down the line, "Rushdie! Here! Rushdie here!" Nobody in Kuwait could understand why the invisible man had manifested himself in their London base: Why was he taking refuge there? Edward had to explain that he had merely invited his friend to dinner. No long-term residence was envisaged.

He slowly came to understand that the protection looked *glamorous*. Men arrived in advance of his own coming, everything was made ready, a sleek Jaguar stopped at the door, there was the moment of maximum risk between car door and front door, then he was whisked inside. It looked like VIP treatment. It looked like *too much*. It made people ask, *Who does he think he is? Why does he deserve to be treated like a king?* His friends didn't ask this but maybe one or two of them wondered too: Was all of this really necessary? The longer it lasted, the longer he went without being killed, the easier it was for people to believe that nobody was trying to kill him, and that he wanted the protection around him to satisfy his vanity, his insufferable self-importance. It was hard to convince people that from where he was standing the protection didn't feel like movie-stardom. It felt like jail.

Meanwhile rumors swirled in the press. The Abu Nidal organization was training a hit team who would enter the United Kingdom "dressed as businessmen, in Westernized clothes." Another assassination squad was supposedly being prepared in the Central African Republic. And as well as these lethal whispers, the ugliness was still blaring from every radio, television and newspaper front page. The Tory minister John Patten eloquently debated the pro-Muslim Keith Vaz, MP, on TV. Kalim Siddiqui was on TV, just back from Iran, saying menacingly, "He will not die in Britain," implying that a kidnapping plot was being hatched. The former pop singer Cat Stevens, recently reincarnated as the born-again Muslim "leader" Yusuf Islam, was on TV, too, hoping for his death and stating that he would be prepared to call in the hit squads if he learned the blasphemer's whereabouts.

He telephoned Jatinder Verma of the Tara Arts theater group and was told of "heavy intimidation [of British Muslims by the campaign organizers] going on at the grass roots" and "political pressure by the Council of Mosques." As depressing as the Islamic campaign were the attacks from the left. John Berger denounced him in *The Guardian.* And the eminent intellectual Paul Gilroy, author of *There Ain't No Black in the Union Jack,* the nearest thing the United Kingdom had to a figure like Cornel West in America, accused him of having "misjudged the people" and therefore of having created his own tragedy. Surreally, Gilroy compared him to the boxer Frank Bruno, who evidently knew how not to "misjudge the people," and was therefore loved. It was not possible, in the thinking of socialist intellectuals like Berger and Gilroy, that the people had misjudged him. The people could not be wrong.

The house problem was becoming acute. Then Deborah Rogers came to the rescue for the second time and offered a solution: a spacious house she knew of in the village of Bucknell in Shropshire that was available for a year. The police checked it out. Yes, it was a possibility. His spirits rose. A home for a year sounded like an unthinkable luxury. He agreed: Joseph Anton would rent it.

One day he asked the protection officer called Piggy: "What would you have done if *The Satanic Verses* had been, say, a poem, or a radio play, and had not been able to generate the income that allows me to rent these places? What would you have done if I had been too poor?" Piggy shrugged. "Fortunately, as it happens," he said, "we don't have to answer that question, do we."

Michael Foot and his wife, Jill Craigie, had persuaded his successor as leader of the opposition, Neil Kinnock, and his wife, Glenys, to meet him for dinner at their house in Pilgrims Lane, Hampstead. The writer and barrister John Mortimer, creator of Rumpole of the Bailey, and his wife, Penny, would also be there. He was driven to London and found himself stuck in a traffic jam right outside the Regent's Park Mosque while the faithful poured out of Friday prayers, having just heard a sermon reviling him. He had to open *The Daily Telegraph* and bury his face in it. After a while he asked, "I assume the doors are locked?" There was a click and a clearing of the throat and Stumpy said, "They are now." He could not help feeling how awful it was to be so segregated from "his" people. When he said this to Sameen she scolded him.

"These mullah-ridden mobs were never your people," she said. "You'd always have opposed them, and been opposed by them, in India or Pakistan also."

At the Foots' house, Neil Kinnock was amazingly friendly, sympathetic and supportive. But he was also worried that it would "get out" that he had been there and that could cause him political problems. He could not have been nicer, but it was a secret niceness. Kinnock was opposed, he said at one point, to state subsidies being given to segregated Muslim schools, but what could he do, he cried, it was Labour Party policy. It was not possible to conceive of his adversary, the formidable Tory prime minister Margaret Thatcher, feebly throwing up her arms like that.

Michael himself had become a passionate ally and friend. Their only disagreement was about Indira Gandhi, whom Michael had known well, and whose years of quasi-dictatorship during the "emergency" of the mid-1970s he was disposed to excuse. When Michael adopted you as a friend, he took the view that you could do no wrong.

Also at the dinner was the poet Tony Harrison, who had made a film-poem for BBC TV called *The Blasphemers' Banquet,* in which he dined in a restaurant in Bradford with Voltaire, Molière, Omar Khayyám and Byron. One chair was left empty. *"That's Salman Rushdie's chair."* They talked about blasphemy being at the very root of Western culture. The trials of Socrates, Jesus Christ and Galileo had all been blasphemy trials and yet the history of philosophy, Christianity and science owed them a mighty debt. "I'm keeping your chair for you," Harrison said. "Just let me know when you can take delivery."

He was driven away into the night. His wisdom teeth exploded.

They had chosen a hospital near Bristol and made all the arrangements. He was smuggled in for examinations and X-rays and had to spend the night before the operation in the morning. Both lower wisdom teeth were impacted and a general anesthetic would be required. The police were concerned that if news of his presence there got out a hostile crowd could gather outside the hospital. They had a plan to cover that eventuality. They had a hearse standing by and would drive it into a hospital bay and bring him out anaesthetized, zipped up in a body bag. This proved to be an unnecessary stratagem.

When he regained consciousness Marianne was holding his hand. He was in a happy morphine haze and the headache, jaw ache and neck ache didn't feel so bad. There was a heated pillow under his neck and Marianne was being very nice to him. There were twenty or thirty thousand Muslims assembling in Hyde Park to demand whatever they were demanding but the morphine made it okay. They had threatened the biggest ever rally in Britain, five hundred thousand people, so twenty thousand felt piffling. Morphine was wonderful. If only he could stay on it all the time he would feel just fine.

Later he had a row with Clarissa because she had allowed Zafar to watch the demonstration on TV. "How could you have done that?" he demanded. "It just happened," she said, adding that he was obviously upset by the demonstration and shouldn't take it out on her. Zafar came on the phone and said that he had seen an effigy with an arrow through its head. He had seen twenty thousand men and boys marching through the streets, not of Tehran, but his own hometown, demanding his father's death. He told Zafar: "People show off for the TV, they think it looks smart." "But it doesn't," Zafar said. "It looks stupid." He could be an astonishing boy.

He spoke to his computer geek friend Gurmukh Singh, who had a brilliant idea: Why didn't he get himself a "cellphone"? There were these "cellphones" now. You charged their batteries and then you carried them around wherever you went and nobody knew where you were calling from. If he had one of these new phones then he would be able to give out a number to family and friends and business colleagues without compromising his location. What a brainwave, he said, that sounds wonderful, almost unbelievable. "I'm going to look into it," Gurmukh told him.

The cellphone—ridiculously bulky, a brick with an antenna—arrived not long afterward and his excitement knew no bounds. He called people and gave them the number and they kept calling him back—Sameen, Pauline, and, several times, his friend Michael Herr, author of the Vietnam War classic *Dispatches*, who was living in London and had been obsessing about him more than anyone else, and who was, if anything, more afraid and paranoid on his behalf than he was himself. Kazuo Ishiguro, whose novel *The Remains of the Day* was just out and enjoying a great triumph, called to say that he thought *The Satanic Verses* should be rereviewed everywhere, this time by novelists, to turn the focus back toward literature. Clarissa called him to make peace. An Irish author represented by A. P. Watt, where she worked, had told her a story about Irish builders he knew in Birmingham who had been working on the foundations of a big new mosque. When nobody was looking they had dropped a copy of *The Satanic Verses* into the wet cement. "So that mosque is being built on your book," Clarissa said.

Michael Holroyd called to say that, in his opinion, the effect of the big march had been to create a huge swing of public opinion against the protesters. People who had been on the fence were coming off it, revolted by what they saw on TV, the posters reading KILL THE DOG, DIE RUSHDIE BASTARD, and WE'D RATHER DIE THAN SEE HIM LIVE, and the twelve-year-old boy explaining to the cameras that he was ready to kill the bastard personally. The appearances by Kalim Siddiqui and Cat Stevens had been helpful as well. The press coverage of these events was indeed very much on his side. "I hate," said a commentator in the London *Times*, "to see a man outnumbered."

There had been sightings of him everywhere that hot, hot May—in Geneva and Cornwall and all over London, and at an Oxford dinner party picketed by Muslims. The South African writer Christopher Hope told Clarissa's colleague Caradoc King that he had actually been at a reception in Oxford also attended by the invisible man. Tariq Ali claimed to have dined with him at a remote location. None of these sightings was accurate, unless there really was a phantom Rushdie on the loose, a runaway shadow like the one in Hans Christian Andersen's great, scary story, performing party tricks while Joseph Anton stayed home. The runaway shadow first glimpsed on the stage of the Royal Court in *Iranian Nights* did crop up again in the title of a second play, by Brian Clark, author of *Whose Life Is It Anyway?* This new work was elegantly titled *Who Killed Salman Rushdie?* He telephoned Clark to point out that the answer to the question was "Nobody, or not yet, anyway, and let's hope it doesn't happen," and Clark offered to change the title to *Who Killed the Writer?* but the premise would remain the same: a writer killed by Iranian assassins because of a book he wrote. "Fiction?" Sure. Could be anybody. Clark told him he intended to offer the work for production. His life and death were both becoming other people's property. He was fair game.

Everyone in England was sunbathing but he remained indoors, growing pale and hairy. He was offered a place on the European "ticket" of the Italian center parties—the Republican Party, the Liberal Party and the Radical Party of one Marco Pannella, who was the person making the offer, which reached him through the office of Paddy Ashdown, the leader of the British Liberal Democrats. Gillon said, "Don't do it; it sounds like a publicity stunt." But Pannella said he felt Europe should make a concrete gesture of solidarity toward him, and if he became a member of the European Parliament (MEP) any attack on him would be considered an attack on the European Parliament itself, which might dissuade some potential attackers. Scotland Yard, whose senior officers seemed determined to hold him incommunicado, feared that such a move might actually increase the danger to him, acting as a red rag to some Muslims; and it might endanger others too. How would he feel if as a result of his decision some "soft targets in Strasbourg" were attacked? In the end he decided against accepting Signor Pannella's invitation. He was not a politician. He was a writer. It was as a writer that he wanted to be defended, as a writer that he wanted to defend himself. He thought of Hester Prynne wearing her scarlet letter with pride. He too had been branded with a scarlet *A* now, standing not for "Adulteress" but for "Apostate." He too, like Hawthorne's great heroine, must wear the scarlet letter as a badge of honor, in spite of the pain.

He was sent a copy of the American magazine *NPQ*, in which he was glad to find an Islamic scholar writing that *The Satanic Verses* stood within a long Muslim tradition of doubting art, poetry and philosophy. One quiet voice of sanity, striving to be heard above the caterwauling of murderous children.

There was a second meeting with Commander Howley, which took place at the Thornhill Crescent, Islington, home of his friend the raunchy Australian comic novelist Kathy Lette and her husband, his lawyer, Geoffrey Robertson QC. Howley reminded him of a nutcracker in the shape of a man's head and arms that his father used to crack walnuts. One placed the nut in the man's jaws and snapped the arms together and the nut gave way with a satisfying crack. The man had a fearsome jawline that Dick Tracy would have envied, and, when the nutcracker was closed, a thin, grim mouth. Any walnut, sighting Commander Howley, would have quaked in its shell. He was a stern and serious man. But on this occasion he had come to provide hope of a kind. It was plainly unreasonable, he conceded, to force on anyone a permanently peripatetic life, requiring him to rent or borrow homes forever. It had therefore been decided—policemen were fond of the passive voice—that he be allowed (there it was again, that strange *allowed*) to start looking for a permanent home to move into "in the middle of the next year, or thereabouts." The middle of next year was a year away, which was disheartening, but the idea of being able to have a home again, and to be protected in it like every other "principal," was cheering, and restorative of his self-respect. How much more dignified that would be than this fretful, scuttling existence! He thanked Commander Howley for that, and added that he hoped he would not be asked to remain buried in the countryside somewhere, far from his family and friends. "No," Howley said. It would be easier for everyone if the house were to be located within the "DPG area." The DPG was the Diplomatic Protection Group, which could offer a rapid-response service in case of need. There would have to be a reinforced safe room and a system of panic buttons but that was presumably acceptable. Yes, he said, of course. "Very well then," Howley said. "We'll aim at that." The nutcracker jaw clamped shut.

He was not able to share the news with anyone, not even his hosts for the day. He had met Kathy Lette in Sydney five years earlier when he was walking near Bondi Beach with Robyn Davidson. There were sounds of a party wafting down from a fourth-floor apartment and when they looked up they saw a woman sitting on the balcony railing with her back to the sea. "I'd recognize that bottom anywhere," Robyn said. That was how his friendship with Kathy began: from the bottom up. Robyn vanished from his life but Kathy remained. She arrived in England after falling in love with Geoffrey, who broke up with Nigella Lawson to be with her, a decision that improved the lives of everyone concerned, including Nigella's. In the Thornhill Crescent house, after the police departed, Geoff held forth on the legal attacks on *The Satanic Verses* and why they would fail. His conviction and strength of feeling were both reassuring. He was a valuable ally.

Marianne came back from an outing in the city. She said she had run into Richard Eyre, the director of the National Theatre, on a subway platform, and when he saw her he burst into tears.

So much was being said by so many people, but the police were asking him not to make further inflammatory statements, their assumption being that any statement by him would be inflammatory simply because he was the one making it. He found himself composing a thousand letters in his head and firing them off into the ether like Bellow's Herzog, half-deranged, obsessive arguments with the world that he could not actually send on their way.

Dear Sunday Telegraph,

Your plan for me is that I should find a safe, secret haven in, perhaps, Canada, or a remote part of Scotland where the locals, ever alert to the presence of strangers, could see the bad guys coming; and once I had found my new home I should keep my mouth shut for the rest of my days. The notion that I have done nothing wrong and, as an innocent man, deserve to be able to lead my life as I choose has evidently been considered and eliminated from your range of options. Yet, oddly, this is the absurd idea to which I cling. Being a big city boy, I have never liked the countryside (except in short bursts) anyway, and cold weather is another long-standing dislike, which rules out both Scotland and Canada. I am also not good at keeping my mouth shut. If someone tries to gag a writer, Sirs, would you not—being journalists yourselves—agree that the best reply is not to be gagged? To speak, if anything, louder and more audaciously than before? To sing (if you are able to sing, which I confess I am not) more beautifully and daringly? To be, if anything, more present? If you can't see it that way, I offer you my apologies in advance. For that is my plan.

Dear Brian Clark,
    Whose life is it anyway?

Dear Chief Rabbi Immanuel Jakobovits,
    I have visited at least one college in which young Jewish men were being taught, rigorously and judiciously, the principles and practices of judicious and rigorous thought. Theirs were some of the most impressive and honed young minds I have ever encountered and I know they would understand the danger and impropriety of making false moral equivalences. It is a shame that a man they might look to as a leader has become neglectful of the proper process of the mind. "Both Mr. Rushdie and the Ayatollah have abused freedom of speech," you say. Thus a novel which, love it or hate it, is in the opinion of at least a few critics and judges a serious work of art is equated with a naked call for murder. This ought to be denounced as a self-evidently ridiculous remark; instead, Chief Rabbi, your colleagues the archbishop of Canterbury and the pope in Rome have said substantially the same thing. You have all called for the prohibition of offenses to the sensibilities of all religions. Now, to an outsider, a person of no religion, it might seem that the various claims to authority and authenticity made by Judaism, Catholicism and the Church of England contradict one another, and are also at odds with the claims made by and on behalf of Islam. If Catholicism is "true" then the Church of England must be "false," and, indeed, wars were fought because many men—and kings, and popes—believed just that. Islam flatly denies that Jesus Christ is the Son of God, and many Muslim priests and politicians openly flaunt their anti-Semitic views. Why then this strange unanimity between apparent irreconcilables? Think, Chief Rabbi, of the Rome of the Caesars. As it was with that great clan, so perhaps it is with the great world religions. No matter how much you may detest one another and seek to do one another down, you are

all members of one family, occupants of the single House of God. When you feel that the House itself is threatened by mere outsiders, by the hell-bound armies of the irreligious, or even by a literary novelist, you close ranks with impressive alacrity and zeal. Roman soldiers marching into battle in close formation formed a testudo, or tortoise, the soldiers on the outside creating walls with their shields while those in the middle raised their shields over their heads to make a roof. So you and your colleagues, Chief Rabbi Jakobovits, have formed a tortoise of the faith. You do not care how stupid you look. You care only that the tortoise wall is strong enough to stand.

Dear Robinson Crusoe,

Suppose you had four Man Fridays to keep you company, and they were all heavily armed. Would you feel safer, or less safe?

Dear Bernie Grant, MP,

"Burning books," you said in the House of Commons exactly one day after the fatwa, "is not a big issue for blacks." The objections to such practices, you claimed, were proof that "the whites wanted to impose their values on the world." I recall that many black leaders—Dr. Martin Luther King, for example—were murdered for their ideas. To call for the murder of a man for his ideas would therefore appear to the bewildered outsider to be a thing which a black member of Parliament might find horrifying. Yet you do not object. You represent, sir, the unacceptable face of multiculturalism, its deformation into an ideology of cultural relativism. Cultural relativism is the death of ethical thought, supporting the right of tyrannical priests to tyrannize, of despotic parents to mutilate their daughters, of bigoted individuals to hate homosexuals and Jews, because it is a part of their "culture" to do so. Bigotry, prejudice and violence or the threat of violence are not human "values." They are proof of the absence of such values. They are not the manifestations of a person's "culture." They are indications of a person's lack of culture. In such crucial matters, sir, to quote the great monochrome philosopher Michael Jackson, it don't matter if you're black or white.

In Tiananmen Square a man holding shopping bags stood in front of a column of tanks, stopping their advance. Half an hour earlier in the supermarket he could not have been thinking of heroism. Heroism came upon him unbidden. This was on June 5, 1989, the third day of the massacre, so he must have been aware of the danger he was in. Yet he stood there until other civilians came and drew him aside. There are those who say that after his gesture he was taken away and shot. The number of the Tiananmen dead was never revealed and is not known. In *One Hundred Years of Solitude* by Gabriel García Márquez the banana company—headed by Mr. Brown, a name belonging in a Tarantino movie—massacred three thousand striking workers in the main square of Macondo. After the killings there was a cleanup so perfect that the incident could be flatly denied. It never took place, except in the memory of José Arcadio Segundo, who saw it all. Against ruthlessness, remembering was the only defense. The Chinese leadership knew this: that memory was the enemy. It was not enough that the protesters be killed. They had to be falsely remembered as deviants and rogues, not as brave students who gave their lives for freedom. The Chinese authorities worked hard on this false version of the past and eventually it took root. The year that began with the small horror of the *fatwa* had acquired a greater horror to tremble at, whose terribleness would grow with the passing years, as the defeat of memory by lies was added to the protesters' useless deaths.

It was time to move out of Porlock Weir. A rental cottage had been found for him by the police, back in Brecon, in a place called Talybont. Maggie Drabble and Michael Holroyd came down to reclaim their home and to celebrate Maggie's fiftieth birthday there. Marianne was not coming to Talybont; she was leaving for America. Lara was graduating from Dartmouth and she naturally wanted to be there. Her departure would be a relief for them both. He could see that she was at the end of her tolerance, more than usually wild-eyed, the tension pouring off her like sweat off a marathon runner. She needed at least a break, probably a way out. He could understand that. She had not bargained for this, and it wasn't her fight. The cliché, *stand by your man,* insisted she had to stay, but everything in her was screaming *Go.* Maybe it would have been different if they had been more in love. But she was standing by a man she wasn't happy to be with. Yes, she needed to go to her daughter's graduation day.

It was a strange dinner the four of them had, half celebratory of Maggie's fiftieth, half shocked by history. Michael told funny stories of his unusual childhood—his mother enlisting his aid to help her leave her many husbands, at least one of those husbands asking him to write the please-come-back notes that might persuade her not to go. The news preoccupied them all. Tiananmen was on everyone's lips. And suddenly Ayatollah Khomeini was dead and being carried through the streets of Tehran to his grave. The police in an adjacent room, waiting for their shift change, were making police jokes. *It's POETS day—Piss Off Early, Tomorrow's Saturday.* Or, more philosophically: *Life is a shit sandwich. The more bread you've got, the less shit you eat.* But the four of them were watching scenes from far away, the immense crowd flailing around the funeral bier, the uncontainable surge and lurch of that many-headed monster, then the bier tilting, the torn shroud, and all at once the dead man's frail, white leg exposed for all to see. He knew, as he watched, that this was a thing he did not understand. It was not enough to say that such crowds were brought in by bus and truck, or paid to mourn effusively, or that many of them were in the kind of trancelike delirium found in some Shia ecstatics on the day of Ashura, the tenth of Muharram, who lashed and scarred themselves to commemorate the death of the Prophet's grandson Hussain ibn-Ali at the battle of Karbala in A.D. 680. It would not do to wonder why a nation whose sons had perished at the dead imam's bidding in a useless war against Iraq should feel such screaming sorrow at his going, to dismiss the scene as a phony performance, put on by an oppressed and fearful people whose fear of the tyrant had not lessened even after his death: not sufficient to dismiss this as terror masquerading as love. The imam had been, for these people, a direct link to their God. The link had snapped. Who would intercede for them now?

The next morning Marianne left for America. He was taken to Talybont. The cottage was tiny and the weather dreadful. There was no privacy to be had here. He and his protectors—affable Fat Jack and a new fellow, highly articulate, clearly an officer with a big future, named Bob Major—would be obliged to live cheek by jowl. Even worse, the cellphone didn't work. There was no signal to pick up. He would have to be driven several miles once a day to a telephone box in the remote countryside to make calls. Claustrophobia hit him hard. "It's all USELESS, USELESS," he wrote in his journal, and then he called Marianne, in Boston, and things got much worse.

He was in a red telephone booth on a Welsh hillside in the rain with a bag of coins in his hand and her voice in his ear. She had had dinner with Derek Walcott and Joseph Brodsky and the two Nobel laureates told her they would not have changed their lives as he had. "I would stay home and do exactly as always," Brodsky had declared, "and let's see what they could do." "I explained it to them," she said on the phone. "I told them, 'the poor man, he's afraid for his life.'" *Thanks a lot, Marianne,* he thought. Joseph Brodsky had given her a foot massage, she said. Hearing that made him feel even better. His wife was with the two alpha males of world poetry getting foot rubs and telling them that her husband was too afraid to live as they would, in the open, courageously. She had been wearing saris everywhere, she said. So, not very low profile, then. He was about to say that perhaps the saris were a little obvious when she dropped her bombshell. She had been approached in her Boston hotel lobby by a CIA agent calling himself Stanley Howard. He had asked to speak with her and they had had a cup of coffee together. "They know where we were," she said in a heightened voice. "They have been inside the house. They took papers from your desk and your wastebasket. They showed them to me as proof that they had entered and looked around. The font and page setup and the work were all definitely yours. The people you live with didn't even know they'd been there. You can't trust the people you have with you now. You need to leave at once. You need to come to America. Mr. Howard Stanley wanted to know if our marriage was real, or if you just wanted to use it as a convenience, to get into America. I stood up for you, so he said then that was okay, you would be allowed to enter. You could live in America like a free man."

Mr. Stanley Howard, Mr. Howard Stanley. Okay, people misremembered and scrambled names, that proved nothing. The stumble might even be proof that she was telling the truth. Let me be clear, he said. You're telling me that the CIA came to see you and told you they had penetrated a major British security operation and broken into the safe house and removed material and nobody noticed a thing. "Yes," she said and then again, "You're not safe, you need to leave, don't trust the people you have around you now." What are you going to do, he asked. She was going to Dartmouth for the graduation ceremony and then going south to visit her sister Johanne in Virginia. Okay, he said, I'll call again tomorrow. But the next day when he called her she did not pick up the phone.

Bob Major and Fat Jack listened gravely when he told them what she had said. Then they asked a number of questions. Finally Bob said, "It doesn't make sense to me." None of the drivers had reported being followed and they were highly trained. None of the sensors they had placed around and inside the Porlock Weir house had been tripped. There was no evidence of any improper entry. "It doesn't add up." But he added, "The trouble is, this is your wife saying this. So we have to take it seriously. It's your wife." They would have to report the matter upward, to the top brass back at the Yard, and then decisions would be taken. In the meanwhile, he said, "I'm afraid you can't stay here. We have to act as if the operation is blown. That means you can't go anywhere you've been or planned to go. We have to change everything. You can't stay here."

"I have to go to London," he said. "It's my son's tenth birthday in a few days."

"You'll have to come up with a place," Fat Jack said.

Afterward people sometimes asked him, *Didn't you lose friends in those days? Weren't people afraid to be seen to be close to you?* And he invariably answered, no, in fact, the opposite happened. His good friends proved themselves to be true friends in need, and people who had not been close to him before drew closer, wanting to help, and acted with astonishing generosity, selflessness and courage. He would remember this, the nobility of human beings acting out of their best selves, far more vividly than the hatred—though the hatred was vivid all right—and would always be grateful to have been the recipient of that bounty.

He had grown close to Jane Wellesley when she produced their documentary *The Riddle of Midnight* in 1987, and their friendship had deepened ever since. In India her surname had opened many firmly locked doors—"*That* Wellesley?" people asked, and then began to fawn a little in the presence of a descendant of Arthur Wellesley, who fought at the battle of Seringapatam and later, as Bonaparte's conqueror, became the first Duke of Wellington, and also of his brother Richard Wellesley, who had become governor-general of India 190 years ago—and she had been more embarrassed than amused. She was a profoundly private woman, sharing her secrets with very few people, and if you told her a secret it would go with her to the grave. She was also a woman of deep feeling, concealed beneath that British reserve. When he called her she instantly offered to move out of her own home, a top-floor apartment in Notting Hill, "for as long as you need it, if you think it will work." It was the sort of place the Special Branch disliked, an apartment, not a house, with only one way in or out, and on the top floor of a building with one staircase and no elevator. Through police eyes it looked like a trap. But he had to be somewhere and there was nowhere else available at such short notice. He moved in.

Mr. Greenup came to see him and suggested that Marianne had made the whole story up. "Do you know what it would take to break an operation like this?" he asked. "Maybe only the Americans would have the resources and it would be a stretch even for them. To pursue your car without being noticed they would have to change the follow car maybe every dozen miles or so, and there would have to be more than a dozen cars rotated to fool your drivers. They might have to use helicopters and satellites too. And to enter your house without disturbing any of the security traps would be quite frankly impossible. And even supposing that they did all this, that they found out where you were and got into the building and out again, taking papers from your study, and got around all the traps—why then would they approach your wife and show her the proof? They would know that she would tell you and you would tell us and the moment we knew that they knew we would change everything, so that all their work and expense would be wasted, and they would be back at square one. They would also know that for the CIA to break a highly sensitive British operation of this sort would be considered a hostile act, something very like an act of war against a friendly nation. Why would they tell her? It doesn't make sense."

Mr. Greenup also said that the cellphone was now considered a security risk and could not be used for the time being at least.

He was smuggled out of the building to make a phone call to Marianne from a phone booth in Hampstead. She sounded distraught. His refusal to accept that he could not trust his protection officers troubled her. She was trying to decide whether to return and if so when.

On the day before his tenth birthday Zafar came to stay. He had asked Clarissa to buy him a train set, but she somehow forgot to send it along, although she did remember to send the bill. It didn't matter. He had his son for the night for the first time in months and that was a thing to be treasured. The police went and bought a cake and on June 17, 1989, they celebrated as best they could. His son's smiling face was the best and most strengthening nourishment in the world. That evening Zafar was taken back to his mother's house, and the next morning Marianne returned.

She was met at Heathrow by the stone-faced double-act of Will Wilson and Will Wilton, the senior men from the Branch and British intelligence, and taken away for questioning for several hours. When she finally arrived at Jane's apartment her face was pale and she was clearly frightened. They didn't speak very much that night. He didn't know how to talk to her, or what to believe.

He wasn't *allowed* to stay in the city any longer. The police had found a place: a bed-and-breakfast inn called Dyke House in the village of Gladestry (*Glades-tree*) in Powys. Back to the Welsh Marches again. Dyke House was a former Edwardian rectory, a modest gabled building with a pretty garden and a little brook babbling nearby, near Offa's Dyke at the bottom of Hergest Ridge. It was run by a retired police officer, Geoff Tutt, and his wife, Christine, and was therefore considered to be secure. Meanwhile in the wider world the Muslim demand that he be tried for blasphemy won a judicial review, and there was another protest rally against him in Bradford and forty-four arrests were made. The bishop of Bradford asked for such protests to cease. It didn't seem likely that they would.

Will Wilson and Will Wilton came to visit him in Gladestry and asked that Marianne not be present at the meeting, which infuriated her. She stomped off for a long walk and they told him that her report had been taken very seriously indeed, that the matter had reached the desks of the British prime minister and the president of the United States, and that after extensive investigation the investigating officers were satisfied that there was no truth in her allegations whatsoever. "I see that this is difficult for you," said Wilson, "because as your wife she would be someone you would wish to believe." They explained the way they had gone about interrogating her. It was nothing like the third-degree treatment beloved of the movies. Instead they relied a great deal on repetition and detail. How did she know that Mr. Stanley Howard or Howard Stanley was a CIA officer? Did he show her ID? What did it look like? Was there a photograph on it, or not? Was it signed? Did it look like a credit card, or did it fold? "Lots of things like that," Will Wilton said. "It's the little things that help." They made her repeat her story many times and, they said, "When there is no variation in the story then we are one hundred percent certain it's a fake." Human beings telling the truth never told the story quite the same way twice.

"It didn't happen," Will Wilson said. "We're as certain of that as we can be."

He was being asked to believe that his wife had invented a CIA plot against him. Why might she have done such a thing? Was her desire to extricate herself from this underground British life so great that she had felt the need to shake his faith in his protectors, so that he would leave England for America, allowing her to do the same? But why would she not have realized that if he believed that the CIA had gone to so much trouble to find him, he might think them even less trustworthy than the Special Branch? After all, why would the CIA do such a thing? Might they plan to exchange him for American hostages being held in Lebanon? And if so, would he not be in greater danger on American soil than in Britain? His head whirled. This was insane. This was actually insane.

"It didn't happen," Will Wilton gently repeated. "No such thing took place."

———

She spoke for a long time to convince him the police were the liars and not she. She used her considerable physical charms to try to persuade him she had told the truth. She grew angry and wept and fell silent and then was voluble again. This performance, her extraordinary last stand, went on for most of the night. But he had made up his mind. He couldn't prove or disprove the truth of her story; but the odds seemed stacked against it. He couldn't trust her anymore. It would be better to be alone than to allow her to remain. He asked her to leave.

Many of her possessions were still at Porlock Weir and one of the drivers took her there to pack. She made phone calls to Sameen and to his friends and everything she told them was untrue. He was beginning to be scared of her now, scared of what she might do or say once she was outside the bubble of the prot. Some months later, when she decided to give her version of their separation to a Sunday newspaper, she alleged that the police had driven her to the middle of nowhere and left her at a phone booth to fend for herself. This was pure fabrication. In reality she had his car and the keys to the Bucknell house, and now that she was considered a security risk he could no longer use any property she knew about. So the reality was that he, not she, had been rendered homeless again by their separation.

There were more bombs—at Collet's bookshop *again,* and later on the street outside Liberty's department store, and then at Penguin bookstores in four British cities—more demonstrations, more court cases, more Muslim accusations of "wickedness," more bloodcurdling noises out of Iran (President Rafsanjani said the death order was irrevocable and supported by the "entire Muslim world") and out of the mouth of the poisonous garden gnome Siddiqui in Britain, more heartening gestures of solidarity by friends and sympathizers in England, America and Europe—a reading here, a play performance there, and twelve thousand people signed the defense campaign's "world statement," *Writers and readers in support of Salman Rushdie.* The defense campaign was run by the respected human rights organization Article 19, named after the free speech article in the Universal Declaration of Human Rights. "Everyone has the right to freedom of opinion and expression," the article declared. "This right includes freedom to hold opinions without interference and to seek, receive, and impart information and ideas through any media and regardless of frontiers." How simple and clear that was. It didn't add, "unless you upset someone, especially someone who is willing to resort to violence." It didn't say, "unless religious leaders decree otherwise and order assassinations." He thought of Bellow again, of Bellow's famous line near the beginning of *The Adventures of Augie March:* "Everybody knows there is no fineness or accuracy of suppression. If you hold down one thing, you hold down the adjoining." John Kennedy, less garrulous than Bellow's Augie, said the same thing in three words. "Freedom is indivisible."

These were ideas he had lived by, almost without knowing it. Artistic freedom had been the air he breathed, and as there had been a plentiful supply of it, it had been unnecessary to make a big deal about the importance of having air to breathe. Then people had started trying to turn off the air supply and it immediately became a matter of urgency to insist on the wrongness of that attempt.

Right now, however, most of his day was spent trying to solve a more basic problem: Where was he going to spend the next week of his life? Again, Jane Wellesley came to the rescue. She had a small house in Ayrshire and offered it with the same immediate grace as before. The Jaguars sped north. In the deep Scottish countryside a problem arose that plagued the protection wherever it went: Concealing the invisible man was easy. Explaining why two Jaguars were parked in the shed next to Jane's house, not so easy. And who were these four large men prowling around the neighborhood? The suspicions of the locals were easily aroused and hard to lay to rest. In addition, the Scottish Special Branch, whose bailiwick this was, didn't feel good about leaving this sensitive matter in the hands of their invading Sassenach counterparts. So they sent a team, too, and now there were four enormous cars in and around Jane's shed, and eight enormous men, gesticulating and arguing, several of them sitting out there in their cars all night. "The problem," he said to his protectors, "is how to hide *you*."

Jane came up to look after him and brought Bill Buford along; Buford, more than half in love with her, was like an eager American puppy at her heels, and she treated him with affectionate, aristocratic amusement. He capered around the house, the happy Fool at the Court of Jane, lacking only motley and a jester's cap and bells. Ayrshire, with the sun breaking out overhead, was briefly a happy island in the storm. Bill said, "You need a nice place, a place you can stay for a while and be comfortable. I'm going to find it for you."

He was a Character, Bill, the capitalization a necessary expression of his amplitude. He was a waver of arms, a hugger, a man who spoke in exclamations and emphases, a self-taught chef, an ex–American footballer, an intellectual reader with deep knowledge of the Elizabethans, an entertainer, part egghead, part Ringling Brothers showman. He had taken a defunct Cambridge student magazine, *Granta,* and reinvented it as the house journal of his gifted generation. Amis fils, McEwan, Barnes, Chatwin, Ishiguro, Fenton, and Angela Carter all flourished in its pages; George Steiner allowed him to publish the whole of his Hitler novella, *The Portage to San Cristobal of A.H.;* he gave the name of "dirty realism" to the work of the Americans Carver, Ford, Wolff, and Joy Williams; his first Travel issue more or less started the craze for travel writing; all this while underpaying his contributors shockingly, enraging many of them by failing to read or decide on their submissions for months at a time, enraging many others by developing an editing style so aggressively intrusive that he needed all his legendary charm to persuade people not to hit him; and hustling subscriptions to a quarterly magazine that never once, during his sixteen years at the helm, ever managed to put out more than three issues a year. He brought great wine with him wherever he went and cooked up a series of feasts involving rich reductions and much ripe game—heart-attack food—and rooms that contained him were usually filled with laughter. He was also a storyteller and gossip and seemed to be the last man on earth to be trusted with the care of the inner sanctum of the secret world of Joseph Anton. Yet every secret was kept. Behind all the gaiety and extroversion, Bill Buford was a man to trust with your life.

"I'm going to get right on it," Bill said. "We're going to get this done."

Two women he didn't know were about to become important characters in his story: Frances D'Souza and Carmel Bedford. Carmel, a big Irishwoman of fierce opinions, was appointed by Article 19 as the secretary of the defense campaign, or to give it its full title, the International Rushdie Defense Committee, and Frances, the new head of Article 19, was her boss. The committee had been set up quite independently of the person it was defending, to fight against "armed censorship," with the support of the Arts Council, PEN, the National Union of Journalists, the Society of Authors and the Writers' Guild, and many other bodies. He had had nothing to do with its origins; but as the years passed he worked more and more closely with Frances and Carmel and they became his indispensable political allies.

They saw him in many moods, depressed, belligerent, judicious, self-pitying, controlled, weak, solipsistic, strong, petty, and determined, and stood by him through them all. Frances—fine-boned, chic, dark, grave in her concentration and whinnyingly joyful in merriment—was a formidable woman. She had worked in the jungles of Borneo and in the Afghan mountains with the mujahideen. She had a fast, sharp mind and a big mothering heart. He was lucky in these *compañeras*. There was a lot to be done.

The cellphone was permitted again and they called him on it, worried. Marianne had showed up unbidden at the Article 19 offices and announced her intention, as his wife, to take a leadership role in the defense campaign. He needed someone to speak for him, she said, and she would be that person. "We just wanted to be sure," Frances said in her careful way, "that this has your backing, that it's what you want." No, he almost yelped. It was the opposite of what he wanted and under no circumstances must Marianne have anything to do with the campaign or be allowed to speak for it, or for him. "Yes," said Frances reflectively. "I thought as much."

Marianne was leaving him angry messages: the banal stuff of marital crisis rendered grotesquely melodramatic by their cloak-and-dagger lives. *Why don't you call me? I'm going to talk to the papers.* He called her, and for a moment she relented. But then she told *The Independent* that although "one is in perfect mental health one is living the life of a paranoid schizophrenic." She did not specify who *one* was.

And Clarissa, too, was on the phone. She wanted him to buy her a new house. She felt she had to move, and that was because of him, and so he should pay the additional cost of the new place. He owed it to her and to his son.

There followed more time spent in guesthouses run by retired police officers (there seemed to be quite a supply of these): at Easton in Dorset and then at Salcombe, in Devon. The view in Devon was beautiful: Salcombe Bay below him in the sunshine, with sailboats cutting across it and gulls wheeling above. Bill was working on a rental in Essex. "Give me a few days," he said.

His friend Nuruddin Farah had offered to mediate with the Islamic intellectual Ali Mazrui as a way of breaking the deadlock over the *fatwa*. "Okay," he told Nuruddin, "but I'm not apologizing or withdrawing the book." After a time Nuruddin admitted failure. "They want more than you're willing to give." Every so often in the *fatwa* years there would be these approaches by people claiming they had the "back-channel" connections that could solve the problem, and offering to act as intermediaries. There was a Pakistani gentleman named Sheikh Matin who approached Andrew in New York, a British-Iranian businessman called Sir David Alliance in London, several others. Every such approach turned out to be a dead end.

Bill called, half amused, half enraged. "Your poem," he said. "The Bradford Council of Mosques wants it banned." In its most recent issue *Granta* had broken with its anti-poetry tradition and published a verse he had written about how he felt, a poem called "6 March 1989." It ended with lines affirming his resolve

> *not to shut up. To sing on, in spite of attacks,*
> *to sing (while my dreams are being murdered by facts)*
> *praises of butterflies broken on racks.*

"You don't want to live with me because I'm a writer," Marianne said in her latest message. "You don't own the franchise on genius." She wanted to publish her "on the lam in Wales story," "*Croeso i Gymru.*" And to write about the Liberty's bomb.

He lived by the telephone but that, too, could bring difficult news.

Anita Desai in Delhi was distressed by how "in-turned" people had become. She had gone to visit her friend the producer Shama Habibullah, and there was Shama's mother, old Attia Hosain, the eminent author of *Sunlight on a Broken Column,* once a friend of his own mother's, and now seventy-six years old. Attia was complaining that the fallout from *The Satanic Verses* had made a lot of trouble for her. "And at my age, it isn't fair."

He was in constant touch with Andrew and Gillon. The relationship with Viking Penguin was deteriorating rapidly. The question of paperback publication had arisen and it looked as if Peter Mayer was looking for a way not to issue a softcover edition. Andrew and Gillon had asked him for a meeting and he had replied by saying that he wanted Penguin's lawyer Martin Garbus to attend any such meeting. This was a novelty: that a meeting between an author and his publisher—between this author and this publisher—could only take place in the presence of an attorney. It was a sign of how wide the rift had become.

He called Tony Lacey, the senior editor at Viking UK, and Tony tried to reassure him that everything would be all right. He called Peter Mayer and received no such reassurance from the publisher. He explained to Peter that he had spoken to the Special Branch and their advice had been that the safest course of action—*the safest course*—was to proceed as normal. Any deviation from the norm would be seen by the book's adversaries as a sign of weakness and would encourage them to redouble their assault. If paperback publication nine months to a year after the hardcover was normal publishing practice, then that was what should happen. "That is not our security advice," Peter Mayer said.

They both knew that for a book to remain in print a paperback edition was essential. If it was not published, a point would come at which the hardcover stopped selling and vanished from the stores. In the absence of a paperback, the novel would effectively have been withdrawn from sale. The campaign against it would have succeeded. "You know what we're fighting for," he told Mayer. "It's all about the long term. So the bottom line is, will you or won't you publish it? Yes or no?" "That is a barbaric attitude," Mayer replied. "I can't think in those terms."

Soon after this conversation, the *Observer* mysteriously got a scoop, a very accurate account of the arguments over the paperback, slanted in favor of Penguin's cautious approach. Penguin executives denied collaborating with the newspaper. However, Blake Morrison, who was the paper's literary editor, told him that the paper had a "source inside Penguin" and believed that the purpose of the piece was to "scupper the paperback." It seemed that a dirty war had begun.

Peter Mayer, a big, cuddly, tousle-headed bear of a man, famously attractive to women, soft-voiced, doe-eyed, much admired by his fellow publishers, and now caught up in the throes of what had become known as the "Rushdie Affair," looked increasingly like a rabbit in the headlights. History was rushing at him like a truck, and there were two entirely contradictory discourses at war within him, bringing him to the point of paralysis: the discourse of principle and the discourse of fear. His sense of obligation was unquestionable. "How we responded to the controversy over *The Satanic Verses* would affect the future of free inquiry, without which there would be no publishing as we knew it but also, by extension, no civil society as we knew it," he told a journalist years later. And when the danger was greatest, the fire at its hottest, he held the line. He received threats against himself and his young daughter. There were letters written in blood. The sniffer dogs and bomb-inspection machinery in the mailroom and the security guards everywhere made the publishing houses in London and New York look like no publishing house had ever looked; like a war zone. There were bomb scares, evacuations of office buildings, menaces and vilifications. And yet there was no retreat. It would come to be remembered as one of the great chapters in the history of publishing, one of the grand principled defenses of liberty, and Mayer would be remembered as the leader of that heroic team.

Almost.

Months of pressure took their toll on Mayer, eroding his will. He began to persuade himself, it seemed, that he had done what he needed to do. The book had been published and kept in print, and he was even willing to guarantee to keep the hardcover in print indefinitely, and the paperback could be issued at some date in the future, some notional date, when safety had returned. There was no need to do any more for the moment and renew the danger to himself, his family and his staff. He was beginning to have union problems. He worried, he said, about the man standing next to him in the urinals at the warehouse. What would he say to that man's family if some calamity were to befall his pissing partner? Letters began to fly back and forth between Andrew, Gillon, Mayer and the author of the beleaguered book. In Mayer's letters it was possible to observe an increasing syntactical convolution that mirrored an apparently knotted inner state. The ceremonial reading aloud of the Mayer letters—in phone calls, or, very occasionally, when they could meet—became a black-comic ritual for Andrew, Gillon and Joseph Anton, a.k.a. Arctic Tern. It was a time when comedy had to be found in dark places.

Mayer was trying to explain why he wanted his lawyer and friend Martin Garbus at the meeting without admitting that he wanted him there for lawyerish, legal reasons: "It is more important for me to meet with you than to insist on any aspect of a meeting for every kind of reason, not the least of which is personal. . . . I know that sometimes people can get trapped in their own positions and I am not saying that of you in an exclusive sense; I am saying that just as equally about me or ourselves. I thought, as sometimes happens, that if there were to be a bog down (out of anyone's best intentions) sometimes a sympathetic third person can propose a way forward, having heard both parties speak, advance an idea useful to everyone. It doesn't always work this way, I know, but the last thing I want to do is to cut ourselves off from such an opportunity, especially when there is someone around as gifted an intermediary as this man is. . . . For the moment, therefore, I am going to ask Marty to fly to London as, if he isn't here, there is no way for him to attend." By this time their laughter had become hysterical and it was difficult to complete the ceremonial reading. "As you can easily spot from the above," came Mayer's punch line, "I'm looking forward to seeing you."

He, the author Peter Mayer was looking forward to seeing, had asked that the paperback be published by the end of 1989, because until publication was complete the tumult about the publication could not die down. Labour MPs like Roy Hattersley and Max Madden had focused on preventing the paperback publication to appease their Muslim constituents, and this was a further reason to proceed. Peace could not begin to return until the publication cycle had been completed. Nor were there any longer any commercial reasons for delay. The hardcover, having sold well, had all but stopped selling, had disappeared from all English-language bestseller lists, and was no longer stocked by many bookstores because of a lack of demand. In ordinary publishing terms this was the right time to publish a cheap edition.

There were other arguments. Translations of the novel were now being published across Europe, in, for example, France, Sweden, Denmark, Finland, the Netherlands, Portugal and Germany. Paperback publication in the United Kingdom and the United States would look like a part of this "natural" process, and, as the police had advised, that would in fact be the safest course of action. In Germany, after Kiepenheuer und Witsch had canceled their contract, a consortium of publishers, booksellers and prominent writers and public figures had been formed to publish the novel under the name Artikel 19, and that publication was to go ahead after the Frankfurt Book Fair. If Peter Mayer wished to construct such a consortium to spread the risk, so to speak, then that might be a possible solution. What he mostly wanted to say to Mayer, and did say when the meeting between them finally took place, was this: "You have done the hard part, Peter. With great steadfastness you, together with everyone at Viking Penguin, have jockeyed this publication around a danger-filled course. Please don't fall at the last fence. If you leap that fence, your legacy will be a glorious one. If you don't, it will always be flawed."

The meeting took place. He was smuggled into Alan Yentob's house in Notting Hill and Andrew, Gillon, Peter Mayer, and Martin Garbus were already there. No agreement was reached. Mayer said he would undertake to "try to convince his people to publish the paperback in the first half of 1990." He would not give a date. Nothing else remotely constructive was said. Garbus, the "gifted intermediary," had proved to be a royal pain in the neck, a person of immense self-satisfaction and imperceptible utility. It had been a waste of time.

Much of what Mayer had to say in other letters was not remotely funny. Some of it was insulting. Andrew and Gillon had told him that a new book, *Haroun and the Sea of Stories*, written for ten-year-old Zafar Rushdie as a gift from his dad, was being worked on whenever the author's unsettled circumstances allowed. Mayer responded that his company was not prepared to consider publishing any new book by Rushdie until a finished text had been examined by them, in case it, too, sparked controversy. Nobody at his company, Mayer said, had known much about the "Koran" when they acquired *The Satanic Verses*. They could not acquire any more work by the author of that novel and then, when the trouble began, admit that they had not read a full manuscript. The author of that novel understood that Mayer had begun to think of him as someone who caused trouble, who was the cause of the trouble that had arisen, and who might cause trouble again.

This view of him went public when Mayer was profiled in *The Independent*. The anonymous profile writer, who had had extensive access to Mayer, wrote: "Mayer, a voracious reader who once said 'every book has a soul,' missed the religious time-bomb ticking inside its covers. Rushdie was asked twice, once before Penguin acquired the book and again afterward, what the now notorious Mahound chapter was supposed to mean. He seemed curiously reluctant to explain. 'Don't worry,' he said at one point. 'It's not terribly important to the plot.' 'My God, this has come back to haunt us,' a Penguin man said later."

Dear Anonymous Profile Writer,
    If I pay you the compliment of assuming you understand the meaning of your sentences, then I must assume you meant to imply that the "religious time-bomb" in my novel is the "soul" that Peter Mayer missed. The rest of this passage clearly suggests that I placed the time-bomb there intentionally and then intentionally misled Penguin about it. This is not only a lie, dear Anonymous, it is a defamatory lie. However, I know enough about journalists, or, let me say, about journalists in the so-called "quality" press, to understand that while you may exaggerate or distort what you have learned, you very rarely print anything for which you have no supporting evidence at all.

Pure fiction is not your game. I therefore conclude that you are reporting, with reasonable accuracy, the impression you gained from your conversations with Peter Mayer and other "Penguin men" and, possibly, women. Did it strike you as plausible, Anonymous, that a writer, after almost five years' work on a book, should say about a forty-page chapter that it was not "important to the plot"? Did it not occur to you, in the spirit of fairness, to inquire of me, through my agents, if I had indeed been asked—twice!—about this "unimportant" chapter and had been "curiously reluctant to explain"? Your neglect suggests, can only suggest, that this is the story you wanted to write, a story of which I am the deceitful villain and Peter Mayer the principled hero, standing by a book whose author tricked him into believing it did not contain a time-bomb. I got myself into trouble and now others must face the music: this is the narrative being constructed for me, a moral prison to add to my more quotidian restrictions. You will find, Sir, that it is a prison I am not prepared to occupy.

He called Mayer, who denied that he had anything to do with the newspaper's insinuations, and did not believe that any other Penguin people had spoken to the journalist. "If you find out who said these things," he said, "tell me, and I will fire that person." He had his sources at the newspaper and one of them confirmed that the executive who had spoken off the record was the managing director of Penguin UK, Trevor Glover. He gave this information to Peter Mayer, who said he didn't believe it. Trevor Glover was not fired, and Mayer still refused to talk about *Haroun and the Sea of Stories* until the book had been read and declared free of time bombs. The relationship between author and publisher was essentially at an end. When an author was convinced that his publishers were briefing the media against him, there was little more to be said.

Bill Buford had nailed down the house in Essex. It was in a village called Little Bardfield. It was expensive, but then everywhere had been expensive. "You'll like it," he said. "It's what you need." He was the "front man," renting the place in his name for six months, with the possibility of an extension. The owner had "gone abroad." It was an old rectory, an early-nineteenth-century, Grade II–listed, Queen Anne building with modern accents. The police liked it because it had a secluded entrance, which would simplify comings and goings, and because it stood on its own land and was not overlooked. There was a mature garden with large shady trees, and a lawn sloping down to a beautiful pond in which a fake heron stood on one leg. After all the cramped cottages and cooped-up boardinghouses it looked positively palatial. Bill would come down as often as he could, to lend credibility to his "tenancy." And Essex was far closer to London than Scotland had been, or Powys, or Devon. It would be easier to see Zafar; though the police still refused to bring Zafar to his "location." He was ten years old and they didn't trust him not to blurt it out at school. They underestimated him. He was a boy with remarkable gifts of self-control, and he understood that his father's safety was at issue. In all the years of the protection he was never guilty of an incautious remark.

A comfortable prison was still a prison. In the living room there were old paintings, one of a lady-in-waiting at the court of Elizabeth I, another of a certain Miss Bastard, whom he liked at once. They were windows into another world but he could not escape through them. He did not have in his pocket the key to the house filled with reproduction antique furniture that he was paying a small fortune to rent, and could not walk out the front gate into the village street. He had to write shopping lists that a police officer would take to a supermarket many miles away so as not to arouse suspicion. He had to hide in a locked bathroom each time the cleaner came to the house, or be smuggled off the premises in advance. The tide of shame rose in him each time such things had to be done. Then the cleaning lady quit, saying that "strange men" were at the rectory. This was worrying, of course. Once again it was proving harder to explain the police's presence than to conceal his. After the cleaner's exit they dusted and vacuumed the house themselves. The police cleaned their own rooms and he cleaned his part of the house. He preferred this to the alternative.

In those years he became aware that people imagined him living in some sort of isolation ward, or inside a giant safe with a peephole through which his protectors watched him, alone, always alone; in that solitary confinement, people asked themselves, would not this most gregarious of writers inevitably lose his grip on reality, his literary talent, his sanity? The truth was that he was less alone now than he had ever been. Like all writers he was familiar with solitude, used to spending several hours a day by himself. The people he had lived with had grown accustomed to his need for such silence. But now he was living with four enormous armed men, men unused to inactivity, the polar opposites of bookish, indoorsy types. They clattered and banged and laughed loud laughs and the thump of their presence in his vicinity was hard to ignore. He shut doors inside the house; they left them open. He retreated; they advanced. It wasn't their fault. They assumed he would like, and need, a little company. So isolation was the thing he had to work hardest to re-create around himself, so that he could hear himself think, so he could work.

The protection teams kept changing and each officer had his own style. There was a fellow named Phil Pitt, a giant of a man who was a crazy gun enthusiast and, even by Branch standards, an ace sharpshooter, which would be valuable in a firefight but was a little terrifying to live with in a vicarage. His nickname in the Branch was "Rambo." There was Dick Billington, the polar opposite of Phil, bespectacled, with a sweet shy smile. Now that was the country parson you expected to find in a vicarage, but this one carried a gun. And there were the Only Fucking Drivers too. They sat in their wing of the Essex house and cooked sausages and played cards and were bored out of their minds. "My friends are really the ones protecting me," he once said to Dick Billington and Phil Pitt in a moment of frustration, "lending me their homes, renting places for me, keeping my secrets. And I'm doing the dirty work of hiding in bathrooms and so on." Dick Billington looked sheepish when he said things like this while Phil Pitt fumed; not a man of words was Phil, and given his size and his love of the firearm it was probably a bad idea to make him fume. They explained tolerantly that their line of work looked like inaction, but that was because the advent of action would be proof that they had made a bad mistake. Security was the art of making nothing happen. The experienced security officer accepted boredom as a part of the job. Boredom was good. You didn't want things to get interesting. Interesting was dangerous. The whole point was to keep everything dull.

They took great pride in their work. Many of them said to him, always using the same words, which were clearly an "A" Squad mantra: "We've never lost anyone." It was a comforting mantra and he often repeated it to himself. The impressive fact was that nobody who had been under "A" Squad's protection had ever been hit, in the long history of the Special Branch. "The Americans can't say that." They disliked the American way of doing things. "They like to throw bodies at the problem," they said, meaning that an American security detail was usually very large indeed, dozens of people or more. Every time an American dignitary visited the United Kingdom, the security forces of the two countries had the same arguments about methodology. "We could take the queen in an unmarked Ford Cortina down Oxford Street in the rush hour and nobody would know she was there," they said. "With the Yanks it's all bells and whistles. But they lost one president, didn't they? And nearly lost another." Each country, he would discover, had its own way of doing things, its own "culture of protection." In the years to come he would experience not only the manpower-heavy American system, but the scary behavior of the French RAID. RAID was "Recherche Assistance Intervention Dissuasion." *Dissuasion,* as a description of how the RAID boys went about their work, seemed like one of the great understatements. Their Italian cousins liked to drive at high speed through urban traffic with Klaxon horns blaring and guns sticking out of the windows. All things considered, he was happy to have Phil and Dick and the softly-softly approach.

They weren't perfect. There were mistakes. There was the time he was taken to Hanif Kureishi's house. At the end of his evening with Hanif he was about to be driven away when his friend sprinted out into the street, looking very pleased with himself, and waving a large handgun in its leather holster above his head. "Oy," Hanif shouted, delightedly. "Hang on a minute. You forgot your shooter."

He began to write. *A sad city, the saddest of cities, a city so ruinously sad that it had forgotten its name.* He too was a man who had lost his name. He knew how the sad city felt. "At last!" he wrote in his journal in early October, and, a few days later, "Completed Chapter One!" When he had written thirty or forty pages he showed them to Zafar to make sure he was on the right track. "Thanks," Zafar said. "I like it, Dad." He detected something a little less than wild enthusiasm in his son's voice. "Really?" he probed. "You're sure?" "Yes," said Zafar and then, after a pause, "Some people might be bored." *"Bored?"* This was a cry of anguish and Zafar tried to mollify him. "No, I'd read it, of course, Dad. I'm just saying that *some* people *might . . .*" "Why bored?" he demanded. "What's the boring bit?" "It's just," Zafar said, "that it doesn't have enough jump in it." This was an astonishingly precise critique. He understood it immediately. "Jump?" he said. "I can do jump. Give me that back." And he almost snatched the type-script out of his worried son's hands, and then had to reassure him, no, he wasn't annoyed, in fact this was very helpful, it might, in fact, be the best piece of editorial advice he had ever received. Several weeks later he gave Zafar the rewritten early chapters and asked, "How is it now?" The boy beamed happily. "Now it's fine," he said.

Herbert Read (1893–1968) was an English art critic—a champion of Henry Moore, Ben Nicholson and Barbara Hepworth—and a poet of the First World War, an existentialist and an anarchist. For many years the Institute of Contemporary Arts on the Mall in London held an annual memorial lecture bearing Read's name. In the autumn of 1989 the ICA sent a letter to Gillon's office asking if Salman Rushdie might be willing to deliver the 1990 lecture.

Mail did not reach him easily. It was collected from the agency and the publishers by the police, put through tests for explosives, and opened. Even though he was always assured that no mail was withheld from him, the relatively small number of abusive letters he received suggested to him that some filtering process had been put in place. There was concern at the Yard over his state of mind—Could he take the pressure? Was he about to crack up completely?—and no doubt it was thought best to spare him the literary onslaught of the faithful. The letter from the ICA made it through the net, and he replied, accepting the invitation. He knew at once that he wanted to write about iconoclasm, to say that in an open society no ideas or beliefs could be ring-fenced and given immunity from challenges of all sorts, philosophical, satirical, profound, superficial, gleeful, irreverent, or smart. All liberty required was that the space for discourse itself be protected. Liberty lay in the argument itself, not the resolution of that argument, in the ability to quarrel, even with the most cherished beliefs of others; a free society was not placid but turbulent. The bazaar of conflicting views was the place where freedom rang. This would evolve into the lecture-essay "Is Nothing Sacred?," and that lecture, once it had been scheduled and announced, would lead to his first serious confrontation with the British police. The invisible man was trying to become visible again, and Scotland Yard didn't like it.

Dear Mr. Shabbir Akhtar,

I have no idea why the Bradford Council of Mosques, of which you are a member, believes it can set itself up as a cultural arbiter, literary critic, and censor. I do know that "the liberal inquisition," the phrase you have coined, and of which you are clearly inordinately proud, is a phrase without any real meaning. The Inquisition, let's remind ourselves, was a tribunal created by Pope Gregory IX, in or around the year 1232; its purpose was the suppression of heresy in northern Italy and southern France, and it became notorious for its use of torture. Plainly the literary world, which is teeming with what you and your colleagues would call heretics and apostates, has little interest in suppressing heresy. Heresy, you may say, is the stock-in-trade of many of that world's members. The Spanish Inquisition, another bunch of torturers, established two and a half centuries later, in 1478, may be what you had in mind, because of its reputation for being anti-Islamic. Actually, however, it most vigorously pursued converts from Islam. Oh, and from Judaism, too. The torture of ex-Jews and ex-Muslims is relatively rare in the modern literary world. My own thumbscrews and rack have seen barely any use in oh, ever so long. However, a sizable percentage of your lot—and here I mean the Council of Mosques, the faithful it claims to represent, and all its allies in the clerisy in the UK and abroad—have been willing to put up their hands when asked if they believed in the execution of a writer for his work. (It's reported that 300,000 Muslim men did this at mosques around Britain just the other Friday.) Four in five British Muslims, according to a recent Gallup poll, believe that some sort of action should be taken against that writer (me). The eradication of heresy, and the use of violence to that end, is a part of your project, not ours. You, Sir, celebrate "fanaticism on behalf of God." You say that Christian tolerance is a reason for Christian "shame." You are in favor of "militant wrath." And yet you call me a "literary terrorist." This would be funny except that you aren't trying to be funny and actually, on reflection, it's not funny at all. You say in The Independent *that works like* The Satanic Verses *and* The Life of Brian *should be "removed from public knowledge," because their methods are "wrong." You may find people to agree with you that my novel is without merit; it is when you take on Monty Python's Flying Circus that, in the words of Bertie Wooster, you make your bloomer. That antic circus and its works are beloved by many, and any attempt to remove them from public knowledge will be met by an army of adversaries armed with dead parrots and walking with silly walks and singing their anthem about always looking on the bright side of life. It is becoming evident to me, Mr. Shabbir Akhtar, that the best way of describing the argument over* The Satanic Verses *may be to call it an argument between those (like the fans of* The Life of Brian) *who have a sense of humor and those (like, I suspect, you) who do not.*

He had begun work on another long essay. For the best part of a year he had not only been invisible but for the most part dumb as well, composing unsent letters in his head, publishing only a few book reviews and one short poem whose publication in *Granta* had displeased not only the Bradford Council of Mosques but, according to Peter Mayer, the staff of Viking Penguin too, some of whom were apparently beginning to believe, like Mr. Shabbir Akhtar, that he should be "removed from public knowledge." Now he would have his say. He spoke to Andrew and Gillon. It would inevitably be a long essay and he needed to know what sort of maximum length would be acceptable to the press. Their view was that the press would publish whatever he wanted to write. They agreed that the best time for such a piece to appear would be on or around the first anniversary of the *fatwa*. It would obviously be important for the context of the essay to be right, so the choice of publication would be crucial. Gillon and Andrew began to make inquiries. He began to think about the essay that would become "In Good Faith," a seven-thousand-word defense of his work, and in thinking about it he made one crucial mistake.

He had fallen into the trap of thinking that his work had been attacked because it had been misrepresented by unscrupulous persons seeking political advantage, and that his own integrity had been impugned for the same reason. If he were a person of base morals, and his work lacking in quality, then it was unnecessary to engage with it intellectually. But, he convinced himself, if he could just show that the work had been seriously undertaken, and that it could honorably be defended, then people—Muslims—would change their minds about it, and about him. In other words, he wanted to be popular. The unpopular boy from boarding school wanted to be able to say, "Look, everyone, you've made a mistake about my book, and about me. It's not an evil book, and I'm a good person. Read this essay and you'll see." This was folly. And yet, in his isolation, he convinced himself that it was achievable. Words had got him into this mess, and words would get him out of it.

The heroes of Greek and Roman antiquity, Odysseus, Jason, and Aeneas, were all sooner or later obliged to sail their ships between the two sea monsters, Scylla and Charybdis, knowing that to fall into the clutches of either would lead to utter destruction. He told himself firmly that in whatever he wrote, fiction or nonfiction, he needed to sail between his personal Scylla and Charybdis, the monsters of fear and revenge. If he wrote timid, frightened things, or angry, vengeful things, his art would be mangled beyond hope of repair. He would become a creature of the *fatwa* and nothing more. To survive he needed to set aside rage and terror, hard though such setting might be, and to try to go on being the writer he had always tried to be, to continue down the road he had defined for himself as his own. To do that would be success. To do otherwise would be dismal failure. This, he knew.

He forgot that there was a third trap: that of courting approval, of wanting, in his weakness, to be loved. He was too blind to see that he was running headlong toward that pit; and that was the trap that ensnared him, and almost destroyed him forever.

They found the Globe Theatre, Shakespeare's glorious wooden O, under a parking lot in Southwark. The news brought tears to his eyes. He had been playing chess against a chess machine and had reached level five but when they found the Globe he couldn't move a pawn. The past had reached out and touched the present and the present was richer for it. He thought of the greatest words in the English language being spoken for the first time at Anchor Terrace and Park Street, the Elizabethan Maiden Lane. The birthplace of Hamlet and Othello and Lear. A lump rose in his throat. The love of the art of literature was a thing impossible to explain to his adversaries, who loved only one book, whose text was immutable and immune to interpretation, being the uncreated word of God.

It was impossible to persuade the Qur'anic literalists to answer a simple question: Did they know that after the Prophet died there was, for some considerable time, *no canonical text*? The Umayyad inscriptions from the Dome of the Rock were at odds with what was now insisted upon as holy writ—a text that was first standardized at the time of the third caliph, Uthman. The very walls of one of Islam's most sacred shrines proclaimed that human fallibility had been present at the birth of the Book. Nothing was perfect on earth that depended on human beings. The Book was orally transmitted around the Muslim world and in the early tenth century there were more than seven variant texts extant. The text prepared and authorized by al-Azhar in the 1920s followed one of these seven variations. The idea that there existed an *ur*-text, the perfect and immutable word of God, was simply inaccurate. History and architecture did not lie, even if novelists might.

Doris Lessing, a writer greatly influenced by Sufi mysticism, called to say that his defense had been "wrongly conducted." Khomeini should have been isolated as un-Islamic, a "Pol Pot figure." "Also," she said, being a plainspoken woman, "I must tell you that I didn't like your book." Everyone had an opinion. Everyone knew what should have been done.

Fear was spreading through the publishing industry. Peter Mayer's fear of his future books had spread to other publishers—he wondered if Penguin executives were trying to recruit support for their position, so that they didn't look too cowardly—and now French and German publishers were saying the same thing. *Publishers Weekly* came out against the publication of a paperback edition and again he smelled a rat, or penguin. Mayer himself continued to refuse to give any date for paperback publication, mentioning the discovery of bombs near his home. These turned out to be the work of Welsh nationalists and had nothing to do with *The Satanic Verses*. That fact did nothing to affect Mayer's position. Tony Lacey told Gillon that Peter had just received a death threat at his home. Bill Buford came to Essex and they cooked duck for dinner. "Don't be bitter," Bill said.

Gillon and Andrew had begun talking to people at Random House—Anthony Cheetham, Si Newhouse—to see if they might be interested in publishing *Haroun and the Sea of Stories*. They said they were interested. But neither they nor Mayer made an offer. Tony Lacey said that Penguin would be "sending a letter." Sonny Mehta called to say he was "doing his best" to get Random House to come through.

At the beginning of November the Penguin letter arrived. It promised no paperback publication date for *The Satanic Verses* and made no offer for the new work. Mayer wanted "months" of complete calm before he would consider publishing the paperback. That seemed improbable in the week that BBC TV showed a documentary about the continuing Muslim "anger." Random House, however, said they wanted to negotiate seriously for future books, and those negotiations began.

He first met Isabel Fonseca at the 1986 PEN Congress in New York. She was smart and beautiful and they became friends. When she moved to London he began to see something of her, though there was never any suggestion of a romance. In early November 1989 she invited him to her London apartment for dinner and it was agreed that he could go. After the usual cloak-and-daggery there he was at her door, holding a bottle of Bordeaux, and there followed the illusion of a pleasant evening dining with a friend, listening to her tales of literary London and John Malkovich and drinking good red wine. Then, late in the evening, calamity struck. A protection officer—shy, parson-like Dick Billington—knocked awkwardly on the door and asked for a word. The apartment was small—a living room, one bedroom—so the team had to come in. The old rectory, he said, blinking rapidly behind his glasses, may have been blown. They were not certain of this, or of how it had happened, but there was beginning to be talk in the village, and his name had been cropping up. "Until we've looked into it," Dick said, "you can't go back there, I'm afraid." He felt an ache in the pit of his stomach, and a feeling of great helplessness came over him. "What," he said, "you mean I can't go back there *tonight*? It's ten o'clock, for goodness' sake." "I know," said Dick. "But we'd rather you didn't. To be on the safe side." He was looking at Isabel. She responded at once. "Well, you can stay here, of course," she said. "That's impossible," he said to Dick. "Can't we go back and then sort this out in the morning?" There was much unhappy body language from Dick. "My instructions are that you can't go back," he said.

There was only one bed, a large double. They slept as far apart as they could and when his restless body accidentally collided with hers he apologized quickly. It was like a black sex comedy: two friends forced by circumstance into bed together and trying to pretend it was nothing special. In a movie they would have given up pretending at some point and made love, and then there would be the embarrassment-comedy of the next morning, and maybe, after much confusion, love. But this was real life and he had just been rendered homeless and she was giving him a roof over his head for the night and he had no idea what the next day would hold and none of that was very sexy at all. He was grateful and miserable and yes, a little desirous of her, wondering what would happen if he did turn toward her, but knowing or believing that such an approach would, in the circumstances, be a boorish exploitation of her kindness. He turned his back toward her and did not sleep very much. In the morning there was Mr. Greenup in Isabel's living room. "You can't go back," he said.

Dev Stonehouse had been off the team for a while, but he had recently been at Little Bardfield, and, perhaps inevitably, had had too much to drink at a local pub and—it seemed almost impossible to believe this when Bob Major told him about it later—had taken out his handgun and started showing off for the other drinkers. The publican, it turned out, used to run the Blind Beggar pub in Whitechapel, the favored watering hole of the notorious Kray twins, where the gangster Ronnie Kray had once murdered a man. A man who had run a pub like that, Bob Major said, "could see the Old Bill coming a mile off." It was a pub to be avoided; but Dev had gone there to celebrate his birthday and after that people had put two and two together and somebody had said *Salman Rushdie* and that was that.

"This is just intolerable," he protested to Mr. Greenup. "I have paid a lot of money to rent that property and you're telling me I can't go back there because one of your officers got drunk? What am I supposed to do? I can't stay here and I have no other possibilities." "You'll have to find somewhere," Mr. Greenup said. "Just like that," he said, a little wildly, snapping his fingers. "Hocus pocus, and here's another place to live." "Many people would say," replied Mr. Greenup stonily, "that you brought this on yourself."

A day of crazy telephony. Sameen had a Pakistani industrialist friend who kept an apartment in Chelsea near the river. Maybe she could get the keys. Jane Wellesley offered her Notting Hill apartment again. And Gillon Aitken offered the services of Lady Cosima Somerset, who was at that time working in the London office. Cosima was utterly reliable and discreet, he said, and she would be wonderful at finding and setting up rentals. Everything could be done through the agency. He spoke to Cosima on the phone and she said briskly, "Right, I'll get started at once." He realized at once that she was indeed the perfect intermediary, intelligent and good-natured; and nobody would suspect this glamorous blue blood of being involved with anything as shady as the Rushdie Affair.

Sameen came to Isabel's later with the keys to her friend's apartment and so, for a few days at least, he had a home. The police—Benny was back—smuggled him into the Chelsea apartment block and said they would take him back to the old rectory at dead of night to pack up his stuff. About the lost rental money there was nothing to be done. It was also Benny's unsolicited opinion that he should withdraw the paperback of *The Satanic Verses*. He said local police officers had been visiting bookshops telling them to tell Penguin not to publish it. That contradicted what Branch officers had told him. Nothing was stable. Nothing could be believed.

After Greenup left and Isabel went to work he made a mistake. In his destabilized condition he called his wife and went to see her. And then there was a bigger mistake: They made love.

He settled into the Chelsea apartment as best he could with everything in his life in turmoil—no permanent abode, no publishing agreements, growing difficulties with the police, and what was to happen now with Marianne?—but when he turned on the TV he saw a great wonder that dwarfed what was happening to him. The Berlin Wall was falling, and young people were dancing on its remains.

That year, which began with horrors—on a small scale the *fatwa*, on a much larger scale Tiananmen—also contained great wonders. The magnificence of the invention of the hypertext transfer protocol, the *http://* that would change the world, was not immediately evident. But the fall of Communism was. He had come to England as a teenage boy who had grown up in the aftermath of the bloody partition of India and Pakistan, and the first great political event to take place in Europe after his arrival was the building of the Berlin Wall in August 1961. *Oh no,* he had thought, *are they partitioning Europe now?* Years later, when he visited Berlin to take part in a TV discussion with Günter Grass, he had crossed the wall on the S-Bahn and it had looked mighty, forbidding, eternal. The western side of the wall was covered in graffiti but the eastern face was ominously clean. He had been unable to imagine that the gigantic apparatus of repression whose icon it was would ever crumble. And yet the day came when the Soviet terror-state was shown to have rotted from within, and it blew away, almost overnight, like sand. *Sic semper tyrannis.* He took renewed strength from the dancing youngsters' joy.

There were times when the rush of events felt overwhelming. Hanif Kureishi was debating Shabbir Akhtar at the ICA and called, afterward, to say what a limp and incompetent adversary Akhtar had been. His friend the writer and Charter 88 founder Anthony Barnett debated Max Madden, MP, on the blasphemy law and Madden, too, proved a weak and craven opponent. Anthony Cheetham and Sonny

Mehta of Random House and Knopf said they wanted to speak to Mr. Greenup before signing any contracts for future books. That was a depressing prospect, but, surprisingly, Greenup said that he had no problems regarding the future and would speak to Cheetham and Sonny and tell them so. Meanwhile Penguin fired Tim Binding, the young editor who had been most passionate about *The Satanic Verses*. Mayer was refusing to return Andrew Wylie's calls. Fred Halliday, the Iran specialist, called to report that he had met with Abbas Maliki, Iran's deputy minister for foreign affairs (and, incidentally, one of the men who had stormed the U.S. embassy in Tehran in 1979). Maliki told Fred that nobody in Iran could go against Khomeini, but if British Muslims were to end their campaign it could let Iran off the hook. "By the way," Fred added, "do you know that pirate Farsi radio stations are beaming readings of the *Verses* in translation into Iran all the time?"

Marianne was still talking about publishing the stories "Croeso i Gymru" and "Learning Urdu" but suddenly decided that they weren't "ready." Her emotional fragility frightened him. Jane was scolding him for renewing contact with Marianne, and so were Pauline Melville and Sameen. What was he thinking about? The answer was that he wasn't thinking straight. It had happened, that was all.

Kalim Siddiqui's latest bloodcurdling remarks were being examined by the Crown Prosecution Service and lawyer Geoff Robertson said the CPS was likely to go ahead with a prosecution. However, it declined to do so, citing "insufficient evidence." Videotape of Siddiqui calling for a man's death was not enough.

There was a house in north London, at 15 Hermitage Lane, that the police liked because it had an "integral garage" that would make it much easier for him to come and go without being seen. John Howley and Mr. Greenup came to meet him at the Chelsea apartment. They were mortified about the "errors" at Little Bardfield and assured him there would be no repetition, and no more Dev Stonehouse. Perhaps because of their mortification they began to make concessions. They appreciated he had lost money on the old rectory and would now have to invest heavily in yet another rental. They were agreeable to him using the old rectory as an "occasional" place until the rental agreement ran out. They were willing to "allow" him to go about a little more and see his friends. And—this was the great breakthrough—they agreed that Zafar could visit and stay with him. Yes, and, if he really insisted, Marianne as well. She was, after all, still his wife.

In early December he went with Bill, his Polish girlfriend, Alicja, Zafar and Marianne to Little Bardfield for the weekend. Zafar was intensely excited and so was he. Marianne however was in a strange state of mind. A few days earlier she had actually apologized for "lying" but now the mad glint was back in her eye and at midnight she dropped another of her bombshells. She and Bill, she said, had become lovers. He asked to talk to Bill alone and they went into the rectory's small TV room. Bill confessed that yes, it had happened once, and he had immediately felt like a fool, and hadn't known how to tell the truth. They spoke for an hour and a half, both of them knowing that their friendship hung in the balance. They said what needed to be said, loudly and softly, in anger and finally with laughter. In the end they agreed to put the matter away and say no more about it. He, too, felt like a fool, who had to make a decision about his marriage all over again. It was like giving up smoking and then starting up again. He had done that too. After five years as a nonsmoker he was back on the drug. He was feeling angry with himself. He had to break both these bad habits soon.

15 Hermitage Lane was a small fortlike building on an anonymous street corner. It was ugly and had almost no furniture. Cosima bullied the landlords into supplying basic furnishings, a worktable and chair, a couple of armchairs, kitchen equipment. But for as long as he stayed there it continued to look like an uninhabited space. This was where he found a way of getting back to work, and *Haroun and the Sea of Stories* began, at last, to progress.

Four Iranian men were arrested in Manchester on December 15, 1989, suspected of being members of a hit squad. One of them, Mehrdad Kokabi, was charged with conspiracy to commit arson and cause explosions in bookshops. After that it was even harder to get Peter Mayer to commit to a publication date for the paperback of *The Satanic Verses*. "Maybe by the middle of next year," he told Andrew and Gillon. And, catastrophically, Random House suddenly got cold feet about signing up his future books. Alberto Vitale, chairman of Random House, Inc., declared that they had made an "underestimate of the danger," and on December 8, Random backed out of the deal. Now he had no paperback and no publisher. Should he just stop writing? The answer was on his worktable, where *Haroun* was insisting on being written. And Bill spoke to him with great sweetness. *Granta* magazine was beginning a publishing venture, Granta Books. "Let us do it," he said. "I'll show you that it's better for us to do it than a big corporation."

The Brandenburg Gate was opened and the two Berlins became one. In Romania, Ceauşescu fell. He agreed to write a review of Thomas Pynchon's silence-breaking novel *Vineland* for *The New York Times*. Samuel Beckett died. He spent another weekend with Zafar at the old rectory, and his son's love lifted his spirits as nothing else could. Then it was Christmas and the novelist Graham Swift insisted he spend it with him and his partner, Candice Rodd, at their south London home. He spent New Year's Eve with friends too: Michael Herr and his wife, Valerie, who had formed the irresistible habit of calling each other "Jim." No *darlings* or *honeys* or *babes* for them. In his low American drawl and her bright English chirp they Jimmed the Old Year out. "Hey, Jim?" "Yes, Jim?" "Happy New Year, Jim." "Happy New Year to you too, Jim." "I love you, Jim." "I love you too, Jim." 1990 arrived with a smile in the company of Jim and Jim.

And Marianne was there too. Yes. And Marianne.

IV

The Trap of Wanting to Be Loved

He had started receiving letters from a woman named Nalini Mehta in Delhi. He did not know anyone by that name, but she was certain she knew him, not just socially, but carnally, pornographically, *biblically*. She knew the dates and places of their assignations and could describe the hotel rooms and the views from the windows. The letters were not only well written but intelligent, and the handwriting, in thin blue ballpoint, was strong and expressive. The photographs were terrible, though: badly taken, poorly lit, the different stages of undress all a little foolish, none of them remotely erotic, though the woman in them was obviously beautiful. He did not reply, not even to try to dissuade her from writing, knowing that would be a bad mistake. The passion with which the writer insisted on their love made him fear for her. Mental illness still bore a stigma in the minds of many Indians. Families denied that such an affliction could have struck one of their members. Any problems were hushed up instead of being properly treated. That Nalini Mehta's letters continued to arrive, that their frequency even began to increase, indicated that she was not being given the loving help she needed.

His own situation exercised her greatly. She "knew" he could not be getting the loving attention *he* needed. Once she had seen in the newspapers that his wife was no longer beside him she pleaded to be allowed to replace her. She would come to him and make him feel good. She would do everything for him and stand beside him and look after him and wrap him in her love. How could he not agree, after everything they had meant to each other—everything they still felt for each other? He had to send for her. "Send for me now," she wrote. "I will come at once."

She told him she had studied English literature at Lady Shri Ram College in Delhi. He remembered that his friend Maria, a Goan writer, had taught there, so he called her to ask if she knew the name. "Nalini," she said sadly. "Of course. My most brilliant student, but completely unbalanced." And he had been right: Her family refused to admit the girl was ill or to get her proper medical care. "I don't know what's to be done," Maria said.

Then the letters changed. I'm coming, she said. I'm coming to England so that I can be there for you. She had met an Englishwoman of her own age in Delhi and had got herself invited to stay with that woman's retired parents in Surrey somewhere. She had her ticket. She was leaving *tomorrow,* then *today.* She had arrived. A few days later she walked unannounced into the London agency and barged into Gillon Aitken's office. Gillon told him afterward, "Well, she is very striking, my dear, and she was quite dressed up, and she said she was a friend of yours, so of course I asked her in." At once she insisted that she be given his address and phone number, because he was expecting her to join him, and the matter was extremely urgent, she had to go to him immediately. That very day, if possible. Gillon saw that something was badly wrong. He did tell Nalini, not unkindly, that he would be happy to pass on a message and if she left a contact number he would pass that on as well. It was at this point that Nalini Mehta offered him sex. Gillon was startled. "My dear, it doesn't happen in my office every day, or even at home." He declined the offer. She became insistent. They could clear the papers off his desk and she would have sex with him right there and then, on the wooden desktop, and then he would give her the phone number and address. Gillon became firm. No, really, that was not an option, he told her. Would she please keep her clothes on. She deflated and became tearful. She had no money, she said. She had spent what little she had getting to the agency from her friend's parents' Surrey home. If he could lend her say a hundred pounds she would repay him as soon as she could. When Andrew Wylie heard the story he said, "She was done for the moment she asked Gillon for money. That was a fatal move." Rising to his great height, Gillon guided her to the door.

Several days passed, perhaps a week. Then at Hermitage Lane the police had a question. Did he know, Phil Pitt asked him, which was to say, had he had any dealings with a lady name of Nalini Mehta? He told the officer what he knew. "Why," he said, "has something happened

to her?" Something had happened. She had disappeared from the home
of her friend's extremely worried parents, to whom she had been talking incessantly about her intimacy with Salman Rushdie, whom she
would soon be going to stay with. When she had been missing for two
days the fretting couple called the police. Given the circumstances surrounding Mr. Rushdie, they said, and considering how loosely she was
talking, somebody might have done her a mischief. It was several more
days before she was found in Piccadilly Circus by a bobby on the beat,
her hair unkempt, wearing the sari she had worn when she left Surrey
five or six days earlier, and telling anyone who would listen that she was
"Salman Rushdie's girlfriend," that they were "in love," and that she
had flown to England at his request, to live with him.

Her Delhi acquaintance's parents didn't really want her back. The
police had no reason to hold her; she hadn't committed any crime. She
had nowhere to go. He called her old English teacher Maria and said,
"Can you help us get in touch with her parents?" And, fortunately, she
could. After some initial reluctance and some defensive remarks to the
effect that there was nothing wrong with his daughter, Nalini's father,
Mr. Mehta, agreed to go to London to bring her home. After that
there were a few more letters, but they eventually stopped coming.
This was, he hoped, a good sign. Maybe she was recovering her health.
Her need to be loved had been very great and it had pushed her into
delusion. He hoped she was now receiving the real, familial love and
care that would allow her to escape from the trap her mind had built
for her.

He did not then understand that before the year was out his mind
would build a trap for him and he, too, desperate for love, would
plunge toward delusion and self-destruction, as though into a lover's
embrace.

He had dreams of vindication. They were detailed dreams, his critics
and would-be murderers coming to him bareheaded and shamefaced,
begging for forgiveness. He wrote them down and for a few seconds
each time they made him feel better. He was working on his
silence-breaking essay and his Herbert Read lecture and the convic-

tion that he could explain, he could make people understand, kept growing. *The Guardian* ran a nasty ad promoting a piece by Hugo Young: a picture of a bandaged Penguin alongside the line DOES SALMAN RUSHDIE HAVE ANY REGRETS? Hugo Young's piece, when it appeared, continued this process of shifting the blame from the men of violence to the target of their attack, saying that he should be "humbled by what he had wrought," and it only made him more determined to stand his ground and demonstrate the rightness of that stand.

It was the first anniversary of the Bradford book burning. A newspaper survey of 100 British bookshops showed that 57 were in favor of the publication of a paperback of *The Satanic Verses,* 27 were against it and 16 had no opinion. The Bradford Council of Mosques' spokesman said: "We cannot let go of this issue. It is crucial to our future." Kalim Siddiqui wrote a letter to *The Guardian* saying that "we [Muslims] have to support the death sentence on Rushdie." A few days later Siddiqui traveled to Tehran and was granted a private audience with Khomeini's successor, Ayatollah Ali Khamenei.

He wrote day and night, pausing only when he could spend time with Zafar. There was a last, charmed weekend at the old rectory under Miss Bastard's gentle supervision. Marianne, who was generally in a bad mood, unable to write, feeling that she had no life, that she was "living a lie," and that her book's publication had been ruined by her association with him, was a little more cheerful than usual, and he found a way not to ask himself why he was with her again. When they left Little Bardfield for good and returned to Hermitage Lane he was visited by Mr. Greenup and told that he would not be permitted to deliver the Herbert Read lecture. There was that word again, *permitted,* which, like its brother *allowed,* turned him into a captive, not a "principal." The police had informed the Institute of Contemporary Arts that they would be unable to protect the event if he were to appear. For him to do so, Greenup said, would be irresponsible and selfish and the Metropolitan Police would not collude with him in his folly.

The ICA people were obviously spooked by the police advice. He told them he was prepared to come and speak even without protection but that was too scary for them. In the end he was obliged to give in. He would find someone else to deliver the lecture on his behalf, he said, and they agreed to that suggestion with relief. The first person he called was Harold Pinter. He explained the situation and made his request. Without a moment's hesitation, and with his usual volubility, Harold replied: "Yes." He was able to go to see Harold and Antonia Fraser at their home in late January and the next day, inspired by their enthusiasm, courage and determination, wrote for fourteen hours without pausing and completed the final version of "Is Nothing Sacred?" Gillon came to Hermitage Lane—as the place had been found by Cosima Somerset and was being "fronted" by the literary agency, Gillon, the "tenant," was allowed to visit, and was brought in by the police after the usual dry-cleaning run—and sat in that bleak beige underfurnished house to read both the lecture and "In Good Faith," an *explication de texte* of *The Satanic Verses,* which was also a plea for a better understanding of it and its author, to be published as a single seven-thousand-word piece in the new *Independent on Sunday.* Gillon took the work away and delivered the ICA lecture to Harold. It was time to restart work on *Haroun.*

"In Good Faith" ran on Sunday, February 4, 1990. The junior minister at the Foreign Office, William Waldegrave, called Harold Pinter to say that it had made him cry. The first Muslim responses were predictably negative, but he detected, perhaps wishfully, a slight change of tone in what Shabbir Akhtar and his sidekick Tariq Modood had to say. There was one piece of bad news: The families of the British hostages in Lebanon planned to issue a statement opposing the *Verses* paperback. Then on Tuesday, February 6, Harold stood up at the ICA and read "Is Nothing Sacred?" The lecture was televised on the BBC *Late Show.* He felt an immense sense of relief. He had said his piece. The storm had been raging for a year, and he had felt that his voice had been too small to be heard above all the other voices bellowing from every corner of the globe, above the howling of the winds of bigotry and history. Now he had proved himself wrong. He wrote in his journal, "The reaction to both IGF and INS? has cheered me immensely. It seems a real shift has taken place. Demonization is in retreat and the attackers seem confused." Friends called, describing the mood at the ICA as "loving," "electric," "exciting." Marianne offered a dissenting view. The atmosphere had been "sterile." She was feeling, she added, "unloved."

Three days after the Read lecture, Ayatollah Khamenei, at Friday prayers, renewed the Iranian mullocracy's death order. It was becoming a familiar pattern in the year-old "Rushdie Affair": An apparent lightening of the clouds, a moment of hope, was followed by a sickening blow—an escalation, an upping of the ante. "Well," he wrote defiantly in his journal, "they haven't got me yet."

Nelson Mandela walked out of the shadows into the sunlight, a free man, and the twelve months of atrocity and wonder acquired another exclamatory moment of joy. He watched Mandela reappear from his long invisibility and understood how little he himself had suffered in comparison. Enough, he told himself. Get back to work.

But Valentine's Day was upon him again. Clarissa sweetly called to wish him well for the anniversary. Harold called. He had met the new Czech president, the playwright and human rights hero Václav Havel, in Prague "and his first question was about you. He wants to do something big." There were more threats, from the Speaker of the Majlis—the Iranian parliament—Mehdi Karroubi (twenty years later an unlikely leader of the opposition to President Ahmadinejad alongside Mir Hossein Moussavi, another enthusiastic supporter of the *fatwa*) and from the "acting commander in chief" of the Revolutionary Guard. Ayatollah Yazdi, Iran's chief justice, said all Muslims with "resources" had a duty to implement the threat, and in London, the garden gnome was having fun, leading a large gathering in "approval" of the threat but adding that its fulfillment was "nothing to do with British Muslims." This was emerging as a new party line. Liaquat Hussain of the Bradford Council of Mosques said that "Is Nothing Sacred?" was a "publicity stunt," and that Rushdie did not need to remain invisible, because he was in no danger from British Muslims—he was just doing so, Hussain said, to keep the controversy going and make more money.

A *New York Times* editorial criticized publishers and politicians for their vacillations and equivocations and supported him for "defending every author's right to publish books that ask troubling questions and open doors to the mind." As the pressure mounted, such sympathetic words had come to mean a great deal.

British Muslim attempts to indict him for blasphemy and under the public order act were heard in court. Geoffrey Robertson argued his case, making the simple point that the consequences of violence were the moral responsibility of those who committed the acts of violence; if people were killed, the fault lay with their killers, not with a faraway novelist. It did not help these Muslims' cause that on the third day of the judicial review the judge started receiving threatening letters. In the end neither of the legal attacks succeeded. This was greeted with "anger" by Muslim leaders, though the "Islamic Party of Great Britain" went so far as to ask for the *fatwa* to be lifted because the author had been "mad" when he wrote the book, quoting as "evidence" the published statement by the director of the mental health charity SANE that *The Satanic Verses* contained one of the best descriptions of schizophrenia she had ever read. Meanwhile, Keith Vaz, who had so enthusiastically joined the Muslim demonstrators a year earlier, now wrote to *The Guardian* to describe the death threat as "odious" and to say that lifting it was now the priority.

A "celebration" dinner was arranged at Jane Wellesley's apartment and Sameen, Bill, Pauline (whose birthday it was), Gillon, Michael and Valerie Herr joined him and Marianne to toast a year of continued life. He was happy to escape the Hermitage Lane house for an evening; he had come to loathe it, for its damp walls, its leaky roof, its low-grade carpentry, above all its lack of furniture. It was expensive and he had never felt so thoroughly ripped off; and he had had to accept it for the sake of being in London and because of its internal garage. The next day Zafar was brought to spend the day at that depressing place and as he watched his son struggle with geometry homework he wished, bitterly, that he could be a proper father again and not miss the boy's childhood. This was the greatest loss.

Marianne came around and scolded him for playing video games. Thanks to Zafar, he had grown fond of Mario the plumber and his brother Luigi, and sometimes Super Mario World felt like a happy alternative to the one he lived in the rest of the time. "Read a good book," his wife told him scornfully. "Give it up." He lost his temper. "Don't tell me how to live my life," he exploded, and she made a grand exit.

Haroun and the Sea of Stories had begun to flow. His notebooks contained many fragments—rhymes, jokes, a floating gardener made out of tough, gnarly roots and vegetables like a painting by Arcimboldo singing *you can chop suey / but you can't chop me*, and a sore-throated warrior whose coughs and throat clearings sounded like novelists, *kafkafka!*, *gogogol!*, and some that didn't make the final cut, *gogh!*, *waugh!*, and (after the unpronounceable narrator of Italo Calvino's *Cosmicomics*) *qfwfq!* Also finally coming to life was the hideous and tone-deaf Princess Batcheat and her caterwauling song about her beloved (and asinine) Prince Bolo, *he don't play polo, he can't fly solo*, all of which could now find their place in that happy current. The magic-lamp creature called Genie Come Lately—"some sort of arriviste upstart"—was discarded, along with her sister, the Genie with the Light Brown Hair. This was fun. It pleased him, then and forever afterward, that in the darkest moments of his life he wrote his brightest and most cheerful book, a book with the genuine, bona fide, well-earned happy ending he had wanted, the first he had ever come up with. As the Walrus told Haroun, such conclusions were not easy to engineer.

Václav Havel was coming to London. It would be his first official trip since assuming the presidency and, Harold Pinter said, he intended to use it to make a major public gesture of support for the author of the *Verses* who, coincidentally, had been wondering if he could put together a pressure group of global eminences led by Havel and perhaps the great Peruvian novelist (and defeated presidential candidate) Mario Vargas Llosa. The idea was to assemble a delegation that the Iranians could say "yes" to: a group of such distinction that agreeing with them would look like a dignified act rather than a retreat.

Sameen had been pushing him to come up with creative options like this. "You have to take charge," she said, "and think of everything you can." Now Havel was coming to London, wanting to be his champion. Maybe there would be an opportunity to meet him and talk things through. "He wants to be photographed with you and have a joint press conference," Harold said. "I'm calling William Waldegrave."

Everyone who knew and loved Harold Pinter knew that he was a good man to have on your side in a scrap. Those who had had the unenviable experience of "being Pintered" knew that the rough edge of Harold's tongue was to be avoided if at all possible. The rage and suppressed violence that burned through his greatest plays were also there in the man, visible in the set of his jaw, the intensity of his gaze, the glittering menace of his smile. Those were qualities you wanted in an ally, not in an opponent. The day after the *fatwa* Harold led a group of writers to Downing Street to demand action. His instant agreement to deliver the Read lecture had given ample proof of his personal courage. If he was calling William Waldegrave, William Waldegrave would know he had been called.

Sure enough, the next day, Harold called back. "It's on." The Havel meeting, which was, Harold said, "the most important thing on Havel's agenda after meeting Thatcher," had been put in the hands of the security team arranging the Czech president's state visit. It felt like—it was—a breakthrough moment; the first time the leader of any government had endorsed him so openly. The British government had been reluctant to allow any minister to meet him, for fear of sending "the wrong messages." Now Havel was going to do what Thatcher would not.

But he was still fortune's fool, and "Joseph Anton" had a bad seven days. Troubles were multiplying at the shoddy house on Hermitage Lane. The central heating had stopped working and a plumber had to come to the house. He had to hide in the bathroom for several hours, drenched in the now habitual sweat of shame. Then the agent for the property arrived to inspect it, and it was back to the bathroom. Finally a builder showed up to repair damp patches in the walls and to replace an area of the ceiling where water leaks had caused serious damage. This time there was nowhere to hide and so, while the builder was working in the living room, poor Joseph Anton had to scurry down the stairs to the garage, protected from discovery by no more than a closed interior door, and be driven hurriedly away. The Jaguar circled the city aimlessly, lost in space, with Dennis the Horse telling him bad jokes until he received word that it was safe to return.

This was what it was like to be invisible. One moment he was talking on the phone to Peter Weidhaas, organizer of the Frankfurt Book Fair, who had just informed Iran that its publishers would not be welcome at the Fair until the *fatwa* was canceled. The next he was hiding from a ceiling repairer. He was an author completing a children's book (and preparing for publication a collection of essays, to be called *Imaginary Homelands* after a piece he had once written about the displaced writer's relationship to place)—and he was also a fugitive cowering in a locked bathroom, fearing discovery by a West Indian plumber.

The day after the close shave with the builder, he finished a good draft of *Haroun and the Sea of Stories,* and his friend John Forrester, a fellow of King's, Cambridge, called to suggest the possibility of an honorary degree, "like the one they gave Morgan Forster long ago." The idea of sharing an honor with the author of *A Passage to India* was very moving. He said he would be delighted if that were to happen. Several months later John called him to say that it would not happen. Too many people at the college were too afraid.

A crisis had arisen at St. Peter's Street. His old home was locked up and uninhabited and things were going wrong. The local police were saying the property was not "secure." There had been a report of a gas leak and the man from the gas board had had to break in. Also, he was told, water was flooding the basement. Somebody needed to go in and take a look. Marianne and he had hardly spoken since their quarrel about the Mario Brothers but she said she would go. The problems turned out to be minor. The gas man had put a ladder up and entered through an unlocked upstairs window so there was no damage to the front door. There had been no gas leak. The water in the basement reported by the gas man turned out not to be a flood but a small drip, easily repaired. Marianne came away from St. Peter's Street in a foul mood and on the phone later she blazed at him about everything. "I bet," she shouted, "you haven't even made the bed."

That evening he was taken to see Edward and Mariam Said at a house on Eton Road in Swiss Cottage. At that time Edward's diagnosis with chronic lymphocytic leukemia was still a year away and he was in the full handsome bloom of health, an expansive talker, a laugher and gesturer, a polymath, flirt, and hypochondriac. In those days if Edward had a cough he feared the onset of serious bronchitis, and if he felt a twinge he was certain his appendix was about to collapse. Amazingly, when he actually did fall ill, he became a hero, rarely complaining, fighting the CLL with all his might and, with the aid of his brilliant physician Dr. Kanti Rai, breaking all records by living for a dozen years after the cancer's first appearance. Edward was a dandy, a little vain about his good looks, and once, years later, they lunched near Columbia University after the end of the *fatwa* business, happy to be meeting in plain sight, without attendant policemen to draw the curtains and do the "dry-cleaning." The cancer was in partial remission and Edward was less gaunt than had sadly become usual. "Edward," said the no-longer-Joseph-Anton, "you're looking healthy again! You've put on weight!" Edward bristled. "Yeah," he said, "but I'm not fat, Salman."

He was a Conrad scholar and he knew about the sailor James Wait aboard the *Narcissus*. He, too, knew that he must live until he died; and he did.

At Eton Road that night in March 1990 Edward told him he had spoken to Arafat about the case—and for Edward to talk to Yasser Arafat, whom he had disliked for so long because of his personal corruption and his sanctioning of terrorism, was no small thing—and Arafat (who was a secularist and an anti-Islamist as well as being corrupt and a terrorist) had replied, "Of course I support him, but the Muslims in the intifada . . . what can I do . . ." "Maybe you should write about the intifada," Edward suggested. "Yours is a very important voice for us and it should be heard again on these issues." Yeah, maybe, he replied. They let the subject drop and spoke of books and music and mutual friends. His appetite for nonstop discussion of the *fatwa* was limited and many of his friends saw that and thoughtfully changed the subject. When he was able to see people it felt like a break from captivity and the last things he wanted to discuss were his chains.

He was forcing himself to focus and spending hours each day polishing and revising the draft of *Haroun*. But the week was not going as planned. He was told by the police that the Havel meeting was off—apparently the Czechs had canceled it because of fears for the president's safety. Instead, he was to telephone Havel's hotel room at 6 P.M. and they would be able to talk. This was a huge disappointment. He was unable to speak for hours. But at six precisely he called the number he had been given. The phone rang for a long time and then a man's voice came on the line. "This is Salman Rushdie," he said. "Am I speaking to President Havel?" The man on the other end of the line actually giggled. "No, no," he said. "Is not here the president. Is secretary." "I see," he said. "But I was told to call at this time to speak to him." Then, after a brief pause, the secretary replied. "Yes. You must please wait some time. The president is in the bathroom."

Now, he thought to himself, *I know there has been a revolution in Czechoslovakia.* The president had already decreed that his motorcades be composed of cars of many colors, just to cheer things up, and had invited the Rolling Stones to play for him, and given his first American interview to Lou Reed because the Czech Velvet Revolution had taken its name from the Velvet Underground (thus making the Velvets the only band in history to help create a revolution instead of just singing about it like, for example, the Beatles). This was a president worth waiting for while he took his time in the toilet.

After several minutes he heard footsteps and then Havel was on the line. He had a very different story about the cancelation of the meeting. He had not wanted the meeting to take place at the Czech embassy. "I do not trust that place," he said. "There are still many people of old regime, many strange people wandering about, many colonels." The new ambassador, Havel's man, had only been in post for two days and had not had time to clean the stables. "I will not go in that place," Havel said. The British had responded by saying that there was nowhere else that they were prepared to allow the meeting to occur. "Imagine this," Havel said. "There is nowhere in Britain they can make safe for you and me." It was plain, he said, that the British government did not want the meeting to occur. Perhaps the image of the great Václav Havel embracing a writer whose own prime minister refused to be seen with him would be a little embarrassing? "It is bad," Havel said. "I have wanted to do this very much."

However, he said, at his press conference he had said many things. "I have told them we are in permanent contact," he said, and laughed. "And maybe it is true, through Harold or such. But I have told them: *permanent contact.* Also, deep solidarity. I have said this too."

He told Havel how much he liked his *Letters to Olga,* written by the celebrated dissident from prison to his wife, and how much they had to say to him in his present situation. "This book," Havel replied, "you know, when we wrote to each other at that time, we had to say many things in riddles, in a kind of code. There are parts of it I don't understand myself. But I have a much better book coming soon." Havel wanted copies of "Is Nothing Sacred?" and "In Good Faith." "Permanent contact," he concluded with another laugh, and said goodbye.

Marianne was still at war with him the next day. "You're obsessed by what happens to you," she blazed, and yes, perhaps that was true. "Every day of your life there's some drama," and yes, unfortunately that was all too often true. He was obsessed with himself, she shouted; he couldn't handle "equality," and he was an "ugly drunk." *Where did that come from,* he wondered, and then she delivered the rest of the blow. "You're trying to repeat your parents' marriage." He was guilty of his father's alcohol abuse. Yes, of course.

Meanwhile, at a Muslim Youth Conference in Bradford, a sixteen-year-old girl called for Rushdie to be stoned to death. The media coverage of the "Affair" had become—for the moment, anyway—sympathetic to him, almost pitying. "Poor Salman Rushdie." "The hapless author." He did not wish to be poor, hapless, pitiable. He did not want to be merely a victim. There were important intellectual, political and moral issues at stake here. He wanted to be a part of the argument: to be a protagonist.

Andrew and Gillon came to see him at Hermitage Lane after meeting the Penguin chiefs at the London home of their colleague Brian Stone, the agent for the Agatha Christie estate. They were a formidable negotiating team because they were such an odd couple: the very tall, languid, plummy-voiced Englishman and the aggressive, bullet-headed American with his checkered past, his fringe membership in the Warhol Factory crew, and his laser-beam eyes. They were a classic hard man–soft man duo, and what made them even more effective was that the people they negotiated with made the mistake of assuming that

Andrew was the tough guy and Gillon the softie. Actually, Andrew was driven by passion and emotion and was entirely capable of amazing you by bursting into tears. Gillon was the killer.

Even Gillon and Andrew found Penguin all but impossible to deal with. This latest meeting was, yet again, inconclusive. Mayer said Penguin would hold to the end-of-June deadline for the paperback but would not give a date. They all agreed with Gillon and Andrew that if the book was not published by June 30, they would insist on getting the publication rights back on July 1 so that they could try to make other arrangements. Gillon said, "I think Mayer may be open to that idea." (Four days later Gillon called to say that Mayer had "half-accepted" the idea of the reversion of rights, but wanted to "negotiate" it—in other words, he wanted money in return. However, his colleague Trevor Glover had said at the meeting with Andrew and Gillon that Penguin's security costs were so high that they had lost money on the hardcover publication, and publishing the paperback would mean an "increased loss," so it was hard for Mayer to argue that he needed to be compensated for doing something—giving up the paperback rights—that would, if Glover was to be believed, actually save him money. "We're pursuing it," Gillon said. "If we reach the first of July and Mayer hasn't published and asks for money," he said, "at that point, I'd go public.")

Andrew believed Penguin was underpaying royalties and withholding a large sum of money that should have been paid. Penguin denied this angrily but Andrew sent in an auditor and discovered a very substantial underpayment indeed. Penguin did not apologize.

The police had suggested a wig. Their best wig man had been to see him and taken a sample of his hair. He was extremely dubious but had been reassured by several of the prot officers that wigs really worked. "You'll be able to walk down the street without attracting attention," they said. "Trust us." He received unexpected confirmation of this from Michael Herr. "In the matter of disguise you don't have to change much, Salman," Michael said, speaking slowly and blinking rapidly. "Just the key signs." The wig was made and arrived in a brown cardboard box looking like a small sleeping animal. When he put it on his head he felt outlandishly stupid. The police said it looked great.

"Okay," he said, dubiously. "Let's take it for a walk." They drove him to Sloane Street and parked near Harvey Nichols. When he got out of the car every head turned to stare at him and several people burst into wide grins or even laughter. "Look," he heard a man's voice say, "there's that bastard Rushdie in a wig." He got back into the Jaguar and never wore the wig again.

Ambassador Maurice Busby was a man who didn't officially exist. As America's head of counterterrorism, his name could not be spoken on radio or television, or printed in any newspaper or magazine. His movements could not be reported and his location was, to use an adjective Vice President Cheney afterward made famous, undisclosed. He was the ghost in the American machine.

"Joseph Anton" had been thinking of going to America when the Hermitage Lane contract expired, to have a few weeks or months out of the cage. The Special Branch had told him from the beginning that their responsibility for him ended at the British frontier. The rules of the game said that whenever a "principal" left the United Kingdom to visit another country the security forces of that country had to be informed so that they could decide what, if anything, they wanted to do about his visit. When the Americans were told about his plans Mr. Maurice Busby asked for a meeting. It would be a nonexistent man's encounter with an invisible man: as if Calvino and H. G. Wells had decided to collaborate on a story. He was taken to an anonymous office building on the south bank of the Thames and led into a large room that was entirely empty except for two straight chairs. He and Ambassador Busby sat facing each other and the American got straight to the point. He was welcome in America, the ambassador said, and he should be in no doubt about that. America sympathized with him and he should know that his case was "on the U.S. agenda vis-à-vis Iran." His wish to visit the United States was in principle approved. However the United States respectfully asked him to consider postponing the trip by "three to four months." Ambassador Busby had been authorized to tell him in deep confidence that there was real movement regarding the American hostages in Lebanon and it was likely that there could be releases soon. He hoped Mr. Rushdie would appreciate the sensitivity of the situation. Mr. Rushdie did appreciate it. He concealed his deep disappointment and agreed to the nonexistent man's request. Gloomily he asked Gillon to extend his tenancy at Hermitage Lane.

Marianne had left to go on her book tour in America. He kept trying to persuade himself that they still loved each other. In his journals he discounted everything that was wrong between them and insisted on their largely imaginary happiness. Such is the need for love. It makes men see visions of paradise and ignore the evidence of their eyes and ears that they are in hell.

Haroun was finished. He shaved off his beard, leaving only a mustache. On Wednesday, April 4, Zafar was brought to Hermitage Lane and his father handed him the manuscript of "his" book. The bright happiness on the boy's face was the only reward the author needed. Zafar read the book quickly and said he loved it. Other early readings by friends were also positive. But who would publish it, he wondered. Would everyone back away? Tony Lacey at Viking Penguin had told Gillon, in confidence, that the paperback of *The Satanic Verses* would "probably" be published on May 28. At last, he thought. Once that hurdle had been crossed maybe that story could begin to end. Lacey also talked to Gillon about *Haroun*. "Now that the paperback is coming out, maybe we could publish the new book as well. We're proud to publish him, you know." Tony was a good, decent man, trying to continue to be a real publisher in an unreal situation.

Alone at Hermitage Lane he reached the end of his Super Mario game, defeating the big bad Bowser himself and rescuing the insufferably pink Princess Toadstool. He was glad Marianne was not there to witness his triumph. On the phone she was ranting again about his alleged *amours* and the untrustworthiness of his friends. He tried not to pay attention. That afternoon Pauline had taken Zafar into the house at St. Peter's Street because there were things of his that he wanted, his boxing gloves, his punch-ball, various games. "My dad and I used to go up on the roof here," he said to Pauline sadly. "It was really hard to get used to him being in hiding. I can't wait for him to come out." She took him for pizza and he spent the meal quoting from *Haroun*. "You can chop liver, but you can't chop me."

He had asked Pauline to bring out a few things for him as well but several of them were missing. All his old photograph albums, five of them, in which his entire life before Marianne was contained, were gone. So was his personal copy, copy number one, of the limited edition of twelve numbered and signed copies of *The Satanic Verses*. (Later, Rick Gekoski, an American antiquarian bookseller based in London, sold him Ted Hughes's copy of this limited edition, copy number eleven. It cost him £2,200 to buy this copy of his own book.) Nobody had keys to the house except Pauline, Sameen, and Marianne. Two years later the journalist Philip Weiss wrote a profile of him in *Esquire* that was shockingly unpleasant about him and pretty nice about Marianne. At least one of the illustrations had clearly come from the missing photograph albums. Under pressure from Andrew *Esquire* admitted that the photograph had been supplied by Marianne. She claimed it had been given to her as a gift. Around the same time a "final typescript" of *The Satanic Verses,* also missing from his study at St. Peter's Street, was being offered to dealers for sale. Rick Gekoski told him that Marianne was saying that this, too, had been a "gift," and had eventually withdrawn the text from the market, unhappy about the prices she was being given. It was the wrong copy; the most valuable manuscript, the "working" text covered in his handwritten annotations and corrections, remained in his possession. The photograph albums were never found or returned.

On April 23 Robert Polhill, a professor at Beirut University, became the first American hostage in Lebanon to be freed by his captors, "Islamic Jihad for the Liberation of Palestine," three years after he was seized. Four days later Frank Reed, who had been a director at the Lebanese International School, was set free by the "Organization of the Islamic Dawn" after four years' captivity. Ambassador Busby had been telling the truth.

Marianne was a woman of many notebooks, and it was a notebook that ended their marriage. He never knew if she left the notebook at Hermitage Lane intentionally, to trigger the final rupture that she claimed not to want. In Junichiro Tanizaki's great novel *The Key*, Marianne's "evil book," a wife and husband each keep "secret" diaries that may in reality be intended to be found and read. In Tanizaki's book the diaries serve as an erotic device. In his own life, the notebook he found served a simpler purpose. It told him the truth he had been trying to hide from himself. She had written, during her American tour, that she had no reason to be in England, but he was forcing her to return, knowing she didn't want to. She had rented a house in America. This was news to him. She knew he could not go to America but she was making plans to leave. She had had enough, which he could very well understand. *Yes, she should go,* he thought, *and let this separation lead gradually to an ending.*

The rest of the journal was darker. She said he feared women. *Yes,* he thought, *at least I am a little afraid of you.* She hated his relationship with his beloved sister Sameen. She made a number of sexual sneers.

She was back in London. He told her he had read the journal and could not continue in the marriage. She became agitated and claimed she did love him and what he had found was her "black journal," which she used to get rid of her worst thoughts, to discard them by writing them down. That was almost plausible. He himself had used writing in this way, committing his fears, weaknesses, lusts, and fantasies to paper and then throwing them in the trash. But the material in the journal was too categorical, too wide ranging, to be just idle anger or resentment. These were no passing feelings. This was what she really thought. He asked her why she had not told him about renting a house and she began to deny she had done so. But he had spoken to Gillon, who said she had told him about the rental. He said, "I don't want to fight with you. What's the point? The war's over." Marianne left.

He called Sameen to ask if there was any truth in Marianne's accusation that he mistreated his sister. She said what he knew: that in the unconditional love they had for each other, nothing could be a problem. He felt disturbed by what he had read, but his main feeling was of relief. This part of his nightmare had come to an end.

The next day the police arranged a treat. Zafar and he were taken on a police speedboat to roar up and down the Thames, all the way to the Barrier and beyond, and then back to River Police HQ at Wapping. Zafar had the time of his life.

Alberto Vitale, the head of Random House, Inc., told Andrew that the last sentence of "Is Nothing Sacred?"—"Wherever in the world the little room of literature has been closed, sooner or later the walls have come tumbling down"—had moved him greatly, and that Random House was once again interested in publishing *Haroun and the Sea of Stories* and Rushdie's future books as well. Vitale said, however, that he would want an "escape clause" in the contract indemnifying Random House against the possibility of anything being written that "caused danger to his staff." In spite of this, Andrew and Gillon thought the move to Random and away from Peter Mayer would be a good thing. "I will not sign anything as humiliating as that 'escape clause,'" he told his agents, adding, for emphasis, "Over my dead body." Andrew felt that this was a point Random House might be willing to concede. Sonny Mehta had finished reading *Haroun* and said he liked it. Within days the deal with Random House was done. But Vitale did not want to announce it. In fact, he wanted to keep it secret as long as possible. But Sonny Mehta and Andrew agreed that a press statement should be drafted.

He was a man without armies obliged to fight constantly on many fronts. There was the private front of his secret life, with its cringings and crouchings, its skulkings and duckings, its fear of plumbers and other repairmen, its fraught search for places of refuge, and its dreadful wigs. Then there was the publishing front, where he could take nothing for granted in spite of all his work. Publication itself was still an issue. It was not certain that he could continue in the life he had chosen, not certain that he would always find willing hands to print and distribute his work. And then there was the harsh and violent world of politics. If he was a soccer ball, he thought, could he be a self-conscious soccer ball and join in the game? Could the soccer ball understand the sport in which it was kicked from end to end? Could the soccer ball act in its own interest and take itself off the field and out of range of the booted, kicking feet?

Here was a man named Peter Temple-Morris, MP, a man with hair like soft vanilla ice cream swirling above the great tub of his face, a fine and prominent man, a Conservative member of the Anglo-Iranian parliamentary group, a man who did not care for him, and now, as the American hostages in Lebanon were being released, decided that the "moral responsibility" for the fate of the British hostages lay with the author of *The Satanic Verses,* who should refrain from publishing his paperback. There followed an avalanche of criticism. The supporters of the hostage John McCarthy said "Rushdie should apologize." In the *Daily Mail,* he was blamed by McCarthy's father, Patrick, for John's continued captivity. His troubles were called "self-enforced" by the hostage Terry Waite's brother David, who added, about the paperback, "One can't always have what one wants." David believed the paperback should be canceled *and* its author should apologize for the offense he had given. All of this hostility had its effect. *The Daily Telegraph* published the results of a Gallup poll: A majority of the respondents agreed that "Salman Rushdie should apologize for *The Satanic Verses.*" And sources told him, though he never knew if it was true, that William Waldegrave privately told Penguin not to publish the paperback, as to do so would affect the fate of the British hostages and the British businessman Roger Cooper, still in Evin prison in Tehran.

This was where Penguin's delays had brought them. This, perhaps, was what Mayer had wanted all along: a respectable reason for nonpublication.

The archbishop of Canterbury, Robert Runcie, met with Mr. Abdul Quddus of the Bradford Council of Mosques. Quddus told the archbishop that on his recent trip to Iran he had been assured by members of the Iranian Majlis that Terry Waite, the archbishop's envoy seized by Lebanese hostage takers, was alive, but would be returned only *if Rushdie was extradited to Iran.* His statement was echoed by Hussein Musawi of the Lebanese Shia group Islamic Amal, who said a British hostage could be freed "if Britain deported Rushdie," and warned that if no action was taken against the author, Terry Waite, John McCarthy and the third British hostage, Jackie Mann, would not come out. This news, reported on the radio in Karachi, greatly alarmed his mother and Sameen had to console her.

He had been trying to arrange a meeting with William Waldegrave to ask what the government planned to do to resolve the crisis. Now Waldegrave told Harold Pinter that the government—which was to say, Margaret Thatcher—was "alarmed" at the idea of such a meeting, and at the possibility of the news of the meeting leaking out to the press. It was well known that he had not been a supporter of the Thatcher government. Now the government's position appeared to be, *Okay, we'll keep him alive, but we don't have to see him or have a plan of action. We'll just keep him in his box, and if he objects there are plenty of people ready to call him ungrateful.*

He was suffering from a great weariness, a kind of nervous exhaustion. He was smoking again five years after he quit, angry with himself for doing so, telling himself he must not let this continue for very long, but smoking nevertheless. "I am fighting the drug," he wrote, "but how powerful it is! I feel the craving all along my arms and in the pit of my stomach." And then in capital letters: "I WILL DRIVE IT OUT AGAIN."

Five Arabs were arrested in Scarborough, allegedly because they were plotting to carry out the *fatwa.* Zafar, who was home sick and hadn't gone to school, saw the report on the lunchtime news and called, pretending not to be worried. The police were saying the story was "media hype" and even though he didn't believe it he gave Zafar that official line to reassure him.

Marianne wrote him a letter. "You went searching for Doubt, and you found it," she said. "And you killed us for that."

"Most of what matters in our lives," he had written in *Midnight's Children,* "takes place in our absence." Death orders, conspiracies to murder, bomb threats, demonstrations, court hearings, and political machinations had not been the things he had in mind, but they had crowded into his own life story to prove his fictional narrator's point. It was moving to know that his plight was of such concern to so many well-wishing strangers. The American novelist Paul Auster, later to become a close friend, wrote a "prayer" for him. *When I sat down to write this morning, the first thing I did was think of Salman Rushdie. I have done this every morning. . . .* And Mike Wallace wanted to help. The legendary *60 Minutes* reporter told a Penguin executive that a "further statement along the lines of 'In Good Faith,' or maybe 'a step or two further' "—whatever that meant—could be carried by him personally to Rafsanjani and that might do the trick and get the *fatwa* lifted.

He talked to Andrew, Gillon and Frances D'Souza and asked them to follow up. "I must not get too excited," he wrote in his journal, "but even the faint possibility of freedom is so exciting that I can't help myself." Andrew spoke to Mike Wallace and then to Kaveh Afrasiabi, a research associate at the Center for Middle Eastern Studies at Harvard. Afrasiabi said he had already spoken to the Iranian ambassador at the United Nations, Kamal Kharrazi, and to "sources leading to Khamenei." He repeated what Wallace had said. If a statement "consistent with your principles" were made then Khamenei would welcome it and cancel the *fatwa*. Iran was looking for a "breaking point" in the crisis and Mike Wallace's involvement was a bonus, important because Khamenei wanted a good media profile in the United States, to "steal Rafsanjani's thunder."

The world always ended up being television.

He was asked to make a statement on video that could be taken by Wallace to Tehran and shown on TV there, and then Khamenei would talk to Wallace on American TV and say what needed to be said. We would be told in a few days, Afrasiabi said, if Iran wanted to go down this route. He had been led to expect a "positive response." Four days later he called Andrew to say he had received the "green light." He proposed a meeting with a Mr. Khoosroo, first secretary of Iran's UN mission, as the next step.

Andrew and Frances spoke to each other and then to him. It was worth going forward cautiously, they decided. Could it be the breakthrough? They did not dare to believe it. And yet they couldn't help themselves. They did believe it.

Mike Wallace and Afrasiabi met Andrew at the agency. Afrasiabi repeated the Iranian demands for a statement of regret *that would be included as a preface in the paperback edition (ugh,* he thought, but on the other hand they were not objecting to the paperback being published), and the setting up of a fund for the families of those who had died in "anti-Rushdie" rioting. Frances D'Souza was worried. On the one hand, she said, there were "signs" that Iran may have stopped funding Siddiqui's Muslim Institute and was trying to install a moderate chief imam in the United Kingdom. On the other hand she feared that the Iranians might be playing a "particularly nasty game." If they canceled the *fatwa*, the protection would end, and then he could be hit by a fundamentalist cell and the Iranians would have acquired "deniability." At some stage, she said, the British government must be involved, to ask for guarantees against that eventuality. Sameen was also worried that he would be killed if he "came out." But what was the alternative? Never to "come out"? He felt shaky, disoriented. Too much was happening. It was hard to know what was for the best.

It began to unravel. The Iranians canceled a meeting with Mike Wallace. They wanted to meet Afrasiabi alone to hear what had been agreed at the meeting with Andrew. And then, pop!, like a bubble bursting, the dream died. The Iranian UN mission said it would have to "consult Tehran." This would take at least two weeks. *It's not serious,* he realized. *It's a joke. They just wanted me to make my statement and then trust them to respond. To trust them. Yes: It's a joke.*

He stopped smoking. Then he started again.

In the next days Iran denied it could lift the *fatwa*. Khamenei said that he "must be handed over to British Muslims to be killed for committing blasphemy" and that would solve the problems between the United Kingdom and Iran. Frances D'Souza went on the BBC program *Newsnight* and was confronted by the spectacle of Siddiqui's "number two," a Scottish convert called James Dickie, who had taken the name of Yaqub Zaki, welcoming hit squads to London. Rafsanjani gave a press conference in which he tried to lower the temperature, but offered no solutions to the *fatwa* crisis. And for the first time the British government offered him a contact man. He was to meet Duncan Slater, a senior Foreign Office type, over the weekend. In the meantime he spoke to the journalist John Bulloch, *The Independent*'s highly respected Middle East expert, who had recently returned from Tehran and confirmed that the Iranians were "desperate to settle issues . . . an acceptable settlement is what's needed." After that the meeting with Slater was a letdown. Slater had no news of any back-channel initiatives, or any government activity to speak of. But it felt good to be in touch with the government and to be assured of its continued support. He had reached the point at which he was grateful for such crumbs.

The Afrasiabi initiative was dead. The Harvard man had written a letter changing the "shopping list" of demands. Publication should be totally suspended for twelve to fifteen months, and "Rushdie should simply go ahead and make his statement first; what does he have to lose?" Also, Andrew said, "I'm afraid he wants to be a novelist and is looking for an agent." A week later Kamal Kharrazi, Iran's man at the United Nations, told Mike Wallace: "It is not the time for this initiative to go forward." Another back channel closed.

He had another meeting with Ambassador Busby, who was accompanied, on this occasion, by Bill Baker of the FBI. They asked him for a few more months' grace before he made any visit to the United States, but remained cordial and sympathetic. Busby had a useful view on the Afrasiabi effort. "Maybe," he said, "the intermediary was wrong for them."

He gave Zafar an electric guitar for his eleventh birthday and spent the afternoon with him at Hermitage Lane, listening to him play it and recording his efforts. Just another ordinary day with the most important human being in his life.

Cosima had found a large, detached house in Wimbledon, much more comfortable than Hermitage Lane: an ample three-story brick home with an octagonal tower on its southern side. The police had looked at it and approved. Hermitage Lane was an awful place but it had given him seven stable months. Now it was time to prepare to move again.

The contract for *Haroun and the Sea of Stories* had not been signed by the publisher. Andrew went to meet Sonny Mehta and Alberto Vitale to ask the reason why. Before the meeting Sonny said to Andrew, "I don't think there's a problem," so clearly there was one. At the meeting, Vitale said he didn't want the contract signed "for insurance reasons." They were negotiating to buy their building and they didn't want this book to become an issue. They were willing to pay two-thirds of the agreed advance to acquire an "option to publish," and would hand over the final third after the author had discussed "editorial issues" with Sonny. "The author should sign," Vitale said, "but we will wait." Andrew called him to give him the news. "No," he said, outraged. "Cancel the deal and tell them I'll sue them for breach of contract. I'd rather go unpublished than be humiliated." Later that afternoon Andrew met with Vitale and Sonny again and they capitulated. Yes, they said, they would sign. He was left with a bitter taste in his mouth, but at least he had won a round.

On his forty-third birthday Gillon brought him the contract to be signed. It contained a "confidentiality clause." He was not to tell anyone about the deal until a later date to be agreed upon with Random House. This clause gave off the unmistakable scent of rat. He signed the contract. Almost at once the rat came out into the open. Sonny Mehta refused to publish *Haroun* unless it was rewritten to his specifications.

He had known Sonny Mehta for ten years, ever since Sonny had published the UK paperback of *Midnight's Children* at Picador Books in London. For all that time he had thought of him as a friend, even though Sonny's famous reserve made him a difficult man to feel close to. Sonny was a man of very few words and even fewer phone calls, given to smiling enigmatically behind his goatee and leaving the talking and socializing to his flamboyant wife, Gita, but he was a man of taste, integrity, deep loyalty to his authors, and elegance (high-quality blazers worn with drainpipe jeans). In the matter of *Haroun and the Sea of Stories,* however, he behaved like a different person entirely. On June 26, 1990, he called Andrew to insist that *Haroun* must be rewritten to change the setting. The "Valley of K," he said, was obviously Kashmir, and Kashmir was a highly contentious place, wars had been fought over it, and Islamic jihadists were active there; so clearly that had to go—maybe, he proposed, the story could be set in Mongolia?—or there would be "bodies everywhere," and "Salman will be in worse trouble than he is now." *Haroun,* he assured Andrew, was a more dangerous and provocative work than *The Satanic Verses.*

He tried to look at his children's fable through that distorted lens. But even with that warped vision the book could surely only be read as "pro-Kashmiri"? The character of "Snooty Buttoo," however, was a satirical portrait of an Indian politician and maybe that was what Sonny, who came from a high diplomatic family and whose wife was the daughter of the chief minister of Orissa, and who moved in Delhi's elite political circles, really objected to? And if Sonny was so scared of a children's book, how would he react to the adult fiction he might be offered in the future?

There was worse to come. Sonny's plan was to go through the entire production process without putting the author's name on the book. Alberto Vitale had bizarrely insisted on secrecy because one of Random House's tenants was the Norwegian consulate, and to announce the publication of a Rushdie novel would make things too dangerous for the Norwegians. A false name would therefore be used and the real name substituted at the last minute, as the book was going to be printed. That was terrible. It looked like frightened behavior—it *was* frightened behavior—and when it leaked, as it would almost certainly leak, that Random House was too scared to name the author of this book, it would give the book a "controversial" aura before anyone had even seen it, and act as a clear invitation to the author's adversaries to start another fight.

Sonny messengered clippings about Kashmir, taken from Indian magazines and newspapers, to Andrew's office to illustrate his concern. There were characters in *Haroun* called Butt and a man called Butt had been hanged in Kashmir recently, "as Salman must have known." So now this "Butt," which had been his mother's maiden name; and which, spelled as "Butt" or "Bhatt," was the most common of Kashmiri names; and which, in *Haroun,* was not the name of a hanged man but of a genial bus driver and then of a giant mechanical hoopoe, had become a politically explosive name? It was absurd, but Sonny was in deadly earnest. Andrew suggested to him that he was not exactly behaving as Salman's old friend and he retorted, "I don't see what this has to do with friendship." Then he added, "Andrew, nobody on earth understands this book as well as I do." Andrew answered, with commendable restraint, "I think Salman believes that he does."

All this Andrew relayed to him from New York while standing in the street after leaving Sonny's office. He told Andrew, "Please go back upstairs and put me on the phone with him." Sonny got on the line and said he was "sure" their disagreements could be sorted out, if he could just fly to London to discuss them. But things had gone too far for that.

"What I need you to answer, Sonny," he said, "is, will you publish my novel as I have written it—yes or no?"

"Let me come and talk to you about it," Sonny repeated.

"There's nothing to talk about," he told Sonny. "Will you publish it as written, that's the only question."

"No," said Sonny, "I will not."

"Then," he told his old friend, "please tear up that contract you have in front of you on your desk."

"Okay," Sonny said, "if that's what you want, Salman."

"It's not what I want," he said. "I want someone to publish *my* book, not some damn book you've got in your head."

"Okay," he said, "then we'll tear it up."

He learned that there had been a Random House UK board meeting some time previously and the possible publication of *Haroun* had been on the agenda. The vote had gone heavily against him.

In another universe, it was time for the World Cup. Bill Buford, who for some time had been writing a book about soccer hooligans, flew to Sardinia for the England-Holland match, not for the soccer but because the battles after the game between the rival gangs of thugs would be too good to miss. That night on the main British evening news the violence in Sardinia was the lead item. An army of British hoodlums was seen advancing on the camera position, brandishing fists and clubs and chanting "England!" In the very center of the first line of British thugs, yelling and chanting with the rest of them, was the editor of *Granta* magazine, taking the participatory techniques of the New Journalism to a level that George Plimpton and Tom Wolfe had perhaps not envisaged. Later that night the Italian police had attacked the British "fans" and many of them were badly beaten, including Bill, who was kicked repeatedly in the kidneys while curled up in a fetal ball on the sidewalk. In spite of his injuries, he dedicated himself, on his return to London, to rescuing his friend's literary career.

Haroun was looking for a publisher. Liz Calder said that Bloomsbury would not wish to compete for it. Christopher Sinclair-Stevenson, who had just launched his own small, independent house, said that his operation was "too fledgling" to take this on. Christopher MacLehose at Harvill was prevented from bidding by Murdoch's HarperCollins, Harvill's majority shareholder. Faber and Faber was a possibility. But it was Bill who wanted it most, for *Granta* magazine's new imprint, Granta Books. "You need someone who will publish you absolutely normally, with all the excitement and pizzazz that a new book from you deserves," he said. "You need to be presented to readers as a writer all over again, and that's what I want to do for you with this book." Until the possibility of publishing *Haroun* arose Bill had been suggesting to him that Blake Morrison be allowed to write his authorized biography, to allow readers to get to know the man, rather than the scandal. Blake was an excellent writer and would do a fine job, he knew that; but he didn't want his private life exposed. And if the time came when the story was ready to be told, he wanted to be the one to do it. *One day,* he told Bill, *it's going to be me.*

Now the biography idea was forgotten. Bill was begging Gillon to be allowed to do *Haroun.* His enthusiasm was gratifying, and persuasive. Granta Books were distributed by Penguin. This, Gillon said, could be an "elegant solution." A breach with Penguin, which could lead to damaging publicity, would be avoided, and yet the Penguin people would not be too directly involved. All of a sudden everyone at Viking Penguin got excited about this. They, too, liked the face-saving aspect. Bill said that the Penguin sales reps' response had been "very positive." Peter Mayer wrote a letter hoping this could be a fresh start and he replied that he, too, hoped it might be. Everyone in the UK office wanted to publish quickly, in September, to be able to benefit from Christmas sales, and Penguin USA agreed. The deal was done and announced almost as soon as it was proposed. The speed was important. If Sonny had had time to explain to his many friends in publishing that he had refused to publish *Haroun* because its author had once again submitted a time bomb without coming clean about its dangers, then that author's ability to publish books would have disappeared forever. Bill Buford, by his courage and determination, had prevented that from happening.

Gita Mehta told a mutual friend, "I think he's a bit off us at the moment."

He missed Marianne. He knew he must not try to go back to her after everything that had happened, after the CIA plot and the black journal, but, mind and body, he missed her. When they spoke on the phone they fought. Conversations that began I wish you well ended with I hope you die. But love, whatever he meant by love, whatever she meant by it, the word "love" still hung in the air between them. His mother had survived decades of marriage to his angry, disappointed, alcoholic father by developing what she called a "forgettery" instead of a memory. She woke up every day and forgot the day before. He, too, seemed to lack a memory for trouble, and woke up remembering only what he yearned for. But he did not act upon his yearning. She had left for America and that was for the best.

He knew that somewhere beneath the constant pressure of events he was deeply depressed and his reactions to the world had grown abnormal. *Pray do not mock me,* as Lear said. *I fear I am not in my perfect mind.* Perhaps he saw in her the physical reality of his old life, the *ordinary* that this present *extraordinary* had usurped. Perhaps this what remained of their love. It was the love of the vanished yesterday, the day-after yearning for the day before.

He was aware that the splitting in him was getting worse, the divide between what "Rushdie" needed to do and how "Salman" wanted to live. He was "Joe" to his protectors, an entity to be kept alive; and in his friends' eyes, when he was able to see them, he read their alarm, their fear that "Salman" might be crushed under the weight of what had happened. "Rushdie" was another matter entirely.

"Rushdie" was a dog. "Rushdie," according to the private comments of many eminent persons, including the Prince of Wales, who made these comments over lunch to his friends Martin Amis and Clive James, deserved little sympathy. "Rushdie" deserved everything he got, and needed to do something to undo the great harm that he had done. "Rushdie" needed to stop insisting on paperbacks and principles and literature and being in the right. "Rushdie" was much hated and little loved. He was an effigy, an absence, something less than human. He—it—needed only to expiate.

Ruthie Rogers, co-owner of London's River Café, gave a birthday party for him. A dozen of his closest friends gathered under the watchful eyes of nine of Andy Warhol's *Mao* screen prints in the huge living room of the Rogers house on Royal Avenue, that brilliantly lit white space with its high curtainless windows that was a Special Branch nightmare. Ruthie and her husband, the architect Richard Rogers, had been no more than friendly acquaintances of his before the *fatwa* but it was in their loving natures to draw closer to friends in time of trouble and do much more than was called for. He was a man in need of hugs and embraces and that evening he received plenty of them. He was glad his friends were huggers and kissers. But he saw himself reflected in their eyes and understood that he was in bad shape.

He was learning the limitations of language. He had always believed in its omnipotence, in the power of the tongue. But language would not get him out of this. "In Good Faith" and "Is Nothing Sacred?" had changed nothing. A Pakistani friend, Omar Noman, wanted to assemble a group of people from "our part of the world" to explain to the Iranians that "they had got the wrong man." An Indian friend, the distinguished attorney Vijay Shankardass, saw a role for Indian Muslims in resolving the affair. Vijay undertook to speak to some leaders, including Syed Shahabuddin, who had managed to get *The Satanic Verses* banned in India, and Salman Khurshid, the "wrong Salman," whom Imam Bukhari of the Delhi Juma Masjid had mistakenly condemned at Friday prayers.

He doubted that reason or argument, the methods of language people, would be very successful. He was battling a greater—or, to use the vocabulary of the godly, a *higher* power, one that scoffed at the merely rational, and commanded a language that far outranked the tongues of mortal men. And this god was not a god of love.

He left Hermitage Lane forever and was driven, with Zafar, to Deborah and Michael's farm in Powys, where they spent a precious weekend together kicking a soccer ball, playing cricket and throwing a Frisbee around a field. Clarissa had wanted the weekend to herself because of a new man she was seeing but that weekend he broke up with her, unwilling to deal with her share of the *fatwa* fallout. She was handling it very strongly. He wished she could be happy.

After the weekend he slipped unnoticed into the Wimbledon house, but then there was trouble. The owner, Mrs. Cindy Pasarell, called several times with nosy questions. Fortunately one of the female protection officers, Rachel Clooney, was on duty, and because a woman's voice was a more reassuring thing to hear than a man's Mrs. Pasarell's curiosity was somewhat assuaged. Then Mr. Devon Pasarell called, apparently unaware of Mrs. Pasarell's calls, saying he needed some things from the garage. Maybe they were separated? The next day a "business associate" of Mrs. Pasarell's showed up at the door for no good reason. Then Cindy Pasarell called again, sounding sterner. She would like to meet the new tenants to satisfy herself that they were "appropriate."

He called Pauline to ask for help. She had played parts in everything from *Far from the Madding Crowd* to *The Young Ones,* and knew all about improv, so she could certainly handle this role. He briefed her on her character and she agreed to spend a day at the house and meet the inquisitive Cindy. The situation was both absurd and fraught. He told Bob Major that he couldn't do this anymore, all this deception and lurking. Some other arrangement would have to be made. Bob made sympathetic, noncommittal noises. He was a foot soldier. A decision like that wasn't his to make.

In the next two days Mr. Pasarell came round again without warning, to "pick up his stuff from the garage," and then *again,* "to drop the garage key through the front door." Rachel Clooney, a tall, elegant blonde with a soft Scottish burr and a big smile, spoke gently to him, but he remained in his black Granada outside the property for quite a while, watching. In an attempt to calm things down, Pauline, as the lady of the house, called Mrs. Pasarell and invited her to tea, but although she accepted the invitation she didn't show up; instead the Pasarells jointly sent a letter of complaint to Gillon's office, protesting about what they called the "multiple occupancy" of the house. The fear of discovery was paralyzing. Would it be Little Bardfield all over again—would he have to move out at once and lose all the rent he had paid and contracted to pay? "This is horrible," he said to Gillon. "It has to end."

It was Gillon who solved the problem. "They're being ridiculous," he said in his haughtiest, most contemptuous tone. "They're getting a great deal of money from you. We need to slap them down a little. Leave it to me, my dear." He faxed them what he called a "fuck-off letter." Soon after he called back, tickled pink. "My dear, I think it worked. They have faxed me back, and agreed to fuck off." The Pasarells had indeed agreed that in return for the excellent amount of rent they were receiving they would cease to bother their tenants. They may even have apologized. And that, for several months, was that.

Nadine Gordimer was collecting the signatures of eminent Europeans on an "appeal to the government of Iran." At the Pinters' home he dined with Carlos and Silvia Fuentes and the great Mexican novelist offered to "round up Latin American heads of state." Meanwhile the garden gnome Siddiqui continued to make his unpleasant gnomic statements, which were echoed in louder voices by the grander gnomes of Qom and Tehran. There had been a huge earthquake near the city of Rasht and forty thousand people had died, and half a million more were homeless, but that did not change the subject. The *fatwa* stood.

Zafar would be away for three whole weeks. He was off to holiday camp with two school friends, and after that Clarissa was taking him to France with Liz Calder and Louis Baum and Louis's son Simon. In his absence, there were Pakistani guerrillas to be dealt with.

The Pakistani film *International Gorillay* (International guerrillas), produced by Sajjad Gul, told the story of a group of local heroes—of the type that would, in the language of a later age, come to be known as jihadis or terrorists—who vowed to find and kill an author called "Salman Rushdie." The quest for "Rushdie" formed the main action of the film and "his" death was the film's version of a happy ending.

"Rushdie" himself was depicted as a drunk, constantly swigging from a bottle of liquor, and a sadist. He lived in what looked very like a palace on what looked very like an island in the Philippines (clearly all novelists had second homes of this kind), being protected by what looked very like the Israeli army (this presumably being a service offered by Israel to all novelists), and he was plotting the overthrow of Pakistan by the fiendish means of opening chains of discotheques and gambling dens across that pure and virtuous land, a perfidious notion for which, as the British Muslim "leader" Iqbal Sacranie might have said, death was too light a punishment. "Rushdie" was dressed exclusively in a series of hideously colored safari suits—vermilion safari suits, aubergine safari suits, cerise safari suits—and the camera, whenever it fell upon the figure of this vile personage, invariably started at his feet and then panned with slow menace up to his face. So the safari suits got a lot of screen time, and when he saw a videotape of the film the fashion insult wounded him deeply. It was, however, oddly satisfying to read that one result of the film's popularity in Pakistan was that the actor playing "Rushdie" became so hated by the film-going public that he had to go into hiding.

At a certain point in the film one of the *international gorillay* was captured by the Israeli army and tied to a tree in the garden of the palace in the Philippines so that "Rushdie" could have his evil way with him. Once "Rushdie" had finished drinking from his bottle and lashing the poor terrorist with a whip, once he had slaked his filthy lust for violence upon the young man's body, he handed the innocent would-be murderer over to the Israeli soldiers and uttered the only genuinely funny line in the film. "Take him away," he cried, "and read to him from *The Satanic Verses* all night!" Well, of course, the poor fellow cracked completely. *Not that, anything but that,* he blubbered as the Israelis led him away.

At the end of the film "Rushdie" was indeed killed—not by the *international gorillay,* but by the Word itself, by thunderbolts unleashed by three large Qur'ans hanging in the sky over his head, which reduced the monster to ash. Personally fried by the Book of the Almighty: There was dignity in that.

On July 22, 1990, the British Board of Film Classification refused *International Gorillay* a certificate, on the fairly self-evident grounds that it was libelous (and because the BBFC feared that if it were to license the film and the real Rushdie were to sue for defamation, the board could be accused of having become party to the libel, and could therefore be sued for damages as well). This placed the real Rushdie in something of a quandary. He was fighting a battle for free speech and yet he was being defended, in this case, by an act of censorship. On the other hand the film was a nasty piece of work. In the end he wrote a letter to the BBFC formally giving up his right of legal recourse, assuring the board that he would pursue neither the filmmaker nor the board itself in the courts, and that he did not wish to be accorded "the dubious protection of censorship." The film should be shown so that it could be seen for the "distorted, incompetent piece of trash that it is." On August 17, as a direct result of his intervention, the board unanimously voted to license the film; whereupon, in spite of all the producer's efforts to promote it, it immediately sank without trace, *because it was a rotten movie,* and no matter what its intended audience may have thought about "Rushdie" or even Rushdie, they were too wise to throw their money away on tickets for a dreadful film.

It was, for him, an object lesson in the importance of the "better out than in" free speech argument—that it was better to allow even the most reprehensible speech than to sweep it under the carpet, better to publicly contest and perhaps deride what was loathsome than to give it the glamour of taboo, and that, for the most part, people could be trusted to tell the good from the bad. If *International Gorillay* had been banned, it would have become the hottest of hot videos and in the parlors of Bradford and Whitechapel young Muslim men would have gathered behind closed drapes to rejoice in the frying of the apostate. Out in the open, subjected to the judgment of the market, it shriveled like a vampire in sunlight, and was gone.

The events of the great world echoed in his Wimbledon redoubt. On August 2, 1990, Saddam Hussein invaded Kuwait and as war with Iraq approached the British Foreign Office began to rush to repair relations with Iran. The British and American military buildup progressed at speed. Suddenly nobody on the British or Iranian side was mentioning the "Rushdie case" at all and Frances D'Souza called to say she was very worried that he would be "bypassed." He called Michael Foot, who said he would find out more. The next day Michael said he had been "reassured," but that didn't sound reassuring. His man at the Foreign and Commonwealth Office, Duncan Slater, asked him to write yet another "mollifying statement" for the FCO to hold and use "when it seemed most useful." It was hard to know, he said, how Iran would "jump." They might use the international crisis as a moment to "solve their problems" with the British, or they might think that they could now push to restore relations without making concessions.

A public library in Rochdale, Lancashire, was firebombed.

He had arranged with Liz Calder to borrow her London apartment while she was on holiday with Clarissa and Zafar, to meet with an American journalist and other friends. She said that a colleague of hers, an editor at Bloomsbury called Elizabeth West, would be visiting the apartment from time to time to feed the parrot, Juju.

"Maybe you should touch base with her before you go," Liz said, "so that nobody gets any nasty surprises." He called Elizabeth and told her his plans. They spoke on the phone for a surprisingly long time and laughed a good deal, and in the end he suggested he could stay on at Liz's place after the journalist left and they could meet there for some quiet parrot maintenance. The police went to a wine store for him and bought, on his instructions, three bottles of wine, including one of the rich Tuscan red Tignanello. And then under the parrot's eye there was dinner by candlelight, salmon, and a salad of nasturtiums, and much too much red wine.

Love never came at you from the direction you were looking in. It crept up on you and whacked you behind the ear. In the months since Marianne's exit there had been some flirtatious telephone calls and, very occasionally, meetings with women, most of whom, he was fairly certain, were moved more by pity than attraction. Zafar's latest *au pair,* an attractive Norwegian girl, said *you can call me if you like*. Most unexpected of all was a clear demonstration of sexual interest from a liberal Muslim journalist. These were the straws he had been grasping at to save himself from drowning. Then he met Elizabeth West and the thing happened that could never be foreseen: the connection, the spark. Life was not ruled by fate, but by chance. If it had not been for a thirsty parrot, he might never have met the future mother of his second son.

By the end of their first evening he knew he wanted to see her again as soon as possible. Was she free the next day, he asked her, and she said yes, she was. They would meet at Liz's apartment again at 8 P.M. and he was shocked by how deep his feelings for her already were. She had long, rich chestnut hair and a brilliant and carefree smile and she bicycled into his life as if there were nothing to it, as if the whole smothering apparatus of fear and protection and restraint simply didn't exist. This was true and exceptional courage: the ability to act normally in an abnormal situation. She was fourteen years younger than he but there was a seriousness beneath the freewheeling exterior that spoke of experience, hinting at the kind of knowledge that comes only from pain. It would have been absurd not to be smitten by her. They quickly discovered a strange coincidence: that he had arrived in England for the first time, accompanied by his father, on his way to Rugby School, on the day that she was born. So in fact they had both arrived on the same day. It felt like an omen, though obviously he did not believe in the ominous. "It was a sunny day," he told her. "And cold." He told her about the Cumberland Hotel and watching television for the first time—*The Flintstones* and then the incomprehensible-to-him northern soap opera *Coronation Street* featuring the ferocious busybody Ena Sharples glowering in her hairnet. He described the chocolate milk shakes at Lyons Corner House and the rotisserie chicken at the Kardomah takeout and he told her what the advertising billboards said, UNZIP A BANANA for Fyffes, and, for Schweppes, TONIC WATER BY SCHHH . . . YOU-KNOW-WHO. She said, "Can you come back again on Monday? I'll cook dinner."

The police were concerned about a third visit in four days to the same address but he put his foot down and they gave in. That evening she told him something about her life though she was guarded about much of it and he sensed again the pain of her childhood, the lost mother, the aging father, the strange Cinderella life with the relatives who took her in. There was a woman she would not name, who had been unkind to her, whom she referred to only as *the woman who looked after me then*. In the end she had found happiness with an older cousin named Carol Knibb, who had become a second mother to her. She had gone to Warwick University and studied literature. And she liked his books. There were long hours of talk and then they were holding hands and then kissing. When he looked at his watch it was three-thirty in the morning, long past pumpkin time, he told her, and in the other room were some extremely grouchy and tired policemen. "Very interested," he wrote in his journal. "She's bright, gentle, vulnerable, beautiful and loving." Her interest in him was unfathomable and mysterious. It was always women who chose, he thought, and men's role was to thank their lucky stars.

She had to go to see her cousin Carol in Derbyshire and then there was a long-planned holiday with a girlfriend, so they couldn't meet again for a couple of weeks. She called from the airport to say goodbye and he wished she wasn't going. He began to tell his friends—Bill Buford, Gillon Aitken—about her, and he told the prot officer Dick Billington that he wanted her added to "the list" so that she could visit him in Wimbledon. As he said the words he knew he had made a big decision about her. "She will have to be vetted, Joe," Dick Billington said. *Negative vetting* was a quicker procedure than *positive vetting*. Checks would be run on her background and as long as no red flags came up she would be cleared. *Positive vetting* took much longer; people had to be interviewed. Legwork was involved. "That won't be necessary in this case," Dick said. Twenty-four hours later Elizabeth had passed the test; there were, apparently, no shady types, no Iranian or Mossad agents, in her past. He called her to tell her. "I want this," he said. "That's wonderful," she replied, and so it began. Two days later she had a drink with Liz Calder (who was back from holiday) to tell her what had happened and then rode her bike up to the front door of the Wimbledon house and stayed the night. That weekend she stayed for two nights. They went to Angela Carter and Mark Pearce's house in Clapham for dinner and Angela, not an easy woman to please, also approved. Zafar was back in London too and he came to stay and he and Elizabeth seemed to hit it off easily.

There was so much to talk about. On her third night at the Wimbledon house they stayed awake until five in the morning, telling each other stories, snoozing, making love. He couldn't remember ever having had a night like it. Something good had begun. His heart was full. Elizabeth had filled it up.

Haroun was going over well among its early readers. This little book, written to keep a promise to a child, might prove to be perhaps his most well-loved work of fiction. Both his emotional and working life had turned a corner, he felt; which made the ridiculous way he was obliged to live feel somehow worse. Zafar said he wanted to go skiing. "Maybe you could go with your mum and I'll pay for it," he said. "But I want to go with you," said his son. The words tore at his heart.

The mail arrived. In it were the first finished copies of *Haroun*. That cheered things up. He signed a dozen personalized copies for Zafar's friends. In Elizabeth's copy he wrote, "Thank you for the return of joy."

It was becoming increasingly acceptable to believe that the "Rushdie case" wasn't worth the trouble it had caused, because the man himself was an unworthy specimen. Norman Tebbit, one of Margaret Thatcher's closest political allies, wrote in *The Independent* that the author of *The Satanic Verses* was "an outstanding villain . . . [whose] public life has been a record of despicable acts of betrayal of his upbringing, religion, adopted home and nationality." The celebrated historian, Tory peer and "authenticator" of the fraudulent "Hitler Diaries," Lord Dacre (Hugh Trevor-Roper) had wiped the egg off his face and declared, also in the *Indy*, "I wonder how Salman Rushdie is faring these days under the benevolent protection of British law and British police, about whom he has been so rude. Not too comfortably I hope. . . . I would not shed a tear if some British Muslims, deploring his manners, should waylay him in a dark street and seek to improve them. If that should cause him thereafter to control his pen, society would benefit and literature would not suffer."

The novelist John le Carré had said, "I don't think it is given to any of us to be impertinent to great religions with impunity," and, on another occasion, "Again and again, it has been within his power to save the faces of his publishers and, with dignity, withdraw his book until a calmer time has come. It seems to me he has nothing more to prove except his own insensitivity." Le Carré also disapproved of the "literary merit" argument: "Are we to believe that those who write literature have a greater right to free speech than those who write pulp? Such elitism does not help Rushdie's cause, whatever that cause has now become." He did not say whether he would also have been against the use of "literary merit" in defense of, say, James Joyce's *Ulysses* or D. H. Lawrence's *Lady Chatterley's Lover.*

Douglas Hurd, the British foreign secretary and "novelist," was asked in the *Evening Standard:* "What was your most painful moment in government?" He replied, "Reading *The Satanic Verses.*"

In early September he met Duncan Slater at Slater's Knightsbridge home. The many Indian pictures and artifacts revealed Slater as an unsuspected Indophile, which perhaps explained his sympathy for the invisible man. "You should use all your media connections," Slater said. "You need positive pieces." Nadine Gordimer had amassed an impressive list of signatories to her appeal to Iran, including Václav Havel, the French minister of culture and many other writers, academics and politicians, and Slater suggested this could be used to prompt a sympathetic editorial in, say, *The Times.* The Gordimer letter was published and made a small stir. Nothing changed. *The Independent* reported that it had received 160 letters criticizing the Tebbit statement, and two in support of it. That was something, at least.

A few days later the Italian foreign minister, Gianni de Michelis, announced that Europe and Iran were "close" to an exchange of letters that would "lift the *fatwa*" and make it possible to normalize relations. Slater said that the report was "a little ahead of the news," but yes, the European Community "troika" of foreign ministers was planning to talk to Iran's foreign minister, Ali Akbar Velayati, in the next few days.

Elizabeth had begun to tell her closest friends about her new relationship. For his part, he spoke to Isabel Fonseca and told her about Elizabeth. Then he heard that Marianne was returning to London.

———

On the publication day of *Haroun and the Sea of Stories,* September 27, 1990, Iran and the United Kingdom renewed partial diplomatic relations. Duncan Slater called from New York to say that "assurances had been received." Iran would do nothing to implement the *fatwa.* However it would not be canceled and the offer of millions of dollars in bounty money (Ayatollah Sanei, who had made the original offer, kept raising the figure) would remain in place because it was "nothing to do with the government." Slater tried to present this as a positive step but it felt like a sellout. Any deal made on his behalf by Douglas Hurd was not a deal he could trust.

The intelligence services and the Special Branch seemed to feel the same way. There was no change in the threat assessment. He would remain at level two, one step behind the queen. There would be no change in the protection arrangements. The house on St. Peter's Street would remain locked and shuttered. He would not be *allowed* to go home again.

But he had made a new beginning. Just then, that was what counted most. *Haroun* was doing well and Sonny Mehta's nightmare scenario remained firmly in the country of his bad dreams. Kashmiris did not rise up, incensed by the name of a talking mechanical hoopoe. There was no trace of blood in the streets. Sonny had been running from shadows and now that daylight had come his bogeymen were exposed as the empty night terrors they were.

He was *allowed* to surface briefly, and unannounced, at a London bookstore, Waterstone's in Hampstead, to sign copies of *Haroun and the Sea of Stories.* Zafar came too and "helped," passing him the books to be signed, and Bill Buford was a benign, grinning presence. For an hour he felt like an author of books again. But there was no escaping the nervousness in the eyes of the protection team. Not for the first time he understood that they, too, were afraid.

At home there was Elizabeth. They were becoming closer by the day. "I'm scared," she told him, "because I've become too vulnerable to you." He did his best to reassure her. *I love you like mad and I'm not going to let you go.* She feared that he was only with her *faute de mieux,* that when the threats ended he would go to America and abandon her. He had told her of his love of New York City and his dream of living there in freedom one day. He, whose life had been a series of uprootings (which he would try to redefine as "multiple rootings"), did not understand how profoundly English she was, how deep her roots went. From those earliest days she felt she was in competition with New York. *You'll bugger off there and leave me behind.* When they had a few glasses of wine this kind of scratchiness developed between them. Neither of them thought these occasional irritations were important. Most of the time they were happy with each other. *I am deeply in love,* he wrote, conscious of how astonishing it was to be able to write those words. His was a heavily guarded life and he himself would not have expected love to find a way past the border controls of his strange internal exile. Yet here it was, most evenings and weekends, bicycling gaily toward him across the Thames.

Hatred was still in the air as well as love. The Muslim Institute's loquacious garden gnome was still ranting, and was being given every opportunity to do so. Here he was on BBC Radio saying that Salman Rushdie "had been found guilty of a capital offense in the eyes of the highest legal authority in Islam and what is left is the application of that punishment." In a Sunday newspaper Siddiqui clarified his thinking. "He should pay with his life." There had been no executions in Britain for a quarter of a century but now the discussion of "legal" killing had been made acceptable again by the "rage of Islam." Siddiqui's views were echoed in Lebanon by the Hezbollah leader Hussein Musawi. *He must die.* Simon Lee, author of *The Cost of Free Speech,* suggested he should be sent to Northern Ireland for the rest of his days, because there was already so much security in place there. The *Sun* columnist Garry Bushell described him as a greater traitor to his country than George Blake. Blake, a Soviet double agent, had been sentenced to forty-two years in prison for espionage, but had escaped from jail and fled to the Soviet Union. Writing a novel could now be described with a straight face as a more heinous offense than high treason.

Two years of attacks by Muslim and non-Muslim adversaries had affected him more than he knew. He had never forgotten the day they brought him a copy of *The Guardian* and he saw that the novelist and critic John Berger was writing about him. He had met Berger and admired, in particular, his essay books *Ways of Seeing* and *About Looking,* and felt that they were on friendly terms. He turned eagerly to the op-ed page to read him. The shock of what he found, Berger's bitter attack on his work and motives, was very great. They had many mutual friends, Anthony Barnett of Charter 88, for example, and over the months and years that followed Berger would be asked by these intermediaries why he had written so hostile a piece. He invariably refused to answer the question.

No woman's love could easily assuage the pain of so many "black arrows." There was probably not enough love in the world to heal him at that moment. His new book had been published and on the same day the British government had climbed back into bed with his would-be assassins. He was being praised on the book pages and reviled in the news. At night he heard *I love you* but the days were shouting *Die.*

Elizabeth received no police protection but, to ensure her safety, it was important to keep her out of the public eye. His friends never mentioned her name, or even her existence, outside the "charmed circle." But inevitably the press found out. No photographs of her were available, and none were made available, but that didn't stop the tabloids from speculating why a beautiful young woman might wish to be with a novelist fourteen years her senior with the mark of death on his brow. He saw a photograph of himself in the paper captioned RUSHDIE: UGLY. Inevitably it was assumed that she was there for low motives, for his money, perhaps, or, in the opinion of a "psychologist" who felt able to judge her without ever having met her, because a certain kind of young woman was turned on by the scent of danger.

Now that the secret was out the police grew more concerned for her safety, and for his. They became uneasy about her cycle route being followed and insisted that she meet them at prearranged locations and be "dry-cleaned." They also issued a notice to the press, warning them off her, because to publicize her would increase the probability of a crime being committed. In all the years that followed the press helped to protect her. No photograph of her was ever taken or printed. Whenever he appeared in public she would be brought to the location separately and taken away afterward in a separate car. He would tell the press photographers that he was happy for them to take his picture and ask, in return, that they leave her alone; and, amazingly, they did. Everyone knew that the *fatwa* was a serious matter, and everyone took it seriously. Even five years later, when his novel *The Moor's Last Sigh* was short-listed for the Booker and he went with Elizabeth to the ceremony, there were no pictures of her. The Booker dinner was live on BBC2 but the cameras were instructed not to look at her, and not a single image of her face was transmitted. As a result of this exceptional restraint she was able, throughout the *fatwa* years, to move around the city freely, as a private person, attracting no attention, friendly or unfriendly. She was intensely private by nature, and this suited her very well.

In mid-October he sat down with Mike Wallace at a hotel to the west of London to be interviewed for *60 Minutes,* and near the top of the interview Wallace mentioned the end of his marriage to Marianne and then asked, "What do you do for companionship? Do you have to lead a celibate life?" He was caught off guard by the question, and could obviously not tell Wallace the truth about his newfound love; he floundered for a second and then as if by a miracle he found the right words. "It's nice," he said, "to have a break." Mike Wallace looked so shocked by this answer that he had to add, "No, I'm not being serious." *Just kidding, Mike.*

Marianne called. She was back from America again. He wanted to talk to her about lawyers and formalizing their divorce but she had something else to discuss. There was a lump in her breast that was thought to be "precancerous." She was very angry with her GP, who should have diagnosed it "six months ago." But there it was. She needed him, she said. She still loved him. Three days later she had worse news. The cancer was there: Burkitt's lymphoma, one of the non-Hodgkin's group of cancers. She was seeing a specialist at Chelsea and Westminster Hospital, a Dr. Abdul-Ahad. In the weeks that followed she told him she was receiving radiotherapy. He didn't know what to say to her.

Pauline Melville had won the Guardian Fiction Prize for *Shape-shifter.* He called her to congratulate her but she wanted to talk about Marianne. She, Pauline, had repeatedly offered to accompany Marianne to the hospital on treatment days. The offer had invariably been refused. She called back some days later and said, "I think you should call this Dr. Abdul-Ahad and speak to him yourself."

The oncologist Dr. Abdul-Ahad had never heard of Marianne, nor, he said, would he treat a cancer such as the one in question. He was a specialist in quite different cancers, primarily in children. This was baffling. Were there other Dr. Abdul-Ahads? Was he talking to the wrong one?

It was the day Marianne had said she was to begin treatment at the Royal Marsden. There were two Royal Marsdens, one on Fulham Road and the other in Sutton. He called them both. They did not know who she was. More bafflement. Perhaps she was using an assumed name. Perhaps she had a Joseph Anton–like pseudonym, too. He had wanted to help, but he had run into a dead end.

He called her GP and asked if she would speak to him. He told her he knew about doctor-patient confidentiality but the oncologist he had spoken to had suggested they talk. "I'm glad you called," the doctor said. "I've lost touch with Marianne—can you give me an address and phone number? I obviously need to speak to her." He was surprised to hear that. The doctor had not seen Marianne for over a year, and added that Marianne had never discussed having cancer with her.

Marianne stopped returning his calls. He never knew if she had been contacted by the doctor or not, never knew if she had moved on to another GP, never knew anything about any of it. They hardly spoke again after that. She agreed to the divorce and made few financial demands, asking for a modest lump sum to help her restart her life. She left London, and moved to Washington, D.C. He never heard anything further about illness, or medical treatment. She continued to live, and to write. Her books were highly regarded and nominated for both the Pulitzer Prize and the National Book Award. He had always thought her a fine writer of high quality and wished her well. Their lives went down separate paths, and did not touch again.

No: That wasn't correct. They touched just once more. He was about to make himself vulnerable to attack, and she took the opportunity, and had her revenge.

He read a novel by the Chilean writer José Donoso about the demolition of the self, *The Obscene Bird of Night*. In his vulnerable state of mind it was probably not the best choice of reading. The title was taken from a letter written by Henry James, Sr., to his sons Henry and William that served as the novel's epigraph: "Every man who has reached even his intellectual teens begins to suspect that life is no farce; that it is not genteel comedy even; that it flowers and fructifies on the contrary out of the profoundest tragic depths of the essential dearth in which its subject's roots are plunged. The natural inheritance of everyone who is capable of spiritual life is an unsubdued forest where the wolf howls and the obscene bird of night chatters."

He lay awake watching Elizabeth sleeping and in his room the unsubdued forest grew and grew, like that other forest in Sendak's great book, the forest beyond which lay the ocean beyond which lay the place where the wild things were, and here was a private boat for him to sail in, and waiting on the beach in the place where the wild things were was a dentist. Maybe the wisdom teeth had been an omen after all. Maybe there were omens and auguries and portents and prophecies, and all the things he didn't believe in were more real than the things he knew. Maybe if there were bat-winged monsters and bug-eyed ghouls . . . maybe if there were demons and devils . . . there could also be a god. Yes, and maybe he was losing his mind. The crazy, stupid, and, finally, dead fish is the one that goes looking for the hook.

The fisherman who caught the crazy fish, the siren who led his private boat onto the rocks was the "holistic dentist" from Harley Street, Hesham el-Essawy. (Maybe he should have listened to the wisdom of the teeth.) Essawy was unlikely casting for the role in spite of his passing resemblance to a fleshier Peter Sellers, but the desperate fish, caught in its tank for two long years, its spirits low, its sense of self-worth badly battered, was hunting for a way out, any way out, and mistook the fisherman's wriggling worm for the key.

———

He had another meeting with Duncan Slater in Knightsbridge and this time there was another man in the room, the Foreign Office highflier David Gore-Booth. Gore-Booth had been present at the conversations with the Iranians in New York and had agreed to debrief him personally. He was haughty, smart, tough and direct and gave the impression, like the Arabist he was, that his sympathies in this matter lay not with the writer but with his critics. Ever since Lawrence of Arabia the FCO had "tilted" toward the Muslim world (Gore-Booth would become an unpopular figure in Israel) and its grandees often exuded a genuine irritation at the difficulties in Britain's relations with that world caused by, of all people, a novelist. However, Gore-Booth said that the assurances received from Iran were "real." They would not seek to carry out the death order. What mattered now was to bring the temperature down at home. If the British Muslims could be persuaded to call off the dogs then things could revert to normal pretty swiftly. "That side of it," he said, "is really up to you."

Frances D'Souza was excitedly optimistic when he called to tell her about the Gore-Booth meeting. "I think we could have a deal!" she said. But the meeting had left him feeling very low because of Gore-Booth's barely disguised contempt for what he had supposedly done. *That side of it is really up to you.* Principle was being recast as obstinacy. His attempt to hold the line, to insist that he was the victim, not the perpetrator, of a great wrong was being received as arrogance. So much was being done for him; why was he being so inflexible? He had started this: He needed to finish it, too.

The weight of such attitudes, which were becoming general, lay heavily upon him, making it progressively harder to believe that he was acting for the best. Some sort of dialogue with British Muslims was perhaps inescapable. Frances told him that Essawy had contacted Article 19 and offered to mediate. Essawy was not very intellectually impressive but he was, she believed, well-meaning, even kindly. This route seemed vital to her now. The defense campaign was short of funds. She needed to raise £6,000 urgently. It was becoming difficult to persuade Article 19 to continue to fund the campaigning work on this issue. They need to show that progress was being made.

He called Essawy. The dentist was courteous toward him, spoke gently, claiming to sympathize with the unpleasantness of his life. He could see that he was being coddled, almost baby-talked toward some sort of acquiescence, but he stayed on the line. Essawy claimed he wanted to help. He could arrange a conference of "very heavyweight" Muslim intellectuals and use that to start a campaign across the Arab world, and even in Iran. "I'm your best bet," he said. "I want you to be a Ghazali figure and return to the faith." Muhammad al-Ghazali, the conservative Muslim thinker, was the author of the celebrated *Incoherence of the Philosophers,* in which he denounced as unbelievers and traducers of the true faith both the great Greeks Aristotle and Socrates, and the Muslim scholars such as Ibn Sina (Avicenna) who had sought to learn from them. Ghazali had been answered by Ibn Rushd (Averroës), the Aristotelian from whom Anis Rushdie had derived the family name, in the equally celebrated work *The Incoherence of the Incoherence.* He himself had always thought of himself as a member of the Ibn Rushd team, not the Ghazalians, but he understood that Essawy was not referring to Ghazali's philosophy itself but to the moment when Ghazali suffered a personal crisis of belief that was overcome by "a light which God Most High cast into my breast." He thought it improbable that his breast would be receiving the light of God Most High anytime soon, but Essawy pressed on. "I don't believe in your god-shaped hole that you wrote about," he said. "You're an intelligent man." As if intelligence and disbelief could not coexist in a single mind. The significance of this alleged god-shaped hole, he was being told, was not just that it was a cavity to be filled up by art and love, as he had written, but that it was *in the shape of God.* Now he should look not into the void, but at that framing shape.

In normal circumstances he would not have wasted his time on such a discussion, but the circumstances were far from normal. He talked to Sameen, who was suspicious. "You need to establish exactly what Essawy expects," his sister said. Essawy had recently written an open letter to Rafsanjani in Iran in which he had referred to "this worthless writer." ("You'll forgive me for that, won't you," he wheedled disingenuously on the phone.) And he had made one demand that would be a major stumbling block: "You mustn't defend the book."

Every time he called Essawy he was aware of being lured further and further into a space from which he would find it hard to withdraw. Yet he continued to call, and Essawy allowed him to take his time, to find his way slowly, at his own speed, with many retreats and evasions, to where the hook waited for his willing mouth. His *South Bank Show* interview had been very helpful, the dentist said. His old stances on Kashmir and Palestine were useful too. They would show Muslims he was not their enemy. He should make a video reiterating his support for Kashmiri and Palestinian aspirations and that could be shown at the Islamic Cultural Center in London, to help change people's minds about him. *Maybe,* he said. *I'll think about it.*

He never learned very much about Essawy the man. The dentist said he was happily married and that, in fact, his wife was so attentively loving that she was cutting his toenails for him as he spoke on the phone. That became the image of the dentist that stuck in his mind: a man making phone calls while a woman knelt at his feet.

Margaret Drabble and Michael Holroyd invited him and Elizabeth down to Porlock Weir for the weekend, along with the playwright Julian Mitchell and his partner, Richard Rosen. They were a merry company but he was in agony, tying his mind in knots, trying to find a way to accommodate his opponents, looking for the words he could say—the words that would be possible for him to say—that might break the impasse. They went for a long walk along the lush green Doone Valley and as they walked he argued with himself. Maybe he could make a statement of belonging to the culture of Islam rather than the faith. There were nonreligious, secular Jews, after all; perhaps he could argue for a kind of secular membership of a Muslim community of tradition and knowledge.

He was after all from an Indian Muslim family. That was the truth. His parents might not have been religious but much of his family had been. He had obviously been profoundly affected by Muslim culture; after all, when he wanted to invent the story of the birth of a fictional religion, he had turned to the story of Islam, because it was what he knew best. And yes, he had argued in essays and interviews for the rights of Kashmiri Muslims, and in *Midnight's Children* he had placed a Muslim family, not a Hindu one, at the heart of the story of the birth of independent India. How could he be called an enemy of Islam when that was his record? He was not an enemy. He was a friend. A skeptical, even a dissident friend, but a friend nevertheless.

He spoke to Essawy from Maggie and Michael's house. The fisherman felt the fish on the line and knew it was time to start reeling it in. "When you speak," he said, "it must be clear. There cannot be equivocations."

The police agreed that he could go to Bernardo Bertolucci's private screening of his new film, *The Sheltering Sky*. After the screening he had no idea what to say to Bernardo. There wasn't a single thing about the film he had enjoyed. "Ah! Salman!" Bertolucci said. "It is very important for me to know what you think of my picture." At that moment the right words came into his head, just as other words had been given to him when Mike Wallace asked him about sex. He put his hand on his heart and said, "Bernardo . . . I can't talk about it." Bertolucci nodded understandingly. "A lot of people have this reaction," he said.

On his way home he hoped for a third miracle, for the right words to come to him at the right moment for a third time, the words that would make British Muslim leaders nod wisely and understand.

He was finalizing his collection of essays, *Imaginary Homelands,* writing the introduction, correcting the proofs, when he was offered an interview on the BBC TV *Late Show.* The interviewer would be his friend Michael Ignatieff, the Russian-Canadian writer and broadcaster, so he was assured of a sympathetic hearing. In this interview he said what he thought everyone wanted to hear. *I am talking with Muslim leaders to try to find common ground.* Nobody wanted to hear about freedom anymore, or about the writer's inalienable right to express his vision of the world as he saw fit, or about the immorality of book burning and death threats. Those arguments were used up. To restate them now would be obdurate and unhelpful. People wanted to hear him making

peace so that the trouble could stop and he could just go away, off their
televisions, out of their newspapers, into well-deserved obscurity, pref-
erably to spend the rest of his life pondering on the evil he had wrought
and finding ways to apologize for it and to make up for it. Nobody
cared about him or his principles or his wretched book. They needed
him to bring the damned thing to an end. *There is a lot of common
ground,* he said, *and the point is to try to make it more solid.*

He bit into the juicy worm and when he felt the point of the hook
he did not stop.

There was a flurry of responses, as if he had been walking through fallen
autumn leaves and kicked them up in the air. Sameen heard on the radio
that "moderate Muslim leaders" were asking Iran to annul the *fatwa*.
However, British Muslim "leaders" to whom he had not spoken denied
that they were negotiating with him. The garden gnome hopped on a
flight to Tehran to urge the leadership of that country not to relent, and
six days later the minister of Islamic culture and guidance, Mohammad
Khatami—the future President Khatami, the great liberal hope of
Iran—declared that the *fatwa* was irreversible. When he heard that he
called Duncan Slater. "I thought you said that the Iranians were going
to let this fade away," he said. "We'll get back to you," Slater replied.

He went on Melvyn Bragg's Monday morning radio show *Start the
Week* and named Essawy as the "major Muslim figure" who had
opened up a dialogue with him. He spoke to Ted Koppel on *Nightline*
and expressed the hope that things would improve. In Iran the offer of
bounty money was raised again: still $1 million for Iranians, but now
$3 million if a non-Iranian did the deed. He spoke to Slater. The New
York agreement was plainly phony. The British government must act.
Slater agreed to pass the message along. The government did not act.
He said, on American television, that he was beginning to be "a little
disturbed by the lack of reaction on the part of the British government" to these new menaces.

The fisherman began to bring the fish to the net. "There must be
a meeting," Essawy said, "and you must be embraced by Muslims once
again."

He consulted nobody, asked for no one's advice or guidance. That alone should have told him he was *not in his perfect mind.* Normally he would have talked through any important decision with Sameen, Pauline, Gillon, Andrew, Bill, Frances. He made no calls. He didn't even discuss it with Elizabeth, not really. "I'm trying to solve this," he told her. But he didn't ask her what she thought.

There was no help coming from any other quarter. It was up to him. He had fought for his book and he would not surrender that. His good name had been destroyed anyway. It didn't matter what people thought of him. They already thought the worst. "Yes," he said to the ever more glutinous dentist, "set up the meeting. I'll come."

Paddington Green station was the most secure police facility in the United Kingdom. Aboveground it was an ordinary cop shop in an ugly office block but the real action was underground. This was where members of the IRA were held and interrogated. And on Christmas Eve, 1990, this was where he was brought to meet Essawy's people. He had been told that no other location could be approved; that was how nervous everyone was. When he entered Paddington Green with its bombproof doors and endless security locks and checks he began to feel nervous himself. Then he walked into the meeting room and stopped dead. He had expected a roundtable discussion, or for everyone to be informally seated in armchairs, perhaps with tea or coffee. That was how naïve he had been. He now saw that there was to be no informality, and not even a pretense of a discussion. They had not come together as equals to talk through a problem and reach a civilized agreement. He was not to be treated as an equal. He was to be put on trial.

The room had been set up by the Muslim worthies as a courtroom. They sat like six tribunal judges in a straight line behind a long table and facing them was a single upright chair. He stopped in the doorway like a horse balking at the first fence and Essawy approached him whispering urgently, telling him he must come in, these were important gentlemen, they had made time in their schedules, they must not be kept waiting. He should please sit. Everyone was waiting.

He should have turned his back then and gone home, away from degradation, back toward self-respect. Every step forward was a mistake. But he was Essawy's zombie now. The dentist's hand gentle on his elbow guided him to the empty chair.

Everyone was introduced to him but he barely registered their names. There were beards and turbans and curious, piercing eyes. He recognized Zaki Badawi, the Egyptian president of the Muslim College in London and a "liberal" who had condemned *The Satanic Verses* but had said that he would shelter its author in his own home. He was introduced to a Mr. Mahgoub, the Egyptian minister of *awqaf* (religious endowments), and to Sheikh Gamal Manna Ali Solaiman of the golden-domed London Central Mosque in Regent's Park and to Sheikh Gamal's associate Sheikh Hamed Khalifa. Essawy was of Egyptian origin and he had brought other Egyptians into this room.

They had him now, so they laughed and joked with him at first. They made rude comments about Kalim Siddiqui, the malevolent garden gnome and Iranian lapdog. They promised to launch a worldwide campaign to lay the *fatwa* issue to rest. He tried to explain the origins of his novel and they agreed that the controversy was based on a "tragic misunderstanding." He was not an enemy of Islam. They wanted to acknowledge him as a member of the Muslim intelligentsia. That was their most earnest desire. *We want to reclaim you for ourselves.* He needed only to make certain gestures of goodwill.

He should distance himself, they said, from the statements made by characters in his novel who attacked or insulted the Prophet or his religion. He said he had frequently pointed out that it was impossible to portray the persecution of a new faith without showing the persecutors doing some persecuting, and it was an obvious injustice to equate his own views with theirs. Well, then, they rejoined, this will be easy for you to say.

He should suspend publication of the paperback edition, they said. He told them that for them to insist on this would be a mistake; they would look like censors. They said a period of time was needed for their reconciliation efforts to work. He needed to create that space. Once the misunderstandings had been cleared up the book would no longer concern anyone and new editions would cease to be a problem.

Finally, he needed to prove his sincerity. He knew what the *shaha-*

dah was, did he not. He had grown up in India calling it the *qalmah* but that was the same thing. *There is no God but God and Muhammad is his Prophet.* That was a statement he needed to make today. That was what would allow them to extend the hand of friendship, forgiveness and understanding.

He said he was willing to express a secular Muslim identity, to say he had grown up in that tradition. They reacted badly to the word "secular." "Secular" was the devil. That word should not have been used. He needed to speak clearly in the time-honored words. That was the only gesture that Muslims would understand.

They had prepared a document for him to sign. Essawy handed it to him. It was ungrammatical and crude. He could not sign it. "Revise, revise," they urged him. "You are the great writer and we are not." In a corner of the room there was a table and another chair. He took the piece of paper there and sat down to study it. "Take your time," they cried. "You should be happy with what you sign."

He was not happy. He was trembling with misery. Now he wished he had asked his friends' advice. What would they have said? What would his father have advised? He saw himself swaying on the edge of a great abyss. But he was also hearing the seductive murmur of hope. If they did what they said . . . if the quarrel came to an end . . . if, if, if.

He signed the corrected document and handed it to Essawy. The six "judges" signed it too. There were embraces and congratulations. It was over. He was lost inside a whirlwind, dizzy, blinded by what he had done, and had no idea where the tornado was taking him. He heard nothing, saw nothing, felt nothing. The police guided him out of the room and he heard the doors open and shut along the underground corridor. Then a car door, open, shut. He was being driven away. When he got back to Wimbledon Elizabeth was waiting, offering him her love. His insides were churning. He went to the bathroom and was violently sick. His body knew what his mind had done and was expressing its opinion.

In the afternoon he was taken to a press conference and tried to sound positive. There were interviews for radio and television, with Essawy and without him. He did not remember what he said. He knew what he was saying to himself. *You are a liar,* he was saying. *You are a liar and a coward and a fool.* Sameen called him. "Have you taken leave of your senses?" she shouted at him. "What do you think you are doing?" *Yes, you have taken leave of your senses,* said his inner voice. *And you have no idea what you have done, or are doing, or can now do.* He had survived this long because he could put his hand on his heart and defend every word he had written or said. He had written seriously and with integrity and everything he had said about that had been the truth. Now he had torn his tongue out of his own mouth, had denied himself the ability to use the language and ideas that were natural to him. Until this moment he had been accused of a crime against the beliefs of others. Now he accused himself, and found himself guilty, of having committed a crime against himself.

Then it was Christmas Day.

He was taken to Pauline's basement apartment in Highbury Hill and Zafar was brought there so that they could spend Christmas morning together. After a couple of hours Zafar went back to his mother's and he and Elizabeth were driven to Graham Swift and Candice Rodd's house in Wandsworth. It was their second Christmas together. They were as friendly as ever and tiptoed around the subject of what had just happened so as not to spoil the Christmas mood, but he could see the worry in their eyes just as they, he was certain, could see the confusion in his. The next day was spent at Bill Buford's little house in Cambridge and Bill had cooked a feast. These moments were islands in the storm. After that his days were busy with journalists and his ears were deafened by the news. He spoke to the British, American and Indian press, and to the BBC World Service's Persian section, and did phone-ins on British Muslim radio stations. He loathed every word he said. He was twisting on the hook he had so willingly swallowed and he made himself sick. He knew the truth: He was no more religious than he had been a few days earlier. The rest was pure expediency. And it wasn't even working.

At first it seemed it just might. The grand sheikh of al-Azhar came out in support and "forgave him his sins" and Sibghat Qadri, QC, asked to meet the attorney general to discuss prosecuting Kalim Siddiqui. But Iran remained intransigent. Khamenei said the *fatwa* would remain in place even "if Rushdie became the most pious man of all time" and a hard-line Tehran newspaper advised him to "prepare for death." Siddiqui duly parroted these statements. And then the Paddington Green Six began to back away from their agreement. Sheikh Gamal demanded the total withdrawal of *The Satanic Verses,* which he and his colleagues had agreed not to do. Gamal and his colleague Sheikh Hamed Khalifa had been strongly criticized by the congregation at the Regent's Park Mosque and under the pressure of that criticism were abandoning their positions. The Saudis and Iranians expressed their "anger" at the Egyptian government's involvement in the peace effort and Mahgoub, in danger of losing his job, also reneged on what he had agreed.

And on January 9, 1991, Elizabeth's thirtieth birthday, he was visited at noon by Mr. Greenup, who told him grimly, "We believe that the danger to you has now increased. Credible intelligence has been received about a specific threat. We are analyzing this and will let you know in due course."

He had fallen into the trap of wanting to be loved, had made himself foolish and weak, and now he was paying the price.

V

"Been Down So Long
It Looks Like Up to Me"

It was Elizabeth's birthday and he was cooking an Indian meal for her. Gillon, Bill, Pauline and Jane Wellesley were coming to Wimbledon for this little celebration dinner. He wanted it to be a special evening for her. She was giving him so much and he could give her very little but at least he could cook this meal. He told nobody about what Greenup had said. There would be time for that another day. This day, January 9, was for the woman he loved. They had been together for five months.

After her birthday he fell ill. He ran a high fever for several days and was confined to bed. As he lay there hot and shivering the news, both private and public, seemed to be an aspect of his sickness. Andrew's assistant Susan had spoken to Marianne, who said she was well, and no doubt she was, but he couldn't pay attention to that now. The police were telling him that because of the "specific threat" his activities would have to be restricted even further. He had been asked to go on various TV programs, *Wogan, Question Time,* but that would not be *allowed.* He had been asked to speak to a House of Commons group but they didn't want to take him to the Palace of Westminster. A few private evenings at the homes of friends might be permitted but that was all. He knew he would refuse to accept this but he was too unwell just then to argue. Late at night as he lay fevered in bed the TV brought him news of the start of the Gulf War, the huge aerial attack on Iraq. Then Iraq attacked Israel with Scud missiles, which miraculously killed nobody and, fortunately, were not armed with chemical warheads. He spent the days in a half delirium of sleep, fever and images of precision bombing. There were phone calls, some answered, some not, many bad dreams, and above all his continuing anguish about his declaration that he had "become a Muslim." Sameen was finding that very hard to take and some of the calls were hers. For two years he had been heading down a road toward the heart of darkness and now he was there, in hell. He had perplexed all his friends and had obliged himself to stand smiling alongside those who had vilified him and threatened others, people who had acquiesced in the threat of murder made by Iran, which Iqbal Sacranie, for one, had called "his divine retribution." The "intellectual" Tariq Modood wrote him a letter saying he must no longer talk about the *fatwa*. "Muslims find it repulsive," Modood said. The West had used the *fatwa* to demonize Muslims, so it would be "repulsive" of him to object to it anymore. This Modood presented himself as a moderate but such hypocrisy made it impossible for him to think in a straight line. And these were the people he could no longer challenge because he had torn out his tongue. Another "moderate," Akbar Ahmed, called to say that the "hard-liners" may slowly be coming around but he must be "very conciliatory," a *sadha* [plain] Muslim." He replied that there was a very limited amount of shit he was willing to eat.

Dear God,

If you exist, and are as they describe You, omniscient, omnipresent, and above all almighty, surely You would not tremble upon your heavenly seat when confronted by a mere book and its scribbler? The great Muslim philosophers often disagreed about Your precise relationship with human beings and human deeds. Ibn Sina (Avicenna) argued that You, being far above the world, were limited to knowing it only in very general and abstract terms. Ghazali disagreed. Any God "acceptable to Islam" would know in detail everything that went on upon the surface of the earth and have an opinion about it. Well, Ibn Rushd didn't buy that, as You would know if Ghazali was right (and not if Ibn Sina or Ibn Rushd were). Ghazali's contention would make You too much like men, Ibn Rushd argued—like men with their foolish arguments, their little dissensions, their petty points of view. It would be beneath You, and would diminish You, to get dragged into human affairs. So, it's hard to know what to think. If you are the God of Ibn Sina and Ibn Rushd then you don't even know what is being said and done right now in your name. However, even if You are Ghazali's God, reading the newspapers, watching TV, and taking sides in political and even literary disputes, I don't believe you could have a problem with The Satanic Verses or any other book, no matter how wretched. What sort of Almighty could be shaken by the work of Man? Contrariwise, God, if by some chance Ibn Sina, Ghazali and Ibn Rushd are all wrong and You don't exist at all, then, too, in that case, too, You would have no problems with writers or books. I conclude that my difficulties are not with You, God, but with Your servants and followers on Earth. A distinguished novelist once told me that she had stopped writing fiction for a time because she didn't like her fans. I wonder if You can sympathize with her position. Thank You for Your attention (unless you're not listening: See above).

"Becoming a Muslim" prompted some Foreign Office types to propose that he speak up for a terrorist. He received a message suggesting that he might usefully intervene in the Kokabi trial. Mehrdad Kokabi, a "student," was charged with arson and causing explosions at bookshops selling *The Satanic Verses*. The prosecution said his fingerprints had been found on the paper wrapping two pipe bombs, and that he had used his credit card to hire cars used in the attacks. Perhaps, it was hinted to him, it would be a nice touch for the author of *The Satanic Verses* to plead for clemency in the case. Outraged by the suggestion, he spoke to Duncan Slater and David Gore-Booth. They both disagreed with the idea. That was faintly reassuring, but two months later all charges against Kokabi were suddenly dropped and he was recommended for deportation to Iran. The government denied that it had twisted the arm of blind Justice. Slater and Gore-Booth said they knew nothing about it. Kokabi returned to Iran, where he was given a hero's welcome and a new job. It became his responsibility to choose "students" who would receive placements abroad.

The page proofs of his collection of essays *Imaginary Homelands* had arrived. Bill said, "Now that you've done this thing maybe we should put your essay into the book." He had published a piece in the London *Times* trying to justify the concessions he had made at Paddington Green. He hated the piece, was already rethinking everything he had done, but having hung the millstone round his neck he was, for the moment at any rate, unable to get it off. He agreed with Bill and the essay went in under the title "Why I Am a Muslim." For the rest of his life he would never see a hardcover copy of *Imaginary Homelands* without feeling a knife of embarrassment and regret.

The war filled everyone's thoughts and when they were not repeating that he must "withdraw the insult" (cease publication of *The Satanic Verses*) the British Muslim "leaders"—Siddiqui, Sacranie, the Bradford mullahs—were expressing sympathy with Saddam Hussein. The second anniversary of the *fatwa* was approaching and the winter weather was bitter and cold. Fay Weldon had sent him a copy of *On Liberty* by John Stuart Mill, perhaps as a rebuke, but its clear, strong words were as inspiring to him as ever. His contempt for the harder-headed of his opponents—for Shabbir Akhtar and his attacks on the nonexistent "liberal inquisition" and his pride in Islam as a religion of "militant wrath"—had been reborn, alongside a new dislike of some of his supposed supporters, who now believed he was not worth supporting. James Fenton wrote a sympathetic piece in *The New York Review of Books* defending him against the phenomenon of the "Dismayed Friends." If the "dream Salman" in people's minds had been let down by the actions of the real Salman, these Dismayed Ones were now beginning to think, then, poof!, to the devil with him, he wasn't worthy of their friendship. Might as well let the assassins have their way.

He was remembering something Günter Grass had once said to him about losing: that it taught you more profound lessons than winning did. The victors believed themselves and their worldviews justified and validated and learned nothing. The losers had to reevaluate everything they had thought to be true and worth fighting for, and so had a chance of learning, the hard way, the deepest lessons life had to teach. The first thing he learned was that *now he knew where the bottom was.* When you hit bottom you knew how deep the water you were in really was. And you knew that you never wanted to be there again.

He was beginning to learn the lesson that would set him free: that to be imprisoned by the need to be loved was to be sealed in a cell in which one experienced an interminable torment and from which there was no escape. He needed to understand that there were people who would never love him. No matter how carefully he explained his work or clarified his intentions in creating it, they would not love him. The unreasoning mind, driven by the doubt-free absolutes of faith, could not be convinced by reason. Those who had demonized him would never say, "Oh, look, he's not a demon after all." He needed to understand that this was *all right*. He didn't like those people either. As long as he was clear about what he had written and said, as long as he felt good about his own work and public positions, he could stand being disliked. He had just done a thing that had made him feel very bad about himself. He would rectify that thing.

He was learning that to win a fight like this, it was not enough to know what one was fighting against. That was easy. He was fighting against the view that people could be killed for their ideas, and against the ability of any religion to place a limiting point on thought. But he needed, now, to be clear of what he was fighting for. Freedom of speech, freedom of the imagination, freedom from fear, and the beautiful, ancient art of which he was privileged to be a practitioner. Also skepticism, irreverence, doubt, satire, comedy, and unholy glee. He would never again flinch from the defense of these things. He had asked himself the question: *As you are fighting a battle that may cost you your life, is the thing for which you are fighting worth losing your life for?* And he had found it possible to answer: *yes*. He was prepared to die, if dying became necessary, for what Carmen Callil had called "a bloody book."

None of his true friends reacted like the Dismayed Ones. They drew closer than ever and tried to help him through what they could see was a profound trauma of the mind and spirit: an existential crisis. Anthony Barnett called, very concerned. "We need to set up a group of friends and advisers for you," he said. "You can't go through this alone." He explained to Anthony that he had, to be frank, lied when he made his assertion of religious belief. He told Anthony, "When I wrote the *Verses* I was saying, *we have to be able to speak like this about religion, we must be free to criticize and historicize.*" And if he now had to pretend that by *we* he meant only *we Muslims*, then he was stuck with that. For the moment. That was the price of what he had done.

"It's precisely this kind of well-intentioned misstatement," Anthony said, "that your friends need to advise you against."

He needed to get away somewhere and think. He put in a request to go quietly to France for a brief vacation but the French didn't want him on their soil. The Americans were still reluctant to have him on theirs. There was no way out of the box. There was one piece of good news, however. The "specific threat" against him was now thought to be a hoax. Mr. Greenup came to tell him, to warn him that the danger was still high—"Iranian-backed elements are still actively looking for you"—and to throw him a bone. He could start looking for a new, permanent home. "Maybe in a few months we will be able to make a more optimistic assessment." That cheered him up a little.

Gillon called him on February 15. The *fatwa* had been renewed. The British government remained silent.

Bill Buford and Alicja had decided to get married and Bill asked him to be best man. The reception was to be at the Midsummer House restaurant on Midsummer Common in Cambridge. Phil Pitt went to "do an advance" and without talking to Bill or to the owner, Hans, declared the restaurant unsuitable. For the first time he lost his temper with the police and told them it was not for them to decide whether or not he could be best man at his friend's wedding. So Phil did speak to Bill and discovered he had had the wrong information—the wrong time, the wrong room—and suddenly the venue was suitable after all. "We're the experts, Joe," he said. "Trust us."

Nigella's sister Thomasina had breast cancer. She had surgery at once. A quadrant of her breast was removed. Radiation therapy would come later. He heard Marianne on BBC Radio Four claiming she loved him but he was so obsessed with "the situation" that there was no room for anyone else, and that was the reason for their split. She described herself as "this brilliant woman." She was asked how she was dealing with life and she replied, "I'm making it up as I go along."

The *fatwa* was damaging more than one life. Zafar's headmaster at the Hall School, Paddy Heazell, was worried about him. "He seems to have a wall around him. Nothing gets through." A visit to a psychiatrist at Great Ormond Street Hospital might be a good idea. He was a bright, lovely boy, but something in him seemed to be asleep. He was shut away inside himself and thought himself a "failure." It was agreed that a female child psychiatrist would see Zafar weekly after school. However, Mr. Heazell was reassuring about Zafar's chances of getting into their preferred secondary school, Highgate, because Highgate stressed the value of interviewing prospective students, and didn't simply rely on Common Entrance results. "Zafar would always win an interview," Mr. Heazell said. But he stressed they needed to bring him out of his present dark place. "He's in a box," Mr. Heazell told Clarissa, "and he won't come out." That weekend Clarissa got Zafar a dog, a border collie–red setter mixture of a pooch called Bruno. The dog was important, and helped. Zafar was very excited.

He had given up smoking again but his resolve was about to be tested. He was told about new security precautions. For some time now a member of the team had been picking up the mail from Gillon's office and bringing it back, but now they wanted it to go via Scotland Yard again because it was too risky to have it driven directly from the agency to Wimbledon. Also they were putting a "double divert" on his phone to make it harder for calls to be traced. It felt as if the lid was being screwed on more tightly but he didn't know why. Then Mr. Greenup came to tell him why. A "team of professionals" had accepted a contract to kill him. Large sums of money were involved. The person behind it was "an Iranian government official outside Iran." The British were not sure if this was an officially sanctioned plan or a maverick operation but they were worried because of the extreme confidence of the hit squad, which had promised to carry out the assassination within four to six months. "Actually, they believe they can kill you in less than a hundred days." The Special Branch did not believe the Wimbledon house had been compromised but under the circumstances it would be preferable if he moved almost immediately. Zafar was a "problem," and a police watch would have to be placed on him. Elizabeth was a "problem" too. It might be necessary to move him onto an army base, to live in an army barracks, for the next half year. If he elected to go to a Security Service safe house he would be sealed away there from all contact with the outside world. However, this did not change the agreement that he could begin to look for a permanent home. Once they had come through the next few months that would be acceptable.

He refused the army base and the sealed-away safe house. If the Wimbledon place had not been compromised there was no reason not to stay there. Why should he lose months of rent and be sent on his travels again if they did not believe that the house had been "blown"? Mr. Greenup's face was its usual expressionless mask. "If you want to live," he said, "you will move."

"Dad," Zafar asked on the phone, "when will we have a permanent place to live?"

If he ever lived to tell the tale, he thought, what a tale of loving friendship it would be. Without his friends he would have been locked up on an army base, incommunicado, forgotten, spiraling downward into madness; or else a homeless wanderer, waiting for the assassin's bullet to find him. The friend who saved him now was James Fenton. "You can have this house," he said as soon as he was asked, "for a month, anyway."

After a rich life spent leaping onto the first Vietcong tank to enter Saigon at the end of the Vietnam War, and joining the crowds looting the Malacañang Palace to celebrate the fall of Ferdinand Marcos and Imelda of the Shoes (he took some monogrammed towels), investing some of the money he received for working on never-used lyrics for the original production of *Les Misérables* in a prawn farm in the Philippines, and journeying a little traumatically into Borneo with the even more adventurous Redmond O'Hanlon (when O'Hanlon later asked Fenton to go with him to the Amazon, James replied, "I would not go with you to High Wycombe")—oh, and coming up with some of the best poetry of love and war to be written in his or any generation—the poet Fenton and his partner, the American writer Darryl Pinckney, had settled into Long Leys Farm, a comfortable country property in Cumnor, outside Oxford, and here James had busied himself with creating the most exquisite of formal gardens under the looming shadow of a giant electricity pylon. This was the home he now offered to his fugitive pal, whose recent Dreadful Mistake he had treated in writing with gentleness and courtesy, describing how when the news of the Mistake was published, "somewhere between six and sixty million newspaper readers around the world set down their coffee cups and said: Oh. But every Oh that was uttered had its own special flavor, its own modifier, its own tinge of meaning. . . . Oh so they got him in the end! Oh how convenient! Oh what a defeat for secularism! Oh what a shame! Oh Allah be praised. For myself the Oh that escaped my lips began life as a vibrant little cerise cloud of wonderment. For a few seconds, as it hung in the air, I thought I detected in the cloud the broken features of Galileo. I looked again, and Galileo seemed to have turned into Patty Hearst. I thought of Oslo . . . no, not Oslo, the Stockholm syndrome." The rest of his long piece, ostensibly a review of *Haroun and the Sea of Stories* for *The New York Review of Books,* offered a portrait of the author as a good man—or at least an enjoyable person to talk to—whose unstated purpose was to restore, ever so delicately and without saying he was doing so, that author's good character in the eyes of the Dismayed Friends. That article had already been ample proof of James's big heart. To leave his home proved something more: his understanding of the need for solidarity in the middle of a war. One did not desert one's friends when they were under fire.

Mr. Greenup grudgingly gave his consent to the move to Long Leys Farm. "Mr. Anton" suspected that the police officer would have quite liked to lock him up on an army base to punish him for all the trouble he had caused, all the public expense he had incurred, but instead the little carnival of Operation Malachite had to pack up and abandon London SW19 for the formal gardens of Cumnor beneath their guardian pylon, which bestrode their narrow world like a colossus.

He saw that Elizabeth was distressed. The strain of the latest developments had muted the brilliance of her smile. The image of an assassination squad so sure of reaching its target that it was willing to give a deadline for the deed would have sent many women running, crying, "I'm sorry, but this isn't my fight." But Elizabeth bore up bravely. She would go on with her job at Bloomsbury and visit him on weekends. In fact she was considering giving up the job so that they didn't need to be separated, and because she wanted to write. She was a poet too, though she was reluctant to show him her work. She had showed him one poem about a man on a unicycle and he thought it pretty good.

He moved to Cumnor and for a time it was impossible to see Zafar or visit any London friends. He was trying to get his head around a new novel provisionally called *The Moor's Last Sigh* but his thoughts were all over the place and he went down a series of blind alleys. He had an instinct that the novel would somehow combine an Indian family story with the Andalusian tale of the fall of Granada, of the last sultan, Boabdil, leaving the Alhambra and, as the sultan's mother contemptuously said, "weeping like a woman for what he could not defend like a man" as he watched the sun set on the last day of Arab Spain, but he could not find the connection. He remembered Mijas, to which Clarissa's mother, Lavinia, had emigrated, and the book he had found there by Ronald Fraser, about the life of Manuel Cortés, mayor of Mijas when the civil war broke out. After the war Cortés returned home and had to be hidden from Franco for *thirty years* until he emerged like Rip van Winkle to witness the tourist ribbon-development devastation of the Costa del Sol. The name of the book was *In Hiding*.

He thought of Picasso and wrote a strange paragraph about the Málaga neighborhood where the great man was born. *In the square the children play, the children with both eyes on the same side of their nose. They play at Harlequin and Pierrot. A bomb like a lightbulb pierces a screaming horse. Newspapers stick to the sides of black guitars. Women turn into flowers. There is fruit. The afternoon is hot. The artist dies. They make him a lopsided coffin, a collage of sky and printed matter. He drinks at his own funeral. His women smile and spit and take his money.*

This artist did not find his way into the novel but in the end understanding came: It would be a novel about artists and the Alhambra of Andalusia would be painted by an Indian woman, standing on top of Malabar Hill in Bombay. The two worlds would meet in art.

He filled a notebook with a Beckettian or perhaps Kafkaesque first-person account written by a man who was regularly beaten, who was kept in a lightless room by unknown captors who entered in the dark to beat him every day. That was not what he wanted to write but these passages about beatings kept coming. One day there was a glimmer of light and he wrote a comic paragraph in which his narrator tried to describe his parents' first lovemaking, but was too embarrassed to include any verbs, *so you will not learn from me,* he wrote, *the bloody details of what happened when she, and then he, and then they, and after that she, and at which he, and in response to that she, and with that, and in addition, and for a while, and then for a long time, and quietly, and noisily, and at the end of their endurance, and at last, and after that . . .* This passage would make it into the finished book. Most of the rest was dross.

Valerie Herr had a cancer scare but the biopsy proved nonmalignant. *Thank goodness, Jim,* he thought. Angela Carter was less fortunate. The cancer had her in its grip and though she fought it hard she would not, in the end, defeat it. All over the world great writers were dying young: Italo Calvino, Raymond Carver, and now here was Angela wrestling with the Reaper. A *fatwa* was not the only way to die. There were older types of death sentence that still worked very well.

Paperback editions of *The Satanic Verses* were published in the Netherlands, Denmark and Germany. Iran held a conference of Muslim scholars that called for the Khomeini death order to be carried out as soon as possible. The 15 Khordad Foundation, the quasi-nongovernmental organization headed by Ayatollah Hassan Sanei that was behind the offers of bounty money, said it would pay $2 million to any friend, relative or neighbor of the author who carried out the threat. (The *bonyads,* or foundations, were originally charitable trusts that, after the Khomeini revolution, made use of the seized assets of the shah and other "enemies of the state" to become gigantic business consortiums headed by senior clerics.) "So many writers are short of money," he said to Andrew. "Maybe we should take this seriously."

There was no news of the assassination squad's whereabouts. The British government had said nothing about the *fatwa* for five months.

He talked to Bill Buford about the problems of finding and acquiring a new long-term home. Bill had a brainwave. Rea Hederman, the publisher of *The New York Review of Books* and *Granta,* employed a sort of personal fixer, a Mr. Fitzgerald, known to everyone as "Fitz," whose efficiency and solid, silver-haired demeanor would make him an ideal front man. Nobody would ever suspect Fitz of getting mixed up in anything as weird as the Rushdie Affair. He asked Hederman if it would be all right to involve Fitz, and Rea agreed at once. Yet again the circle of friends found solutions the authorities were unable or unwilling to offer. Fitz began the hunt and soon came up with a house in Highgate, north London, with a gated forecourt, an integral garage, enough room for both protection officers and both drivers to sleep on the premises, and a substantial and secluded garden, which would allow him to feel a little less like a mole in a hole. He would be able to go outside—into the sunlight, or even the rain, or the snow. The house, on Hampstead Lane, was immediately available for rent and the owners, whose name was Bulsara, were willing to negotiate a sale as well. The police looked at it and pronounced it ideal. The rental agreement was completed at once, in Rea Hederman's name. Joseph Anton was put into mothballs for a while.

All that mattered was that he would have a place to go. It was the end of March. He moved out of Long Leys Farm, hugging James and Darryl gratefully as he gave them back their home, and he and Elizabeth went for the weekend to Deborah Rogers and Michael Berkeley's farm in Wales. Here he was with friends for the first time in weeks. Deb and Michael were there, welcoming as ever, and Ian McEwan had come over with his two young sons. They walked in the hills and ate delicious beef lasagna. On Monday he would move into the new house. But first there was Sunday. Michael went out in the morning and got the papers. He came home looking upset. "I'm sorry," he said. "It's pretty bad."

Marianne had given an interview to *The Sunday Times*. The newspaper had put it on the front page. RUSHDIE'S WIFE SAYS HE IS SELF-OBSESSED AND VAIN, by Tim Rayment. "Salman Rushdie's wife yesterday denounced him as a weak, self-obsessed man who had failed to live up to the role history had given him. . . . 'All of us who love him, who were devoted to him, who were friends of his, wish that the man had been as great as the event. That's the secret everyone is trying to keep hidden. He is not. He's not the bravest man in the world, but will do anything to save his life.' " There was much, much more. She said he had told her he intended to meet with Colonel Gadhafi, and that was when she knew "I didn't want to be married to him at all." Interestingly, she now denied her previous allegation that when they separated the Special Branch had left her stranded in the English countryside next to a phone booth. No, that hadn't happened, but she wouldn't say what had. She accused him of leaving "screaming messages" on her phone, of manipulating the press, and of being uninterested in the broader issue of free expression. He was concerned only about himself. "The great fallacy he committed was to think he was the issue. He never was. The issues were free expression and the racist society in Great Britain, and he did not come forward and speak. What he's been speaking for during the past two years is Salman Rushdie's career."

She was an articulate speaker and it was a wounding attack. He understood what she was doing. People knew that he had been the one to end their marriage, and she had calculated that if she called him a weak cowardly Gadhafi lover and careerist, if she could erase his years of involvement on issues of free speech and liberty with British PEN and other groups, if she could wipe away the image of the young Booker Prize winner who, on the morning after his victory, was standing with a placard outside Downing Street to protest the arrest of the great Indonesian writer Pramoedya Ananta Toer, then she could make him, in the public's already jaundiced eye, a man not worth staying with, a man any decent woman would have to leave. She was delivering her exit lines.

He thought: *I gave her the weapons to strike me with. It's not her fault. It's mine.*

His friends—Michael Herr, Alan Yentob, Harold Pinter—called or wrote to her to express their anger and disappointment. She saw that the interview was not playing as she had hoped it would, and attempted the usual excuses, she had been misquoted, she had been "betrayed" by the newspaper, she had been publicizing her new collection of stories, she had wanted to talk about the work of Amnesty International; and she added that her husband had "ruined her career." These arguments did not go over well.

Imaginary Homelands had been published and for the most part it had been treated with respect, even admiration, but almost everyone lamented the final essay about his supposed "conversion." They were right to do so. He thought: *I have to undo the Dreadful Mistake. I have to unsay what I said. Until I do that I can't live with honor. I am a man without religion pretending to be a religious man.* "He will do anything to save his life," *Marianne says. Right now that sounds true. I have to make it untrue.*

All his life he had known that there was a small enclosed space at the center of his being that nobody else could enter, and that all his work and best thoughts flowed from that secret place in a way he did not fully understand. Now the bright light of the *fatwa* had blazed through the curtains of that little habitation and his secret self stood naked in the glare. *Weak man. Not the bravest man in the world. So be it,* he thought. Naked, without artifice, he would salvage his good name; and he would try to perform once again the magic trick of art. That was where his true salvation lay.

It was a big house, full of ugly furniture, but solid feeling, durable. It was possible to imagine a future. If Zafar got into Highgate School he would be nearby. Elizabeth, who loved Hampstead Heath above all things, was happy to be living at its northern rim. He began to be able to do a little good work and that April he wrote a short story, "Christopher Columbus and Queen Isabella of Spain Consummate Their Relationship," his first short story in a very long while, and the fog of unknowing that had concealed *The Moor's Last Sigh* from him began to dissipate. He wrote down names. Moraes Zogoiby, known as Moor. His mother, Aurora Zogoiby, was the painter. The family was from Cochin, where the West first met the East. The Western ships came not to conquer but to trade. Vasco da Gama was looking for pepper, the Black Gold of Malabar. He liked the idea that the whole, complex connection of Europe and India grew out of a peppercorn. He would grow his book out of a peppercorn too. The Zogoibys would be a family of spice traders. Half-Christian, half-Jewish, a "cathjew nut," the Moor would be almost a minority of one. But the book would try to show that the entire Indian reality could be grown out of that tiny peppercorn. "Authenticity" did not belong to the majority alone, as the Hindu majoritarian politics of India was beginning to insist. Every Indian person, every Indian story, was as authentic as every other.

But he had his own problem of authenticity. He could not go to India. How then could he write a true book about it? He remembered what his friend Nuruddin Farah had told him—Nuruddin, whose exile from Somalia had lasted twenty-two years, because the dictator Mohammed Siad Barre had wanted to see him dead. Every book Nuruddin wrote in exile had been set in a naturalistically portrayed Somalia. "I keep it here," Nuruddin said, pointing to his heart.

In May the two Regent's Park imams who had been at the Paddington Green meeting declared that he was not a true Muslim because he refused to withdraw his book. Other "leaders" announced their "disappointment," and said "we are back to square one." He wrote a sharp reply and published it in *The Independent*. That felt a good deal better. He felt himself rise an inch or two off the bottom and begin the long journey back toward himself.

Article 19 had been wondering if it was worth continuing to fund work on behalf of the International Rushdie Defense Committee. But Frances and Carmel were determined to go on, and, if anything, take the campaign to a new, more public level. As the British government slipped toward apathy on the issue, which encouraged Britain's European partners to follow suit, it would be the defense campaign that would have to take up the fight. Frances took Harold Pinter, Antonia Fraser and Ronnie Harwood with her to a meeting at the Foreign Office with Douglas Hurd, who told them that when the Tory minister Lynda Chalker visited Iran in April she had not raised the *fatwa* with anyone. To do so, Hurd said, would "not necessarily be helpful for Mr. Rushdie." Rumors that a "hit squad" had entered the country to hunt Mr. Rushdie down had begun to be reported in the press but Mr. Hurd was grimly determined to be helpful by keeping his mouth shut. Douglas Hogg, who had taken over from William Waldegrave as Hurd's deputy, also said that for the British government to make a loud noise about the *fatwa* would be a mistake, and would make it harder to obtain the release of the remaining British hostages in Lebanon.

One month later the failure of this kind of quietism became clear. Ettore Capriolo, the translator of the Italian edition of *The Satanic Verses,* was visited at his home by an "Iranian" man who, according to Gillon, had made an appointment to discuss "literary matters." Once the man was inside Capriolo's home he demanded to be given "Salman Rushdie's address" and when he didn't get it he attacked the translator violently, kicking and stabbing him repeatedly, then running away and leaving Capriolo bleeding on the floor. By great good fortune, the translator survived.

When Gillon told him the news he was unable to avoid the feeling that the attack was his fault. His enemies had been so good at shifting the blame onto his shoulders that now he believed it too. He wrote to Mr. Capriolo to express his sorrow and his hope that the translator's recovery would be full and quick. He never received a reply. Afterward he heard from his Italian publishers that Capriolo was not well disposed toward him and refused to work on any of his future books.

This was as close as the *fatwa* had come to its mark. And after the black arrow struck Ettore Capriolo it flew on to Japan. Eight days later, at the University of Tsukuba to the northeast of Tokyo, the Japanese translator of *The Satanic Verses,* Hitoshi Igarashi, was found murdered in an elevator near his office. Professor Igarashi was an Arabic and Persian scholar and a convert to Islam, but that did not save him. He was stabbed over and over again in the face and arms. The murderer was not arrested. Many rumors about the killer reached England. He was an Iranian who had recently entered Japan. A footprint had been found in a flowerbed and the shoe type was only to be found in mainland China. Names of visitors entering Japan from Chinese ports of departure were correlated against the names and known work names of Islamic terrorists, and there was a match, he was told, but the name was not released. Japan produced no fuel of its own and received much of its crude oil from Iran. The Japanese government had actually tried to prevent the publication of *The Satanic Verses,* asking leading publishers not to produce a Japanese edition. It did not want the Igarashi murder to complicate its dealings with Iran. The case was hushed up. No charges were brought. A good man lay dead but his death was not allowed to become an embarrassment.

Japan's Pakistan Association did not remain silent. It rejoiced. "Today we have been congratulating each other," it said in a statement. "God made sure that Igarashi got what he deserved. Everyone was really happy."

He wrote an agonized, apologetic letter to Hitoshi Igarashi's widow. There was no reply.

All over the world terrorist assassins were hitting their targets. In India, Rajiv Gandhi was assassinated while campaigning for reelection in the southern town of Sriperumbudur. He had been defeated in the election of 1989 in part, he believed, because the heavy security around him had created an aloof, distant image. This time he was determined to be closer to the people. As a result the Tamil Tigers' suicide bomber, a woman known as Dhanu, was able to come right up to him and detonate the belt of explosives around her waist. A photographer standing next to Rajiv was also killed but his camera remained intact and there were pictures of the assassination on the film inside. It was difficult to find enough of the former prime minister to cremate. In London, he was trying to make some sort of livable life. He mourned Hitoshi Igarashi and asked every day for news of Ettore Capriolo's health and hoped that if his turn came he did not take anyone with him because they were standing too close.

Joseph Anton, you must live until you die.

Zafar's visits to the school's recommended counselor, Clare Chappell, had helped. He was doing better at school and proud of his teachers' pleasure at his improvement. But now it was Elizabeth's well-being that had become a thing to worry about. They had done their best to keep their relationship a secret, known only to the inner circle of their friends, but the story was leaking out. "Everyone at the office knows about it," she said. "I spent all day shaking with the shock." Bloomsbury Publishing employed relatively few Islamic terrorists but she decided she wanted to leave. She would be with him full-time and write her poetry and not have to worry about loose talk. She did not make it sound like a sacrifice but he knew it was a big one, and that she made him feel that *it was really what she wanted, so he needn't feel badly about it,*

was further proof of her generosity of spirit. She walked out of Bloomsbury without a qualm and never spoke a word of accusation or regret.
Sections of the British tabloid press had begun to run entirely untrue
stories about what "Rushdie's new love" was costing the country, in-
sinuating that Elizabeth's entry into the story had upped the security
budget by hundreds of thousands of pounds. As the government ceased
to pursue his case, the press focus was changing to the cost of the protection. He was costing the country a fortune and was, of course, arrogant and ungrateful. And now the country had to pay for his
girlfriend too.

Elizabeth knew she wasn't costing the country anything and her
contempt for the fabricated stories was admirable.

Most of the time the house on Hampstead Lane felt worry-free
and permanent. It felt *there*. He didn't spend half his day worrying
about it being "blown" and having to make another sudden move.
Even when tradesmen came to the house things were calm. The place
was large enough for him to get on with his work while the gardener
mowed the lawn or the plumber plumbed or some piece of kitchen
equipment got repaired. The Bulsaras were relatively incurious landlords. Fitz was very convincing, and portrayed his boss as a high-flying
international publisher, often away, sometimes there; in other words,
not unlike the real Rea Hederman, even though the real Rea would
never have rented an eight-bedroom house on Hampstead Lane. Fitz
began to talk to them about the possibility of buying the house and
Mrs. Bulsara proposed a ridiculous price. "I've tried to negotiate her
down, sir," said Fitz, "but she's got pound signs in her eyes."

Then a new property came on to the market, very nearby in the
northern (and less pricey) reaches of Bishop's Avenue. It needed work
but the asking price was relatively reasonable. The owner wanted a
quick sale. Elizabeth went to see it, accompanied by Fitz and a member of the protection team, and they all liked it. "We can definitely
make it work," Elizabeth said and the police gave it the thumbs-up
too. Yes, he could have a permanent base again; it had been agreed at
the highest level, they said. He drove by the house twice but there was
no way for him to go inside. It stood behind a double-gated forecourt,
a mansion with a high-gabled roof and a whitewashed façade, anony-

mous and, yes, inviting. He took Elizabeth's word for it and moved as fast as he could. Ten days after Elizabeth saw 9 Bishop's Avenue for the first time they had exchanged contracts and the house was his. He couldn't believe it. He had a home again. "You should understand," he said to his new protection officer, a posh chap known to his colleagues as CHT (for Colin Hill-Thompson), "that once I move in there I'm never going to go on my travels again." Colin was perhaps the most sympathetic of all the officers he'd had on the team so far. "Quite right," he said. "Stick to your guns. They've approved it, and that's that."

The new house needed a lot of work. He called an architect friend, David Ashton Hill, and drew him into the heart of the secret. David, the next in the long sequence of Friends Without Whom Life Would Have Been Impossible, set to work at once; the construction workers were not allowed into the secret but were told "the story." 9 Bishop's Avenue was the intended London home base of Joseph Anton, international publisher of American origin. His English girlfriend, Elizabeth, was in charge of the works and would make all necessary decisions. The building contractor, Nick Norden, was the son of the comedy writer Denis Norden, and nobody's fool. It was difficult to explain to Nick why a publisher like Mr. Anton required bulletproof glass in the ground-floor windows, or a safe room upstairs. It was odd that Mr. Anton was never there for meetings, not even once. Elizabeth's good-natured Englishness was reassuring, of course, and Mr. Anton's Americanness could be blamed for a lot of his skittishness about security—Americans, as all Englishmen knew, were scared of everything; if a car backfired in Paris, everyone in America canceled their French holidays—but the truth, Mr. Anton suspected, was that Nick Norden and his builders knew perfectly well whose house they were doing up. But they didn't say so, preferring to act as if they had swallowed the story, and nobody ever leaked a word to the press. It took nine months to prepare the house for Mr. Anton, who lived there for the following seven years, and the secret was kept throughout that time. At the very end, one of the senior officers of "A" Squad confessed that they had expected the house to become public knowledge in a few months, and that everyone at the Yard had been amazed that it remained "covert" for eight years and more. Once again, he had reason to be grateful to the seriousness with which people responded to his plight. Everyone understood that this was an important secret to keep; and so, quite simply, they kept it.

He asked Fitz to prolong the rental period at Hampstead Lane. Fitz took it upon himself to negotiate the rent down—"They've been robbing you blind, sir"—and he succeeded, even though Mrs. Bulsara implored him, "Please, Mr. Fitz, you must persuade Mr. Hederman to pay more." He pointed out the problems with the property—there were two ovens in the kitchen, both out of order—and she said, as if it were a full and sufficient explanation, "But we are Indian, we cook on gas rings." Mrs. Bulsara bemoaned the loss of the sale, but continued to have an absurd idea of the value of the property. However, she agreed to lower the rent. Then out of the blue there were bailiffs at the door: High Court bailiffs, arriving to "seize the Bulsaras' assets."

The protection team, when faced with the unexpected, sometimes developed headless-chicken behavioral traits. Um, Joe, what's the story we're telling again? In whose name is the house rented? Joseph Anton, right? Oh, *not* Joseph Anton? Oh, that's right. Rea who? How do you spell that? Who are we saying he is? Oh, he actually *is* a publisher? Oh, okay. And, Joe, what is Fitz's full name? Okay, somebody had better answer the door. He said, "You guys have to get better at this." Later that day he wrote out the narrative and pinned it to their sitting-room door.

The bailiffs had showed up because the Bulsaras had defaulted on a monthly payment of just £500. Fitz took charge, calling the Bulsaras's lawyer, who faxed a letter to the bailiffs saying the check was in the mail. So in theory the bailiffs could show up every month? And they could be back tomorrow if the check turned out not to be in the mail? What was wrong with the Bulsaras' finances? This was awful; his solid-seeming house could melt away because of the landlord's money troubles, and in the months that would be needed to get the new place ready he would be homeless yet again. Fitz was unfazed. "I'll speak to them," he said. The bailiffs never returned.

There was the question of health and the related question of fear. He went to the doctor—a Dr. Bevan of St. John's Wood, known to the Special Branch, who had treated people receiving protection before—and his heart, blood pressure and other vital signs were all in excellent shape, surprising even the physician. His physiology had apparently not noticed that he was living in stressful circumstances. It was doing just fine, and the usual guardian angels of the stress sufferer, Ambien, Valium, Zoloft and Xanax—were not called upon. He had no explanation for his good health (and he was sleeping well, too) except that the soft machine of his body had somehow come to terms with what had happened. He had begun to write *The Moor's Last Sigh,* whose central character was a man aging at twice the normal speed. "Moor" Zogoiby's life was going by too fast and so death was approaching more swiftly than it should. The character's life relationship with fear was also his author's. *I'll tell you a secret about fear,* said the Moor. *It's an absolutist. With fear, it's all or nothing. Either, like any bullying tyrant, it rules your life with a stupid blinding omnipotence, or else you overthrow it, and its power vanishes in a puff of smoke. And another secret: the revolution against fear, the engendering of that tawdry despot's fall, has more or less nothing to do with "courage." It is driven by something much more straightforward: the simple need to get on with your life. I stopped being afraid because, if my time on earth was limited, I didn't have seconds to spare for funk.*

He didn't have time to sit in a corner and quake. Of course there was much to be afraid of, and he could feel the gremlin of fear stalking him, the bat-winged fear monster sitting on his shoulder nibbling eagerly at his neck, but he had understood that if he was to function he had to find a way of shaking the beasties off. He imagined himself trapping the gremlins in a small box and putting the locked box in a corner of the room. Once that was done, and sometimes it had to be done more than once a day, it was possible to proceed.

Elizabeth dealt with fear more simply. As long as the Special Branch teams were with them, she told herself, they would be safe. She never gave any sign of being afraid until the very end of the protection. It was freedom that made her fearful. Inside the bubble of the protection, she felt, for the most part, fine.

He was offered the chance to buy a newer, more comfortable car than the aging Jaguars and Range Rovers in the police fleet. It was an armored BMW sedan whose previous owner was the rag-trade millionaire Sir Ralph Halpern, the founder of Topshop, but better known as "five-times-a-night Ralph," after a young lover sold her story to the tabloids. "Who knows what happened in that backseat," mused Dennis the Horse. "But it's quite a catch, Sir Ralph's bimbomobile." It was worth £140,000 but was being offered for £35,000, "a steal," Dennis the Horse declared. It might even be permissible, the police hinted, if they were out of London and driving down country roads, for him to be allowed to drive the car himself. And the bulletproof windows could open, unlike the windows in the police Jaguars. Fresh air could, when it was deemed safe, be breathed.

He bought the car.

The first time he was driven anywhere in it was when he was taken to Spy Central. The headquarters of the British Secret Intelligence Service (SIS), familiar to fans of James Bond movies, sat across the Thames looking toward Random House as if it were an author in need of a good publisher. John le Carré in his Smiley books called SIS "the Circus" because its offices were supposedly at Cambridge Circus, which meant the spooks would have being looking out at Andrew Lloyd Webber's Palace Theatre. In parts of the Civil Service the SIS was called "Box 850," a PO box address once used by MI6. At the heart of Spyland sat the person who was not, in real life, called M. The head of MI6—this was no longer a secret—was called C. On those rare occasions when Mr. Anton of Hampstead Lane and later of 9 Bishop's Avenue was allowed to pass through those heavily guarded doors he never made it to the spider's lair, never met C. He was dealt with by officers from elsewhere in the alphabet, lowercase officers, one might say; though he did just once address a gathering of many of the service's capital letters. And he did, twice, meet the heads of MI5, Eliza Manningham-Buller and Stephen Lander.

On this first occasion, he was taken into a room that might have been a conference room in any London hotel to be given good news. The "specific threat" against him had been "downgraded." So the deadline for the assassination no longer stood? It did not. The operation, he was told, had been "frustrated." That was an odd and interesting word. He wanted to ask about this "frustration." Then he thought, *Don't ask*. Then he asked anyway. "Since this is my life we're talking about," he said, "I think you should tell me a bit more about why things are better now." The young executive across the shiny wooden table leaned forward with a friendly expression. "No," he said. That was the end of the discussion. Well, *no* was a clear answer, at least, he thought, unexpectedly amused. Source protection was an absolute priority in the SIS. He would be told only what his case officer believed necessary. Beyond that lay the Land of No.

The "frustration" of his enemies made him, for a moment, light-headed with delight, but back at Hampstead Lane, Mr. Greenup brought him down to earth. The threat level was still high. Certain restrictions would continue. He would not, for example, *allow* Zafar to be brought to the house.

He received an invitation to speak at an event at Columbia University, in the Low Memorial Library, to celebrate the two hundredth anniversary of the Bill of Rights. He had to start accepting such invitations, he thought; he had to emerge from invisibility and reclaim his voice. He talked to Frances D'Souza about trying to get Václav Havel to invite him to Prague so that the meeting the British had made impossible in London could take place on Havel's own turf. If Her Majesty's Government was giving up on the case they would have to internationalize the defense campaign and embarrass Thatcher and Hurd into making an effort. He would use any platforms that were offered to point out that his case was by no means unique, that writers and intellectuals across the Islamic world were being accused of exactly the same thought crimes as himself, blasphemy, heresy, apostasy, insult and offense, which meant that either the best and most independent creative minds in the Muslim world were degenerates, or else that the accusations masked the accusers' real project: the stifling of heterodoxy and dissent. To say this was not, as some people hinted, special pleading to attract more sympathy to his own case, or to justify his "outrages." It was just the truth. To make this argument effectively, he told Frances, he would also have to un-say what he had said, to un-make his Great Mistake, and he needed to un-say it loudly on the most visible platforms, at the best-reported events. Frances had strong protective feelings for him and worried that to do that might be to worsen his situation. No, he said, it would be worse to remain in the false situation he had created for himself. He was learning the hard way that the world was not a compassionate place, but there was no reason to expect it to be otherwise. Life was ungenerous to most people and second chances were hard to find. The comedian Peter Cook in the classic sixties revue *Beyond the Fringe* had advised people that the best thing to do in the event of a nuclear attack "was to be out of the area where the attack is about to occur. Keep right out of that area," he warned, "because that's the danger area, where the bombs are dropping." The way to avoid the world's lack of compassion for one's errors was to avoid making the errors in the first place. But he had made his error. He would do whatever it took to make that right.

"There will be repercussions even if it means death," said the spokesman of the Bradford Council of Mosques. "In sentencing the author of *The Satanic Verses* to death the judgment of the imam was flawless," said the garden gnome. Meanwhile in Paris a death squad entered the home of the exiled ex-president of Iran, Shapur Bakhtiar, an opponent of the ayatollahs' regime, and murdered him and an aide with knives in what was described as a "ritual killing."

There was a coup in Moscow against Mikhail Gorbachev and for three days he was under house arrest. When he was freed and flew back to Moscow there were reporters waiting by the plane to ask him if he would now abolish the Communist Party. He looked horrified by the question and at that moment, precisely then, history (in the form of Boris Yeltsin) rushed by him and left him trailing in its wake. Yet he, not Yeltsin or Reagan or Thatcher, was the man who changed the world by forbidding the Red Army to fire on demonstrators in Leipzig and elsewhere. Many years later the formerly invisible man would meet Mikhail Gorbachev at a fund-raising event in London. "Rushdie!" cried Gorbachev. "I totally support all your positions." There was even a small hug. *What, all of them?* he asked the man with the map of Antarctica tattooed on his forehead. "Yes," said Gorbachev, through his interpreter. "Total support."

He was writing a monograph about the film *The Wizard of Oz* for his friend Colin MacCabe at the British Film Institute. The two great themes of the film were home and friendship and he had never felt the need for both more strongly. He had friends every bit as loyal as Dorothy's companions on the Yellow Brick Road, and he was about to have a permanent home again, after three years on the road. He wrote a dystopian short story, "At the Auction of the Ruby Slippers," as a companion piece to the essay. The slippers that could take you home whenever you wanted them to: What was the value of such things in a violent science-fiction future in which everything was for sale and home had become a "scattered, damaged" concept? The essay pleased Bob Gottlieb at *The New Yorker* and he published a large piece of it before the BFI booklet was published. The actor who played the Munchkin coroner, Meinhardt Raabe, read it in a retirement home in Fort Lauderdale and sent in a fan letter, accompanied by a gift: a color photograph of his big scene from the movie. He stood on the steps of the Munchkin town hall holding up the long scroll, at the top of which were the large Gothic letters reading CERTIFICATE OF DEATH. Under that legend Raabe, using a blue ballpoint pen, had carefully inscribed the words *Salman Rushdie*. When he saw his name on the Munchkin death certificate his first thought was, *How funny is that, really?* But then he thought, *No, I get it, Mr. Raabe in his retirement home shoots letters off to people all over America, all over the world, he's another Herzog blasting his words into empty space, except that he also has a big stack of these pictures by his bedside and sends one of them with every letter. It's his calling card. He doesn't think, Oh, but this particular guy actually has a death order out on him, maybe I should be a little more sensitive. He writes, signs, mails. That's what he does.*

After the booklet was published Colin MacCabe told him that many people at the BFI had been terrified to be associated with a book by the notorious Mr. Rushdie. Colin had managed to assuage at least some of their fears. The book came out and there were no rivers of blood. It was just a little book about an old movie. But he had understood that before he could be free again he would have to overcome other people's fears as well as his own.

———

The British hostage John McCarthy was released in Lebanon.

The "A" Squad chiefs decided it was time to *allow* Zafar to visit his father at Hampstead Lane. Mr. Greenup at first suggested that the boy should be blindfolded so that the location was not compromised but that was out of the question and Greenup did not press the point. That afternoon Zafar was brought to the house and his happiness lit up its ugly interior and made it beautiful.

Frances called him, excited. She had been asked to tell him in confidence that *Haroun and the Sea of Stories* had won a Writers' Guild Award for the best children's book of the year. "They would love it if you could somehow come to collect your prize." Yes, he told her, he too would very much like to be there. He went to see Michael Foot who said, "Good. The mood has changed. We have to see Hurd again and be much tougher in our demands." He loved Michael's appetite for the fight, undiminished by his advancing years. That, and his head for whiskey, only rivaled by that of Christopher Hitchens. When drinking with Michael it had more than once been necessary to pour his Scotch surreptitiously into a potted plant.

He told the police about the Writers' Guild Award. The ceremony would be at the Dorchester Hotel on September 15. The protection team made sharp-intake-of-breath noises of demurral. "Don't know how that'll go down at the office, Joe," said Benny Winters, looking, in his sharp tan leather jacket, a little like Lenny Kravitz with shorter hair. "But we'll run it by them for sure." The result of running it by them was a visit from Mr. Greenup at his grimmest, accompanied by another senior police officer, a woman, Helen Hammington, who didn't say much at first.

"I'm sorry, Joe," said Mr. Greenup. "I can't *allow* that."

"You won't *allow* me to go to Park Lane to collect my literary award," he replied, slowly. "You won't *allow* this even though only one person, the event organizer, would have to know in advance, and we could arrive after people are seated for dinner, be there perhaps ten minutes before the award ceremony, collect the prize and then leave before the ceremony ends. This is what you won't *allow*."

"For security reasons," Mr. Greenup said, setting his jaw. "It's most unwise."

He inhaled deeply. (His reward for giving up smoking was the arrival of late-onset asthma, so he was sometimes short of breath.) "You see," he said, "I was under the impression that I am a free citizen of a free country, and it's not really for you to *allow* or not *allow* me to do anything."

Mr. Greenup lost his composure. "It is my view," he said, "that you are endangering the citizenry of London by reason of your desire for self-aggrandizement." This was an astonishingly composed sentence—*citizenry, by reason of, self-aggrandizement*—and he never forgot it. A pivotal moment—what Henri Cartier-Bresson had called *le moment décisif*—had arrived.

"You see," he said, "here's the thing. I know where the Dorchester Hotel is and as it happens I have the money to pay for a taxi. So the question is not whether or not I'm going to the awards. I *am* going to the awards. The only question you have to answer is, are you coming with me?"

Helen Hammington joined the conversation and told him that she was replacing Mr. Greenup as the senior case officer at the Yard. This was extraordinarily good news. She then said to Mr. Greenup, "I think we can probably handle this." Greenup went bright pink but said nothing. "It has been decided," Hammington went on, "that we should probably *allow* you to go out a bit more."

Two days later he was at the Dorchester in the bosom of the book world and received his award, a glass inkwell on a wooden plinth. He thanked the people in the room for their solidarity and apologized for materializing and dematerializing in the middle of dinner. "In this free country," he said, "I am not a free man." The standing ovation actually brought tears to his eyes, and he was not a man who cried easily. He waved at the audience and as he left the room he heard John Cleese at the mike saying, "Oh, *great*. I'm supposed to follow *that*." It had been a harmless little bit of self-aggrandizement after all. The citizenry of London were safe in their tuxedos, their homes, their beds. And he never saw Mr. Greenup again.

The angel of death never seemed to be far away in those strange days. Liz called: Angela Carter had been told she had no more than six months to live. Zafar called him in tears. "Hattie is dead," he said. Hattie was May Jewell, Clarissa's Anglo-Argentine grandmother, a fan of wide-brimmed hats and the model for the character of Rosa Diamond in *The Satanic Verses,* outside whose house in Pevensey Bay, Sussex, Gibreel Farishta and Saladin Chamcha had landed on sand after falling out of an exploding jumbo jet, and lived. Some of May Jewell's favorite stories—in London, in Chester Square Mews, she had once seen the ghost of a stableboy who looked as if he was walking on his knees until she realized that he was walking on the old, lower street level and so was visible only from the knees up; in Pevensey Bay the invading fleet of the Norman Conquest would have sailed through her living room, because the coastline had changed since 1066; in Argentina the bulls at her *estancia* of Las Petacas would come and lay their heads in her lap as if they were unicorns and she a virgin, neither of which was the case—had found their way into his pages. He had been very fond of her stories, of her hats, and of her.

Helen Hammington came to see him again to tell him what the police felt would be all right for him to do under the new, liberalized rules. They could take him, by arrangement, to shop for clothes and books after hours. Perhaps he would like to make a shopping expedition out of London, to somewhere like Bath, for example, in which case he could even go when the shops were open. If he wanted to do book signings that might be possible as long as they too were away from London. His friend Professor Chris Bigsby had invited him to read at the University of East Anglia, and perhaps he could accept invitations of that sort. Occasional outings to the Covent Garden Opera House or the English National Opera, or to the National Theatre, could be made to work. She knew that Ruthie Rogers, co-owner of the River Café in Hammersmith, was his close friend, so maybe he could go to dinner there, or at the Ivy, where the owners, Jeremy King and Chris Corbin, would also be helpful. Oh: and Zafar would now be *allowed* not only to visit, but also to spend the night at Hampstead Lane. Mr. Greenup's departure had certainly altered things.

(What he was *not allowed* to do: to live publicly, to move freely, to pursue the ordinary life of a writer or of a free man in his forties. His life was like a severe diet regime: Everything that was not expressly *allowed* was forbidden.)

On November 11 it would be one thousand days since Bruce Chatwin's memorial service and the declaration of the *fatwa*. He talked to Frances and Carmel about how to use the moment politically. They agreed to hold a twenty-four-hour "vigil" in Central Hall Westminster. When news of this was published he was called by Duncan Slater. Douglas Hurd, Slater said, was asking for the vigil to be canceled and threatening that if it was not, the Rushdie defense campaign would be blamed—perhaps even by the government—for delaying the release of the British hostage Terry Waite. Michael Foot was furious when he was told this. "Giving in to threats encourages hostage taking," he said. But in the end the event was canceled at the *fatwa* victim's request. Terry Waite's human rights had to be given precedence over his own.

The head of the Frankfurt Book Fair, Peter Weidhaas, had wanted to reinvite Iranian publishers, but uproar in Germany prevented him from doing so.

The thousandth day arrived. He completed an essay, "One Thousand Days in a Balloon," to mark its arrival. PEN American Center held a rally and delivered a protest letter to the United Nations. His British friends, their vigil canceled, read letters of support at a bookstore on Charing Cross Road. However, *The Independent* newspaper, which was becoming a sort of house journal for British Islam, carried an article by the "writer" Ziauddin Sardar, who said, "The best course for Mr. Rushdie and his supporters is to shut up. A fly caught in a cobweb does not draw attention to itself." The fly in question called the editor of that newspaper to tell him that he would no longer write reviews for its books pages.

On November 18 Terry Waite was freed by his captors. There were no more British hostages in Lebanon. How, he wondered, would the authorities try to silence him now? He had his answer soon enough. On November 22, the archbishop of Canterbury, George Carey, decided to attack *The Satanic Verses* and its author. The novel, Carey said, was an "outrageous slur" on the Prophet Muhammad. "We must be more tolerant of Muslim anger," the archbishop declared.

He fought back in a radio interview, and the British press came down heavily against the archbishop. Carey backed down and apologized and invited the man whose work he had condemned to tea. The invisible man was driven to Lambeth Palace and there was the prim figure of the archbishop and a dog asleep in front of a fire and here was a cup of tea: one cup and, disappointingly, no cucumber sandwiches. Carey was clumsy and stumbling and didn't have much to say. When asked if he would try to intercede with Khamenei to have the *fatwa* revoked, as one man of the cloth to another, he replied feebly, "I don't think he would pay much attention to me." The purpose of the tea was no more than damage limitation. It was soon over.

And there were rumors that the British were preparing to exchange ambassadors with Iran and resume full diplomatic relations. He needed a public platform urgently. The date of the event at Columbia University was fast approaching and it seemed very important indeed that he be there, that his voice be heard. But there were still two American hostages in Lebanon and it was not clear that he would be allowed to enter the United States. And how would he travel? No commercial airline was willing to have him as a passenger. The police told him that there were military passenger planes flying between the United Kingdom and the United States most weeks. Maybe he could get a seat on that. They made inquiries and yes, he would be allowed to travel on a military flight. But it was still not clear that he could make the trip.

Duncan Slater called to apologize for the "confrontation" over the thousandth-day vigil and said there was "no hurry" to exchange ambassadors. He was being sent on a posting abroad, he said, and David Gore-Booth would take his place as the FCO's liaison man. He had liked Slater and felt supported by him. Gore-Booth was a very different proposition: darker, brusquer, more abrasive.

Joseph Cicippio was freed on December 1 and the last American hostage, Terry Anderson, was released a week later. The Americans kept their word and lifted their embargo on his journey. The trip to the Low Library was on.

He would cross the ocean on a Royal Air Force flight to Dulles International Airport in Washington, D.C. A private plane, belonging, he was told, to the head of Time Warner, would be made available for his journey to New York and back. In New York he would be met by an

NYPD security detail. As the date of his departure approached these plans kept altering, agonizingly. The private plane from D.C. to Manhattan turned into a car, then a helicopter, and then became a plane again. Andrew had planned a dinner at which he could meet influential New Yorkers, and an "arts lunch" with, perhaps, Allen Ginsberg, Martin Scorsese, Bob Dylan, Madonna, Robert De Niro. It sounded too fanciful, and it was. He was told he would not be allowed to leave his hotel at all except to speak at Columbia. He would not be allowed to join the diners in the Low Library, but would go there to make his speech and then immediately leave. He would fly back to D.C. that same night and take the RAF flight back to the United Kingdom. U.S. embassies worldwide had been put on high alert and had taken on extra security in case there were Islamic reprisals against America for allowing him into the country. Everyone he or Andrew spoke to was very, very nervous—the RAF, the Ministry of Defence, the U.S. embassy, the U.S. State Department, the British Foreign Office, the NYPD. He said to Larry Robinson on the phone, "It's easier to get into the Garden of Eden than the United States. To enter Paradise all you need to do is be good."

As the date approached the United States kept pushing back the departure hour. Finally, on Tuesday, December 10, International Human Rights Day, and the day before his speech at Columbia, he boarded the RAF transport and, with his back to the direction of travel, left British soil for the first time in three years.

He was met on the tarmac at Teterboro Airport in New Jersey by a nine-car motorcade with motorcycle outriders. The central car was an armored white stretch limo. That was his car. In charge of the very large number of NYPD officers involved was Lieutenant Bob Kennedy, known, for the day, as "Hudson Commander." Lieutenant Bob introduced himself and explained the "scenario," often breaking off to speak into his sleeve. *Roger Hudson Lookout this is Hudson Commander over. Roger that. Over and out.* Policemen nowadays spoke the way they had seen policemen speak on TV. Lieutenant Bob, it was clear, thought he was in a major movie. "We'll be moving you through the city to the hotel in this vehicle right here," he said redundantly as the motorcade set off.

"Lieutenant Bob," he said, "this is a lot. The nine vehicles, the motorbikes, the sirens, the flashing lights, all of these officers. Wouldn't it actually be safer just to drive me through the backstreets in a used Buick?"

Lieutenant Bob looked at him with the pitying look people reserve for the chronically stupid or insane. "No, sir, it would not," he replied.

"Who else would you do something on this scale for, Lieutenant Bob?"

"Sir, this right here is what we'd do for Arafat." It was something of a shock to be bracketed with the leader of the Palestinian Liberation Organization.

"Lieutenant Bob, if I was the president, how much more would you do?"

"Sir, if you were the president of these United States, we'd close down a whole bunch of these side streets here, and, sir, we'd have snipers on the rooftops along the route, but in your case we didn't think that was necessary because it would look too conspicuous."

The inconspicuous nine-vehicle motorcade rolled toward Manhattan with motorcycle sirens blaring and lights flashing, attracting no attention at all.

Andrew was waiting for him at the hotel. In the presidential suite there were bulletproof padded mattresses covering all the windows even though they were on the top floor, and there were perhaps two dozen men holding gigantic science-fiction weapons scattered through the rooms. Andrew had arranged for him to have two visitors. Susan Sontag came first to hug him and tell him everything that PEN American Center had done and would do on his behalf. Then Allen Ginsberg arrived at one door and Susan had to be shown out through another so that the two American giants did not meet. He was not sure why this was necessary, but Andrew said it would be for the best, so the clash of literary egos was avoided, and when Ginsberg came in wearing sandals and carrying a little rucksack he sized up the situation and said firmly, "Okay, we're going to meditate now." He began pulling cushions off the sofas and putting them on the floor. The Indian writer thought, *This is unusual, here's an American teaching me how to say* om shantih om. Aloud he said, to be mischievous, "I'm not meditating unless Andrew Wylie meditates as well." And then there they were all sitting cross-legged on the floor chanting about *shantih,* peace, while the army of men with science-fiction weaponry looked on and the bulletproof padding shut out the cold December sun. When he had finished his meditation session Ginsberg handed out several booklets about Buddhism and left.

A little while later Elizabeth arrived unannounced and Lieutenant Bob brought her in to see him, surrounded by armed men. "It's okay, Lieutenant Bob," he said. "Elizabeth's cool. Elizabeth's with me."

Kennedy narrowed his eyes. "If I wanted to kill you, sir," he said insanely, wearing his best Crazy Jack Nicholson look, "she's exactly who I'd send."

"How so, Lieutenant Bob?"

Kennedy gestured toward a table on which there was an arrangement of fruits and cheeses as well as cutlery and plates. "Sir, if she were to take one of those forks there and stab you in the neck, I'd lose my job. Sir."

Andrew Wylie was finding it difficult to keep a straight face and Elizabeth was known as the Mad Forkist for the rest of the trip.

That evening they were in the armored white stretch limo in the middle of the nine-vehicle motorcade with the motorcycle outriders and the sirens and flashing lights, zooming down 125th Street toward the Columbia campus at sixty miles an hour with the whole of Harlem out on the sidewalk watching the low-profile operation ghost almost imperceptibly by, and Andrew was screaming with delight at the outrageousness of it all, "This is the best day of my *life!*"

Then the fun, the slightly hysterical, black-comedy fun, was over. He was concealed behind a curtain at the Low Library and when his name was announced there was a shocked gasp and he moved forward, out of invisibility into the light. Then there was welcoming, affectionate applause. The lights were in his eyes and he couldn't see the room, he had no idea who was out there, but he had his speech to make, his one thousand days in a balloon to describe. He asked his audience to think about religious persecution, and the question of what a single human life was worth, and he began the long business of unmaking his Mistake, unsaying what he had said, restoring himself to the ranks of the advocates of liberty and leaving God behind. He would have to unsay the Mistake over and over again for many years but that night when he admitted his error to the distinguished audience at Columbia and stood up again for what he most passionately believed—*free speech is the whole ball game,* he said, *free speech is life itself*—he felt cleaner, and in the audience's sympathetic response he heard compassion. If he had been a religious man he would have said he felt shriven, absolved of his sins. But he was not religious and would never again feign religiosity. He was a proudly irreligious man. *Don't pray for me,* he had said to his mother. *Don't you get it? That's not our team.*

Once the speech was over America unceremoniously threw him out. There was no time to say goodbye to Andrew or Elizabeth. Lieutenant Bob sat in the front of the white limo while it rushed through the night to MacArthur Airport at Islip on Long Island and there was the plane waiting to take him to Dulles, where he boarded the RAF transport along with all the military personnel and then he was back in his cage. But he had traveled, and he had spoken. The first time was the hardest, and all the difficulties had been overcome, and ahead of him lay the second time, and the third, and the fourth. There might not be light at the end of the tunnel yet, but at least he was in the tunnel now.

The "Balloon" essay replaced the "conversion" text in the paperback edition of *Imaginary Homelands* and at last he could stop cringing every time he saw a copy of that book. *At last,* he thought when the paperback arrived. *This is the real book. Its author is the real me.* His burden felt less heavy. He made his break with the dentist Essawy and left those well-manicured toenails behind forever.

Dear Religion,

Can I raise the question of first principles? Because, strangely, or not so strangely, the religious and nonreligious can't agree on what these are. To the reasonable Greek man approaching the question of truth, first principles were starting points (arche) and we perceived them because we possessed aware-

ness / consciousness (nous). By the use of pure reason, and relying on our sensory perception of the world, Descartes and Spinoza believed that we could arrive at a description of truth that we recognized as true. Religious thinkers, on the other hand—Aquinas, Ibn Rushd—maintained that reason existed outside human consciousness, that it hung out there in space like the northern lights or the asteroid belt, waiting to be discovered. Once discovered it was fixed and immutable, because it was preexisting, see, it didn't rely on us to exist, it just was. This idea of disembodied reason, absolute reason, is a little hard to swallow, especially when you, Religion, join it to the idea of revelation. Because then thinking is over, isn't it? Everything that needs to be thought has been revealed and we're stuck with that, eternally, absolutely, without hope of appeal. God, one might well cry, help us. I'm with the other team, which believes that unless first principles of this type can be challenged by first principles of the other type—by finding new starting points, applying our consciousness and sensory awareness of what-is to those starting points, and so coming up with new conclusions—we're done for, our brains will rot, and men in turbans and long beards (or men in frocks pretending to be celibate while molesting young boys) will inherit the earth. However, and this may confuse you, in cultural matters I am not a relativist and I do believe in universals. Human rights, for example, human freedoms, human nature and what it wants and deserves. Consequently I do not agree with Professor S. Huntington's notion that reason belongs to the West and obscurantism to the East. The heart is what it is and knows nothing of compass points. The need for liberty, like the inevitability of death, is a universal. It may not preexist, being a consequence of our essential humanity, but it is not negotiable. I understand, Religion, that this may confuse you, but I am perfectly clear about it. I asked my nous and it gave me the thumbs-up. Discuss. By all means. Discuss. Oh. P.S. What's up with those Pakistani official forms (all of them, for everything) that insist you state your religion, and won't accept "none" for an answer? "None" is considered as "spoiling" the form and you have to fill out another one or risk the consequences, which might well be dire. I don't know if this is the case in other Muslim countries but I kind of suspect it might be. That's a little extreme, Religion, don't you think? Borderline fascistic, even? What sort of club is it that makes it compulsory to be a member? I thought the best clubs were exclusive and tried their damnedest to keep the riffraff out.

Discuss this also. Please.

Dear Reader,

Thank you for your kind words about my work. May I make the elementary point that the freedom to write is closely related to the freedom to read, and not have your reading selected, vetted and censored for you by any priesthood or Outraged Community? Since when was a work of art defined by the people who didn't like it? The value of art lies in the love it engenders, not the hatred. It's love that makes books last. Please keep reading.

He made new year's resolutions. To lose weight, to get his divorce, to write his novel, to have *The Satanic Verses* published in paperback, and to get the *fatwa* canceled. He knew that he would be unable to keep all these promises to himself. But three or four out of five would be good. He lost fifteen pounds in the next six weeks. That was a good start. He bought his first computer. Like many old-technology people he worried that it might change his writing. Many years earlier he and Fay Weldon had done a joint reading in Kentish Town and during the Q & A a woman had asked, "When you're typing and you x-x-x out a sentence, do you go on writing, or do you take the sheet of paper out of the typewriter and start the page all over again?" Both he and Fay had answered that they took the paper out and started all over again, *obviously.* Like many writers he had a fetish for clean copy, and the ease of "cleaning up" a page on this miraculous gadget was enough to convince him of its value. The less time he spent on retyping, the more time he would have for doing the actual writing. *The Moor's Last Sigh* would be the first novel he wrote on a computer.

The house at St. Peter's Street needed to be sold. His expenses were huge and the money would be very useful. While the tabloid press continued to complain that he was costing the United Kingdom too much money, his own resources were near breaking point. He had bought (and was refurbishing) a large house, where he and the protection team could live happily ever after, and a bulletproof bimbomobile. He was buying a two-bedroom flat in Hampstead so that Elizabeth could have a "public" home address, buying it in her name as a gift. Fortunately, Robert McCrum of Faber and Faber wanted to buy the Islington house and they quickly agreed terms. But the sale stalled when the sale of Robert's existing home fell through. He said there were other people interested, however, and hoped to be able to go ahead soon.

He met Duncan Slater for the last time. Slater was off to be British ambassador to Malaysia. They spoke for three hours and the upshot was that "HMG" had been affected by the louder noises he had begun to make, especially at Columbia. "Hurd recognizes you have a large constituency," Slater told him. "It's not necessarily his, but it's large and impossible to ignore." The foreign secretary had understood that the Rushdie case couldn't be swept under the carpet. "We might be able to get the bounty money canceled," Slater said. Well, that would be a good start, he replied. "The FCO isn't pleased about your plans for the paperback, though."

On Elizabeth's birthday, a few days later, they heard that Angela Carter's cancer was in both lungs. It was hard for her to breathe and she had only a few weeks left. Her beautiful little boy, Alex, had been told. The idea of losing her was unbearable, but as his mother used to say, *what can't be cured must be endured.* Two weeks later, Angela invited him to tea. It was the last time he saw her. When he got to the old familiar Clapham house he found that she had hauled herself out of bed and dressed up for him and was sitting upright in an armchair pouring tea like a formal hostess. He could see what an effort it was for her, and how much it mattered to her to do this, so they had a proper afternoon tea together and laughed as much as they could. "The insurance people will be furious," she cackled, "because I've only paid three years' premiums on a *huge new plan* and now they have to pay up, so my boys will be all right." Her boys were her husband, Mark, who sat silently with them as was his wont, and her son, Alex, who wasn't there. After a short time she was exhausted and he got up to go and kissed her goodbye. "You take care," she said, and that was that. Four weeks after their tea she was dead.

His closest friends—Caroline Michel, Richard and Ruth Rogers, Alan Yentob and Philippa Walker, Melvyn Bragg and others—were planning a public event to take place on the third anniversary of the *fatwa,* with many leading writers attending. Günter Grass said yes, he would come, and so did Mario Vargas Llosa and Tom Stoppard, and those who couldn't come—Nadine Gordimer, Edward Said—promised to send video messages. What was not being publicly announced was that he himself would make a "surprise" appearance. The venue was the Stationers' Hall, the old guildhall where many years earlier, in another life, he had received his Booker Prize.

That young writer would not have had to listen to his publishers refusing to publish his paperback, but the golden years were over. He met Peter Mayer at Gillon's home and Mayer was finally clear. No, he didn't see the day when Penguin would publish a paperback edition of *The Satanic Verses,* though he would personally guarantee that the hardcover would be kept in print; and yes, he would, therefore, allow paperback rights to revert to the author so that some kind of consortium publication could be put together. Everyone tried to be polite and gracious even though it was a shocking moment. Mayer's lawyer Martin Garbus was present again and opined that in America a consortium led by the American Booksellers Association, PEN American Center and the Authors Guild might be possible. The next day he called Frances D'Souza and, without any authority to do so, claimed that *he* was setting up a consortium, and asked her if Article 19 would be willing to serve as the book's UK publishers. (Garbus would later claim in *The New York Times* that he had indeed been behind the creation of the consortium that published the book, a claim so much the opposite of the truth that it had to be swiftly refuted.)

His life was like a day of high winds that sent clouds rushing across the sun: first darkness, then sudden light, then gloom again. The day after the Penguin meeting Sameen's second child was born in the Florence Ward of Northwick Park Hospital in Harrow: a second daughter, Mishka. She would grow up to be a piano virtuoso, bringing music into a family which, until her arrival, had been comically unmusical.

He was told by Special Branch that the latest intel suggested that Hezbollah units were still actively trying to hunt him down and kill him. There was no change in the threat assessment, which remained at Ludicrously High.

Andrew met in New York with the United Nations' Giandomenico Picco, the negotiator who had engineered the release of many of the Lebanon hostages, including John McCarthy. Picco said, of the Rushdie case, "I have worked on this and am working on it." Some months later, in Washington, D.C., the invisible man was able to meet with the secret negotiator, and Picco gave him a piece of advice he would always remember. "The trouble with negotiating such a deal," Picco said, "is that you spend a lot of time waiting for the train to arrive at the station, but you don't know at which station it will arrive. The art of the negotiation is to be standing at as many stations as possible, so that when the train arrives, you are there."

In Berlin the newspaper *Die Tageszeitung* began a campaign of "Letters to Salman Rushdie." The letters would be reprinted in two dozen newspapers across Europe and the Americas, and Peter Carey, Günter Grass, Nadine Gordimer, Mario Vargas Llosa, Norman Mailer, José Saramago, and William Styron were among the great writers who had agreed to contribute. When Carmel Bedford called Margaret Atwood to ask her to write a letter, the mighty Peggy said, "Oh, my, what could I possibly say?" To which Carmel with steely Irish ballsiness, answered, "Use your imagination." And there was one great novelist who called him who did not contribute but was perhaps the most exciting of all to hear from. It was Thomas Pynchon, another famous invisible man, calling to thank him for his review of *Vineland* in *The New York Times Book Review,* and asking solicitously how he was doing. He replied by quoting the title of the cult classic by Pynchon's friend Richard Fariña, the dedicatee of *Gravity's Rainbow:* "Been down so long it looks like up to me." Pynchon suggested that whenever next they were both in New York together they might meet for dinner. "Oh my goodness," he said, sounding like a spotty schoolboy with a crush, "ooh, yes, please."

Putting together a consortium of publishers, booksellers, industry organizations and prominent individuals in the book world had not been difficult in Germany and Spain. Everyone had wanted to be part of what they saw as an important defense of free expression. Mysteriously, it was proving to be a very different matter in the United States. Andrew had taken advice from Justice William Brennan, one of the

American "Supremes," from the celebrated constitutional lawyer Floyd Abrams, and from the former attorney general Elliot Richardson, and they had all agreed that the paperback publication of *The Satanic Verses* was a major First Amendment issue. America's eight leading publishers all disagreed. One after the other the great figures of U.S. publishing denied that freedom of expression was an issue in this matter, murmuring that to join a consortium would be an "implicit criticism" of Peter Mayer and Penguin. Sonny Mehta said to him, "What if people just don't want to do it, Salman—if they just want it to go away?" Andrew heard that the Association of American Publishers was actually forming an unofficial anti-publication cartel to support Peter Mayer (whom they liked) and to oppose his own efforts, because, to be frank, they didn't much care for the notorious Andrew Wylie, whose client was reputed to be pretty unpalatable as well. People were not returning his calls. Doors were being shut in his face. *The New York Times* reported that efforts to form a consortium were "faltering." But Andrew—and Gillon in London—remained grimly determined. "We can publish this paperback," they said, "and we will."

One single publisher broke ranks with the rest. George Craig of HarperCollins told Andrew he would—quietly—help. He could not authorize HarperCollins to join the consortium but he could and would bankroll the printing of the first one hundred thousand copies, and provide a designer to create a paperback jacket; and he would show Andrew how to set up the printing, warehousing and distribution system the consortium would need to keep publication going. But even Craig was nervous; he didn't want it known that he was doing anything. And so, covertly, surreptitiously, a publishing plan came together, like the planning of a crime by men in snap-brim hats and outsized overcoats grouped around a wooden table in a basement under a single naked lightbulb. The company, named *The Consortium, Inc.,* was incorporated in Delaware. There were three members of the Consortium: Gillon Aitken, Salman Rushdie and Andrew Wylie. Not a single American, or indeed British, publisher added his name officially or—George Craig honorably excepted—gave the project any financial or organizational support. Andrew and Gillon poured their money into the project too and reached an agreement with their author about how any profits might be divided. "We're doing this," Andrew said. "We're just about ready to go."

He had bought Elizabeth's flat and was still waiting for Robert McCrum to complete the purchase of the house on St. Peter's Street. The building works at 9 Bishop's Avenue were costing a small fortune and money was tight. If for some reason Hampstead Lane were to be "blown," he thought, he probably couldn't afford another high-priced rental. It might have to be the army base after all.

Valentine's Day was almost upon him and the usual unpleasant noises were being made. The *fatwa* was restated, of course. An Iranian newspaper described the order as a "divine command to stone the devil to death." Iran's British lackey Kalim Siddiqui spoke up from under his toadstool. "Rushdie is Islam's Enemy Number One." But this time there were a few answering cries. One hundred and fifteen European MPs signed a motion expressing "deep sympathy for the continuing difficulties experienced by the author," and calling upon all member states to press Iran to withdraw the threats. David Gore-Booth told him that Douglas Hogg and the Foreign Office were taking a "very positive" line, but wanted to wait until after the April elections to the Iranian Majlis. Then they could seek to have the bounty revoked and to get the *fatwa* formally "ring-fenced"—that is, to get the Iranians to declare it to be valid only inside Iran—as a first step toward its final cancelation.

He was a little encouraged. At least the defense campaign's pressure was obliging the government to come up with new ideas about the case.

Then a very surprising thing happened. Frances and Article 19's Middle East expert Saïd Essoulami wrote to the Iranian *chargé d'affaires* asking for a meeting to discuss the case—and the Iranians agreed. On the morning of February 14, 1992, Frances and Saïd met Iranian officials and discussed the *fatwa* and the bounty money. The Iranians gave very little away, but they had plainly been rattled by the pro-Rushdie publicity, Frances thought. They insisted to her and Saïd that the British government was not interested in the case. (When news of this meeting got into the press, the Iranians tried to deny that it had taken place, and then claimed that only a "local employee" and not any of the mission's diplomatic staff had been present.)

There were protests and statements in his support all over the world that day. In France seventeen million people watched a TV interview he had recorded: the largest audience ever measured in France for a program other than the main evening news. That evening at the Stationers' Hall in London he spoke to an audience of writers and friends, telling them, "I refuse to be an un-person. I refuse to forgo the right to publish my work." The event was sympathetically covered in all the British newspapers except *The Independent*, which failed to mention it at all.

Angela Carter died on February 16, 1992. When the phone call came he stood in his living room and wept. Then he was wanted for the *Late Show*, to talk about her. A media appearance was the last thing on his mind, but Alan Yentob said, "Angela would have wanted it to be you," so he wrote something and was taken to the studio. When he got there he said, "I'm doing exactly one take of this. I'm not going to be able to do two." He got through it somehow and went home. Another version of his piece ran in *The New York Times*. He had just finished his essay about *The Wizard of Oz* and he remembered that it was Angela who had first told him the tales of the Munchkins' dreadful behavior in Hollywood, their drunkenness and promiscuity. She had particularly loved the story of the boozed-up Munchkin who got stuck in a toilet bowl. He dedicated his little book to her. Unlike that old fraud, Oz, the Great and Terrible, she had been *a very good wizard,* as he wrote in his newspaper piece, *and a very dear friend.*

She had made detailed arrangements for her funeral service and he was commanded to participate and to read Andrew Marvell's poem "On a Drop of Dew":

> *So the Soul, that Drop, that Ray*
> *Of the clear Fountain of Eternal Day*
> . . . .

Does, in its pure and circling thoughts, express
The greater Heaven in an Heaven less.

On the day before the funeral the tabloids ran more unpleasant stuff about Elizabeth and her "expense" to the nation. They had no photograph of her, however, and the police warned him that if they went to the service the paparazzi would hound them and get the picture that would place her in greater danger. He said they would go separately then and Helen Hammington's sympathetic mask slipped. He was making too many demands on the Branch, she said, because of his public appearances. "Every other principal you protect," he pointed out, "has a full daily program of events and you don't complain. I want to go to my friend's funeral and you say it's too much." "Yes," she said, "but every other principal is performing or has performed a service to the nation. You, in my opinion, have not."

In the end Elizabeth did not go to the service at Putney Vale Cemetery. There was not a single press photographer at the event. The police had been wrong about that. They did not say so, of course. They were planning for the worst-case scenario as they always did. He would not live his life by the worst-case scenario. That would turn him into their prisoner. He was nobody's prisoner. He was an innocent man trying to lead a free man's life.

Michael Berkeley told him afterward that the presence of so many policemen in the crematorium grounds on the day of the funeral had provoked the following exchange among the congregation emerging from the previous cremation: "Must be someone really important on next." And, just as Michael was about to interject, yes, someone *really* important, Angela Carter, he heard the reply. "Nah. Probably just some villain let out of the Scrubs for the morning to bury his mother."

The protection officers themselves continued to be as friendly, sympathetic and helpful as they could. When Zafar wanted to demonstrate his prowess at rugby the new guy, Tony Dunblane—he of the dashing mustache and tweed jackets, like a pirate from the suburbs—took father and son to the police sports ground at Bushey and the guys lined up like a three-quarter line so that Zafar could run and pass the rugby ball. (Zafar had done his entrance exam and interview for Highgate School and, to his parents' great joy and infinite relief, won himself a place. He knew he had achieved a big thing for himself and his confidence soared, just as his mother and father had hoped.) Elizabeth was methodically going about the business of choosing furniture and wallpaper for the new house as if they were any couple setting up home together and Tony brought back pictures of the latest, state-of-the-art sound systems and TV sets and offered to assemble everything they selected once they had all moved in. And when Robert McCrum finally did exchange contracts and the deal to sell 41 St. Peter's Street was done the police took him back to what was no longer his home and helped him box up his possessions and take them out to a waiting van to be stored at a police lockup until they could be brought to the new house. The ordinary human kindness of these men toward a fellow human being in "one hell of a jam," as Tony Dunblane put it, never ceased to move him.

It took almost five hours, with Elizabeth's help, to pack up Marianne's effects. Hidden among her belongings he found all the pictures he had taken on his trip to Nicaragua in 1986, about which he had written his short book of reportage, The Jaguar Smile. And all the negatives, too. (Later, Gillon's colleague Sally Riley, appointed by Marianne to receive her possessions, returned other discoveries—an antique stone Gandhara civilization head that his mother had given him, and a bag of his photographs—not the ones from the missing albums, but the spares, rejects and double prints. At least these few reminders of his life before Marianne had been salvaged. Images of Zafar's birth and early moments were especially good to regain. The main body of the missing photographs, the ones pasted into the lost albums, was never recovered.)

The difficulties of the everyday—or that calamitous distortion of the quotidian that had become "everyday" to him—continued, like an invader, to occupy him. Andrew Wylie had been trying to buy a new apartment; when the co-op board learned that he was the literary agent for the author of The Satanic Verses, it turned him down. Communicating this news, trying to sound as if it didn't matter, Andrew had never sounded so low. It was a poor reward for all he had done, and was doing, on his author's behalf. This story, at least, had a happy ending. Not long after his rejection, Andrew found a better apartment, and this time the co-op board did not refuse him.

Then, a bombshell. Helen Hammington came to visit and the iron fist emerged from the velvet glove. After he and Elizabeth had settled into the new house, she said, police protection would be withdrawn, because Deputy Assistant Commissioner John Howley was not willing to risk the safety of his men in what would inevitably become an overt protection.

It was a breathtaking betrayal of trust. From the first day of the protection he had been assured that it would continue until the intelligence services' threat assessment came down to an acceptable level. That had not happened. Moreover, it had been Howley and his henchman Greenup who had suggested that the time had come when he should buy a place. They had specifically assured him that if the proper security systems were installed the protection could continue in that location even if it became known as his house. They had obliged him to buy a detached property, with a forecourt and two separate gates, one electronic and one manually operated (in case of power cuts), an integral garage whose automatic wooden door would conceal a sheet of bulletproof metal; he had been obliged to install the expensive bulletproof windows and alarm systems they had insisted upon, and, most of all, had had to buy a house more than double the size he and Elizabeth needed for themselves, so that four police officers—two protection officers and two drivers—could sleep on the premises, and have their own living room as well. He had spent a huge amount of money and effort satisfying every requirement, and now that he had spent that money and was nailed to the spot they were saying, "Okay, we'll be off, then." The immorality of it was almost impressive.

The real reason was cost, he knew that; cost, and the tabloid mentality that believed he didn't deserve what it might cost to protect him properly, overtly, as they protected everyone else.

Certain things about the *fatwa* were known at that time: not publicly known, but known among the people who needed to know, including himself and Deputy Assistant Commissioner Howley. The threat was not merely theoretical. There was a special task force inside the Iranian intelligence ministry whose duty was to make and carry out a plan to put the Khomeini order into effect. The task force had a code name, and there was a chain of approval in place. A plan would be developed, then approved by different levels up to and including the president, and finally signed off on by the religious leadership. That was the normal Iranian modus operandi. The task force that had executed Shapur Bakhtiar had almost certainly operated the same way. That Howley should be prepared to withdraw protection knowing what he knew, and so soon after the Bakhtiar killing, revealed a lot about his thinking. *We've never lost anyone,* the members of his protection team had told him, proudly, but Howley was telling him something different. *We don't care if we lose you.* That felt . . . bad.

He said to Elizabeth that she should consider her own safety. If the police left there was no saying how dangerous life might become. "I'm not leaving you," she replied.

Somehow he managed to do a little work. He completed a synopsis of *The Moor's Last Sigh* that finally made some sort of sense. It had taken him a long time to get right. Now all he needed was the peace of mind that would allow him to write it.

He had been invited by the writer Scott Armstrong to speak at the Freedom Forum in Washington, D.C., in late March, and he wanted to go. It seemed probable that meetings with senior American politicians and journalists could be arranged while he was in D.C. He decided he would use the platform to express his doubts about the British commitment to his safety—to begin the fightback in a place where the media were more likely to give him a sympathetic hearing. Andrew told him he would do everything in his power to get him a copy of the paperback of *The Satanic Verses* in time for the forum. That would be a reply to the censors that the forum might very well wish to hear. The book was actually at the printer at last. It had been delayed by Penguin, who had somehow failed to sign the reversion document until the eleventh hour, and had then argued that the now-famous cover image of the two grappling, tumbling figures, a prince and a demon, belonged to them (it had actually been taken from an old Indian miniature, *Rustam Killing the White Demon,* from the *Shahnama,* or Book of Kings, the original now preserved in a Clive Album at the Victoria & Albert Museum). Eventually Penguin had given up being obstructive and signed on the required dotted lines and the printing and binding machines had been turned on. After all these years, paperbacks were actually beginning to exist.

After much reluctance the RAF agreed to fly him to Dulles and back on one of their regular transport flights—just this one more time. The service would not be available to him in the future. Also, on this occasion they would ask him to pay not only for his own seat but for the seats of the two RAF security personnel who would travel to America and back with him. Humbly, having no alternative, he paid up. He thought often of a line from a song by John Prine: *There's a hole in Daddy's arm where all the money goes.* The *fatwa* was his heroin. It made him spend everything he earned and, though it might end up killing him, it didn't even give him a high.

Before he left for America, Fat Jack "wanted a word" on behalf of the lads. They were all worried about proposed changes in the status of "A" Squad that, if put into effect, would push them out of Special Branch and strip them of their detective status. Some of their Tory principals were working to have these changes scrapped but there was a general election imminent and what if the Labour Party got back into power? The latest polls showed Labour leading the Tories by 3 percent. Might he perhaps be able to talk to his chum Neil Kinnock on their behalf if Kinnock became prime minister? "Frankly," he said, "vis-à-vis Labour, you're just about all we've got."

The alarm rang at half past five in the morning and they creaked out of bed. The protection team took Elizabeth to Swiss Cottage so that she could catch a train to Heathrow and then he was driven to RAF Brize Norton through the pretty Cotswolds dressed in early morning mist and began his second trip abroad in three years.

At Dulles he was met by a private security firm hired by the Freedom Forum at the shocking cost, he later learned, of $80,000. His detail chief was a sweet-natured fellow who asked if he could have copies of the paperback edition for himself and his team. The total number of copies he wanted was over fifty. That was alarming: How big *was* this team? "Sure," he said. "I'll get them for you."

He met Elizabeth and Andrew at a conference center called Westfields six miles from Dulles. He was to do his interviews in the Windsor suite. He had grown up in Bombay in a house called Windsor Villa, a part of the Westfield Estate. The coincidence made him smile. Long days of interviews followed, and all the journalists were excited, even aroused, by the cloak-and-daggery. They had been brought to this location by security and had not known where they were going in advance. A big thrill. The *fatwa* was the only subject that interested most of the media. Only Esther B. Fein of *The New York Times* actually wanted to talk about his writing, and how he managed to do it in these extraordinary conditions.

Scott Armstrong, burly, businesslike, every inch the D.C. insider, had bad news: The meeting with congressmen planned for the next day had been canceled after, according to his information, an intervention by Secretary of State James Baker himself. Why was Baker doing this? The answer became clearer in the following days, when the George H. W. Bush administration refused all requests for meetings and declined to make a statement on the case. The White House press secretary, Marlin Fitzwater, said, "He's just an author on a book tour."

Andrew lost his temper and accused Scott of having tricked them. Voices were raised. Scott was furious with Andrew but rightly suggested they shelve their anger and see what could be salvaged. They had dinner with Mike Wallace and a few others. Here, in confidence, and to enlist the sympathies of these august journalists, the true nature of the Consortium was revealed, as well as the hostility of the U.S. administration and the possibility of the British withdrawing protection.

It was time for his speech. He was wearing a burgundy linen suit that was by now spectacularly crumpled but there was no time to change. He looked like a nutty professor but maybe that was okay. He was more worried about his words than his appearance. The language of political speeches was alien to him. He believed in pushing language, making it mean as much as he could make it mean, listening to the meaning of its music as well as its words; but now he was supposed to speak plainly. *Say what you really mean,* he had been told; *explain yourself, justify yourself, don't hide behind your fiction.* Did it matter if a writer was denuded in this way, stripped of the richness of language? Yes, it did, because beauty struck chords deep within the human heart, beauty opened doors in the spirit. Beauty mattered because beauty was joy and joy was the reason he did what he did, his joy in words and in using them to tell tales, to create worlds, to sing. And beauty, for now, was being treated as a luxury he should do without; as a luxury; as a lie. Ugliness was truth.

He did the best he could. He asked for American support and help, for America to show itself to be "the true friend of liberty," and spoke not only of the freedom to write and publish but also of the freedom to read. He spoke of his fears that the British were prepared to abandon him to his fate. Then he announced that after many adversities it had finally been possible to publish a paperback of *The Satanic Verses,* and he held up a copy of the book. It was not an attractive edition. It had a hideous gold cover with large thick black and red lettering that looked a little too much like Nazi typography. But it existed, and that felt very good. Three and a half years after the novel was first published he had managed to complete the process of publication.

There were journalist friends in the audience, Praful Bidwai from *The Times of India* and Anton Harber, whose *Weekly Mail* had tried to invite him to South Africa in 1988. But he was not able to linger and chat. The security team spoke of the "risk of snipers." The building across the street "had Libyan connections." *Ah, yes, Colonel Gadhafi, my old friend,* he thought. He was spirited away.

Elizabeth had been "looked after" by Scott's wife, Barbara, and she told him the security people had not let her enter the conference room, and made her sit in a garage. She was graceful about it, but now it was his turn to get furious. They were taken to stay at the welcoming home of an extremely talkative seventy-five-year-old gentleman named Maurice Rosenblatt, a powerful liberal lobbyist who had played

an important part in the downfall of Senator Joseph McCarthy. While
Rosenblatt soliloquized Andrew was still fuming with rage about the
canceled Congress meeting. Then Scott called and Andrew went for
him. "I'll tell you what an asshole you are later," Scott said, and asked
to speak to Mr. Rushdie, to whom he said, "I don't owe Andrew an
explanation, but I do owe you one." As they were talking Peter Galbraith, a senior staff member for the U.S. Senate Committee on Foreign Relations, whom he had never met, but knew as the son of John
Kenneth Galbraith and, more salaciously perhaps, as the young university lover of Benazir Bhutto, came through on the other line to say that
the meeting was on again. There would be a lunch at the senators'
private dining room hosted by Senators Daniel Patrick Moynihan and
Patrick Leahy, and many other senators would come. The temperature
came down rapidly. Andrew calmed down and apologized to Scott,
Scott felt vindicated, and there was much relief. They went to bed
exhausted but feeling a good deal better.

It was their first time in Washington and the next day he and
Elizabeth had their first sight of the citadels and fortresses of American
might. Then Elizabeth was left to explore the Smithsonian and the
Botanical Gardens and he was taken to the Capitol and Senator Leahy
was advancing toward him, big and avuncular and bear-pawed. And
here were Senators Simon, Lugar, Cranston, Wofford, Pell, and the
great man himself, Daniel Patrick Moynihan, skyscraper tall as befitted
the senior senator from New York, bow-tied, with that professionally
puckish grin. They listened carefully as he went through the situation
and then it was Senator Simon who leaped in first, insisting that the
Senate pass a resolution of support. Soon they were all coming up with
proposals, and it was exciting, no doubt about that, to have these men
rallying to his flag. By the end of lunch (chicken salad, no possibility
of alcohol) Moynihan had taken charge and suggested that he and
Leahy draft a resolution and put it to the Senate. It was a huge step.

Andrew had arranged for everyone at the meeting to be given copies of the *Satanic Verses* paperback, but now, amazingly, the senators
pulled out multiple copies of earlier books and wanted them personalized and signed for themselves and their families too. He was not often
impressed by book signings but this one was an astonishment.

Then another surprise. The senators led him to an antechamber of the Foreign Affairs Committee and there was a huge throng of journalists and photographers waiting for them. Scott had been "working his ass off" and Andrew owed him an apology. Andrew did in fact apologize later that day. "I don't really do this," Scott said. "I'm a writer not a publicist. Normally I'm trying to break down security around a story, not maintain it." But his affability returned.

And so now here was the author of *The Satanic Verses,* "just an author on a book tour," giving a press conference at the heart of America's power with the senators standing behind him like a backup group, all holding copies of The Paperback in their hands. If they had broken out into a little *doo-wop, shang-a-lang* chorus it would not, on that day of amazements, have been very surprising.

He spoke about this being one battle in a larger war, about the assault on creative and intellectual freedoms across the Muslim world, and expressed his gratitude to the gathered senators for their support. Moynihan took the microphone and said it was an honor to be standing beside him. He was plainly no longer in England. That was not what politicians said about him there.

They had dinner—in a restaurant!—with Scott and Barbara Armstrong and Christopher and Carol Hitchens. Marianne was living in D.C., Christopher said, but he didn't think she would say anything hostile because it would mess up her "connections" with "the people she wants to know." She did indeed remain silent, which was a blessing. The next day he recorded a one-hour special with Charlie Rose and in the afternoon did a one-hour phone-in program with John Hockenberry for NPR. A nine-year-old girl called Erin called to ask, "Mr. Rushdie, do you have fun writing your books?" He said he had had a lot of fun writing *Haroun.* "Oh, *sure,*" Erin said, "I've read *that* book. *That's* a *good* book." Later a Muslim called Susan came on the air and wept a lot and when Hockenberry asked her if she thought Mr. Rushdie should be killed she said, "I'd have to read up on that."

Scott had called his friend Bob Woodward for help and was very struck, he said, "by the depth of Bob's commitment." Woodward had arranged something pretty special: a tea with the legendary Katherine Graham, owner of *The Washington Post.*

In the car on the way to Mrs. Graham's house he felt so tired that he almost fell asleep. But adrenaline was a helpful little biochemical and once he was in the great lady's presence he was alert again. The op-ed columnist Amy Schwartz was there. She wrote the editorials about him, he was told. Not all of them had been friendly. David Ignatius, the foreign editor, was there too, and wanted to discuss the approaching Iranian elections. Don Graham, Mrs. Graham's son, was "one hundred percent on board," Scott told him.

He had to do almost all the talking. The *Post* journalists asked questions and he answered. Mrs. Graham hardly spoke, except when he asked her directly why she thought the U.S. administration had acted so offhandedly. "This is such a strange government," she said. "It has so few power centers. Baker's one. He's a funny man, always seems to have his own private agenda." Ignatius chipped in to echo something Woodward had also said. "The best route to the administration might be through Barbara Bush." After the meeting he said to Scott that he would just have to hope that the *Post* would back him now. "Kay Graham wouldn't have seen you," Scott said, "if the decision to support hadn't already been taken." So it was work well done. *The New York Times* had already said it would back him if other papers came in too. If Graham was in, so would Sulzberger be, and Andrew thought he could bring in Dow Jones and Scott believed he could deliver Gannett. He would draft a two-part statement for them all to sign: support for the paperback publication and support for its author against the *fatwa,* and, at the end, a demand that the U.S. administration join in and lend its support as well.

In fact, *The New York Times* didn't wait to sign a support statement. As if energized by his meeting with its Washington rivals, the *Times* ran an editorial on the morning after his tea with Queen Kay, attacking the White House and State Department for their hands-off approach. *"This is sadly consistent with three years of official waffling ever since Ayatollah Khomeini denounced* The Satanic Verses *as blasphemous and called for the death of its author and publishers. Mr. Rushdie has since lived in hiding. His Japanese translator was stabbed to death, his Italian translator wounded in a knife attack. Meanwhile exiled opponents of the Iranian regime were assassinated in France and Switzerland. If this is not state-sponsored ter-*

rorism, what is? Yet the West's response has been shamefully squeamish. . . . Far more than Mr. Rushdie's life is at risk if Western states do not jointly warn Iran that it cannot win the trade it covets until it ceases exporting and exhorting terrorism." Nations acted in their own self-interest. For Iran to cancel the *fatwa* it would be necessary to show Iran that it was in its interest to do so. This was what he had said to Mrs. Graham and to Mike Wallace before her. Now *The New York Times* was saying it too.

Elizabeth was taken to her plane and a few hours later he was on an RAF flight out of America. The high life was over. In London the police didn't want to take him to Angela Carter's memorial event at the Ritzy cinema in Brixton. He came down to earth with a bump, and argued for a long time until they agreed he could go. Elizabeth went separately as usual. The Ritzy, gaudy, down-at-the-heels, seemed perfect for Angela. On the stage there was a large three-panel screen painted by Corinna Sargood in very bright colors, featuring macaws. And a big spray of flowers. On the walls there were panels showing movie scenes. Nuruddin Farah embraced him and said, "There is a woman I am very serious about I want you to meet." He replied, "There is a woman I am very serious about I want *you* to meet." Eva Figes hugged him too. "It's so nice to have you to touch instead of seeing you on TV." Lorna Sage spoke, wonderfully describing Angela's laugh—the mouth opened wide in a great rictus and then her silent shaking for several minutes before the noise came. She had met Angela after reading *Heroes and Villains* and had praised her writing effusively. "I must have sounded very strange," she said, "because after a while Angela drew herself up and said, 'I'm not gay, you know.' " After the ceremony the police made him leave at once. Clarissa and Zafar were there too but he wasn't allowed to say hello to them. "I came after you but you'd gone," Zafar told him later. He had followed his father out of the side door and watched him being whisked away.

41 St. Peter's Street was empty, most of the furniture in storage, or given away to Sameen and Pauline, or used to furnish Elizabeth's new flat near Hampstead Heath. The keys were sent to Robert McCrum and then the sale was complete. A chapter of life was closing.

On April 9 Melvyn Bragg and Michael Foot threw a joint election-night party at Melvyn's Hampstead house. The night began in a celebratory mood with high expectations of an end to the long years of "Tory misrule." But as the evening went on it became plain that Kinnock had lost. He had never seen a party die so fast. He left early because it was just too sad to stay there among all the broken hopes.

One week later Helen Hammington asked for another meeting. He told her he would want his lawyer present, and his solicitor Bernie Simons was brought to Hampstead Lane. Helen Hammington looked uneasy and embarrassed as she told him of the "revised plans" for his protection. As she spoke it became clear that she, and Howley behind her, were climbing down completely. The protection would continue until the threat level dropped. If the new house "went overt" then they would take that in their stride.

He would always believe that he had America—the senators, the newspapers—to thank for this little success. America had made it impossible for Britain to walk away from his defense.

VI

Why It's Impossible
to Photograph
the Pampas

ON A VISIT TO MIJAS LONG AGO—MIJAS, WHERE MANUEL CORTÉS HAD hidden from Franco for three decades, spending his days in an alcove behind a wardrobe and, when his family had to move house, dressing up like an old woman to walk the streets of the town whose mayor he had been—he had met a photographer of German origin named Gustavo Thorlichen, a tall, handsome man with aquiline features, sleek silver hair, and three good stories to tell. The Mijas expat tribe whispered that he was probably an ex-Nazi because he had ended up in South America. In fact he had fled Germany in the 1930s to Argentina to escape the Nazis. One day in Buenos Aires he had been summoned to take photographs of Eva Perón, "one of four photographers," the Perón aide told him on the phone, "to be so honored." He took a deep breath and replied, "Thank you for the honor, but when you ask me to take photographs, you should ask me to come by myself, and in these circumstances I must respectfully decline." There was a silence, and then the aide said, "You can be thrown out of Argentina for what you have just said." "If I can be thrown out for saying that," Gustavo answered, "then it's not worth staying." He put down the phone, went into the bedroom and told his wife, "Start packing." Twenty minutes later the phone rang again and the same aide's voice said, "Evita will see you tomorrow morning at eleven, alone." After that he became the personal photographer of both Eva and Juan Perón, and the famous photograph of Evita's face in death was, he said, his.

That was the first good story. The second involved hanging out with the young Che Guevara in La Paz and being called a "great photographic artist" in Che's "motorcycle diaries." The third was about being in a bookstore in Buenos Aires as a young photographer, just starting out, and recognizing the much older man shuffling into the store as Jorge Luis Borges. He screwed up his courage, approached the great writer, and said he was working on a book of photographs that would be a portrait of Argentina and he would be very proud if Borges were to write a foreword. To ask a blind man to write the preface to a book of images was crazy, he knew that, but he asked anyway. Borges said to him, "Let's go for a walk." As they strolled through the city Borges described the buildings around him with photographic accuracy. But every so often there was a new building in the place of a demolished old one. Then Borges would stop and say, "Describe it. Start on the ground floor and go up." As Gustavo spoke he could see Borges putting up the new building in his mind and fixing it in its place. At the end of the walk Borges agreed to write the foreword.

Thorlichen had given him a copy of the *Argentina* book and even though it was boxed away somewhere now with almost all his possessions he still remembered what Borges had written about the limits of photography. Photography only saw what was in front of it, and that was why a photograph could never capture the truth of the great Argentinian pampas. "Darwin observed, and Hudson corroborated him," Borges wrote, "that this plain, famous among the plains of the world, does not leave an impression of vastness on one regarding it from the ground, or on horseback, since its horizon is that of the eye and does not exceed three miles. In other words, the vastness is not in each view of the pampas (which is what photography can register) but in the imagination of the traveler, in his memory of days on the march and in his prevision of many to follow." Only the passage of time revealed the infinite vastness of the pampas, and a photograph could not capture duration. A photograph of the pampas showed nothing more than a large field. It could not capture the delirium-inducing monotony of traveling on, and on, and on, and on through that unchanging, unending void.

As his new life stretched out into its fourth year he felt very often like that imaginary Borgesian traveler, marooned in space and time. The movie *Groundhog Day* had not yet been released but when he saw it he identified strongly with its protagonist, Bill Murray. In his life, too, each step forward was canceled by one going back. The illusion of change was undone by the discovery that nothing had changed. Hope was erased by disappointment, good news by bad. The cycles of his life repeated themselves over and over. Had he known that another six years of sequestration still stretched out in front of him, far beyond the horizon, then indeed dementia might have set in. But he could see only as far as the rim of the earth and what lay beyond it remained a mystery. He attended to the immediate and let infinity take care of itself.

His friends told him afterward that they saw the burden slowly crushing him, making him look older than his years. When it was finally lifted a sort of youth returned, as if at the end of the unendingness he had somehow made time reverse to the point at which he had entered the vortex. He would look younger in his fifties than he had in his forties. But his fifties were still half a decade away. And in the meantime many people, when his story was mentioned, grew impatient, or irritated, or bored. It was not a patient age, but a time of rapid change, in which no subject held the attention for very long. He became an annoyance to businessmen because his story got in the way of their desire to develop the Iranian market, and to diplomats trying to build bridges, and to journalists for whom, when there was nothing new to say, there was no news. To say that it was the unchangingness that was the story, the intolerable eternity of it, was to say a thing people could not or would not hear. To say that he woke up every day in a house full of armed strangers, that he was unable to stroll out of his door to buy a newspaper or pick up a cup of coffee, that most of his friends and even his family were unaware of his home address, and that he could do nothing and go nowhere except with the agreement of strangers; that what everyone else took for granted, air travel, for example, was a thing he had constantly to negotiate for; and that somewhere in the vicinity, always, was the threat of violent death, a threat that, according to the people whose job it was to assess such things, had not diminished in the slightest . . . this was dull. What, he was still traveling through the pampas, and everything was the same as before? Well, everyone had heard *that* story and didn't want to hear it anymore. *Tell us a new story,* that was the general opinion, *or else please go away.*

There was no point telling the world it was wrong. No mileage in that approach. So, yes, a new story. If that was what was wanted, that was what he would provide. Enough of invisibility, silence, timidity, defensiveness, guilt! An invisible, silenced man was an empty space into which others could pour their prejudices, their agendas, their wrath. The fight against fanaticism needed visible faces, audible voices. He would be quiet no longer. He would try to become a loud and visible man.

It was not easy to be thrust onto so public a stage. It took time to find one's bearings, to know how to act under all that light. He had fumbled and stumbled, had been stunned into silence and said the wrong things when he spoke. But there was more clarity now. At the Stationers' Hall he had refused to be an unperson. America had allowed him to begin his journey back to personhood, first at Columbia and then in Washington. There was more dignity in being a combatant than a victim. Yes; he would fight his corner. That would be the story from now on.

If he ever wrote a book about these years, how would he do it? He could change names, obviously—he could call these people "Helen Hammington" and "Rab Connolly" and "Paul Topper" and "Dick Wood," or "Mr. Afternoon"and "Mr. Morning"—but how could he convey what these years had been like? He began to think of a project provisionally called "Inferno" in which he could try to turn his story into something other than simple autobiography. A hallucinatory portrait of a man whose picture of the world had been broken. Like everyone he had had a picture of the world in his head that had made a kind of sense. He had lived in that picture and understood why it was the way it was, and how to find his way around inside it. Then like a great hammer swinging the *fatwa* smashed the picture and left him in an absurd formless amoral universe in which danger was everywhere and sense was not to be found. The man in his story tried desperately to hold his world-picture together but pieces of it came away in his hand like mirror shards and cut his hands until they bled. In his demented state, in this dark wood, the man with the bleeding hands who was a version of himself made his way toward the daylight, through the inferno, in which he passed through the numberless circles of hell, the private and public hells, into the secret worlds of terror, and toward the great, forbidden thoughts.

After a while he abandoned this idea. The only reason his story was interesting was that it had actually happened. It wouldn't be interesting if it wasn't true.

The truth was that the days were hard but, in spite of his friends' fears, he was not crushed. Rather, he learned how to fight back, and the immortal writers of the past were his guides. He was not, after all, the first writer to be endangered or sequestered or anathematized for his art. He thought of mighty Dostoyevsky facing the firing squad and then, after the last-minute commutation of his sentence, spending four years in a prison camp, and of Genet unstoppably writing his violently homoerotic masterpiece *Our Lady of the Flowers* in jail. The French translator of *Les Versets Sataniques,* unwilling to use his own name, had called himself "A. Nasier" in honor of the great François Rabelais, who had published his first book, *Pantagruel,* under the anagrammatic nom de plume of "Alcofribas Nasier." Rabelais too had been condemned by religious authority; the Catholic Church had been unable to stomach his satirical hyperabundance. But he had been defended by the king, François I, on the grounds that his genius could not be suppressed. Those were the days, when artists could be defended by kings *because they were good at what they did.* These were lesser times.

His Mistake had opened his eyes, cleared his thoughts and stripped him of all equivocation. He saw the gathering danger ahead because he had felt its dreadful demoralizing force within his own breast. For a time he had given up his language and been forced to speak, haltingly and with many contortions, using a tongue that was not his own. Compromise destroyed the compromiser and did not placate the uncompromising foe. You did not become a blackbird by painting your wings black, but like an oil-slicked gull you lost the power of flight. The greatest danger of the growing menace was that good men would commit intellectual suicide and call it peace. Good men would give in to fear and call it respect.

Before anyone else was interested in the ornithology of terror he saw the gathering birds. He would be a Cassandra for his own time, cursed to be unheard, or if listened to, then blamed for what he pointed at. Snakes had licked his ears and he could hear the future. No, not Cassandra, that wasn't right, for he was not a prophet. He was just listening in the right direction, looking toward the advancing storm.

But it would be hard to turn men's heads. Nobody wanted to know what he knew.

Milton's *Areopagitica* sang against the shrieking blackbirds. *He who destroys a good book, kills reason itself. . . . Give me the liberty to know, to utter, and to argue freely according to conscience, above all liberties.* He had read the ancient texts on liberty long ago when they struck him as fine, but theoretical. He didn't need the theory of freedom when he had the fact of it. They didn't strike him as theoretical anymore.

The writers who had always spoken to him most clearly were members of what he thought of as a rival "Great Tradition" to set against the Leavisite canon, writers who understood the unreality of "reality" and the reality of the world's waking nightmare, the monstrous mutability of the everyday, the irruption of the extreme and improbable into the humdrum quotidian. Rabelais, Gogol, Kafka, these and their ilk had been his masters and their world, too, no longer felt to him like fantasies. He was living—trapped—in the Gogolian, the Rabelaisian, the Kafkaesque.

In the photographs that survived of that time, assiduously preserved in large albums by Elizabeth, Mr. Joseph Anton was not well-dressed. His habitual daily attire was tracksuit trousers and a sweatshirt. The trousers were often green and the sweatshirt maroon. His hair was too long and his beard too shaggy. To dress like this was to say, *I am letting myself go. I am not a person to take seriously. I am just some slob.* He should have shaved daily and worn crisp, cleanly pressed clothes, Savile Row suits, perhaps, or at least a smart shirt and slacks. He should have sat at his desk like Scott Fitzgerald in his Brooks Brothers suit, or Borges, nattily turned out in a stiff collar and cuff-linked shirt. Maybe his sentences would have been better if he had taken more care of his appearance. Though Hemingway in his cotton shorts and sandals wasn't so bad. He would like to have seen fancy shoes on his feet in those photographs, possibly two-tone oxfords, or white leather. Instead he slouched around the house in Birkenstocks, the uncoolest of all possible footwear, except for Crocs. He looked at himself in the mirror and loathed what he saw. He trimmed his beard and asked Elizabeth to cut his hair—chic Elizabeth, whose personal style had been Late Student when they met, and who had taken to designer clothes with the eagerness of a beached mermaid discovering the sea—and asked the police to take him out to buy new clothes. It was time to take himself in hand. He was going into battle and his armor needed to shine.

When a thing happened that had not happened before, a confusion often descended upon people, a fog that fuddled the clearest minds; and often the consequence of such confusion was rejection, and even anger. A fish crawled out of a swamp onto dry land and the other fish were bewildered, perhaps even annoyed that a forbidden frontier had been crossed. A meteorite struck the earth and the dust blocked out the sun but the dinosaurs went on fighting and eating, not understanding that they had been rendered extinct. The birth of language angered the dumb. The shah of Persia, facing the Ottoman guns, refused to accept the end of the age of the sword and sent his cavalry to gallop suicidally against the blazing cannons of the Turk. A scientist observed tortoises and mockingbirds and wrote about *random mutation* and *natural selection* and the adherents of the Book of Genesis cursed his name. A revolution in painting was derided and dismissed as mere *impressionism*. A folksinger plugged his guitar into an amp and a voice in the crowd shouted "Judas!"

This was the question his novel had asked: *How does newness enter the world?*

The arrival of the new was not always linked to progress. Men found new ways of oppressing one another, too, new ways of unmaking their best achievements and sliding back toward that primal ooze; and men's darkest innovations, as much as their brightest ones, confused their fellow men. When the first witches were burned it was easier to blame the witches than to question the justice of their burning. When the odors from the gas ovens drifted into the streets of nearby villages and the dark snow fell from the sky it was easier not to understand. Most Chinese citizens did not understand the fallen heroes of Tiananmen. They were guided toward false understanding by the perpetrators of the crime. When tyrants rose to power across the Muslim world there were many who were ready to call their regimes *authentic* and the opposition to such regimes *Westernized* or *deracinated*. When a Pakistani politician defended a woman falsely accused of blasphemy he was murdered by his bodyguard and his country applauded the murderer and threw flower petals over him when he was brought to court. Most of these dark newnesses were innovations that came into being in the name of a totalizing ideology, an absolute ruler, an unarguable dogma, or a god.

The attack on *The Satanic Verses* was in itself a small thing, though it had garnered a lot of headlines, so it was hard to persuade people that it was extraordinary enough, that it meant enough to warrant an exceptional response. As he began his long trek around the world's corridors of power, he was obliged, over and over again, to restate the case. *A serious writer had written a serious book. The violence and menace of the response was a terrorist act that had to be confronted.* Ah, but his book had offended many people, had it not? *Perhaps, but the attack on the book, its author, publishers, translators and booksellers, was a far greater offense.* Ah, so, having made trouble, he opposed the trouble that came at him in return, and wanted the world's leaders to defend his right to be a troublemaker.

In seventeenth-century England Matthew Hopkins, the "Witch Finder Generall," developed a test for witchcraft. You weighted the accused woman down—with stones, or by tying her to a chair—and then threw her into a river or a lake. If she floated, she was a witch, and merited burning; if she sank and drowned, she was innocent.

The accusation of witchcraft was often the same thing as a "guilty" verdict. Now he was the one in the crucible, trying to persuade the world that the witch finders were the criminals, not he.

Something new was happening here: the growth of a new intolerance. It was spreading across the surface of the earth, but nobody wanted to know. A new word had been created to help the blind remain blind: *Islamophobia*. To criticize the militant stridency of this religion in its contemporary incarnation was to be a bigot. A *phobic* person was extreme and irrational in his views, and so the fault lay with such persons and not with the belief system that boasted over one billion followers worldwide. One billion believers could not be wrong, therefore the critics must be the ones foaming at the mouth. When, he wanted to know, did it become irrational to dislike religion, any religion, even to dislike it vehemently? When did reason get redescribed as unreason? When were the fairy stories of the superstitious placed above criticism, beyond satire? A religion was not a race. It was an idea, and ideas stood (or fell) because they were strong enough (or too weak) to withstand criticism, not because they were shielded from it. Strong ideas welcomed dissent. "He that wrestles with us strengthens our nerves and sharpens our skill," wrote Edmund Burke. "Our antagonist is our helper." Only the weak and the authoritarian turned away from their opponents and called them names and sometimes wished to do them harm.

It was Islam that had changed, not people like himself, it was Islam that had become phobic of a very wide range of ideas, behaviors, and things. In those years and in the years that followed Islamic voices in this or that part of the world—Algeria, Pakistan, Afghanistan— anathematized theater, film and music, and musicians and performers were mutilated and killed. Representational art was evil, and so the ancient Buddhist statues at Bamiyan were destroyed by the Taliban. There were Islamist attacks on socialists and unionists, cartoonists and journalists, prostitutes and homosexuals, women in skirts and beardless men, and also, surreally, on such evils as frozen chickens and samosas.

When the history of the twentieth century was written the decision to place the House of Saud on the Throne That Sits Over the Oil might well look like the greatest foreign policy error of the Western powers, because the Sauds had used their unlimited oil wealth to build schools (madrassas) to propagate the extremist, puritanical ideology of their beloved (and previously marginal) Muhammad ibn 'Abd al-Wahhab, and as a result Wahhabism had grown from its tiny cult origins to overrun the Arab world. Its rise gave confidence and energy to other Islamic extremists. In India the Deobandi cult spread outward from the seminary of Darul Uloom, in Shia Iran there were the militant preachers of Qom, and in Sunni Egypt the powerful conservatives of Al-Azhar. As the extremist ideologies—Wahhabi, Salafi, Khomeini-ite, Deobandi—grew in power and the madrassas funded by Saudi oil turned out generations of narrow-eyed men with hairy chins and easily clenched fists, Islam moved a long way away from its origins while claiming to be returning to its roots. The American humorist H. L. Mencken memorably defined puritanism as "the haunting fear that someone, somewhere may be happy," and very often the true enemy of the new Islam seemed to be happiness itself. And this was the faith whose *critics* were the bigots? "When I use a word," Humpty Dumpty told Alice, in Wonderland, "it means just what I choose it to mean—neither more nor less." The creators of "Newspeak" in Orwell's *1984* knew exactly what Humpty Dumpty meant, renaming the propaganda ministry the Ministry of Truth and the state's most repressive organ the Ministry of Love. "Islamophobia" was an addition to the vocabulary of Humpty Dumpty Newspeak. It took the language of analysis, reason and dispute, and stood it on its head.

He knew, as surely as he knew anything, that the fanatical cancer spreading through Muslim communities would, in the end, explode into the wider world beyond Islam. If the intellectual battle was lost—if this new Islam established its right to be "respected" and to have its opponents excoriated, placed beyond the pale, and, why not, even killed—then political defeat would follow.

He had entered the world of politics and was trying to make arguments from principle. But behind closed doors, in the rooms in which decisions were made, principles very rarely made policy. It would be an uphill fight, made harder because he also had to struggle to regain a freer private and professional life. The battle would have to be fought simultaneously on both fronts.

Peter Florence, who ran the Hay-on-Wye literary festival, got in touch to ask if there was any chance that he might take part in that year's event. The great Israeli novelist David Grossman had been scheduled to take part in a conversation with Martin Amis, but had had to cancel. It would be so great, Peter said, if you could step in. We wouldn't have to tell anyone in advance. The audience would be so thrilled to see you and welcome you back to the world of books. He wanted to accept; but first he had to discuss Peter's invitation with the protection team, who had to discuss it with the senior officers at the Yard, and, as the proposed event was outside the Metropolitan Police's jurisdiction, the chief constable of the Powys police force would have to be informed, and local uniformed officers would have to be involved. He could imagine the senior policemen rolling their eyes, *here he goes, making demands again,* but he was determined not to succumb to their desire that he lie low and say nothing. In the end it was agreed that he could go and stay at Deborah Rogers and Michael Berkeley's farm near Hay and make the proposed appearance, as long as news of it didn't get out before the event. And so it was done. He walked out on stage at Hay to find that he and Martin were wearing identical linen suits and for a happy hour and a half he was a writer among readers again. The paperback of *The Satanic Verses,* imported from America, was on sale at Hay and everywhere else in the United Kingdom, and after all that difficulty this was what happened: nothing. Things did not improve, but things did not get worse, either. The moment Penguin Books had feared so greatly that they had given up publication rights passed off without a single unpleasant incident. He wondered if Peter Mayer had noticed that.

Each of his campaigning trips took days—weeks—to prepare for. There were arguments with local security forces, problems with airlines, politicians' broken agreements, the interminable yes-and-no, up-and-down work of political organization. Frances and Carmel and he talked constantly, and the campaign was becoming his full-time job as well. In later years he would say that he had lost one, maybe two full-length novels to the *fatwa;* that was why, once the dark years came to an end, he plunged into writing with renewed determination. There were books piled up inside him, demanding to be born.

The campaign began in Scandinavia. In the years that followed he would fall in love with the Nordic peoples because of their adherence to the highest principles of freedom. Even their airlines had morals and carried him without argument. The world was a strange place: In the hour of his greatest adversity, a boy from the tropics found some of his closest allies in the frozen north, even if the Danes were worried about cheese. Denmark exported a very large quantity of its feta cheese to Iran and if it was seen to be cozying up to the blasphemer, apostate and heretic, the cheese trade might suffer. The Danish government was obliged to choose between cheese and human rights, and at first it chose cheese. (There were rumors that the British government had urged the Danes not to meet with him. Ian McEwan's Dutch publisher, Jaco Groot, had heard that the Brits were telling their European colleagues that they didn't want to be "embarrassed" by "too public a show of support.")

He went anyway, as the guest of Danish PEN. Elizabeth traveled a day earlier with Carmel, and then he was taken to Heathrow through a security entrance and driven onto the tarmac and was the last passenger onto the plane. He had been very worried that the other passengers might panic when they saw him, but these passengers were almost all Danes, and he was greeted by smiles and handshakes and genuine, fearless pleasure. As the plane lifted off from the runway he thought, *Maybe I can begin to fly again. Maybe it will be all right.*

At Copenhagen airport, the reception committee somehow missed him. He was evidently less recognizable than he thought. He went through the airport and walked out beyond the security barrier and spent almost half an hour in the arrivals hall looking for someone who knew what was happening. For thirty minutes he had slipped through the safety net. He was tempted to get in a taxi and make a run for it. But then the police came sprinting toward him and with them was his host Niels Barfoed of Danish PEN, huffing and puffing and apologizing for the confusion. They went to the waiting cars and the net closed around him again.

His presence—this became "normal" for a while—had not been announced in advance. The PEN members gathered at the Louisiana Museum of Modern Art that evening were expecting the guest of honor to be Günter Grass, and Grass was indeed there, one of the sequence of great literary figures who agreed to act, in those years, as his "beard." "If Salman Rushdie is a hostage then we are hostages too," Grass said, introducing him, and then it was his turn. A few weeks earlier, he said, fifty Iranian intellectuals had published a declaration in his defense. "To defend Rushdie is to defend ourselves," they said. To fail against the *fatwa* would embolden authoritarian regimes. This was where the line had to be drawn and there could be no retreat from it. He was fighting his fellow writers' fight as well as his own. The sixty-five Danish intellectuals gathered at Louisiana pledged to join him in that fight, and to lobby their own government to do the right thing. "If the British Government feels unable to confront Iran's unacceptable threat to the democratic process," said Frances D'Souza, "the defense committee must seek the commitment and support that has been offered in Europe."

At one point he saw a battleship cruising by outside the windows of the museum. "Is that for me?" he asked, meaning it as a joke; but it was indeed for him: his personal battleship, to guard him against a naval attack, and to keep a lookout for Islamic frogmen swimming up toward the museum with cutlasses between their teeth. Yes, everything had been thought of. They were a thorough people, the Danes.

His Norwegian publisher, William Nygaard of H. Aschehoug & Co., insisted that he follow up on his Danish trip by visiting Norway. "Here I think we can do even better," he said. Government ministers were ready to meet him. Every summer Aschehoug threw a big garden party at the beautiful old villa at Drammensveien 99, which at the turn of the last century had been the Nygaard family home. This party was one of the highlights of the Oslo season, attended by many of the best-known Norwegian writers as well as business and political leaders. "You must come to the party," William said. "In the garden! With more than one thousand people! It will be fantastic. A gesture of freedom." William was a charismatic figure in Norway: a dashing skier, strikingly handsome, scion of one of the oldest families, and head of the leading publishing house. He was also as good as his word; the visit to Norway was a success. At the Drammensveien garden party he was guided through the throng by William Nygaard and met, well, *le tout* Oslo. The response to his visit, William told him later, was immense.

This trip made William his most "visible" European publisher. They did not know it then, but his work on his author's behalf had placed his life in great danger. Fourteen months later the terror would come knocking at William's door.

In London the Labour spokesman for the arts, Mark Fisher, MP, arranged a press conference at the House of Commons, attended by Labour and Tory MPs, and he was given a sympathetic hearing inside the Palace of Westminster for the first time. There was one sour note. The ultrarightist Conservative Rupert Allason stood up and said, "Please don't misinterpret my presence here as support. To conceal what you were up to, your publishers say, you misled them about your book. It is quite wrong for public money to be used to protect you." This nasty little attack upset him less than it once would have. He no longer hoped to be universally loved; he knew that wherever he went he would find adversaries as well as friends. Nor were all the adversaries on the right. Gerald Kaufman, the Labour MP who had been vocal about his dislike of Mr. Rushdie's writing, publicly rebuked his fellow Labourite Mark Fisher for inviting the author to the House of Commons. (The Iranian Majlis agreed with Kaufman that the invitation had been "disgraceful.") There would be more Kaufmans and Allasons along the road. What was important was to press the case.

He spoke to David Gore-Booth at the Foreign Office and asked him directly about the rumors that the British government was opposed to his new, higher-profile campaigning and had been working behind the scenes to sabotage it. Gore-Booth had an excellent poker face and no emotion flickered across it. He denied the rumors. "HMG supports your meetings with other governments," he said. He offered to help with police liaison so that the security forces of countries he visited didn't "overdo" it. It was hard to know what to think. Perhaps he had begun to drag the government along with him.

He was invited to Spain by the Complutense University of Madrid to converse with Mario Vargas Llosa at the Escorial Palace. He took Elizabeth and Zafar with him and they spent three quiet days in Segovia before the conference. The Spanish police maintained a very discreet presence and he was able to walk in the streets and eat in the restaurants of that beautiful little town and feel almost like a free man. He lunched in Ávila with Mario and his wife, Patricia. These were precious hours. Then at the Escorial the rector of the Complutense University, Gustavo Villapalos, said he had excellent connections in Iran and offered to mediate. Khomeini, he said, had once called him a "very holy man." This latest offer of mediation proved as futile as the others. He was horrified to read Villapalos's announcement in the Spanish press that he had agreed to alter and cut "offending" passages from *The Satanic Verses* to make a settlement possible. He denied this vehemently and after that Villapalos became unavailable and all contact with him ceased.

You must be at all the platforms, Giandomenico Picco had said, *so that you are standing there when the train arrives.* But some of the platforms didn't have any tracks running past them. They were just places to stand.

From the moment they landed in Denver they could see things were going badly wrong. The local police were treating the event as a trailer for World War III, and as he and Elizabeth made their way through the airport there were men brandishing enormous assault weaponry running in several directions, and police officers manhandling members of the public out of his way, and there was shouting, and pointing, and an air of imminent calamity. It scared him, terrified the bystanders, and alienated the airline, which refused to allow him on board any of its planes ever again, because of *his behavior.* The antics of the security forces became "his."

They were driven to Boulder, where he spoke at a pan-American literary conference along with Oscar Arias, Robert Coover, William Styron, Peter Matthiessen and William Gass. "Latin American writers have known for a long time that literature is a life and death matter," he said in his speech. "Now I share that knowledge with them." He lived in an age in which literature's importance seemed to be fading. He wanted to make it a part of his mission to insist on the vital importance of books and of protecting the freedoms necessary to create them. In his great novel *If on a Winter's Night a Traveler,* Italo Calvino said (speaking through his character Arkadian Porphyrich): "Nobody these days holds the written word in such high esteem as police states do. What statistic allows one to identify the nations where literature enjoys true consideration better than the sums appropriated for controlling it and suppressing it?" Which was certainly true of, for example, Cuba. Philip Roth once said, speaking about Soviet-era repression,

"When I was first in Czechoslovakia, it occurred to me that I work in a society where as a writer everything goes and nothing matters, while for the Czech writers I met in Prague, nothing goes and everything matters." What was true of police states and Soviet tyranny was also true of Latin American dictatorships, and of the new theocratic fascism that was confronting him and many other writers, but in the United States—in the liberal, if thin, air of Boulder, Colorado—it was not easy for people to feel the lived truth of repression. He had made it his task, he said, to explain the world in which "nothing goes and everything matters" to the world of "everything goes and nothing matters."

It took the personal intervention of the president of the University of Colorado, Boulder, to persuade another airline to fly him home. After he finished his speech he and Elizabeth were taken immediately back to the Denver airport and almost pushed onto a flight to London. The police operation was not as out of control as it had been when they arrived, but it was still big enough to spook anyone who was watching. He left America feeling that the campaign had just taken a step backward.

Terror was knocking on many doors. In Egypt the leading secularist Farag Fouda had been murdered. In India, Professor Mushirul Hasan, vice chancellor of Delhi's Jamia Millia Islamia University and a distinguished historian, was menaced by "angry Muslims" for daring to oppose the banning of *The Satanic Verses*. He was forced to climb down and condemn the book but the mob demanded that he also approve of the *fatwa*. He refused to do so. As a result he would be unable to return to the university for five long years. In Berlin, four Kurdish-Iranian opposition politicians attending the Socialist International were murdered at the Mykonos restaurant, and the Iranian regime was suspected of being behind the killings. And in London, Elizabeth and he were asleep in their bedroom when there was a very loud explosion and the whole house shook. Policemen rushed into the room with their weapons and dragged the sleepers onto the floor. They remained prone among armed men for what felt like hours until it was confirmed that the explosion had been some distance away at the Staples Corner roundabout, under the overpass for the North Circular Road. It was the Provisional IRA at work; nothing to do with them. It was a non-Islamic bomb. They were left alone to go back to sleep.

Islamic terror wasn't far away. Ayatollah Sanei of the 15 Khordad Foundation increased the bounty money to include "expenses." (Keep your receipts, assassins, you can reclaim that business lunch.) Three Iranians were expelled from the United Kingdom because they had been conspiring to kill him: two embassy employees, Mehdi Sayed Sadeghi and Mahmoud Mehdi Soltani, and a "student," Gassem Vakhshiteh. Back in Iran, the Majlis—the supposedly "moderate" Majlis elected by voters in the recent Iranian elections!—"petitioned" President Rafsanjani to uphold the *fatwa,* and the pro-Rafsanjani Ayatollah Jannati responded that the "time was right to kill the filthy Rushdie."

He went to south London to play table tennis with the painter Tom Phillips at his studio. It seemed like the right thing to do. Tom had begun to paint his portrait—he told Tom he looked too gloomy in it, but Tom said, "Gloomy? What do you mean? I call it *Mr. Chirpy*"— so he sat for that for two hours before losing at Ping-Pong. He did not enjoy losing at Ping-Pong.

That day the 15 Khordad Foundation announced that it would soon begin to send assassination teams to the United Kingdom to carry out the *fatwa.* Losing at Ping-Pong was bad, but he was trying not to lose his mind.

Zafar left the Hall School for the last time—the Hall, which had done so much to shield him from the worst of what was happening to his father, the teachers and boys allowing him, without the sentiment ever being expressed in words, to have a normal childhood in the midst of the insanity. Zafar's parents had much to be grateful to the school for. It was to be hoped that the new school would look after him as lovingly as the old one.

Highgate was mostly a day school but there were houses for weekly boarders and Zafar had been keen to board. Within days, however, he discovered he hated boarding. At thirteen, he was a boy who liked his private space and in a boys' boardinghouse there wasn't any. So he was immediately miserable. Both his parents agreed he should stop boarding and the school accepted their decision. Zafar immediately began to radiate happiness and started to love the school. And now his father had a home near Highgate so he could come and stay on school nights and their relationship could regain what it had lost for four years: intimacy, continuity, and something like ease. Zafar had his own room in the new house and asked for it to be furnished entirely in black and white. He couldn't bring his friends around, but understood why, and said he didn't mind. Even without visits from other boys, it was a big improvement over boarding. He had a home with his father once again.

In India, extremist Hindus destroyed one of the oldest mosques in India, the Babri Masjid at Ayodhya, built by the first Mughal emperor. The destroyers claimed that the mosque was built over the ruins of a Hindu temple marking the *Ramjanmabhoomi,* the birthplace of Lord Rama, the seventh avatar of Vishnu. Mayhem was not the prerogative of Islam alone. When he heard the news of the destruction of the Babri Masjid he was possessed by a complex grief. He was sad that religion had again revealed that its power for destruction far exceeded its power for good, that a series of unprovable propositions—that the modern Ayodhya was the same place as the Ayodhya of the *Ramayana,* where Rama was king at an unknowable date in the remote past; that the alleged birthplace was the true birthplace; that gods and their avatars actually existed—had resulted in the vandalization of an actual and beautiful building whose misfortune was to have been constructed in a country that passed no strong laws to protect its heritage, and in which it was possible to ignore such laws as did exist if you were sufficiently numerous and claimed to be acting in the name of a god. He was sad, too, because he still had feelings of affection for the same Muslim culture of India that was preventing Mushirul Hasan from going to work, and preventing him from being given a visa to visit the country of his birth. The history of Muslim India was inescapably his history too. One day he would write a novel about Babar's grandson

Akbar the Great, who tried to make peace between the many gods of India and their followers, and who, for a time, succeeded.

The wounds inflicted by India were the deepest. There was no question, he was told, of his being given a visa to visit the country of his birth and deepest inspiration. He was not even welcome at the Indian cultural center in London because, according to the center's director (and grandson of the Mahatma) Gopal Gandhi, his presence there would be seen as anti-Muslim and would prejudice the center's secular credentials. He set his jaw and went back to work. *The Moor's Last Sigh* was as secular as a novel could be but its author was thought of as a divisive sectarian in the country about which he was writing. The clouds thickened over his head. But he found that his bloody-mindedness was equal to the pain, that his sentences could still form, his imagination still spark. He would not allow the rejections to break his art.

He became, having no alternative, in part an ambassador for himself. But politicking did not come easily to him. He made his speeches and argued his cause and asked the world's dignitaries to set their faces against this new "remote-control terrorism," this pointing of a lethal finger across the world, *Him, you see him? Kill him, the bald one holding the book;* and to understand that if terrorism-by-*fatwa* was not defeated it would surely be repeated. But often the words sounded stale in his own ears. In Finland, after he spoke at a meeting of the Nordic Council, resolutions were passed, subcommittees were created, promises of support were given; but he couldn't shake the feeling that nothing substantial was being gained. He was more delighted by the beauty of the autumn woodland outside the window, and he had a chance to walk in it with Elizabeth, and breathe the crisp air, and feel briefly at peace; and that, to his mind, at that moment, was a greater blessing than all the resolutions in the world.

With the help of Elizabeth's gentle encouragement, his disillusion faded. He was finding his voice again, she told him, and his Mistake was fading into the past, though he would have to go on unsaying it for years. He was being listened to with respect, and that undeniably felt good after so many people's ugly dismissals of his character and work. Gradually he became more practiced at making his case. During the worst excesses of Soviet Communism, he argued, Western Marxists had tried to distance "actually existing Socialism" from the True Faith, Karl Marx's vision of equality and justice. But when the USSR collapsed, and it became plain that "actually existing Socialism" had fatally polluted Marxism in the eyes of all those who had helped bring the despots down, it was no longer possible to believe in a True Faith untainted by the crimes of the real world. Now, as Islamic states forged new tyrannies, and justified many horrors in the name of God, a similar separation was being made by Muslims; so there was the "actually existing Islam" of the bloody theocracies and then there was the True Faith of peace and love.

He found this hard to swallow, and tried to find the right words to say why. He could easily understand the defenders of Muslim culture; when the Babri Masjid fell it hurt him as it did them. And he too was moved by the many kindnesses of Muslim society, its charitable spirit, the beauty of its architecture, painting and poetry, its contributions to philosophy and science, its arabesques, its mystics, and the gentle wisdom of open-minded Muslims like his grandfather, his mother's father, Dr. Ataullah Butt. Dr. Butt of Aligarh, who worked as a family physician and was also involved with the Tibbya College of Aligarh Muslim University, where Western medicine was studied side by side with traditional Indian herbal treatments, went on the pilgrimage to Mecca, said his prayers five times a day every day of his life—and was one of the most tolerant men his grandson ever met, gruffly good-natured, open to every sort of childish and adolescent rebellious thought, even to the idea of the nonexistence of God, a damn fool idea, he would say, but one that should be talked through. If Islam was what Dr. Butt believed, there wasn't much wrong with that.

But something was eating away at the faith of his grandfather, corroding and corrupting it, making it an ideology of narrowness and intolerance, banning books, persecuting thinkers, erecting absolutisms, turning dogma into a weapon with which to beat the undogmatic. That thing needed to be fought and to fight it one had to name it and the only name that fit was *Islam*. Actually existing Islam had become its own poison and Muslims were dying of it and that needed to be said, in Finland, Spain, America, Denmark, Norway and everywhere else. He would say it, if nobody else would. He wanted to speak, too, for the idea that liberty was everyone's heritage and not, as Samuel Huntington argued, a Western notion alien to the cultures of the East. As "respect for Islam," which was fear of Islamist violence cloaked in Tartuffe-like hypocrisy, gained legitimacy in the West, the cancer of cultural relativism had begun to eat away at the rich multicultures of the modern world, and down that slippery slope they might all slide toward the Slough of Despond, John Bunyan's swamp of despair.

As he struggled from country to country, hammering on the doors of the mighty and trying to find small moments of freedom in the clutches of this or that security force, he tried to find the words he needed to be not only an advocate for himself but also of what he stood for, or wanted to stand for from now on.

One "small moment of freedom" came when he was invited to a U2 concert at Earls Court. This was during the *Achtung Baby* tour with its pendant psychedelic Trabants. The police said yes at once when he told them: Finally, something they wanted to do! It turned out that Bono had read *The Jaguar Smile* and, as he had visited Nicaragua at about the same time, was interested to meet its author. (He never ran into Bono in Nicaragua but one day his shining-eyed blond interpreter Margarita, a Jayne Mansfield look-alike, had cried excitedly, "Bono's coming! Bono's in Nicaragua!" and then, without any change in vocal inflection or any dimming of the eyes, had added, "Who is Bono?") And so there he was at Earls Court, standing in the shadows, listening. Backstage, after the show, he was shown into a trailer full of sand-wiches and children. There were no groupies at U2 gigs; just crèches. Bono came in and was instantly festooned with daughters. He was keen to talk politics—Nicaragua, an upcoming protest against unsafe nuclear waste disposal at Sellafield in northern England, his support for the cause of *The Satanic Verses*. They didn't spend long together, but a friendship was born.

Nigella Lawson and John Diamond got married in Venice. Like all her friends he was made very happy by the news. Where John was there would always be laughter. At the party they gave at the Groucho Club to celebrate their wedding, the cake was made by Ruthie Rogers and designed, Ruthie said, by her husband, the great architect himself. John said, innocently, "Surely not? If it's a Richard Rogers design, shouldn't all the ingredients be on the outside?"

Germany was Iran's largest trading partner. He had to go there. A tiny, fierce member of the German Bundestag named Thea Bock intended, she said, to make sure he saw "everybody." But first he had to get to Bonn, and he could not fly Lufthansa or British Airways. Thea Bock came up with a small private aircraft, bright red, like something out of a World War I story: "Biggles and the *Fatwa*." The plane was so small and old-fashioned that *the windows opened*. It flew so low that he feared they might bump into a hill, or a steeple. It was like riding an Indian scooter-rickshaw through the sky. Fortunately the weather was good, a sunny, calm day, and his pilot was able to fly his little phut-phut uneventfully to the German capital, where the meetings went so well, thanks to the efforts of Thea Bock, that the Iranians got badly rattled, because here, all of a sudden, was Rushdie being greeted warmly by Björn Engholm, the leader of the Social Democrats, and by Rita Süssmuth, the Speaker of the German Parliament, and by many of the most prominent German MPs; and, in the absence abroad of Foreign Minister Klaus Kinkel, here was Rushdie at the German Foreign Ministry being received by the head of its cultural section, Dr. Schirmer. The Iranian ambassador spoke angrily on German television and said he was certain that Germany would not jeopardize its relations with Iran on account of this man. He also said that American or Israeli assassins might be about to assassinate the apostate, pretending to be Muslim killers, just to make Iran look bad.

Ambassador Hossein Musavian was hauled into the German Foreign Ministry the next day. "We will protect Mr. Rushdie," said the deputy foreign minister. "After our very frank exchange, he [the Iranian ambassador] knows this is the case." The suggestions about a killing by U.S. or Israeli intelligence were called "absurd." Ambassador Musavian said that his remarks had been "misquoted."

So there was *momentum,* as Frances said; but had *critical mass* (one of her favorite terms) been achieved? Not yet. The Bradford Council of Mosques made another nasty statement alleging that the campaign was making things worse and that the author should not expect any "reprieve" from the Muslim community. The council's president, Liaquat Hussein, clearly believed he was an important man saying an important thing. But he sounded like a voice from the past. His fifteen minutes of fame were up.

He was in Stockholm to receive the Kurt Tucholsky Prize, given to writers resisting persecution, and to address the Swedish Academy. Iran condemned the award, of course. The Iranian chief justice spoke up, and so did the bountiful Ayatollah Sanei. *Dear Chief Injustice,* he began, but then abandoned the imaginary letter. Some people did not deserve to be written to, not even in the imagination. *My dear Sanei of the Bounty, may I draw your attention to the possibility of a mutiny? Maybe you and your pals will end up as Bligh spirits, adrift in a small boat, hoping for the coast of Timor.*

The Swedish Academy met in a beautiful rococo room on the upper floor of the old Stockholm Stock Exchange Building. Around a long table were nineteen chairs upholstered in pale blue silk. One was for the king, just in case he showed up; it stood empty if he did not, which was always. On the backs of the other chairs were Roman numerals from I to XVIII. When an academician died a new member was elected to fill his chair and sat in that chair until he or she moved on to the greater academy in the sky. He thought at once of G. K. Chesterton's lively thriller *The Man Who Was Thursday,* about an anarchist cell whose seven leaders were code-named after the days of the week. He was not, however, in the presence of anarchists. He had been granted permission to enter literature's holy of holies, the room in which the Nobel Prize was awarded, to address a gravely friendly gathering of gray eminences. Lars Gyllensten (XIV) and Kerstin Ekman (XV), the academicians who had withdrawn from this table to protest their colleagues' pusillanimous lack of response to the *fatwa*, did not attend. Their chairs were a vacant rebuke. That saddened him; he had hoped to bring about a reconciliation. The academy's invitation had been offered as a way of compensating for their earlier silence. His presence among them indicated their support. A twentieth, numeral-free chair was drawn up to the table next to the empty seat of the king, and he sat in it and spoke and answered questions until the academicians were satisfied. Elizabeth, Frances and Carmel were allowed to watch, seated in other chairs lined up against a wall.

At the heart of the dispute over *The Satanic Verses,* he said, behind all the accusations and abuse, was a question of profound importance: *Who shall have control over the story?* Who has, who should have, the power not only to tell the stories with which, and within which, we all lived, but also to say in what manner those stories may be told? For everyone lived by and inside stories, the so-called grand narratives. The nation was a story, and the family was another, and religion was a third. As a creative artist he knew that the only answer to the question was: *Everyone and anyone has, or should have that power.* We should all be free to take the grand narratives to task, to argue with them, satirize them, and insist that they change to reflect the changing times. We should speak of them reverently, irreverently, passionately, caustically, or however we chose. That was our right as members of an open society. In fact, one could say that our ability to re-tell and re-make the story of our culture was the best proof that our societies were indeed free. In a free society the argument over the grand narratives never ceased. It was the argument itself that mattered. The argument was freedom. But in a closed society those who possessed political or ideological power invariably tried to shut down these debates. *We will tell you the story,* they said, *and we will tell you what it means. We will tell you how the story is to be told and we forbid you to tell it in any other way. If you do not like the way we tell the story then you are an enemy of the state or a traitor to the faith. You have no rights. Woe betide you! We will come after you and teach you the meaning of your refusal.*

The storytelling animal must be free to tell his tales.

At the end of the meeting he received a gift. Across the way from this room was a well-known restaurant, Den Gyldene Freden (The

Golden Peace), owned by the academy. At the end of their weekly meetings the Eighteen, or however many of them had showed up, retired to a private room at the Golden Peace for dinner. Each of them paid, on arrival, with a silver coin bearing the academy's motto, *Snille och smak*. Talent and taste. When they left the restaurant the coins were returned to them. These coins were never given out to the general public, but he left the academy that day with one in his pocket.

In New York, this time, there was no motorcade waiting, no Lieutenant Bob worrying about what Elizabeth might do with a fork. (He had flown on Scandinavian Airlines, taking the long way round, via Oslo.) There were security personnel to guide him through the airport, but that was all. There was no public appearance planned and so the American police were willing to leave him largely to his own devices. He was allowed to have a few days of near-freedom, the closest to it he'd come in almost four years. He stayed in Andrew Wylie's apartment and the NYPD remained in their cars in the street below. During those days he made peace with Sonny Mehta. And he had dinner with Thomas Pynchon.

One of Andrew's best qualities was his unwillingness to bear a grudge. "You and Sonny should patch things up," he said. "You've been friends too long. It's the right thing to do." And there were good business reasons for offering an olive branch. In the long term, Random House was the most likely publisher to take over the paperback publication of *The Satanic Verses*. Penguin would never do it, and as Penguin was the distributor of Granta Books that made a long-term relationship with Granta difficult to contemplate, in spite of Bill's extraordinary friendship and heroism. "We can't lose sight of the goal," Andrew said, "and the goal is normal publication for all your books, including the *Verses*." Now that the Consortium edition had leaped the paperback hurdle it would be possible, he believed, to persuade Sonny to take on new books without fear, and also to accept long-term responsibility for the backlist. "Not right away," Andrew said, "but maybe after they have published the next novel. I really think they will do it. And that's what should be done." He and Gillon had gone ahead and negotiated a deal with Sonny and Knopf for *The Moor's Last Sigh*. They had also placated Bill, who had been very upset when he was told their plan. But Bill was a friend first and a publisher second and he had a big enough heart to see Andrew's point. He had saved *Haroun* from Sonny and now agreed to surrender *Moor* back to him without rancor.

Before the deal could be signed he and Sonny needed to bury the hatchet and that was the real purpose of the New York trip. Andrew also contacted Pynchon's agent (and wife), Melanie Jackson, and the reclusive author of *Gravity's Rainbow* agreed to meet. In the end the two meetings were combined. He and Pynchon dined with Sonny at the Mehtas' midtown apartment. The rift with Sonny was repaired with a hug and the matter of *Haroun* left undiscussed. That was Sonny's taciturn way of doing things—to leave awkward things unsaid and move forward—and maybe it was for the best. Then Pynchon arrived, looking exactly as Thomas Pynchon should look. He was tall, wore a red-and-white lumberjack shirt and blue jeans, had Albert Einstein white hair and Bugs Bunny front teeth. After an initial half hour of stilted conversation Pynchon seemed to relax and then spoke at length on American labor history and his own membership, dating from his early days working as a technical writer at Boeing, of the trade union of technical writers. It was strange to think of those authors of user's manuals being addressed by the great American novelist, whom they perhaps thought of as that fellow who used to write the safety newsletter for the supersonic CIM-10 Bomarc missile, without knowing anything about how Pynchon's knowledge of that missile had inspired his extraordinary descriptions of the World War II V-2 rockets falling on London. The conversation went on long past midnight. At one point Pynchon said, "You guys are probably tired, huh," and yes, they were, but they were also thinking *It's Thomas Pynchon, we can't go to sleep.*

When Pynchon finally left, he thought: *Okay, so now we're friends. When I visit New York maybe we'll sometimes meet for a drink or a bite to eat and slowly we'll get to know each other better.*

But they never met again.

———

Exhilarating days. He took a buggy ride with Gita in the park and although one old woman cried "Wowie!" nobody else turned a hair. He breakfasted with Giandomenico Picco, who said, "The U.S. is the key." He walked in Battery Park and through Lincoln Center. At Andrew's office he had an emotional reunion with Michael Herr, who had moved back to America and was living upstate in his childhood town of Cazenovia, New York, a stone's throw from Chittenango, the birthplace of L. Frank Baum, author of *The Wizard of Oz*. And Sonny threw a party for him, and Paul Auster and Siri Hustvedt, Don DeLillo, Toni Morrison, Susan Sontag, Annie Leibovitz and Paul Simon were all there. His favorite moment of that evening of liberation, when he felt again a part of the only world he had ever wanted to inhabit, was when Bette Bao Lord said to Susan Sontag, straight-faced, really wanting to know the answer: "Susan, do you have any interesting quirks?"

He and Elizabeth went out to Long Island with Andrew and Camie Wylie to their house in Water Mill, and were joined there by Ian McEwan, Martin Amis, David Rieff, Bill Buford and Christopher and Carol Hitchens. Andrew gave a party at which Susan Sontag revealed one of her interesting quirks. She was really two Susans, Good Susan and Bad Susan, and while Good Susan was brilliant and funny and loyal and rather grand, Bad Susan could be a bullying monster. A junior Wylie agency employee said something about the Bosnian conflict that was not to Susan's liking and Bad Susan came roaring out of her and the junior Wylie agent was in danger of being devoured. It wasn't a fair fight, Susan Sontag versus this young girl, who wasn't able to fight back anyway because Sontag was a valued client of the Wylie Agency. It was necessary to save the young agent's life, and he and Bill Buford went across and silenced the mighty Sontag by bombarding her with trivia. "Hey, Susan, how do you like the Yankees' rotation?" "What? What are you talking about? I don't give a *damn* about the Yankees' rotation, I'm just telling this young woman . . ." "Yeah, but Susan, you've gotta admit, El Duque, he's quite something." "No, this is important, this young woman here thinks that in Bosnia . . ." "What do you think of the wine, Susan? I think the red may be a little corked." And in the end Sontag fell silent, defeated by inconsequentiality, and the young agent was allowed to live.

It was cold November weather but they ran on the beach throwing a football around and skipped stones across the water and played their foolish word games (the game of Titles That Weren't Quite Good Enough, for example: *Mr. Zhivago*, *A Farewell to Weapons*, *For Whom the Bell Rings*, *Two Days in the Life of Ivan Denisovich*, *Mademoiselle Bovary*, *The Story of the Forsytes*, *The Big Gatsby*, *Cab Driver*, *Love in the Time of Influenza*, *Toby-Dick*, *Snag-22*, *Raspberry Finn*) and security officers were nowhere in sight. In those days of friendship he saw a glimmer of hope for the future. If America would let him come and stay quietly on American soil and take his chances then maybe that was the best possibility of finding some freedom in the short term; maybe he could achieve a part-time freedom at least, for a month a year, or two, or three, while he was fighting for an end to the threats. What was he, after all, but a huddled mass yearning to breathe free? He heard the song of the statue in the harbor, and she seemed to be singing to him.

His Canadian publisher, Louise Dennys, president of PEN Canada, Graham Greene's niece and the best editor in Toronto as well as being one half of the tallest and best-looking happy marriage he knew of (to the even taller and just as gorgeous Ric Young), wanted him to make one of his surprise entrances at the annual benefit event for Canadian PEN. She was confident that meetings with leading politicians would follow and that Canada could be persuaded to "come on board" enthusiastically. A private plane had been found. It was quite a plane, with an interior designed by Ralph Lauren, and it was the most comfortable transatlantic flight of his life. But he would have preferred to be standing in line at Heathrow like any other passenger, flying as everyone flew. When life was a series of crises and emergency solutions, it was normality that felt like a luxury—infinitely desirable, yet unobtainable.

In Toronto they were met by Ric Young and the novelist John Ralston Saul, representing PEN, and were driven to the home of Michael Ondaatje and Linda Spalding. The next day the work began. He was interviewed, among many others, by the leading Canadian journalist Peter Gzowski, who asked, on his radio show, about his sex life. "No comment," he said. "But," pressed Gzowski, "that doesn't mean no sex?" At lunch he met the premier of Ontario, Bob Rae, whose help had been the crucial factor in getting the plane. Rae was youthful, friendly, blond, wore sneakers, and said he had agreed to come on stage at the benefit even though his wife was afraid he would be killed. It turned out that Canadian security had warned all politicians against meeting him; or that may have been a convenient excuse. For whatever reason, the meetings were proving to be difficult to arrange. That evening he and Elizabeth dined at the home of John Saul and the TV journalist and future governor-general of Canada, Adrienne Clarkson, and after dinner Adrienne stood up and sang "Hello, Young Lovers" to them in a good, strong voice.

The next evening they were all backstage at the Winter Garden Theatre and he put on the PEN T-shirt that Ric had brought for him. John Irving arrived, grinning. Peggy Atwood rushed in wearing a cowboy hat and fringed jacket and kissed him. Then the "Rushdie" part of the program began and it felt like the highest of literary honors, as writer after writer spoke a part of the *fatwa*'s dire chronology and then took a seat on the stage. John Irving spoke sweetly about their first meeting long ago and read the beginning and the end of *Midnight's Children* and then it was Atwood who introduced him and he went out onto the stage and twelve hundred people gasped and then began to roar their solidarity and love. This business of being turned into an icon was very odd, he thought. He didn't feel iconic. He felt . . . *actual*. But right now it might just be the best weapon he had. The symbolic icon-Salman his supporters had constructed, an idealized Salman of Liberty who stood flawlessly and unwaveringly for the highest values, counteracted and might just in the end defeat the demon version of himself constructed by his adversaries. He raised his arm and waved and when the roar subsided spoke lightly of witch hunts and the dangerous power of comedy and then read his story "Christopher Columbus and Queen Isabella of Spain Consummate Their Relationship." Louise had wanted him to do this, to be there as a writer among literary folk, and to offer them his writing. When the story was over Louise came out and read a message of support from Canada's secretary of state for external affairs, Barbara Macdougall, and then Bob Rae came out and embraced him—the first head of a government in the world to do so—and the roar began again. It was an evening he would never forget.

The Iranian embassy in Ottawa had protested to the Canadian government that it had not been told about his visit in advance. That was the best joke of the week.

And before and in between and after these journeyings he and Elizabeth moved into their new house. It was a house he would never have chosen, in an area he would never have wished to live in; it was too big, because of the policemen who had to live with him, too expensive, too conservative. But David Ashton Hill had done a wonderful job, and Elizabeth had furnished it beautifully, and he had a terrific work room, and above all it was his home, not rented for him by helpful surrogates, not found for him by policemen or loaned to him by friends out of the goodness of their hearts; and so he loved it, and entered it in a sort of ecstatic state. *There's no place like home.* The bimbomobile drove in through the electronic gates, the armored garage door rose and then closed behind him, and there he was. No policeman would ever force him to leave it. *Brother, I am too old to go again to my travels,* King Charles II had said after the Restoration, and the king's sentiments were also his. Martin Luther was in his thoughts too. *Hier stehe ich. Ich kann nicht anders.* Martin Luther wasn't talking about real estate, obviously. But this was how he also felt. Here I stand, he told himself. Here I also sit and work and ride my exercise bike and watch TV and bathe and eat and sleep. I can do no other.

Bill Buford had asked him to be one of the judges for the Best of Young British Novelists, 1993. In 1983 he had been on the first of those lists along with Ian McEwan, Martin Amis, Kazuo Ishiguro, Graham Swift and Julian Barnes. Now he was reading the work of younger writers: Jeanette Winterson, Will Self, Louis de Bernières, A. L. Kennedy, Ben Okri, Hanif Kureishi. His fellow judges were A. S. Byatt, John Mitchinson of Waterstone's booksellers, and Bill himself. There were pleasant discoveries (Iain Banks) and also disappointments (Sunetra Gupta was not a British citizen so couldn't be considered). They agreed quickly about more than half the writers included in the final twenty and then the interesting disagreements began. He argued with Antonia Byatt about Robert McLiam Wilson and lost. She favored D. J. Taylor, but that was a battle she, in her turn, did not win. There was a disagreement about which of the daughters of Lucian Freud they might include, Esther Freud or Rose Boyt. (Esther made it, Rose didn't.) He was a great admirer of A. L. Kennedy's work and managed to marshal enough support for it to override Antonia Byatt's opposition. It was a passionate, serious debate and at the end there were sixteen writers about whom all the judges were in total agreement and a final four about whom they all disagreed equally strongly. Then the list was published and the piranhas of the little pond of the London literary scene went after it.

Harry Ritchie in *The Sunday Times,* after getting exclusive rights to reveal the names of the chosen twenty writers and agreeing to support the promotion properly, took it upon himself to trash the list. He called Ritchie and said, "Have you read all of those writers? Because I certainly hadn't until I took on this job." Ritchie admitted that he had read only about half the writers on the list. That hadn't stopped him from disparaging them. Apparently you could no longer count on even your allotted fifteen minutes of grace before the bludgeoning began. You got whacked on the head as soon as you were out of the egg. Three days later James Wood, the malevolent Procrustes of literary criticism, who tormented his victims on the narrow bed of his inflexible literary ideologies, pulling them painfully apart or else cutting them off at the knees, gave the twenty the treatment in *The Guardian.* Welcome to English literature, boys and girls.

On Christmas Day he and Elizabeth were able to invite Graham Swift and Candice Rodd to spend the day with them. On Boxing Day, Nigella Lawson and John Diamond and Bill and Alicja Buford came to dine. Elizabeth, who loved the festival and all its rituals—he had begun to call her, affectionately, a "Christmas fundamentalist"—was very happy to be able to "do Christmas" for everyone. After four years they could spend the holidays in their own home, with their own tree, repaying their friends' years of hospitality and kindness.

But the beating wings of the death angel were never far away. Nigella's sister Thomasina was doing badly in her battle against breast cancer. Antonia Fraser's son Orlando had a bad car accident in Bosnia, broke many bones and had a perforated lung. But he survived. Ian McEwan's stepdaughter Polly's boyfriend was caught in a burning house in Berlin. He did not survive.

Clarissa called, in tears. She had been given a six months' layoff notice by the A. P. Watt literary agency. He spoke to Gillon Aitken and Liz Calder. This was a problem that had to be solved.

He was photographed in a sort of cage by Terry O'Neill for the London *Sunday Times*. This picture would run on the cover of the Sunday magazine, to illustrate an essay by him that would be given the title "The Last Hostage." He wondered as he clutched the rusting bars O'Neill had found for him to stand behind if the day would ever again come when journalists and photographers were interested in him as a novelist. It didn't seem likely. He had just heard from Andrew that in spite of the agency's best efforts Random House had declined to take on the publication of the paperback of *The Satanic Verses*. The Consortium could not be dissolved just yet. However, Andrew added, many senior figures at Random House—Frances Coady and Simon Master in the London office, and Sonny Mehta in New York—professed to be "very angry" about this refusal by the top brass (the same top brass who, when refusing to join the paperback consortium, had said they "weren't going to be pushed around by any damn agent") and promised they were working to "turn it around."

A political trip to Dublin. Elizabeth and he were invited to stay at Bono's place in Killiney. There was a beautiful little guest house at the bottom of the Hewsons' garden with CinemaScope views of Killiney Bay. Guests were encouraged to sign their names and scribble messages or drawings on the bathroom wall. On the first evening he met Irish writers at the home of the *Irish Times* journalist Paddy Smyth, whose mother, the eminent novelist Jennifer Johnston, told the story of how Tom Maschler at Jonathan Cape had told her, after reading her first novel, that he thought she wasn't a writer and would never write another book, which was why he wasn't going to publish the one she had written. So there was literary gossip but also political work. The former prime minister Garret Fitzgerald was one of several politicians present, all of whom pledged their support.

President Mary Robinson received him at her official residence, Phoenix Park—his first meeting with a head of state!—and sat twinkling-eyed and silent while he made his case. She said little, but murmured, "It's no sin to listen." He spoke at the "Let in the Light" free-speech conference at Trinity and afterward at the drinks for the speakers a small sturdy woman came up to him and told him that because he had opposed the ordinance called Section 31, which banned Sinn Féin from Irish TV, "you have removed all danger to yourself from us." "I see," he said, "and who's *us*?" The woman looked him in the eye. "You know fockin' well who we are," she said. After being given this free pass by the IRA he was whisked to the legendary talk-show host Gay Byrne's *Late Late Show,* and because Gay said he had read and liked *The Satanic Verses,* just about the whole of Ireland decided that it and its author must be okay.

In the morning he visited Joyce's Martello tower, where stately, plump Buck Mulligan had lived with Stephen Dedalus and walking up the stairs to the turreted roof he felt as many had felt before him as if he were stepping into the novel. *Introibo ad altare Dei,* he said under his breath. Then at the Abbey Theatre a lunch with writers and the new arts minister, the poet Michael D. Higgins, and all of them wearing I AM SALMAN RUSHDIE button badges. After lunch two of the other Salman Rushdies, Colm Tóibín and Dermot Bolger, took him for a walk out to the lighthouse on Howth Head (the Garda following at a polite distance) and the lighthouse keeper, John, allowed him to switch on the light. On Sunday Bono smuggled him out to a bar in Killiney without telling the Garda and for half an hour he was giddy with the unprotected freedom of it and maybe thanks to the unprotected Guinness too. When they got back to the Hewson house the Garda looked at Bono with mournful accusation but forbore to speak harsh words to their country's favorite son.

———

In *The Independent on Sunday* he was being attacked from the right and the left; the Prince of Wales called him a bad writer who cost too much to protect, while the left-wing journalist Richard Gott, an old Soviet sympathizer who was eventually forced to resign from *The Guardian* when it was proven that he had "taken Red gold," attacked his political opinions and his "out of touch" writing. He suddenly felt, with the force of an epiphany, the truth of what he had written in "In Good Faith": that freedom was always taken, never given. Maybe he should refuse protection and just live out his life. But could he take Elizabeth and Zafar into that risky future? Would that not be irresponsible? He should discuss this with Elizabeth and Clarissa too.

A new president had his inauguration in Washington. Christopher Hitchens called. "Clinton is definitely pro-you," he said. "That's a sure thing." John Leonard published a piece in *The Nation* recommending that the incoming president, who was known to be a serious reader and had said that his favorite book was García Márquez's *One Hundred Years of Solitude,* should read *The Satanic Verses.*

The Secret Policeman's Balls were fund-raising benefits for Amnesty International in the 1980s, but the comedians and musicians who took part were almost certainly not informed that the secret policemen really did have a ball—or at least a sizable bash. Every winter, in February or so, the "A" Squad's annual party took over Peelers, the large bar/restaurant space on an upper floor of New Scotland Yard, and the guest list was unlike any other in London. Everyone who was receiving or had ever received protection was invited, and all of these "principals" did their best to attend, as a way of thanking the officers who had looked after them. Prime ministers past and present, Northern Ireland secretaries of state, defense ministers, foreign secretaries of both major parties gossiped and boozed with prot officers and OFDs. In addition the protection teams were allowed to invite a few of their principals' friends and associates who had been especially helpful. It made for quite a room.

He would say in those years that if he ever wrote the story of his life he would call it *Back Doors of the World*. Anybody could walk in the front door. You really had to be somebody to get in through the kitchen door, the staff entrance, the rear window, the garbage chute. Even when he was taken to New Scotland Yard for the Secret Policemen's Ball he went in through the underground parking garage and was spirited upstairs in an elevator locked off for his use. The other guests used the main entrance but he was the rear-entry guy. But once at Peelers he was a part of that happy throng—happy, in part, because the only drinks on offer appeared to be enormous glasses of scotch or gin—and all "his" team members came up to greet him with a cheery "Joe!"

The protection officers took especial delight in putting together principals who would never ordinarily meet, just to see what happened. They steered him through the crowd to where a frail old man with the remnants of a famous mustache stood, slightly stooped, beside his solicitous wife. He had in fact once run into Enoch Powell before, back in the 1970s when he had been living in Clarissa's house on Lower Belgrave Street. He had gone into the local newspaper shop, Quinlan's, to buy a paper and there was Powell coming out toward him, Powell at the height of his demon-eyed fame, just a few years after the anti-immigrant "rivers of blood" speech that destroyed his political career. *Like the Roman I seem to see the river Tiber foaming with much blood,* he had said, expressing every British racist's fear of dusky foreigners. That day at Quinlan's newspaper shop the nonviolent young immigrant facing the notorious Enoch had seriously considered punching him in the nose, and had always been a little disappointed with himself that he had not. But Lower Belgrave Street was full of people in need of a bloody nose—Madame Somoza, the Nicaraguan dictator's wife, next door at number 35 and those nice Lucans at number 46 (Lord Lucan, at that time, had not yet tried to murder his wife, killing the nanny instead; but he was working up to it). Once you started punching people it would be hard to know where to stop. It had probably been a good idea to walk away from Enoch of the glittering eyeballs and post-Hitlerian upper lip.

And twenty years later here Powell was again. "No," he said to his protectors. "On the whole, I'd prefer not to." Then came cries of "Oh, go on Joe, he's an old geezer now," and the one that got through his defenses, "Mrs. Powell, you see, Joe," said Stanley Doll, "it's a hard life for her, looking after the old boy. She really wants to meet you. It would mean a lot." So it was Margaret Powell he and Elizabeth agreed to meet. She had lived in Karachi as a young person, in the same neighborhood as members of his own family, and wanted to chat about the old days. Old Enoch stood beside her stooped and nodding and silent, too decrepit to be worth punching anymore. After a courteous interval he made his excuses, took Elizabeth by the elbow, turned away, and there was Margaret Thatcher looking right at him with her handbag and lacquered hair and her crooked little smile.

He would never have guessed that the Iron Lady was a touchy-feely person. Throughout their brief conversation the former prime minister was putting her hands on him. *Hello, dear,* her hand resting lightly on the back of his hand, *how are you getting along,* her hand beginning to caress his forearm, *are these wonderful men taking good care of you?,* her hand on his shoulder now, he had better speak, he told himself, before she started caressing his cheek. "Yes, thank you," he said, and she ducked her head in that famous bobble-head nod. *Good, good,* the hand was caressing his arm again, *well, you look after yourself,* and that would have been it, except that Elizabeth interrupted to ask, very firmly, what the British government proposed to do to end the threats. Lady Thatcher looked mildly surprised to find such tough words emerging from the mouth of this pretty young thing, and her body stiffened just a little. *Oh, my dear,* and now it was Elizabeth she was caressing, *yes, it must be very worrying for you, but I'm afraid nothing will really change until there's a change of regime in Tehran.* "That's it?" Elizabeth said. "That's your policy?" The Thatcher hand withdrew. The sharp gaze wandered off and focused on infinity. There was a vague nod and a trailing *Mmm* noise and then she was gone.

Elizabeth was angry for the rest of the evening. *That's it? That's their whole plan?* But he thought of Margaret Thatcher caressing his arm, and smiled.

The fourth anniversary of the *fatwa* was as heated as ever. The usual blood-curdling noises emanated from Tehran, where Ayatollah Khamenei, President Rafsanjani, Nateq-Nouri, the Speaker of the Majlis and others were plainly rattled by the increasing volume of official objections to their murderous little plan. Their menaces were answered in the U.S. Congress, at the UN Commission for Human Rights, and even by the British government. Douglas Hurd spoke up in Strasbourg and his deputy Douglas Hogg spoke in Geneva, identifying the Rushdie case as a "human rights issue of great importance." An oil deal with Iran was being blocked in Norway; a billion-dollar line of credit promised by Canada to Iran had also been blocked. He himself was in an unexpected place: delivering the sermon—or, since he was not a man of the cloth, the address—from the pulpit of King's College Chapel.

Before he began to speak the dean of King's warned him about the echo. "Leave gaps after every few words," he said, "or the reverberations will make you inaudible." He felt that he was being let into a mystery: So *that* was why sermons always sounded like that. "To stand—in this house—is to be reminded—of what is most beautiful—about religious faith," he began, and thought, *I sound like an archbishop.* He pressed on, to speak in the house of God about the virtues of the secular, and to lament the loss of others who had fought the good fight—Farag Fouda in Egypt, and now Turkey's most popular journalist, Ugur Mumcu, assassinated by a bomb in his car. The ruthlessness of the godly invalidated their claims of virtue. "Just as King's Chapel—may be taken—as a symbol—of what is best—about religion," he said in his best ecclesiastical diction, "so the *fatwa*—has become—a symbol—of what is worst. The *fatwa* itself—may be seen—as a set—of modern satanic verses. In the *fatwa*—once again—evil—takes on the guise—of virtue—and the faithful—are—deceived."

On February 26, 1993, the World Trade Center in New York was bombed by a group led by a Kuwaiti man called Ramzi Yousef. Six people died, over a thousand were injured, but the towers did not fall.

Friends were telling him the campaign was becoming very effective and he was doing very well but he was too often in the grip of what Winston Churchill had called the "black dog" of depression. Out there in the world he could fight, he had taught himself to do what had to be done. When he got home he often fell apart and it was Elizabeth who had to deal with the wreckage. David Gore-Booth told him that the Foreign Office had talked to British Airways but the airline was determinedly refusing to carry him. Tom Phillips had finished his portrait of Mr. Chirpy and offered it to the National Portrait Gallery, which decided not to acquire it "at this time." Sometimes when news of this sort arrived he drank too much—he had never been a big drinker before the *fatwa*—and then his demons could not be resisted and there was a certain amount of booze-induced bad temper. Tom Phillips had given him the *Mr. Chirpy* portrait, and when he tried to hang it, and found his toolbox missing, he burst into an excessive rage that Elizabeth found unbearable, and she collapsed in floods of tears. And she told him that the idea of giving up the protection was crazy and she would not live with him in an unprotected house. If he gave up the protection he would live there alone.

After that he was more careful of her feelings. She was a brave, loving woman and he was lucky to have her and he would not allow himself to screw things up. He decided to cut out alcohol altogether, and though he didn't succeed entirely the nights of excess came to an end and moderation returned. He would not fulfill Marianne's curse and turn into his alcoholic father. He refused to turn Elizabeth into another version of his own long-suffering mother.

Doris Lessing was writing her memoirs and called to discuss them. Rousseau's way, she said, was the only way; you just had to tell the truth, to tell as much truth as possible. But scruples and hesitations were inevitable. "At that time, Salman, I was a pretty good-looking woman and there are implications in that fact which you may not have considered. The people with whom I had or almost had affairs . . . many of them were very well known and several of them are still alive. I do think of Rousseau," she added, "and I hope this book is an emotionally honest work, but is it fair to be honest about other people's emotions?" Anyway, she concluded, the real problems would be in volume two. She was still doing volume one, whose personages were all dead or "don't care anymore." With much giggling she went off to write, encouraging him to do the same. He wanted to say, but did not, that he was again imagining a life of not being a writer, thinking of the peace and stillness, perhaps even the joy, of that life. But he was resolved to finish the book he was writing. This one last sigh at least.

And the book was slowly progressing. In Cochin, Abraham Zogoiby and Aurora da Gama were falling in "pepper love."

In mid-March he finally managed to fly to Paris. The fearsome men of the RAID surrounded him as he got off the plane and informed him that he had to do exactly, *exactly,* as they said. They took him at high speed to the Grande Arche de la Défense and there was Jack Lang, minister of culture and number two in the French government, waiting to greet him with Bernard-Henri Lévy and bring him to the auditorium. He tried not to think about the mammoth security operation all around the arche and to concentrate, instead, on the extraordinary gathering waiting for him, which appeared to be the entire French intelligentsia and political elite of the right as well as the left. (Except Mitterrand. Always, in those years in France, *sauf Mitterrand.*) Bernard Kouchner and Nicolas Sarkozy, Alain Finkielkraut and Jorge Semprún, Philippe Sollers and Elie Wiesel rubbed shoulders and behaved cordially to one another. Patrice Chéreau, Françoise Giroud, Michel Rocard, Ismail Kadare, Simone Veil—this was a mighty room.

Jack Lang, introducing the proceedings, said, "We must thank Salman Rushdie today, because he has united French culture." That got a big laugh. Then for two hours there was an intense period of questioning. He hoped that he had made a good impression, but there was no time to find out if he had, because as soon as the meeting ended the RAID team hustled him out of the room and drove him away as fast as they could go. They were taking him to the British embassy, which, being technically British soil, was the only place in Paris where he was allowed to spend the night. One night. The British ambassador, Christopher Mallaby, greeted him with great friendship and courtesy and had even read some of his books. But it was also made clear that this was a one-off invitation. He could not think of the embassy as his hotel in Paris. The next morning he was driven to the airport and dismissed from France.

On his way to and from the embassy he was shocked to notice that *the Place de la Concorde was closed to traffic.* All the roads in and out of Concorde were blocked by policemen so that he, in his RAID motorcade, could rush across the place unimpeded. It made him sad. He did not want to be the person for whom Concorde was closed off. The motorcade passed a little café-bistro and everyone drinking coffee under its awning was staring in his direction, with curiosity and a little resentment mingling on their faces. *I wonder,* he thought, *if I will ever again be one of those people drinking a cup of coffee on the sidewalk and watching the world go by.*

The house was beautiful but it felt like a gilded cage. He had learned how to withstand the Islamic attacks on him; it was after all not surprising that fanatics and bigots should continue to behave like bigots and fanatics. It was harder to handle the non-Muslim British criticisms, which were mounting in volume, and the apparent duplicity of the Foreign Office and John Major's government, which consistently promised one thing and did another. He wrote a furious article letting all the rage and disappointment show. Cooler heads—Elizabeth, Frances, Gillon—persuaded him not to publish it. He thought, looking back, that he had been wrong to take their advice. Every time he chose to remain silent during this period of his life—for example, during the year between the *fatwa* and the publication of "In Good Faith"—the silence afterward felt like a mistake.

On Monday 22nd February, the prime minister's office announced that Mr. Major had agreed in principle to a meeting with me, as a demonstration of the government's determination to stand up for freedom of expression and for the right of its citizens not to be murdered by thugs in the pay of a foreign power. More recently a date was set for that meeting. Immediately a vociferous Tory backbench campaign sought to have the meeting canceled, because of its interference with Britain's "partnership" with the murderous mullahs of Tehran. The date—which I had been assured was "as firm as can be"—has today been postponed without explanation. By a curious coincidence, a proposed British trade delegation to Iran in early May can now take place without embarrassment. Iran is hailing this visit—the first such mission in the fourteen years since the Khomeini revolution—as a "breakthrough" in relations. Its news agency states that the British have promised that lines of credit will be made available.

It is becoming harder to retain confidence in the Foreign Office's decision to launch a new "high profile" international initiative against the notorious fatwa. For not only are we scurrying off to do business with the tyrannical regime that the U.S. administration calls an "international outlaw" and brands as the world's leading sponsor of terrorism, but we also propose to lend that regime the money with which to do business with us. Meanwhile, I gather I am to be offered a new date for my little meeting. But nobody from No. 10 Downing Street has spoken or written to me.

The Tory "anti-Rushdie" pressure group—its very description demonstrates its members' desire to turn this into an issue of personality rather than principle—includes Sir Edward Heath and Emma Nicholson, as well as that well-known apologist for Iranian interests, Peter Temple-Morris. Emma Nicholson tells us that she has grown to "respect and like" the Iranian regime (whose record of killing, maiming and torturing its own people has recently been condemned by the United Nations as being among the worst in the world), while Sir Edward, still protected by Special Branch because, twenty years ago, the British people suffered under his disastrous premiership, criticizes the decision to offer similar protection to a fellow Briton who is presently in greater danger than himself. All these persons agree on one point: The crisis is my fault. Never mind that over two hundred of the most prominent Iranians in exile have signed a statement of absolute support for me. That writers, thinkers, journalists and academics throughout the Muslim world—where the attack upon dissenting, progressive and above all secularist ideas is daily gathering force—have told the British media that "to defend Rushdie is to defend us." That The Satanic Verses, *a legitimate work of the free imagination, has many defenders (and where there are at least two views why should the book burners have the last word?), or that its opponents have felt no need to understand it.*

Iranian officials have admitted that Khomeini never so much as saw a copy of the novel. Islamic jurisprudents have stated that the fatwa contradicts

*Islamic law, never mind international law. Meanwhile, the Iranian press is of-
fering a prize of sixteen gold pieces and a pilgrimage to Mecca for a cartoon
"proving" that* The Satanic Verses *is not a novel at all, but a carefully engineered Western conspiracy against Islam. Does this whole affair not feel, at
times, like the blackest of black comedy—a circus sideshow enacted by murderous clowns?*

*In the last four years I have been slandered by many people. I do not in-
tend to keep turning the other cheek. If it was proper to attack those on the
left who were the fellow travelers of Communism, and those on the right who
sought to appease the Nazis, then the friends of revolutionary Iran—
businessmen, politicians or British fundamentalists—deserve to be treated
with equal contempt.*

*I believe we have reached a turning point. Either we are serious about de-
fending freedom, or we are not. If we are, then I hope Mr. Major will very
soon be willing to stand up and be counted as he has promised. I should very
much like to discuss with him how pressure on Iran can be increased—in the
EC, through the Commonwealth and the UN, at the World Court. Iran
needs us more than we need Iran. Instead of quaking when the mullahs
threaten to cut trade links, let us be the ones to turn the economic screws. I
have discovered, in my conversations across Europe and North America, widespread all-party interest in the idea of a ban on offering credit to Iran, as a
first stage. But everyone is waiting for the British government to take a lead.
In today's newspaper, however, Bernard Levin suggests that fully two-thirds
of all Tory MPs would be delighted if Iranian assassins succeeded in killing
me. If these MPs truly represent the nation—if we are so unconcerned about
our liberties—then so be it: Lift the protection, disclose my whereabouts and
let the bullets come. One way or the other. Let's make up our minds.*

The much-postponed meeting with John Major finally took place
on May 11 at his office in the House of Commons. He had spoken to
Nigella Lawson before he went and her levelheadedness was a great
help. "He can't possibly refuse to back you," she said. "The bad state
of the economy helps you, because if he can't point to economic success he's going to have to go for some moral strength." She also had
good news; she was pregnant. He told Elizabeth this, knowing that she
very much wanted to be pregnant herself. But how could they think

about bringing a child into this nightmare, into their soft prison? And then there was the simple translocated chromosome, which turned pregnancy into biological roulette. A baby didn't seem like the wisest option for a man who was about to beg the prime minister to help him save his life.

The prime minister was not wearing his trademark nice-guy grin and did not talk about cricket. He seemed closed off, maybe even a little defensive, a man who knew he was going to be asked to do things he might not want to do. He said bluntly that there would be no photographs taken at this meeting because he wanted to "minimize the reaction from Iran and from his own backbenchers." That was an inauspicious start.

"I'd like to thank you for the four years of protection," he told Major. "I'm immensely grateful to the men who look after me, risking their own lives." Major looked shocked. This was not the Rushdie he had expected, the one the *Daily Mail* described as "bad-mannered, sullen, graceless, silly, curmudgeonly, unattractive, small-minded, arrogant and egocentric." It immediately became plain that the prime minister had the *Daily Mail* in his head. (It had printed an editorial opposing this meeting.) "Maybe you should say things like that more often," he said, "in public, to correct the impression people have of you." "Prime Minister," he said, "I say it every time I talk to a journalist." He nodded vaguely but seemed more relaxed and affable. The meeting went well from then on. It was not the first or last time that people discovered, once he had managed to wipe away the tabloid cartoon-Rushdie from their eyes, that he was actually quite companionable. "You've put on weight," Major suddenly said. "Thanks a lot, Prime Minister," he replied. "You should do my job," the prime minister told him, "and you'd lose it in no time." "Fine," he answered, "I'll do your job if you'll do mine." After that they were almost pals.

Major expressed his agreement with the high-profile approach. "You should go to Japan and shame them into action," he said. They discussed getting a resolution from the Commonwealth so that Iran could not characterize the issue as a difference of opinion between East and West. They talked about the International Court of Justice; Major did not want to take the case there because he didn't want to "paint Iran into a corner." And they agreed on the value of a meeting with President Clinton. He told the prime minister what the UN hostage negotiator Picco had said. *The U.S. is the key.* Major nodded and looked at his aides. "Let us see what we can do to help," he said.

When the news of the meeting was released, along with a statement by the prime minister condemning the *fatwa,* the Iranian regime's official newspaper *Kayhan* reacted angrily. "The author of *The Satanic Verses* is literally going to get it in the neck." This was high-stakes poker. He was deliberately trying to up the ante, and so far the Iranians were hanging tough and refusing to fold. But there was only one way to go now. He had to raise again.

Clarissa called him to say there was a lump in her breast, "and it's four out of five on the cancer probability scale." She was having the lumpectomy in six days and the result would be available a week later. There was a tremble in her voice but there was her usual stoic courage too. He was very shaken. He called her back a few minutes later and offered to pay for private treatment, whatever she needed. They talked about whether it was possible to avoid a full mastectomy and he passed on such information as he had gleaned from Nigella and Thomasina about the high quality of the breast cancer unit at Guy's Hospital and the name of the specialist, Mr. Fentiman. There had been a *Sunday Times* magazine cover story about breast cancer and there was Fentiman again. He thought, *She must beat it. She doesn't deserve it. She will beat it.* He and Elizabeth would do whatever they could. But in the face of fatal illness one was always alone. And Zafar would have to face this too; Zafar, who had already spent four years fearing for one parent. The blow had not come from the direction in which he was looking. It was the "safe" parent who was now in danger. He couldn't help thinking ahead. How could he make a livable life for Zafar if the boy lost his mother? He would have to live in this secret house but what of his school, his friends, his life in the "real" world? How could he help him heal the wound of so terrible a loss?

He said to Elizabeth, it feels as if half your life is a sort of struggle toward the sunlight. Then you get five minutes in the sun and after that you're dragged down into the darkness again and you die. No sooner had he said it than he heard the character of Flory Zogoiby saying it too, Abraham's mother in *The Moor's Last Sigh*. Were there no limits to the shamelessness of the literary imagination? No. There were no limits.

He told the prot officer Dick Billington about Clarissa and the possibility of cancer, and Dick said, "Oh, women are always getting ill."

Sameen told him she'd had a long talk with Clarissa, who wanted to reminisce about the old days. She had been brave but said she felt she'd "had her share of bad luck." Clarissa's illness had made Sameen think about her own mortality. She wanted to ask him if he would assume guardianship of her daughters if she and their father died.

He said yes, of course, but she should have a backup plan, considering the danger to his own life.

The test results came in from Bart's—St. Bartholomew's Hospital— and they were very bad indeed. Clarissa had an *invasive ductal carcinoma,* and it had been undetected for perhaps eighteen months. Radical surgery would be required. The cancer had "probably" spread to the lymphatic system. She would have to have blood tests, and her lungs, liver and bone marrow would have to be tested too. She was speaking in her most controlled voice but he could hear the terror under the words. Zafar hugged her very tightly, she said, and was close to tears. She had already, with huge strength, accustomed herself to the need for the mastectomy but what would she do, she said, if there was bad news about the liver and the bone marrow? How did one face the inevitability of death?

He called Nigella. There was a man she knew who was trying new techniques with liver cancer and having some success. That was a straw to clutch at, but no more than a straw.

Zafar came to spend the night. He was suppressing his feelings. His mother had always done the same thing in the face of adversity. "How's Mum?" "Fine." It was better to let him deal with the news slowly, at his own speed, rather than sit him down and terrify him. Clarissa had spoken to him and used the word "cancer." He replied, "You told me that already." But she hadn't.

The new test results arrived. Clarissa's blood, lungs, liver and bone were all cancer-free. But it's a "bad cancer," she was told. The mastectomy was unavoidable, and ten lymph nodes would also have to be removed. She wanted a second opinion. He wanted her to get one. He would cover all her costs. She went to a highly recommended oncologist named Sikora at Hammersmith Hospital and Sikora didn't think the mastectomy was necessary. Now that the lump had been removed she could have chemotherapy and radiotherapy and that would handle it. When she heard she could keep her breasts she brightened enormously. She was a beautiful woman and the mutilation of that beauty had been hard for her to bear. Then she had to meet the surgeon who would perform the lumpectomy, a man named Linn, and he turned out to be a creep. *Darling,* he called her oleaginously, *sweetheart, why do you object to this op so much?* He told her she should have the mastectomy, directly contradicting the head of oncology, Sikora, wrecking her newfound confidence and removing her justification for having switched to Hammersmith Hospital from Bart's, where she had had counseling she valued and doctors she actually liked. She began to panic and was close to hysteria for two days until she could speak to Sikora again. He reassured her that his proposed course of action was the one they would follow. She calmed down, and took Zafar away for a week's cycling holiday in France.

Sameen said that her friend Kishu, a surgeon in New York, had told her that with an invasive cancer of this sort one shouldn't mess about but go ahead and have the mastectomy. Yet the no-mastectomy route had lifted Clarissa's spirits immeasurably. It was so hard to know how to advise her. She did not want his advice.

His lawyer Bernie Simons called. The *decree nisi* had gone through and the divorce from Marianne would be complete in a few weeks when they received the decree absolute. Oh, yeah, he remembered. I'm still getting divorced.

He received a message from Bernard-Henri Lévy. It was good news: He was to be offered the *très important* Swiss award, the Prix Colette, the prize of the Geneva Book Fair. He should come to Switzerland the following week and receive the prize at a grand ceremony at the fair. But the Swiss government declared him an unwelcome visitor and said they would refuse to provide police protection for his visit. He thought of Mr. Greenup saying he was endangering the citizenry by reason of his desire for self-aggrandizement. On this occasion the Swiss Greenups had won. There would be no self-aggrandizement. The citizenry of Switzerland would be safe. All he could do was to make a phone call to the room at the Geneva Book Fair in which the prize was being awarded. BHL made a speech saying that the award had been the unanimous decision of the jury. The jury president, Mme Edmonde Charles-Roux, said that the award was faithful to the "spirit of Colette," who "fought against intolerance." However, Colette's heirs were furious about the award, presumably not agreeing with Mme Charles-Roux that to select Salman Rushdie was "in the spirit of Colette." They expressed their anger by refusing to allow Colette's name to be used in future. Thus he became the final winner of the Prix Colette.

He had a nosy neighbor to deal with, an elderly gentleman named Bertie Joel. Mr. Joel came to the gate and said, on the intercom, that he wanted someone to come to his house "in the next fifteen minutes." Elizabeth was out so one of the team had to go around. Everyone was tense; had Mr. Anton's secret identity been discovered? But it was just a question of a blocked drain that ran between the two properties. The new head of the protection team, Frank Bishop, was an older, well-spoken, cheerful man, and a cricket-mad member of the Marylebone Cricket Club. It turned out that Bertie Joel was a member too and had known Frank's father. The cricket connection erased all suspicions. "The builders told me that the whole house was being steel plated, so I suspected Mafia connections," said Bertie Joel, and Frank laughed it off and put him at his ease. When he came back and told everyone what had happened the team was almost hysterical with relief. "Got a result there, Joe," Frank said. "It's a result, that is."

There were other such moments. The electric gates jammed open one day and a man looking exactly like the poet Philip Larkin wandered in and peered around the forecourt. On another day there was a man on the sidewalk with a stepladder, trying to take pictures of the house over the hedge. It turned out he was doing a newspaper story about repossessions of houses on the street. On yet another day there was a man on a motorbike and a Volvo parked across the street containing three men who were "acting strangely." On such days he thought, *Maybe there really are killers in the neighborhood and I really am about to be killed*. But all of these were false alarms. The house was not "blown."

Bernie Simons was suddenly dead; sweet, indispensable Bernie, solicitor to a whole generation of the British left, the wisest and warmest of human beings, who had helped him fight the Muslim cases against him and been an invaluable ally in the battle against Howley and Hammington's threat to withdraw protection. Bernie was only fifty-two. He had been at a conference in Madrid and had just finished dinner, gone upstairs, had an enormous heart attack and plunged face-first toward the rug. A quick end after a good meal. That, at least, was appropriate. All over London people were calling one another to mourn. He spoke to Robert McCrum, Caroline Michel, Melvyn Bragg. To Robert he said, "It's so terrible—it makes me want to call Bernie and ask him to fix it."

It was too early to start finding his contemporaries in the obituary pages but the next day Bernie was there, as Angela had been, and as he feared Clarissa might soon be. And Edward Said had CLL, chronic lymphocytic leukemia, and Gita Mehta had a cancer too and was being operated on. The wings, the beating wings. He was the one who was supposed to die but people were dropping all around him.

In early June, Elizabeth drove Clarissa to Hammersmith Hospital for another bout of exploratory surgery. The outcome was hopeful. The surgeon, Mr. Linn, said he could "see no more cancer." So maybe they had caught it early enough, and she would live. Clarissa was very sure that it was good news. Radiotherapy would zap any cells that remained and since "only one, the smallest one" of the lymph nodes was infected she could do without chemotherapy, she thought. He had his doubts but held his tongue.

Edward Said told him that his white count was going up and he might need chemotherapy soon. "But I'm a walking miracle," he said. His doctor was the man who had "written the book" on CLL, a Long Island physician of Indian origin named Dr. Kanti Rai; the stages of the illness were known as the "Rai stages" because of his work on defining the nature of the disease. So Edward, who had been something of a hypochondriac until he got really sick, where-upon he immediately became a courageous hero, had the best of all possible doctors and was fighting the illness with all his might. "You're a walking miracle, too," he said. "The two of us have no right to be alive but here we are." He said he had seen an interview with Ayatollah Sanei of the Bounty in *The New York Times*. "He has a cartoon of you burning in hell on the wall behind his head. He said, *The road to Paradise will be easier when Rushdie is dead.*" Edward's huge giggle of a laugh erupted as his arms waved to dismiss the Bountiful One's remark.

On his forty-sixth birthday he had friends to the house for dinner. By this time there was a list of people the Special Branch approved of, close friends they had come to know over the years, and knew to be closemouthed and trustworthy. Bill Buford brought an excellent Côtes du Rhone and Gillon brought Puligny-Montrachet. There was a ham-mock from Pauline Melville and a very nice blue linen shirt from Ni-gella. John Diamond was lucky to be alive after a bus jumped a red light and hit his car at 40 mph right on the driver's door. Fortunately, the door had held.

Antonia Fraser and Harold Pinter brought a limited edition of Harold's poems. (If Harold had your fax number these poems would arrive from time to time and needed to be praised as soon as possible. One of the poems was named "Len Hutton" after the great England batsman. *I saw Len Hutton in his prime / Another time / Another time.* That was it. Harold's great friend and fellow playwright Simon Gray neglected to comment on this piece and Harold called him up to re-proach him. "I'm sorry, Harold," Simon said. "I haven't had time to finish it." Mr. Pinter didn't see the joke.)

The prominent Algerian writer and journalist Tahar Djaout was shot in the head and died, the third major intellectual, after Farag Fouda in Egypt and Ugur Mumcu in Turkey, to be murdered in a year. He tried to draw attention to their cases in the Western media but there was only a little interest. His own campaign seemed to be stalling. Christopher Hitchens had heard from the British ambassador in Washington, Sir Robin Renwick, that any meeting with Clinton would not take place before the autumn at the earliest. Frances and Carmel quarreled often and then they both quarreled with him. He expressed his near-despair to them and insisted that they get their own show back on the road and they rallied.

He made a second trip to Paris to speak at a gathering of the Académie Universelle des Cultures in a grand chamber at the Louvre full of gilt, frescoes, and writers: Elie Wiesel, Wole Soyinka, Yashar Kemal, Adonis, Ismail Kadare, Cynthia Ozick . . . and Umberto Eco. He had just given Eco's novel *Foucault's Pendulum* the worst review he had ever given any book. Eco bore down upon him and then behaved with immense good grace. He spread his arms and cried, "Rushdie! I am the boolsheet Eco!" After that they were on excellent terms. (In times to come they joined forces with Mario Vargas Llosa to form a literary triple act that Eco named the Three Musketeers, "because first we were enemies and now we are friends." Vargas Llosa had criticized Salman for being too left-wing, Eco had criticized Mario for being too right-wing, and Salman had criticized Eco's writing, but when they met they got on famously. The Three Musketeers performed successfully in Paris, London and New York.)

The security arrangements were insanely excessive. The good men of the RAID had forced the Louvre Museum to close for the day. There were vast numbers of men with machine guns everywhere. He was not allowed to stand near a window. And at lunchtime when the writers walked across to the I. M. Pei glass pyramid to go downstairs for lunch the RAID forced him to sit in a car that drove perhaps one hundred yards to the pyramid from the wing of the Louvre where the Académie had met, with armed men in mirrored sunglasses walking all around it, heavy weaponry at the ready. It was worse than crazy; it was embarrassing.

At the end of the day the security forces informed him that the interior minister, Charles Pasqua, had refused him permission to spend the night in France, because it would be too expensive. But, he argued, he had been offered private accommodation at the homes of Bernard-Henri Lévy, Bernard Kouchner and Christine Ockrent, and Jack Lang's daughter Caroline, so it would cost nothing at all. *Well, then, it is because we have identified a specific threat against you so we cannot guarantee your safety.* Not even the Special Branch believed that lie. "They would have shared that information with us, Joe," said Frank Bishop, "and they did not." Caroline Lang said, "If you want to defy the RAID order we will all squat here in the Louvre with you, and bring in beds and wine and friends." That was a funny and touching idea but he refused. "If I do that they will never let me enter France again." Then Christopher Mallaby refused to allow him to stay at the embassy; but someone, the British or the French, managed to persuade British Airways to fly him back to London. So for the first time in four years he flew, without any problems from crew or passengers—many of whom came up to express their friendship, solidarity and sympathy—on a BA plane. After the trip, however, British Airways said that the flight had been agreed to under French pressure "at the local operational level" and they had taken steps "to ensure that it would never happen again."

U2's giant *Zooropa* tour arrived at Wembley Stadium, and Bono called him to ask if he'd like to come out on stage. U2 wanted to make a gesture of solidarity, and this was the biggest one they could think of. Amazingly the Special Branch did not object. Maybe they didn't think there would be many Islamic assassins at a U2 gig, or perhaps they just wanted to see the show. He took Zafar and Elizabeth with him and for the first half of the show they sat in the stadium and watched it. When he got up to go backstage Zafar said, "Dad . . . don't sing." He had no intention of singing, and U2 were even less keen on letting him, but to tease his teenage son he said, "I don't see why not. It's quite a good backing band, this Irish band, and there are eighty thousand people out here, so . . . maybe I'll sing." Zafar looked agitated. "You don't understand, Dad," he said. "If you sing, I'll have to kill myself."

Backstage he found Bono in his MacPhisto outfit—the gold lamé suit, the white face, the little red velvet horns—and in a few minutes they worked out a little bit of dialogue for them to do. Bono would pretend to call him on his cellphone and while they were "talking" he would walk out on stage. When he went on he understood what it felt like to have eighty thousand people cheering you on. The audience at the average book reading—or even at a big gala night like the PEN benefit in Toronto—was a little smaller. Girls tended not to climb onto their boyfriends' shoulders, and stage diving was discouraged. Even at the very best literary events, there were only one or two supermodels dancing by the mixing desk. This was bigger.

When he wrote *The Ground Beneath Her Feet* it was useful to have some sense of what it felt like to be out there under the weight of all that light, unable to see the monster that was roaring at you from the dark. He did his best not to trip over any of the cables. After the show Anton Corbijn took a photograph for which he persuaded him to exchange glasses with Bono. For one moment he was allowed to look godlike in Mr. B's wraparound Fly shades, while the rock star peered at him benignly over his uncool literary specs. It was a graphic expression of the difference between the two worlds that had, thanks to U2's generous desire to help him, briefly met.

A few days later Bono called, talking about wanting to grow as a writer. In a rock group the writer just became a sort of conduit for the feelings in the air, the words didn't drive the work, the music did, unless you came from a folk tradition like Dylan, but he wanted to change. *Would you sit down and talk about how you work.* He wanted to meet new people, different people. He sounded hungry for mind food and for what he called *just a good row.* He offered his house in the south of France. He offered friendship.

He had, he told his friends, been cursed with an interesting life, which sometimes resembled a bad novel by himself. One of its worst bad-novel characteristics was that major characters who were unconnected to the rest of the story could show up at any moment, without prefiguration, elbowing themselves into the narrative and threatening to hijack it.

May 27 was the date on which, four years later, his second son, Milan, would be born, taking possession of the date for good, but in 1993 it signaled the entry of a very different individual, the Turkish writer, newspaper publisher and provocateur Aziz Nesin.

He had met Nesin just once, seven years earlier, when the Turkish writer was the one in trouble. Harold Pinter invited a group of writers to the Campden Hill Square house to organize a protest because Nesin had been told that Turkey had decided to confiscate his passport. He wondered if Nesin remembered that the future author of *The Satanic Verses* had willingly signed the protest, and suspected he did not. On May 27 he was told that unspecified extracts from *The Satanic Verses* had been published in the leftist newspaper *Aydinlik*, of which Nesin was editor in chief, without any agreement being sought from the author, in a Turkish translation he had not been sent (it was normal practice for translations to be independently read for quality and accuracy before publication), to challenge the ban on the book in Turkey. The headline over the excerpts read SALMAN RUSHDIE: THINKER OR CHARLATAN? In the following days there were more extracts, and Nesin's commentary on those extracts made it clear that he was firmly in the "charlatan" camp. The Wylie Agency wrote to Nesin to tell him that piracy was piracy and, if he had, as he said, fought for the rights of writers for many years, would he be willing to object to Ayatollah Khomeini's infringement of those rights? Nesin's reply was as petulant as possible. He printed the agency's letter in his newspaper, and commented, "Of what concern is Salman Rushdie's cause to me?" He said he intended to continue publishing, and if Rushdie objected, "you may take us to court."

Aydinlik was harassed, its staff arrested, its distribution halted and copies seized. In an Istanbul mosque an imam declared a jihad against the newspaper. The Turkish government, defending Turkey's secularist principles, decreed that the paper must be distributed, but the controversy continued and the mood remained ugly.

He felt that yet again he and his work had become pawns in somebody else's game. His friend the Turkish writer Murat Belge said that Nesin had been "childish" but, nevertheless, the forces attacking him could not be allowed to succeed. Most painful of all is that he, too, was a committed secularist, and might have expected better treatment from secularists in Turkey. A rift in the forces of secularism could only be good news to secularism's foes. Those foes reacted to the *Aydinlik* excerpts soon afterward, and with extreme violence.

At the beginning of July, Nesin went to a secularist conference in the town of Sivas in Anatolia (Anatolia was the part of Turkey where extreme Islamism had most adherents). They unveiled a statue to Pir Sultan Abdal, a local poet who had been stoned to death for blasphemy in the sixteenth century. Nesin, it was afterward said, made a speech declaring his atheism, and made certain criticisms of the Qur'an. This may or may not have been true. That night the Madimak Hotel, where all the delegates were staying, was surrounded by extremists chanting slogans and threats, and then set on fire. Thirty-seven people died in the flames—writers, cartoonists, actors and dancers. Aziz Nesin was saved, helped out of the building by firemen who did not recognize him. When they realized who he was they began beating him, and a local politician shouted "This is the devil we should really have killed."

The horror of the Sivas massacre was called, in the world's press, a "Rushdie riot." He went on television to denounce the murderers, and wrote angry articles for the *Observer* in London and also for *The New York Times*. That the riot bore his name was unfair, but it wasn't the point. The killings of Farag Fouda, Ugur Mumcu, Tahar Djaout and the Sivas dead were eloquent proof that the attack on *The Satanic Verses* was no isolated incident, but part of a global Islamic assault on freethinkers. He did everything in his power to demand action, from the Turkish government, from the G7 meeting then taking place in Tokyo, from the world. There was a vicious attempt in, of all places, *The Nation,* to accuse him of "spiteful abuse" of Turkish secularists (written by Alexander Cockburn, one of the great contemporary masters of spiteful abuse), but that didn't matter either. Aziz Nesin and the author whose work he had stolen and denigrated would never be friends, but in the face of such an attack he stood shoulder to shoulder with all Turkish secularists, including Nesin.

In the Iranian Majlis and press, inevitably, there were speeches supporting the murderers of Sivas. This was the way of that world: to applaud assassins and vilify men who lived (and sometimes died) by the word.

Horrified by the Sivas atrocity, the celebrated German "undercover journalist" Günter Wallraff, who, in his hugely successful book *Lowest of the Low* had impersonated a Turkish guest worker to expose the terrible treatment of those workers by German racists and even by the German state, got in touch and insisted that the Nesin-Rushdie "misunderstanding" had to be put right. Nesin had continued to give interviews attacking the author of *The Satanic Verses* and his dreadful book, and Wallraff and Arne Ruth, the editor of the Swedish daily *Dagens Nyheter,* had been trying hard to stop him. "If I can persuade Nesin to visit me here at home, would you please come also so we can fix this?" asked Wallraff. He replied that that depended on the spirit in which Nesin was willing to approach such a meeting. "So far he has been insulting and dismissive and that would make it hard for me to be there." "Leave this to me," Wallraff said. "If he says he will come with a positive attitude, will you do the same?" "Yes, okay."

He flew from Biggin Hill to Cologne, and at Günter's home the great journalist and his wife were loud, jovial and welcoming, and Wallraff insisted they play Ping-Pong at once. Wallraff turned out to be a strong player and won most of the games. Aziz Nesin, a small, stocky, silver-haired man, did not come to the Ping-Pong table. He looked like what he was; a badly shaken man who was also unhappy with the company he was in. He sat in a corner and brooded. This was not promising. In the first formal conversation between them, with Wallraff acting as interpreter, Nesin continued to be as scornful as he had been in *Aydinlik*. He had his own fight, against Turkish fanaticism, and didn't give a damn about this one. Wallraff explained to him that they were the same fight. After Ugur Mumcu was killed it had been said in Turkey that "those who condemned Salman Rushdie have now killed Mumcu." A defeat in one battle between secularism and religion was a defeat in all such battles. "Salman has supported you in the past, and he has spoken out everywhere about Sivas," he said, "so you must support him now." It was a long day. Nesin's *amour-propre* seemed to be getting in the way of a reconciliation, because he knew he would have to climb down and admit he had been ungracious. But Wallraff was determined not to let things end badly and in the end Nesin, muttering and grumbling, extended his hand. There was a brief hand clasp followed by an even briefer hug and a photograph in which everyone looked ill at ease and then Wallraff cried, "Good! Now we are all friends!" and took them all for a motorboat ride on the Rhine.

Wallraff's people had filmed the whole event and put together a news item featuring Nesin and himself in which they jointly denounced religious fanaticism and the weakness of the West's responses to it. In public at least, the rift was healed. Aziz Nesin and he had no further contact. Nesin lived on for two years, until a heart attack bore him away.

Dear Harold,

Thanks for arranging for Elizabeth, me and the lads to see your production of Mamet's Oleanna, *and for dinner at the Grill St. Quentin afterward. It was probably wrong of me to mention my reservations about the play, though I did, I thought, say several nice things about your production of it. It was clearly wrong of me to change the subject and start talking to Antonia about her book on the Gunpowder Plot. (I confess I'm interested, these days, in people who want to blow things up.) I saw out of the corner of an eye that you had begun to emit steam from your ears and that your nuclear core had begun to melt down. The China Syndrome was a definite possibility. To prevent it, I said, "Harold, did I forget to mention that your production of* Oleanna *was a work of absolute fucking genius?" "Yes," you said, your teeth glittering mirthlessly. "Yes, as a matter of fact you did forget to mention that." "Harold," I said, "your production of* Oleanna *was a work of absolute fucking genius." "Well, that's more like it," you said, and the nuclear calamity was averted. I have long taken pride in being able to say truthfully that I have never been "Pintered." I am relieved to have found a way of preserving that record.*

He traveled to Prague to see President Václav Havel and Havel greeted him with immense warmth, *finally, we meet!* and spoke of him publicly with such generosity that his great rival, the right-wing prime minister, Václav Klaus, "distanced" himself from the meeting, saying it was a "private" encounter and he had had no knowledge of it (though the Czech police had borrowed one of Klaus's cars for their visitor to use). Klaus said he hoped it would not "hurt" Czech relations with Iran.

He took part in an International PEN conference at Santiago de Compostela—Iberia made no difficulties—and was asked about recent press reports that Prince Charles had attacked him. He replied quoting what Ian McEwan had said to Spanish journalists on a book-publication visit to the country the week before: "Prince Charles costs much more to protect than Rushdie and has never written anything of interest." He returned to London to find the *Daily Mail* vilifying him for something like treachery because he had dared to make a joke about the heir to the throne. "He is abusing the freedom we are paying for," their columnist Mary Kenny declared. Five days later *Midnight's Children* was declared the "Booker of Bookers," the best book to win the prize in its first twenty-five years. He had barely a day to relish the honor before the pendulum swung, and dreadful calamity struck again.

The morning after getting home to Oslo from the Frankfurt Book Fair, William Nygaard was about to set off for work when he saw that his car had a flat rear tire. He did not know that the tire had been slashed by a gunman hidden in the shrubbery behind the car. The gunman had calculated that William would come toward him to open the trunk and get the spare tire out, and once he was in that position he would be a sitting duck. But William was the head of a big publishing company and had no intention of changing the tire himself. He got out his cellphone and called a car service. That gave the gunman a problem: Should he break cover and show himself in order to get a clear shot at his target, or should he fire from where he was, even though William was not where he wanted him to be? He decided to shoot. William was hit three times and fell to the ground. A group of thirteen-year-old kids saw a man with "dark, bad skin" running away, but the gunman was not caught.

If William had not been an athletic man he would almost certainly have died. But the former skiing ace had remained physically fit and that saved his life. What was more extraordinary was that once William was out of intensive care the doctors were able to say that he would make a full recovery. The trajectories of the bullets through his body, they told him, were the only three paths the bullets could have taken without either killing or paralyzing him. William Nygaard, a great publisher, was also a lucky man.

When he heard that William had been shot he knew that his friend had taken bullets that had been meant for him. He remembered William's pride on the day of the Aschehoug garden party the year before. William's hand had been on his shoulder as the publisher shepherded him through the surprised throng, introducing him to this novelist, that opera singer, a business mogul here, a political figure there. *A gesture of freedom,* William had said, and now he lay at death's door because of it. But, thanks to his unwillingness to change his own flat tire, and then to the miracle of the trajectories, he survived. The day came when the wounded publisher was well enough to speak briefly on the telephone. His colleague Halfdan Freihow of Aschehoug called Carmel to say that William was anxious to speak to Salman and could he call the hospital. *Yes of course.* A male nurse answered the phone and warned that William's voice was very weak. Then William was put on the phone and even after the warning it was a shock to hear how feeble he sounded; he was gasping for breath, his usually impeccable English faltering, distress in every syllable.

He hadn't even understood at first that he had been shot, had remained conscious until the police arrived and gave them his son's telephone number. "I screamed like hell," he said, "and I rolled over and over down a small hill, and that is what saved me, I think, because I was out of sight." He would have to stay in the hospital a long time, but, he wheezed, yes, a full recovery was possible. "They missed all the organs." Then he said, "I just want you to know that I am really proud to be the publisher of *The Satanic Verses,* to be part of the Affair. Maybe now I will have to live something like you, unless they catch the man." *I'm so sorry, William, I have to tell you that I feel responsible for this. . . .* William broke into the apology and said, feebly, "Don't say that. It is not right that you say that." *But how can I not feel . . .* "You know, Salman, I am a grown-up person, and when I agreed to publish *The Satanic Verses* I understood that there were risks, and I took those risks. The fault is not yours. The person to blame is the man who fired the gun." *Yes, but I . . .* "One other thing," said William. "I just ordered a big reprint." Grace under pressure, Hemingway called it. True courage allied to high principle. A union a bullet could not destroy. And the bullets had been big bastards, .44s, soft-nosed, meant to kill.

The Scandinavian press was up in arms about the Nygaard shooting. The Norwegian publishers' association demanded to know what the Norwegian government's response to Iran would be. And a former Iranian ambassador who had defected to the opposition group Mujahideen-e Khalq, or PMOI ("People's Mujahideen of Iran"), announced that he had told the Norwegian police four months earlier that a hit was being planned against William.

The Nordic governments were angry, but the shooting had frightened people. The Dutch Ministry of Culture had been planning to invite him to Amsterdam but now it was backing away, and so was Royal Dutch Airlines. The Council of Europe, which had agreed to a meeting months earlier, canceled it. Gabi Gleichmann, who was leading the "Rushdie campaign" in Sweden—though he and Carmel Bedford were constantly at odds—had been given police protection. In Britain, the *ad hominem* attacks continued. An article in the *Evening Standard* called him "conceited" and "mad," derided him for wanting so much attention, and sneered that he wasn't worth it because he had conducted himself so poorly. London's LBC radio station was running a poll to ask the British public "if we should support Rushdie anymore," and in *The Telegraph* there was an interview with Marianne Wiggins in which her ex-husband was called "doleful, foolish, cowardly, vain, farcical, and morally ambiguous." Clive Bradley at the British Publishers Association said that Trevor Glover at Penguin UK was blocking a statement about William. He called Glover, who at first pretended he hadn't done it, thought it was "just a casual conversation," but, "Gosh, we are all a bit more nervous now and should we make a public noise?" and then finally agreed to call Bradley to lift the Penguin veto.

He received a threatening letter, the first for a long while, warning him that his "time was drawing near," because "Allah saw all things." The letter was signed by D. Ali of the "Manchester Socialist Workers Party and Anti-Racist League." Their members were watching all the airports, he said, and they had people in all neighborhoods—"Liverpool, Bradford, Hampstead, Kensington"—and as the winter darkness was "better for them to do their work," he would soon be "back in Iran."

There was an evening at Isabel Fonseca's apartment with Martin Amis, James Fenton, and Darryl Pinckney, and Martin depressed him by telling him that George Steiner believed he had "set out to make a lot of trouble," and Martin's father, Kingsley Amis, had said that "if you set out to make trouble you shouldn't complain when you get it," and Al Alvarez had said that he had "done it because he wanted to be the most famous writer in the world." And to Germaine Greer he was a "megalomaniac" and John le Carré had called him a "twerp" and Martin's ex-stepmother Elizabeth Jane Howard and Sybille Bedford thought he had "done it to make money." His friends were ridiculing these assertions but by the end of the evening he felt very upset and only Elizabeth's love brought him back. Maybe they should marry, he wrote in his journal. Who could love him better, be braver, sweeter-natured, or give more of herself? She had committed herself to him, and deserved no less in return. At home, celebrating their first year at 9 Bishops' Avenue, they had a loving evening and he felt better.

In his Beckettian moods, hunched over in his wooden study, he was a man lost in a mocking void: both Didi and Gogo, playing games against despair. No, he was their antithesis; they hoped for Godot, whereas he was waiting for what he hoped would never come. Almost every day there were moments when he allowed his shoulders to slump, then pushed them back again. He ate too much, gave up smoking, wheezed, quarreled with the empty air, rubbing his fists against his temples, and always thinking, thinking like a fire, as if thinking could burn away his ills. Almost every day was like this: a battle against hopelessness, often lost, but never lost forever. "Inside us," José Saramago had written, "there is something that has no name. That something is what we are." The something that had no name within him always came to his rescue in the end. He clenched his teeth, shook his head to clear his thoughts, and ordered himself to get on with it.

William Nygaard took his first steps. Halfdan Freihow said that William had decided to move house because of the "danger of the bushes," which would prevent him "taking a late-night piss in the garden." They were finding him a high-security apartment building to live in. The hit man had not been found. William had "nowhere to aim his anger." But he was getting better. The novel's Danish publisher, Johannes Riis, said that things were calm in Denmark, and he had "the advantage of a calm wife." He thought of the danger as comparable to crossing the road, he said, and his author, hearing this, was again humbled in the presence of real courage. "I am furious," Johannes added, "that such an obscenity should continue to be part of the frame in which we live."

At the first meeting of the so-called "International Parliament of Writers" in Strasbourg he worried about the name, because they were unelected, but the French shrugged and said that in France *un parlement* was just a place where people talked. He insisted that the statement they were drafting against Islamist terror should include references to Tahar Djaout, Farag Fouda, Aziz Nesin, Ugur Mumcu and the newly embattled Bangladeshi writer Taslima Nasreen as well as himself. Susan Sontag swept in, embraced him, and spoke passionately in fluent French, calling him *un grand écrivain* who represented the crucial secularized culture the Muslim extremists wished to suppress. Strasbourg mayor Catherine Trautmann wanted to give him the freedom of the city. Catherine Lalumière of the Council of Europe promised that the council would take up his cause. That evening there was a party for the visiting writers and he was accosted by a crazily passionate Iranian woman, "Hélène Kafi," who rebuked him for not making common cause with the Mujahideen-e Khalq. "I am not being aggressive, Salman Rushdie, but *je suis un peu déçu de vous,* you should know who your real friends are." The next day she claimed in the media that she, and through her the PMOI, had joined the French "Rushdie committee" and the grenades that had been thrown at the French embassy and

Air France offices in Tehran were because of that. (In fact they were because of France's decision to give asylum to the PMOI leader Maryam Rajavi, and unrelated to the "Rushdie Affair.")

He sat on a small red sofa with Toni Morrison, who had just won the Nobel Prize, and Sontag, who shouted, "My God, I'm sitting between the two most famous writers in the world!"—whereupon both he and Toni began assuring her that her day in Stockholm would surely come very soon. Susan asked him what he was writing. She had put her finger on the thing that was worrying him most. To lead the campaign against the *fatwa* he had had almost to stop being a working writer. This was the flattening effect of becoming involved in politics. His thoughts had been full of airlines and ministers and feta cheese and had turned away from the sweet recesses of the mind where fiction lurked. His novel had stalled. Was this campaign, which people told him was working so well, actually a way of diminishing himself in the world's eyes as well as his own? Was he actually helping to turn himself into nothing more than the flattened, two-dimensional caricature at the heart of the "Rushdie Affair" and abdicating his claim to art? He had gone from *Salman* to *Rushdie* to *Joseph Anton* and now, perhaps, he was making a nobody of himself. He was a lobbyist lobbying for an empty space that no longer contained a man.

He told Susan, "I've sworn an oath that next year I'll stay home and write."

To reach the summit—a meeting with a president—it was necessary to approach him from many directions at once. The approach to Mount Clinton had been made by him personally, by the Rushdie defense committee and Article 19, by the British ambassador in Washington on behalf of the British government, by PEN American Center. Aryeh Neier of Human Rights Watch, Nick Veliotes of the Association of American Publishers and Scott Armstrong of the Freedom Forum were among those pushing for the meeting. In addition, Christopher Hitchens had been urging his White House contacts to make it happen. Christopher was not an admirer of Bill Clinton, but he was on friendly terms with the president's close adviser George Stephanopoulos, and spoke to him several times. It seemed that Clinton's people were divided between those who were telling him the *fatwa* was not America's affair and those, like Stephanopoulos, who wanted him to do the right thing.

Two days after his return to London the "green light from Washington" came through. At first Nick Veliotes was told that the president would not be at the meeting. It would be with the national security adviser, Anthony Lake, with Vice President Gore "dropping in." At the U.S. embassy in Grosvenor Square, his contact person Larry Robinson confirmed that it would be a meeting with Lake and Gore. He would be given "portal to portal protection," that was to say, from the aircraft to the Massachusetts Institute of Technology (where he was to be honored—Alan Lightman, author of *Einstein's Dreams,* who taught at MIT, had called him to make the offer of an honorary professorship), from MIT to D.C., and in D.C. until he left the country again. Two days later Frances was told that Gore would be in the Far East and Lake might be unavailable so the meeting would be with Secretary of State Warren Christopher and Lake's "number two." The meeting with Warren Christopher would be in the Treaty Room with photographers. He spoke to Christopher Hitchens, who feared this was a case of Clinton "funking it." That evening the deal changed again. The meeting would be with Anthony Lake and Warren Christopher and the assistant secretary of state for democracy, human rights and labor, John Shattuck. The president was "not confirmed." It would be the day before Thanksgiving, and the president had a great deal to do. He had to pardon a turkey. He might not have time to help out a novelist as well.

At JFK there were eight cars waiting instead of the lower-key three he had been promised. The officer in charge, Jim Tandy, was a big improvement on Lieutenant Bob, gently spoken and helpful, a tall, thin, mustachioed man with a wide-eyed, serious face. He was taken first to Andrew's apartment, where the police were making a big deal out of his arrival, even preventing the other residents of the building from using the elevators. That would be popular, he thought. He was supposed to be a Pakistani diplomat called Dr. Ren, but nobody was being fooled.

Inside Andrew's apartment there were friends to greet him. Norman Mailer wished him luck, and Norris Mailer said, "If you see Bill, tell him I said hello." As a young woman she had worked on Clinton's campaign when he was running for governor of Arkansas. "I got to know him very well," she said. Okay, he told Norris politely, I'll mention it. "No," she said, putting her elegant hand on his arm like Margaret Thatcher at her most touchy-feely. "You don't understand. I mean I got to know him *very well.*" Oh. Right. Yes, Norris. In that case I'll *definitely* give him your best.

He met Paul Auster and Siri Hustvedt, who were very affectionate; it was the beginning of what would become one of his closest friendships. Don DeLillo was there too. He was working on a "huge and sprawling book," he said. It would be called *Underworld.* "I know something about underworlds," he replied. Paul and Don wanted to produce a leaflet with a text about the *fatwa* that would be inserted into every book sold in America on February 14, 1994, but they had been told it would cost over $20,000 to produce and that was unrealistic. Peter Carey arrived and said with his usual dry comedy, "Hello, Salman, you look like shit." Susan Sontag, who had agreed to be his "beard" at MIT, was looking forward to their little plot. David Rieff was full of sadness about Bosnia. Annie Leibovitz talked a little about her Bosnia photographs, but seemed oddly reluctant to push herself forward in Susan's presence. Sonny and Gita Mehta arrived and Gita looked ill and drained. They said she was fine now, recovering from the cancer, and he hoped they were telling the truth. And suddenly Andrew said, "Oh my God, we've forgotten to invite Edward Said." That was very bad. Edward would certainly mind.

Elizabeth and he slept at Andrew's place and awoke to find a line of black limos parked in the street, as well as a large, unsubtle blue van labeled BOMB SQUAD. Then came the road trip to Concord, Massachusetts, where they would be the guests of Alan and Jean Lightman. Alan took them for a walk around Walden Pond and when they came to the remains of Thoreau's hut he said to Alan that if he ever wrote up this trip he would call it "From a Log Cabin to the White House." The hut was disappointingly close to the town, and Thoreau could easily have strolled in for a beer if he wanted one. It wasn't exactly a wilderness retreat.

The next morning he was driven to a Boston hotel and Jean Light-man took Elizabeth off to see the city. Andrew and he worked the phones to see what progress had been or could be made. It became obvious that Frances and Carmel were at odds with Scott Armstrong, though Christopher Hitchens spoke up for him. Within the White House, Hitch added, Stephanopoulos and Shattuck were on his side and working on the president, but there was nothing definite to report. A U.S. official, Tom Robertson called to say that the meeting had been pushed back half an hour, from 11:30 A.M. to noon. What did this mean? Did it mean anything? Scott and Hitch said later that the change happened right after George Stephanopoulos and others went to see the president's scheduling person . . . so . . . maybe. Fingers crossed.

In the afternoon he went with Andrew Wylie to see Andrew's childhood home. The new owner, a fiftysomething lady with a big smile called Nancy, looked at the motorcade and said, "Who are all those *people* outside?" Then she said "Oh," and asked him if he was who he looked like. At first he said, "No, unfortunately," and she replied, "You mean 'fortunately.' The poor man doesn't have a very nice life, does he?" But she had all his books, so he owned up, and she was thrilled and wanted them signed. The house evoked many memories for Andrew because much of it, even the wallpaper upstairs, was unchanged from thirty years ago, and the letters *AW* were still scratched into the wood of the bookcases in the library, and on the edge of a door the three-foot height of the young Andy Wylie was still marked and named.

They had dinner at MIT hosted by a spectacularly cross-eyed provost and then it was time for the Event. He had never received even an honorary degree before, so he was a little overcome by this honorary professorship. MIT did not like handing out honorary doctorates, he was told, and it had only once in its history bestowed an honorary professorship on anyone else. That person was Winston Churchill. "Pretty exalted company for a scribbler, Rushdie," he told himself. The Event was billed as an evening with Susan Sontag, but when Susan stood up to speak she told the audience that she was only there to introduce another writer whose name could not be announced in advance. She then spoke about him with fondness and described his work in language that meant more to him than the professorship. Finally he entered the lecture theater through a small door at the rear. He spoke briefly and then read parts of *Midnight's Children* and the "Columbus and Isabella" story. Then he and Elizabeth were whisked away, and there was a late-night flight to Washington. They arrived in a state of some exhaustion at the Hitchens apartment sometime after midnight. He met Hitch and Carol's daughter, Laura Antonia, for the first time and was asked to be an "ungodparent." He agreed at once. With him and Martin Amis as ungodly mentors, he thought, the little girl had no chance. His throat felt sore, and he had a rough tooth that had cut his tongue. The latest on Clinton was no better than a maybe. Hitch confessed to loathing Carmel, who was messing things up by being clumsy, he said. It was time to sleep and fix things in the morning.

The morning brought a fight among the friends. Scott Armstrong came by to say that the White House had decided not to offer Clinton or Gore. He had been told "Nice try, but no." Carmel had launched a telephone campaign involving Aryeh Neier and others and that had been "counterproductive." When Carmel and Frances arrived the tension exploded and everyone was yelling at everyone else, accusation and counteraccusation, Frances claiming that Scott was the one who had fouled things up. Finally he had to call a truce. "We have something to achieve here and I need your help." Scott arranged for the post–White House press conference to be at the National Press Club, so that was one thing done, at least. Then the quarrel flared up again. Who would go with him to the White House? He was allowed to bring only two people with him. Voices were raised once more, tempers ran high. *I called so-and-so. I did such and such.* Andrew quickly withdrew himself from the contest and Christopher said he had no reason to be one of the chosen but the NGOs were locking horns.

Once again, he put an end to the dispute. "Elizabeth is going with me," he said, "and I'd like Frances to come too." Sulking, cloudy faces retreated to corners of Christopher's apartment or beyond it. But the quarrel was over.

The motorcade was waiting to drive them to 1600 Pennsylvania Avenue. Once they were in their appointed car the three of them were laid low by an infection of nervous giggles. They wondered if, in the end, Clinton's duties with Tom the Turkey would keep him away from their meeting, and if so what the next day's headlines would say. "Clinton Pardons Turkey," he improvised. "Rushdie Gets Stuffed." Ha ha ha ha ha ha ha ha ha! Then they were at the "diplomats' entrance," the side door, and were allowed inside. World politics, the great dirty game, inevitably funneled back in the end to this smallish white mansion in which a big pink man in an oval room made yes-no choices in spite of being deafened by the babbling maybes of his aides.

At twelve noon they were taken up a narrow staircase to Anthony Lake's smallish office, past a flurry of smiling, excited aides. He told the national security adviser it was exciting to be at the White House at last and Lake, twinkling, said, "Well, hang on, because it's about to get a little more exciting." POTUS had agreed to meet him! At 12:15 P.M. they would walk across to the Old Executive Building and find Mr. Clinton there. Frances began to talk quickly and managed to persuade Lake that she should come along as well. So poor Elizabeth was to be left behind. There were many books waiting to be autographed in Lake's outer office and as he was signing them Warren Christopher arrived. Elizabeth was left to entertain the secretary of state while Lake and he walked toward the president. "This should have happened years ago," Lake said to him. They discovered Clinton in a hallway under an orange cupola and George Stephanopoulos was there too, grinning broadly, as well as two female aides who also looked delighted. Bill Clinton was even bigger and pinker than he had anticipated and very affable, too, but he got right to the point. "What can I do for you?" the president of the United States wanted to know. The year of political campaigning had prepared him for the question. *When you're the Supplicant, you must always know what you want from the meeting,* he had learned, *and always ask them for something that is in their power to give.*

"Mr. President," he said, "when I leave the White House I have to go to the Press Club and there will be a lot of journalists waiting to find out what you had to say. I'd like to be able to tell them that the

United States is joining the campaign against the Iranian *fatwa* and supports progressive voices around the world." Clinton nodded and grinned. "Yes, you can say that," he replied, "because it's true." *End of meeting,* the Supplicant thought, with a little lilt of triumph in his heart. "We have friends in common," the president said. "Bill Styron, Norman Mailer. They have been bearding me about you. Norman's wife, Norris, you know, worked on my first political campaign. I got to know her pretty well."

The Supplicant thanked the president for the meeting and said it was of immense symbolic importance. "Yes," Clinton said. "It should send a message around the world. It's intended to be a demonstration of American support for free speech and of our desire that First Amendment–style rights should grow all around the world." There was no photograph. That would be too much of a demonstration. But the meeting had happened. That was a fact.

As they walked back to Anthony Lake's office he noticed that Frances D'Souza was wearing an enormous goofy grin. "Frances," he asked, "why are you wearing that enormous goofy grin?" Her voice had a distant, pensive quality. "Don't you think," she asked languorously, "he held on to my hand just a little too long?"

Warren Christopher was more than a little in love with Elizabeth when they got back. Christopher and Lake at once agreed that the *fatwa* was "right at the top of the American agenda with Iran." Their desire to isolate Iran more than equaled his own. They too were in favor of a credit freeze and were working to achieve one. The meeting was an hour long and afterward, returning to the Hitchens apartment, all the Supplicants felt giddy with success. Christopher said that Stephanopoulos, who had pushed hard for the Clinton encounter, was also elated. He had called Hitch as soon as it had happened. "The eagle has landed," he said.

The press conference—seventy journalists on the day before Thanksgiving, better than Scott Armstrong had feared—went well. Hitch's friend Martin Walker of *The Guardian* said it was "perfectly done." Then came the quid pro quo, the exclusive interview with David Frost, who could not have been a happier chap and *super*-ed and *thrilling*-ed and *darling*-ed and *wonderful*-ed him for simply *ages* when it was done, and *absolutely* wanted to have a *drinkie* in London before Christmas.

Jim Tandy, the chief of the security detail, introduced a jarring note. A suspicious "Mideastern man" had been lurking around the building. He had made a call and then left in a car with three other men. Tandy asked: "Do you want to stay, or should we move you someplace else?" He said, "Stay," but the final decision had to be Christopher and Carol's. "Stay," they said.

The British ambassador had a reception for them. They were met at the embassy door by a plummy-voiced Amanda, who told them it was the only Lutyens building in America and then, "Of course, he built so much of New Delhi. . . . Have you ever been to India?" He let it pass. The Renwicks were gracious hosts. Sir Robin's French wife, Annie, at once fell in love with Elizabeth, who was making many conquests in D.C. "She is so warm, so direct, so calm; she makes you feel you've known her a long time. A very special person." Sonny Mehta came, and said Gita was okay. Kay Graham came and said almost nothing.

They spent Thanksgiving with the endlessly hospitable Hitchenses. The English journalists and documentary filmmakers Andrew and Leslie Cockburn came with their very smart nine-year-old daughter, Olivia, who said with great fluency exactly why she was a fan of *Haroun and the Sea of Stories* and then went away to grow up into the actress Olivia Wilde. There was a red-haired teenage boy there—much more tongue-tied than Olivia, even though he was several years older—who said he had wanted to be a writer but now he didn't anymore, "because look what happened to you."

The Clinton meeting was front-page news everywhere, and the coverage was almost uniformly positive. The British press seemed to be playing down the significance of the Clinton meeting, but the predictable fundamentalist responses to it were given plenty of ink. That, too, was predictable.

After Thanksgiving Clinton seemed to wobble. "I only met him for a couple of minutes," he said. "Some of my people didn't want me to. I hope people won't misunderstand. No insult was intended. I just wanted to defend free speech. I think I did the right thing." And so on, pretty gelatinously. It didn't sound like the Leader of the Free World taking a stand against terrorism. *The New York Times* felt the same way and wrote an editorial titled "Hold the Waffles, Please," encouraging the president to stick by his good deed without feeling the need to apologize for it; to have the courage of his (or perhaps George Stephanopoulos's and Anthony Lake's?) convictions. On *Crossfire* Christopher Hitchens was confronted by a screaming Muslim and Pat Buchanan saying "Rushdie is a pornographer" whose work was "filthy" and attacking the president for meeting such a person. Watching the program was depressing. He called Hitch late at night and was told that the host, Michael Kinsley, felt that the opposition had been "trounced," that the "foregrounding" of the issue again was a good thing, and that Clinton was "holding the line" even though there was a backstage battle between the Lake-Stephanopoulos grouping and the security-minded aides. Christopher had wise words for him too. "The fact is, you will never get anything for nothing. Every time you score a hit, the old arguments against you will be dragged out and deployed again. But this also means that they will be shot down again, and I detect an increasing unwillingness among the foes to come out and play. Thus you wouldn't have got a *Times* editorial if there hadn't been a waffle, and the overall effect of that is to invigorate your defenders. Meanwhile you still have the Clinton statement and the Christopher-Lake meeting, and that can't be taken away from you. So *cheer up.*"

Christopher had quickly become—with Andrew—the most dedicated friend and ally he had in the United States. A few days later he called to say that John Shattuck at State had suggested forming an informal group of himself, Hitch, Scott Armstrong at the Freedom Forum and maybe Andrew Wylie to "progress" the U.S. response. Hitch had spoken to Stephanopoulos at a reception, where people were listening, and George had said firmly, "The first statement is the one we stand by; I hope you don't think we tried to take anything back." A week later he faxed a note—ah, the days of faxes long ago!—about an "amazingly" good meeting with the new counterterrorism boss, Ambassador Robert Gelbard, who was raising the case at various G7 forums but facing "reluctance" from the Japanese and, guess who, the Brits. Gelbard promised to raise the airline issue with the Federal Aviation Authority, whose new chief of security, Admiral Flynn, was a "pal." Also, Christopher reported, Clinton had told someone that he'd have liked to spend longer with the author of *The Satanic Verses,* only Rushdie had been in "such a hurry." That was funny, and showed, Hitch thought, that he was glad the meeting had happened. Tony Lake was telling people that the meeting had been one of the high points of his year. Scott Armstrong was really helping too, Hitch said. Neither of them was impressed by Frances and Carmel, which was worrying; and which, almost at once, precipitated a crisis.

An account of the Washington adventure appeared in *The Guardian* and in the article Scott Armstrong and Christopher Hitchens had both voiced their doubts about Frances and Carmel's usefulness to the cause. "You have seriously undermined Article 19 in the United States," Frances said on the phone in tones of extreme, righteous anger. "Armstrong and Hitchens would never have spoken as they did without your tacit approval." He tried to tell her that he hadn't even known such a piece was in the works, but she said, "I'm sure you're behind it all," and told him that as a result of what he had done the MacArthur Foundation might withdraw essential funding from Article 19. He took a deep breath, wrote a letter to *The Guardian* defending Frances and Carmel, and called Rick MacArthur in confidence. MacArthur said, not unreasonably, that he paid for half Frances's budget. It was the foundation's policy to bring organizations to the point at which they could "diversify their funding base" and that meant developing a high profile in the United States. It was Frances's fault, he said, that she had failed to get attention for Article 19's leadership role in "the most important human rights case in the world." He went on talking to Rick until MacArthur agreed not to make the cuts for the moment.

When he put down the phone he was very angry himself. He had just taken Frances with him to the White House, and had praised Article 19's work at all subsequent press conferences, and felt unjustly accused. Carmel Bedford's follow-up fax—"Unless we can undo the damage these self-seekers have brought about is there any point in us continuing?"—made matters worse. He faxed Frances and Carmel a note telling them what he thought of their accusations and why. He said nothing about his confidential call to Rick MacArthur, or its result. After a few days Carmel changed her tone and sent him mollifying faxes but from Frances there was nothing. She sulked like Achilles in her tent. The shock of her accusations did not fade.

Carmen Balcells, the legendary all-powerful Spanish literary agent, called Andrew Wylie from Barcelona to say that the great Gabriel García Márquez was writing a "novelization based on Mr. Rushdie's life." It would, she added, be "completely written by the writer, who is a well-known author." He didn't know how to respond. Should he be flattered? Because he was not flattered. He was to be someone else's "novelization" now? If the roles were reversed he would not have felt he had the right to come between another writer and his own life story. But his life had perhaps become everyone's property, and if he tried to stop the book he could just imagine the headlines. RUSHDIE CENSORS MÁRQUEZ. And what was meant by a "novelization"? If García Márquez was writing about a Latin American writer who had fallen foul of Christian religious fanatics then good luck to him. But if Márquez proposed to climb inside his head then that would feel like an invasion. He asked Andrew to express his concerns and a long silence from Balcells ensued, followed by a message saying that the Márquez book was not about Mr. Rushdie. Then what, he wondered, had this whole strange episode been about?

Gabriel García Márquez never published a "novelization" or anything bearing any resemblance to what Carmen Balcells had proposed. But the Balcells approach had rubbed salt in his self-inflicted wound. García Márquez had wanted, or didn't want, to write either a work of fiction or nonfiction about him, but he himself hadn't written a word of fiction all year—no, for much more than a year. Writing had always been at the center of his life but now things from the margins had flooded in to fill up the space he had always kept free for his work. He recorded a TV introduction to a film about Tahar Djaout. He was offered a monthly column to be distributed worldwide by the *New York Times* syndicate and asked Andrew to accept.

Christmas was coming. He was exhausted and, in spite of all the year's political successes, at a low ebb. He talked to Elizabeth about the future, about having a child, about how they might live, and realized that she could not imagine feeling safe without police protection. He had met her in the middle of the spider's web and the web was the only reality she trusted. If one day he reached a point at which the "prot" could end, would she feel too frightened to stay with him? It was a small cloud on the horizon. Would it grow to fill the sky?

Thomasina Lawson died aged just thirty-two. Clarissa was having chemotherapy. And Frank Zappa died too. The past leaped out at him when he read that, ambushing him with powerful, unexpected emotions. On one of their first dates Clarissa and he had gone to hear the Mothers of Invention at the Royal Albert Hall and in the middle of the show a stoned black guy in a shiny purple shirt climbed up onto the stage and demanded to play with the band. Zappa was unfazed. "Uh-huh, sir," he said, "and what is your instrument of choice?" Purple Shirt mumbled something about a horn and Zappa cried, "Give this man a horn!" Purple Shirt began to tootle tunelessly. Zappa listened for a few bars and then, in a stage aside, said, "Hmm. I wonder what we can think of to accompany this man on his horn. I know! The mighty, majestic Albert Hall pipe organ!" Whereupon one of the Mothers climbed up to the organ bench, pulled out all the stops, and played "Louie Louie," while Purple Shirt tootled on tunelessly and inaudibly below. It was one of their early happy memories, and now Zappa was gone, and Clarissa was fighting for her life. (At least her job had been saved. He had called her bosses at A. P. Watt, and pointed out how bad it would look to lay off a woman who was fighting cancer and was the mother of Salman Rushdie's son. Gillon Aitken and Liz Calder called too, at his request, and the agency relented. Clarissa didn't know he had had anything to do with it.) He invited her to spend Christmas Day with them. She came with Zafar, smiling weakly, looking hunted, and seemed to enjoy the day.

———

People were writing him letters too, like the imaginary letters in his head. One hundred Arab and Muslim writers jointly published a book of essays written in many languages and published in French, *Pour Rushdie,* to defend freedom of speech. One hundred writers who mostly understood what he had been talking about, who came from the world out of which his book had been born, and who, even when they didn't like what he said, were willing to defend, as Voltaire would have defended, his right to say it. *With him the prophetic gesture has been opened up to the four winds of the imaginary,* wrote the book's editors, and then came the cavalcade of the great and small voices of the Arab world. From the Syrian poet Adonis: *Truth is not the sword / Nor the hand that holds it.* And Mohammad Arkoun of Algeria: *I would like to see* The Satanic Verses *made available to all Muslims in order that they might be able to reflect in a more modern fashion on the cognitive status of revelation.* And Rabah Belamri of Algeria: *The Rushdie Affair has very clearly revealed to the entire world that Islam . . . has now demonstrated its incapacity to undergo with impunity any serious kind of examination.* And from Turkey, Fethi Benslama: *In his book Salman Rushdie went the whole way, once and for all, as if he really wanted to be, all by himself, all the different authors who had never been able to exist in the history of his tradition.* And Zhor Ben Chamsi of Morocco: *We should really be grateful to Rushdie for having opened up the imaginary for Muslims once again.* And Assia Djebar, the Algerian: *This prince of a writer . . . is nothing else but perpetually naked and alone. He is the first man to have lived in the condition of a Muslim woman (and . . . he is also the first man to be able to write from the standpoint of a Muslim woman).* And Karim Ghassim of Iran: *He is our neighbor.* And Émile Habibi, Palestinian: *If we fail to save Salman Rushdie—God forbid!—the shame will haunt global civilization as a whole.* And the Algerian Mohammed Harbi: *With Rushdie, we recognize the disrespect, the principle of pleasure that is freedom in culture and the arts, as a source of fruitful examination of our past and present.* And the Syrian Jamil Hatmal: *I choose Salman Rushdie over the murderous turbans.* And Sonallah Ibrahim of Egypt: *Every person of conscience must go to the aid of this great writer in hardship.* And the Moroccan-French writer Salim Jay: *The only truly free man today is Salman Rushdie. . . . He is the Adam of a library to come: one of freedom.* And Elias Khoury of Lebanon: *We have the obligation to tell him that he personifies our solitude and that his story is our own.* And the Tunisian Abdelwahab Meddeb: *Rushdie, you have written what no man has written. . . . Instead of condemning you, in the name of Islam, I congratulate you.* And Sami Naïr, French-Algerian: *Salman Rushdie must be read.*

Thank you, my brothers and sisters, he silently replied to the hundred voices. Thank you for your courage and understanding. I wish you all a happy new year.

VII

A Truckload of Dung

HIS BIGGEST PROBLEM, HE THOUGHT IN HIS MOST BITTER MOMENTS, WAS that he wasn't dead. If he were dead nobody in England would have to fuss about the cost of his security and whether or not he merited such special treatment for so long. He wouldn't have to fight for the right to get on a plane, or to battle senior police officers for tiny increments of personal freedom. There would no longer be any need to worry about the safety of his mother, his sisters, his child. He wouldn't have to talk to any more politicians (*big* advantage). His exile from India wouldn't hurt. And the stress level would definitely be lower.

He was supposed to be dead, but he obviously hadn't understood that. That was the headline everyone had set up, just waiting to run. The obituaries had been written. A character in a tragedy, or even a tragic farce, was not meant to rewrite the script. Yet he insisted on living, and, what was more, talking, arguing his case, believing himself not to be the wronger but the wronged, standing by his work, and also—if one could believe such temerity—insisting on getting his life back, inch by inch, step by painful step. "What's blond, has big tits, and lives in Tasmania? Salman Rushdie!" was a popular joke, and if he had agreed to go into some sort of witness protection program and lived out his tedious days somewhere obscure under a false name then that, too, would have been acceptable. But Mr. Joseph Anton wanted to get back to being Salman Rushdie and that was, frankly, unmannerly of him. His was not to be a success story, and there was certainly no room in it for pleasure. Dead, he might even be given the respect due to a free-speech martyr. Alive, he was a dull and unpleasantly lingering pain in the neck.

When he was alone in his room, trying to convince himself that this was no more than the familiar solitude of the writer at work, trying to forget the armed men playing cards downstairs and his inability to walk out of his front door without permission, it was easy to slide toward such bitterness. But fortunately there seemed to be a thing in him that woke up and refused that unattractive, self-pitying defeat. He instructed himself to remember the most important rules he had made for himself: Not to accept the descriptions of reality made by security people, politicians or priests. To insist, instead, on the validity of his own judgments and instincts. To move toward a rebirth, or at least a renewal. To be reborn *as himself*, into his own life: That was the goal. And if he was a "dead man on leave," well, the dead went on quests, too. According to the ancient Egyptians death was a quest, a journey toward rebirth. He too would journey back from the Book of the Dead toward the "bright book of life."

And what could be a finer affirmation of life, of the power of life over death, the power of his will to defeat the forces arrayed against him, than to bring a new life into the world? All of a sudden he was ready. He told Elizabeth that he agreed; they should try to have a child. All the problems remained, the security issues, the simple translocated chromosome, but he didn't care. The newborn life would make its own rules, would insist on what she or he needed. Yes! He wanted to have a second child. In any case it would not have been right to prevent Elizabeth from becoming a mother. They had been together for three and a half years and she had loved and put up with him with all her heart. But now she was not the only one who wanted a baby. After he said *Yes, let's do it* she could not stop beaming at him, hugging him, kissing him all evening. They had a bottle of Tignanello to celebrate at dinnertime, in memory of their first "date." He had always teased her that on that evening at Liz Calder's place she had "thrown herself at him" after dinner. "On the contrary," was her view, "*you* threw yourself at *me*." Now, three and a half strange years later, they were in their own home, at the end of a good meal and near the bottom of a bottle of fine Tuscan red wine. "I guess you can throw yourself at me again," he said.

The year 1994 began with a rebuff. *The New York Times* withdrew its offer of a syndicated column. The French syndication bureau had complained that its staff and offices would be endangered. It was at first unclear if the newspaper's owners were aware of, or had approved, the decision. Within a couple of days it was plain that the Sulzbergers did know and that the offer was definitively withdrawn. Gloria B. Anderson, the New York syndication chief, was regretful but powerless. She told Andrew that she had initially made the offer purely for commercial reasons, but since then had started reading Rushdie and was now a fan. That was nice, but useless. More than four years would pass before Gloria called again.

Malachite was the coolest prot. The other members of "A" Squad called it a "glory job" and even though the Malachite veterans Bob Major and Stanley Doll modestly pooh-poohed the notion it was plainly true. The Malachite team was, in the opinion of its fellow officers, doing the most dangerous job and the most important one. The others were "just" protecting politicians. Malachite was defending a principle. The police officers understood this clearly. It was a shame the nation was more confused. In London there were two Tory MPs ready to ask questions in the House of Commons about the cost of the protection. It was plain most Conservative MPs believed the protection was a waste of money and wanted it ended. So did he, he wanted to tell them. Nobody was more eager to get back to ordinary life than he. But the new man in charge of Operation Malachite, Dick Wood, told him that Iranian intelligence was "still trying as hard as ever" to find their target. Rafsanjani had approved the hit long ago and the killers no longer needed to refer to him. It remained their number one concern. Soon afterward, Stella Rimington, head of MI5, said in the BBC's annual Dimbleby lecture that "the determined efforts to locate and kill the author Salman Rushdie seem likely to go on."

It was time for the Special Branch party again. Elizabeth tried to charm John Major but he didn't pay attention, "gave her no lift," to use one of Sameen's favorite phrases. She was upset and said "I feel I've failed you," which was ridiculous, of course. Major did promise Frances D'Souza he would make a statement on February 14, so that was something gained from the evening, at least. And the home secretary, Michael Howard, was friendly too. In the middle of the party their protectors gave them a tour of the Special Branch floors. They saw the "reserve room," where the duty officer let him look in the "Cranks Book" and answer a filthy phone call from one Crank. They saw the records office on the nineteenth floor, with a great view of London, and the secret files, which they couldn't open, and the book containing the current IRA code words that, when used, meant the anonymous caller was warning of a real bomb. It was interesting that in spite of computerization so much was still kept in little box files.

After the party the team took him and Elizabeth for a drink at a favorite police wine bar, the Exchange. He realized they had all become very close. At the end of the evening they warned him that there was "quite a senior rogue" in town, they "wanted to be straight" with him and tell him that they would need to be "extra careful" for a few days. A week after that he heard that the "rogue" had been briefing other rogues on how to kill him, activating them from their roguish sleep. So now there were several rogues actively looking for him, to do to him what rogues were activated to do.

The fifth anniversary of the *fatwa* was approaching. He called Frances and made peace with her and Carmel but had very little appetite, just then, for talk of more campaigning. This year his friends did their best to pick up some of the load. Julian Barnes wrote a terrific piece for *The New Yorker,* witty and well-researched, an analysis of what was happening by someone who knew and liked him. Christopher Hitchens wrote in the *London Review of Books,* and John Diamond wrote in a tabloid paper to fight back against the tabloids' attempts at character assassination on their own turf. The playwright Ronald Harwood met UN secretary-general Boutros Boutros-Ghali on his behalf. "Boo-Boo was very sympathetic," Ronnie told him. "He asked if the Brits have tried back-channel diplomacy through the Indians or the Japanese, because the Iranians pay attention to them." He didn't know the answer but he suspected it was *No.* "He said if the Brits want *him* to try then Douglas Hurd will have to request it formally." He wondered why this had not been done.

Meanwhile, all over Europe, as the anniversary approached, the coverage was sympathetic. Outside Britain he was seen as likable, funny, brave, talented, and worthy of respect. He was photographed by the great William Klein and afterward Klein mentioned to Caroline Michel how much he enjoyed the shoot: "He's so nice and funny." "If I could only meet everyone in the world in small groups," he said to Caroline, "maybe I can put an end to all the hatred and scorn. There you are—a solution—maybe a little intimate dinner for me, Khamenei and Rafsanjani." "I'll work on it right away," said Caroline.

The International Parliament of Writers in Strasbourg had elected him president and asked him to write a sort of declaration of intent. "We [writers] are miners and jewelers," he wrote, in part, "truth-tellers and liars, jesters and commanders, mongrels and bastards, parents and lovers, architects and demolition men. We are citizens of many countries: the finite and the frontiered country of observable reality and everyday life, the united states of the mind, the celestial and infernal nations of desire, and the unfettered republic of the tongue. Together they comprise a territory far greater than that governed by any worldly power; yet their defenses against that power can seem very weak. The creative spirit is all too frequently treated as an enemy by those mighty or petty potentates who resent our power to build pictures of the world which quarrel with, or undermine, their own simpler and less openhearted views. The best of literature will survive, but we cannot wait for the future to release it from the censor's chains."

The Parliament of Writers' great achievement was the foundation of the International Cities of Refuge Network, which in the next fifteen years would grow to include three dozen cities from Ljubljana to Mexico City by way of Amsterdam, Barcelona, and Las Vegas. Nations often had reasons not to give refuge to persecuted writers—foreign ministries inevitably feared that, say, welcoming a Chinese writer in trouble might derail a trade deal—but at the urban level, mayors often saw this as an initiative with no downside. It didn't cost much to provide a threatened writer with a small apartment and a basic stipend for a couple of years. He was proud of having been involved in the genesis of the scheme, and there was no doubt that his signature on the letters the parliament sent out made a difference. He was glad to be able to send his name, which had gained such a strange, dark kind of fame, out to work on behalf of other writers who needed help.

On February 14 his "declaration" appeared in *The Independent*. He had worried that that newspaper, with its track record of Islamic appeasement, would contrive to put some sort of negative spin on the piece, and so it did. He woke up on Valentine's Day to find his text on page three next to the news story about the anniversary while the entire op-ed page was given over to the egregious Yasmin Alibhai-Brown's piece about how the *fatwa* had led to many good, positive outcomes, allowing the British Muslim community to find an identity and a public voice. "Had it not been for that fateful 14 February 1989," she wrote, "the world would be hurrying, unchallenged, toward the inalienable right to wear blue jeans and eat McDonald's hamburgers." How good of Khomeini to stimulate a new debate about Islamic and Western values, he thought; that was worth turning a few writers into hamburgers for.

"Happy anniversary!" It had become a black-comic tradition that his friends called to congratulate him on his special day. Elizabeth made him an elaborate Valentine's card intertwining her own face with Frida Kahlo's. Hanif Kureishi was off to Pakistan and agreed to take a letter to the anniversary boy's mother in Karachi. Caroline Lang called from Paris to say that the tough-guy interior minister, Charles Pasqua, had been persuaded to agree that M. Rushdie could spend nights in France, not only at private residences but even at hotels. (Pasqua was later found guilty of making illegal arms sales to Angola and received a one-year jail sentence. The Belgian foreign minister, Willy Claes, was convicted for bribery. Such was the political world. Relatively few novelists were ever found guilty of the more lucrative forms of corruption.)

The campaigns of the previous two years bore fruit in the form of declarations by world leaders. This time John Major made a strongly worded statement, *We all want to make clear to the Iranian government that they cannot enjoy full and friendly relations with the rest of the international* community *unless and until* . . . and the leader of the opposition, John Smith, said *I totally condemn* . . . *it is intolerable that* . . . *I call upon the Iranian government to* . . . and Ase Kleveland, the Norwegian minister of culture, said *We will intensify our efforts against* and *we demand that the* fatwa *be repealed* and Dick Spring in Ireland said *unacceptable* and *serious violation* and the Canadian foreign minister, André Ouellet, said *the fact that Rushdie has survived is a hope for freedom in the world.*

Half a million copies of the Auster-DeLillo leaflet (for which, in the end, the money had been raised) were distributed that day. *Pour Rushdie* was published in the United States as *For Rushdie*. And Frances and Carmel took Michael Foot, Julian Barnes and others to the Iranian embassy to deliver a letter of protest, but failed to arrange for any journalists to be there. Carmel also told BBC Radio that the *fatwa* had been extended to cover his family and friends. That was a clumsy and inaccurate misstatement that could potentially place the people closest to him at risk. Clarissa was on the phone one minute after it went out on the news to ask what was going on. John Diamond called him next, and he had to work hard for the rest of the day to persuade the BBC to put out a retraction.

Gillon had been trying to set up British printing and distribution for the *Verses* paperback and now reported success. Bill Norris, boss of the distribution company Central Books, of which Troika Books was the literary division, was happy to take on the task, excited about it, and unafraid. Central distributed antifascist literature and, Norris said, was always receiving threats because of that. Their building already had protection. But their interest was in promoting the book, not the scandal. He took a deep breath and said yes. *Let us do this thing. Let us defy the bastards.*

It struck him forcibly that literature was a country he had not inhabited for some time. Almost four years had passed since he finished *Haroun and the Sea of Stories,* and his writing was still going badly, he couldn't focus or concentrate and was beginning to panic. Panic could be a good thing, it had driven him to work before now, but this had been the longest—yes, he would use the term—*writing block* of his life.

It scared him and he knew he must break through it. March would be a make-or-break month. Frances Coady, his UK editor at Random House, had suggested "maybe a wee book of stories to tide people over," and that could be a way back. What mattered was to write, and he was not writing. Not really. Not at all.

He tried to make himself remember what it was to be a writer, willed himself to rediscover the habits of a lifetime. The inward inquiry, the waiting, the trust in the tale. The slow or quick discovery of how to slice through the body of a fictional world, where to enter it, what journey to make through it, and how to leave. And the magic of concentration, like falling into a deep well or a hole in time. Falling into the page, searching for the ecstasy that came too rarely. And the hard work of self-criticism, the harsh interrogation of his sentences, using what Hemingway had called his "shit detector." The frustration of bumping up against the limits of talent and understanding. "Open the universe a little more." Yes; he was Bellow's dog.

There was strange news: It was revealed that he had been awarded the Austrian State Prize for European Literature *two years earlier,* but the Austrian government had prevented the information from being released. Now there was a hue and cry in the Austrian media. The Austrian culture minister, Rudolf Scholten, admitted he had been naïve and asked to speak to Dr. Rushdie on the phone. When Dr. Rushdie called him, the minister was friendly and apologetic: It had been a mistake, and all the arrangements would soon be made. The mystery of the "secret" Austrian prize was widely reported all over Europe. No English newspaper thought it worth mentioning, however. But the good old *Independent* ran a piece contrasting Taslima Nasreen's courageous decision to live "openly" (i.e., she couldn't go out of her heavily guarded apartment all day, only venturing out under cover of darkness in a car with blackened windows) with *The Satanic Verses'* author's craven wish to remain "in hiding" (which involved fighting for his freedom against police restraints, and going out nevertheless in broad daylight to public places, while being criticized for doing so).

In the shadow world of the phantom killers the Iranian foreign minister, Ali Akbar Velayati, was saying the *fatwa* could not be rescinded. In fact, Velayati was speaking in Vienna, and almost at once the police were telling the *fatwa*'s prime target that his plan to visit that city to receive his State Prize was "too dangerous." Too many people already knew too much about it. Dick Wood told him that the official Foreign Office view was that he would be foolish to go. But they were leaving the final decision to him, even though they "knew" that "something was being planned." He said he didn't want to be scared off, didn't want to run from shadows, and Dick, speaking personally, said he agreed. "It takes time to set up a hit, and they really haven't had enough time."

In Vienna Rudolf Scholten and his wife, Christine, a doctor, greeted them like old friends. The security detail chief said that "certain activities" at the Islamic cultural center were suspicious and so his freedom would unfortunately have to be restricted. They could not walk in the streets, but were shown the city from the roof of the Burgtheater, whose director, Claus Peymann, a burly, bohemian fellow, invited him to come back soon and do an event there. They were driven through the Vienna woods—lovely, dark and deep, like the woods in Robert Frost's famous "hallucinatory" poem—but he was not allowed to get out of the car, which made the woods feel even more like a hallucination. After dinner Elizabeth stayed at the Scholtens' but he was taken by helicopter to the headquarters of the Austrian Special Branch, outside Vienna, and had to spend the night there. *Miles to go before I sleep.* A man who had been watching the Scholtens' apartment building was followed back to the Iraqi, not the Iranian, embassy. So he was probably from the PMOI, whose headquarters were in Iraq. (Saddam Hussein willingly provided a safe haven for his enemy Khomeini's enemies.) The next day the Austrian police surrounded him in phalanx formation and led him into the hall where the award ceremony was to be held. Police helicopters buzzed in the sky overhead. But everything went off without incident. He received his award and went home.

Back in London, he had a late-night conversation with the American counterterrorism chief Robert Gelbard, who said he had "disturbing and specific" information about continued "efforts" against him by the Iranians, "a sign of their frustration," he said, "but as this is something new you should hear about it." *Finish your damn novel, Salman,* he told himself. *You may not have very long left.* The *Observer* ran a story describing a quarrel between Rafsanjani and Khamenei about the Rushdie case. Rafsanjani wanted to abolish the 15 Khordad Foundation, the power base of Sanei of the Bounty, and to ban the use of death squads. But Khamenei had prevented both moves and reiterated the *fatwa*. Nothing changed.

In Norway the writers' union announced that it would invite him to be its guest of honor at its annual conference in Stavanger. The head of the local Muslim association, Ibrahim Yildiz, immediately said that if Rushdie came to Stavanger he would kill him. "If I can find the weapons and have the opportunity, I will not let him go."

He had been missing smallish sums of money from the desk drawer where he kept the petty cash—and this was in a house containing four armed police officers!—and didn't know what to think. Then Clarissa called to say that Zafar's bank statement showed far too much money, and high expenditure. Zafar told her there was a boy at school (he wouldn't name him) who had "sold something from home that he shouldn't have taken" and had asked him to bank the money. This was clearly a lie. He also told Clarissa he had "gone through the list of incomings and outgoings with Dad," but he had done no such thing. A second lie.

They decided to institute major sanctions. The account was to be closed, he would have none of the money from it and no more pocket money until he said what was really happening. Half an hour later—who said economic sanctions didn't work?—Zafar confessed. He had been pilfering the cash from his dad's desk drawer. The dinghy he wanted had cost much more than he thought, £250 not £150, and there were other expenses, things he needed to have on board the boat, and it would have taken forever to save the money, and he really wanted the boat. He was quite severely punished—there would be no TV, the bank account was closed, he would have to repay £30 a month out of his £50 pocket money, and he couldn't use the boat (a Mirror dinghy, which he had already bought, as his parents now discovered) until it had been honestly paid for. Clarissa and he hoped that this episode would shock Zafar back into honesty. But he also had to learn that his parents had trusted him completely and now he had to earn back that trust. At the same time he must not doubt their love, which was unconditional. Zafar looked terrified and ashamed. He didn't argue with the punishment.

Five days later Elizabeth discovered that her most treasured piece of jewelry, a gold charm bracelet that had belonged to her mother, was missing from its hiding place, a box inside another box inside her clothes closet. Nothing else had gone. He asked her to search, but she seemed to have decided that Zafar had taken it. She made a half-hearted search and found nothing. Zafar was asleep in his room and she insisted he be woken up and asked about it. He begged her to turn the house upside down first, but she said she had looked and it wasn't there. So he had to wake his child and accuse him, even though every instinct he possessed told him this boy of his could not have done this thing, he didn't even know where Elizabeth kept her jewels, it didn't make sense. Zafar was very upset and denied having done anything. And when the boy was lying wide awake and wretchedly unhappy in his bed in the middle of the night Elizabeth found the bracelet, which had been there all the time.

Now it was he who was ashamed in front of his son. And between Elizabeth and himself a shadow fell that did not quickly fade.

They were at the home of Ronnie and Natasha Harwood, whose thirty-fifth wedding anniversary it was, and Judge Stephen Tumim, Her Majesty's chief inspector of prisons, a laughing, rubicund gent, whom the IRA had recently promised to kill, was talking about "prot," and what it was like to be made to leave your home of thirty years by the Special Branch. His wife, Winifred, said she had suffered a nervous collapse. She would go to the house, with a police escort, to collect things they needed, and seeing the beds made up and knowing they would never be slept in again was, she said, like visiting a corpse. They had both been grief-stricken, and the worst part was not knowing when it would end. "It's the same for lifers," Judge Tumim said. "When you're held *at Her Majesty's pleasure* you don't know how long you'll be in for. This is a life sentence too, or something very like it."

Stephen and Winifred had had to stay in the military barracks on Albany Street near Regent's Park, which was where he and Elizabeth so nearly got dumped. But things were done for Stephen that had never been offered to them. The state had agreed to value and buy his home from him, because, as the good judge put it, "protected people can't find anyone foolish enough to buy their homes." "I did," he replied, and Ronnie Harwood said, grinning wickedly, "Yes, it's my publisher, Robert McCrum."

Tumim was a marvelous talker. He had met the notorious serial killer Dennis Nilsen when doing a prison visit and had been "a bit alarmed" when Nilsen asked to speak to him alone. "But he only wanted to show off how well-read he had become." Nilsen had been caught when his household drains got blocked with human flesh and entrails. He murdered at least fifteen men and boys and had sex with their dead bodies. Tumim had found Nilsen "very sinister," which sounded probable. They had shared some protection officers and gossiped about them for a while. "The perfect job for covering up an extramarital affair," Tumim agreed. "*Can't tell you where I'm going, darling, or when I'll be back, it's all top secret, you know.* They all have affairs, naturally. We'd probably do the same." He told Tumim the story of the bigamist protection officer. "They're very attractive men, you know," the judge said understandingly.

In the end Tumim had begun to feel safe when the governor of the Maze prison at Long Kesh in Northern Ireland, where the IRA man Bobby Sands had died on hunger strike against conditions in the "H Blocks," told him that he was off the IRA hit list. He had been on it, but now he had been taken off. "The intelligence people don't know much, really," he said. "But if I'd refused to leave home I probably would have been shot. I was in the habit of sitting in a window, looking down toward the river, and just across the river were some bushes, perfect for a sniper. I'd have been a sitting duck. The prot boys told me, *Every time you go into the garden you'll wonder if there's a gunman in the bushes.* But it's all right now."

Ronnie told him the next day that the judge made jokes about those days now, but it had been an awful time for him and his family. One of Tumim's daughters, disliking being in a house full of armed men, starting leaving notes in each room, NO SMOKING, and other instructions. The loss of privacy and spontaneity: These were the hardest things to deal with. It had been very good to talk to someone else who had been through what he was going through, and to hear that such a story could have a happy ending. Elizabeth and Winifred Tumim complained to each other about the weight of the doors of the bulletproof cars. There weren't many people with whom one could have such a chat. "It makes you much fonder of the police," said the judge, "and much less tolerant of the bastards. The IRA in my case. You have different bastards to deal with, not all of them Muslim."

Mr. Anton detected a change in police attitudes toward Operation Malachite. On the one hand, they planned to institute occasional "covert surveillance" of Zafar and Clarissa's home, and he was glad of that, having always been worried that Burma Road was left entirely unsupervised. Dick Wood said he might have to "change teams" when he went out, even to the cinema, because he didn't want the faces of people who stayed at the Bishops' Avenue house to become too well known. On the other hand, a better attitude toward the principal himself was emerging. The protection officer Tony Dunblane confided, "I personally feel that we, the Branch, shouldn't do the Iranians' job for them by keeping you locked up." Soon afterward, his senior officer, Dick Wood, agreed. "I have the impression," Dick said, "that for more than three years you were treated like a naughty child." Many of the restrictions Mr. Greenup had insisted on had been unnecessary. *Well, now you tell me,* he replied. *Three years and more of my life made more unpleasant than they had to be because Greenup didn't like me. I had to fight for every inch of space.* "I don't know how you stood it," Dick said. "None of us could have."

Helen Hammington had softened, too, and was prepared to help the Malachite principal have a slightly better life. Perhaps all his meetings with world leaders had helped to change her attitude. Perhaps his own arguments had finally had some effect. He didn't ask.

———

In 1982 he had visited the old synagogue in Cochin, Kerala, a small gem tiled in blue ceramics from China (TILES FROM CANTON & NO TWO ARE IDENTICAL, a sign read). The story of the almost-extinct community of Keralan Jews caught his imagination and he approached the synagogue's tiny caretaker, an elderly gentleman with the fine South Indian name of Jackie Cohen, and peppered him with questions.

After a few minutes Mr. Cohen grew impatient. "Why you asking so much?" the querulous old caretaker demanded. "Well," he replied, "I'm a writer, and maybe I could write something about this place." Jackie Cohen waved a bony, dismissive arm. "There is no need," he said, just a little haughtily. "We already have a leaflet."

He had kept a journal of his visit to Kerala and some writerly instinct had told him not to waste it. Now that journal, which had been retrieved from St. Peter's Street, showed him the way back to his work. He pored over it day after day, remembering the beauty of Cochin harbor, the pepper warehouses storing the "Black Gold of Malabar," and the great punkah fans in the church where Vasco da Gama had been buried. As he walked through the streets of the Jewtown district in his mind, the Cochin section of *The Moor's Last Sigh* began to come alive. Aurora Zogoiby and her son Moraes the Moor guided him into their world.

His nightmare had been long and literature had been hard to reclaim. He thought every day of William Nygaard and his bullet holes, of Ettore Capriolo kicked and stabbed, of Hitoshi Igarashi dead in a pool of blood by an elevator shaft. Not only he, the shameless author, but the world of books—literature itself—had been vilified, shot, kicked, knifed, killed, and blamed at the same time. Yet the true life of books was profoundly other than this world of violence, and in it he rediscovered the discourse he loved. He emerged from his alien everyday reality and sank into Aurora, her glamour, her bohemian excess, her painterly contemplations of languor and desire, devoured her, like a starving man at a feast.

He had read a story about Lenin hiring look-alikes to travel the Soviet Union to deliver speeches he had no time to give, and thought it would be funny if, in Kerala, where Communism was popular, the local Leninists decided to hire Indian Lenins to do the same thing. The

Too-Tall Lenin, the Too-Short Lenin, the Too-Fat Lenin, the Too-Skinny Lenin, the Too-Lame Lenin, the Too-Bald Lenin, and Lenin the Too-thless marched into his pages and with them came lightness and brio. Perhaps he could write a good book, after all. *The Moor's Last Sigh* would be his first novel for adults since *The Satanic Verses*. There was a lot riding on its reception. He tried to put such thoughts out of his mind.

His daily life was less disrupted now than it had been when he wrote *Haroun and the Sea of Stories* but the gift of deep concentration proved harder to recapture. The imperative of his promise to Zafar had driven *Haroun* forward through all the house moves and uncertainties. Now he had a place to live and a pleasant room to write in but he was distracted. He forced himself back into his old routines. He got up in the morning and went straight to his desk, without showering or dressing for the day, sometimes without even cleaning his teeth, and forced himself to sit there in his pajamas until he had begun the day's work. "The art of writing," Hemingway said, "is the art of applying the seat of the pants to the seat of the chair." *Sit down,* he ordered himself. *Don't stand up.* And slowly, slowly, his old power returned. The world went away. Time stood still. He fell happily toward that deep place where unwritten books wait to be found, like lovers demanding proof of utter devotion before they appear. He was a writer again.

When he wasn't writing the novel he was revising old stories and thinking of new ones for the collection he was calling *East, West*—a title in which, he thought, the comma represented himself. He had the three "East" stories and the three "West" stories too and was working on the three tales of cultural crossover that would form the final part of the collection. "Chekov and Zulu" was about Indian diplomats obsessed by *Star Trek* at the time of Mrs. Gandhi's assassination, and his friendship with Salman Haidar at the Indian High Commission gave him some useful material. "The Harmony of the Spheres" was an almost-true story based on the suicide of a close Cambridge friend, Jamie Webb, a writer on occult themes who developed acute schizophrenia and eventually shot himself. And the longest story, "The Courter," was still being written. In the midsixties, when his parents moved from Bombay to Kensington, they brought his old Mangalorean *ayah* Mary Menezes with them for a time to look after his youngest sister, then just two years old. But Mary grew horribly homesick, her heart breaking with longing for another place. She actually started having heart troubles and in the end returned to India. The moment she got back the heart troubles stopped and never came back. She lived to be well over one hundred years old. The idea that you might actually be in danger of dying from a broken heart was something to write about. He joined Mary's story to the tale of an Eastern European janitor he once met at the Ogilvy & Mather advertising agency in London, an elderly man who could barely speak English and was suffering from the aftereffects of a stroke, but who played chess with a fluency and force that very few opponents could resist. In his story the silenced chess player and the homesick *ayah* fell in love.

The police had planned a special treat for him and Elizabeth. They were taken to the legendary Black Museum in Scotland Yard, which was not normally open to the public. The temperature in the museum was kept very low so he shivered as he went inside. The curator, John Ross, who oversaw this bizarre collection of actual murder weapons and other true-crime memorabilia, said he wished that the British police were allowed to kill people. Perhaps his long proximity to these instruments of death had affected his thinking. In the Black Museum there were many disguised weapons—umbrella guns, truncheons that were guns, knives that shot bullets. All the fantasy weapons of crime novels and spy movies were here, laid out on tables, and every weapon on display had killed a man or woman. "We use this to train young officers," Mr. Ross said. "Just so they understand, you see, that anything can be a gun." Here was the gun used by Ruth Ellis, the last woman to be hanged in England, to kill her lover David Blakely. Here was the gun with which, at Caxton Hall in Westminster in 1940, the Sikh assassin Udham Singh had murdered Sir Michael O'Dwyer, the former governor of the Punjab, to avenge the Indians shot down in the Amritsar massacre twenty-one years earlier, on April 13, 1919. Here was the cooker and bath in which the serial killer John Reginald

Christie had boiled and filleted his victims at 10 Rillington Place in west London. And here was Heinrich Himmler's death mask.

Dennis Nilsen had served briefly in the police force, Mr. Ross said, but was kicked out after a year for being a homosexual. "We couldn't do that now, could we," reflected Mr. Ross. "Ho no, we could not."

In a pickle jar was a pair of human arms severed at the elbow. They belonged to a British killer who had been shot dead when on the run in Germany. Scotland Yard had asked their German colleagues to send them the corpse's fingerprints so that they could formally identify it and close the case. The Germans sent over the killer's arms instead. " '*You* take der fingerprints,' " Mr. Ross said, affecting an accent. "Spot of the old German sense of humor there." And he was a man whom people were trying to kill, and so he had been invited into the world of murder as a special treat. Spot of the old British sense of humor there, he thought. Ho yes.

That night, with images of the Black Museum still vivid in his imagination, he took part at the Royal Court Theatre in a memorial reading for Anthony Burgess, along with John Walsh, Melvyn Bragg, D. J. Enright and Lorna Sage. He read the part of *A Clockwork Orange* in which Alex and his droogs attack the author of a book called *A Clockwork Orange*. He had been thinking a good deal about what Burgess called "ultraviolence" (including violence against authors); about the glamour of terrorism, and how it made lost, hopeless young men feel powerful and consequential. The Russian-based slang Burgess had created for his book had defined that kind of violence, glorified it and anaesthetized responses to it, so that it became a brilliant metaphor of what made violence hip. To read *A Clockwork Orange* was to gain a better understanding of the enemies of *The Satanic Verses*.

He had finished "The Courter," so the *East, West* collection was complete. He had also finished part one of *The Moor's Last Sigh*, "A House Divided," about forty thousand words long. The block had been broken at last. He was deeply inside the dream. He was no longer in Cochin. Now in his mind's eye he saw the city of his youth, which had been forced to adopt a false name, just as he had. *Midnight's Chil-*

dren had been his novel of Bombay. This would be the book of a darker, more corrupt, more violent place, seen not through the eyes of childhood but using adulthood's more jaundiced gaze. A novel of Mumbai.

He had begun to fight a court case in India to recover a piece of ancestral property, his grandfather's summer cottage at Solan in the Shimla Hills, which had been seized illegally by the state government of Himachal Pradesh. When this news reached London the *Daily Mail* ran an editorial suggesting that if he would like to go and live in Solan his passage there could be paid for by public subscription because it would be so much cheaper than continuing the protection. If any other Indian immigrant to Britain had been told to go back where he came from it would be called racism, but it was apparently permissible to speak of this particular immigrant any way one chose.

At the end of June he traveled to Norway to meet William Nygaard, who was recovering well, but slowly, from his wounds, and gave him a hug. In July he wrote the first of a series of open letters to the beleaguered Bangladeshi writer Taslima Nasreen for the Berlin daily *Die Tageszeitung.* After him came Mario Vargas Llosa, Milan Kundera, Czesław Miłosz and many others. On August 7 the *fatwa* had been in place for two thousand days. On August 9 Taslima Nasreen arrived in Stockholm with the help of Gabi Gleichmann of Swedish PEN, and was given asylum by the Swedish government. Nine days later she received the Kurt Tucholsky Prize. So she was safe; exiled, deprived of her language, her country and her culture, but alive. "Exile," he had written in *The Satanic Verses,* "is a dream of glorious return." He had been writing about the exile of a Khomeini-like imam, but the line boomeranged back and described its author, and now Taslima as well. He could not return to India, and Taslima could not go back to Bangladesh; they could only dream.

Slowly, carefully, he had arranged for a few weeks of escape. He, Elizabeth and Zafar went by night train to Scotland and were met by the prot vehicles, which had been driven up the day before. On the small private island of Eriska near Oban there was a quiet hotel and they spent a week's holiday there doing ordinary holiday things—island walks, skeet shooting, mini-golf—that felt unutterably luxurious. They visited Iona and in the graveyard where the ancient kings of Scotland lay at rest—where Macbeth himself was interred—they saw a fresh grave, the earth upon it still moist, in which John Smith, the Labour leader, had recently been buried. He had met Smith once and admired him. He stood by the grave and bowed his head.

And after Scotland came the real escape. Elizabeth and Zafar flew from London to New York. He had to go the long way around again. He flew to Oslo, waited, then caught the Scandinavian Airlines flight to JFK and arrived in pouring rain. The U.S. authorities had asked him to stay on board and after all the other passengers had deplaned they came aboard and went through all the immigration formalities. He was taken off the aircraft and driven off the airfield to the appointed meeting place with Andrew Wylie. Then he was in Andrew's car, and the world of security retreated and set him free. No protection had been asked for and none had been offered or insisted upon. The promise of the statue in the harbor had been kept.

Freedom! Freedom! He felt a hundred pounds lighter and in the mood to sing. Zafar and Elizabeth were waiting at Andrew's place and that evening Paul Auster and Siri Hustvedt, Susan Sontag and David Rieff stopped by, all of them filled with happy disbelief at seeing him free of his chains. He took Elizabeth and Zafar on a helicopter ride around the city with Andrew Wylie and Elizabeth and Andrew screamed with terror—Andrew loudly, Elizabeth silently—the whole time. After the ride they rented a car at Hertz. The round pink face of the blond Hertz girl, Debi, showed no flicker of recognition as she typed his name into the computer. Then they had a Lincoln Town Car of their own! He felt like a child with the keys to the toy store. They went out to eat with Jay McInerney and Erroll McDonald of Random House. Everything felt intensely exciting. Willie Nelson was there! And Matthew Modine! The maître d' looked concerned, but so what. Zafar, fifteen now, was at his grown-up best. Jay treated him like a man, talked to him about girls, and Zafar loved it. He went to bed grinning and woke up with the grin still in place.

They were going to Cazenovia, New York, to stay with Michael and Valerie Herr. They had been sent elaborate directions, but he called Michael before setting off, just to be clear. "The only bit I'm not sure of," he said, "is how to get out of New York." With perfect comic timing Michael drawled, "Yeah, people have been trying to work that out for years, Salman."

Every instant was a gift. Driving up the interstate felt like space travel, past the Albany galactic cluster and the Schenectady nebula toward the constellation of Syracuse. They paused in Chittenango, which had been turned into an Oz theme park: yellow brick sidewalks, Aunt Em's Coffee Shop, awful. They pressed on to Cazenovia and then Michael was blinking at them from behind his little pebble glasses and smiling his ironic lopsided smile and Valerie was looking vaguely beatific and *well*. They were in the world of Jim and Jim. The Herrs' daughters were home and there was a corgi called Pablo who came and laid its head in his lap and would not be moved. Behind the ample wooden house a pond was surrounded by wilderness. They took a night walk below a big old moon. In the morning there was a dead deer in the pond.

He learned to pronounce "Skaneateles" on the way to the Finger Lake where the writer Tobias Wolff owned a cabin. They ate in a fish bar, walked out to the end of the pier, *behaved normally,* felt abnormally light-headed with joy. In the evening they stopped by a bookstore and he was recognized instantly. That made Michael nervous but nobody made a fuss and he reassured Michael, "I'll just stay away from the bookstore tomorrow." On Sunday they stayed home with the Herrs and Toby Wolff came to lunch and he and Michael swapped stories of Vietnam.

The drive to John Irving's place in Vermont was about three hours long. They stopped near the state line for lunch. The restaurant was run by an Algerian named Rouchdy, who inevitably grew very excited. "Rushdie! We have the same name! I always getting mistaken for you! I say, no, no, I am much better looking!" (On another visit to America an Egyptian maître d' at Harry Cipriani in midtown New York waxed similarly lyrical. "Rushdie! I like you! That book, your book, I read it! Rushdie, I like your book, that book! I am from Egypt! Egypt! In Egypt, that book is banned! Your book! It is *totally banned!* But everyone has read it!")

John and Janet Irving lived in a long house on a hillside above the town of Dorset. John said, "When we talked to the architect we just put napkin squares down in a line, some of them set at angles, like this. We told him, build it this way, and he did." There was a *New York Times* bestseller list framed on a wall, with *The Satanic Verses* one place above John's book. There were other framed bestseller lists and in all of them John stood at number one. Local writers came for dinner and there were shouts and arguments and drinks. He recalled that when he first met John he had had the temerity to ask him, "Why all the bears in your books? Were there bears that were important in your life?" No, John answered, and anyway—this was after *The Hotel New Hampshire*—he was done with bears now. He was writing the book for a ballet for Baryshnikov, he added, and there was only one problem. "What problem?" "Baryshnikov doesn't want to wear the bear suit."

They went to a state fair and failed dismally to guess the weight of the pig. *Some pig,* he said, and Elizabeth answered, *Radiant.* They looked at each other, finding it hard to believe that all this was really happening. After two days he bundled Elizabeth and Zafar into the Lincoln Town Car and drove to New London to get the ferry to Orient Point on the North Fork of Long Island. As the ferry left New London a black nuclear submarine like a giant blind cetacean was coming into harbor. That night they reached Andrew's house in Water Mill. The simplest things brought them close to ecstasy. He horsed around in Andrew's pool with Zafar and had rarely seen his teenage son so happy. Zafar Rollerbladed down the leafy lanes and he followed on a borrowed bike. They went to the beach. Zafar and Andrew's daughter Erica got Chevy Chase's autograph in a restaurant. Elizabeth bought summer dresses in Southampton. Then the spell broke and it was time to go home. Elizabeth and Zafar flew home on one of the many airlines that were forbidden to him. He flew to Oslo and changed planes. *We are going to do this again, for much longer,* he promised himself. America had given him back his liberty for a few precious days. There was no sweeter narcotic, and, like any addict, he immediately wanted more.

His new contact at the Foreign Office was an Arabist called Andrew Green, but when Green offered him a meeting, he and Frances agreed to decline it because Green had nothing new to discuss. "Is Salman very depressed?" Green asked Frances. "Is this an analytical or an emotional response?" No, he's actually not depressed, Mr. Green, he's just tired of being jerked around.

Frances had written to Klaus Kinkel, who now held the rotating presidency of the European Union. Kinkel sent back a stonewalling reply. No, no, no. And a member of the conservative German Christian Democratic Union was the new head of the human rights committee of the European Parliament, which was bad news too. The Germans sometimes felt very like Iran's agents in Europe. They had their brooms out and were sweeping him under the carpet once again.

His nine stories were finding favor. Michael Dibdin in *The Independent on Sunday* wrote that this book did him more good and won him more friends than any number of speeches or statements, and that sounded right. Then Cat Stevens—Yusuf Islam—bubbled up in *The Guardian* like a fart in a bathtub, still demanding that Rushdie withdraw his book and "repent," and claiming that his support of the *fatwa* was in line with the Ten Commandments. (In later years he would pretend that he had never said any of these things, never called for anyone's murder, never justified it on the basis of his religion's "law," never appeared on TV or spoken to the papers to spout his uneducated bloodthirsty garbage, knowing he lived in an age in which nobody had a memory. Repeated denials could establish a new truth that erased the old one.)

Dick Wood's new sidekick Rab Connolly, a sharp, fiery, slightly dangerous red-haired man who was taking a degree course in postcolonial literature in his spare time, called to panic about a cartoon in *The Guardian* showing an "establishment network" with lines connecting Mr. Anton to Alan Yentob, Melvyn Bragg, Ian McEwan, Martin Amis, Richard and Ruthie Rogers, and the River Café. "All those people visit you at your residence and this could prejudice the covert nature of the prot." He pointed out that the media in London had known for a long time who his friends were, so this was nothing new, and after a while Connolly agreed that his friends would still be allowed to visit him in spite of the cartoon. He sometimes felt he was caught in a trap of perceptions. If he tried to come out of his hole and be more visible, the press concluded he was no longer in danger, and acted accordingly, sometimes (as in the case of the *Guardian* cartoon) making the police feel that they had increased the risk to the Malachite principal. Then he was pushed back into the hole. On this occasion, at least, Rab Connolly did not lose his nerve. "I don't want to stop you from going anywhere," he said.

Out of the blue Marianne sent him a note, which was faxed to him by Gillon. "Against my will I watched you on *Face to Face* tonight, and I'm glad I did. There you were, as I once knew you—sweet and good and honest, discoursing about Love. Let's bury what we made together, please." On letterhead paper, and unsigned. He wrote to her saying he would be happy to bury the hatchet if she would just return his photographs. She did not reply.

At home, there were many tiny irritations caused by cohabiting with four policemen. Two teenagers in the street stared at the house and the police at once decided that Zafar must have told his school friends where it was. (He had not, and the teenagers were not from Highgate School.) More and more electronic security systems were brought into the house and fought with one another. When they set the alarms the police radios didn't work and when they used the radios they jammed the alarms. They put an "outer rim" perimeter alarm system around the edges of the garden and every squirrel that ran by, every leaf that fell, triggered the alarm. "It's like the Keystone Cops around here sometimes," he said to Elizabeth, whose smile was forced, because the pregnancy she longed for had not happened. Tension rose in their bedroom. That did not help.

Elizabeth and he had dinner with Hitch, Carol, Martin and Isabel after a *London Review of Books* party and Martin was at his most emphatic. "Of course Dostoyevsky's no fucking good." "Of course Beckett's no fucking good *at all*." Too much wine and whiskey had been drunk and he began to argue fiercely with his friend. As their voices rose Isabel tried to intervene and he turned to her and said, "Oh, fuck off, Isabel." He hadn't meant to say that but the drink let it out. At once Martin bridled. "You can't talk to my girlfriend like that. Apologize." He said, "I've known her twice as long as you, and she isn't even offended. Are you offended, Isabel?" Isabel said, "Of course I'm not offended," but Martin had become dogged: "Apologize."

"Or what? Or else what, Martin? Or else we go outside?" Isabel and Elizabeth both intervened to put a stop to the idiocy but Christopher said, "Let it play itself out." "All right," he said, "I apologize. Isabel, I apologize. Now, Martin, there's something you have to do for me." "What's that?" "You have to never speak to me again as long as you live."

The next day he felt awful and did not feel better until he had spoken to Martin and put the quarrel away, agreeing with him that such things could happen from time to time and did not affect the love they felt for each other. He told Martin that there had built up inside him a huge unscreamed scream and last night a bit of it had come out in the wrong place, at the wrong time.

In November he went to Strasbourg to the meeting of the Parliament of Writers. The men of the RAID had taken over the entire top floor of the Hotel Regent Contades to protect him. They were tense because the trial of the murderers of Shapur Bakhtiar was in progress, and the subject of the conference was the tense situation with the Islamists of the FIS and GIA in Algeria, and his presence in the city cranked up the volume considerably.

He met Jacques Derrida, who made him think of Peter Sellers in *The Magic Christian,* walking through life with an invisible wind machine permanently ruffling his hair. He soon realized that he and Derrida would not agree about anything. In the Algeria session he made his argument that Islam itself, Actually Existing Islam, could not be exonerated from the crimes done in its name. Derrida disagreed. The "rage of Islam" was driven not by Islam but by the misdeeds of the West. Ideology had nothing to do with it. It was a question of power.

The RAID people were getting twitchier by the hour. They announced a bomb scare at the opera house, where the writers were meeting. There was a suspicious canister and they carried out a controlled explosion. It was a fire extinguisher. The bang happened during

Günter Wallraff's speech and unnerved him for a moment. He had been ill with hepatitis and had made a special effort to come to Strasbourg "to be with you."

That night on Arte he was asked to take the Proust questionnaire. What was his favorite word? "Comedy." And his least favorite? "Religion."

On the flight back, a German woman, quite young, had hysterics when he boarded the Air France flight, and left the plane, white and weeping. An announcement was made to calm things down. The passenger had left because she was not feeling well. Whereupon a mousy Englishman stood up and roared. "Oh, well, *none* of us are feeling *well. I'm* not feeling well *myself.* Let's *all* get off." He and his wife, a bottle blonde with big hair, an electric blue Chanel suit and much gold jewelry, got off the plane like Mr. and Mrs. Moses leading the Exodus. Fortunately, nobody followed them. And Air France agreed to go on flying him.

Ayatollah Jannati said in Tehran that the *fatwa* "sticks in the throats of the enemies of Islam but it cannot be revoked until that man dies."

Clarissa was feeling better. On Christmas Day she insisted on having Zafar to herself. He and Elizabeth went to Graham and Candice's and, in the evening, visited Jill Craigie and Michael Foot, who had been in the hospital with something unmentionable but made a big effort to make light of it. Finally Jill admitted he had had a hernia in the bowel. He had been throwing up, couldn't eat, and they had feared cancer, so the hernia was a huge relief. "All his organs are okay," she said, though of course at his age the operation was a major setback. "He kept telling me what to do if he was *no more* and of course I wouldn't listen," Jill said in her best no-nonsense voice. (Nobody could then have guessed that he would outlive her by eleven years.)

Michael had presents for them both, a second edition of Hazlitt's *Lives of the Poets* for Elizabeth and a first edition of *Lectures on the English Comic Writers* for him. Michael and Jill treated them both with great love and he thought, "If I had had my choice of parents these would have been the finest I could imagine having."

His own mother was well and safe and far away and seventy-eight years old, and he missed her.

My darling Amma,

Another year is on its last legs but we, I'm happy to say, are not. Speaking of legs, how's your "arthur-itis"? When I was at Rugby your letters to me always began with the question "Are you fat or are you thin?" Thin meant they weren't feeding your boy properly. Fat was good. Well, I'm getting thinner, but you should be happy. Thin is better, on the whole. In my letters from school I always tried to conceal how unhappy I was there. They were my first fictions, those letters, "scored 24 runs at cricket," "having a great time," "I am well and happy." When you found out how miserable I'd been you were horrified, of course, but by then I was on my way to college. That was thirty-nine years ago. We have always concealed bad news from one another. You did it too. You'd tell Sameen everything and then say, "Don't tell Salman, it would upset him." What a pair we are. Anyway, the house we live in has "settled down," to use the police parlance. It isn't attracting any attention from the neighbors. We seem to have pulled it off, and inside this cocoon things sometimes feel almost calm, and I'm able to work. The book is going well and I can see the finish line. When a book is going well everything else in life feels tolerable; even in this strange life. I've been taking stock of the year. In the "minus" column, I've developed "late-onset" asthma, a little reward from the universe for having broken my cigarette habit. Still, at least I can never smoke again now. Inhaling smoke is plain impossible. "Late-onset" asthma is usually pretty mild, but it's also incurable. Incurabubble, to paraphrase my old ad campaign. And as you always taught us, "What can't be cured must be endured." Among the "plusses": the new leader of the Labour Party, Tony Blair, said some nice things in an interview with Julian Barnes. "I absolutely one hundred percent support him. . . . You can't muck around with something like this at all." Absolutely one hundred percent is good, na, Amma? Let's hope the percentage doesn't drop as and when he becomes PM. European Muslims seem to be getting almost as sick of the fatwa as I am. Dutch Muslims and French Muslims have come out against it. The French Muslims actually supported free speech and freedom of

conscience! In Britain of course we still have Sacranie and Siddiqui and the
Bradford clowns, so there are plenty of laughs. And in Kuwait an imam
wants to ban the "blasphemous" Barbie doll. Would you ever have thought
that poor Barbie and I would be guilty of the same offense? An Egyptian
magazine published parts of The Satanic Verses *alongside banned work by*
Naguib Mahfouz and demanded that religious authorities be deprived of the
right to say what may or may not be read in Egypt. By the way, Tantawi, the
grand mufti of Egypt, has come out against the fatwa. *And in his opening*
address to the Organization of the Islamic Conference meeting in Casablanca,
King Hassan of Morocco said nobody had the right to declare people infidels
or launch fatwas *or jihads against them. This is good, I think. The funda-*
mental things apply as time goes by. Be well. Come and see me soon. I love
you.

Oh, P.S.: That woman Taslima is causing a lot of trouble for Gabi G. in
Sweden, denouncing him (for what?) and saying she has nothing good to say
about him. She's quite a piece of work, I'm afraid, and has been alienating
her defenders all over Europe. Poor Gabi did as much as anyone to get her
out of danger. No good deed goes unpunished, as they say.

Happy new year!
I am well and happy.

He had finished his novel. Seven years had passed since Saladin Chamcha turned away from the window looking out upon the Arabian Sea;
it was five years since Haroun Khalifa's mother, Soraya, began to sing
again. Those were endings he had had to discover during the writing
process, but he had had the end of *The Moor's Last Sigh* almost from
the beginning. Moor Zogoiby's graveyard requiem for himself: *I'll lay*
me down upon this graven stone, lay my head beneath these letters RIP, and
close my eyes, according to my family's old practice of falling asleep in times of
trouble, and hope to awaken, renewed and joyful, into a better time. It had
been helpful to know the last notes of the music, to know the target
toward which all the book's arrows—narrative, thematic, comic, symbolic—were flying. Outside the pages of books the question of a satisfying ending was mostly unanswerable. Human life was rarely shapely,
only intermittently meaningful, its clumsiness the inevitable conse-

quence of the victory of content over form, of *what* and *when* over *how* and *why*. Yet with the passage of time he became more and more determined to shape his story toward the ending everyone refused to believe in, in which he and his loved ones could move beyond a discourse of risk and safety into a future free of danger in which "risk" became once again a word for creative daring and "safe" was the way you felt when you were surrounded by love.

He had always been post-something according to that mandarin literary discourse in which all contemporary writing was mere aftermath—postcolonial, postmodern, postsecular, postintellectual, postliterate. Now he would add his own category, post-*fatwa,* to that dusty post-office, and would end up not just po-co and po-mo but po-*fa* as well. He had been interested in reclamation ever since he wrote *Midnight's Children* to reclaim his Indian heritage for himself, and even before that, in fact, for was he not a Bombay boy, and was that megalopolis not itself a city built on land reclaimed from the sea? Now once again he would set out to reclaim lost ground. His completed novel would be published, and with that act he would reclaim his place in the world of books. And he would plan an American summer, and negotiate little increments of liberty with the police chiefs, and yes, he would continue to think about political pressure, about the defense campaign, but he didn't have time to wait for a political solution, he needed to start grabbing those fragments of freedom that were within his reach, to start moving toward the happy ending he was determined to write for himself, step by lightening step.

Andrew on the phone talking about *The Moor* was almost moved to tears. Gillon's upper lip was stiffer but he, too, was moved. He was happy to hear their excitement, even if he was already beginning to feel that the ending needed work, that the character of the villain of the final act, Vasco Miranda, wasn't quite there yet. Elizabeth finished it and was happy about the dedication, *For E.J.W.,* and full of much praise and some sharp editorial commentary, but she also imagined that the Japanese woman in the book's last movement, Aoi Uë, her name all vowels, contained a bit of her, and Moor Zogoiby's comparison of her with his previous, deranged lover, Uma—he called Aoi "a better woman whom he loved less"—was really a comparison of herself and Marianne. He had to talk for an hour to persuade her that this was not so, that if she wanted to find herself in the novel she should look at the writing, at the tenderness and lovingness there, which was what he had learned from being with her, and which was her true mark on the book.

He was telling the truth. But when he had told it he felt that he had diminished the novel, because he had once again been forced to explain his work and its motives. The joy of finishing was a little dimmed, and he began to fear that people would be able to read the book only as a coded version of his life.

That evening they met Graham Swift and Caryl Phillips at Julie's restaurant in Notting Hill and Dick Wood, who had come out with the protection team for once, and who didn't like staying out late, sent him a note at midnight ordering him to leave because the drivers were tired. He had done this once before, at Billy Connolly's birthday party, and this time an angry altercation took place, with the Malachite principal pointing out that he would not have sent such an infantilizing note to any other principal, and that grown-ups did sometimes dine until after the witching hour. Dick changed his tune, saying that the real reason for the note had been that a waiter had been making a suspicious, whispered phone call. Caz Phillips investigated—the restaurant was a favorite haunt of his—and reported that the waiter had been calling his girlfriend, but none of the protection team, not even Dick's sidekick Rab, had believed the waiter story anyway. "Oh, we all know it was nothing to do with the phone call," Rab said with a laugh. "Dick was tired, that's all." Rab offered him a "group apology on behalf of the whole team" and promised it would not happen again. But he felt, gloomily, that his hopes for an increasingly "ordinary" social life had been dashed. Dick, after all, had been the one who had told him that he had been treated too harshly by the police, who had limited his freedom of movement unnecessarily.

Helen Hammington came to see him to try to set things right, and a day later Dick came, too, entering with the words "I don't expect you to apologize," which made matters considerably worse. During their meeting, however, it was agreed that greater "flexibility" was needed. Dick blamed the departed Tony Dunblane for the old rigidities. "Now that he's gone you'll find the people you have will be more amenable." But Mr. Anton had liked Dunblane and always found him helpful.

He received two pieces of hate mail, a photograph of otters with an added speech balloon inside which were the words YOU SHOULDN'T "OTTER" DONE IT, and a greetings card that said HAPPY FATWAH—SEE YOU SOON—ISLAMIC JIHAD. On the same day Peter Temple-Morris of the "anti-Rushdie" Tory group made a speech at a seminar on Iran at the School of Oriental and African Studies in which he said in the approving presence of the Iranian *chargé d'affaires,* Ansari, that Mr. Rushdie was to blame for the whole affair and should now keep silent, because "silence is golden." This was an interlingual pun: In Iran the author of *The Satanic Verses* had sometimes been called a "golden man," which was a Farsi idiom for a dishonest person, a shyster. Also on the same day, Frances called to say that Article 19 had spent £60,000 on the defense campaign in 1994 but had only raised £30,000 in funding for it, so from now on they would have to cut their efforts in half.

At the annual "A" Squad party he was touched to discover that the Malachite prot team was feeling decidedly proprietorial about his new novel and were resolved that it "must" win the Booker Prize. "Okay," he told the lads, "we'll be in touch with the jury and let them know that quite a few heavily armed men have a strong interest in the result." After that he and Elizabeth were *allowed* to have dinner at the Ivy. (The prot team sat at a table near the door and people-watched like everyone else.) He was feeling very emotional, he told her, because the completion of *The Moor's Last Sigh,* even more than *Haroun and the Sea of Stories,* felt like his victory over the forces of darkness. Even if they killed him now they could not defeat him. He had not been silenced. He had continued.

There were paparazzi outside and they all knew who Elizabeth was; but when he came out of the restaurant he said, "You can have me but not her, please," and every one of them respected the request.

Clarissa was well again. The words "full remission" were heard for the first time. There was a broader smile on Zafar's face than his father had seen there for some time. She was also up for a new job as literature officer of the Arts Council, a job he had encouraged her to try for. He called Michael Holroyd, who was on the interviewing panel, and made a passionate pitch for her. The difficulty might be her age, Michael said; the Arts Council might prefer someone younger. He said, She's only forty-six, Michael, and she's perfectly suited for the job. She went for her interview and performed impressively. A few days later the job was hers.

The Moor's Last Sigh was making new friends every day. His French editor, Ivan Nabokov, wrote enthusiastically from Paris. Sonny Mehta, characteristically uncommunicative, hadn't read the book yet. "Yes," his assistant told Andrew, "he's been worrying about that." The nightmare scenario was that Sonny might panic over the book's portrait of a Bombay political party called "Mumbai's Axis," a satirical portrait of the thuggish Shiv Sena, and that, consequently, Random House would cancel their contract, as they had at the time of *Haroun*. But eventually, after long anxious days in which, after receiving a message that Sonny "wants you to call him," he was repeatedly told that the great man was not available, they finally spoke, and Sonny said he liked the book. There would be no contract-ripping moment this time around. Another small step forward.

And then a bigger step. After long discussions between himself and Scotland Yard, Rab Connolly told him that when *The Moor's Last Sigh* was published he would be *allowed* to do public readings and signings, and that these could be advertised six days in advance, avoiding Fridays, so that the Muslim opposition couldn't use Friday prayer meetings to organize. "Announcement on Saturday, event the following Thursday," Rab said. "That has been agreed." It was a breakthrough. His editor, Frances Coady, and Caroline Michel, who was in charge of publicity, were thrilled.

The step backward, when it came, took him completely by surprise. Clarissa was healthier by the day, and excited about her new job, and Zafar's schoolwork was improving with his mother's health, and his confidence grew every week. Then in mid-March she called to say that she had been thinking, and had also been advised, that she needed more money. (When they divorced he had lacked the funds to make a clean-break settlement, and had been paying her a mixture of alimony and child support for ten years.) Her lawyers had told her she could get huge amounts, she said, admitting for the first time that lawyers were involved, but she would accept £150,000. "Okay," he said. "You win. £150,000. Okay." It was a lot of money, but that wasn't it. Hostility, like love, came at you from the direction you weren't looking in. He had not expected her to pursue him after all these years, after his immense concern for her during her illness, after his behind-the-scenes efforts on her behalf at A. P. Watt and the Arts Council. (In fairness, she didn't know about those phone calls.) There was no concealing from Zafar the sudden strain between his mother and father. The boy was very worried, but insisted on knowing what was going on. Zafar was almost sixteen, and watching both his parents fiercely. It was impossible to keep the truth from him.

The Iranian deputy foreign minister, Mahmud Va'ezi, was contradicting himself, promising in Denmark that Iran would send no assassins to carry out the death order, and then, in Paris the next day, affirming "the need for the implementation" of that order. The policy of "critical dialogue" between the EU and Iran, initiated in 1992 to improve Iran's record on human rights, support for terrorism and the *fatwa,* was exposed as an utter failure. It wasn't critical enough, and as the Iranians weren't interested in it, there was no dialogue.

After Va'ezi's remarks in Paris, this was what the British government said: nothing. Other countries protested, but from the United Kingdom, there wasn't a peep. He spent some days fuming about Va'ezi's forked tongue, and then he had an idea. He suggested to Frances D'Souza that if they were to take Va'ezi's Danish statement as a sort of "cease-fire" declaration they might be able to get the French to push Iran to disown the minister's subsequent remarks in Paris and agree to a public promise of non-implementation of the *fatwa,* which would have to be closely monitored by the EU for a stipulated period, et cetera et cetera, before any upgrade of relations to full ambassadorial level could occur. The idea of a "French initiative" excited Frances. She had been depressed by her recent meeting with Douglas Hogg, at which he had told her that nothing could be done except to continue with the protection; Khamenei was in charge and so Iranian terrorism continued. Hogg said to Frances that he had been told by the Iranians *eighteen months earlier* that they would not carry out the *fatwa* in Britain but had felt no need to mention the fact because it "meant nothing." So HMG's policy was inertia as usual. Frances agreed to try to rouse their French allies. She contacted Jack Lang and Bernard-Henri Lévy and they began to plan. He himself even called Jacques Derrida, who wanted him to be photographed with French parliamentarians and warned him, "Whoever you meet with will be interpreted as a political sign, and you should be careful of certain persons." Derrida meant BHL, no doubt, a divisive figure in France. But Bernard had been staunch in his support and he would not disown so loyal a friend.

On March 19, 1995, he took the Eurostar to Paris, was immediately devoured by the RAID and taken to see a group of the courageous French Muslims who had signed a declaration in his support. The next day he met all the leading French political figures *sauf Mitterrand*: the president-in-waiting Jacques Chirac, big, shambling, comfortable in his body, with a killer's dead eyes; the prime minister, Édouard Balladur, a man with a little pursed mouth of whose stiff-backed demeanor the French liked to say that *il a avalé son parapluie,* he has swallowed his umbrella; Alain Juppé, the foreign minister, a quick, clever little bald guy who later joined the list of politicians of the era who were convicted of a crime (mishandling public funds); the Socialist Lionel Jospin, who felt like Calvino's *cavaliere inesistente,* an empty space in a loose suit. Frances and he proposed the "cease-fire plan" and they all went for it. Juppé guaranteed to put the idea on the agenda of the EU foreign ministers' meeting, Balladur gave a press conference announcing "their" initiative, Chirac said he had spoken to Douglas Hurd and Hurd was "for it." He himself gave a press conference at the National Assembly and went home believing that something might just have begun to move. Douglas Hogg sent a message wanting a meeting in the next few days. "I guess he will say that if HMG follows the 'French initiative' there will be enormous pressure from Tory backbenchers to end the protection if the initiative succeeds," he wrote in his journal. "I must therefore be absolutely clear in my mind what I want, and must make HMG accept the language of 'cease-fire' and 'monitoring' that we have sold to the French. And he must promise to break the BA ban." Rab Connolly said: "Hogg is going to tell you that the threat remains very high and so the French initiative is useless." *Well,* he thought, *that remains to be seen.*

He went to meet Hogg with the history of the Foreign Office's mixture of inertia and hostility at the ready, and in no mood to be mollified. He and his work had both been attacked by two foreign secretaries, Howe and Hurd; then there had been the period of years when no diplomat or politician was prepared to meet him, followed by the equally unsatisfactory period of secret, "deniable" meetings with Slater and Gore-Booth. He had had to create pressure from other governments to "wake up" the Brits, and even then their backing had been halfhearted: John Major had allowed no photograph to be taken of their meeting, and although he had promised a "high-profile campaign" no such campaign had materialized. Hogg himself had made clear that the only British policy was to wait for "regime change" in Iran, which wasn't a probability. Who, he would ask, was telling the British media that there was a "high cost" to the British when he went abroad, when in fact there was no cost at all? Why were the constant falsehoods about costs never corrected or denied?

Douglas Hogg gave him a sympathetic hearing. He was prepared to "go along" with the "French initiative" or "cease-fire plan" but said, "I have to tell you that there is still a very real risk to your safety. We believe the Iranians are still actively trying to find you. And if we go down this route the French and Germans will improve links with Iran fast and so, eventually, will HMG. The political pressure will end. Also, I will have to send you a pompous letter so that I can say afterward that you were warned of the dangers."

Afterward. Meaning, after he was murdered.

"We are trying to improve the language of the *démarche,*" he said. "It should include your associates, that is, all those threatened by the *fatwa,* translators, publishers, booksellers and so on. And we want Balladur to send this straight to Rafsanjani and get Rafsanjani's own signature on it if possible, because the higher the signature the greater the chances that they will actually call the dogs off."

That night he wrote in his journal: "Am I committing suicide?"

Larry Robinson, the contact man at the U.S. embassy, called Carmel Bedford to find out what was going on. He was worried. "You can't trust the Iranians," he said. "It would wreck our whole strategy." Carmel responded outspokenly. "What have you done for us? Is there a strategy? If there is, tell us what it is, make us an offer. If we get a deal through the EU, we'll take it, after six and a half years of nobody lifting a finger to help." Larry Robinson said, "I'll get back to you."

On April 10, the crucial day of the EU foreign ministers' meeting, Hogg's assistant Andy Ashcroft called to say that Hurd and Major were now both "on side," and that the French initiative was now British government policy. Mr. Anton stressed the need for the monitoring period, to make sure the Iranians were doing what they promised to do, and Ashcroft said, "That is certainly how we will play it." When he got off the phone he called the editor of *The Times,* Peter Stothard, and the editor of *The Guardian,* Alan Rusbridger, and told them to expect developments. He called Larry Robinson and said, "This isn't an alternative to canceling the *fatwa.* Nor is it intended to create a '*fatwa*-free zone,' ring-fencing Europe and the USA; it's a frontierless agreement." Robinson voiced the sensible reservations. "It could let Iran off the hook." But he hadn't yet heard from D.C., so didn't know if the administration was, on balance, "pro or anti." He himself felt that the bounty-hunter risk had faded, but the threat from the regime had not.

"Well, it's a risk," he told Larry. "But then, what isn't?"

He talked to Richard Norton-Taylor at *The Guardian.* There was a draft text and the EU would ask Iran to sign it. It would contain an absolute guarantee of non-implementation and could be a step on the way to canceling the *fatwa* later.

The foreign ministers' meeting had gone well, Andy Ashcroft told him. The reference to "associates" had not been added to the text but the French had agreed that the foreign ministers' troika would discuss it with the Iranians orally. He agreed that it was important to talk to the press and emphasize the important points.

They had managed to get people's attention. The story was on the front page in every newspaper. *The Times* wanted to do a follow-up story. Why had HMG not thought of anything like this before? It was being understood that he had had to come up with this initiative himself and had sold it to the French without much effort by the British Foreign Office. Okay, he thought, *good*.

A statement on Tehran radio said, *It is illogical for the EU to ask for a formal guarantee of non-implementation as the Iranian government has never said it will implement the* fatwa. That sounded halfway to a guarantee. Then on April 19, at 10:30 in the morning (London time), the troika ambassadors in Tehran (French, German and Spanish) together with the British *chargé d'affaires*, Jeffrey James, presented the European Union's demands to the Iranian Ministry of Foreign Affairs.

The *démarche* had been made, and the news was on the wire services at once. The head of the Iranian judiciary, Yazdi, derided the initiative and Sanei of the Bounty said, "It will only ensure that the *fatwa* is carried out sooner," and maybe he was right. But Richard Norton-Taylor at *The Guardian*'s foreign desk told Carmel that Rafsanjani, at the end of his visit to India, had said at a press conference that Iran would not implement the *fatwa*.

Zafar wanted to know what was going on. When he was told, he said, "*Excellent. Excellent.*" His eyes lit up with hope, and his father thought, *If the* démarche *is signed we will have to try and make it mean what it says.*

The "French initiative" was making its way through the labyrinthine intestines of the Iranian mullocracy, being digested and absorbed according to the slow mysteries of that arcane organism. Every so often there would be pronouncements of some sort, positive or negative. These he came to think of as flatulence. They were odorous but they were not the point. Even a loud, shocking rumor—*the head of Iranian intelligence has defected, bringing with him documents that prove the regime's involvement in international terrorism*—was no more than a belch rising from the stomach of this many-headed ecclesiastical Gargantua to roar briefly through one of its many and contradictory mouths. (This rumor unsurprisingly turned out to be untrue; a gassy nothing.) The full, official response would come at its own pace.

In the meantime he again went with Elizabeth to Austria for a few days at the invitation of Christine and the minister of culture, Rudolf Scholten, who were quickly becoming their good friends and wanted to give them a few days "out of the cage." When they arrived they found themselves in the midst of family tragedy.

Rudolf's father had been run down by a car that morning and killed. "We shouldn't stay," he said at once, but Rudolf insisted they should. "It will help to have you here." Christine, too, said, "Really, you should stay." Once again he learned from others a lesson in grace and strength.

They had dinner at the art-filled home of Scholten's close friend André ("Franzi") Heller, the polymathic writer, actor, musician, producer, and above all the creator of extraordinary public installations and spectacular art-theater events around the world. Heller was excited about the great rally, the *Fest für Freiheit* or Freedom Festival, that he was staging at the Heldenplatz in two days' time. It was in the Heldenplatz in 1938 that Adolf Hitler had announced the *Anschluss* of Austria. To hold an anti-Nazi rally in that same place was to perform an act of reclamation, cleansing the Heldenplatz of the stain of the Nazi memory, and by doing so to strike a blow against the rising neo-Nazism of the present. Nazi undertones were always there in Austria, and the neo-Nazi right, led by Jörg Haider, was growing in popularity. The Austrian left knew its adversary was strong, and became more progressive and passionate in response. "You must stay," Franzi Heller suddenly said. "You must be there, it's very important that you speak from that stage about liberty." He was reluctant at first, not sure if it was right to insert himself into other people's narratives, but he saw that Heller was adamant. So he scribbled a brief text in English and Rudolf and Franzi translated it and he had to practice, over and over, parrot-fashion, speaking words in a language he did not know.

On the day of the Heldenplatz rally the heavens opened and a flood fell upon Vienna, giving rise to the thought that if there was any sort of God he was probably a neo-Nazi like Jörg Haider. Or perhaps Haider had some kind of quasi-Wagnerian access to the Nordic weather-god Freyr and had asked him in operatic prayer for this world-destroying Ragnarok-rain. Franzi Heller was very concerned. If the crowd was small it would be a catastrophe, a propaganda gift to Haider and his followers. He need not have worried. As the morning hours passed the square began to fill. The crowd was young, wrapped in plastic and carrying inadequate umbrellas, or simply surrendering with a shrug to the irrelevant monsoon. Fifty thousand and more of them packed the wicked old square with their hopes for a better future. On the stage there were people making music and speeches but the crowd was the star of the evening, the soaked, undimmed, magnificent crowd. He said his few sentences of German and the soaked crowd cheered. His chief security officer, Wolfgang Bachler, was gleeful, too. "This is just the way to attack Haider," he exulted.

Across the border at the Frankfurt Book Fair, the eminent Islamic scholar Annemarie Schimmel was awarded the Peace Prize of the German Book Trade and to widespread dismay spoke in enthusiastic support of the *fatwa* against the author of *The Satanic Verses,* a book she had previously denounced. In the resulting uproar she tried the "Cat Stevens defense"—she said hadn't said it—but then, as many people told the press they were prepared to swear affidavits confirming that they had heard her say it, she briefly said she wanted to apologize for saying it, but then declined to apologize. She was undoubtedly a great scholar and a *grande dame* of seventy-three but that didn't mean she wasn't a member of the Cat Stevens Stupid Party.

Article 19 had arranged a trip to Denmark to meet the prime minister and foreign minister and in spite of his growing feeling that such meetings were useless, he went. His soft-spoken, kindly, principled publisher Johannes Riis was with him, and William Nygaard came from Oslo, too. They were *allowed* to walk in the Copenhagen streets and at night, amazingly, to visit the Tivoli Gardens, where they rode the bumper cars for a few blissful, carefree minutes, shouting and smashing into one another like little boys. He watched William and Johannes driving their bumper cars maniacally around the Tivoli track and thought, *I have been given a lesson, in these years, in the worst of human*

nature, but also in the best of it, a lesson in courage, principle, selflessness, de-
termination and honor, and in the end that's what I want to remember: that I
was at the center of a group of people behaving as well, as nobly, as human
beings can behave, and beyond that group at the center of a larger narrative filled
with people I didn't know, would never know, people as determined as my
bumper-car friends not to allow the darkness to prevail.

All of a sudden the "French initiative" came to life. Jill Craigie
called in a state of high excitement to say that news of "the Iranians
backing down" had been all over the radio. He couldn't get any confirmation from anyone that evening, but Jill's excitement was conta-
gious. And the next morning the story was all over the news. Amit
Roy, author of *The Telegraph*'s front-page lead story, told Frances
D'Souza privately that he had spent three hours with the Iranian *chargé*
d'affaires, Gholamreza Ansari, who had been saying "incredible things."
We'll never enforce the fatwa, *we will withdraw the bounty money.* He kept
calm. There had been too many false dawns. But Zafar was thrilled.
"That's wonderful," he kept saying, moving his father almost to tears.
In the midst of the media noise they sat together and worked on his
school English text, *Far from the Madding Crowd,* to help him prepare
for his GCSE exams. Instead of Khamenei and Rafsanjani they spoke
of Bathsheba Everdene, William Boldwood and Gabriel Oak.

Frances had heard that Western journalists, including five Brits,
were on their way to Tehran at the invitation of the regime. Maybe an
announcement was imminent. "Keep your hat on," he told Frances.
"The fat mullah isn't singing yet." But the next morning there was a
big story in *The Times.* He remained calm. "I know the reality," he told
his journal. "When will I be able to live without policemen? When
will airlines carry me, states allow me to visit without RAID-style
hysteria? When will I be able to go back to being a person? Not yet
awhile, I suspect. The 'secondary *fatwas*' imposed by other people's
fears are harder to overturn than the mullahs'." But he also found himself asking, *Can it be that I have moved this fucking mountain?*

Andy Ashcroft called from Hogg's office to say that the Foreign
Office had been "completely surprised" by the media hoo-hah.
"Maybe the Iranians are engaged in a softening-up process." Ashcroft
thought the official response would not come for another month. The

"critical dialogue" meeting between Iran and the EU was on June 22 and that was when they expected to hear the official reply to the *démarche*.

On May 30, after the EU foreign ministers' meeting, the Danish government said it was "confident" that Iran would "make a satisfactory answer to the *démarche* before the end of the French EU presidency." The French were pressing hard, the Iranians were taking the matter seriously, pushing for concessions in return, but the EU was standing firm. "It is coming," he wrote in his journal. "It is coming."

Peter Temple-Morris, MP, said on BBC Radio, "Rushdie has been behaving himself for a while, keeping his mouth shut, and that's why improvements are possible." But Robert Fisk's interview with the Iranian foreign minister, Velayati, was full of the old garbage, *can't cancel the* fatwa, *the bounty offer is "free speech,"* all of that. Belches and flatulence. For reality, he had to wait.

The police were losing their nerve about the publication of *The Moor's Last Sigh*. A reading had been arranged at Waterstone's in Hampstead but now Scotland Yard was reneging on its agreement to allow it to be publicized. The deputy assistant commissioner was "jumpy," said Helen Hammington, and the local "uniforms" would be jumpier. She feared they would "over-police" the event but she also said the public order "experts" feared a violent demonstration by a group called Hizb ut-Tahrir, whom Helen described as "wearing suits" and "talking on mobile phones" and being smart and fast enough to organize a rapid-response attack. Rab Connolly came to see him and said, "There are people in the force who are very hostile toward you and want the reading to go wrong." He also said that in conversations with Cathay Pacific Airways about the proposed Australasian book tour he heard that at meetings of airline operators British Airways had been "proselytizing their ban" and encouraging other airlines to back it.

As the publication day of *The Moor's Last Sigh* approached the battle between himself and the senior officers at Scotland Yard, which increasingly embarrassed the Malachite team, burst into open war.

Rab Connolly called to say that Commander Howley was out of the office, and in his absence another ranking officer, Commander Moss, had sided with the "jumpy" local deputy assistant commissioner, Skeete, against him. The police were backing out of their agreement to allow advertised readings, Connolly said, *because it's you.* Margaret Thatcher was going on a book tour too and all her events would automatically receive the police's maximum efforts because—the old Greenup line again—she had performed a service to the state; but Mr. Rushdie was a troublemaker and didn't merit their assistance. The officers who dealt with him most frequently—Connolly, Dick Wood, and Helen Hammington (who was at home nursing a broken leg)—were all on his side but their bosses were adamant. "If he goes to that bookshop," Moss said, "he goes alone." Howley was back after the weekend, Rab Connolly said, and, "talking out of school," he added, "I have asked to see him. If he does not back me I will resign from the prot and probably be returned to uniform duties." That simple statement was a heartbreaker.

He told Frances Coady and Caroline Michel, who were stunned. They had planned the book launch on the basis of the agreement with the police that was now, at the last minute, being broken. He told Frances D'Souza also. "I'm at the end of my rope," he said. "I won't put up with this anymore." If he was to receive protection it could not be of this judgmental, ungenerous kind. If this *diktat* was confirmed he would go to war in public. The tabloids would vilify him, but they did that anyway. Let England decide.

He was at war with policemen who believed he had done nothing of value in his life. Perhaps not all of Scotland Yard thought this way, however. Dick Wood reported that Assistant Commissioner David Veness, the most senior officer to enter the story so far, had "green-lighted" the Hampstead reading, saying he would "tell the fussers to calm down." Rab Connolly was at home, perhaps brooding about losing his job when he delivered his ultimatum. But in the end there was no ultimatum. On Monday Howley ordered Connolly to cancel the event and Connolly called the bookstore and did so without telling either the publishers or the author himself.

This was no longer just a battle that could be won using conventional weapons. It was about to go thermonuclear. He demanded a meeting at Scotland Yard the next morning and took Frances Coady and Caroline Michel with him to represent Random House, to point out that their publishing plan was being severely damaged by the police. They met the shamefaced members of the Malachite team—Helen Hammington had come in on her broken leg, and Dick Wood and Rab Connolly were there, all of them raw and aggrieved because they had been fighting with their boss, who wasn't accustomed to such insubordination, and the results had not been pretty. They were senior officers, but Howley had "shouted at them." The commander's decision, Helen said, her face grim and set below her close-cropped hair, was "absolute." The meeting was over.

This was when he, in a calculated strategy, deliberately went off the deep end and began to shout. He knew nobody in this office was to blame for what was happening, and that, in fact, they had laid their careers on the line for him; but if he couldn't get past them, he had lost, and he had just decided not to lose. So cold-bloodedly, knowing it was his only chance, he blew his stack. If Helen couldn't change the decision, he yelled, then she had bloody well better get him into a room with somebody who could, because Random House and he had acted strictly in accordance with what the police had said was possible, *months ago,* and this last-minute high-handedness just damn well wouldn't do, it wouldn't do *at all,* and if he didn't get into that room *right now* he would go public in the loudest and most aggressive way, so get me in there, Helen, or else. Or fucking *else.* Five minutes later he was alone in an office with Commander John Howley.

If he had been fire with Helen, now he would be ice. Howley was giving him his best cold stare but he could out-freeze him. The policeman spoke first. "Because of your renewed high profile," Howley said—meaning the *démarche*—"we believe that the news media will pick up the story of the reading and put it on the main news." And after that there would be screaming hordes of Muslims outside the store. "That can't be allowed." He kept his voice low as he replied. "The decision is unacceptable," he said. "I do not believe your public-order argument. You are also being discriminatory. On the same page of today's *Times* that has a story about the possible Iranian thaw is an advertisement for a Thatcher book-related event, and you are protecting that. In addition, because Mr. Veness gave the green light just yesterday, everyone at Waterstone's and Random House knows what's going on, so this will become public even if I do nothing. And I must tell you that I'm not going to do nothing. If you don't reverse your decision I will call a press conference and give interviews to every major newspaper, radio program and TV channel denouncing you. I have never done anything but thank the police up to now, but I can and will change my tune."

"If you do that," Howley said, "you will look very bad."

"Probably," he replied, "but guess what? *You will look very bad as well.* So here's the choice. You let the event go ahead, and neither of us looks bad, or you prohibit it, in which case we both do. You choose."

"I'll think about what you've said," Howley said in his gray, clipped voice. "I'll let you know by the end of the day."

Andy Ashcroft called at 1 P.M. The G7 had joined the campaign and agreed to call for an end to the *fatwa*. The EU was pushing hard for Rafsanjani's signature and for all the conditions of the French *démarche*. "You mustn't settle for just a *fatwa*-free Europe," he told Ashcroft. "And the Iranians, in commentary after the announcement, should enjoin Muslims in the West to abide by local laws." Ashcroft said he was "pretty optimistic." "I've been having a row with the Special Branch," he told the Foreign Office aide, "and it would be good if you could give things a nudge, because it wouldn't look good to be having a public row right now." Ashcroft laughed. "I'll see what I can do."

Two and a half hours later Dick Wood called to say that Howley had backed down. The reading was two days away. It wasn't to be advertised until the morning of the event. That was the compromise being offered.

He took it.

All the seats at Waterstone's were sold by lunchtime. "Imagine if we'd advertised on Monday as planned," said the Hampstead branch manager, Paul Bagley. "We'd have sold thousands." Hampstead High

Street was swarming with uniformed police officers, and there wasn't a single demonstrator in sight. Not a single gentleman with a beard, placard and righteously outraged expression. Not one. Where were the suits and mobile phones, the "thousand violent fanatics" of the Hizb ut-Tahrir? Not there, that was where. If it hadn't been for the hordes of police in the street it would have looked like a completely ordinary literary event.

It wasn't, of course. It was his first preannounced public reading in almost seven years. It was the publication day of his first adult novel since *The Satanic Verses*. The Waterstone's people told Caroline Michel afterward that it was the best reading they had ever heard, which was nice; for the reader himself it felt like a miracle. He was with his own audience again, after so very long. To hear their laughter, to feel that they were moved: extraordinary. He read the opening of the novel, and the bit about the Lenins, and the "Mother India" passage. Afterward hundreds of copies of the book rushed out into the London night, held in happy hands. And not a single demonstrator ever showed up.

He had crossed his Rubicon. There could be no turning back. The Cambridge Waterstone's people had been there and wanted to go ahead with their event, this time with two days' prior advertising. Dick Wood said that "everyone at the office was very pleased." He wondered if that included Commander Howley. One day, then two days, then more. Step by step, back toward his real life. Away from Joseph Anton, in the direction of his own name.

He sent bottles of champagne to the officers who had fought for him against the bigwigs of Scotland Yard.

The noise about the "French initiative" was getting louder by the day. *The Independent* reported that the head of the Iranian Revolutionary Guard's European-based cells of hit men had written to Khamenei complaining that he had been ordered to call all his dogs off, a straw in the wind that hinted both that the dogs were indeed being called off and that Khamenei might not be opposed to their kenneling. Then Arne Ruth of *Dagens Nyheter* reported a "very exciting" meeting in Stockholm. Along with other Swedish journalists he had met the Iranian minister, Larijani, who had said, extraordinarily, that he wanted articles written stressing Iran's "admiration for Salman Rushdie's work" because they wanted to "change the psychological attitudes." Even more astounding was Larijani's on-the-record statement that the *fatwa* did not need to be enforced as it was not in Iran's best interests. This was the same Larijani who had frequently demanded Mr. Rushdie's death. On the matter of Sanei of the Bounty, however, Larijani did not budge. The government couldn't do anything about that. Then, a witticism. Why didn't Mr. Rushdie sue Sanei under Iranian law? *Oh, werry good,* he thought, lapsing briefly into Dickensian vowels. *Werry werry good indeed.*

The wind was swirling. The straws were blowing in many directions. If there was an answer blowing in that wind, he had no idea what it was.

Elizabeth was upset that there were no signs of a pregnancy. She told him he should have a "sperm test." There were these moments of strain between them. It worried them both.

Caroline Michel said, "Yes, media excitement is at a great height, and it can be used to make a better life for you." He did not want to remain forever trapped in a shadow world of diplomats, intelligence spooks, terrorists and counterterrorists. If he gave up his own portrait of the world and accepted this one then he would never escape. He was trying to understand how to think and act in response to what might be about to happen. It would be quite a tightrope act. If the Swedish diplomat Jan Eliasson was right about the need for a positive response in the media then he should perhaps say that things were better but not over; that it was the beginning of the end, but not the end; a cease-fire, but not yet a final peace. Ayatollah Meshkini had recently said that *any* fatwa *could be annulled, and many had been.* Should he mention that? Probably not. The Iranians would probably not be thrilled if he quoted their ayatollahs back at them.

Andrew Green of the Foreign Office called to brief him about what was planned. The Iranian text would take the form of "a letter from Foreign Minister Velayati stating that his deputy Va'ezi was authorized to give the Iranian view," which would not be stated in Velayati's letter, but in an "annexe" to it, and which would also be published in the Iranian press. Was that acceptable to him or not, Green wanted to know. It sounded as if the Foreign Office thought it wasn't enough. This was a long way from Rafsanjani's signature, after all.

Larry Robinson called from the U.S. embassy. He felt that the Europeans were pushing for acceptance, but the United States and United Kingdom did not want to. He was worried that Iran was setting up a "deniable assassination." (Elizabeth, too, felt he might be killed at one of his hard-won readings, but Rab Connolly said that the "spies" were saying that the "bad guys" weren't planning to do that.)

What to do? He really didn't know. What on earth should he do?

The media were treating this moment as if it was the end of the *fatwa* story, but maybe it wasn't, in which case he would lose everyone's attention, but the danger would remain. Or, alternatively, by going for it, by bouncing things forward, perhaps he could use the media to create an atmosphere in which the threat really would come to an end.

If the EU rejected the Iranian reply to the *démarche,* it could allow Iran to accuse the EU of bad faith and hairsplitting, and to suggest that the West did not want to solve the *fatwa* problem—that he was being used by the West as a pawn in a larger game. And maybe he was. The U.S. administration and, to an extent, the British government wanted to tighten the political screws on Iran and in that effort the *fatwa* was useful to them, no doubt of it. But if he accepted the Iranian reply then the defense campaign would fizzle, and the *fatwa* and bounty offer would remain in place. He felt out of his depth.

The day of the Iranian reply was also the day of the Cambridge reading. Two days' notice had created an enormous audience, and of course the shop was nervous, he was told he had to come in the back door, if he tried to walk in the front door the event would be canceled. But it was happening, and once again there was no sign of a demonstration.

His own instinct, backed by his conversations with artists and journalists in the British Asian community, was that the energy had long gone out of the British Muslim protests. That phase was over.

At 12:45 P.M. there was shocking and unexpected news. The deputy foreign minister, Va'ezi, had told IRNA, the Iranian news agency, that Iran had rejected the European *démarche,* and the French initiative was dead. That very morning Iran had been briefing the media that Va'ezi's piece of paper would satisfy all the EU's demands, and now here he was saying that no written guarantee had been given, and none would be.

Just like that.

It was impossible to know what had happened in Tehran. Somebody had lost a fight and someone else had won it.

Elizabeth burst into tears. He became oddly calm. He must use the planned press conference to go back onto the attack. By refusing to say that they would not engage in terrorism, the Iranians had revealed that they might well do so. The collapse of this initiative left Iran naked in the bright light of the world's attention. This was what he had to say, as loudly as he could.

Strangely he was not afraid for himself, but he did not know how to talk to those who loved him, how to tell Zafar the disappointing news, what to say to Sameen. He did not know how to give weeping Elizabeth strength, or where to find hope. It felt as if there might not be any hope. But he knew that he had to—that he would—continue, taking his lead from Beckett's mighty Unnamable. *I can't go on. I'll go on.*

And of course life did go on. One thing had become clearer than ever: He had to take his freedom where he could get it. An "official" end was no longer looking possible, but America beckoned him for another summer break. The uninterest of U.S. policemen in his protection was just fine, in fact it was a real boon. That year Elizabeth, Zafar and he were able to have twenty-five happy summer days of American freedom. Zafar and Elizabeth flew out together on a direct flight; he used Rudolf Scholten's friends at Austrian Airlines to bring him to JFK via Vienna: a very long way around, but no matter, he was there!

And Andrew was there! And they drove straight out to Water Mill for nine wonderful days on Gibson Beach, and at friends' homes, doing nothing and everything. The simplicity of it—and the contrast with his sequestered British life—brought tears to his eyes. And after Water Mill they went by car and ferry to Martha's Vineyard, where they would be the guests of Doris Lockhart Saatchi on her Chilmark property for eight days more. His main memory of that trip would be of William Styron's genitalia. Elizabeth and he visited the Styrons at their Vineyard Haven home and there on the porch was the great writer in khaki shorts, sitting with his legs splayed and wearing no underpants, his treasures generously and fully on display. This was more than he had ever hoped to know about the author of *The Confessions of Nat Turner* and *Sophie's Choice,* but all information was useful, he supposed, and he duly filed it away for later use.

Then three nights at the Irvings', and three at the Herrs', and three more at the Wylie place on Park Avenue. Zafar got his GCSE results on their last night and they were, thank goodness, good. In the years that followed he often wondered how he would have survived without these annual American safety-valve journeys, when they could pretend to be normal literary folk going about their normal business unaccompanied by men with guns, and it didn't seem that hard. He became certain, very quickly, that when the day came it would be America that would make it easiest for him to reclaim his freedom. When he said this to Elizabeth she frowned and became irritable.

In the darkness that followed the collapse of the French initiative there was one unexpected shaft of light. Lufthansa cracked under public pressure. There was a lunch with Mr. and Mrs. Lufthansa, CEO Jürgen Weber *und frau.* Frau Weber turned out to be a *big fan,* or so she told him. And, yes, they were *delighted* to carry him, her husband said. They were *proud* to do it. It was just as easy as that. After over six years of refusals—pouf!—they'd *love* to have him on their planes, *any time.* They admired him *so much.* "Thank you," he said, and everyone looked very pleased, and of course there were many books to be autographed.

The BBC made a documentary about *The Moor's Last Sigh* and commissioned his friend the Indian painter Bhupen Khakhar to paint his portrait for the film. It was a novel about painters and painting and his friendships with a generation of gifted Indian artists—with Bhupen himself above all—had allowed him to think of writing it. They had first met in the early 1980s and each of them had at once seen himself in the other and they had quickly become friends. Soon after their first meeting he went to Bhupen's show at the Kasmin Knoedler gallery in London. In his pocket was a check for a story he had just sold to *The Atlantic Monthly*. At the show he fell in love with Bhupen's *Second Class Railway Compartment* and when he discovered that the price tag was exactly the same as the figure on the check in his pocket (Indian art was cheaper then) he had happily turned his story into his friend's painting, and it had remained one of his most prized possessions ever since. It was hard for contemporary Indian artists to escape the influence of the West (in an earlier generation M. F. Husain's famous horses had leaped straight out of Picasso's *Guernica,* and the work of many of the other big names—Souza, Raza, Gaitonde—was too deeply indebted for his liking to modernism and Western developments in abstraction). Finding an Indian idiom that was neither folkloric nor derivative had not been easy, and Bhupen had been one of the first to succeed, looking at the street art of India, the movie posters, the painted shop fronts, and at the figurative and narrative traditions of Indian painting, and creating out of that visual environment an oeuvre of idiosyncrasy, originality and wit.

At the heart of *The Moor's Last Sigh* was the idea of the palimpsest, a picture concealed beneath another picture, a world hidden beneath another world. Before he was born his parents had hired a young Bombay painter to decorate his future nursery with fairy-tale and cartoon animals and the impoverished artist Krishen Khanna had accepted the commission. He had also painted a portrait of the unborn Salman's beautiful young mother, Negin, but her husband, Anis, hadn't liked it and refused to buy it. Khanna stored his rejected canvas at his friend Husain's studio and one day Husain painted a picture of his own over it, and sold it. So somewhere in Bombay there was a portrait of Negin Rushdie by Krishen, who of course grew up to be one of the leading artists of his generation, concealed beneath a picture by Husain. Krishen said, "Husain knows where every picture of his has ended up, but he won't say." The BBC tried to get him to say, but the old man angrily tapped his cane on the floor and denied that the story was true. "Of course it's true," Krishen said. "He's just worried that you want to destroy his painting to find your mother's portrait, and he's offended that you're looking for my picture and you don't care about his." In the end he had come to think that the portrait was more evocative lost than found—lost, it was a beautiful mystery; found, it might have proved that Anis Rushdie's artistic judgment had been correct, and that the then apprentice Khanna hadn't done a very good job—and he called off the search.

He sat for Bhupen in a studio in Edwardes Square, Kensington, and told him the story of the lost picture. Bhupen giggled delightedly and worked away. His portrait was being painted in profile in the tradition of Indian court portraits, and like a good *nawab* he wore a see-through shirt, only his, as painted by Bhupen, looked more like nylon than sheer cotton. Bhupen began by drawing, in a single movement, a charcoal profile that caught an exact likeness with effortless skill. The painting that covered this single charcoal line looked in some ways less like its subject and more like the character of Moor Zogoiby in the novel. "It's a painting of you both," Bhupen said. "You as the Moor and the Moor as you." So there was a lost portrait beneath this portrait too.

The completed painting was eventually acquired by the National Portrait Gallery, and Bhupen became the first Indian artist to have a work hanging there. Bhupen died on August 8, 2003, on the same day as Negin Rushdie. There was no escape from coincidence, though the meaning of such synchronicity remained elusive. He lost a friend and a mother on the same day. That was meaning enough.

The novel was published. He continued to push out his boundaries. He took part in his largest pre-announced appearance yet, at the *Times* Writers' Forum in Central Hall Westminster, along with Martin Amis,

Fay Weldon and Melvyn Bragg. He read a passage from *The Moor's Last Sigh* and thanked the audience for being at his "little coming-out party." Yes, there was security, and yes, he had to come and go by the back door in an armored car, but he was publishing his book. And no, there were no demonstrations, and the police bigwigs at the Yard began, at last, to relax.

He was planning something very ambitious. His South American publishers asked if he would visit Chile, Mexico and Argentina in December, and he decided he could do that and then go on to New Zealand and Australia. It would be a mammoth journey and he became determined to pull it off. Many airlines had to be spoken to, but now that he had Lufthansa as well as Iberia, Air France, Austrian and Scandinavian Airlines on his side, it was easier to make the case. Slowly the route was worked out, approvals sought and received; the Mexican ambassador in London, Andrés Rozental, met him with Carlos Fuentes and helped to arrange the Mexican leg of the journey; and then, amazingly, improbably, the plans were set. They were cleared to go.

They went to Oslo for the Norwegian publication of *The Moor's Last Sigh* and he read in the great hall of Oslo University, the Aula, with murals by Edvard Munch. It was the first pre-announced reading outside the United Kingdom and both he and William Nygaard felt that they had taken a big step forward. *A victory over our oppressors,* William said, *and we have done it together.* William was still a little slowed by his injuries, still a little in pain, but full of life. That night in Oslo, to everyone's amazement, the northern lights filled the sky. They were rarely seen in Oslo, which was too far south, or in October, which was too early, but there they were, the green aurora showing up "in honor," William said, "of your Aurora." The heroine of *The Moor's Last Sigh* was Aurora Zogoiby, and it was as if she was up there, dancing in the sky, somewhere among the giant green curtains that arced and rippled wildly from horizon to horizon. Everyone in Oslo was calling their friends, saying *go outside, look up, it's amazing.* The aurora was in the sky for an hour or more, and it felt like a sign of better times.

Robert McCrum had had a stroke in the house at 41 St. Peter's Street. He and Sarah Lyall had been married for just two months and while she was away he had almost died. Robert had survived, but an arm was paralyzed, he could walk only a couple of steps at a time, and it was impossible to say how bad the long-term damage might be. He was improving a little and both he and Sarah clung to that as a sign of hope. The Curse of St. Peter's Street had struck again.

He went with Christopher Hitchens to see Robert and Sarah and, in a way, to apologize for the Curse. It was strange to be back in his old home, where he had been when, as he had begun to say, the excrement hit the ventilation system. Various ghosts flitted in and out of the room as he and Hitch talked to their stricken friend. They didn't stay long. Robert needed to rest.

In the snapshots his memory kept of his life in those years, the police were often absent, erased from history's photos like the Communist leader Clementis at the beginning of Milan Kundera's *The Book of Laughter and Forgetting*. To help him get through the days, he tried to make himself forget he was always surrounded by security and that security considerations loomed so large in his daily life. He forgot the small daily privations. He could not get his own mail or pick up his morning paper from the forecourt of his home. There were pajamaed collisions in the kitchen that never stopped feeling embarrassing. There was *Joe*, the increasingly hated pseudonym. (Was it really necessary to avoid calling him by his own name in his own house?) There was the loss of all spontaneity. *I'd like to go for a walk, please. Okay, Joe, give us an hour to set it up. But in an hour I won't want to go for a walk.* And every time he did go out they took him to a "changeover point" and made him get out of one car, the car associated with the house, and into another, the car associated with his public appearances. For the rest of his life he would hate these changeover points, Nutley Terrace, Park Village East, he would wince inwardly every time he passed them, but at the time he made himself *not experience them,* he detached himself from the body of the man scuttling from vehicle to vehicle, and when he reached his destination he refused to think about the prot, he was just out with his friends, being himself.

For his friends it was the opposite, the security was so unusual for them, so odd and thrilling, that it was just about all they remembered. When he asked them for their memories of those days they gave him memories of policemen, *Do you remember the one who seduced our nanny, Do you remember the two really good-looking guys, everyone had a crush on them,* they remembered drawn curtains and locked garden doors. Even in his friends' eyes he was becoming a sideshow and the police were the main event. But when he tried to recall those days the police often weren't there. They had been there, of course, but his memory had decided they weren't.

But sometimes it was impossible to perform his little mind trick. In the snapshots his memory preserved of his South American trip, the policemen of Chile were right in the center of the frame, frightening, unforgettable, *loud.*

Snapshot of Chile. There were two different police forces in Chile, the uniformed Carabineros and the plainclothes Policía de Investigaciones, and while he and Elizabeth were in the air, flying to Santiago, these two great institutions quarreled about the decision to allow him into the country. He was supposed to speak at a literary fair, but when they got off the plane on a hot glaring airless day they were surrounded by uniformed police and taken to a stifling shed somewhere on the airport tarmac while people shouted in Spanish all around them. Their passports were taken away. No English speaker was produced to interpret, and when he tried to ask what was going on he was shouted at and ordered, with unmistakable gestures, to back off and shut up. *Welcome to Sudamerica,* he thought, sweating a good deal.

In 1993 Augusto Pinochet was no longer president but he was still commander-in-chief of the armed forces and even in the autumn of the patriarch nobody was in any doubt about his continued power and influence. In Pinochet's Chile the security forces were omnipotent. Except that in this case the two police systems were in a dogfight, and he was the bone. He was reminded of the passage in Ryszard Kapuściński's *The Emperor* in which Kapuściński described Haile Selassie's two entirely separate intelligence services, whose chief job was to spy on each other. He also reminded himself, less amusingly, that this was a country in which disappearances and unexplained murders had until recently been commonplace. Had they perhaps been "disappeared"?

After being held in the shed for perhaps two hours they were taken to a police facility described as a hotel. It was not a hotel. The door of their room did not open from the inside. There were armed guards posted outside it. He asked repeatedly for their passports to be returned, for his publisher to be called, and to speak to the British ambassador. The guards shrugged. They did not speak English. More hours ticked by. There was nothing to eat or drink.

His captors grew careless. The door of their room was left open and though the "hotel" was full of uniformed men there was no guard at their door. He took a deep breath and said to Elizabeth, "I'm going to try something." He put on his sunglasses, walked out of the room, and set off down the stairs toward the front door.

Nobody realized what he was doing until he was two floors down, and then there were shouting, gesticulating men around him on the stairs, but he continued to walk. *What you do. Where you go. Not possible.* He was at the front desk now and there was a little cloud of braided, mirror-shaded men around him; men with guns, he noted, but then he had grown accustomed to that. *Where you go? Stop. You stop.* He smiled as sweetly as he could. "I'm going for a walk," he said, indicating the front door and making a walking gesture with his fingers. "I've never been to Santiago before, you know. It looks beautiful. I just thought I'd take a little stroll." The Carabineros didn't know what to do. They menaced and shouted but nobody put a hand on him. He kept walking. He was out of the front door now, his feet hit the sidewalk, he had no idea what he was doing, really, but he turned left and marched on. "Sir, it is necessary you stop at once, please." An interpreter had appeared as if by magic. "I see they finally pulled the rabbit out of the hat," he said, still smiling, still walking. "Sir, what are you doing, please, this is not allowed." He made his smile even broader. "Tell them, if I am committing a crime, then they must arrest me and take me to jail," he said. "Otherwise, I want the British ambassador on the phone within the next two minutes." Two minutes later he was talking to the embassy. "Thank goodness," said the official on the other end. "We've been trying all day to find out what happened to you. You just dropped completely off the map."

The man from the embassy arrived at the police facility a few minutes later. No diplomat had ever been a more welcome sight. "You have no idea of the argument that's been going on," he said. "They almost ordered your plane to turn around and fly back." Now that international diplomacy was in on the act Elizabeth and he were *allowed* to go to a real hotel, where they met a delegation of Chilean writers, including Antonio Skármeta, author of the 1985 novel *El Cartero de Neruda,* which had recently been filmed as *Il Postino (The Postman).* Skármeta, a big man with a big heart, greeted him with open arms and a flood of apologies. *A scandal. A shame upon us Chileans. Now we will make everything better, now that we know you are here, and safe.*

There were things that were not possible and others that were possible. It was already too late to keep the appointment at the book fair. But the next day there would be a gathering of writers, artists, and journalists in a small theater space, and he would be *allowed* to address it. After that he and Elizabeth would be shown the true hospitality of Chile at the Concha y Toro vineyard and at a beautiful estancia to the south of Santiago. These were good things, but the snapshots of those pleasures faded and vanished. The pictures of their brief "disappearance" in the care of the Carabineros did not fade. Chile did not feel like a country to which it would be good quickly to return.

Snapshots of Argentina. In the mid-1970s he went to a lecture by Jorge Luis Borges in central London and up there on the podium beside the great writer, who looked like a more lugubrious, Latin American version of the French comedian Fernandel, was a beautiful young Japanese-looking woman, who's *that?,* he remembered thinking, and now, all these years later, here was María Kodama walking toward them to welcome them to Buenos Aires, Borges's legendary widow, María K, with her zebra hair, and they were having lunch in the restaurant that bore her name. And after lunch she took them to her Fundación Internacional Jorge Luis Borges, not actually located in Borges's old house but in the house next door, because the owner of the actual house didn't want to sell; the fundación house was a mirror image of the "real" house, and it seemed appropriate for Borges to be memorialized in a mirror image. On the upper floor of the building was an exact re-creation of the writer's workroom, a spare narrow monastic cell with a simple table, an upright chair and a cot in one corner. The

rest of the floor was full of books. If one had never had the good fortune of meeting Borges, then meeting his library was the next best
thing. Here on these polyglot shelves were the writer's beloved copies
of Stevenson, Chesterton and Poe, along with books in half the languages of the human race. He remembered the story of the meeting
between Borges and Anthony Burgess. *We have the same name,* Burgess
had told the Argentinian master, and then, searching for a common
language to converse in that would be unintelligible to the listening
ears all around them, they settled on Anglo-Saxon, and chattered away
happily in Beowulf's tongue.

And there was an entire room filled with encyclopedias, encyclopedias of everything, from whose pages had been born, no doubt, the
famous fallaciously named *Anglo-American Cyclopedia,* a "literal but de-
linquent reprint of the *Encyclopedia Britannica* of 1902," in whose
forty-sixth volume the fictional characters "Borges" and "Bioy Casa-
res" had discovered the article about the land of Uqbar in the great
ficción "Tlön, Uqbar, Orbis Tertius," and also, of course, the magical
encyclopedia of Tlön itself.

He could have spent all day with these numinous books, but he
had only an hour. As they left María presented Elizabeth with a precious gift, a stone "desert rose," one of the first gifts Borges had given
her, she said, *and I hope you will be as happy as we were.*

"Do you remember," he asked María, "an essay Borges wrote as
preface to a book of photographs of Argentina by a photographer
named Gustavo Thorlichen?"

"Yes," she said. "The essay in which he speaks of the impossibility
of photographing the pampas."

"The unending pampas," he said, "the Borgesian pampas, which
are made of time, not space: That is where we live."

In Buenos Aires there was security but it was manageable, *erasable.*
News of the Chilean police madness had preceded him and the Argentine cops wanted to look better than that, so they gave him a little
breathing room. He was able to do his work for *The Moor's Last Sigh,*
and even to fit in a little tourism, visiting the family vault in the Re-
coleta Cemetery where Eva Perón had come to rest, and where a little
Lloyd Webber–ish plaque enjoined passersby not to cry for her. *No me*

llores para mi. Okay, then, I won't, he told her silently. Whatever you say, lady.

He had been asked to meet with Argentina's foreign minister, Guido di Tella, and on his way to the meeting the British embassy official who was accompanying him mentioned that Alan Parker's film of *Evita,* starring Madonna, had been refused permission to shoot at the Casa Rosada. "If you could say something about that," the diplomat murmured, "it would be helpful. If you could just find a way of dropping it into your chat." So he did. After Señor di Tella had asked about the *fatwa* and di Tella had made the now-traditional (and largely empty) supportive noises, he asked the foreign minister about the movie's problems. Di Tella made a what-can-I-do gesture. "The Casa Rosada, you know, it is the seat of government, it is difficult to allow a movie there."

"You know," he replied, "this is a pretty big budget movie, and they are going to make it, and if you don't let them film at the Casa Rosada they will find another building to play the part of the Casa, in, maybe, I don't know . . . Uruguay?"

Di Tella stiffened. "Uruguay?" he cried.

"Yes. Maybe. Maybe Uruguay."

"Okay," di Tella said. "Excuse me one moment please. I have to make a phone call."

Shortly after this conversation, *Evita* was given permission to film at the Casa Rosada. When the movie came out he read that Madonna herself had personally lobbied the president of Argentina for permission, so maybe that was the real reason for the change of heart. But maybe Uruguay had something to do with it too.

Snapshot of Mexico. Yes, there were policemen everywhere, and yes, he managed to launch his book and talk about free speech and see the relics of the bloody Aztecs and the home of Frida Kahlo and Diego Rivera in Coyoacán and the room in which the assassin Mercader drove the ice pick into Trotsky's skull, and yes, he was able to take part in the Guadalajara book fair with Carlos Fuentes, and was flown by helicopter over the hills where the blue agave grew to the town of Tequila for lunch at one of the old tequila haciendas with the other writers who had spoken at the fair and there was even a mariachi band

and everyone drank too much Tres Generaciones tequila and then there were headaches and other familiar aftereffects. And yes, his visit to Tequila gave him the setting for a scene near the beginning of *The Ground Beneath Her Feet* in which the town is shaken by an earthquake and the vats crack and tequila runs like water in the streets. And after Tequila he and Elizabeth were guests, with Carlos and Silvia Fuentes, at an astonishing house called Pascualitos that was really an archipelago of *palapa*-thatched cabanas overlooking the Pacific Ocean and was featured in fancy books about contemporary architecture, and yes, he realized that he loved Mexico. But all of that was beside the point.

The point was that one evening in Mexico City Carlos Fuentes said, "It's crazy that you have never met Gabriel García Márquez. It's too bad that he's in Cuba right now, because of all the writers in the world you and Gabo are the two who need to meet." He got up and walked out of the room and came back a few minutes later to say, "There's somebody on the phone that you have to talk to."

García Márquez claimed not to be able to speak English but in fact he understood it pretty well. As for himself, his spoken Spanish was lamentable but again, he could understand some of what people were saying as long as they didn't use a lot of slang or speak too rapidly. The only language the two of them had in common was French, so they tried using that, except that García Márquez—of whom it was impossible to think of as "Gabo"—kept sliding back into Spanish; and he heard more English than he intended coming out of his own mouth. But strangely, in the snapshot his memory took of their extended conversation, *there was no language problem.* They were just talking to each other, warmly, affectionately, fluently, saying things about each other's books and about the worlds from which they sprang. He talked about the many aspects of Latin American life that chimed with the South Asian experience—these were both worlds with a long colonial past, worlds in which religion was alive and important and often oppressive, in which generals and civilians vied for power, in which there were great extremes of wealth and poverty to be found and a good deal of corruption in between. It wasn't surprising, he said, that the literature of Latin America found such a ready audience in the East. And Gabo said—"Gabo!" It seemed presumptuous, like calling a god by his intimate family nickname—that the writing of South American writers had been greatly influenced by the wonder tales of the East. So they had much in common. And then García Márquez paid him the greatest compliment he had ever been paid. *Of all the writers outside the Spanish language,* he said, *the two I try always to follow are J. M. Coetzee and you.* That sentence alone made the whole trip worthwhile.

Only when he had put the phone down did he realize that García Márquez hadn't asked a single question about the *fatwa*, or about the way he had to live now. He had spoken writer to writer, about books. That was a high compliment as well.

Snapshot of the collapse of time, before the day when. They flew from Mexico to Buenos Aires to Tierra del Fuego and up along the Chilean coast toward New Zealand. When they crossed the international date line his brain gave up. You could have told him it was four-thirty last Tuesday and he would have believed you. The date line was so bewildering that time crumbled in your hands like stale bread and you could say anything about it and people would say okay, sure, why not. The date line revealed time as a fiction, a thing that wasn't real, it made you think that anything could happen, the days could run backward if they felt like it, or your life could unspool like a reel of film spilling crazily onto the floor from a broken projector. Time might be staccato, a series of disconnected moments, random, without meaning, or it might simply throw up its hands in despair and come to an end. This sudden chronological bewilderment made his head swim and he almost fainted. When he came to his senses he was in New Zealand, and back in the English language, which was comforting. But a greater bewilderment lay ahead. He didn't hear the wings of the exterminating angel, but they were up there, above him, coming lower all the time.

Snapshot of the days before the day when. In New Zealand and Australia the security was more sensible, less intrusive, easier to accept. But there was something they didn't know. As they drove across the North Island past Mount Ruapehu, which had been erupting for months, and from which a column of smoke leaned angrily across the sky, they weren't thinking of signs or portents. In Australia they spent a weekend at the aptly named "Happy Daze" property in the Blue Mountains near Sydney as the guests of Julie Clarke and Richard Neville, the

great post-hippie, ex-editor of *Oz,* one of the defendants in the famous *Oz Schoolkids Issue* obscenity trial, and chronicler of the sixties
counterculture in the seminal memoir *Hippie Hippie Shake,* and in that
blissed-out zone (they slept in a tree house) it was not possible to think
about much except peace and love. They could not have guessed that
they were two days away from coming as close as they ever came to
being killed, the most nearly lethal moment in all those menacing
years.

Snapshot of the day when. They had decided to stay on after the
working part of the trip was completed and have Christmas in the sun,
and the police had agreed that they could do without protection as
nobody would know they were still in the country. The novelist Rodney Hall, who lived in a beautiful, secluded seaside property at Bermagui, New South Wales, four hours' drive south of Sydney, had invited
them to come and stay. Christmas in Bermagui, Rodney assured them,
would be totally private, and idyllic too. Zafar flew out from London
and joined them in Sydney after his school broke up. Zafar at sixteen
and a half was a tall, broad-shouldered young man with remarkable
physical confidence. On the morning when the police backed off and
left them alone they had a celebratory coffee in a place near Bondi
Beach, and an Arab-looking man shot odd looks at them and then
went to stand on the sidewalk and made urgent, gesticulating phone
calls. Zafar got up and said, "Maybe I'll just go and have a word," and
his father had the strange and likable feeling of being protected by his
son, but asked him not to bother. The man making phone calls turned
out to be unimportant and they headed to where their rented Holden
saloon car was parked to begin the long drive south.

Elizabeth had brought along a multi-cassette audiobook of Homer's *Iliad* and put it into the car's cassette player and as they drifted
through southern New South Wales on the Princes Highway, past
Thirroul, the suburb of Wollongong where D. H. Lawrence wrote
Kangaroo, and on down the coast, the didgeridoo music of Australian
place-names counterpointed the martial, tragic proper nouns of ancient Greece and Troy, Gerringong, Agamemnon, Nowra, Priam,
Iphigenia, Tomerong, Clytemnestra, Wandandian, Jerrawangala, Hec-
tor, Yatte Yattah, Mondayong, Andromache, Achilles; and Zafar, lulled

by the ancient tale of the wine-dark, fish-rich sea, stretched out on the backseat and fell deeply asleep.

At just about the halfway point of their journey they came to the little town of Milton, and he had been driving for two hours by then, and he should probably have stopped and handed over the wheel to Elizabeth, but no, he insisted, he was fine, he was happy to drive on. The tape ended and for an instant—for a fraction of an instant—his eyes flicked down to the *eject* button and then a number of things happened very quickly, though at the time, Time, which had felt unreliable ever since the date line crossing, seemed to slow and almost come to a halt. An enormous, articulated container truck swung out of a side road and made a wide left turn, and he would always say that the driver's cab crossed the white line, though Elizabeth remembered that he himself had veered slightly to his right, but for whatever reason all of a sudden there was a gigantic, tearing noise, the horrible death-noise of metal on metal, as the cab hit the Holden smack on the driver's door, crumpling it inward, and the slow-motion time got even slower, he seemed to be dragging against the truck for an eternity, twenty seconds maybe, or an hour perhaps, and when the truck finally let them go the Holden slid sideways across the blacktop, heading for the grassy verge, and just beyond the verge, coming toward them, was a substantial, spreading tree, and at a certain moment, as he wrestled with the steering, the thought slowly formed in his slow-motion mind, *I'm not going to be able to avoid that tree, we're going to hit that tree, oh, here it is, we're hitting the tree, we're hitting it . . . now,* and he looked at Elizabeth as she jerked forward against her seat belt, her eyes wide, her mouth open, and a white puff of vapor came out of her mouth like a little speech-bubble, and at that moment he feared that he might be seeing her life leave her body and he shouted in a voice that wasn't his own voice *are you all right,* and he wondered what he would do with the rest of his life if he didn't hear a reply.

Zafar woke up. "Did something happen?" he asked sleepily. "What's going on?" Well, yes, Zafar, you see that tree that's now in the middle of the car, that's what would appear to be going on.

They were all alive. It was an accident that, nine times out of ten, would have killed everyone in the car, but this was the tenth time and

SALMAN RUSHDIE

nobody had even broken a bone. The car could have been dragged
under the truck, in which case they would all have been decapitated,
but instead it had bounced off a wheel. And on the floor in the back,
next to his sleeping son, there had been an open case of wine that they
were taking to Rodney as a gift. When the car hit the tree the bottles
were launched forward like missiles and smashed into the windshield.
If those bottles had hit Elizabeth or himself their skulls would have
been broken. But the missiles flew over their shoulders and missed.
Elizabeth and Zafar got out of the car unaided, without a scratch on
their bodies. He was a little less lucky. The driver's door had been
crushed and needed to be opened from the outside, and he had heavy
bruising and several deep cuts on his bare right forearm and sandaled
right foot. Standing up from the forearm was an egg-shaped swelling,
which he took to be a sign of a fracture. The good people of Milton
came out to help and he was guided to a patch of grass where he sat
down, unable to speak, lost in relief and shock.

Another lucky chance: There was a small medical facility nearby,
the Milton-Ulladulla Hospital, so an ambulance was quickly with
them. The men in white, running up, stopped and stared. "Excuse me,
mate, but are you Salman Rushdie?" At that moment he really didn't
want to be. He wanted to be an anonymous person receiving medical
treatment. But yes, he was. "Oh, okay, mate, now this is probably a
terrible time to ask you this, but could I get an autograph?" *Give the
man an autograph,* he thought. *He's the one with the ambulance.*

The police arrived and went to question the driver of the truck,
who was still sitting in his cab, scratching his head. The truck looked
as if nothing had happened to it. The Holden had been swatted away
by this behemoth and the monster didn't have a visible scratch. The
police were giving the driver a hard time, though. They too had
worked out that the man sitting dazed and wounded on the grass was
Salman Rushdie, and so they wanted to know, what was the driver's
religion? The driver was bewildered. "What's my religion got to do
with anything?" Well, was he a *Muzlim?* An *Islammic?* Was he
Eye-ray-nian? Is that why he had tried to kill Mr. Rushdie? Maybe one
of the Ayatoller's fellers? Was he carrying out the whatever it was
called, the *fatso?* The poor driver shook his confused head. He didn't
know who the guy was he had hit. He had just been driving this truck

and didn't know about any *fatso*. In the end the police believed him and sent him on his way.

The truck's container had been full of fresh fertilizer. "You mean," he said to Zafar and Elizabeth, a little hysterically, "we were almost killed by a truckload of *shit*? We almost died under a mountain of *manure*?" Yes, that was the case. Having eluded professional assassins for almost seven years, he and his loved ones had almost met their end under a mighty avalanche of dung.

In the hospital a series of careful tests established that everyone was fine. His arm wasn't broken, just heavily bruised. He called Rodney Hall, who said he would drive up to fetch them right away, but that meant he wouldn't be there for two hours. In the meanwhile, the media arrived in numbers. The hospital staff did a magnificent job of keeping the journalists at bay, refusing to comment on who might or might not be receiving treatment on the premises. But the media knew what they knew and hung around. "You can stay here until your friend arrives if you like," the doctors and nurses told them. So they stayed in the emergency ward and waited, looking at one another carefully as if to reassure themselves that the others were really still there.

Rodney arrived, urgent and full of solicitude. The press were still outside, he said, so how should we do this? Just march past them, let them snap away, and leave? "No," he told Rodney. "In the first place, I don't want a picture of me looking beaten up with my arm in a sling all over the papers tomorrow. And in the second place if I leave in your car it won't take them long to work out where I'm staying, and that would ruin Christmas."

"I could take Elizabeth and Zafar," Rodney suggested, "and meet you a couple of miles south of here. Nobody knows what Zafar and Elizabeth look like so we should be able to stroll out without attracting attention."

Dr. Johnson, the kindly young physician who had been taking care of them, had a suggestion. "My car is in the staff car park," he said. "The press won't be there. I could drive you down the road to join your friends."

"That's incredibly nice of you," he said. "Are you sure?"

"Are you kidding?" Dr. Johnson said. "This is the most exciting thing that's happened in Milton ever, probably."

Rodney's home was on a small headland next to an almost deserted stretch of beach surrounded by eucalyptus forest, and it was as secluded and as idyllic as he had promised. They were made welcome, cared for, wined and dined; they read books aloud and walked and slept, and slowly the shock of the accident receded. On Christmas Day they swam in the Tasman Sea in the morning and then ate Christmas dinner al fresco on the lawn. He sat silent, staring at Elizabeth and Zafar, and thought, *We're still here. Look at us. We're all still alive.*

VIII

Mr. Morning and
Mr. Afternoon

THE SUBJECT ALWAYS CHANGES, HE HAD TOLD HIMSELF MANY TIMES. *WE live in accelerating times, and the subject changes faster than ever.* But seven years of life were gone, seven years of his forties, the prime of a man's life, seven years of his son's childhood that he could never have back, and the subject hadn't changed. He was having to face the possibility that this might not just be a phase of his life—that the rest of his life might be like this. That was a hard lump to swallow.

They were all feeling the strain. Zafar was frustrated by the secrecy—*Can't I bring a couple of friends home?*—and was doing badly at school. Clarissa was making a name for herself at the Arts Council, becoming one of its most loved figures, a sort of patron saint of little magazines around the country, and he was happy to see her find her place in the world; but ever since the money squabble their relationship had soured. It wasn't hostile, but it wasn't friendly anymore either, and that was a bad, sad thing. Elizabeth wasn't pregnant and that often affected her mood. She went to see a gynecologist and discovered that for various internal reasons she might find it hard to conceive. So there was this problem to overcome as well the simple chromosome translocation, and if and when a baby was conceived there would be security problems. These she closed her mind to and ignored.

A new year began. Caroline Michel called to say that UK hardcover sales of *The Moor's Last Sigh* were already at almost two hundred thousand copies. However, there was trouble in India. In Bombay the Shiv Sena had taken exception to its portrayal in the novel as "Mumbai's Axis." A few other people hadn't thought it funny that one of the characters in the novel had a stuffed pet dog on wheels called Jawaharlal after the country's first prime minister. The sixty-eight-year-old Urdu novelist Qurratulain Hyder, author of the celebrated novel of partition *Aag ka Darya (River of Fire)*, announced that this piece of fictional taxidermy proved that the author should "never be forgiven."

As a result of the "controversy" the Indian government, with its traditional commitment to freedom of expression, halted the book's import in customs on some flimsy pretext. He called his Indian attorney Vijay Shankardass, a soft-spoken, high-principled man and one of the most able lawyers in India, and Vijay said that if they could get India's book trade organizations to join with the book's Indian publishers, Rupa, they could get into court quickly with a "show cause injunction" and force the government's hand. There was a wobble from Rupa's boss, Rajan Mehra, who at first timidly feared that taking on the government could have unpleasant repercussions for his business, but Vijay helped him stiffen his resolve and in the end Mehra "did the needful." On the day the case was lodged the government backed down, the blockade was lifted, and *The Moor's Last Sigh* entered India and was freely published without any trouble whatsoever. At the Delhi Book Fair the unbanning of the novel was a huge event, "a great victory," he thanked Vijay. But *The Satanic Verses* remained banned in India, and so did its author.

The other bit of Indian trouble concerned his little house in Solan up in the Shimla Hills. His paternal grandfather, Mohammed Din Khaliqi Dehlavi, whom he had never known, had long ago bought the place as a summer retreat from the Delhi heat, a six-room stone cottage on a small plot of land, but with a sweeping view of the mountains. He had left it to his only son, Anis, and Anis Rushdie before his death had gifted it to *his* only son. It had been requisitioned by the state government of Himachal Pradesh under the Evacuee Property Act, which allowed India to seize the property of anyone who had gone to settle in Pakistan. But he had never done that, so the house had been taken illegally. Vijay Shankardass was fighting this case for him too, but even though Vijay had managed to establish Anis's title to the property his own inheritance of it had not yet been accepted, and the Himachal government had said, curtly, that it "didn't want to be seen to be doing favors for Salman Rushdie."

It would be another year before the diligent researches of Vijay's team turned up the hidden document that won the case—the document in which a high officer of the Himachal government had perjured himself in a sworn affidavit stating that he knew that Salman

Rushdie had become a citizen of Pakistan. But Salman Rushdie had never held any citizenship other than Indian and British. Perjury was a serious crime, carrying a mandatory jail sentence, and when they knew that Vijay Shankardass had the untruthful affidavit in his possession the Himachal authorities would suddenly become extremely cooperative. In April 1997 the house would once again be in his name, vacated in reasonable condition by the government officer who had squatted there, and Vijay collected the keys.

His favorite comments about *The Moor's Last Sigh* were those from Indian friends who got in touch after reading the now-unbanned book to ask how he'd managed to write it without visiting India. "You sneaked in, didn't you?" they suggested. "You came quietly and soaked stuff up. Otherwise how would you have known all those things?" That put a big smile on his face. His greatest worry had been that his "novel of exile" would read like a foreigner's book, disconnected from the Indian reality. He thought of Nuruddin Farah carrying Somalia in his heart wherever he traveled, and was proud that he had managed to write his book from the private India he carried everywhere with him.

The novel was getting some of the best notices of his life, confirmations that the long derailment had not crippled him. There was a little U.S. book tour, but it was expensive. A small aircraft had to be hired. U.S. police forces insisted on the need for security, so a private security firm headed by an experienced fellow named Jerome H. Glazebrook had to be engaged. It was generous of Sonny Mehta to absorb most of these costs, though the venues contributed, and so did he. Sonny came with him on the tour and threw lavish parties in Miami (where everyone seemed to be a thriller writer, and where, after he asked Carl Hiaasen to fill him in about Miami, Hiaasen took a deep breath and stopped talking two hours later, giving a high-speed master class on Floridian political shenanigans) and in San Francisco (where Czesław Miłosz, Robin Williams, Jerry Brown, Linda Ronstadt and Angela Davis were among the guests). These were slightly furtive events, with the guests not being told the truth about the author's identity or the location of the bash until the last minute.

Miami and San Francisco's finest were frisked by security guards in case they were thinking of making a little extra cash by going after the bounty.

Sonny and he even had time for a weekend in Key West, where they were joined by Gita Mehta, who was looking well and was back to her buoyant, loquacious best. He thought of this unusual and costly book tour as Sonny's silent way of apologizing for the problems he had caused at the time of *Haroun and the Sea of Stories,* and was happy to let bygones be bygones. The day after he got back to London *The Moor's Last Sigh* won him a British Book Award, a "Nibbie," as the "author of the year." (The book of the year Nibbie went to the cookbook writer Delia Smith who, in her acceptance speech, unusually referred to herself in the third person, "Thank you for honoring a Delia Smith book.") A great cheer went up when his award was announced. *I mustn't forget that there is an England that's on my side,* he told himself. Given the continued attacks on his character in the papers he had come to think of collectively as the *Daily Insult,* it would have been easy, but wrong, to forget that.

Back in the house on Bishop's Avenue, life with the police was hard to readjust to. They locked doors at night but never unlocked them in the morning. They compulsively closed curtains but they never opened them again. The chairs they sat upon broke under their weight and the wooden floor in the entrance hall cracked under their heavy feet. It was the seventh anniversary of the *fatwa.* No British newspaper published a sympathetic or appreciative word. It was an old, boring story that didn't seem to be going anywhere; not news. He wrote a piece for *The Times* in which he tried to argue that the purposes of the *fatwa* had been defeated, even if the *fatwa* itself was still extant: The book had not been suppressed and nor had its author. He thought of the era of fear and self-censorship that the *fatwa* had brought into being—in which the Oxford University Press had refused to publish an extract from *Midnight's Children* in an English-language teaching text on the grounds that it was "too sensitive"; in which the Egyptian writer Alaa Hamed (together with his publisher and printer) had been sentenced to eight years in prison for writing a novel, *A Distance in a Man's Mind,* that was judged to be a threat to social peace and national unity; in which Western publishers spoke openly of avoiding any text that might be thought critical of Islam—and he didn't believe his own article. He had had a few small successes, but the real victory had by no means been won.

He kept trying to talk to Elizabeth about America. In America they wouldn't have to live with four policemen or the constant accusation of costing the nation a fortune without having performed any service to it. They had had a taste of that freedom in the last couple of summers; they could have much more of it. Whenever he raised the subject she scowled mutinously and wouldn't discuss it. He began to see that she had a fear of freedom, or at least of freedom with him. She felt safe only inside the bubble of the protection. If he insisted on stepping outside it, she might very well be unwilling to take that step with him. For the first time (shocking himself) he began to imagine a life without her. He left for Paris to launch the French edition of *The Moor's Last Sigh;* the tension between them had not died down.

In Paris *les gentilhommes du RAID* were up to their usual tricks. They closed down the entire street in front of the Hôtel de l'Abbaye near Saint-Sulpice. They refused him permission to appear in any public place. "If he doesn't like it," they had told his publishers, "he doesn't have to come." But the good news was that the book was getting a great welcome, fighting for the top spot in the bestseller lists against Umberto Eco's latest and *The Horse Whisperer.* There were also political meetings with the foreign minister, Hervé de Charette, and the minister of culture, Philippe Douste-Blazy. *Chez* Bernard-Henri Lévy he met the grand old man of the cinema and the *nouveau roman,* Alain Robbe-Grillet, whose novel *La Jalousie* and screenplay for *L'Année Dernière à Marienbad* he greatly admired. Robbe-Grillet was planning to make a film in Cambodia at the end of the year, starring Jean-Louis Trintignant and BHL's wife, Arielle Dombasle. Trintignant was to play a pilot who crashed in the Cambodian jungle and then saw fantasies of Arielle in his subsequent delirium while being tended to in a jungle village by *un médecin assez sinistre.* The part of the sinister doctor, Robbe-Grillet enthused, is perfect for you, Salman. Two weeks in Cambodia in December! Philippe Douste-Blazy will arrange everything! (Douste-Blazy, present at the occasion, nodded agreeably, and apologized, also, for the RAID overreaction. "On your next visits we will use only two security guards.") He asked Robbe-Grillet if he could see a script and Robbe-Grillet nodded impatiently, yes, of course, of course, but you must do it! It will be fantastic! The doctor, it is you!

No screenplay was ever sent to him. The film was never made.

One other thing happened in Paris. Caroline Lang, Jack Lang's brilliant and beautiful daughter, came to keep him company at the Hôtel de l'Abbaye one afternoon, and because of her beauty, and the wine, and the difficulties with Elizabeth, they became lovers; and immediately afterward decided not to do that again, but to remain friends. After their few hours together he had to appear live on TV, on Bernard Pivot's *Bouillon de Culture,* and felt that the emotional upheaval caused by his infidelity meant that he gave a poor account of himself.

Andrew Wylie and Gillon had come to the end of the road and had decided to end their association. Andrew came to the house, very upset, raging a little, but mainly grieving. "It became plain to me," Andrew said, at once sorrowful and outraged, "that Gillon has never been my partner. Brian Stone is Gillon's partner." Brian was their associate, the agent who controlled the Agatha Christie estate. "The nameplate at the London agency," Andrew said bitterly, "still reads Atken and Stone." Their fight had been about money, but also about their different visions. Andrew had grand, expansionist dreams; Gillon was cautious and, always, financially prudent. It had not been a pleasant split; an ugly divorce, like most divorces. Andrew was like a jilted lover, simultaneously contemptuous and in despair.

He was deeply troubled by his agents' split-up. Gillon and Andrew had been twin pillars of strength in the past years, and he had relied on them absolutely. Neither of them had flinched for a moment in the face of the Islamic attack, and their courage had shamed many publishers into being braver than they might otherwise have been. He couldn't imagine doing without either of them, but now he would have to choose, although Gillon gracefully made the choice easier by calling the next day to say, "My dear, it's obvious you must go with Andrew. He was your agent first, he brought you to me, and of course you must stay with him, that's absolutely right."

They had gone through so much, done so much together. Their relationship had deepened far beyond the normal author-agent cordiality. They had become close friends. And yet now he would have to lose Gillon. He had never imagined such a day, had always thought that both Gillon and Andrew would be his agents forever. "Okay," he said to Gillon. "Thank you. But as far as I'm concerned nothing has changed between us."

"We'll have lunch soon," said Gillon, and that was that.

Italy had assumed the rotating presidency of the European Union and was in the process of persuading all EU member states to accept a letter, to be signed by the EU and Iran jointly, that accepted that the *fatwa* was eternally valid, in return for a short statement from Iran that it would not carry it out. Frances D'Souza's sources told her that the EU troika of foreign ministers was going to Tehran to discuss terrorism, and was refusing even to bring up the *fatwa* unless this text was agreed to—which means, she said, agreed to by him. The British government was holding out, but was worried about its isolation. He asked Frances to inform her sources that he had not fought for seven years to have the European Union agree on the validity of an extraterritorial murder order. He would not agree to such a statement in a million years. "Fuck them, the expedient bastards," he said. He would not collaborate in this hideous piece of amorality.

The "Italian letter" was never signed or sent.

He spoke to Gail Rebuck at Random House about getting her to take over paperback publication of *The Satanic Verses*. She said that Alberto Vitale now seemed "receptive" but she needed some reassurances about security. He suggested to Gail and to Caroline Michel that they get reports from all European publishers of the *Verses* paperback in translation, and from Central Books, the Consortium's UK distributors, about their security measures, if any, and arrange a meeting with Helen Hammington, Dick Wood and Rab Connolly to get their view. *Inch by inch,* he thought. *We'll get there, but it's so painfully slow.*

Elizabeth heard that Carol Knibb, her cousin who had raised her after her mother died, was suffering from chronic lymphocytic leukemia, the same CLL that Edward Said was fighting in New York. Elizabeth was overwhelmed by the news. Carol was the closest thing she had to a family. He, too, was profoundly saddened. Carol was a sweet, kind woman. "It's a fightable cancer," he said to Elizabeth. "We can help her fight. She should talk to Edward's doctor Kanti Rai on Long Island."

Death came indiscriminately to the sweet and the sour. Two weeks after hearing about Carol's cancer he had news of a death he could not mourn. The malevolent gnome Kalim Siddiqui had issued his last threat. He had been attending a conference in Pretoria, South Africa, when a heart attack killed him. It emerged that he had recently had bypass surgery but had gone on ranting and raving when a wiser man would have opted for a quieter life. So he could be said to have chosen his end. *It couldn't have happened to a nicer man,* he thought, but made no public comment.

Michael Foot called, very pleased. "What's the name of the Muslim God? Their God, what's the fellow called?" Allah, Michael. "Oh yes, Allah, of course that's right. Well, he's clearly not on old Siddiqui's side, eh? Eh?" *Come in Dr. Siddiqui your time is up.*

Elizabeth had gone to visit Carol in Derbyshire. When she came back she was happy to hear of Siddiqui's last exit. She also read the just-completed twenty-page synopsis of the new novel, *The Ground Beneath Her Feet,* and loved it so much that the gulf between them closed and was forgotten. And the next day—the universe didn't like him to be happy for too long—he was taken to Spy Central to be told some genuinely frightening news.

It was never comforting to approach the large sand-colored fortress on the river, even if it was improbably decorated with Christmas trees; he never came here to be cheered up. Today in an anonymous boardroom he was faced with the afternoon and the morning, Mr. P—— M—— and Mr. A—— M——, the head of counterterrorism for the

Middle East and the man on the Iran desk. Rab Connolly and Dick Wood were there too, in a "listening capacity." "The security services now know," AM said, "that Iran, by which we mean Khamenei the supreme leader and intelligence minister Fallahian, have set in motion a long-term plan to find and assassinate you. They are prepared to take a long time and spend a lot of money. The plan may have been in place for as long as two years already, but we have only become sure of its existence in the last few months." "It is our duty to tell you this," said PM. "This is why we are meeting you today under our real names."

While he was receiving the bad news from Mr. Morning and Mr. Afternoon, he was waiting tensely for them to say that his home had been located by the enemy. But that was not the case. However, if it did become known, Mr. Morning said, that would be very alarming. At the very least it would require him to receive police protection for the rest of his life.

He expressed his fears for Zafar, Elizabeth, Sameen, his mother in Karachi. "There is no evidence that any of your family or friends have been targeted," said Mr. Afternoon. "Not even as a route to you. You, however, remain target number one."

"Deniability is considered to be of paramount importance by the Iranians," Mr. Morning said. "This is because of the political flak they've been getting after attacks of recent years." *Shapur Bakhtiar, the Mykonos killings.* "They would probably not use Iranian personnel." "But," Mr. Afternoon said, to make him feel a little better, "the stage of them sending weapons through the diplomatic mail, or sending people into the country, is still months or even years away."

It was the worst thing he had feared, a long-term Bakhtiar-style assault. Mr. Morning and Mr. Afternoon could not say what effect a political settlement with Iran might have on such a plot. They believed the Iranian Foreign Ministry might be unaware of its existence. "It's being kept to a very small group inside the Ministry of Information," Mr. Morning said. "There may even be others in the ministry who would wish to thwart such a plan," said Mr. Afternoon, "but Fallahian and Khamenei seem determined to carry out the *fatwa,* and Rafsanjani probably knows too."

The good news was that he had not been located, and that, in the opinion of Afternoon and Morning, the threat from the "community at large" had evaporated. "And now," said Mr. Morning, revealing a flash of steel under his courteous manner, "we can do our level best to disrupt the plot—to put a bloody great fist into the middle of it. To disrupt it with such heavy political fallout that it will be impossible to set up such a scheme again."

Maybe he's just trying to make me feel better, he thought, *but it's working. I like the thought of that fist.*

As far as the wider world was concerned, the *fatwa* story was fading away. It wasn't in the papers anymore, and he himself was being seen here and there, visiting his friends, eating in the occasional restaurant, cropping up in various countries to promote his new book. It was obvious to most people that the threat had receded, and it seemed likely to many commentators that the protection was continuing only because he was insisting on it—insisting not because it was necessary but to satisfy his monumental egotism. And at this moment, when whatever little shred of public sympathy still existed was blowing away in the wind, he was being told that the danger was greater than it had ever been, the attack on his life more serious than any that had previously been identified. And he couldn't even say so. Mr. Morning and Mr. Afternoon had been very clear about that.

Andrew had found him a Long Island house to rent, very secluded, on Little Noyac Path in the hills above Bridgehampton. It would be rented in Elizabeth's name and they could have it for two months. Yes, he said, let's go ahead. He had decided to continue with his plan of retrieving his freedom piece by piece. To behave as if he had not heard what he had heard in the Christmas tree fortress. The only alternative was to go back to being a prisoner, and he wasn't prepared to do that. So: Yes, please, Andrew. Let's do the deal. A few days later Rab Connolly told him that Mr. Morning and Mr. Afternoon now believed that the assassins had decided he was too well protected in the United Kingdom, so they might try to kill him while he was on a foreign trip. And he was planning to spend two months on Long Island without protection, and was bringing Elizabeth and Zafar with him. He felt, once again, like the driver of that Holden, being hit by a truckload of shit and heading straight for a tree, with the people he loved most in the car beside him. He talked to Elizabeth. She still wanted to go. So, damn it, they would do it, and by doing it prove that it could be done.

He went to make a speech in Barcelona. He flew to America and delivered the commencement address at Bard College. Nobody tried to kill him. However, an Iranian dissident in exile, Reza Mazlouman, an ex–minister of education from the days of the shah, who had been living quietly in the Parisian suburb of Créteil, was found dead. Two shots to the head and one to the chest. The world, which had briefly brightened when *The Moor's Last Sigh* was published, darkened again. In his imagination he kept trying to write a happy ending to his own story, but couldn't come up with one. Maybe there wasn't going to be one. *Two shots to the head and one to the chest.* There was that possible ending, too.

Elizabeth wasn't pregnant and the tension between them grew again. If she didn't get pregnant soon she was insisting on trying the in vitro fertilization route even though his chromosome problem greatly reduced the chances of success. If she did get pregnant it was probable that her closely protected anonymity would be lost, and that the location of the Bishop's Avenue house would become public knowledge. That would turn the place into an armed camp; and, anyway, how were they to bring up a child in the nightmare they were obliged to inhabit? What kind of life would such a child have? But against all logical arguments she set her overwhelming need, and he his determination that they should be able to lead a real life, and so they would go ahead, they would keep trying, they would do whatever they had to do.

Vijay Shankardass called from India to give him hopeful news. The new Indian government's foreign minister, Inder Gujral, was in favor of allowing him to visit India again, and the home affairs minister agreed. So there was a possibility that his long exile could soon end.

Andrew was showing around his synopsis of *The Ground Beneath Her Feet* and it was going over well with his publishers, but the issue of the long-term paperback publication of *The Satanic Verses* still needed to be resolved, and Andrew wanted to make it a condition of any English-language deal that the publisher should take on the *Verses* as well. There were paperbacks in print everywhere else by now, and the Consortium edition was still available in English, but that was essentially a form of self-publication and couldn't be the long-term answer. In England, Gail Rebuck and Random House UK were moving toward agreeing to republish the paperback as a Vintage book, but in America the Random House boss, Alberto Vitale, was not inclined to do so. The solution, Andrew suggested, might be Holtzbrinck, whose German arm, Kindler Verlag, had already published the German-language paperback without difficulties, and whose American house, Henry Holt, under the leadership of the flamboyant publisher Michael Naumann, seemed ready to do the same. He told Andrew he would like to stay with Random House in the United Kingdom, and Andrew said he had come to the same view, so they were "on the same page."

At the end of the last ice age the glaciers retreated from Long Island leaving behind the terminal moraine that created the wooded hills in which he and Elizabeth spent that summer. The low, roomy white house was owned by an elderly couple named Milton and Patricia Grobow, whom he was not at first able to meet, since he theoretically didn't exist, and Elizabeth was there for the summer by herself "to write and see friends." Afterward, when the Grobows worked out what was going on, they were genuinely happy to be providing him with a summer refuge. They were fine, ethical, liberal people with a daughter working at *The Nation* and they were proud, they said, to be able to help. But even before he was revealed he was happy there, in a place where the biggest danger they had to face was Lyme disease. They told their closest friends where they were staying, kept away from the Hamptons "scene," walked on the beach at sunset, and he felt, as he always felt in America, the slow rebirth of his true self. He began to write his new novel and the Grobow house, surrounded by fields and woods, turned out to be a perfect place to work. The book, which he was beginning to understand would be a long one, began slowly to unfold. Elizabeth was a keen gardener and spent happy hours tending the Grobows' plants. Zafar went to Greece with his mother and then came out to join them and loved the place and for a while they could just be a family summering together by the sea. They shopped in the stores and ate in the restaurants and if people recognized him they were too discreet to intrude on his privacy. One evening Andrew and Camie Wylie took them to Nick & Toni's for dinner and the artist Eric Fischl, stopping by their table on his way out to say hello to Andrew, turned to him and asked, "Should we all be scared because you're in here with us?" All he could think of to say was, "Well, you don't need to be, because you're leaving anyway." He knew Fischl meant no harm, it was just a joke, but in these special months when he escaped from the bubble of his unreal real life he didn't like being reminded that the bubble was still there, waiting for him to return.

They went back to London in early September and soon after their return Elizabeth's dearest wish came true. She was pregnant. He at once began to fear the worst. If one of his faulty chromosomes had been selected then the fetus would not form and she would miscarry very soon, probably at the end of the next menstrual cycle. But she was joyfully confident that everything was fine, and her instincts were right. There was no early miscarriage, and soon enough they could see an ultrasound image of their living, healthy child.

"We're going to have a son," he said.

"Yes," she said, "we're going to have a son."

It was as if the whole world was singing.

The Moor's Last Sigh had been awarded the European Union's Aristeion Prize for Literature along with the Austrian novelist Christoph Ransmayr's novel Morbus Kitahara, but the Danish government announced that he would not be allowed to attend the awards ceremony in Copenhagen on November 14, 1996, for security reasons. They claimed to be aware of a "specific threat" to his life, but the Special

Branch told him they were not aware of any such threat, and if there had been one, the Danes would have been obliged to inform them. So it was just a pretext. As usual his first feeling was of humiliation, but his second feeling was of outrage, and he decided that this time he would not stand for it. He issued a statement through Article 19. "It is scandalous that Copenhagen, the present EU 'capital of culture,' refuses to permit the winner of the EU's own literature prize to attend the award ceremony. It is a cowardly decision which is exactly the opposite of what one should do in the face of threats such as the Iranian *fatwa*. If one wishes to ensure that such threats are not repeated, it is important to demonstrate that they are not effective." Danish politicians of all parties, including the ruling party, attacked the decision, and the Danish government gave in. On November 13 he flew to Denmark and the award ceremony took place at the new Arken Museum of Modern Art, which was ringed by armed policemen and looked like a prison camp, except that all the inmates were in full evening dress.

After the ceremony his publisher Johannes Riis suggested that they go with a few friends to a nice Copenhagen bar for a drink, and while they were in the bar the "Christmas beer" arrived. Men wearing red Santa hats came in bearing cases of the traditional winter ale, and he was given one of the first bottles, as well as one of the Santa hats, which he put on. Somebody took a photograph: the man who had been thought too dangerous to allow into Denmark sitting like anyone else in an ordinary bar, drinking a beer and wearing a party hat. This defiantly unthreatened picture almost brought down the Danish government when it was on every front page the next morning. The prime minister, Poul Nyrup Rasmussen, had to apologize publicly for his earlier veto. Then there was a meeting with Rasmussen, who congratulated him on his little victory. "I just decided to fight," he told the confounded prime minister. "Yes," said Rasmussen shamefacedly, "and you did it very well."

He wanted to think about other things. As he entered the year in which he would turn fifty and become a father for the second time he knew that he was sick of fighting for seats on airplanes, of being upset by name-calling in the newspapers, of policemen sleeping in his house, of lobbying politicians, and of secret Mr. Mornings and Mr. Afternoons speaking of assassination. His new book was alive in his head and new life had stirred in Elizabeth's womb. For the book he was reading Rilke, listening to Gluck, watching on blurry VHS the great Brazilian movie *Orfeu Negro,* and being happy to discover, in Hindu mythology, an Orpheus myth in reverse: the love god Kama slain by Shiva in a moment of anger and brought back to life only because of his wife Rati's entreaties, Eurydice rescuing Orpheus. A triangle was rotating slowly in his mind's eye, at whose three points were art, love and death. Could art, fueled by love, transcend death? Or must death, in spite of art, inevitably consume love? Or perhaps art, meditating on love and death, could become greater than them both. He had singers and songwriters on the brain because in the Orpheus myth the arts of music and poetry were united. But the quotidian could not be kept at bay. He worried constantly about what sort of life he could offer to the boy who was coming to see them, entering this world out of the void of unbeing to find . . . what? Helen Hammington and her troops dogging his every move? It was unthinkable. Yet he had to think it. His imagination wanted to soar but he had lead weights tied to his ankles. *I could be bounded in a nutshell and count myself a king of infinite space,* Hamlet alleged, but Hamlet hadn't tried living with the Special Branch. If you were bounded in a nutshell along with four sleeping policemen then, for sure, O Prince of Denmark, you would have bad dreams.

In August 1997 it would be the fiftieth anniversary of India's independence, and he had been asked to edit an anthology of Indian writing to mark the occasion. He asked Elizabeth to help him. It would be something they could do together, something to think about together other than the difficulties of their lives.

He had been talking to the police about changing the system. Elizabeth and he needed to prepare a room for the baby and perhaps also find a live-in nanny. They could no longer offer accommodation to four police officers a night, and anyway, how much good were they if they were all asleep? For once he found the Yard receptive to his ideas. It was agreed that police officers would no longer sleep at his residence. He would have a daytime team and then a night shift of two officers who would remain in the "police living room," awake, monitoring their array of video screens. Under this arrangement, he was told, he could finally have a "dedicated team," not made up of part-timers from other teams but allocated to himself alone, and that should simplify his life. The new deal was in place by early January 1997 and he noticed that all the protection officers were glum and grumpy. *Oh,* he thought in a lightbulb moment, *it's because of the overtime.*

One of the great benefits of being on a "covert prot" like Operation Malachite, and living with the principal twenty-four hours a day, was that the overtime was terrific. On all other, "overt" prots the protection teams went home at night and the principal's residence was protected by uniformed officers. Now all of a sudden their nocturnal overtime payments had vanished. No wonder they were *a bit cheesed off, to be honest with you, Joe,* and no wonder the bigwigs at the Yard had so quickly acceded to his suggestion. He had saved them a pile of cash.

The very next weekend he discovered that the "extra convenience of a dedicated team" was a fiction. He had been invited to Oxford to Ian McEwan's home but was abruptly informed by Hammington's deputy Dick Stark, whose self-satisfaction had begun to be a constant irritation, that no drivers were available, so he would have to stay indoors all weekend. There was a "manpower shortage," though "obviously," if Elizabeth needed to go to hospital, they would find a way. From now on there would "always be more difficulty at weekends." He would need to tell them by Tuesday if he wanted any "movements" on Saturday or Sunday. The Oxford trip seemed, he was told, like "a lot of manpower for not very much."

He tried to argue his case. There were now three officers at his house all day, so if he wanted to go to a private event like a dinner at a friend's house they needed to find only one more driver—was that really so difficult? But as usual, at Scotland Yard, there was only a minimal desire to be helpful to him. There was a general election coming, he thought, and if the Labour Party won it he would have friendlier people in high places. He had to get guarantees that he would be assisted to lead a livable life. He would not accept imprisonment, with outings at the police's pleasure.

Meanwhile Elizabeth had become obsessed by secrecy. She didn't want anyone outside their inner circle to know she was pregnant until the baby was born. He did not know how to keep such secrets anymore. He wanted to be allowed to live an honest life with his family. He even spoke to her about marriage but when he mentioned a prenup the conversation became a quarrel. He tried to speak about the greater ease of being in America and the quarrel got worse. They were going crazy, he thought. Locked up and insane. Two people who loved each other were being smashed by the stresses imposed on them by the police, the government, and Iran.

The *Daily Insult* carried a story on its women's page about a German psychologist who said that ugly men did well with pretty women because they were more attentive. "That must be welcome information in Salman Rushdie's hideout," the *Insult* hypothesized.

He spoke to Frances D'Souza about setting up a group of sympathetic MPs to take up his cause, and maybe even adding a couple of friendly lords like Richard Rogers. (He had no constituency MP of his own because his location could not be disclosed.) She thought it was a good idea. A week later Mark Fisher, Labour's arts spokesman, invited him to the House of Commons to have a drink with Derek Fatchett, the deputy to Robin Cook, Labour's foreign affairs spokesman and the probable foreign secretary in a Labour government. Fatchett heard him out with mounting rage and said, "I promise you, when we come to power, it will be a high priority for us to sort this out." Mark promised to stay on every aspect of the case. *Why,* he wondered as he left, kicking himself, *didn't I think of this adopt-an-MP scheme before?*

He went to the annual "A" Squad party, in a bad mood with the senior officers, and left as soon as was polite. Afterward he was *allowed* to have dinner with Caroline Michel and Susan Sontag in a restaurant. He told Susan about the baby and she asked if they were going to get married. Um, he stumbled, we're doing fine, lots of people don't get married these days. "Marry her, you bastard!" Susan shouted. "She's the best thing that ever happened to you!" And Caroline agreed. "Yeah! What are you waiting for?" Elizabeth seemed very interested in his answer to that question. When he got home he stood in the kitchen leaning against the Aga range, and said, wryly, "We'd better get married, then." The next morning Elizabeth asked him as soon as he woke up, "Do you remember what you did last night?" He found that he was feeling good about it, which amazed him. After the Wiggins catastrophe he had thought he would never risk another marriage. But here he went again, as the song had it, taking a chance on love.

She didn't want to be married looking pregnant. So maybe they would do it in the summer, after the baby arrived, in America. A few weeks earlier they had been *allowed,* as a sort of Christmas treat, to accept Richard Eyre's invitation to see his production of *Guys and Dolls* at the National Theatre, and now Elizabeth could spend a few months in the role of Adelaide, "the well-known fiancée." No sooner had he made this joke than the person developed a cold.

BBC TV was trying to adapt *Midnight's Children* as a five-part miniseries but the project had run into script difficulties. The writer Ken Taylor, who had so successfully adapted Paul Scott's *The Jewel in the Crown,* was finding the very different *Midnight's Children* a harder task. Alan Yentob called to say, "If you want this series to be made I'm afraid you're going to have to step in." Kevin Loader, the series producer, promised to give Ken Taylor the bad news but never did so, and Ken, not surprisingly, was angry when he found out. However the new scripts had been drafted and the director, Tristram Powell, told him that Mark Thompson, the new controller of BBC2, was delighted with them and was now "100 percent behind the project." That was good. But the real problems this project would face would not come from within the BBC.

Rab Connolly came to see him, in a conciliatory frame of mind. He denied that Labour MPs had been putting any pressure on Scotland Yard, but it seemed probable. "I think we can say that you won't have problems about things like the McEwan visit again," he said.

It was the week of the *fatwa* anniversary and the "super-secret" information he had been given by Mr. Morning and Mr. Afternoon was all over the papers. "Security had been stepped up" around him, The *Guardian* reported, which wasn't true, "because MI5 knows of a specific threat," which was. Meanwhile Sanei of the Bounty had increased the money by another half a million dollars. *The Times* made the bounty offer its lead story and, in an editorial, demanded that Britain lead the EU in taking a new, tougher line with Iran. He himself wrote a piece that was widely published around the world, and did interviews with CNN and the BBC to back it up, suggesting that if such an attack had been launched against someone thought to be "important"—Margaret Thatcher, Rupert Murdoch, Jeffrey Archer—the world community would not have sat on its hands for eight years, bleating impotently. The lack of a solution therefore reflected a widespread belief that some people's lives—the lives of troublesome writers, for example—were worth less than others'.

But he was more worried about Zafar than Iran. Zafar had passed his driving test and had been bought a small car but adulthood seemed some distance away. The thrill of the car was encouraging some wild behavior. There was a girl, Evie Dalton, and Zafar was playing truant. He left home early saying that his whole class had been called in for extra English to go through coursework—what a fluent liar he had become! This was the *fatwa*'s damage, and if it proved to be long-term damage that would be unbearable. A girl had called the school pretending to be Clarissa, to say he had a doctor's appointment and would be in later. The school, smelling a rat, called Clarissa to check, and the lie was discovered. Clarissa spoke to Evie's mother, Mehra, and of course that nice Indian lady was deeply shocked.

Zafar turned up at school at lunchtime and was in a good deal of trouble. His parents grounded him, and he would not have the use of the car for quite some time. That he could simply disappear, knowing the panic it would unleash in his father about his safety, was a sign of how far off the rails he was getting. He had always been a kind and thoughtful boy. But he was a teenager now.

He took Zafar out for dinner, just the two of them, and that helped. He understood it was important to do this regularly and felt foolish not to have understood that before. Zafar was worried on his new brother's behalf, he said. *You're an older parent, Dad, and as he grows up he will have a very strange life, like me.* He wanted very much to bring his Evie to the Bishop's Avenue house. But two weeks later he was heartbroken. Evie, to whom he felt so close because they were both half-Indian, had left him for his best friend, Tom. "But I can't stay angry with anyone for more than a few hours," he said, movingly. He was trying to remain friends with them both (and he succeeded; Evie and Tom remained two of his very closest pals). But the situation preyed on his mind and seriously affected his schoolwork. He had to buckle down. A levels would be upon him very soon.

Two weeks later Zafar was given permission to use his car again and almost at once had an accident. He called at a quarter past nine in the morning; the accident had happened just around the corner from Bishop's Avenue on Winnington Road, but his jailbird father wasn't *allowed* to do what any father would do—to rush to the scene and make sure his son was all right. Instead he had to stay in his jail, fretting, while Elizabeth went to find Zafar. The young fellow had been lucky: a nosebleed and a cut lip, no whiplash injuries or broken bones. The accident had been his fault. He had tried to overtake a car that had indicated it was turning right, and he hit the car and then demolished a low garden wall. The local police told him he could have killed someone and that he might be prosecuted for unsafe driving (though in the end he wasn't). Meanwhile, at the Bishop's Avenue house, his father's protectors were saying helpfully, "Well, he has been driving too fast; he was an accident waiting to happen."

He called Clarissa and she called the school. Then he called the badly shaken Zafar and tried to give him love and support on the phone, telling him all the usual things about learning from it, becoming a better driver as a result, and so on. "It will probably be all over school by the time I get there," he said gloomily. "Some guys drove past and saw me." He was a chastened fellow that weekend, and wrote a nice letter to the lady whose garden wall he had knocked down, and for whose repair his dad, inevitably, would pay.

Zafar's "mock A-level" results came in and his performance in this important dummy run was very poor. Two C grades and a D in English. He told Zafar, furiously, "If you don't do something about this right now you aren't going to any university. You're going down the drain."

———

The Indian anthology was done. He had written an introduction that he knew would be argued with in India because it was so politically incorrect, arguing that the most interesting writing being done by Indian writers was now being done in English. He had spent an evening with Anita and Kiran Desai wondering if this was true. They had been looking, they said, for a contemporary Hindi text to translate into English, and hadn't found anything worth doing. Others he spoke to said, of course there are some people, Nirmal Verma, Mahasveta Devi, in the south maybe O. V. Vijayan and Anantha Moorthy, but in general it's not a rich moment for literature in the Indian *bhashas.* So maybe his point was valid, or at least worth offering up as a debating point, but he suspected it would be attacked; and it was.

Two days after Elizabeth and he delivered the anthology, the police almost killed someone.

He was working in his study on *The Ground Beneath Her Feet* when he heard a very, very loud noise and ran downstairs to find all the protection team in the entrance hall looking shocked and, it had to be said, guilty. One of the nicest of the present bunch of prot officers, a gray-haired, well-spoken beanpole of a fellow called Mike Merrill, had fired his gun by mistake. He had been cleaning the weapon and hadn't noticed that there was a bullet in the magazine. The bullet had crossed the police living room, blasted a hole in the closed door, rocketed across the entrance hall and made quite a mess of the wall on the far side. It was the purest good luck that nobody had been there at the time. The Special Branch–approved cleaning lady Beryl (who was also, he discovered, Dick Stark's lover; he was married, too, of course) wasn't there; it wasn't one of her days. And Elizabeth had gone out, and Zafar was at school. So everyone was safe. But the incident changed something for him. What if Elizabeth or Zafar had been passing by? There was going to be a new baby in this house in a few months and there were bullets flying around it. His friends visited him here. This could have happened at any time. "These guns," he said aloud, "have to get out of my house."

Mike was mortified and apologized over and over again. He was taken off the protection and never reappeared, and that was a loss. One of the other new protection officers, Mark Edwards, said, in an attempt at reassurance, "In the future, the cleaning and checking procedure will take place against the far wall of the house, never near the inner door. What was done was against regulations." Oh, he said, so the next time you'll blow a hole in the side of the house and perhaps kill one of the neighbors? No, thank you. He had been so trusting that he had never even dreamed of such an error, but now it had happened and his trust would not easily be renewed. "The simple fact is," he said, "that I can no longer have armed men in my home." There was a new bigwig on his case at Scotland Yard, Detective Superintendent Frank Armstrong (who would later become Tony Blair's personal protection officer and then temporary assistant commissioner "in charge of the operations portfolio," which meant, essentially, that he would be the person running the Metropolitan Police). A meeting with Armstrong had been scheduled in a month's time. "I can't wait that long," he told his shamefaced team. "I want that meeting now."

He got Rab Connolly, who came up to the house to make his official report. He told Rab he had no wish to make a complaint against Mike or anyone else but the event had created a new imperative for him. The guns had to leave the house, and that had to happen right away. Rab gave him the usual line about what would happen if the house became known, the "very heavy uniform operation," the whole street closed to traffic, and there would be no protection anymore because "everyone would refuse to do it." Then he said, "If someone else had been in charge at the beginning, and had taken a proper decision, you wouldn't have had to hide at all, and you'd be in a completely different situation now." Well, that made him feel a *lot* better. This was how the police talked to him. If he wanted this, they wouldn't do that. If he wanted that, then they would get tough about this. Oh, and if this whole thing had been done right from the get-go then it wouldn't be wrong now, but because it was wrong it couldn't be put right.

He was in shock. A gun had been fired in his home. Elizabeth would be back soon. He had to calm down before she arrived so that he could talk to her about it properly. It would not help if they were both hysterical. He had to control himself.

Frank Armstrong, a man of thick eyebrows and a professionally cheery smile, a man of burliness, accustomed to command, came to the house with Rab and Dick Stark.

He was worried about something. Mr. Anton's friend Ronnie Harwood was an old pal of the home secretary, Michael Howard, and had asked for a meeting to talk about the Rushdie protection. "What's it about?" Frank Armstrong wanted to know. "I would suppose it's about allowing me to live with some dignity," he replied. "And to say, we must have a strategy for what happens if this house becomes known. That has to be a political decision as well as an operational one. I need everyone to focus on this subject and think it through. That's what I've been saying to the Labour leadership, and that's what Ronnie's going to tell Michael Howard."

Everything was political. Now that Armstrong saw that he had some political "muscle" he became cooperative, even deferential. The Branch was sympathetic to his request for armed personnel to be withdrawn from the property, he said. He had a proposal to make. *If you were prepared to hire a retiring Branch officer or driver to work with you, maybe even one of the officers you have come to know, we might perhaps withdraw from the house and allow that person to be in charge of all your private movements, and offer you protection only when you move into public spaces.*

Yes! He thought at once. *Yes, please.* "All right," Armstrong said. "That gives us something to work on."

He spoke to Frank Bishop, Whispering Frank the cricket lover, the kindly protection officer with whom Elizabeth and he had forged the closest relationship. Frank was on the verge of retiring and was "up" for this new job. Dennis the Horse, also close to retirement, could be paid an additional retainer as a "backup man," to stand in for Frank when he was unwell or on holiday. "I'll have to run it by the wife, of course," Frank said, and that seemed only fair.

Frances D'Souza had a "chum in MI6" who told her that the spooks were well aware of Elizabeth's pregnancy and knew that as a result they had "three years maximum to sort this out." The idea that their baby was making policy made him smile. MI6, Frances's chum said, had been showing the Foreign Office evidence of the extent of Iranian terrorism, "ten times as much as anyone else, the Saudis, the Nigerians, whoever" and as a result the British government now agreed there was no point in being nice to Iran, the "critical dialogue" was garbage, and all investment in and trade with that country had to cease. The French and Germans were stumbling blocks, but MI6 believed that the new "tough line" would "bring the mullahs to their knees in about two years." *I'll believe it when I see it,* he thought.

And always the wings of that giant blackbird, the exterminating angel, beating close at hand. Andrew called to say that Allen Ginsberg had inoperable liver cancer and a month to live. And even worse news. Nigella called. John Diamond had throat cancer. Doctors were trying to be reassuring. It was "curable, like skin cancer on the inside," with radiation therapy. They had successfully treated Sean Connery for it seven years earlier. "I feel very unsafe," Nigella sadly said.

Unsafe was a feeling he was familiar with.

Isabel Fonseca had spoken to Elizabeth and offered her mother's beautiful garden in East Hampton, with the dazzling field of pink, lilac, purple and white cosmos behind it, as a place for the wedding, and that sounded perfect. But a few days later Elizabeth did what people always did and read his journal when he wasn't there and found out about his day in Paris with Caroline Lang and then they had the painful conversation people always had and Elizabeth was the one feeling wretched and *unsafe* and it was his fault.

They talked for the next two days and slowly, with setbacks, she began to be able to put it away. "Once I felt so confident with you," she said, "I felt nothing could come between us." And, at another time, "I don't want any more trouble in our relationship. I think it would kill me." And, later still, "It's become really important to me to be married, because then you won't have been unfaithful." "You mean, in our marriage?" "Yes."

She dreamed about his infidelity and he dreamed about meeting Marianne in an organic supermarket and asking her for the return of his possessions. "I'll never give them back," she said, and wheeled her cart away.

The shock, the pain, the weeping, the anger came in waves, and then subsided. She was only a month away from giving birth. She decided the future was more important than the past. And forgave him, or at least agreed to forget.

"What was it you said your mother had instead of a memory, which helped her put up with your father?"

"A forgettery."

"I need one of those as well."

The general election had been called and apart from one rogue poll Labour were maintaining a 20 percent lead over the Conservatives. After the long sullen Tory epoch there was an excitement in the air. In the last days before the Blair victory Zafar began to do his A levels and his parents crossed their fingers, and Rab Connolly announced that he was off to look after Mrs. Thatcher and would be replaced by Paul Topper, who seemed smart and nice and eager and a bit less prickly than Rab. Meanwhile the European Union was offering to send ambassadors back to Iran without even bothering to get the slightest assurance about the *fatwa*. Iran, ever the more cynically skillful player, retaliated by not sending *its* ambassadors back, and barring the German envoy "for the time being," just because it felt like doing so. He turned his thoughts away from politics and went to the first, and very cheering, table reading of his *Midnight's Children* scripts at the BBC.

Journalists were nosing around the baby story, many of them convinced the child had already been born. The *Evening Standard* called Martin Amis. "Have you been around to see it yet?" He found it ridiculous to be asked to keep the secret, but in this matter Elizabeth agreed with the police. Meanwhile, a favored name was emerging. "Milan," like Kundera, yes, but it was also a name with an Indian etymology, from the verb *milana,* to mix or mingle or blend; thus, *Milan,* a mingling, a coming together, a union. Not an inappropriate name for a boy in whom England and India were united.

Then it was election day and nobody was thinking about their baby. He sat at home and could not vote, because he was still unable to register without giving a home address. He read in the papers that even homeless people had been given a special dispensation that allowed them to cast their ballots; but there was no special dispensation for him. He put bitter thoughts aside and went to his friends' election night parties. Melvyn Bragg and Michael Foot were having one again, and this time there would be no awful anticlimax. The lawyer Helena Kennedy and her surgeon husband, Iain Hutchison, were having one too. The results came in: It was a big victory for Blair's "New Labour." Joy was unconfined. Party guests told stories of strangers talking happily to one another on the Tube—in England!—and of taxi drivers bursting into song. *The skies above were clear again.* Optimism, a sense of infinite possibility, was being reborn. Now there would be much-needed welfare reform, and £5 billion for new council housing to help replace the public housing stock that had been sold off to the private sector during the Thatcher years, and the European Convention on Human Rights would finally be incorporated into British law. Some months before the election at an arts award show he had challenged Blair, who was rumored to be uninterested in the arts, and by his own admission read books only about economics and political biographies, to recognize the arts' value to British society, to understand that the arts were "the national imagination." Blair had been at that ceremony and had responded that it was New Labour's job to excite the nation with *its* imagination, and tonight, in the glow of the election victory, it was possible not to see that reply as an evasion. Tonight was for celebration. Reality could wait until morning. Years later on the night of Barack Obama's election to the American presidency, he would feel those feelings again.

The three-thousandth day of the *fatwa* arrived two days later. Elizabeth was looking exceptionally beautiful, and the due date was very close. Clarissa's car was broken into and her briefcase with all her credit cards in it was stolen, along with a pair of Zafar's sunglasses, to which the thief had obviously taken a shine. And that night they went to a victory party given by the *Observer* for Tony Blair in a place called Bleeding Heart Crypt, a gathering that the newspaper's Will Hutton called "a laying on of hands." At the party the new Blairite elite welcomed him and treated him like a friend— Gordon Brown, Peter Mandelson, Margaret Beckett, the two Tessas,

Blackstone and Jowell. Richard and Ruthie Rogers were there, and Neil and Glenys Kinnock. Neil drew him close and whispered into his ear, "Now we've got to make the buggers do it." Yes indeed. "His" side was in power again. As Margaret Thatcher liked to say: *Rejoice.*

On the way to the victory party Dick Stark handed him a letter from Frank Armstrong asking him to "rethink" all his plans. He didn't want the new child's existence to be publicly acknowledged, he didn't think the wedding was a good idea, he didn't want Elizabeth's name to be on the book she had coedited. It was a shaming aspect of his life that policemen felt able to talk to him like this. He sent a restrained reply to Armstrong. Police strategy, he said, must be based on what was humanly and decently possible.

He made the mistake of going on *Q&A with Riz Khan* on CNN, and the questions were uniformly hostile. From Tehran he was asked for the millionth time if he had "known what he was doing," and from Switzerland a man asked, "After insulting the Brits, Thatcher and the queen, how can you still live in England?" and from Saudi Arabia a woman called in to say, "Nobody should pay you any attention, because we all know who God is," and to ask, repeatedly, "But what did you gain from your book? What did you gain?" He tried to answer all these questions lightly, with good humor. This was his fate, to face hostility with a smile.

His phone rang. A woman from the *Daily Express* said, "I hear congratulations are in order, and your partner is expecting a baby." *The Sunday Times* sent him a fax. "We hear you have had a baby! Congratulations! Notable development! Of course we won't name the mother or child for security reasons but (a) how are you going to manage to be a parent? (b) will there have to be more security now?" Armstrong's desire to keep the baby secret was an absurdity and he wished Elizabeth wasn't feeling secretive as well. Damn it, he thought, they should just be open about it, and then there would be less of a story. When the press thought something was being hidden from them, it only made them hungrier. The next day the *Express* ran the story, although it omitted Elizabeth's name. Who cares? he thought. He was glad it was out in the open, and the story was perfectly pleasant and well-wishing. One less secret. *Good.* But Elizabeth was angry, and the stress levels rose. They were not understanding each other's sentences, misunderstanding each other's tone of voice, squabbling over nothings. He woke up at 4 A.M. to find her crying. She was fearful about Carol's health. She was alarmed about having her name in the papers. She was sad about his infidelity. She was worried about everything.

And here, right on cue, was Helen Hammington, singing the same old song. If the house was blown the cost of the protection would be tripled, she said. "But in the final analysis, and on the basis that it's at your request, Joe, and as long as you understand that it's irreversible, we are prepared to go ahead with your plan to remove the protection team, and the choice of Frank Bishop as your man has been approved." That part, at least, was reasonably constructive. But from that point on things took a turn for the worse. "We don't want Elizabeth's name to be on this anthology of yours," she said. "That, to be frank, horrifies us. Can it be changed, even now? Can it be blotted out?" He said, if you want a public scandal, that's how to create one. "She could be followed," said Paul Topper, the new guy. "If I was told that Elizabeth was living with you I could find you in one or two weeks using one or two men." He tried to remain cool. He pointed out that when the protection started he had had a wife, whose name was very well known, whose picture had been on the front pages of every newspaper, and yet she had come and gone freely from his various bolt-holes, and the police had not thought it a problem. So now he had a fiancée whose name was not very widely known, whose photograph had never been published. It was unreasonable to turn her into a problem.

Then he said a whole lot more. He said, "All I am asking is that this British family be allowed to lead its life and raise its child." And he also said, "You can't ask people not to be the people they are and not to do the work they do. You can't expect Elizabeth not to put her name on her own work, and you must accept that our child is going to be born, and will grow up, and have friends, and go to school; he will have a right to a livable life."

"All this," Helen said, "is being discussed at very high levels of the Home Office."

On May 24, 1997, Ali Akbar Nateq-Nouri, the "official candidate" in the Iranian presidential election, was heavily defeated by the "moderate," "reform" candidate Mohammad Khatami. On CNN young Iranian women were demanding freedom of thought and a better future for their children. Would they get it? Would he? Would the new people in Iran and England finally solve the problem? Khatami seemed to be positioning himself as a Gorbachev figure, who could provide reform from within the existing system. That might well be inadequate, as *glasnost* and *perestroika* had been. He found it hard to be too excited about Khatami. There had been too many false dawns.

On Tuesday, May 27, Elizabeth went to see her gynecologist, Mr. Smith, at 4 P.M. As soon as she got home, around a quarter past six in the evening, very rapid contractions began. He alerted the protection team and grabbed the bag that had been packed and ready in their bedroom for over a week and they were driven to the Lindo Wing of St. Mary's Hospital, Paddington, where they were given an empty corner room, Room 407, which was, they were told, where Princess Diana had had both her babies. Labor progressed rapidly. Elizabeth wanted to try to do it without drugs, and, with her usual determination, managed it, though the demands of childbirth made her uncharacteristically cranky. Between contractions she ordered him to massage her back but the instant they began he wasn't allowed to touch her and she wanted him out of her field of vision. At one point she exclaimed comically at a midwife named Eileen, "Your perfume makes me sick, I hate it!" Eileen very sweetly and uncomplainingly went away to wash and change.

He looked at the time and suddenly thought, *He's going to be born at midnight.* But in the event the boy arrived eight minutes early. At eight minutes to midnight Milan Luca West Rushdie was born, seven pounds, nine ounces, with huge feet and hands, and a full head of hair. Labor had taken just five and a half hours from start to finish. This boy had wanted to get out, and here he was, slippery on his mother's stomach, the long grayish umbilical cord looped loosely around his neck and shoulders. His father took off his shirt and held him against his chest.

Welcome, Milan, he told his son. *This is the world, with all its joy and horror, and it waits for you. Be happy in it. Be lucky. You are our new love.*

Elizabeth called Carol and he called Zafar. The next day, Milan's first day of life, he was visited by his brother, and by his "extra uncles," Alan Yentob (who canceled his schedule at the BBC to come to the hospital) and Martin Amis, who came with Isabel, their daughter, Fernanda, and Martin's son Jacob. It was a sunny day.

The Special Branch officers were excited, too. "It's our first baby," they said. Nobody had ever become a parent before while under their protection. This was Milan's first "first": He was the "A" Squad Baby.

He had been helping Bill Buford put together a special "India issue" of *The New Yorker* and a special group photograph of Indian writers had been arranged. He found himself in an Islington studio with Vikram Seth, Vikram Chandra, Anita Desai, Kiran Desai, Arundhati Roy, Ardashir Vakil, Rohinton Mistry, Amit Chaudhuri, Amitav Ghosh, and Romesh Gunesekera (nobody was sure why a Sri Lankan writer had been included, but oh well, Romesh was a nice fellow and a good writer). The photographer was Max Vadukul and it wasn't an easy picture for him to take. As Bill wrote afterward, Vadukul had been "desperate to herd an edgy group into his frame. The results are illuminating. In the pile of pictures [Vadukul took] there are variations on a theme of muted panic. There are looks of self-consciousness, of curiosity, of giddiness." He himself remembered the group as pretty good-natured on the whole, even though Rohinton Mistry (mildly) and Ardu Vakil (more stridently) took Amit Chaudhuri to task for the stereotypical views about the Parsi community Amit had expressed in a review of one of Rohinton's books. Amit was the only one of the eleven writers who didn't come to the lunch afterward, at Granita restaurant on Upper Street, scene of the legendary Blair-Brown leadership pact. He told Bill afterward, "I realized I didn't belong in that group. Not my sort of people." Years later in an interview with Amitava Kumar, Arundhati Roy felt they hadn't been her sort of people either. She "chuckled," she told Kumar, when remembering that day: "I think everybody was being a bit spiky with everybody else. There were muted arguments, sulks, and mutterings. There was brittle politeness. Everybody was a little uncomfortable. . . . Anyway, I don't think anybody in that photograph felt they really belonged in the same 'group' as the next person." He remembered her as having been pretty friendly and happy to be there with the rest of them. But that was probably a mistake.

A few days after the photo session he went to the launch party for *The God of Small Things* because he had enjoyed meeting its author and wanted to help her celebrate her big moment. He found Miss Roy in an icier mood. That morning a review of her novel had appeared in *The New Yorker,* written by John Updike, and it was a largely positive review, not quite ten out of ten but eight and a half, perhaps. Anyway, an excellent review for a first novel in an important place, written by a giant of American letters. "Did you see it?" he asked her. "You must be very pleased." Miss Roy shrugged prettily. "Yes, I saw it," she said. "So what?" That was surprising and, in a way, impressive. But, "No, Arundhati, that's too cool," he told her. "A wonderful thing is happening to you. Your first novel is having a magnificent success. There is nothing quite like first success. You should enjoy it. Don't be so cool." She looked him straight in the eye. "I am pretty cool," she said, and turned away.

After an effusive introduction from her publisher, Stuart Proffitt, she gave a long, gloomy reading and Robert McCrum, who was happily recovering from his stroke, whispered, "Five out of ten." In the car home the protection officer Paul Topper said, "I'd been thinking of buying the book after her publisher's speech but then she read from it and I thought, perhaps not."

Elizabeth and Milan came home from the hospital and Caroline Michel came over, bringing "your second baby," the finished copy of the *Vintage Book of Indian Writing* (later published in the United States as *Mirrorwork*). Outside the bubble of the protection, the news of Milan's birth was breaking. The *Evening Standard* ran the story, including Milan's name. The police were still very worried about Elizabeth's name getting into the papers and were working hard to prevent it. For the time being her name did not appear. He was taken back to the spy fortress where Mr. Afternoon and Mr. Morning were worried about Elizabeth and Milan too. But, they said, a "specific threat" had been "disrupted." No more details. He remembered the *bloody great fist* and hoped it had done its work well. Did this mean he no longer had to worry about the assassination plan? "We didn't say that," Mr. Afternoon demurred. "There are still strong reasons for concern," Mr. Morning confirmed. *Can you tell me what those reasons are?* "No," said Mr. Afternoon. *I see. No, you say.* "That is correct," Mr. Morning said. "But the specific threat that we became aware of at the time of your Danish trip," Mr. Afternoon said, "that threat has been frustrated." *Oh, you mean there actually* was *a specific threat in Copenhagen?* "There was," said Mr. Afternoon. *Then why didn't you tell me?* "Source protection," said Mr. Morning. "We couldn't have you telling the media that you knew." Given the choice between protecting him and the source, the spies had chosen the source.

Meanwhile the *Daily Insult* was preparing to run stories about the increased cost to the nation of Milan's birth. (There was no such increase.) He braced himself for RUSHDIE BABY COSTS TAXPAYERS A FORTUNE. But a different story ran instead: RUSHDIE HOLDS BBC TO RANSOM. He was apparently prejudicing the *Midnight's Children* project by making ridiculously high financial demands. The figures quoted were more than double what he was being paid. He instructed his lawyers to pursue the *Insult,* and after some weeks its bosses caved in and apologized in print.

They went to Marylebone registry office and no sooner had they registered his birth and name than Elizabeth broke down completely because his surname was not hyphenated, not West-Rushdie but plain Rushdie. Only a day earlier she had told him how nice it was to tell everyone his name was Milan Rushdie, so he was caught completely off guard. They had discussed the question of the surname many times and had, he thought, agreed on it months ago. She now said she had suppressed her true feelings because "you wouldn't have liked it." For the rest of the day she was inconsolable and distraught. The next day was Friday the thirteenth and she was still angry, miserable, accusatory. "What a good job we are making of destroying the great happiness we have been given," he wrote in his journal. He was shaken and wretchedly upset. That so levelheaded a woman should have gone into so complete an emotional meltdown suggested that it was about much more than what it seemed to be about. This near-hysterical Elizabeth was not the woman he had known for seven years. All the uncertainty, fear and anxiety she had bottled up seemed to be pouring out of her. The missing hyphen was just a MacGuffin—the pretext that had unleashed the real, hidden story of how she felt.

She had a pinched nerve and was suddenly in great pain. She ignored all his pleas that she see a doctor until the pain got so bad that she literally couldn't move. Tension was crackling between them and he said, too sharply, "This is your way of dealing with pain. You tell anyone who wants to help you to shut up and get out of your sight." She shouted back at him, furious, "Are you going to criticize the way I gave birth?" *Oh, no, no,* he thought. *No, we shouldn't be doing this.* A serious rift had grown up between them just when they should have been closer than ever.

On Father's Day he was given a card: an outline of Zafar's hand, eighteen years old, and inside it an outline of Milan's hand, aged eighteen days. It became one of his most prized possessions. And after that Elizabeth and he made up their quarrel.

Zafar was eighteen years old. "My pride in this young fellow is absolute," he wrote in his journal. "He has grown into a fine, honest, brave young man. The essential sweetness with which he was born, his gentleness, his calm, that is still there, unscathed. He has a genuine gift for life. He has greeted Milan's birth with grace and, it seems, genuine interest. And we still have a relationship good enough for him to trust me with his private feelings—an intimacy my father and I failed to maintain. Will he earn his university place? His destiny is in his own hands. But at least he knows, has always known, that he is deeply loved. My adult son."

The birthday boy came over in the morning and was given his birthday present—a car radio—and a letter telling him of his father's pride in him, in his courage and grace. He read it and said, moved, "*That's* very nice."

He wrote and talked, argued and fought. Nothing changed. Well, the government did change. He had an excellent meeting with Derek Fatchett, now Robin Cook's understudy at the Foreign Office, and there was a big difference in mood from the old Tory days. "We will push the case hard," Fatchett promised, and he said he would help with the Indian travel ban, he would help with British Airways, he would, in general, help. Suddenly he felt the government was on his side. Who could say what a difference that might make? The new regime in Iran wasn't making promising noises. A birthday message came in from the new "moderate" president, Khatami: "Salman Rushdie will die soon."

Laurie Anderson had called to ask if he had a text about fire. She was curating an evening of performances to raise money to build a children's hospital for the charity War Child, and she had an amazing fire video and needed words to go with it. He edited together passages from the "London's burning" part of *The Satanic Verses*. Laurie had persuaded Brian Eno to record several loops of sound, which she was going to mix from a little desk in the wings while he read. There was no time to rehearse anything so he just went out on stage and started reading with the fire video flaming behind him and Laurie mixing the Enomusic, the sound swelling and fading without warning, and he had to ride those waves like a surfer or skateboard daredevil, his own voice rising and falling, gleaming the cube. It was one of the most enjoyable things he had ever done. Zafar came to watch him with a girl called Melissa, the first time he had heard his dad read, and afterward he said, "You stuttered a couple of times and you move around too much; it's distracting," but he seemed to have liked it, on the whole.

They had dinner at Antonia Fraser and Harold Pinter's house and Harold held Milan on his lap for a long time. Finally he handed him back to Elizabeth and said, "Tell him when he grows up that his Uncle Harold enjoyed his cuddle."

The boss of British Airways, Robert Ayling, went to speak at Zafar's school, and Zafar questioned him about his airline's refusal to fly his dad, and criticized and scolded him for several minutes. Afterward, when BA finally changed their no-fly policy, Ayling spoke of how moved he had been by Zafar's intervention. It was Zafar who softened the airline boss's heart.

Summer in America! As soon as Milan was old enough to fly they traveled to their annual weeks of summer freedom . . . on a British airline this time, a direct flight, and the three of them together! Virgin Atlantic had agreed to carry him, giving him a direct route to the United States. No more trips to Oslo, Vienna or Paris to catch a friendly plane. A brick fell out of the prison wall.

The Grobow house was welcoming, their friends were all around them—Martin and Isabel were in East Hampton, Ian McEwan and Annalena McAfee had rented a house in Sag Harbor, many other good people visited them from the city—and they had a new baby and a wedding to plan. This was their annual shot in the arm, the time that gave them the strength to survive the rest of the time. There were birds in the trees and deer in the woods and the sea was warm and Milan was two months old, as sweet and smiling and mischief-faced and miraculous as he could be. Everything was perfect except for one thing. Four days after they arrived he heard from Tristram Powell that the Indian government had refused to allow the BBC to film *Midnight's Children* on Indian soil. "It would be prudent to avoid the misapprehension," a government statement explained, "that we in any way endorsed the author." That statement engraved itself on his heart. "The producer, Chris Hall, is on his way to Sri Lanka to see if we can shoot there," Tristram said in his gentle way. "Everyone at the Beeb feels so much effort has been put in and the scripts are so good that they want to try to save it." But he felt sick at heart. India, his great love, had told him to fuck off because it didn't want to endorse him in any way. *Midnight's Children,* his love letter to India, had been deemed unfit to be filmed anywhere in that country. That summer he would be working on *The Ground Beneath Her Feet,* a novel about people without a sense of belonging, people who dreamed of leaving, not of home. He would use the way he felt now, dreadful, disconnected, spurned, as fuel for his book.

The story broke in the British press but he turned away from it. His friends were all around him and he was writing his book and soon he would be married to the woman he had loved for seven years. Bill Buford came to stay with his girlfriend, Mary Johnson, a sparky Betty Boop look-alike from Tennessee, and the Wylies and Martin and Isabel came around for a mighty barbecue cooked by Bill, who had become quite a chef. He took Elizabeth out for a pre-wedding date at the American Hotel in Sag Harbor. The avant-garde director Robert Wilson invited him to watch rehearsals of a new piece he was making, and wanted him to provide a text for it. He listened to Bob explain the piece for over half an hour and then had to admit he hadn't understood a word of what the great man had said. Robert McCrum came to stay for a night. Elizabeth spoke to the people at Loaves & Fishes, the outrageously expensive deli, and arranged the wedding food and drink. They went to the East Hampton town hall and got a wedding license. He bought himself a new suit. Zafar called from London with grand news: His A level results had been good enough to get him his place at Exeter University. Happiness and wedding plans cushioned the Indian blow.

Then, a second Indian rebuff. Bill Buford had been invited to the big New York celebration of the fiftieth anniversary of Indian independence to be held at the Indian consulate in Manhattan on independence day, August 15, 1997. He told the consulate folks that Mr. Rushdie was in town, but they backed away as if confronted by a rattlesnake. A woman called Bill and gave a stammering explanation. "In the light of everything surrounding him . . . we felt . . . not in his best interests . . . a very big event . . . lots of publicity . . . the consul-general can't . . . not in our best interests . . ." On India's fiftieth birthday, Saleem Sinai's birthday, Saleem's Cinderella creator would not go to the ball. He would not allow his love of the country and its people to be destroyed by Official India, he promised himself. Even if Official India never allowed him to set foot in his homeland again.

Again he took refuge in the good stuff. He went to the city for a few days and found Elizabeth a wedding present at Tiffany. He did interviews for the *Mirrorwork* anthology and went to hear David Byrne sing "Psycho Killer" at Roseland. He had dinner with Paul Auster and Siri Hustvedt. Paul was writing and directing a film called *Lulu on the Bridge* and wanted him to play a sinister interrogator who would give Harvey Keitel the third degree. (A sinister interrogator after Robbe-Grillet's offer of *un médecin assez sinistre:* Was this typecasting?) Zafar flew out to join him and they took the jitney back to Bridgehampton in hundred-degree heat. He got back to Little Noyac Path to find Elizabeth in a suspicious, mistrustful mood. What had he been up to in New York? Who had he been seeing? The damage done by his brief infidelity was still there. He didn't know what to do except to tell her he loved her. It made him fear for their marriage. But five minutes later she shrugged off her misgivings and said she was fine.

He went with Ian McEwan to get Thai takeout for dinner. At the restaurant, Chinda's, the Thai lady said, "You know who you rook rike, you rook rike that man who wrote that book." Yes, he admitted, that's me. "Oh good," she said. "I read that book, I rike it, then you wrote another book but I did not read. When you phone your order you order beef and we think, maybe it's Birry Joel, but no, Birry Joel he come on Tuesdays." At dinner Martin spoke of going off to visit Saul Bellow. He envied Martin this: his closeness to the greatest American novelist of their time. But he had bigger fish to fry. He was getting married in four days, and it was about to be the end of the world, or at least the world according to Arnold Schwarzenegger. The day after their wedding day, August 29, 1997, was used in *Terminator 2* as the date of "Judgment Day," the day the machines, guided by the supercomputer Skynet, launched their nuclear holocaust against the human race. So they were getting married on the last day in the history of the world as they knew it.

The weather was excellent and the field of cosmos was as brilliant as the sky. Their friends assembled at Isabel's family's compound and he went to fetch the judge. Then in a circle stood Paul and Siri and little Sophie Auster too, and Bill and Mary, and Martin and Isabel and the two Amis boys and Martin's daughter Delilah Seale and Isabel's sister Quina, and Ian and Annalena and the two McEwan boys, and Andrew and Camie and their daughter Erica Wylie, and Hitch and Carol and their daughter, his "ungoddaughter," Laura Antonia Blue Hitchens, and Isabel's mother, Betty Fonseca, and Betty's husband, Dick Cornuelle, in whose garden they were standing, and Milan cradled in Siri's arms, and Zafar, and Elizabeth with roses and lilies in her hair. There were readings. Bill read a Shakespeare sonnet, the usual one, and Paul unusually but thoughtfully read William Carlos Williams's "The Ivy Crown," about love that came later in life:

> At our age the imagination
>   across the sorry facts
>   lifts us
> to make roses
>   stand before thorns.
>   Sure
> love is cruel
>   and selfish
>   and totally obtuse—
> at least, blinded by the light,
>   young love is.
>   But we are older,
> I to love
>   and you to be loved,
>   we have,
> no matter how,
>   by our wills survived
>   to keep
> the jeweled prize
>   always
>   at our finger tips.
> We will it so
>   and so it is
>   past all accident.

They rejoiced that night in their seven years of improbable happiness, these two who had found each other in the middle of a hurricane and had clung to each other, not in fear of the storm but in delight at the finding. Her smile had brightened his days and her love his nights, and her courage and care had given him strength, and of course, as he confessed to her and all his friends in his wedding night speech, it had been he who had flung himself at her and not the other way around. (When he conceded this after seven years of insisting on the opposite she laughed out loud in astonishment.) And the world did not end, but began again the next day, refreshed, renewed, past all accident. *We are only mortal,* the poet said, *but being mortal / can defy our fate.*

> The business of love is
>   cruelty which,
> by our wills,
>   we transform
>   to live together.

And on the day on which the world continued Ian and Annalena got married too, at East Hampton town hall. They had planned a party on the beach, but the weather turned against them, so everyone came to Little Noyac Path and there were more wedding festivities all afternoon and evening. The day brightened and they played incompetent, un-American baseball in the field at the back of the house and then he and Ian went again to Chinda's for Thai takeout and he still wasn't Birry Joel.

The British papers got the story of his marriage at once—the East Hampton town hall staff had leaked the news almost as soon as the ceremony was complete—and all of them ran it, with Elizabeth's full name. So there she was, visible at last. For a moment she wobbled badly, then recovered and got used to it, as was her determined, sanguine way. As for himself, he felt relieved. He was very tired of "hiding."

That night, after a barbecue on Gibson Beach, they were at John

Avedon's house when David Rieff called to say that there had been a car crash in Paris and Princess Diana had been badly injured and her lover, Dodi al-Fayed, was dead. It was on all the TV channels but nothing substantive was being said about the princess. Later when they were going to bed he said to Elizabeth, "If she was alive they would have told us so. If they are not giving us news of her condition it's because she's dead." And in the morning there was the confirmation on the front of *The New York Times* and Elizabeth wept. All that day the story rolled out. The paparazzi chasing her on their motorbikes. The car going very fast, the drunk driver pushing it to 120 miles per hour. *That poor girl had no luck,* he thought. Her unhappy ending arrived just as happier beginnings had become possible. But to die because you didn't want your photograph taken, that was folly. If they had paused for a moment on the steps of the Ritz and let the paparazzi do their work maybe they would not have been pursued and it would have not been necessary to drive at that insane speed and die in a concrete underpass, wasting themselves for nothing.

He remembered J. G. Ballard's great novel *Crash* about the deadly mingling of love, death and automobiles and thought, maybe we are all responsible, our hunger for her image murdered her, and at the end, as she died, the last thing she saw would have been the phallic snouts of the cameras coming toward her through the smashed car windows, clicking, clicking. He was asked to write something for *The New Yorker* about the event and he sent them something of this nature and in England the *Daily Insult* called it a "Satanic version," in bad taste, as if the *Insult* had not been willing to pay a fortune for the photographs for which the paparazzi were chasing her, as if the *Insult* had the good taste not to publish the pictures of the wreck.

Milton and Patricia Grobow knew everything now; they had read about the wedding in the local papers. They were delighted, and "proud," and happy for the arrangement to continue in future years. Patricia had been the Kennedy children's nanny, she said, she was "used to being discreet." Milton was almost eighty and very frail. The Grobows said they might consider selling the Rushdies the house.

A few days after they got back to London he flew to Italy to take part in the Mantova literary festival, but nobody seemed to have cleared his visit with the local police, who barricaded him in his hotel and refused to allow him to attend the festival sessions. Finally, with many of the other writers as a sort of honor guard, he tried to repeat his Chilean trick by just walking out into the street, and was taken to the police station and held for several hours in a "waiting room" until the mayor and the police chief decided to avoid a scandal by allowing him to do what he had come to their town to do. After the weeks of ordinary life in the United States this return to European skittishness was dispiriting.

In London, the Labour home secretary, Jack Straw, always keen to ingratiate himself with his Islamic constituents, announced new legislation that would extend the archaic, obsolete, and fit-to-be-repealed blasphemy law to cover religions other than the Church of England, thus making it possible, among other things, for *The Satanic Verses* to be prosecuted again, and probably banned. So much for the "government of his friends" coming to power, he thought. Straw's attempt would eventually fail but the Blair government continued to try to find ways of making it illegal to criticize religion—i.e., Islam—for several years. At one point he went to the Home Office to protest against this, accompanied by Rowan Atkinson ("Mr. Bean Goes to Whitehall"). Rowan, in real life a quiet-spoken, thoughtful man, asked the faceless men and junior minister about satire. They were all his fans, of course, and wanted him to love them back, so they said, *Oh, comedy, we love it, satire, that's no problem at all.* He nodded lugubriously and said that recently, in a TV sketch, he had used footage of Muslims kneeling at Friday prayers in, he thought, Tehran, together with a voiceover that said, "And the search goes on for the ayatollah's contact lens." Would that be okay under the new law, he wanted to know, or would he in fact go to jail? Oh, yes, that would be *fine,* they told him, *completely* fine, no problem at all. Hmm, said Rowan, but how would he be able to be sure of that? It's easy, they answered, you'd just submit the script to a government department for approval, and *of course you'd get it,* and then you'd know. "Why," Rowan wondered mildly, "am I not reassured by that, I wonder." On the day this appalling bill came before the House of Commons for the final vote, the Labour whips, believing the revolt against it was so great that it was lost, told Tony Blair there was no need for him to stay until the votes were counted. So the prime minister went home and his bill failed *by one vote.* If he had stayed the votes would have been tied, and the Speaker would have cast his vote for the government as he was obliged to do, and the bill would have become the law of the land. It was that close a thing.

Life moved forward by small steps. Barry Moss, the head of Special Branch, came to see him to tell him that the new deal, under which he would employ Frank Bishop with Dennis Le Chevalier as backup, and the police would withdraw completely from the Bishop's Avenue house, had been approved. From January 1, 1998, his home would be his own, and he would be able to make all "private movements" by himself with Frank's help. He felt a great weight vanish from his shoulders. He, and Elizabeth and Milan, were about to have a private life in England, for the first time.

Frances D'Souza called to say that the much-feared Iranian minister of intelligence, Fallahian, had been replaced by a certain Mr. Najaf-Abadi, a supposed "liberal, pragmatic type." Well, let's just see, he replied.

Gail Rebuck agreed that Random House UK would take the Consortium paperback edition of *The Satanic Verses* into their warehouse immediately and put the Vintage colophon on it at the next reprint, which would probably be needed around Christmas. That was actually a very big step; the long-anticipated "normalization" of the novel's status in the United Kingdom, nine long years after it was first published.

Miss Arundhati Roy won the Booker Prize, as expected—she had been the odds-on favorite—and the next day she told *The Times* that his writing was merely "exotic" whereas hers was truthful. That was interesting, but he decided not to respond. Then news came from Germany that she had said much the same thing to a journalist there.

He called David Godwin, her agent, to say that he did not believe it would be a good thing for two Indian Booker winners to be seen attacking each other in public. He had never said publicly what he thought of *The God of Small Things,* but if she wanted a fight, she could certainly have one. No, no, David said, I'm sure she was misquoted. Soon afterward he received a mollifying message from Miss Roy that made the same claim. *Let it rest,* he thought, and moved on.

Günter Grass was seventy, and the Thalia Theater in Hamburg was planning a big celebration of his life and work. He flew to Hamburg with his new best friends, Lufthansa, and took part in the event along with Nadine Gordimer and just about every important German writer. After the public part of the evening was over there was music and dancing and he discovered that Grass was a great dancer. Every young woman at the after-party wanted to be twirled by him and Günter tirelessly waltzed, gavotted, polkaed and fox-trotted the night away. So now he had two reasons to envy the great man. He had always envied Grass's skill as an artist. How liberating it must be to finish a day's writing, walk over to an art studio and begin to work in a completely different way on the same themes! How great to be able to create one's own dust-jacket images! Grass's bronzes and etchings of rats, toads, flounders, eels, and boys with tin drums were things of beauty. But now there was his dancing to admire as well. It really was too much.

The Sri Lankan authorities were sounding positive about the BBC *Midnight's Children* project but, according to one of the BBC producers, Ruth Caleb, they were making it a condition of giving permission that he not attend the shoot. Okay, he said, nice to be so popular, and a few days later Tristram faxed him from Sri Lanka. "I am holding the permission document in my hand." That was a happy moment. But as things turned out, it was another in the long series of false dawns.

Milan was beginning to say, with great emphasis, "Ha! *Ha!* HA." When his parents said it back to him, he was delighted and said it again. Was this his first word—the word representing laughter, not just laughter itself? He looked desperate to speak. But of course it was much too early.

Elizabeth was going to see Carol for a few days and they had not made love since their wedding, not for many, many months. "I'm tired," she said, and then stayed up until 2 A.M. sticking wedding photos in an album. But things between them were good, mostly very good, and that thing, too, stopped being ungood soon enough. *The business of love is cruelty, which by our wills we transform to live together.*

When he looked back at the record he had made of his life, he understood that it was easier to make a note of an unpleasantness than a moment of felicity, easier to record a quarrel than a loving word. The truth was that for many years Elizabeth and he had got on easily and lovingly almost all the time. But not long after their marriage the ease and happiness began to diminish and the cracks to appear. "Trouble in a marriage," he later wrote, "is like monsoon water accumulating on a flat roof. You don't realize it's up there, but it gets heavier and heavier, until one day, with a great crash, the whole roof falls in on your head."

A woman named Flora Botsford was the BBC's Colombo correspondent, but it was her mischief-making that, in the opinion of the producer, Chris Hall, was "the thing that dished us." It was sometimes easy to believe that media people preferred things to go wrong, because EVERYTHING GOES WELL was not a catchy headline. Botsford's willingness, as a BBC employee, to stir up trouble for a major BBC production was surprising, or, more depressingly, not surprising. She took it upon herself to call a number of Sri Lankan Muslim MPs, looking for hostile quotes, and she found one, and one was all it took. Writing in *The Guardian*, Botsford began: "At the risk of offending local Muslims, the BBC is to film a controversial five-part serial of Salman Rushdie's book *Midnight's Children* in Sri Lanka, officials confirmed last week." Then her carefully unearthed MP had his moment of glory. "At least one Muslim politician in Sri Lanka is doing his best to put a stop to the project, raising the issue in parliament. 'Salman Rushdie is a very controversial figure,' said A. H. M. Azwar, an opposition MP. 'He has defiled and defamed the Holy Prophet, which is an unforgivable act. Muslims the world over detest even the mention of his name. There must be a strong reason for India to ban the film, and we should beware of raising communal feelings here.' "

The ripples spread quickly. In India there were many columns calling it a scandal that India had refused permission, but in Tehran the
Iranian Foreign Ministry called in the Sri Lankan ambassador to protest. Chris Hall had written permission to film from President Chan-
drika Bandaranaike Kumaratunga herself, and for a moment it seemed
the president might keep her word. But then a group of Sri Lankan
Muslim MPs demanded that she reverse her decision. Islamic attacks of
quite remarkable venom were launched against the author of *Midnight's Children* in the Sri Lankan media. He was a cowardly race traitor, and *Midnight's Children* was a book that insulted and ridiculed his
own people. A junior minister announced that permission to film had
been revoked, but was contradicted by his seniors. The deputy foreign
minister said, "Go ahead." The deputy defense minister guaranteed
"the full support of the military." However, the downward spiral had
begun. He could smell the approach of catastrophe, even though the
Foreign Ministry of Sri Lanka and the film production board both
confirmed that permission had been given to film. There was what
Chris Hall described as a boozy meeting of local intellectuals at the
BBC production office, and all of them were supportive. The Sri
Lankan press was almost uniformly behind the production too. But the
feeling of impending doom remained. One week later, permission to
film was revoked without any explanation, just six weeks after written
permission had been given by the president. The government was trying to pass politically tricky devolution legislation and needed the support of the small handful of Muslim MPs. Behind the scenes, Iran and
Saudi Arabia had threatened to expel their Sri Lankan workers if the
production went ahead.

There had been no public outcry against the production in either
India or Sri Lanka. But in both places, the project had been killed. He
felt as if somebody had just hit him very hard. "I must not fall down,"
he thought, but he was crushed.

Chris Hall remained convinced that Flora Botsford's article had lit
the fire. "The BBC did not serve you well," he said. President Kumaratunga wrote him a letter personally apologizing for the cancellation.
"I have read the book titled *Midnight's Children* and liked it very much.
I would have liked to see it as a film. However, sometimes political
considerations outweigh perhaps worthier causes. I hope there would

soon arrive a time in Sri Lanka when people would begin once again to think rationally and when the true and deeper values of life will prevail. Then my country will once again become the 'Serendib' it deserves to be." In 1999 she survived an assassination attempt by the Tamil Tigers, but was blinded in one eye.

The final act of the tale of the filming of *Midnight's Children,* the act with the happy ending, began eleven years later. In the fall of 2008 he was in Toronto for the publication of his novel *The Enchantress of Florence* and having dinner, on an evening off from book promotion, with his friend the film director Deepa Mehta. "The book of yours I'd really like to film," Deepa said, "is *Midnight's Children.* Who has the rights?" "As it happens," he replied, "I do." "Then can I do it?" she asked. "Yes," he said. He gave her an option for one dollar and for the next two years they worked on raising the money and writing a screenplay. The scripts he'd written for the BBC now looked wooden and stilted and he was actually glad they had never been filmed. The new screenplay felt properly cinematic and Deepa's instincts about the film were very close to his own. In January 2011 *Midnight's Children,* now a feature film, not a TV series, returned to India and Sri Lanka to film, and thirty years after the publication of the novel, fourteen years after the collapse of the BBC TV series, the film was finally made. On the day principal photography was completed in Colombo he felt as if a curse had been lifted. Another mountain had been climbed.

Halfway through the shoot the Iranians tried to stop it again. The Sri Lankan ambassador was hauled into the Foreign Ministry in Tehran to be told of Iran's displeasure about the project. For two days permission to film was again revoked. Again, they had a letter of permission from the president, but he feared that this president too would prove spineless under pressure. However, this time the outcome was different. The president told Deepa, "Go ahead and finish your film."

The film was finished, and scheduled for a 2012 release. What a cascade of emotions that bald sentence concealed. *Per ardua ad astra,* he thought. The thing had been done.

In mid-November 1997 John le Carré, one of the few writers who had spoken out against him when the attack on *The Satanic Verses* began, complained in *The Guardian* that he had been unjustly "smeared" and "tarred with the anti-Semitic brush" by Norman Rush in *The New York Times Book Review,* and described "the whole oppressive weight of political correctness" as a kind of McCarthyite movement in reverse.

He should have kept his feelings to himself, of course, but he couldn't resist replying. "It would be easier to sympathize with him," he wrote in a letter to the newspaper, "had he not been so ready to join in an earlier campaign of vilification against a fellow writer. In 1989, during the worst days of the Islamic attack on *The Satanic Verses,* le Carré rather pompously joined forces with my assailants. It would be gracious if he were to admit that he understands the nature of the Thought Police a little better now that, at least in his own opinion, he's the one in the line of fire."

Le Carré rose grandly to the bait: "Rushdie's way with the truth is as self-serving as ever," he replied. "I never joined his assailants. Nor did I take the easy path of proclaiming him to be a shining innocent. My position was that there is no law in life or nature that says great religions may be insulted with impunity. I wrote that there is no absolute standard of free speech in any society. I wrote that tolerance does not come at the same time, and in the same form, to all religions and cultures, and that Christian society too, until very recently, defined the limits of freedom by what was sacred. I wrote, and would write again today, that when it came to the further exploitation of Rushdie's work in paperback form, I was more concerned about the girl at Penguin Books who might get her hands blown off in the mailroom than I was about Rushdie's royalties. Anyone who had wished to read the book by then had ample access to it. My purpose was not to justify the persecution of Rushdie, which, like any decent person, I deplore, but to sound a less arrogant, less colonialist, and less self-righteous note than we were hearing from the safety of his admirers' camp."

By now *The Guardian* was enjoying the fight so much that it was running the letters on the front page. His reply to le Carré ran the next day: "John le Carré . . . claims not to have joined in the attack against me but also states that 'there is no law in life or nature that says great religions may be insulted with impunity.' A cursory examination of this lofty formulation reveals that (1) it takes the philistine, reductionist, radical Islamist line that *The Satanic Verses* was no more than an 'insult,' and (2) it suggests that anyone who displeases philistine, reductionist, radical Islamist folk loses his right to live in safety. . . . He says that he is more interested in safeguarding publishing staff than in my royalties. But it is precisely these people, my novel's publishers in some thirty countries, together with the staff of bookshops, who have most passionately supported and defended my right to publish. It is ignoble of le Carré to use them as an argument for censorship when they have so courageously stood up for freedom. John le Carré is right to say that free speech isn't absolute. We have the freedoms we fight for, and we lose those we don't defend. I'd always thought George Smiley knew that. His creator appears to have forgotten."

At this point, Christopher Hitchens joined the fray unbidden, and his reply would drive the spy novelist to greater heights of apoplexy. "John le Carré's conduct in your pages is like nothing so much as that of a man who, having relieved himself in his own hat, makes haste to clamp the brimming *chapeau* on his head," opined Hitch with his characteristic understatement. "He used to be evasive and euphemistic about the open solicitation of murder, for bounty, on the grounds that ayatollahs had feelings, too. Now he tells us that his prime concern was the safety of the girls in the mailroom. For good measure, he arbitrarily counterposes their security against Rushdie's royalties. May we take it, then, that he would have had no objection if *The Satanic Verses* had been written and published for free and distributed gratis from unattended stalls? This might have at least satisfied those who appear to believe that the defense of free expression should be free of cost and free of risk. As it happens, no mailroom girls have been injured in the course of eight years' defiance of the *fatwa*. And when the nervous book chains of North America briefly did withdraw *The Satanic Verses* on dubious grounds of 'security,' it was their staff unions who protested and who volunteered to stand next to plateglass windows in upholding the reader's right to buy and peruse any book. In le Carré's eyes, their brave decision was taken in 'safety' and was moreover blasphemous toward a great religion! Could we not have been spared this revelation of the contents of his hat—I mean head?"

The next day it was le Carré's turn: "Anyone reading yesterday's letters from Salman Rushdie and Christopher Hitchens might well ask himself into whose hands the great cause of free speech has fallen. Whether from Rushdie's throne or Hitchens's gutter, the message is the same: 'Our cause is absolute, it brooks no dissent or qualification; whoever questions it is by definition an ignorant, pompous, semi-literate unperson.' Rushdie sneers at my language and trashes a thoughtful and well-received speech I made to the Anglo-Israel Association, and which The Guardian saw fit to reprint. Hitchens portrays me as a buffoon who pours his own urine on his head. Two rabid ayatollahs could not have done a better job. But will the friendship last? I am amazed that Hitchens has put up with Rushdie's self-canonization for so long. Rushdie, so far as I can make out, does not deny the fact that he insulted a great religion. Instead he accuses me—note his pre-posterous language for a change—of taking the philistine reductionist radical Islamist line. I didn't know I was so clever. What I do know is, Rushdie took on a known enemy and screamed 'foul' when it acted in character. The pain he has had to endure is appalling, but it doesn't make a martyr of him, nor—much as he would like it to—does it sweep away all argument about the ambiguities of his participation in his own downfall."

In for a penny, in for a pound, he thought. "It's true I did call [le Carré] pompous, which I thought pretty mild in the circumstances. 'Ignorant' and 'semiliterate' are dunces' caps he has skillfully fitted on his own head. . . . Le Carré's habit of giving himself good reviews ('my thoughtful and well-received speech') was no doubt developed because, well, somebody has to write them. . . . I have no intention of repeating yet again my many explications of The Satanic Verses, a novel of which I remain extremely proud. A novel, Mr. le Carré, not a gibe. You know what a novel is, don't you, John?"

Oh, and so on. His letters, le Carré said, should be required read-ing for all British high school students as an example of "cultural in-tolerance masquerading as free speech." He wanted to bring the fight to an end but felt obliged to respond to the allegation of *taking on a known enemy and then screaming "foul."* "I presume our Hampstead hero would say the same to the many writers, journalists and intellectuals in and from Iran, Algeria, Egypt, Turkey and elsewhere, who are also battling against Islamism, and for a secularized society; in short, for freedom from the oppression of Great World Religions. For my part, I have tried, in these bad years, to draw attention to their plight. Some of the best of them—Farag Fouda, Tahar Djaout, Ugur Mumcu—have been murdered because of their willingness to 'take on a known enemy.' . . . I happen not to feel that priests and mullahs, let alone bombers and assassins, are the best people to set the limits of what it is possible to think."

Le Carré fell silent, but now his friend William Shawcross leaped into the ring. "Rushdie's claims are outrageous and . . . carry the stink of triumphalist self-righteousness." This was awkward, because Shawcross was the outgoing chairman of Article 19, which then had to write a letter distancing itself from his allegations. *The Guardian* was reluctant to let the story die and its editor, Alan Rusbridger, called to ask if he would like to reply to the Shawcross letter. "No," he told Rusbridger. "If le Carré wants to get his friends to do a little proxy whingeing, that's his business. I've said what I had to say."

Several journalists traced le Carré's hostility back to that old, bad review of *The Russia House,* but he was suddenly overcome with sadness about what had happened. The le Carré of *Tinker, Tailor, Soldier, Spy* and *The Spy Who Came in from the Cold* was a writer he had long admired. In happier times they had even shared a comradely stage on behalf of the Nicaragua Solidarity Campaign. He wondered if le Carré might respond positively if offered an olive branch. But Charlotte Cornwell, le Carré's sister, was expressing her rage to Pauline Melville, whom she ran into in a north London street—"Well! As for your friend!"—so maybe feelings in the Cornwell camp were running too high for a peace initiative to succeed just yet. But he regretted the fight, and felt that nobody "won" the argument. Both of them had lost.

Not long after this spat he was invited to Spy Central to address a bunch of British intelligence station chiefs, and the redoubtable Eliza Manningham-Buller of MI5, a woman who looked exactly like her name, halfway between Bertie Wooster's Aunt Dahlia and the queen, was furious about le Carré. "What does he think he's doing?" she demanded. "Does he understand nothing? Is he a complete fool?" "But," he asked Eliza, "wasn't he one of you lot back in the day?" Eliza Manningham-Buller was one of those rare and valuable women who could actually snort. "Hah!" she snorted, like a true Wodehouseian aunt. "I suppose he did work for us in some sort of minor capacity for about five minutes, but he never, my dear, reached the levels you've been talking to tonight, and let me tell you, after this business, he never will."

Eleven years later, in 2008, he read an interview with John le Carré in which his former adversary said of their old contretemps, "Perhaps I was wrong. If so, I was wrong for the right reasons."

He had written almost two hundred pages of *The Ground Beneath Her Feet* when Paul Auster's hopes of casting him in his film *Lulu on the Bridge* were dashed. The Teamsters union—"Can you imagine it, the big, tough Teamsters?" he mourned—declared themselves too scared to have Mr. Rushdie in the picture. They wanted more money, of course, danger money, but this was a shoestring operation and there wasn't any more money. Paul and his producer Peter Newman fought hard to make it happen, but in the end they had to admit defeat. "On the day I realized we couldn't do it," Paul told him, "I went into a room by myself and wept."

His part went at short notice to Willem Dafoe. Which was, at least, flattering.

He went to hear Edward Said speak at the offices of the *London Review of Books,* and a young man named Asad came up and confessed that in 1989 he was the leader of the Islamic Society in Coventry and had been the "West Midlands convener" of demonstrations against *The Satanic Verses.* "But it's all right," he burst out in embarrassment, "I'm an atheist now." Well, that was progress, he told Asad, but the young man had more to say. "And then recently," Asad cried, "I read your book, and I couldn't see what all the fuss was about!" "That's good," he replied, "but I should point out that you, who hadn't read the book, were the person organizing the fuss." He remembered the old

Chinese proverb, sometimes ascribed to Confucius: *If you sit by the river for long enough, the body of your enemy will float by.*

Milan was seven months old, smiling at everyone, babbling constantly, alert, good-natured, beautiful. A week before Christmas he began to crawl. The police were taking down their surveillance equipment and moving out. On New Year's Day, Frank Bishop came to work for him, and after a few weeks of "transition" they would have their home to themselves, and because of that both he and Elizabeth felt, in spite of all the year's disappointments, that it was ending well.

At the beginning of the year of the beginning of the end, when he closed the door for the last time on the four policemen who had lived with him under many different names and in many different places for the previous nine years, and thus brought to a close the period of round-the-clock protection that Will Wilson and Will Wilton had offered him in Lonsdale Square at the end of an earlier life, he asked himself if he was regaining freedom for himself and his family or signing everyone's death warrant. Was he the most irresponsible of men, or a realist with good instincts who wanted to rebuild, in private, a real private life? The answer could only be retrospective. In ten or twenty years he would know if his instincts had been right or wrong. Life was lived forward but was judged in reverse.

So, at the beginning of the year of the beginning of the end; and without knowing the future; and with a baby boy who was attending to the things that it was a baby's business to attend to, the business of sitting up by himself for the first time, straight-backed, the business of trying to pull himself up to a standing position in his crib, and failing, and trying again, until the day came when he ceased being a crawling thing and became *Homo erectus,* well on his way to being *sapiens;* and while the baby boy's older brother was going away on a gap year adventure in Mexico, where he would be arrested by policemen and watch whales at play and swim in pools below high waterfalls in Taxco and watch the fire-torch-bearing divers plunge off the cliffs of Acapulco and read Bukowski and Kerouac and meet his mother and go with her to Chichen Itza and Oaxaca and frighten his father by staying out of touch for alarmingly long periods, his father who could not help fearing the worst, who had silently feared for his son's safety ever since the day of the unanswered telephone calls and the wrongly identified house with the front door open nine years ago; a journey from which the eighteen-year-old boy would return so slim, so tanned, so handsome that when he rang the doorbell and his father saw him on the entry phone monitor screen he didn't recognize him, *Who's that?*, he cried in wonderment and then realized that this young god was his own child; while all the ordinariness of ordinary life continued, as it was right that it should continue, even in the midst of another, engulfing existence that continued to be extraordinary, the day came, on Monday, January 26, 1998, when they slept alone in their home, and instead of being scared by the silence around them, by the lack of security technology and the absence of large sleeping policemen, they could not stop smiling and went to bed early and slept like the dead; no, not the dead, like the happy, unencumbered living. And then at 3:45 A.M. he woke up and couldn't go back to sleep.

But the world's unkindness was never far away. "There is no question of Rushdie being allowed to visit India in the foreseeable future," said an Indian government official. The world had become a place in which his arrival in a land that he loved *could lead to a political crisis.* He thought of the boy Kay in Hans Christian Andersen's story *The Snow Queen* who has cold splinters of a devil's mirror in his eye and heart. His sadness was that splinter and he feared it would change his personality and make him see the world as a place full of hatefulness filled with people to scorn and loathe. Sometimes he met such people. At a birthday party for his friend Nigella he had just absorbed the unbearable news that her husband, John, had a new lump, and that the signs looked bad, when he was confronted by a journalist whose name he could not bring himself to write down even a dozen years later, who, having had perhaps a glass of wine too many, began to abuse him in language so extreme that in the end he had to leave Nigella's party. For days after that encounter he was unable to function, unable to write, unable to go into other rooms in which a man might come up to him and call him names, and he canceled engagements and stayed home and felt the splinter of the cold mirror in his heart. Two of his journalist friends, Jon Snow and Francis Wheen, told him that the same journalist had abused them too, and in very similar language, and because misery loved company he cheered up when he heard that. But for another week he was unable to work.

Maybe it was because he was losing faith in the world he was obliged to live in, or in his ability to find joy in it, that he introduced into his novel the idea of a parallel world, a world in which fictions were real while their creators didn't exist, in which Alexander Portnoy was real and not Philip Roth, in which Don Quixote had once lived but not Cervantes; and of a variant to that world in which Jesse Presley had been the twin that survived while Elvis died; in which Lou Reed was a woman and Laurie Anderson was a man. As he wrote the novel the act of inhabiting an imagined world seemed somehow nobler than the tawdry business of living in the real one. But down that road lay the madness of Don Quixote. He had never believed in the novel as a place to escape into. He must not begin to believe in escapist literature now. No, he would write about worlds in collision, about quarreling realities fighting for the same segment of space-time. It was an age in which incompatible realities frequently collided with one another, just as Otto Cone had said in *The Satanic Verses*. Israel and Palestine, for example. Also, the reality in which he was a decent, honorable man and a good writer had collided with another reality in which he was a devil creature and a worthless scribe. It was not clear that both realities could coexist. Maybe one of them would crowd the other one out.

It was the night of the "A" Squad party at Peelers, the Secret Policemen's Ball, and this year Tony Blair was there and the police brought them together. He spoke to the prime minister and made his pitch and Blair was friendly but noncommittal. After that Francis Wheen did him a great favor. He wrote a piece in *The Guardian* attacking Blair for his passivity in the Rushdie case, his refusal to stand beside the writer and show support. Almost at once there was a call from Fiona Millar, Cherie Blair's right-hand person, who sounded very apologetic and invited him and Elizabeth to dinner at Chequers on the ninth anniversary of the *fatwa*. And yes, it would be okay to bring Milan too, it would be an informal family-and-friends occasion. Milan, to celebrate his invitation, learned how to wave.

Dear Mr. Blair,

Thanks for dinner. And Chequers! Thanks for letting us have a look at it. Nelson's diary, Cromwell's death mask—I was a history student, so I liked all that. Elizabeth loves gardens so she was delighted by the beech trees etc. To me all trees are "trees" and all flowers are "flowers," but yeah, I liked the flowers and trees. I liked it, too, that the furnishings were just slightly faded, faintly genteel-dowdy, which made the place look like a house people actually lived in and not a small country-house hotel. I liked it that the staff were dressed up so much more smartly than the guests. I'd bet Margaret Thatcher never wore blue jeans when entertaining.

I remember meeting you and Cherie for dinner at Geoffrey Robertson's house not long after you became party leader. Boy, were you tense! I thought: Here's a fellow who knows that if he blows the next election his entire party may very well disappear down the plug-hole. Meanwhile, Cherie was relaxed, confident, cultured, every inch the successful QC with broad artistic interests. (This was the night you admitted you didn't go to the theater or read for pleasure.) Well, what a difference getting the job makes! At Chequers your grin was almost natural, your body language comfortable, your whole self at ease. Cherie, on the other hand, looked like a nervous wreck. As she showed us around the house—"and this of course is the famous Long Room, and here, do just have a look, is the famous blah, and hanging on that wall is the famous blah blah blah"—we got the feeling that she'd rather hang herself than do this good-wife second-fiddle châtelaine-of-Chequers shtick for the next five or ten years. It was as if you'd exchanged characters. So interesting.

And at dinner your family was delightful and Gordon Brown and his Sarah, and Alastair Campbell and his Fiona, very pleasant indeed. And Cameron Mackintosh! And Mick Hucknall! And Mick's hot girlfriend what's-her-name! We couldn't have asked for more. It cheered us up no end, I can tell you, because we'd had a bit of a tough day, Elizabeth and I, absorbing the annual felicities coming our way from Iran. Sanei of the Bounty offered a bonus if I was killed in the United States, "because everybody hates

America." And the chief prosecutor Morteza Moqtadaie announcing "the shedding of this man's blood is obligatory," and state-run Tehran radio speculating that "the destruction of this man's worthless life could breathe new life into Islam." A little upsetting, you know? I'm sure you can understand if my mood was a little off.

But I'm getting very fond, I must say, of Robin Cook and Derek Fatchett. It meant a lot on this unwished-for anniversary to hear the foreign secretary demand the end of the fatwa, demand that Iran open a dialogue about canceling it. There have been foreign secretaries, let me tell you!, who . . . but it's best not to dwell on the past. Just wanted to say I felt grateful for the new management and its willingness to battle religious fanaticism.

Oh, I hear you're both devoutly religious by the way, yourself and Cherie. Congratulations on doing a really excellent job of hiding that.

I remember one striking moment at dinner. Well, two. I remember you dandling little Milan on your knee. That was kind. And then, as I recall, you began to talk about freedom and I thought, I'm interested in that, so I turned away from Mick Hucknall's hot girlfriend to listen to you, and there you were talking about the freedom of the market as if that was what you meant by liberty, which couldn't have been true, because you're a Labour prime minister, aren't you?, so I must have misunderstood, or perhaps this was a New Labour thing, freedom = market freedom, a new concept, perhaps. Anyway, quite the surprise.

And then we were leaving and the staff were cooing over Milan and saying how nice it was for them to have little children in the house, because prime ministers had tended to be older and their children to be grown up, but now there was the frequent patter of the little feet of the younger Blairs and it brought the old house to life. We liked that, Elizabeth and I, and we liked seeing the enormous teddy bear in the front hall, a gift from a foreign head of state, the president, perhaps, of Darkest Peru, "What's it called," I asked, and Cherie said you hadn't thought of a name yet, and without pausing to think I said, "You should call it Tony Bear." Which I admit may not have been brilliant, but it was quick, at least, so perhaps it merited just a tiny smile?, but no, your face was stone and you said, "No, I don't think that's a good name at all," and I left thinking, Oh, no, the prime minister doesn't have a sense of humor.

But I didn't care. Your government was on my side and that meant the *small jarring notes could be ignored, and even later in your premiership, when the jarring notes became louder and more discordant and it really was hard not to pay attention to them, I always had a soft spot for you, I could never hate you the way so many people began to hate you, because you, or at least your Mr. Cook and Mr. Fatchett, set out sincerely to change my life for the better. And, in the end, they succeeded. Which may not quite cancel out the invasion of Iraq, but it weighed in my personal scales, that's for sure.*

Thanks again for a lovely evening.

On the day after the Chequers dinner—the day the news of it was released—Iran announced that it was "surprised" by Robin Cook's call for the end of the *fatwa*. "It will last for ten thousand years," the Iranian statement asserted, and he thought, *Well, if I get to live for ten thousand years, that will do just fine.*

And on the day after that, in the Ambassadors Waiting Room at the Foreign Office, he and Robin Cook stood side by side and faced the press and photographers, and Cook made a number of tough, uncompromising remarks, and another loud, clear message was sent to the Khatami government in Iran. His protection officer Keith Williams murmured to him as they left the building, "They've done you proud, sir."

The newly assertive British government position seemed to be having some effect.

Mary Robinson, the ex-president of Ireland and the new UN commissioner for human rights, went to Tehran and met high-ranking officials and announced after her visit that Iran "in no way supported" carrying out the *fatwa*. The UN special *rapporteur* on Iran was told there "might be some progress possible on the *fatwa*." And Italy's foreign minister, Lamberto Dini, met with his Iranian counterpart, Kamal Kharrazi, and was told that Iran was "completely prepared to cooperate with Europe to solve existing political problems."

Now they had a family home. One of the policemen's bedrooms was being turned into Milan's room, and their "living room," where the furniture was all but worn out, could be a playroom, and then there were two spare bedrooms. "If the house is blown it will be a huge problem," they were constantly told, but the truth was this: *The house was never blown.* It never became known, never got into the newspapers, never became a security problem, never required the threatened "colossal" expenditure on security equipment and man-hours. That didn't happen, and one of the reasons, he came to believe, was the good nature of ordinary people. He remained certain that the builders who had worked on the house knew whose house they were working on, and didn't buy the "Joseph Anton" story; and not long after the police moved out and Frank started working for him there was a problem with the garage door—a suspiciously heavy wooden door with steel plating hidden inside, whose weight meant its opening mechanism often developed a fault—and the company that had installed the door sent a mechanic over, who chattily said to Frank as he went to work, "You know whose house this used to be, don't you? It was that Mr. Rushdie. Poor bastard." So people had known who "shouldn't" have known. But nobody gossiped, nobody went to the papers. Everyone knew it was serious. Nobody talked.

And for the first time in nine years he had a "dedicated team" of protection officers for his "public" adventures (meals in restaurants, walks on Hampstead Heath, the occasional movie, and every so often a literary event—a reading, a book signing, a lecture). Bob Lowe and Bernie Lindsey, the handsome devils who became the heartthrobs of the London literary scene, alternating with Charles Richards and Keith Williams, who didn't. And the OFDs, Russell and Nigel alternating with Ian and Paul. These officers were not just "dedicated" in the sense of working only on Malachite and on no other prot. They were also committed to his cause, totally on his side, ready to fight his battles. "We all admire your endurance," Bob told him. "We really do." They took the view that there was no reason why he shouldn't have as rich a life as he wanted to have, and that it was their job to make it possible. They persuaded the security chiefs of several reluctant airlines, who had been put off by the continued British Airways refusal to fly him, that they should not follow BA's lead. They wanted his life to get better, and they were ready to help. He would never forget, or cease to value, their friendship and support.

They remained on their guard. Paul Topper, the team's supervisor at the Yard, said that intelligence reports indicated "activity." It was not a time to be careless.

There was some sad news: Phil Pitt—the officer known to his colleagues as "Rambo"—had been forced into retirement by a degenerative disease of the spine, and might end up in a wheelchair. There was something very shocking about the fall of one of these large, fit, strong, active men. And these men were professional protectors. It was their job to make sure other people were all right. They weren't supposed to crumble. It was the wrong way around.

Elizabeth wanted another child, and she wanted it right away. His heart sank. Milan was such a great gift, such a great joy, but he did not want to take any more spins on the roulette wheel of genetics. He had two beautiful sons and they were more than enough. But Elizabeth was a determined woman when there was something she really wanted—one might even use the word "mulish"—and he feared he would lose her, and with her Milan, if he refused. His own need was not for another baby. It was for freedom. That need might never be met.

This time she conceived quickly, while she was still breast-feeding Milan. But this time they were not lucky. Two weeks after the pregnancy was confirmed the chromosomal tragedy of the early miscarriage occurred.

After the miscarriage Elizabeth turned away from him and devoted herself exclusively to little Milan. A nanny was found, Susan, the daughter of a Special Branch officer, but she resisted employing her. "I just want someone for an hour or two a day," she said. "Just a bit of child-minding help."

Their lives became very separate. She didn't even want to travel in the same car as him, preferring to be in her own car with the baby. He hardly saw her during the day and in the big empty house he felt his life becoming empty too. Sometimes they had an omelet together at around 10 P.M. and then she was "too tired to stay awake," while he was too wakeful to sleep. She didn't want to go anywhere with him, do anything with him, spend the evening with him, and she grew resentful if he suggested going out without her. So the imprisonment-by-baby continued. "I want two more children," she said flatly. There wasn't much more conversation than that.

Their friends began to notice the growing distance between them. "She never looks at you anymore," Caroline Michel said, worried. "She never touches you. What's the matter?" But he didn't want to say what the matter was.

Milan began to walk. He was ten and a half months old.

Random House took the paperback of *The Satanic Verses* into their warehouse, and at once the British press did its best to stir things up. *The Guardian* ran a provocative front-page story suggesting that Random House's decision would "revive" the trouble, and at once it did revive. The *Evening Standard* threatened to run a piece saying that Random House had gone ahead without taking police advice. Dick Stark called them to say that that was incorrect, so instead the paper threatened a story saying that Random House had published *in spite of* police advice. Dick Stark checked with the men in the Christmas tree fortress and they said there was "minimal" risk, which reassured Gail Rebuck. Andrew, Gillon and he had kept the Consortium paperback edition in print for five years now, so this change of warehousing arrangements should not have been news. Paperback publication had been "normalized" across Europe and in Canada and even in the United States, where Henry Holt's Owl imprint had taken over distribution without any trouble. But a few hostile news stories might make the British experience very different. Random House and the Special Branch worked hard to reassure the *Standard* and in the end its story did not run. And in *The Telegraph* there was a balanced, measured, wholly sensible piece. The risk diminished. However, Random House brought bomb scanners into their mailroom and warned their staff. All the senior executives were still worried about the press stirring up a big Islamist reaction. But to their great credit they were readying themselves to reprint and to issue the Vintage edition. "I'm sure the worst thing we can do is flinch or delay," said Simon Master. "If we have a good weekend, we'll print." In Russia the publishers of *The Satanic Verses* were being threatened by local Muslims. That was alarming. But as things turned out, nothing happened in England, and at long last paperback publication of *The Satanic Verses* was taken over by Vintage Books, and normal service was resumed. The Consortium was dissolved.

There were some more small, good things. Gloria B. Anderson of the *New York Times* syndication department came back four years after her bosses had prevented her from following through on her offer to give him a syndicated column to say that this time everyone was very keen that he should write for the paper. There was nothing to be gained by bearing a grudge. This was *The New York Times,* and it would give him a monthly platform all around the world. And it would probably pay for Whispering Frank and Beryl the cleaning lady and maybe a nanny too.

His niece Mishka, a pale, stick-thin little girl of six, had been revealing astonishing musical gifts in a largely tone-deaf family. Now the Purcell School and the Menuhin School were fighting over her. Sameen chose the Purcell because Mishka was not just a musical virtuoso, she was years ahead of her age group academically as well, and the Purcell was better at providing their students with a good general education. The Menuhin was a one-track-minded musical hothouse. Mishka's extraordinary precocity came at a price. She was too bright for her own age group and too young for her academic equals, so it was and would be a lonely childhood. But she had knocked them flat at the Purcell and Menuhin and already at her tender age it was clear that this, a life in music, was what she wanted. One day in the family car when her parents were arguing out the pros and cons of the two schools, little Mishka piped up from the backseat, "Shouldn't that be my decision?"

The Purcell School told Sameen that Mishka was exceptionally gifted, and that they would be privileged to have her. She could start in September, because they were not insured to teach students younger than that, and she would be the youngest person ever to be given a full scholarship at the school. High excitement! A bright new star was rising in the family and they would have to protect and guide her until she was old enough to shine by herself.

He was awarded the Budapest Grand Prize for Literature and went to receive it. In Budapest the mayor, Gábor Demszky, who had been a leading publisher of samizdat texts during the Soviet era, opened up the glass-fronted cabinet in his office to reveal the precious books, formerly illegal, which were now the emblems of his greatest pride. They had been printed on a portable printing press from Huddersfield that they moved secretly from apartment to apartment at night to prevent it from falling into the wrong hands; a machine so important that they never mentioned it in conversation, using a woman's name instead. "Huddersfield was an important part of the fight against Communism," Demszky said. Then they got onto the mayoral motorboat and zoomed up and down the Danube at speed. The grand prize itself was a surprise: a small engraved metal box that, when opened, was filled with crisp new U.S. dollars. Very useful.

Zafar went to do an Italian course in Florence, and was very happy. There were several new girls in his life, an opera singer with whom he broke up "because she suddenly began to remind me of my mum," and a tall, somewhat older blonde. Evie was now his best friend and he had grown so close to her family the Daltons that his mother and father were sometimes almost jealous of them. But Zafar was having a ball, planning excursions to Siena, Pisa, and Fiesole. He had not had the easiest of childhoods and it was a fine thing to see him growing up into this great fellow, so full of confidence, stretching his wings.

Harold Pinter and Antonia Fraser came to dinner at Bishop's Avenue. Robert McCrum, a little slower than he used to be, with a sweet, vague smile on his face, and his wife, Sarah Lyall, were the other guests, and when Harold discovered that Robert worked for the *Observer*, with which he had some unmemorable political quarrel, and that Sarah worked for the hated, because American, *New York Times*, he launched into one of his loudest, longest, least attractive bouts of Pintering.

Dear Harold,

You know my admiration for you and, I hope, that I value our friendship highly; but I can't let the events of last night pass unremarked upon. Robert, a good man bravely fighting back from a stroke, is simply not able to speak and argue as freely as he once did, and retreated under your assault into a miserable silence. Sarah, whom I like very much, was almost reduced to tears and, worse, amazed to find herself in the position of defending U.S. Zionism-imperialism as embodied by The New York Times. Elizabeth and I both felt that our hospitality had been abused and our evening ruined. The grand slam, in fact. I can't help saying that I mind very much about all this. It happens all the time, and as your friend I must ask you to STOP IT. On Cuba, on East Timor, on so many issues you are much more right than wrong, but these tirades—when you appear to assume that others have failed to notice the offenses that outrage you—are just plain tiresome. I think you owe us all an apology.

With much love, Salman

Dear Salman,

Your letter was very painful for me to read but I am grateful to you for it. You write as a true friend. What you say is absolutely true and in this case the truth is bitter. There is no justification for my behavior and I have no defense. I can only say this: I hear myself bullying and boring but it's like a St. Vitus' dance, a fever, an appalling sickening—and of course drunken—descent into incoherence and insult. Lamentable. Your letter was really a whip of iced water and has had a great effect on me. I have to believe it's not too late for me to grow up. I do send heartfelt apologies to you and Elizabeth. I care for you both so much. I have written to the McCrums.

With my love, Harold.

Dear Harold,

Thank you for your letter. We love you very much. Water under the bridge.

Salman

———

The day after Milan's first birthday they flew to America to spend three months—*Three months!* It would be their longest stretch of freedom—in the house on Little Noyac Path. It was a year since they had been at John Avedon's house and heard about Diana's death and then there had been the global phenomenon of her death and the miracle of the flowers and so on and now he was back in Bridgehampton with his imaginary Ormus and Vina and the ground was opening up beneath Vina's feet and she was swallowed by the earth and turned into a global phenomenon, too. He was approaching the end of his novel, finishing the chapter "Beneath Her Feet" and writing the chapter "Vina Divina" and of course Diana's dying had affected Vina's and it felt right that he wrote this passage in the place where he'd been when he heard the news. He wrote a song for Ormus, the song Ormus wrote for her, his Orphic hymn to lost love, *what I worshipped stole my love away, it was the ground beneath her feet,* and pressed on toward the Lennonesque end of his unending book

In the months that followed the book was completed, revised, polished, printed, and given to others to read. On the day he finished working on it, in the little study up its own staircase that had become his summer aerie, he made himself a promise. *The Ground Beneath Her Feet* was one of his three really long books, along with *The Satanic Verses* and *Midnight's Children*. "No more 250,000-word monsters," he told himself. "Shorter books, more often." For more than a decade he kept that promise, writing two short and two medium-length novels between 2000 and 2009. Then he got to work on his memoir, and realized that he had fallen off the wagon.

It was the Summer of Monica and it was not clear that President Clinton would survive the attempt to impeach him. Dreadful black-comic jokes were circulating.

The stains on the dress couldn't provide an incontestable ID because everyone from Arkansas has the same DNA.

"Happiness writes white," Henry de Montherlant wrote. "It doesn't show up on the page." Happiness that summer was a low white house surrounded by green fields amid hills and woods, and walking with Elizabeth and his sons on the beach in the late afternoon as the sun fell low in the sky and a haze obscured the horizon. It was going to the copy shop near Bridgehampton Commons and waiting while copies of his novel were made. "You can come back later," the woman in the store told him, but he waited. It was a first wedding anniversary dinner with Elizabeth in Sag Harbor at the American Hotel. It was a trip to Yankee Stadium with Don DeLillo to watch the Yanks play the Angels, even if they did lose the game. And it was a letter from his new editor, Michael Naumann at Henry Holt, that spoke of *The Ground Beneath Her Feet* in language so exalted that he couldn't quote it to anyone. Just six days after this letter arrived, however, Michael Naumann resigned from Holt and went off to be the new German minister of culture. *Oh well,* he thought. It was still a wonderful letter.

Nigella called from London. John's cancer was definitely back. He had to have a large section of his tongue removed. John Diamond, one of the most articulate, quickest-witted, funniest, most verbal men he had ever met, deprived of the power of speech. That was a sad, bad thing.

And Susan Sontag had cancer too.

They returned to London and as usual it was like walking into a closed door. The National Theatre's production of *Haroun and the Sea of Stories* was in rehearsal, but the police said it would be too dangerous for him to go to the opening night because "the enemy would expect you to be there," and it would necessitate a police operation of immense magnitude and expense. So, at once, he went back to war. He was taken to the spies' Christmas tree fortress and Mr. Morning and Mr. Afternoon told him that no, there was no evidence of any specific activity, but yes, the threat assessment remained as high as ever. On September 22, 1998, he had a clear-the-air meeting with Helen Hammington's successor, Bob Blake, and Blake conceded that his desire to be at the opening of *Haroun* was natural, and that the risk attached wasn't really very great.

The boss of British Airways, Bob Ayling, had finally agreed to see him. He talked about his encounter with Zafar and how deeply it had moved him. A crack appeared in the closed door. He went to Clarissa's house on Burma Road after a long time. Zafar was having a party to celebrate the imminent beginning of his life as a university student at Exeter. His son was delighted to hear what Ayling had said, to feel that he had helped his father. And then, that evening, the television, radio and telephone all went insane.

CNN broke the story. President Khatami of Iran had declared the death threat "over." After that he was on the phone all night. Christiane Amanpour told him that she was "certain that it's happening," and that she had off-the-record quotes from Khatami that more would happen soon, and that he had reached a "consensus" with Khamenei about it. At 9:30 P.M. "his" new man at the Foreign Office, Neil Crompton, called and asked for a meeting at 10:30 the next morning. "Something's clearly happening," he said. "It's probably good news. Let's put our heads together."

At the Foreign Office there was a feeling of mounting excitement. "Okay," he said, "but we must have unequivocal language on the *fatwa* and the bounty. The British government must be able to make a clear statement that it's over. Otherwise we'll be letting Iran off the hook and allowing a deniable hit by hard-liners or Hezbollah. If it's good news then Mr. Blair should say so. Their top man is speaking, and so ours should as well." The UN General Assembly was in session in New York. British and Iranian officials were meeting that afternoon to discuss the case. The two foreign ministers, Robin Cook and Kamal Kharrazi, were to meet the next morning. It seemed that Iran really wanted to make a deal.

Robin Cook called him at 9 A.M. on the twenty-fourth—four A.M. in New York!—and told him what he thought could be achieved. "We'll get a guarantee, but the *fatwa* will not be formally revoked, because they say it can't be now that Khomeini is dead. There seems to be no hard-liner activity in Iran. This is the best deal we're likely to get. This is the strongest language we've ever heard from them." So here he was at last between the rock and the hard place. The bounty and *fatwa* would stay but the Iranian government would "dissociate" itself from them, and "neither encourage nor permit" anyone to carry out the threat. Robert Fisk in *The Independent* was saying that this was no longer a matter of interest in Iran. Was that true? In the best-case scenario, Cook was right, the Iranians were making a genuine commitment and really wanted to put this matter behind them, to draw a line under it, and the British government, too, would be putting its prestige on the line by accepting the deal, and any betrayal of that deal would make both sides look foolish. The main threat to his life had always come from the MOIS, the Iranian Ministry of Intelligence and Security, and if they were being "stood down" then that was something Mr. Afternoon and Mr. Morning could presumably confirm. And a high-profile public agreement would make everyone *feel* that the story was over. De facto would lead to de jure.

And in the worst-case scenario, the hard-liners would go on trying to kill him, and, once his protection had been withdrawn, they would succeed.

That afternoon at 4 P.M. he met Frances D'Souza and Carmel Bedford at the Article 19 offices in Islington, and all three of them were very worried. The deal sounded inadequate, not enough was being offered, but if he did not react positively he could be portrayed as obstructive, while if he did then the defense campaign would lose all bargaining power. His only hope, he told Frances and Carmel, was that both governments' credibility rested on the deal.

The three of them went to the Foreign Office to meet Derek Fatchett at 5:20 P.M. He had always liked Fatchett, a decent, straightforward man, and now Fatchett was looking him in the eye and saying, "The deal is genuine, the Iranians are committed, all segments of the leadership have agreed. I'm asking you to trust the British government. You should know that Neil Crompton and his colleagues here at the FCO have been negotiating this for months, being as tough as they can. They are all sure that Iran is serious." "Why should I believe it?" he asked Fatchett. "If they aren't canceling anything, why shouldn't I conclude that this is all bullshit?" "Because," Fatchett said, "in Iran nobody bullshits about the Rushdie case. These politicians are risking their careers. They would not do it unless they were certain of support from the highest level." Khatami had just returned to Tehran from the general assembly, where he had declared that "the Salman Rushdie issue was completely finished," and was greeted and embraced at the airport by Khamenei's personal representative. That was a meaningful sign.

He asked about the security briefing he'd just had from Mr. Morning and Mr. Afternoon, in which he had been told there was no reduction in the threat to his life. "That's out of date," Fatchett said. He asked about Hezbollah in Lebanon and Fatchett said, "They aren't involved." He went on asking questions for a while and then suddenly something opened up inside him, a great emotion welled up, and he said, "Okay." He said, "In that case, hurray, and thank you, thank you all, from the bottom of my heart." The tears rose and the huge emotion silenced him. He hugged Frances and Carmel. The TV was turned on and there were Cook and Kharrazi side by side in New York, live on Sky News, announcing the *fatwa*'s end. He sat in Fatchett's office in the Foreign Office and watched the British government do its level best to save his life. Then he went outside with Derek Fatchett and the cameras were waiting and he went up to them and said, "It seems it's over." "What does it mean for you," asked the nice young woman holding the microphone. "It means everything," he said, choking back the tears. "It means freedom."

When he was in the car Robin Cook called from New York and he thanked him too. Even the police were moved. "It's very exciting," said Bob Lowe. "A historic moment."

At home it took Elizabeth time to believe it but gradually the mood of rejoicing grew. Martin Bache, one of her oldest friends from her college days, was there, and Pauline Melville rushed over, so they each had one of their closest people with them, which felt right. And Zafar was there, more visibly moved than his father had ever seen him. And there was the phone, the phone. So many friends and well-wishers. William Nygaard called; perhaps the most important call of all. Andrew, weeping. He called Gillon to thank him too. He called Clarissa to thank her for her care of Zafar during these long hard years. One after another his friends telephoned. *The ceremonies of joy*, he thought. The day he had never expected had come. And yes, it was a victory, it had been about something important, not just his life. It had been a fight for things that mattered and they had prevailed, all of them, together.

He called Christiane Amanpour and gave her a quote. Everyone else would have to wait for the press conference the next day.

And if he had been living in a fairy tale he would have gone to bed and woken up a free man and the clouds would have been banished from the sky and he and his wife and children would have lived happily ever after.

He was not living in a fairy tale.

There are some people for whom this cannot be a great day. I would like to particularly think of the family of Professor Hitoshi Igarashi, the Japanese translator of The Satanic Verses, *who was murdered. I would like to think about the Italian translator, Dr. Ettore Capriolo, who was knifed and happily recovered; and my distinguished Norwegian publisher, William Nygaard, who took a number of bullets in his back and mercifully has made a full recovery. Let us not forget that this has been a dreadful event, a dreadful event, and I would like to say also how sorrowful I feel about all the people who died in demonstrations, particularly in the subcontinent of India. It's emerged that in many cases they didn't even know who they were demonstrating against or why and that was a shocking and terrible waste of life and I regret that equally with everything else that happened.*

The reason we're here is to recognize the end of a terrorist threat by the government of one country against the citizens of other countries and that is a great moment and we should recognize it as such. The reason why we have been able to fight this campaign, why so many people created defense committees around the world, the reason why this issue has been kept alive is not just that somebody's life was in danger—because the world is full of people whose lives are in danger—the reason is that some incredibly important things were being fought for here: the art of the novel, and beyond that, the freedom of the imagination and the overwhelming, overarching issue of freedom of speech, and the right of human beings to walk down the streets of their own countries without fear. Many of us who were not politicians by inclination have been prepared to become political animals and fight this fight because it was worth fighting, not just for myself, not just to save my skin, but because it represented many things in the world that we most care about.

I don't think it's a moment to feel anything except a serious and grave satisfaction that one of the great principles of free societies has been defended.

I'd like to thank all the people who have helped in that fight. Frances and Carmel and Article 19 and the defense committees in the United States, Scandinavia, Holland, France, Germany and elsewhere have been essential. This is a fight which ordinary people have fought. At the end of it there has been a political negotiation which has resulted in this happy ending. But the struggle succeeded because of ordinary people readers, writers, booksellers, publishers, translators and citizens. It is everybody's day, not just my day. I think we should just recognize that behind the issues of terrorism and security and Special Branch protection and how much it costs and all that, there is this fundamental thing that we have tried to defend, and it has been a privilege to be allowed to defend it.

He spoke without notes, extempore, to the press thronging the Article 19 offices and he also thanked Elizabeth and Zafar for their love and support. He was filmed walking down Upper Street in Islington by himself, a "free man," and he lifted a sheepish, doubtful fist into the air. Then there was a day of interviews. He got home thinking that the day had gone well and found waiting for him an editorial in the *Evening Standard* describing him as a social irritant and a nasty piece of work. And on the BBC and ITN news programs the angle was "No apology." That was the British media's spin on the day's events. This social irritant and nasty piece of work had refused, after everything, to apologize for his awful book.

That Sunday he took Zafar to Exeter University, and Elizabeth and Clarissa came too. As Zafar entered his room in Lopes Hall his face fell and misery overcame him. They tried to give him comfort and support but soon it was time to leave. It was a hard moment for Clarissa. "He doesn't need us anymore," she said, and had to lower her head to hide her tears. "But he does," he told her. "He isn't going anywhere. He loves us both and will stick around. He is just growing up."

They got back to London late to find that the "no apology" British TV stories had been translated in Iran as "insulting remarks," and here was the Iranian ambassador-elect Muhammadi restating the *fatwa* and the Iranian papers were calling for him to be murdered and saying that if he believed himself safe he would just be easier to kill. Had he been sold out, he wondered, and at the same time knew that he had to continue to free himself of the shackles of security, even if that did make him easier to assassinate.

Two days later he was back at Spy Central for a joint meeting between Mr. Morning and Mr. Afternoon representing the security services, a certain Michael Axworthy representing the Foreign Office, and himself. To his horror Mr. Afternoon and Mr. Morning both said that they could not guarantee his safety from either the Iranian Revolutionary Guards (the feared *pasdaran,* the ruthless "protectors" of the Islamic revolution), or the proxy killers of the Lebanon Hezbollah, and as a result they refused to reduce the level-two threat assessment. These were issues on which he had specifically pressed Derek Fatchett and had been given categorical guarantees, Fatchett even saying that the security services' information was out of date. It became clear that the security services, as well as Scotland Yard, were furious with the Foreign Office for rushing into a settlement. They said it would take them until Christmas at least to verify the Iranian position and there was no guarantee that they would come up with a good result.

It was at this point that he began to shout at Michael Axworthy, who began to sweat and shake. He had been lied to, he yelled, he had been given the lie direct, and the Foreign Office was full of tricksters and duplicitous bastards. Axworthy left the room to make a call and returned to say, with commendable self-control, that Robin Cook would call him the next day at 11:40 A.M. exactly.

Then a meeting at Scotland Yard at which there was much police sympathy for his anger. Richard Bones, the Special Branch officer who had been at the meeting with the intelligence scervices, sitting quietly in the background, said, "You've been treated terribly. Your analysis is spot-on. I will bear witness for you if you ever need it." The police agreed that they would continue his protection as before until the situation had been clarified. And as he calmed down it did occur to him that things in Iran might settle down after the initial shock of the deal. So far the senior mullahs had not condemned the agreement. Maybe he just needed to give it time, and by Christmas he would be free.

In the morning Robin Cook called to reassure him of the government's commitment to making sure the problem was solved. "I'm disappointed in the security analysis you were given," he said. "I've asked for an SIS reading by the end of the week." Cook agreed with him that there could, should, be a positive result by Christmas: in three months' time.

More than three years would elapse before Mr. Morning and Mr. Afternoon started feeling positive.

The backlash against the Cook-Kharrazi declaration became more and more severe. Half the Iranian Majlis signed a petition calling for the *fatwa* to be carried out. A mysterious new group of "radical students" offered a new £190,000 bounty for his death. (This turned out to be an error; the actual figure was £19,000.) The Khordad *bonyad*, or foundation, run by Sanei of the Bounty increased its offer by about $300,000. The Iranian *chargé d'affaires*, Ansari, was brought into the Foreign Office to receive a British protest, and blamed British press coverage and statements by British ministers and by Rushdie, which had "put the ministry of foreign affairs in Tehran under a lot of pressure—they hadn't expected the news to be so big." But he did renew Iran's commitment to the New York agreement. Whatever that meant.

Clarissa was worried. Two "Muslim-looking men" had come to the house asking for Zafar by name, but he was away in Exeter, of course. She thought it might be because he was now on the electoral roll.

Alun Evans, the British Airways executive who had been asked to liaise with him, and who was very much "on his side," called to say that he believed BA was "on its way to change," and that after a few "comparatively minor" matters were resolved they should be able to make a positive decision. "In a few weeks." And he was right. A few weeks later, after nine and a half years of being banned from flying on the national carrier, he was welcomed back on board.

The play of *Haroun and the Sea of Stories* opened, and it was an exceptional production, in which a suitably magical atmosphere was created at minimal expense, the sea made of billowing silk scarves, the actors all performing small magic tricks as they went about their business; and at the climactic moment when Haroun discovered the source of all stories, a torch played on the faces of the audience and identified it, the audience itself, as that treasured source. Once again, as had happened at the Hampstead book signing about which Commander Howley had made such a fuss, there were no demonstrations or security problems. It was just a good night out at the theater.

He had sent the typescript of *The Ground Beneath Her Feet* to Bono to see what he thought of it, and to point out any obvious music-industry howlers that needed correcting. What happened was entirely unexpected. Bono telephoned to say that he had taken some of the lyrics from the text of *The Ground Beneath Her Feet* and written "a couple of melodies." "One of them is very beautiful," he said. "The one from the title track in the book. It's one of the most beautiful things we've ever done." He grinned. He hadn't known, he said, that novels had title tracks, but yeah, he knew which song Bono meant. *All my life I worshipped her, / Her golden voice, her beauty's beat.* Bono wanted him to go to Dublin so he could play it for him. This was a novel about the permeable borderline between the imaginary and the real worlds, and here was one of its imaginary songs crossing that borderline and becoming a real song. A few weeks later he did go to Ireland and at Paul McGuinness's place in Annamoe, County Wicklow, Bono made him go and sit in his car and listen to the demo CD there. The sound system in Bono's car was not like the sound system in anyone else's car. It was a major sound system. Bono played the track three times. He liked it the first time. It was nothing like the tune he had imagined in his head but it was a haunting ballad, and U2 was good at haunting ballads. He said he liked it but Bono kept playing it to make sure he wasn't bullshitting, and when at last he was sure he said, "Let's go in the house and play it to everyone else."

India announced it was lifting the ban on his visits. It was on the BBC *Six O'Clock News*. Vijay Shankardass was triumphant. "Very soon," he said, "you will have your visa." When he heard the news his feeling of sadness was at first greater than his joy. "I never thought," he wrote in his journal, "that I would not anticipate going to India with pleasure, yet that is now the case. I almost dread it. Yet I will go. I will go to reclaim my right to go. I must maintain the connection for my sons' sake. So that I can show them what I loved and what belongs, also, to them." And yes, it was a Hindu nationalist BJP (Bharatiya Janata Party) government that was letting him in, and inevitably it would be said that his being given a visa was an anti-Muslim act, but he refused to inhabit the role of demon that had been constructed for him. He was a man who still loved the country of his birth in spite of his long exile and the banning of his book. He was a writer for whom India had been the deepest wellspring of his inspiration, and he would take the five-year visa when it was offered.

His initial melancholic reaction faded. He spoke happily, excitedly, about returning to India at a dinner with a group of writers with whom he had participated in a charity reading organized by Julian Barnes. Louis de Bernières took it upon himself to instruct his excited, happy colleague not to go under any circumstances, because by showing up there he would grievously insult India's Muslims again. De Bernières then delivered a short lecture on the history of Hindu-Muslim politics to a writer whose entire creative and intellectual life had engaged with that subject and who, just possibly, knew more about it than the author of a novel that had notoriously distorted the history of the Greek Communist resistance to the World War II Italian invasion forces on the island of Cephalonia. It was the closest he ever came to punching another novelist in the nose. Helen Fielding, another member of the party, saw the blood rising in his eyes and leaped to her feet, smiling as gaily as she could. "Well! *Lovely* evening. Just *lovely*. I'm off!" she cried, and that saved the day, allowing him to get up and excuse himself too, and Mr. de Bernières's nose remained smugly unpunched.

———

He had a private meeting with Derek Fatchett, who said again, *Trust me.* All the intelligence coming out of Iran was uniformly positive. All parties had signed on to the agreement, all the dogs had been called off. Sanei was a loose cannon, but he didn't have the money, anyway. "We will go on working on all the issues," he said. "It matters now to keep our nerve." Fatchett said that his own statement calling the agreement "a diplomatic success for Britain" had been a problem in Iran. "As was your statement, 'It means freedom.'"

He was being asked to do something difficult: to hold his tongue. If he did so, the angry voices would gradually fall silent, and the *fatwa* would fade away.

Meanwhile in Tehran, one thousand Hezbollah students were marching, saying they were ready to carry out attacks on the author and his publishers, ready to strap bombs to their bodies, and so on; singing the terrorists' old, sad song.

He went to meet Robin Cook at the House of Commons. Cook said he had received confirmation that Khamenei and the whole Expediency Council had "signed up to the New York agreement." So it should follow that all the killers had been called off. He was certain, he said, about MOIS and Hezbollah-Lebanon. Their assassins had been stood down. As far as the Revolutionary Guards were concerned it was a case of "negative intelligence": There was no sign that any attack from that quarter was under way. "A guarantee has been received from the Iranian government that it will prevent anyone leaving Iran to attack you. They know that their prestige is on the line." The symbolic meaning of the Cook-Kharrazi "shoulder to shoulder" appearance had been carefully weighed and had been on TV in every Muslim country in the world, "and if you are killed, frankly, their credibility collapses." He also said, "This is not finished business for us. We will exert further pressure and we expect further results."

Then the foreign secretary of the United Kingdom asked a question that was not easy to answer. "Why do you need a defense campaign against me?" Robin Cook wanted to know. "I'm prepared to offer you full access to me, and regular briefings. I'm fighting on your behalf."

He replied, "Because many people think I'm being sold out by you, that a weak agreement is being presented as a strong one, and that I'm being shunted aside for commercial and geopolitical reasons."

"Oh," Cook said scornfully. "They think Peter Mandelson is telling me what to do." (Mandelson was the trade and industry minister.) "That is not so," he said, and then, echoing Derek Fatchett, "You're going to have to trust me."

He was silent for a long moment, and Cook made no attempt to hurry his decision. Was he being duped? he asked himself. It was only a few days since he had yelled at Michael Axworthy about being betrayed. But here were two politicians whom he liked and who had fought harder for him than any others had in a decade, and they were asking him to have faith, keep his nerve, and above all, for a while, to keep quiet. "If you attack the Khordad foundation it will be great news for them, because then the Iranian government won't be able to move against them without seeming to be run by you."

He thought and thought. The defense campaign had been started to combat the inertia of governments. Now here was his own government promising to work energetically on his behalf. Maybe this was a new phase: working with the government instead of against it.

"Okay," he said, "I'll do it."

He went to see Frances D'Souza at Article 19 and asked her to dissolve the defense campaign. Carmel Bedford was in Oslo at a meeting of representatives of several of the defense committees and when he called her to tell her his decision she exploded with rage, blaming Frances for the decision. "She's short-listed for a job at the Foreign Office! It's in her interest to wind this up!" Frances and Carmel had stopped getting along. He became certain that he had made the right decision.

So the Rushdie Defense Campaign ended. "Let us hope," he wrote in his journal, "I am justified in my decision. But at any rate it is mine. I can't blame anyone else."

IRANIAN VILLAGERS OFFER RUSHDIE BOUNTY Residents of an Iranian village near the Caspian Sea have set a new bounty, including land, a house and carpets, on Salman Rushdie. "Kiyapay village will give 4,500 square metres of farmland, 1,500 square metres of fruit gardens, a house and 10 car-

pets as a reward," said a village official. The 2,000 villagers have also opened a bank account to collect donations.

It wasn't always easy to keep calm, keep silent, and keep his nerve.

He went to New York to make a TV film about *The Ground Beneath Her Feet* for French TV. At once the world opened up. He walked the city streets by himself and did not feel at risk. In London he was trapped by the caution of the British intelligence services, but here in New York his life was in his own hands; he could decide for himself what was sensible and what was dangerous. He could recapture his freedom in America before the British agreed it was time to give it back to him. *Freedom is taken, never given.* He knew that. He had to act on that knowledge.

Bill Buford, wearing a *Mars Attacks* head, took him to a Halloween dinner uptown. He wore a *keffiyeh,* held a baby's rattle in one hand and a crusty bread roll in the other, and went as "Sheikh, Rattle and Roll."

Back in London, it was Jeanne Moreau's seventieth birthday and he was invited to a lunch in her honor at the French ambassador's residence. He sat between Moreau, still glamorous and even sexy at seventy, and the great ballerina Sylvie Guillem, who wanted to come and see the play of *Haroun.* Moreau turned out to be a terrific *raconteuse.* Also at the table was an embassy apparatchik whose job was to lob softball questions at her: "Now you mus' tell 'ow you meet our great Franch film director François Truffaut" and then she was off and running. "Ah, François. It was at Cannes, you know, and I was there with Louis"—"That is our also great Franch director, Louis Malle . . ." "Yes, Louis, and we are at the Palais du Cinéma, and François, he come up and greet Louis, and then for some time they walk together and I am behind with another man, and then afterward I am walking with François, and it is very strange because he will not look me in the face, he look always down at the floor and sometimes quickly up, and then down again, until finally he look at me and he say, 'Can I have your telephone number?' " "And," said the apparatchik, "you give eet to 'eem." He took over the questioning himself and asked her about working with Luis Buñuel on *Diary of a Chambermaid.* "Ah, Don Luis," she said in her deep, throaty cigarette voice, "I love him. I say to him one day, 'Oh, Don Luis, if only I was your daughter!' And he say me, 'No, my dear, you should not wish it, because if you were my daughter I would lock you up and you would not be in the movies!' "

"I have always loved the song you sing in *Jules et Jim,*" he told her as they sipped their Château Beychevelle. " 'Le Tourbillon.' Is that an old song or was it written for the movie?" "No," she said. "It was written for me. It was an old lover, you know, and after we break up he wrote that song. And then when François say he want me to sing I propose the song to him and he agree." "And now," he asked, "now that it's such a famous movie scene, do you still think of it as the song your former lover wrote for you, or is it 'the song from *Jules et Jim'?*" "Oh," she said, shrugging, "now it is the song from the movie."

Before he left the *résidence* the ambassador drew him aside and told him he had been awarded the highest rank, *commandeur,* in the Ordre des Arts et des Lettres; an immense honor. The decision was made several years ago, the ambassador said, but the previous French government sat on it. But now there would be a party for him here at the *résidence* and he would get his medal and ribbon. That was wonderful news, he said, but within days the back-pedaling began. The woman responsible for sending out the invitations said she was "holding fire" because she was "waiting for approval from Paris," and then oddly neither the ambassador nor the cultural attaché, Olivier Poivre d'Arvor, could be reached. After several days of being stonewalled he called Jack Lang, who told him that the president of Iran was scheduled to visit France in ten days and that was why the Quai d'Orsay was stalling. Lang made some calls and that did the trick. Olivier called back. Would it be possible to choose a date on which M. Lang himself could come and do the honors? Yes, he said. Of course.

Zafar gave a party and wanted him to be there. The protection team hustled him into the nightclub and then tried to turn a blind eye to the things that usually happened in such clubs. He found himself at a table with Damon Albarn and Alex James of Blur, who had heard about his collaboration with U2 and wanted to record a song with him too. Suddenly his services as a lyricist were in demand. Alex had drunk the best part of a bottle of absinthe, which had perhaps been unwise. "I've got a fucking great idea," he said. "I'll write the words and you write the music." But, Alex, he said mildly, I don't write music and I can't play a musical instrument. "Nothing to it," Alex said. "I'll teach you how to play the guitar. It'll only take half an hour. Fucking nothing to it. Then you write the music and I'll write the words. It'll be fucking amazing." The collaboration with Blur did not take place.

He met Bob Blake, who was now the head of "A" Squad, at Scotland Yard to talk about the future. A new novel would be published in the new year, he said, and he must be free to promote it properly, with proper announcements of appearances and signings. They had by now done enough of these to be confident that there would not be problems. Also, he wanted to scale the protection back even further. He understood that airlines still felt happier if he was brought to the plane by the protection team, and that public venues also appreciated police involvement in his appearances, but other than that, he and Frank could handle most things. Interestingly Blake seemed open to all his proposals, which suggested that the threat assessment was changing, even if he hadn't yet been informed of the change. "All right," Blake said, "let's see what we can do." He was worried about India, though. It was the view of Mr. Morning and Mr. Afternoon that if he were to travel to India in January or early February there was the risk of an Iranian attack. Could he know on what their fears were based? "No." "Well, anyway, I wasn't planning to go to India at that time." When he said that he saw the policeman visibly relax.

He arrived at the foreign secretary's office in the House of Commons to find Stephen Lander, the director general of MI5, waiting for him along with Robin Cook, who had bad news to deliver. Intelligence

reports had been received, Cook said, of a meeting of the Iranian Supreme National Security Council—just saying that name earned Cook
a disapproving look from Lander, but he said it all the same—at which
Khatami and Kharrazi had failed to pacify the hard-liners. Khamenei
was "not in a position" to call off the Revolutionary Guards or Hezbollah. So the danger to his life persisted. But, Cook said, he "personally" and the Foreign Office were committed to resolving the problems,
and there was no evidence of any planned attack, except for the worry
about India. There was no great likelihood of an attack in any Western
country, Lander said. *No great likelihood* was cold comfort, but that was
all he was going to get. "I did let Kharrazi know," Cook said, "that we
knew about the SNSC meeting, and Kharrazi was pretty shocked. He
tried to say that the deal was still on. He knows his reputation, and
Khatami's, is at stake."

Keep your nerve.

Nothing was ever perfect, but this was a level of imperfection that was
hard to take. Still, he remained resolved. He had to take his life back
into his own hands. He couldn't wait any longer for the "imperfection
factor" to drop to a more acceptable level. But when he spoke to
Elizabeth about America she wasn't listening. She was listening to
what Isabel Fonseca was saying. "America is a dangerous country, and
everyone in it has a gun." Her antagonism to his New York dream was
growing. Sometimes he actually seemed to see a jagged rip or tear
between them, getting wider, as if the fabric of the world were a sheet
of paper and they were on opposite halves of it, falling apart from each
other, as if it was inevitable that sooner or later their stories would
continue on separate pages, in spite of the years of love, because when
life began to speak in imperatives the living had no choice but to obey.
His greatest imperative was liberty, and hers was motherhood, and no
doubt it was in part because she was a mother that a life in America
without police protection struck her as unsafe and irresponsible, and in
part it was because she was English and didn't want her son to grow up
American, and in part it was because she hardly knew America, because her America was not much larger than Bridgehampton, and she

feared that in New York she would be isolated and alone. He understood all her fears and doubts, but his own needs were like commands, and he knew that he would do what had to be done.

Sometimes love was not enough.

It was his mother's eighty-second birthday. When he told her on the phone that he had a new book due out in 1999 she said, in Urdu, *Is dafa koi achchhi si kitab likhna.* "This time, write a nice book."

IX

His Millenarian Illusion

SOMETIMES LOVE WAS NOT ENOUGH. IN THE YEARS AFTER HER HUSBAND'S death Negin Rushdie discovered that her first husband, the handsome youth who had fallen in love with her when she was pretty young Zohra Butt, was still alive. Theirs had not been an arranged marriage but a true "love match" and they did not fall apart because they had stopped being in love but because he was unable to father children and motherhood was an imperative. The sadness of exchanging the love of a man for the love of her unborn children was so profound that for many years she did not speak his name, and her children, as they arrived and grew, were not even told of his existence, until in the end she blurted it out to Sameen, her eldest daughter. "His name was Shaghil," she said, and blushed, and wept, as if she were confessing an infidelity. She never mentioned him to her son, never said what he did for a living or in what town he made his home. He was her ghost, the phantom of lost love, and out of loyalty to her husband, her children's father, she suffered the haunting in silence.

After Anis Rushdie died her brother Mahmood told Negin that Shaghil was still alive, had never remarried, still loved her, and wanted to see her again. Her children encouraged her to get in touch. There was nothing standing between the old lovers. The imperative of motherhood was, obviously, no longer an obstruction. And it would be a foolishness to allow illogical feelings of betraying the dead Anis to stand in her way. It was not required of her to live alone and lonely for the rest of her life—and she lived on for sixteen years after Anis died—when there was the possibility of renewing an old love and allowing it to illuminate her later years. But when they spoke to her in this way she gave a small, mutinous smile and shook her head like a girl. In those years of the *fatwa* she visited London several times and stayed at Sameen's house and he visited her when he could. The first husband, Shaghil, was still no more than a name to him. She still refused to discuss him, to say if he was a funny or a serious man, or what he liked to eat, or if he could sing, or whether he was tall like her ramrod brother Mahmood or short like Anis. In *Midnight's Children* her son had written about a mother with a first husband who could not give her children, but that sad poet-politician, "Nadir Khan," was created out of the author's imagination alone. No trace of Shaghil could be found in him except for the biological problem. But now the real man was writing her letters and when she was not smiling like a foolish girl she was pressing her lips tightly together and shaking her head sharply and refusing to discuss it.

In *Love in the Time of Cholera,* the great novel by Gabriel García Márquez, the lovers Fermina Daza and Florentino Ariza parted when they were still very young but came together again in the sunset of their lives. Negin Rushdie was being offered just such a sunset love but for reasons she never gave she resisted it. For this resistance, too, there was a literary antecedent, in Edith Wharton's *The Age of Innocence:* Newland Archer in his later years, accompanied by his adult son, sits paralyzed in a little French square below the awning and balcony of his old love the Countess Olenska's apartment and unable, after all the lost years, to walk up the stairs to see her. Perhaps he did not want her to see him as an old man. Perhaps he did not want to see her as an old woman. Perhaps the memory of what he had not had the courage to grasp was too overwhelming. Perhaps he had buried it too deep and could no longer exhume it, and the horror of being with Countess Olenska and no longer feeling what he had felt was too much for him to bear.

"It's more real to me here than if I went up," he suddenly heard himself say; and the fear lest that last shadow of reality should lose its edge kept him rooted to his seat as the minutes succeeded each other.

Negin Rushdie had read neither book but if she had she would not have believed in Fermina and Florentino's happy reunion, or rather there was a thing in her that was not allowing her to believe in such an ending. She was frozen as Newland Archer had been frozen, the passage of the years had stymied her, and even though an expression of love seized hold of her face every time his name was mentioned she could not act on what she felt. It was more real to her without him than it would be if he returned. So she never responded to his letters, never called him, and never saw him in the sixteen years that remained. She died as her husband's widow and her children's mother and could not, or would not, write a new last chapter to her story. Sometimes love was not enough.

Anis Rushdie had been married once before Negin as well. They were unusual in this, in their class and place and time, that theirs was a second marriage for them both. About Anis's first wife his children were told only that she was bad-tempered and that they quarreled all the time. (The children knew that their father had a bad temper too.) And they also knew about a great tragedy. Anis and the first wife had had a daughter, their half sister, whose name they were never told. One night the first wife called Anis and said that the girl was very sick and might die, and he thought that she was lying, that she was telling the story as a ruse to draw him back toward her, so he ignored the message, and the little girl died. When he heard that his daughter was dead he rushed to his first wife's house but she would not let him in, though he beat his fists on the door and wept.

The marriage of Anis and Negin remained a mystery to their son. To their growing children it looked like an unhappy life, in which his growing disappointment expressed itself in nightly whiskey rages from which she tried to shield her children. More than once the older children Sameen and Salman tried to persuade their parents to divorce, so that they, the children, could enjoy each parent's company without having to endure the side effects of their unhappiness. Anis and Negin did not take their children's advice. There was something they both thought of as "love" below the misery of the nights and as they both believed in it, it could be said to have existed. The mystery at the heart of other people's intimacy, the incomprehensible survival of love at the heart of unlovingness: that was a thing he learned from his parents' lives.

Also: If both your parents had been previously divorced, and then lived unhappily "loving" lives, you grew up with a belief in the impermanence of love, a belief that love was a darker, harsher, less comfortable, less comforting emotion than the songs and movies said. And if that was true, then he, with his many broken marriages—what was the lesson he was teaching his sons? A friend of his once said to him that remaining in an unhappy marriage was the tragedy—not the divorce. But the pain he caused to the mothers of his children, the two women who loved him better than anyone else, haunted him. Nor did he blame his parents for setting him a bad example. This was his own doing and his own responsibility. Whatever wounds his life had inflicted on him, the wounds he inflicted on Clarissa and Elizabeth were worse. He had loved them both but his love had not been strong enough.

He had loved his sisters, and they had all loved one another, but most of those relationships, too, had come apart. Sameen and he had remained very close. When they were children he was the good boy and she the naughty girl. He would get her out of trouble with his parents and she would beat people up for him. Once the father of one of the boys she had punched, a certain Mohan Mathan, came to their home, Windsor Villa, to complain to Anis. "Your daughter knocked down my son!" he cried in outrage and Anis began to laugh. "If I were you," he said, "I'd lower your voice before everyone in the neighborhood hears that."

The bond between them never weakened, but they gradually became aware that their sister Bunno—her real name was Nevid, but she was always Bunno in the family—resented it. She was five years younger than he was, four years younger than Sameen, and her experience of her childhood was of being excluded from the intimacy of her older siblings. In the end she quarreled dreadfully with them, and with her parents, and went to California to be far away from them all. He felt the pain of his "lost sister" often, but then she would explode into his life so violently that he backed away again. At one point she became crazily convinced that he and Sameen had somehow defrauded her of her inheritance, and threatened to expose and denounce him in public. He had to ask lawyers to warn her off and after that they did not speak for a very long time. The youngest of the family, Nabeelah, known as Guljum, began brightly as a great beauty and a gifted structural engineer, but then the mental unbalance that destroyed her work, her marriage, her relationships with her family and eventually her life began to make its presence felt, she began to chew tobacco and to abuse prescription medication and to eat until her beauty was buried under a mountain of fat, and then, shockingly, she was found dead in her bed and that was how it happened that the youngest of them was the one to go first.

Love, in his family, had usually not been enough.

It was the tenth anniversary of the Bradford book burning and then the tenth anniversary of the *fatwa*—*Ten years!*, he thought, *doesn't time fly when you're having fun*—and the usual people were making their usual noises. Mr. Shabbir Akhtar, whom *The Independent* described as a "brilliant" thinker, said that they wouldn't burn *The Satanic Verses* now because they no longer felt "excluded." (In the years that followed many British Muslims, including some of the most zealously hostile ones, would suggest that the campaign about the novel had been a mistake. Some only meant that it was a mistaken tactic, because it had made its author more famous and increased the book's sales, but others went so far as to say they had learned the importance of defending freedom of speech.) On Valentine's Day the Iranian Revolutionary Guards said in Tehran that the *fatwa* "would be fulfilled" and Sanei of the Bounty confirmed that his "annihilation" was still planned. But there were no marches, no rallies at mosques, no senior ayatollahs delivering bloodthirsty sermons. So it was quieter than he had feared it might have been.

He continued to press the police for more freedom. Now that Frank Bishop was working for him, on his payroll, surely Frank could take over more of their duties and, by the way, save them a lot of money? He had learned enough about the difference between "threat" and "risk" to know that the risk attached to him turning up unannounced to a private party, restaurant, theater, or cinema, was almost nil. There was no reason for a whole protection team to be involved. Frank could do it. But they were reluctant to scale the protection back. They asked that he leave things as they were until after his summer visit to Long Island, and he reluctantly agreed.

The first furor of 1999 followed the granting of his Indian visa. At the last minute a visa officer at India House tried to say he could have only a regular six-month visitor visa, and Vijay Shankardass had to go into India House and see the high commissioner, Lalit Mansingh, as well as the foreign minister, who happened to be in London, and they agreed to "do the right thing" and grant the full five-year visa to which persons of Indian origin were entitled. It was also agreed that if he visited India he would be entitled to the protection of the Indian police.

At once the Indian Muslim "anger" began. Fierce old Imam Bukhari at the Juma Masjid in Delhi (who, ten years earlier, had condemned the "wrong Salman") raged against the visa decision before a crowd of three thousand believers at Friday prayers. He was "prepared to die," he said, to prevent a visit by Mr. Rushdie. Two days later the *Tehran Times* predicted he would be assassinated in India. "Perhaps Providence has decreed that this shameless person will meet his end where he was born." In India the only non-BJP leader to support the visa decision was the general secretary of the Communist Party of India (Marxist). Mani Shanker Aiyar of Congress said his party had been "quite right" to ban *The Satanic Verses* and its author, and if the BJP had agreed to a visa it must "take the consequences." But then he added, oddly, that if Mr. Rushdie did come to India "he will be a guest and must be welcomed." Imam Bukhari said that Muslims would "object according to the Constitution" but if some devout Muslim decided to kill the blasphemer he would have the support of all Muslims. The writer Githa Hariharan sent him a series of didactic, ideological emails that were simply annoying. It was plain that a trip to India would have to wait until tempers cooled.

Theresa from Bono's office called. "Hello, Salman? Have you got a copy of the lyrics of yer song, what is it now, 'The Ground Beneath Her Feet'?" Why, yes, as a matter of fact he did have a copy. "Only could you fax them over to the studio right away, because they're about to record the vocals, and Bono's lost them?" Yes, I could do that. Right away. Yes.

Then for a time it was all illness and doctors and the beating wings of the exterminating angel. Elizabeth's cousin Carol Knibb and her husband, Brian, came to stay at Bishop's Avenue for several days and late at night he had his first sight of Carol's bald chemotherapy head. It reminded him, without his wanting it to, of the scene in Roald Dahl's *The Witches* of the witches peeling off their worldly, "humanizing" garb. He was very fond of Carol and was angry with himself for his reaction, which was, to say the least, inglorious. She had been to see Kanti Rai in America, and he was treating her, but she wasn't reacting to the treatment as well as Edward Said had, and the prognosis wasn't good. But there were still things to try, she said, determinedly cheerful.

Iris Murdoch died. He had attended an Arts Council lunch in her honor not long after the publication of her last novel, *Jackson's Dilemma,* a book that had received a critical mauling. Iris had been in low spirits, he recalled, and had told him that she thought she should stop writing. "Surely not because of a few bad reviews," he said to her. "You're *Iris Murdoch.*" "Yes," she said sadly, "but sometimes people stop liking your work and you run out of ideas and you should perhaps just stop." Only a few months later the onset of Alzheimer's disease was diagnosed.

And Derek Fatchett died. He had a sudden heart attack in a pub and that was the end of him. Nobody had worked harder or with more determination to solve the problem of the *fatwa.* He was only fifty-four years old.

He was suffering from a condition called ptosis. His eyelids didn't open properly and the droop was getting worse, particularly in the right lid. It was beginning to interfere with his eyesight. If he didn't have an operation the day would come when he wouldn't be able to open his eyes at all. His hooded, Sleepy LaBeef eyes were often used as metaphors of his villainy, but it turned out they were just a medical affliction.

The top man for ptosis operations was Mr. Richard Collin. He was booked in at the King Edward VII Hospital for Officers, "where all the Royal Family goes for its operations," Mr. Collin told him, but just before he went in he was told that the "matron" had refused to have him as a patient on security grounds. The team went to see her and, fortunately, was able to pacify her, and the operation was on again. It always distressed him to be so much at the mercy of other people's fear, it felt like being slapped in the face, and he could never slap back. Then the day before the operation Clarissa called. Zafar was determined to drop out of college. He hated it. It was a "shithole." He had been offered the opportunity to manage a London nightclub, and he hoped to promote concerts and had a friend with whom he thought he could put on an event at Wembley Stadium and that was the life he wanted. He was overdrawn at the bank, too, and that had to be dealt with. They were both very worried that he was living, as Clarissa said, in "cloud cuckoo land," and their worry brought them close once again. Zafar needed strong, united parents now. They spoke to him and he agreed to give up the Wembley concert idea. He wasn't happy about it.

When he regained consciousness after the operation there was a bandage over his eyes. He called out and nobody answered. "Hello?" He called again and then once again and there was no reply. He didn't know where he was and he was blind and nobody was speaking to him. Maybe something had gone badly wrong. Maybe he had been kidnapped. Or maybe he was in some anteroom of hell waiting for the Devil's attention. *Hello hello hello* no reply *can you hear me* no they couldn't *is anybody here is anybody there* well if they were there they weren't saying so. A few minutes, or weeks, of (literally) blind panic ended when a nurse's voice said yes, she was there, she was sorry, Elizabeth had just gone home to sleep, it was 3 A.M., and she just had to go to the bathroom. *Perfect timing,* he thought, *I come out of anesthesia exactly when the nurse has to take a leak.*

In the morning the bandage was removed and there was another bizarre moment when his eyelids didn't respond properly to the commands of his brain, fluttering crazily and independently of each other, and then everything settled down, he hadn't been blinded by an accidental knife, and they brought him a mirror and his eyes were open wide. Perhaps the right eye a little too wide. "Yes," said Mr. Collin, "let's leave it a week and then maybe a small adjustment."

His new eyelids made their debut at a sad but determinedly upbeat occasion, a party at Ruthie and Richard Rogers's house to celebrate Nigella Lawson and John Diamond's tenth anniversary. The news on John was bad, worse than bad, there was no point in doing any more surgery, chemotherapy might buy him some time, but that was all. His friends gathered to celebrate his life and John made a "speech" by writing it down and having it simultaneously projected onto a high white wall, a speech whose most remarkable characteristic was that it made the assembled company laugh a great deal.

Meanwhile the new eyelids were having quite an effect on people. *Are you wearing new glasses? You look so well! Have you got a suntan? You look so . . . happy!* Later, when the press got hold of the story, *The Sunday Times* had a piece that was almost apologetic about the way it had seen him over the years. Suddenly the paper understood that his "aloof, arrogant, sinister hoodlum's gaze" was just the product of a deteriorating eyelid condition. He looked "revitalized, reborn," said the article. "How the eyes deceive."

He had to go to Torino, Italy, to receive an honorary doctorate before Richard Collin had a chance to adjust his excessively starey right eye and in the photographs of that occasion he looked slightly deranged. The trip went well; this time the Italian police were friendly, eager to please, nonobstructive, very different from their colleagues in Mantova. His cohonoree, John Beumer III, was a mouth cancer doctor from UCLA who made a notably grisly speech about new techniques in the treatment of oral carcinomas, tongues being sewn onto cheeks and the like, and while he listened to Beumer he was thinking, "None of that saved my friend."

By coincidence President Khatami of Iran was visiting Rome on the same day, and the press were excited by the synchronicity and made a good deal of it. Khatami, inevitably, didn't believe it was a coincidence, and "strongly criticized" Europe for supporting the novelist. "Support for Rushdie means support for war among civilizations," he said. "I very much regret that a person who has insulted the sanctities of over one billion Muslims is currently being praised in European

countries." This was a man who said he didn't want a clash of civilizations but then characterized everything he disliked as "war"; a man
who said he was "against terrorism" but exempted such acts of violence as the *fatwa* by saying that was not terrorism, it was justice. And
this was the "moderate" man whose word he had been asked by the
British government to rely on.

The publication date of *The Ground Beneath Her Feet* was approaching
and the U.S. tour was a problem. Most European airlines were now
willing to carry him but the American carriers still refused. He could
get to New York, and by using Air Canada could make it to the West
Coast, but the rest of the country would have to be covered by hiring
a private plane. And there would be the additional cost of Jerry Glazebrook's security services. They somehow had to find $125,000 for a
two-week tour, and the publishers were prepared to put in only around
$40,000. He spoke to Andrew Wylie and Jerry Glazebrook and they
managed to wrangle the security costs down by $10,000, and the vari-
ous venues were prepared to contribute, in total, around $35,000 in
speaking fees plus security costs. If he kicked in the fees he was being
paid by *The New Yorker* for their extract from the book, and the last
three or four months of income from his syndicated *New York Times*
columns, they would be able to pay the bills. He was determined that
the tour should go ahead and so he told Andrew to agree, even though
it meant he was sacrificing around $80,000 in income. The English
reviews were in, and they were mostly very positive, and he didn't
want the American publication to suffer.

There was no point dwelling on what the critics said, they liked
the book or they didn't, but the strange case of James Wood merited a
small footnote. Mr. Wood reviewed *The Ground Beneath Her Feet* in
The Guardian, which also published the first UK extract from the
book, and his notice was splendid. "His spectacular new novel . . . a
considerable achievement, inventive and complex . . . this brilliant
novel . . . buoyant, bonhomous, punning, [it] imparts a creative joy,
the most generous in such free pleasure since *Midnight's Children.* I
suspect that it will deservedly become Rushdie's most enjoyed book."

Well, thank you, James, he thought. When the novel was published in the United States, Mr. Wood delivered a harsher judgment. He wrote another review, in *The New Republic,* a revised version of the *Guardian* piece, in which the "deservedly" fell out of his praise. The book was now a "characteristic postmodern defeat," whose "seductive ribaldry lacks the ground beneath its feet." The two notices were published just seven weeks apart. A critic who contradicted himself according to the literary predilections of his paymasters had, perhaps, some explaining to do.

He flew to New York to do interviews and almost at once began to feel extremely ill. He did his best to keep going through the arduous schedule but in the end the high fever forced him to see a doctor. He was told he had a severe chest infection, near pneumonia, and if he had left it one more day he would almost certainly have been hospitalized. He was put on powerful antibiotics and somehow made it through the interviews. After the work was done, he felt shaky but better, and went to a reception at Tina Brown's house, where he found himself standing in a small circle of guests whose other members were Martin Amis, Martin Scorsese, David Bowie, Iman, Harrison Ford, Calista Flockhart and Jerry Seinfeld. "Mr. Rushdie," Seinfeld said, nervously, "did you ever see the episode of the show we did about you?" This was the episode in which Kramer claimed to have seen "Salman Rushdie" in the steam room and he and Jerry interrogated the man whose name, "Sal Bass," they thought might be code for, well, *Salmon.* When he reassured Mr. Seinfeld that he had thought the episode very funny, the comedian visibly relaxed.

The eight-city U.S. tour went off without alarms, except that the big trade fair, the BEA in Los Angeles, refused to have him on the premises. However, while he was in L.A. he was invited to the Playboy Mansion, whose owner was plainly braver than the organizers of BookExpo America. Morgan Entrekin, the publisher at Grove/Atlantic, had published a Hugh Hefner volume, *The Century of Sex:* Playboy's *History of the Sexual Revolution,* and as a result was allowed to host a party for bookish folk at the mansion. The bookish folk duly trooped up into the Holmby Hills and excitedly drank warmish champagne in a tent on the lawn of Hefnerland under the disdainful gaze of terminally bored Bunnies. Halfway through the evening Morgan came bounding toward him accompanied by a young blond woman with a nice smile and an improbable body. This was Heather Kozar, the newly elected Playmate of the Year, a very young girl with excellent manners who disappointingly insisted on calling him *sir*. "I'm sorry, sir, I haven't read any of your books," she apologized. "To tell you the truth, I don't read a lot of books, sir, because they make me feel tired and go to sleep." Yes, yes, he agreed, he often felt exactly the same way. "But there are some books, sir," she added, "like *Vogue*, which I feel I have to read to keep up with what's going on."

He flew back to London and had his eyelids adjusted until they looked normal, and celebrated Milan's second birthday and Zafar's twentieth and then he was fifty-two. On his birthday Sameen and her two girls came to dinner, and Pauline Melville and Jane Wellesley too, and a few days later he took Zafar to Centre Court at Wimbledon to watch Sampras beat Henman in the semifinal. If it hadn't been for the policemen life might almost have felt normal. Perhaps the old clouds were slowly lifting, but new clouds were forming. "The gulf between E. and me about living in NY is threatening our marriage," he wrote in his journal. "I can't see a way out. We will have to spend time apart, me in a Manhattan apartment, she in London. But how to bear the separation from this sweet little boy whom I love so much?"

In mid-July they went to the Grobow house in Bridgehampton for nine weeks, and it was during this time that he succumbed to his millenarian illusion.

Even if one did not believe that the approaching millennium would see the Second Coming of Christ, it was possible to be seduced by the romantic, "millenarian" idea that such a day, which came only once in a thousand years, could inaugurate a great transformation, and that life—the life of the world, but also of individuals within it—would be better in the new millennium that was dawning. *Well, one can hope,* he thought.

In early August 1999 the millenarian illusion that would overpower him and change his life presented itself to him in female form on, of all places, Liberty Island. It was laughable, really, that he met her under the Statue of Liberty. In fiction the symbolism of such a scene would have felt ponderously overweight. But real life sometimes rammed its point home just to make sure you got it, and in his real life Tina Brown and Harvey Weinstein gave a lavish party on Liberty Island to launch their short-lived *Talk* magazine, and there were fireworks in the sky and Macy Gray singing *I try to say goodbye and I choke, I try to walk away and I stumble,* and a guest list that ranged all the way from Madonna to himself. He didn't meet Madonna that night, or he might have asked her about what her assistant Caresse had said to a TV producer who sent her a copy of *The Ground Beneath Her Feet* in hopes of getting a favorable comment from the great lady—after all the book was about a major, if imaginary, female rock star. "Oh, no," Caresse said, "Madonna didn't *read* the book. She *shredded* it." (When he did meet Madonna with Zadie Smith several years later at the *Vanity Fair* Oscars bash she spoke only of real estate values in the Marble Arch area of London and he didn't bother to bring up the shredding, because he and Zadie were trying too hard to contain their laughter at the tall, gorgeous young Italian stallion whose murmured pickup line seemed to impress Ms. Ciccone: "You are Italian, no?" he asked her, leaning in close. "I can tell. . . .")

Elizabeth had stayed in Bridgehampton with Milan and he drove into the city with Zafar, Martin and Isabel. There were lights hanging from the trees on Liberty Island and a cool summer breeze came off the water and they didn't know anyone and as the daylight failed it was hard to see who was there anyway, but that was all right. Then under a Chinese lantern beneath the great copper lady he came face-to-face with Padma Lakshmi and at once he realized he'd seen her before, or her picture anyway, in an Italian magazine in which he, too, had been featured, and he remembered thinking, "If I ever meet this girl my goose is cooked." Now he said, "You're that beautiful Indian girl who had a show on Italian TV and then came back to America to be an actress." The Illusion couldn't believe that he would know anything about her, so she began to doubt that he was who she thought he was and made him say his full name, and then the ice was broken. They talked for only a few minutes but managed to exchange phone numbers and the next day when he called her the line was busy because at that exact moment she was calling him. He was sitting in his car by

Mecox Bay and smelled, wafting toward him across the shining water, the strong aroma of oven-roasted goose.

He was a married man. His wife and their two-year-old child were waiting for him at home, and if things had been different there he would have grasped the obvious truth that an apparition who seemed to embody everything he hoped for from his future, a Lady Liberty made of flesh and blood, had to be a mirage, and that to plunge toward her as if she were real was to court disaster for himself, inflict unconscionable pain upon his wife, and place an unfair burden upon the Illusion herself, an American of Indian origin who had grand ambitions and secret plans that had nothing to do with the fulfillment of his deepest needs.

Her name was an oddity, one name broken into two by her mother's divorce. She had been born Padmalakshmi Vaidyanathan in Delhi (though most of her "Tam Bram," or Tamil Brahman, family lived in Madras), but her father, Vaidyanathan, had abandoned her and her mother, Vijayalakshmi, when she was one year old. Vijayalakshmi promptly discarded her ex-husband's name, bisecting her own name and her daughter's instead. Soon after that she left to take up a senior nursing appointment at Sloan-Kettering in New York, and later moved to Los Angeles and remarried. Padma did not meet her father until she was almost thirty years old.

Another woman with a missing parent. The pattern of his romantic life continued to repeat itself.

"You saw an illusion and you destroyed your family for it," Elizabeth would tell him, and she was right. The Phantom of Liberty was a mirage of an oasis. She seemed to contain his Indian past and his American future. She was free of the caution and worry that had bedeviled his life with Elizabeth and which Elizabeth could not leave behind. She was the dream of leaving it all behind and beginning again—an American, pilgrim dream—a *Mayflower* fantasy more alluring than her beauty, and her beauty was brighter than the sun.

At home there was another great quarrel about the things that had become the things they always fought about. Elizabeth's demand that they immediately have more babies, which he didn't want, went to war with his half-realized dream of freedom in America, which she feared, and drove him, a week later, to New York City, where in a suite at the Mark Hotel Padma said to him, "There's a bad me inside me and when she comes out she just takes whatever she wants," and even that warning didn't send him sprinting home to his marital bed. The Illusion had become too powerful to be dispelled by all the evidence that reality could provide. She could not be the dream he dreamed of her. Her feelings for him—he would learn—were real, but they were intermittent. She was ambitious in a way that often obliterated feeling. They would have a sort of life together—eight years from first meeting to final divorce, not a negligible length of time—and in the end, inevitably, she broke his heart as he had broken Elizabeth's. In the end she would be Elizabeth's best revenge.

It was just one night. She went back to Los Angeles and he returned first to Little Noyac Path and then to London. He was working on an eighty-page book proposal, treatments for four novels and a book of essays, that he hoped would bring in enough money up front to allow him to buy his Manhattan home, and things between Elizabeth and himself continued to be rough-edged; but he saw his friends and received an honorary doctorate in Liège and was happy that Günter Grass was given the Nobel Prize at last and if he managed not to mind too much that he was not on the Booker Prize short list (and neither were the much praised Vikram Seth and Roddy Doyle) it was because he was calling Padma at her apartment in West Hollywood late at night and being made to feel better than he had felt in years. Then he went to Paris for the publication of *La terre sous ses pieds* and she joined him for a week of intoxicating pleasure punctuated by hammer blows of guilt.

Zafar had not returned to Exeter, but whatever feelings his parents might have had on the subject suddenly became irrelevant because Clarissa was admitted to the hospital with over a liter of liquid in her lungs caused by a serious infection in the region of her ribs. She had been complaining of acute discomfort to her GP for some time but he had not sent her for any tests and told her it was all in her head. Now she wanted to sue him for malpractice but behind her angry words there surged a dreadful fear. It had been almost exactly five years since she had been declared cancer-free, and after five years one was supposed to be able to relax, but now she was very afraid that the terrible thing had returned. She called him to say, "I haven't told Zafar, but there may be a secondary cancer in the lung or on the bone. The X-ray is next week and if there's any shadow it's probably inoperable." Her voice trembled and broke but then she steadied herself. She was being strong but after the weekend her brother Tim called to confirm that the cancer was back. There were cancer cells in the fluid removed from her lungs. "Will you tell Zafar?" Yes, he would.

It was the hardest thing he ever had to tell his son. Zafar had not been expecting it, or had managed to close his mind to the possibility, and so he was horribly shocked. In many ways he was more like his mother than his father. He had her inward temperament and her green eyes and her liking for adventure; they went four-wheeling in the Welsh hills and spent weeks together on cycling holidays in France. She had been there for him every day through the crisis of his father's life and had helped him have a childhood and to grow up without going crazy. She wasn't the parent Zafar was supposed to lose.

"Oh my sweet loving son," he wrote in his journal, "what pain I must help you to face." The X-rays showed that the cancer had reached the bone and that, too, was something only Zafar's father could tell him. The young man's eyes brimmed with tears and he began to tremble and allowed himself briefly to be held. The doctors had said that if Clarissa responded to treatment she could perhaps expect to have a few more years. He didn't believe it and decided he had to tell his son the grim probabilities. "Zafar," he said, "the one thing I know about cancer is that when it gets a grip on the body it goes very fast." He was thinking of his own father, the speed with which his myeloma killed him at the end. "Yes," Zafar said, pleading to be agreed with, "but she's still got months and months at least, right?" He shook his head. "I'm afraid," he said, "that it may be a question of weeks, or even days. At the end it can be like falling off a cliff." Zafar looked as if he'd been slapped hard across the face. "Oh," he said, and again, "oh."

She was in Hammersmith Hospital and was getting rapidly worse. Tim said they had found that the cancer was in her lungs as well and

JOSEPH ANTON 581

she had an oxygen face mask to help her breathe and she couldn't eat solids. The speed of her decline was terrifying. The doctors at Hammersmith were at a loss because of her weakness.

They couldn't operate or begin chemotherapy until they fixed the problem of the fluid filling her lungs, and she just kept getting weaker.

She really was dying, he understood. She was fading fast.

Zafar called Mr. Waxman, the senior consultant at Hammersmith, and Waxman told him it wasn't appropriate to discuss the case on the phone but agreed to speak to Zafar if he came into the hospital. "That means nothing good," Zafar said, and he was right. Then Zafar went to see Clarissa's GP, who admitted to having made "two serious mistakes." He had not taken her chest pains seriously when she first mentioned them, and he hadn't rethought his position when she complained about the pains repeatedly. "Eighty-five percent of chest pains are caused by stress," he said, "and I went with the statistics." Also, she had had a mammogram less than two months earlier and it had been clear. But the cancer hadn't come back in her breast. She had been complaining of pain since June or early July, Zafar said, and the doctor had done nothing. Now, this insensitive man crassly and cruelly said to the dying woman's son, "She had a very serious cancer before, you know, and I'm not sure she ever accepted that. Now, her days are numbered."

"I will get this bastard," he wrote in his journal. "I will get him."

He went with Zafar to Clarissa's bedside on the afternoon of Tuesday, November 2, 1999. She was gaunt and yellow and so weak, so scared. She could hardly sign her name on the checks she said she had to send. She did not want to sign her will, but in the end she signed it. Waxman talked about starting the chemotherapy at once because it was her only chance and he said there was a 60 percent chance of success, but he didn't sound convinced. Zafar's face was heavy with despair and though his father tried to sound as positive as he could it didn't do any good.

The next morning Waxman said that Clarissa had very few days to live. They had started the chemotherapy but she had had a negative reaction to it and they had had to stop. There was nothing else to be done. "There is," said Zafar, who had spent the night scouring the

Internet and had come up with a wonder drug. Mr. Waxman told him, kindly, that it was too late for all that.

The "Internet." That was a word they were learning to use. That was the year someone had first used the word "Google" in his presence. Now there were these new electronic horizons, this new "terra incognita that spreads out in every gaze," in which Bellow's Augie had once located the human adventure. If this "Google" had existed in 1989 the attack on him would have spread so much faster and wider that he would not have stood a chance. He had been lucky to be attacked just before the dawn of the information age. But today he was not the one who was dying.

She had less than twenty-four hours, they told him, and he was sitting by her bedside holding her hand and Zafar's, and Zafar held her other hand and his. Tim and his wife, Alison, and Clarissa's close friends Rosanne and Avril were there. Then at one point she slid into something worse than sleep and Zafar drew him aside and asked, "You said that at the end it happens very fast—is this it? It looks like all the life has drained from her face." He thought, yes, it might be, and he went to her to say goodbye. He leaned over her and kissed her three times on the side of the head—and *bang,* she sat up straight and opened her eyes. *Wow, that was quite a kiss,* he thought, and then she turned and looked him right in the face and asked with terror in her gaze, "I'm not dying, am I?" "No," he lied, "you're just resting," and for the rest of his life he wondered if he had been right to lie. If he asked such a question on his deathbed he would hope to be told the truth but he had seen the terror in her and had not been able to say the words. After that for a time she seemed stronger and he made another appalling mistake. He took Zafar home to rest for a few hours. But while they were sleeping she faded again and went beyond the Orphic power of love to recall her. This time she did not return. At 12:50 A.M. the phone rang and he heard Tim's voice and understood his folly. Zafar, that great big young man, wept in his arms all the way to the hospital while the police drove them to Hammersmith like the wind.

Clarissa died. She died. Tim and Rosanne had been with her at the end. Her body lay curtained in a ward. Her mouth was slightly open, as if she were trying to speak. She was cool to the touch but not yet completely cold. Zafar couldn't stay with her. "That's not my mother," he said, and left the room, and didn't look at her in death again. He himself couldn't stay away from her. He sat beside her and talked to her through the night. He talked about their long love and his gratitude to her for their son. He thanked her again for mothering him through these hard times. It was as if the years of their separation had fallen away and he had full emotional access once again to an earlier self, an old love, at the very moment when those things had been lost forever. He was overcome by grief and sobbed uncontrollably and blamed himself for many things.

He had worried that Zafar would try to lock his grief away, as Clarissa herself might have done, but instead his son talked for days, remembering all the things she and he had done together, the bike rides, the yachting holidays, their time in Mexico. He was wonderfully mature and brave. "I am very proud of my boy," his father wrote in his journal, "and will enfold him in my love."

Clarissa was cremated on Saturday afternoon, November 13, 1999, at Golders Green crematorium. Following the hearse was unbearable. Her mother, Lavinia, seeing her daughter beginning her last journey, broke down completely and he put his arm around her while she cried. They made their way through Clarissa's London, the London they had lived in together and apart—Highbury, Highgate, Hampstead. Oh, oh, he howled inwardly. There were over two hundred people waiting for her at the crematorium and the grief was on everyone's face. He spoke by her coffin of their beginnings, how he first saw her bringing tea to Mama Cass Elliot onstage at a charity event, how their friends Connie Carter and Peter Hazell-Smith had arranged a dinner *à quatre* to introduce them, how he had waited for her for two years. "I fell in love quickly, she slowly," he said. How their son was born, their greatest treasure, on a Sunday in June. After the birth the midwife had thrown him out while they cleaned and dressed the young mother and he wandered the empty Sunday streets looking for flowers and gave ten pounds to a news vendor for a copy of the *Sunday Express* just so he could say, "Keep the change, I've just had a son." *We never disagreed about you, Zafar, and now she lives in you. I look into your face and see her eyes.*

The months that followed were perhaps Zafar's lowest time because as well as mourning his mother his home in Burma Road was sold and he had to look for a new place to live. Also, his reason for leaving Exeter, a music tour featuring a pair of DJs called Phats and Smalls that he was promoting, fell apart and his business partner Tony disappeared leaving him responsible for some large-ish debts and his father lost a sum of money bailing him out, so he felt, briefly, that he had lost everything, his mother, his work, his home, his confidence, his hope, and here was his father telling him that he was probably separating from Elizabeth and going to live in America, and, well, that was just great.

It was good to be able to say, from a dozen or so years in the future, that Zafar went on to prove that his chosen path had been the right one for him, that he worked astonishingly hard at making his way and developed a successful career in the entertainment, PR and event management world, that he was universally liked and respected, and that the time came when people stopped saying to him, "Oh, you're Salman's son," and instead began saying to his father, "Oh, you're Zafar's dad."

Dear Self, aged 52,

Really? Your older son is in pieces on the floor with the grief of mother loss and also existential dread of the future, and your younger son is just two years old, and there you are in New York, apartment hunting, and then in Los Angeles chasing your pipe-dream who always dressed as Pocahontas on Halloween, your downfall? That's who you are? Boy, I'm glad you grew up into me.

Sincerely,

Self, aged 65.

Dear 65,

You grew up?

Sincerely,

52

"We are the same person," she said to him, "we want the same things." He began to introduce her to his New York friends, and to meet hers, when he was in New York with her he knew that a new life in the New World was what he wanted; a life with her. But there was a question that wouldn't go away: How cruel was he prepared to be in the pursuit of his own happiness?

There was another question as well. Would people just be too damn afraid of the cloud over his head to sell him a place to live? In his own opinion the cloud was evaporating, but the opinion of others was another matter. There were apartments he liked, in TriBeCa and in Chelsea, which fell through because the buildings' developers panicked and said that if he moved into the building nobody else would want to live there. Real estate brokers said they saw the developers' point. He became grimly determined to defeat such objections.

He flew to Los Angeles to see Padma and on his first night there she provoked a bewildering quarrel. The world could not have told him more clearly that he was in the wrong place with the wrong woman in the wrong city on the wrong continent at the wrong time. He moved out of her apartment into the Bel-Air Hotel, booked an earlier flight back to London, and called Padma to say that the spell had been broken, he had come to his senses, and he was going back to his wife.

He called Elizabeth and told her that his plans had changed, but within hours Padma was at his hotel door begging for forgiveness. By the end of the week she had turned him around again.

It was clear to him at the time and afterward that these months of vacillation inflicted greater pain on Elizabeth than anything else. He tried to say goodbye and he choked. He tried to walk away and he stumbled. And as he swung back and forth he hurt her more and more. He went back to London and the Illusion sent him emails of blistering desire. *Just wait. I only want to please you. I'm just waiting until I can kill you with happiness.*

Meanwhile, a few days before Christmas, the Bishop's Avenue house was burgled.

Beryl the housekeeper arrived to find the front door wide open and one of their suitcases and Zafar's toolbox standing in the forecourt.

All the ground floor interior doors were open, which was unusual also. They were in the habit of locking them at night. She thought she heard movement upstairs, called out, got no reply, got scared, decided not to go inside and called Frank Bishop. Frank called him on his mobile but he was asleep and the call went to voice mail. Then Frank called the landline and woke Elizabeth, who snapped at him, "Get out of bed." Upper-story windows had been opened too and blinds and curtains as well. He began to rush around the house. He woke Zafar, who had heard nothing. He found another wide-open window. In his study his French Ordre des Arts et des Lettres medal was gone, and a camera. His laptops, passport, video camera were all untouched. His watch and some U.S. currency had been taken but his American Express card, which had been right next to the cash, was still there. None of Elizabeth's jewelry was missing; a diamond ring, in plain view, was still in its place. Zafar's stereo was gone, and some living-room ornaments, a white-metal Ganesh, a carved ivory tusk bought in India in the early 1970s, a silver box, an antique magnifying glass, and a little octagonal illuminated Qur'an given to him by Clarissa's grandmother May Jewell before their wedding. And in the dining room all their cutlery was gone in its wooden canteen. That was all.

The master bedroom window was wide open. This had been a skillful cat burglar. He came in through the bedroom window and left muddy footprints on the floor and woke nobody. It was a chilling thought. The man had crept right past them and none of the three of them had opened their eyes. Did the burglar know whose house he had entered, whose medal he had stolen? Did he recognize the sleeper in the bed? Did he know his own danger? If there had still been policemen in the house he would probably have been shot dead.

Everyone was all right. That was the main thing. But had the house been blown? Frank Bishop arrived, Beryl came inside, and officers came up from the Yard to assess the situation. If this was a Christmas sneak thief, as was most likely, it was extremely improbable that he would disclose the location to Islamic terrorists, or even go to the press, which would be self-incriminating. So, stay put, hope for the best. Yes. That was what they would do.

Elizabeth took Milan and went to see Carol and he was left with his agonized self-questioning. The millennium celebrations were approaching and he was being torn apart. Oh, and in Iran, it was reported that five hundred "hard-liners" had pledged to sell a kidney each to raise the money for his killing, which might solve the problem. *A sure cure for all diseases,* as Sir Walter Raleigh had said of the executioner's ax.

Joseph Heller died, and a great good humor went with him. Jill Craigie died, and a great kindness left with her.

On New Year's Eve the PR guru Matthew Freud and his fiancée, Rupert Murdoch's daughter Elisabeth, invited them to the Millennium Dome. He took Elizabeth, Zafar, Martin and Isabel, and Susan the new nanny stayed at the house to babysit Milan. In the dome, Tony Blair stopped by to shake hands with Matthew and Elizabeth and shook his hand as well. When it was time to sing "Auld Lang Syne" the queen had to hold Blair's hand and the expression on her face was one of faint distaste. Elizabeth held his hand and the expression on her face was of terrible love and anguish. *Should auld acquaintance be forgot and never brought to mind,* they sang, and then it was midnight and church bells were pealing all across England and the Y2K bug failed to bite and there were no terrorist attacks and the new age dawned and nothing was different. There was no magic in moments. Only human beings could bring about transformations, magnificent or diabolical. Their fate was in their own hands.

Dear Millennium,

Anyway, you're a fake. The 1999/2000 changeover would only be the millennium if there had been a Year Zero A.D. before a Year 0001, and there wasn't, which means that two thousand years will be completed at the end of the two thousandth year and were not completed at the beginning of it. These bells and fireworks and street parties are all a year early. The real transformative moment is yet to arrive. And, as I'm writing this from my know-it-all place in the future, I can tell you with complete authority that, what with the U.S. election in November 2000 and the well-known subsequent events of

September 2001, a year from this faux-millennium was when the change did come.

On Twelfth Night, just a couple of weeks after Elizabeth took Milan to see his "grandma," Carol Knibb tried to commit suicide, leaving letters for a number of people including Elizabeth. She said she had no faith in her treatment and preferred to "end it." She didn't succeed because she didn't take enough morphine. Her husband, Brian, woke her up, and though she said that she wished he hadn't, she would probably have woken up anyway. She was in an isolation ward now because in this condition the slightest infection could bear her away. Her white corpuscle count was down to two (it should have been twelve), and the red count was also very low. The chemotherapy had had a very destructive effect. Brian called Edward Said's doctor Kanti Rai, who said yes, there were other treatments available in America, but he couldn't swear that they were better than the attention she was receiving. Elizabeth was badly hit by Carol's suicide attempt. "She was like a rock to me," she said, and then added, "But in a way I've been my own rock ever since my mother died." He hugged her to comfort her and she said, "Do you still . . ." but then broke off and left the room. Something wrenched hard at his heart.

Then it was her birthday and he took her and Zafar and five of her oldest friends to dinner at the Ivy. But when they came home she confronted him and demanded to know what he was going do. He spoke to her about the destructive effect of the battle between her desire for more babies and his for New York and he uttered for the first time the word "divorce."

At the end of a marriage there was no originality. The one who was ending it slowly dragged himself away, while the one who did not want it to end swung between sorrowing love and vengeful anger. There were days when they remembered the people they had always been and found a way to be generous and understanding, but those

days became rarer. Then there were lawyers and after that both people were angry and the one who was ending it stopped feeling guilty,
*you came into my life riding a bicycle and working as a junior editor and
living in someone's attic as their lodger and you want to leave it as a multi-
millionairess,* and the one who had not wanted it to end did everything she could have sworn she would never do and made it difficult
for the one who was ending it to see his son, *I will never forgive you,
you have ruined his life, I'm not thinking about you, I'm thinking of him,*
and they had to take that to court and the judge had to tell them that
they should not be in his courtroom because they owed it to their
child to work it out. These were not the people they truly were.
Those people would reemerge in time, after the name-calling and
greed and destructiveness had passed, after the one who was being
left met the Illusion face-to-face in New York and abused her in a
vocabulary nobody had realized she even possessed, after they worked
out how to share their son, somewhere in that future after the war
was over and the pain had begun to fade they recaptured themselves
and remembered that they liked each other and that beyond liking
each other they needed to be good parents to their child, and then a
little imp of cordiality crept back into the room, and pretty soon they
were discussing things like adults, still disagreeing, disagreeing quite
a lot, in fact, and still sometimes losing patience with each other, but
managing to speak, even to meet, finding their way back not so
much to each other as to themselves, and even managing, just sometimes, to smile.

And what took even longer, but happened in the end, was the
return of a friendship, which allowed them to do things as a family
once again, to eat in each other's homes, to go out to dinner and a
movie with the boys, even to take vacations together in France, in
India, and, yes, in America too. In the end it would be a relationship
to be proud of, one that had been broken and stomped on and broken
again, but then rebuilt, not easily, not without moments of destructiveness, but slowly, seriously, by the people they truly were, who had
reemerged from the science-fiction armor, the wild monster-movie
bodysuits, of the people the divorce made them be.

It would take years for this to happen, and it would require his Illusion to stab him in the heart and vanish from his life, not in a green puff of smoke like the Wicked Witch of the West but in some ancient Scrooge McDuck's private jet, into his private world at Dismal Downs and other places filled with wretchedness and cash. After eight years during which she had told him once a week on average that he was too old for her she ended up with a duck who was two hundred years older, because Scrooge McDuck could open the enchanted door that allowed her into her own secret dreamworld of infinite entitlement, of life lived with no limits on the Big Rock Candy Mountain with the birds and the bees and the cigarette trees; and because in a private room of a private pleasure dome in Duckburg, USA, there was a swimming pool filled with golden doubloons and they could dive off the low springboard there and swim for hours as Uncle Scrooge liked to swim, in the soothing liquidity of his money; and so what if he was Duck Cheney's close friend and John McDuck (no relation) would tell him he could have his choice of U.S. ambassadorships after the defeat of Barack Obama?, that didn't matter, because in the basement of his private castle was the Diamond as Big as the Ritz, and in the cave at the heart of Duck Mountain, which he had bought in a venture-capitalist coup long ago in the Jurassic era when he was just a young duckling of seventy summers or so, his tame tyrannosaurus flanked by his loyal velociraptors guarded from all marauders his fabled dragon hoard, his private uncountable stash.

Once she had gone away into the world of make-believe where she truly belonged, reality returned. Elizabeth and he did not remarry, nor did they become lovers again, because that would have been unrealistic, but they were able to be better parents, and also the best of friends, and their true characters were shown not in the war they fought but in the peace they made.

In the year 2000 that old story, the *fatwa,* did resurface now and then. He was in Manhattan standing on a Barrow Street sidewalk after looking at a possible place to rent when the British foreign secretary called him on his cellphone. *How bizarre this is,* he thought. *I'm standing here unprotected and going about my everyday life while Robin Cook tells me that*

his Iranian counterpart, Kharrazi, has promised that everyone in Iran is be-
hind the deal, but British intelligence still isn't convinced, and by the way
Kharrazi says the story about the men selling their kidneys isn't true, blah
blah blah. He had thrown a switch in his head and wasn't waiting to be
given the green light by the British government or Iran anymore, he
was building his freedom by himself right here on the sidewalks of
New York, and if he could just find a place to live that would really,
really help.

There was an apartment on Sixty-fifth Street and Madison across
the street from the Armani store. The ceilings weren't high enough
and it wasn't that beautiful but he could afford it and the owner was
ready to sell it to him. It was a co-op, so he had to be approved by the
co-op board, but the seller was the chairman of that board and promised it would not be a problem, which proved that even chairmen of
Upper East Side co-op boards could be ignorant of what people really
thought of them, because when it was time for the interview, the hostility of the board toward the candidate could not wholly be explained
by the cloud over the candidate's head. He arrived at a glossy apartment populated by lacquered ladies whose faces didn't move, as if they
were masked characters in a Greek tragedy, and he was ordered to take
off his shoes to protect the fluffy white rug on the floor. There followed an interview so perfunctory that it could only mean one of two
things: the masked goddesses had already decided to say yes, or they
had already decided to say no. At the end of the appointment he said
he would be grateful for a quick decision, at which the grandest of the
grande dames shrugged eloquently and said through the Oresteian im-
mobility of her face that the decision would happen when it happened, and then added, "New York's a very tough town, Mr. Rushdie,
and I'm sure you understand why." "No?" he wanted to say. "No, as a
matter of fact I don't understand, Mrs. Sophocles, could you explain
that?" But he knew what she was really saying. "No. Over my dead
Botoxed liposucked rib-removed colonically irrigated body. Never in
a million years."

In the years that followed he occasionally wished he had remembered that lady's name because he owed her a big thank-you.
If he had passed the board he would have been obliged to buy the

apartment he didn't really like. He failed, and that very afternoon he found his new home. Sometimes it was hard not to believe in Fate.

The U2 song—"his" song—was being played on the radio and DJs seemed to like it. "In the film," Padma said to him, "I have to play Vina Apsara. I'm perfect casting for her. Obviously." *How she made me feel, how she made me real.* "But you're not a singer," he said, and she lost her temper. "I'm taking singing lessons," she said. "My coach says I have real potential." The film rights to the novel had recently been acquired by the piratically dashing Portuguese producer Paulo Branco and the film was to be directed by Raúl Ruiz. He met Branco and proposed Padma for the female lead. "Of course," said Branco. "That will be perfect." In those days he had not learned how to translate producer-speak into English. He did not realize that Branco was really saying, "Of course not."

He had lunch in London with Lee Hall, the acclaimed, Oscar-nominated screenwriter of *Billy Elliot,* who loved *The Ground Beneath Her Feet* and was eager to work on the screenplay. When Ruiz refused even to meet Hall the project began to go rapidly downhill. Ruiz hired an Argentinian screenwriter, Santiago Amigorena, a Spanish speaker who would write the screenplay in French, after which it would be translated into English. The first draft of this Chimera, this Pushmi-Pullyu of a screenplay, was predictably appalling. "Life is a carpet," one of the characters was asked to say, "and we can only see the full design in our dreams." That was one of the better lines of dialogue. He protested to Branco and was asked if he would be prepared to work with Amigorena on a revised version. He agreed and flew to Paris and met Santiago, a nice man and no doubt an excellent writer in his own language. After their discussions, however, Amigorena sent him a second draft that was as opaquely mystical as the first. He took a deep breath and told Branco he would like to write a draft himself. When he sent this screenplay to Branco, he was told that Raúl Ruiz had refused to read it. "He won't even read it? Why?" he called Branco to ask. "You have to understand," Branco replied, "that we are here in the Universe of Raúl Ruiz." "Oh," he said, "I thought we were in the universe of my novel." The project broke down irretrievably within a few days, and Padma's dream of playing Vina Apsara came to an early end.

"New York is a tough town, Mr. Rushdie." He woke up one morning to find a full-length photograph of Padma on page one of the *Post,* and beside her, below a small inset picture of himself, was the headline, in letters two inches high, TO DIE FOR.

And the next day in the same newspaper there was a cartoon in which his face was seen through the crosshairs of a sniper's rifle. The caption read, DON'T BE SILLY, PADMA, THOSE KOOKY IRANIANS WOULD NEVER COME AFTER ME IN NEW YORK. And again a few weeks later, in the *Post* again, there was a photograph of the two of them together walking down a Manhattan street, and the headline WORTH DYING FOR. The story was out everywhere, and in London one newspaper editor claimed his office was being "flooded" with letters demanding that Rushdie's royalties be seized because he was "laughing at Britain" by living openly in New York.

Now she was scared. Her picture had been in all the papers in the world and she felt vulnerable, she said. He met, in Andrew Wylie's office, with officers from the intelligence division of the NYPD, who were surprisingly reassuring. In a way the *Post* had done him a favor, they said. They had announced his arrival in the city so loudly that if any of the "bad guys" they were monitoring had been interested there would have been an immediate response. But there had been no disturbance in the Force. Everything was calm. "We don't think anyone is interested in you at this point," they told him. "So we have no problem with your plans."

Those plans included a deliberate policy of being seen in public. There would be no more "hiding." He would eat at Balthazar, Da Silvano and Nobu, he would go to movie screenings and book launches and be seen enjoying himself at late-night hot spots such as Moomba, at which Padma was well known. He would inevitably be jeered at in some quarters for turning into some sort of party monster but it was the only way he could think of to demonstrate to people that they didn't have to be afraid, that things were going to be different now, that it was *okay.* Only by living openly, visibly and fearlessly, and being written about for doing so, could he reduce the climate of fear around him, which was now, in his opinion, a bigger obstacle than whatever Iranian threat still remained. And in spite of her frequent moodiness, her capacity for brattish "model behavior," and her not infrequent coldness toward him, Padma, to her great credit, agreed that this was how he should live, and was prepared to stand next to him while he did so, even if, in Besant Nagar, Madras, her grandfather K. C. Krishnamurti—"K.C.K."—was giving interviews to the press saying he was "horrified" by this Rushdie's presence in his granddaughter's life.

(In their years together he visited Padma's Madras relatives several times. K.C.K. soon gave up his opposition to the relationship, being unable, he said, to deny his beloved granddaughter whatever she said was making her happy. "This Rushdie," in turn, came to think of Padma's family as the best part of her, the Indian part in which he wanted so much to believe. He became especially close to her mother's much younger sister Neela, who was more like a big sister to Padma than an aunt, and that was almost like having a new sister himself. When Padma was with her Madras family, who were good-humored, no-nonsense people, she became a different person, simpler, less affected, and the combination of that Madrasi simplicity with her astonishing beauty was utterly irresistible. Sometimes he thought that if she and he could build a family life that made her feel as safe as this little Besant Nagar world, she might feel able to be her unassuming best self always, and if she could do that then they could certainly be happy. But that was not what life had in store.)

The *Oresteia* was playing at the National Theatre in London and as the media unpleasantness went on and on (and there had been the usual we're-going-to-kill-you *fatwa*-anniversary noises out of Iran, making him wonder for the thousandth time about the wisdom of what he was doing) he wondered if he too would be pursued by the Furies all his days, the three Furies of Islamic fanaticism, press criticism and an angry abandoned wife; or might he, like Orestes, one day break the curse upon his house, be acquitted by some modern Athena's justice, and be allowed to live out his days in peace?

He was writing a novel called *Fury.* He had been invited to write it for the Dutch Book Week "gift," the first non-Dutch author to be so honored. Every year during Dutch Book Week the "gift" was given away to everyone who bought a book in a bookstore. Hundreds of thousands of copies were distributed. Mostly these were short books, but *Fury* was growing into a full-length novel. In spite of everything that was happening in his life it was pouring out of him, insisting on being written, demanding to exist with an urgency that almost scared him. He had actually been working on another novel—the book that would eventually become *Shalimar the Clown*—but *Fury* had barged in and pushed *Shalimar* temporarily off his desk.

At the heart of the book was the idea that he had arrived in Manhattan when it believed itself to be experiencing a golden age—"the city boiled with money," he wrote—and he knew that such "pinnacle moments" were always of brief duration. He decided he wanted to take the creative risk of capturing the moment while he was living through it, to abandon the perspective of history and push his nose right up against the present, to set it down on paper while it was still happening. If he got it right, he thought, then the book's contemporary readers, especially in New York City, would experience recognition pleasure, the satisfaction of saying to themselves *Yes, that's the way it is,* and in the future the book would bring the moment back to life for readers who were too young to have lived through it, and they would say *Yes, that's the way it must have been, the way it was.* If he got it wrong . . . well, where there was no risk of failure there was also no possibility of success. Art was always a risk, always made at the edge of possibility, and it always put the artist in question, and that was the way he liked it.

Moving through the city was a man he created to be both like him and unlike; like him in that he was of the same age, of Indian origin, with a British history and a broken marriage; a newcomer to New York. He wanted to make it clear that he could not and would not try to write about the city as a born-and-bred New Yorker might. He would write another kind of characteristic New York story, a tale of arrival. But his Malik Solanka's *anomie* and grouchiness was intentionally developed to separate him from his creator. Solanka's somewhat sour and disenchanted take on the city to which he had come to save himself was deliberately, comically contradictory; he was against what he was for, he grumbled about the very things that had drawn him to this town. And the Fury was not a creature pursuing Malik Solanka, clawing at his head, but the thing he feared most within himself.

Saladin Chamcha in *The Satanic Verses* had been another attempt to create an anti- or opposite-self, and it was puzzling that in both cases these characters whom he had written to be other than himself were read by many people as simple self-portraits. But Stephen Dedalus was not Joyce, and Herzog was not Bellow, and Zuckerman was not Roth, and Marcel was not Proust; writers had always worked close to the bull, like matadors, had played complex games with autobiography, and yet their creations were more interesting than themselves. Surely this was known. But what was known could also be forgotten. He had to rely on the passage of the years to clear things up.

The Ground Beneath Her Feet had been declared the winner of the "Eurasian region" of the Commonwealth Writers' Prize for Best Book. The overall winner would be declared at a ceremony in New Delhi in April. He decided he would go. He would take Zafar with him and go. He would reclaim India after all the lost and sometimes angry years. (The Indian ban on *The Satanic Verses* was, of course, still in place.)

Vijay Shankardass called him before he left London. The Delhi police were extremely nervous about his impending arrival. Could he please avoid being spotted on the plane? His bald head was very recognizable; would he please wear a hat? His eyes were also easily identified; would he please wear sunglasses? His beard, too, should be concealed. He should wear a scarf around it. Too hot? Oh, but there were cotton scarves. . . . "Salman," Vijay said, carefully, "there's a lot of tension out here. I'm feeling fairly anxious myself."

He didn't know what to expect. Would he be welcomed or spurned? There was only one way to find out.

When he got off the plane in Delhi he felt an urge to kiss the ground, or, rather, the blue rug in the airport jetway, but was too embarrassed to do it beneath the watchful eyes of a small army of security guards. The hot day enfolded him and Zafar like an embrace. They climbed into a cramped, white Hindustan Ambassador. Its air-conditioning system wasn't working. He was back.

India rushed in from every direction. BUY CHILLY COCKROACH TRAPS! DRINK HELLO MINERAL WATER! SPEED THRILLS BUT KILLS! shouted the hoardings. There were new kinds of message, too. ENROLL FOR ORACLE 8I. GRADUATE WITH JAVA AS WELL. And, as proof that the long protectionist years were over, Coca-Cola was back with a vengeance. When he was last in India Coke was banned, leaving the field clear for the disgusting local imitations, Campa-Cola and Thums Up. Now there was a red Coke ad every hundred yards or so. Coke's slogan of the moment was written in Hindi transliterated into Roman script: *Jo Chaho Ho Jaaye.* Which could be translated, literally, as "Whatever you desire, let it come to pass." He chose to think of this as a blessing.

HORN PLEASE, demanded the signs on the backs of the one million trucks blocking the road. All the other trucks, cars, bikes, motor scooters, taxis and auto rickshaws enthusiastically responded, welcoming them to town with an energetic rendition of the symphony of the Indian street. *Wait for Side! Sorry-Bye-Bye! Fatta Boy!*

It was impossible to tempt Zafar into Indian national dress. He himself put on a cool, loose kurta-pajama outfit the moment he arrived, but Zafar insisted, "It's just not my style," preferring to stay in his young Londoner's uniform of T-shirt, cargo pants and sneakers. (By the end of the trip he was wearing the white pajamas, but not the kurtas; still, progress of a kind had been made.)

There were signs at the Red Fort advertising an evening *son et lumière* show. "If Mum was here," Zafar said suddenly, "she'd insist on coming to that." *Yes,* he thought, *she would.* "Well," he answered his son, "she was here, you know." He began to tell Zafar about their trip in 1974, and what his mother thought of this or that—how much she liked the serenity of this spot, or the hubbub over there. The journey acquired a new dimension.

He had known that the first visit would be the trickiest. If it went well, things would ease. The second visit? "Rushdie returns again" wasn't much of a news story. And the third—"Oh, here he is once more"—barely sounded like news at all. In the long slog back to "normality," habituation, even boredom, was a useful weapon. He planned to bore India into submission.

His protectors had a nightmare scenario in their heads, involving rioting mobs. In Old Delhi, where many Muslims lived, they were especially on edge, particularly whenever a member of the public committed the faux pas of recognizing him. "Sir, there has been exposure! Exposure has occurred! Sir, they have said the name, sir! The name has been spoken! Sir, please, the hat!"

The Official Brits kept their distance from him. The head of the British Council in India, Colin Perchard, refused him permission to use the council's auditorium for a press conference. The British high commissioner, Sir Rob Young, had been instructed by the Foreign Office to stay away from him. He tried not to care, reminding himself why he was really there. The Commonwealth Writers' Prize was only a pretext. This trip with Zafar was the real victory. India itself was the prize.

They went on a road trip: Jaipur, Fatehpur Sikri, Agra, Solan. There were more trucks than he remembered, many more, blaring and lethal, often driving straight at them down the wrong side of the carriageway. There were wrecks from head-on smashes every few miles.

Look, Zafar, that is the shrine of a prominent Muslim saint; all the truckers stop there and pray for luck, even the Hindus. Then they get back into their cabs and take hideous risks with their lives and ours as well. Look, Zafar, that is a tractor-trolley loaded with men. At election time the *sarpanch,* or headman, of every village is ordered to provide such trolleyloads for politicians' rallies. For Sonia Gandhi, ten tractor-trolleys per village is the requirement. People are so disillusioned with politicians these days that nobody would actually go to the rallies of their own free will. Look, those are the polluting chimneys of brick kilns smoking in the fields.

Outside the city the air is less filthy, but it still isn't clean. But in Bombay between December and February, think of this, aircraft can't land or take off before 11 A.M. because of the smog.

Every hundred yards or so they saw a sign reading STD-ISD-PCO. PCO was personal call office, and now anyone could pop into one of these little booths, make calls to anywhere in India or, indeed, the world, and pay on the way out. This was the first communications revolution of India. A few years later there would be a second, and hundreds of millions of cellphones would put Indians in touch with one another and with the world as never before.

Zafar was almost twenty-one. Going with him to Solan, to their reclaimed villa, was an emotional moment. One day it would belong to Zafar and little Milan. They would be the fourth generation of the family to come here. Theirs was a far-flung family and this little acre of continuity stood for a lot.

The air freshened, tall conifers leaned from steep slopes. As the sun set the lights of the first hill stations glowed above them in the twilight. They passed a narrow-gauge railway train on its slow, picturesque way up to Shimla. They stopped at a *dhaba* near Solan for dinner and the owner was happy he was there. Someone else ran up for an autograph. He ignored the worried frown on the police team chief Akshey Kumar's face. He hadn't been to Solan since he was twelve years old, but it felt like home.

It was dark when they reached Anis Villa. From the road they had to climb down 122 steps to reach it. At the bottom there was a little gate and Vijay formally welcomed him to the home he had won back for the family. The *chowkidar* Govind Ram ran up and astonished Zafar by stooping down to touch their feet. The sky was on fire with stars. He went into the back garden by himself. He needed to be alone.

He was woken at 5 A.M. by amplified music and chanting from a Hindu temple across the valley. He got dressed and walked around the house in the dawn light. With its high-pitched pink roofs and little corner turrets it was more beautiful than he remembered, more beautiful than it looked in Vijay's photographs of it, and the view of the hills was stunning. It was a very strange feeling to walk around a house he didn't know that somehow belonged to him.

They spent most of the day mooching around the premises, sitting in the garden under the shade of big old conifers, eating Vijay's special scrambled eggs. The trip had been worthwhile: He knew it from the expression on Zafar's face.

———

Rumors of his presence in India were rife. A couple of Islamic organizations had vowed to make trouble. At dinner in Solan's Himani restaurant, he was tucking into the spicy Indian version of Chinese food when he was spotted by a Doordarshan reporter called Agnihotri who was on vacation with his family. Within moments a local press reporter arrived and asked a few friendly questions. None of this was very unexpected, but as a result of these chance encounters the jitteriness of the police reached new heights, and boiled over into a full-scale row. Back at Anis Villa, Vijay received a call on his cellphone from a police officer named Kulbir Krishan in Delhi. This call made Vijay lose his composure for the first time in all the years of their friendship. He was almost trembling as he said, "We are accused of having called those journalists to the restaurant. This man says we have not been gentlemen, we have not kept our word, and we have, if you can believe the phrase, 'talked out of turn.' Finally the fellow says, 'There will be riots in Delhi tomorrow, and if we fire on the crowds and there are deaths, the blood will be on your heads.' "

He was horrified. This was becoming a matter of life and death. If the Delhi police had become so trigger-happy that they were preparing to kill people, they had to be stopped before it was too late. No time now for niceties. Zafar looked on, dazed, while he deliberately blew his stack at poor, decent Akshey Kumar (who was not at all to blame) and told him that unless Kulbir Krishan got back on the phone at once, apologized to Vijay personally, and gave an assurance that there were no plans to murder anybody tomorrow, he would insist on driving through the night back to New Delhi so that he could be waiting at Prime Minister Vajpayee's office door at dawn to ask him to deal with the problem personally. After a certain amount of this kind of raging Kulbir did call back to speak of "misunderstandings" and promised that there would be no shootings or deaths. "If I spoke out of context," he memorably concluded, "then I am very sorry indeed."

He burst out laughing at the sheer absurdity of this formulation and put down the phone. But he did not sleep well. The meaning of his Indian journey would be defined by what happened in the next two days, and even though he hoped and believed that the police were being unnecessarily nervous, he couldn't be sure. Delhi was their town, and he was Rip van Winkle.

At half past twelve the next day they were back in Delhi and he was closeted in a meeting with R. S. Gupta, the special assistant commissioner in charge of security for the whole city, a calm, forceful man. He painted a dark picture. A Muslim politician, Shoaib Iqbal, planned to go to Friday midday prayers at Juma Masjid and seek Imam Bukhari's help to start a demonstration against him, and against the Indian government for allowing him to enter the country. The numbers could be huge and bring the city to a standstill. "We are negotiating with them," Gupta said, "to keep the numbers small, and the event peaceful. Maybe we will succeed." After a couple of hours of high-tension waiting, during which he was effectively confined to quarters—"Sir, no movements, please"—the news was good. Less than two hundred people marched—and two hundred marchers, in India, was a number smaller than zero—and it had all gone off without a hitch. The nightmare scenario had not come to pass. "Fortunately," Mr. Gupta said, "we have been able to manage it."

What really happened? The security worldview was always impressive and often persuasive, but it was just one version of the truth. It was one of the characteristics of security forces everywhere in the world to try and have it both ways. Had there been mass demonstrations, they would have said, "You see, all our nervousness has been amply justified." But there were no such marches; and so, "We were able to prevent the trouble because of our foresight and skill." Maybe so, he thought. But it might also be the case that for the vast majority of Indian Muslims, the controversy over *The Satanic Verses* was old hat, and in spite of the efforts of the politician and the imam (both of whom made blood-and-thunder speeches) nobody could really be bothered to march. *Oh, there's a novelist in town to go to a dinner? What's his name? Rushdie? So what?* This was the view taken, almost without exception, by the Indian press in its analysis of the day's events. The small demonstration was noted, but the private political agendas of its organizers were also pointed out. The script in people's heads was being rewritten. The foretold catastrophe—riots, killings—had not come to pass. What happened instead was extraordinary, and, for Zafar and himself, an event of immense emotional impact. What burst out in the city was not violence, but joy.

At a quarter to eight in the evening, he and Zafar walked into the Commonwealth Writers' Prize reception at the Oberoi Hotel and from that moment until they left India the celebrations never stopped. Journalists and photographers surrounded them, their faces wreathed in most unjournalistic smiles. Friends burst through the media wall to embrace them. The actor Roshan Seth, recently recovered from serious heart problems, hugged him and said, "Look at us, *yaar,* we're both supposed to be dead but still going strong." The eminent columnist Amita Malik, a friend of his family's from the old days in Bombay, at first mistook Zafar for his father's bodyguard (to Zafar's great delight) but then reminisced wonderfully about the past, praising Anis Rushdie's wit, his quick gift for repartee, and telling tales of Negin's beloved brother Hameed, who died too young, too long ago. Gifted young writers—Raj Kamal Jha, Namita Gokhale, Shauna Singh Baldwin—came up to say generous things about the significance of his writing for their own work. One of the great ladies of English-language Indian literature, the novelist Nayantara Sahgal, clasped his hands and whispered, "Welcome home." And there was Zafar being interviewed for television and speaking touchingly about his own happiness at being there. His heart overflowed. He had not really dared to expect this, had been infected by the fears of the police, and had defended himself against many kinds of disappointment. Now the defenses fell away and happiness rose like a tropical dawn, fast and brilliant and hot. India was his again. It was a rare thing to be granted one's heart's desire.

He did not win the Commonwealth Writers' Prize, which went to J. M. Coetzee. But this was a homecoming party more than an awards ceremony. RUSHDIE IN INDIA: THERE IS ONLY JOY, LOTS OF JOY. As *The Indian Express*'s hyperbolically affectionate front-page headline demonstrated, the party spirit was spilling into the media, drowning the few, muted negative voices. In all his conversations with the press he tried to avoid reopening old wounds, to tell Indian Muslims that he was not and had never been their enemy, and to stress that he was in India to mend broken links and to begin, so to speak, a new chapter. *The Asian Age* concurred: "Let's turn a page."

Elsewhere, in *Outlook,* there was pleasure that India had "made some amends for being the first to ban *The Satanic Verses* and subjecting him to the persecution and agony that followed." *The Pioneer* expressed its satisfaction that India was, once again, standing up for "democratic values and the individual's right to express himself." It also, in a less elevated mood, improbably but delightfully accused him of "turning the city's sophisticated party women into a bunch of giggling schoolgirls" who told their men, "Dahling, [he] could send Bollywood hunks back to school." Dilip Padgaonkar of *The Times of India* put it most movingly. "He is reconciled with India and India with him. . . . Something sublime has happened to him which should enable him to continue to mesmerize us with his yarns. He has returned to where his heart has always been. He has returned home." In the *Hindustan Times,* there was an editorial headed RECONSIDER THE BAN. This sentiment was echoed right across the media. In *The Times of India* an Islamic scholar, among other intellectuals, backed an end to the ban. On the electronic media, opinion polls ran 75 percent to 25 percent in favor of allowing *The Satanic Verses* to be freely published in India at long last.

Vijay threw a farewell party for him. His two actress aunts, Uzra Butt and her sister Zohra Segal, were there, with his cousin Kiran Segal, Zohra's daughter and one of the country's foremost exponents and teachers of the Odissi school of Indian classical dancing. This was the zany wing of the family, sharp of tongue and mischievous of eye. Uzra and Zohra were the grand dames of the Indian theater, and everyone had been a little in love with Kiran at one time or another. Zohra and Kiran lived in an apartment in Hampstead in the 1960s, and during his Rugby days he had sometimes spent vacations in their spare bedroom, next to Kiran's bedroom door, on which there was a large, admonitory skull and crossbones sign. Vijay Shankardass and Roshan Seth both stayed in the same spare room in the same period. All three of them had looked wistfully at the skull and crossbones and none of them ever got past it.

"I haven't seen you dance for years," he said to Kiran.

"Come back soon," she said. "Then I'll dance."

———

Once upon a time a boy named Milan and his father lived together by the shore of a magic river. If you went up the river toward its source you grew younger the farther you went. If you went downriver you got older. If you went sideways down one of the many tributaries of the river, look out! You could turn into someone else entirely. Milan and his father traveled downriver in a small boat and he grew up into a man but when he saw how old his father had become he didn't want to be a man anymore, he wanted to be a boy again. So they went back home and he grew young again and his father went back to normal too. When Milan told his mother she didn't believe his story, she thought the magic river was just a river and she didn't care where it came from or where it went or what happened to those who moved upon its waters. But it was true. He and his father both knew it was true, and that's what counted. The end.

"I like you, Daddy. I told you you could put me to sleep."

He was still living at the Bishop's Avenue house when he was in London, sleeping in one of the bedrooms vacated by the police, but that had to change. "Let's get on with this. I'm sick of living with you," Elizabeth said, but she also said, "You know we could easily make this work if you wanted it to." They fought and then she wanted to hold his hand and then they fought again. This was a very bad time. *You don't have the upper hand in this. You have created this situation and now you must face the consequences.* And on another day, *I still love you. I don't know what to do with all this feeling.* But one day in the future they would walk together on a beach in Goa, and wander down the *route de Cézanne* in France, and she would come to New York and stay in his home and dress up as Morticia Addams (Milan was Michael Jackson and he was Tony Soprano) and they would go to the Village for Halloween.

Carol Knibb died ten days after Milan's third birthday but he never forgot her. His only "real" grandmother was far away and refusing to fly anymore no matter how often she was asked, and he never met her. Carol was the nearest thing he had and now he had lost her. He was too young to become so closely acquainted with death.

Helen Fielding called. "Hello, Salman. How would you like to make a fool of yourself?" They were making a film of *Bridget Jones's Diary* and she wanted him to be in a scene at a book party at which Bridget asked a writer the way to the toilet. "Okay," he said, "why not?" Acting was his unscratched itch. At school he had played (in hunchbacked, woolen-stockinged drag) the mad doctor Fräulein Mathilde von Zahnd in Dürrenmatt's *The Physicists*. At Cambridge he had been cast in a few modest roles in undergraduate productions, a frightened judge in Bertolt Brecht's *Private Life of the Master Race,* a statue that came to life in Eugène Ionesco's *The Future Is in Eggs,* and Pertinax Surly, the skeptical sidekick of the easily duped Sir Epicure Mammon, in Ben Jonson's *The Alchemist*. Then after Cambridge there had been the Oval House. He had sometimes dreamed with Bill Buford of running away one year and signing up with an obscure summer stock company in the Midwest and performing happily in absurd comedies and dreadful melodramas, but that was out of the question now. A couple of days making a fool of himself on *Bridget* would have to do.

The party scene took two days to film. Renée Zellweger stuck to her English accent all the time, even off-camera, so that he had the odd feeling of meeting Bridget Jones, not the actress playing her. Colin Firth was funny and welcoming. "I secretly hope you're going to be lousy at this, because I can't write books." And Hugh Grant kissed him. There was a scene in which he and Hugh were supposed to greet each other as long-lost friends, and before one of the takes Hugh asked, "Do you mind if I kiss you in this one?" and then planted a major smacker right on his amazed mouth. The scene didn't make it into the final cut of the movie. His first screen kiss, he thought, and it was with Hugh Grant!, and it ended up on the cutting-room floor. (The only other man who ever kissed him was the film director Abel Ferrara, who once embraced him in a New York nightclub and used his gristly tongue. On that occasion, fortunately, there were no cameras rolling.)

It was harder than he expected to play a character called Salman Rushdie whose dialogue was written by someone else. If he had been at a book party when an inexperienced PR girl was being clumsy and foolish his instinct would have been to be nice to her, and he tried to play it that way, but it wasn't funny. The snootier he acted the more comic Bridget's confusion became. Jeffrey Archer was in the party scene too, and was very annoyed that he didn't have anything to say. "I've taken the trouble to turn up," he kept telling the producers. "The least you could do is write me a line or two." They didn't. Richard Curtis's script was the script and that was that. He himself tried to write a bit of extra dialogue for "Salman Rushdie"—obviously—but it was all cut out of the finished film, except for one exchange that could be heard in the background, faintly. Somebody asked him how autobiographical his books were and he replied, "You know, nobody's ever asked me that before."

Now they had a place to live in New York and at close quarters the Illusion was becoming real. She was capable of saying things of such majestic narcissism that he didn't know whether to bury his head in his hands or applaud. When the Indian movie star Aishwarya Rai was named the most beautiful Indian woman in the world in some glossy magazine or other, for example, Padma announced, in a room full of people, that she had "serious issues with that." Her moodiness was unpredictable and extreme. About him, she was guarded. "I'm just giving it the summer and then we'll see." She blew cold and hot and he was beginning to be unsure if the hot made the cold worthwhile. She was dark and closed off for days at a time and then one morning the sunlight streamed out of her face. His journal was full of his own doubts. "How long can I stay with this woman whose selfishness is her most prominent characteristic?" One night they sat in Washington Square Park after a quarrelsome dinner and he told her, "This isn't working for me." After that for several days she was her sweetest self and he forgot why he had said what he said. She met some of his women friends and most of them approved. When he told her what they had said the positive remarks about her character mattered less to her than the comment about her perfect breasts. French *Playboy* found nude photographs of her and ran one on the cover, calling her his "fiancée." She didn't care about the words and she didn't mind the picture being there, but she wanted to be paid for it, and he had to hire a French lawyer to work for her. *This is what I'm doing now,* he thought, bewildered. *My girlfriend is on the cover of* Playboy *in the nude and I'm negotiating the fee.*

Her mother called, weeping, in a marital crisis. She wanted to get away from her husband, Padma's stepfather. "Of course," he said at once, "she must come and stay with us." "That was the day I knew I loved you," Padma told him afterward. "When you immediately agreed to look after my mom." And yes, they loved each other. There were many years when he thought of it as a great love affair, a grand passion, and so, he believed, did she. Yes, it was unstable, and yes, perhaps it was doomed; but while it was happening he did not think of it as illusory. He thought of it as the real thing.

Zafar came to New York and met her. He liked her, he said, but found it odd that she was closer to his own generation than his father's, and said it was an "odd fit, the intellectual and the model." But he thought she was "very nice" and "if that's what you want, I support it." He certainly saw, as everyone saw, the importance to his father of his new undefended life in New York, and that there could be no going back from that.

That summer he didn't want to return to Little Noyac Path, but Joseph Heller's widow, Valerie, offered him their house on Skimhampton Road on the East Hampton–Amagansett border. She had been invited to Italy and needed the break. "I haven't packed it up, Joe's clothes are still in the closets, so I want somebody I know to look after it." The idea of writing at Joseph Heller's desk was at once exciting and disorientingly strange. "His shirts would fit you," Valerie added. "Feel free to wear anything you like." *No,* he thought. *That would be going too far. No, thank you.*

He was by himself a lot because Padma was acting in a Mariah Carey movie that was shooting in Toronto, and by summer's end he had completed a draft of *Fury*. When he came back to the city and gave it to the woman with whom he was trying to make a new life she had almost nothing to say about it, except about the character who looked like her. *All right,* he told himself, *nobody gives you everything.* He set the typescript aside and they went out for the evening. In the small hours of the morning a thought occurred to him. "I am actually enjoying myself." "Which, folks," he wrote in his journal, "I am allowed to do."

There was extraordinary news. The British intelligence services had at long last downgraded the threat assessment. He was no longer at level two. He was now merely at level three, which was a big step toward normality, and if things continued to go well, they said, then in six months or so he might well be down at level four. Nobody at level four received Special Branch protection, so when that happened they could call it a day. He said, "Isn't it already a little overcautious? When I'm in America I hail cabs, take the subway, go to the ball game, picnic in the park. Then I come back to London and I have to be in the bulletproof car again." This is how we'd like to do it, they said. Slow and steady. We've been doing this too long to want to make a mistake with you now.

Level three! It made him feel that his instincts had been justified. He had been trying to show everyone that he could take back his life, and there were friends who thought he was being a fool; Isabel Fonseca had written him long, worried emails telling him that if he didn't "come to his senses" and hire bodyguards, "the obvious" was "inevitable." But now, very slowly, too slowly for his liking, the safety net of the security world was beginning to release him. He had to go on proving he was right and the doom-mongers were wrong. He would regain his freedom. Level four couldn't come soon enough.

Soon after this news came another huge concession. The condition of his marriage had been discussed, the Special Branch told him, and it was understood that at some point he would wish, and very probably need, to move out of the marital home. The higher-ups at the Yard, after discussions with Mr. Morning and Mr. Afternoon, had agreed that he could have an "overt" protection for six months at a new address. After that, assuming there was no negative change in the threat assessment, they would confirm the end of the danger to his life and the protection would cease. There it was at last. The finishing line had come into view.

Even though many of his women friends were being very supportive (not all of them; the critic Hermione Lee saw him in a restaurant and called him, only half-affectionately, a "scoundrel"), his worries about

Milan continued. And then there was another piece of crazy behavior from the real woman behind the Illusion, a quarrel woven out of thin air, and he found himself thinking, *I'll go back, I'll do it for Milan's sake,* and he made the stupid mistake of mentioning that possibility to Elizabeth, who reacted with hostility, interested—understandably enough—only in her own pain, not in his problems. He tried a second time and then a third. But she was so hurt, so guarded, that she could not respond. And in the meantime, in New York, the beautiful woman who had him in thrall pleaded with him not to go, and finally admitted that everything he'd been saying was true, all his criticisms were justified, but she wanted to make it work, and she would. He believed her. He couldn't help it. She was his dream of the future and he couldn't give it up. So he turned away from Elizabeth again. It was his last vacillation, and the cruelest, the weakest. He detested what he had done.

The lawyers went to war. Ten years had passed since he had eaten lamb and nasturtiums with Elizabeth at Liz Calder's apartment. A year had passed since the thunderbolt on Liberty Island.

After two false starts, two apartments whose owners were spooked by the security issues, he agreed to rent, for a year, a small Notting Hill mews house belonging to the pop star Jason Donovan, former star of *Joseph and the Amazing Technicolor Dreamcoat.* When the news got out the *Daily Insult* was predictably furious that this man, who "hated Britain," should now have uniformed policemen at his door around the clock because he no longer wanted to "hide." *You've got a nerve, Mr. Rushdie,* the *Insult* told him. Elizabeth didn't want Milan to come to the new house. It wasn't safe, she said. It would upset him terribly. "You're a selfish person who goes through life ruining other people's lives," she told him. "Who have you ever made happy? How can you live with yourself?" He had no good reply. But in the end Milan would come and stay with him. In the end he and Milan made and maintained a close, loving relationship, and Milan grew up to be an unusually mature, composed, strong-minded, sweet-natured, exceptional young person. In the end it was plain that Milan's life had not been ruined, and that he was a happy, openhearted fellow. Yes, in the end, in the end. But before the end, unfortunately, there had to be the middle.

Mr. Joseph Anton, international publisher of American origin, passed away unmourned on the day that Salman Rushdie, novelist of Indian origin, surfaced from his long underground years and took up part-time residence in Pembridge Mews, Notting Hill. Mr. Rushdie celebrated the moment, even if nobody else did.

X

At the Halcyon Hotel

UNTIL HE BEGAN HIS LIFE WITH PADMA HE KNEW VERY LITTLE ABOUT THE city of Los Angeles except the conventional wisdom that it was the place where illusions were born. For a long time he believed that the Twentieth Century–Fox logo was a real building, and he didn't know that the MGM lion was yawning, not roaring, and he wanted to know in which mountain range the Paramount mountain was located. In other words he was as gullible as most film fanatics even though he had been raised in a movie city as important as Hollywood and should by rights have been a hard-bitten insider-cynic who wanted only to debunk the industry's self-promotion, vanity, cruelty and deceit. Instead he fell for all of it, the whole Chinese Theatre concrete footprint hocus-pocus, he knew that the shaping influence on his own imagination of Fellini and Buñuel, but also of John Ford and Howard Hawks and Errol Flynn, and *Seven Brides for Seven Brothers* and *Knights of the Round Table* and *Scaramouche*—was as profound as that of Sterne or Joyce, and the street names, Sunset Boulevard, Coldwater Canyon, Malibu Colony, quickened his pulse, and this was where Nathanael West had lived when he wrote *The Day of the Locust,* and that was where Jim Morrison was living in the early days of the Doors. He wasn't a complete rube; his Nicaraguan friend Gioconda Belli was living in Santa Monica and introduced him to another, smarter, more political L.A., and so did his friend Roxana Tynan, who was working on the election campaign of the future mayor Antonio Villaraigosa, and one day he ran into the academic Zachary Leader in the Rexall drugstore on Beverly and La Cienega and Leader told him that this was where Aldous Huxley had first dropped mescaline, "so those," he said, pointing to the sliding glass doors of the pharmacy, "are the doors of perception."

Padma's immediate family (her mother had gone back to her stepfather after a couple of months' separation) lived in deeply unfashionable West Covina and she had attended La Puente High School—in a neighborhood so unsafe, she told him, that every day after school she ran all the way home and didn't stop until she got there—so that was yet another version of the city for him to explore. Even in Hollywood he remembered the sadness of F. Scott Fitzgerald's Pat Hobby stories about a broken-down screenwriter, and had enough of the ghoul in him to go looking for Cielo Drive and the ghost of Sharon Tate. He was still feeling like a convict recently sprung from the pen and so for him one of the great treats of the city was the thing that many other people hated about it: driving. He hadn't been able to drive himself for years so he rented a car and drove for hours, learning the city streets and the labyrinthine canyons, going up the Pacific Coast Highway and down to the Million Dollar Hotel, and if the freeways were jammed he drove the back roads and anyway was happy to sit in traffic and hum the old Pointer Sisters song "Fire" (*I'm ridin' in your car / you turn on the radio . . .*), which he remembered because it had been a hit when he came here as a young advertising copywriter to make commercials for Clairol's Nice 'n Easy and rode around the city escorted by a couple of Beverly Hills cops in mirror shades who thought they were Starsky and Hutch ("You want me to stop the traffic for you? You sure you don't? Because I could stop the traffic real easy, you know!"). Now there were no cops and he was living with a beautiful woman in her West Hollywood apartment on Kings Road between Beverly and Melrose while their New York place was being fixed up, and there were days when life felt very, very good.

The apartment was small, so he often worked at the library in Beverly Hills, happily anonymous, and because he loved local history he plunged into the city's past and found out that the angels in the city's name were the ones in Saint Francis of Assisi's first, very small church, the Porziuncola, and learned about the fabled Lizard People, who had lived in tunnels under the city thousands or hundreds of years ago or maybe just last week. For a brief moment he wanted to write about G. Warren Shufelt, who in 1934 invented some sort of vibration machine that actually *found the tunnels,* which could be accessed from a basement in the central library and ran all the way to Dodger Stadium and then, after his great discovery, and before he could show the tunnels to anyone else, the great Shufelt *mysteriously totally disappeared!, and was never seen again!, I mean, what* happened *to him?* Hmm, he thought, on second thought, maybe writing about old G. Warren wasn't such a good idea.

Hollywood was a small town inside a big city and for five minutes a new arrival such as himself became the flavor of the month. The film director Michael Mann invited him to dinner and they discussed a project for a movie about the Mexican border. The movie star Will Smith told him about being taught by Muhammad Ali to do the "Ali Shuffle." The producer Brian Grazer invited him to his office to ask if he wanted to write a movie about his life. A few years earlier he had heard from Christopher Hitchens that Milos Forman thought a Rushdie movie could be a great companion piece to his other free-speech film, *The People vs. Larry Flynt,* but that hadn't sounded right, and nor did this. If he told his story, he said to Grazer, he would do it in a book first. (He also liked being in Hollywood without being in the business. It was, well, *cooler.* The moment he signed a screenwriting deal he would be just another employee.)

He had lunch with Christopher Hitchens and Christopher's big fan Warren Beatty at the Beverly Hills Hotel. "Can I say," Warren Beatty said to him, "that when I saw you at dinner at Mr. Chow the other day you were with a woman so beautiful that it made me want to faint?" In those days he trusted her completely, so he replied, "I'll call her. Maybe she can join us." "Will you please tell her," Beatty said, "that Warren Beatty is here and he thought she was so beautiful that it made him want to faint." She was in her car, impatient, when he called. (She hated driving.) "I'm having lunch with Warren Beatty," he said, "and he says to tell you that he thinks you're so beautiful that it makes him want to faint." "Shut up," she said, "I don't have time for your jokes."

Once he had convinced her that he was telling the truth she did join them, and deliberately did nothing to doll herself up, arriving in sweatpants and tank top and looking, of course, as if she might make Warren Beatty faint. "You'll excuse me," the legendary lover said to him, "if I make a fool of myself over your lady for five minutes. After that we can go on having lunch." It was probably just as well that Annette Bening existed, he told himself, otherwise . . . well, never mind. They went on having lunch and that was that.

Carrie Fisher, his closest friend in Hollywood, sharp-witted and sharp-tongued, was uncertain about Padma. She gave a party so that he could meet, in particular, Meg Ryan, who might be more suitable, and whom he liked very much, even if she did keep saying (three times), "You know, people are *so wrong* about you!" But then the subject turned to the spiritual life and Meg talked about her many visits to ashrams in India and her admiration for Swami Muktananda and Gurumayi. That got in the way, especially because he told her of his skepticism regarding the guru industry, and suggested she might profitably read Gita Mehta's book *Karma Cola*. "Why are you so cynical?" she asked him, as if she genuinely wanted to know the answer, and he said that if you grew up in India it was easy to conclude that these people were fakes. "Yes, of course there are lots of charlatans," she said, reasonably, "but can't you discriminate?" He shook his head sadly. "No," he said. "No, I can't." That was the end of their chat.

The commute between West Hollywood and Pembridge Mews was brutal and the divorce, which had become too ugly to describe, the great difficulties being made about his access to his little boy, which drove him insane, the escalating cost of fixing the New York place, which turned out to be in much worse shape than he had thought, and Padma's changes of mood, which were so frequent that he was happy if things stayed good between them for two days consecutively, all had to be dealt with through a dull glaze of jet lag. And one day in L.A. he heard the news he had been awaiting with dread for some years. John Diamond had died. He buried his face in his hands and when the woman who said she loved him asked him what the matter was, and he told her, she answered, "I'm sorry you're sad, but you're just going to have to be sad until you're not." At such moments he thought he couldn't stay with her for another two seconds.

But he stayed. He stayed for another six years. When he looked back on those days through the disillusioned eyes of his post-divorce self he didn't fully understand his own behavior. Perhaps it had been a form of obstinacy, or a refusal to destroy the relationship for which he had destroyed a marriage, or an unwillingness to emerge from his dream of a happy future with her, even if it was a mirage. Or she was just too goddamn gorgeous to leave.

At the time, however, he had a simpler answer. He stayed with her because he loved her. Because they loved each other. Because they were in love.

They did break up several times in those years, for short periods, and often he was the one pulling away from her; but finally he asked her to marry him, and soon after their wedding she was the one who left. After her exit Milan, who had been the ring bearer at the ceremony, asked him, "Dad, how can such a beautiful day have meant nothing?" He had no answer. He felt the same way.

There were good moments, of course. They made a home together, decorated and furnished it as happily as any couple. "I built it with you with love and a pure heart," she told him years later, when they were speaking again, and he believed her. There was love and passion between them and when it was good it was very good indeed. They went together to the Book Ball in Amsterdam for the publication of *Woede,* which was *Fury* in Dutch, and she was a big hit; everyone was dazzled by her beauty, the national news set its film of her arrival at the airport to the tune of Charles Aznavour singing "Isn't She Lovely," and then there was a panel discussion of her extraordinary looks by four salivating critics. So she was happy, and treated him lovingly, and was the perfect girlfriend. However, there were also lower, and lowering, moments, and those were becoming more frequent. He slowly understood that she was becoming competitive with him and thought he was blocking her light. She didn't like playing second fiddle. "Don't come with me," she told him near the end of their time together, when they were invited to a movie awards event honoring his friend Deepa Mehta, "because when you're there people only want to talk to you." He told her she couldn't choose the days of the week on which she was married. "I've always been proud to be standing next to you," he said, "and I'm sad that you don't feel the same way about me." But she was determined to get out of his shadow, to strike out for herself; and in the end she did.

In the Age of Acceleration a newspaper column could not be written even a couple of days in advance. He had to wake up on the day his monthly piece for the *New York Times* syndicate was due, read the news, work out what subject or subjects people were most anxious about, think of something he legitimately had to offer on one of those subjects, and write a thousand words by 5 P.M. at the latest. Deadline journalism was a very different craft than that of the novelist and it took him a while to acquire it. At a certain point it became almost exhilarating to have to think at this sort of speed. It was a privilege, too, to have been allowed into the commentariat, that smallish group of columnists who had been anointed as the world's opinion formers. He had already discovered how hard it was to have opinions, especially the kind of opinions that "worked" in such columns—strong opinions, intensely argued. He had trouble coming up with one strong opinion a month and he was therefore in awe of those colleagues— Thomas Friedman, Maureen Dowd, Charles Krauthammer et al.— who could have two such opinions *every week*. He was in his third year, and had already written about anti-Americanism, Charlton Heston and the National Rifle Association, Kashmir, Northern Ireland, Kosovo, the attack on teaching the theory of evolution in Kansas, Jörg Haider, Elián González, and Fiji. He felt he might be on the verge of running out of things to feel strongly about, and suggested to Gloria B. Anderson at the *New York Times* syndicate that the time to give up the column might be approaching. She tried hard to dissuade him. Several of his columns had made an impression, she said. At the beginning of the year 2000 he had written that "the defining struggle of the new age would be between Terrorism and Security." That was something he was well qualified to write about, she told him, and if he was right, and she was sure he was, then, as she put it, "the news agenda will be coming around to you, and people will want to know what you have to say."

Gloria didn't know, and neither did he, how suddenly and emphatically the shift she predicted in the news agenda would happen. Nobody was looking out of the classroom window toward the winged storm gathering in the playground. He didn't know, and neither did Gloria, that the birds had massed on the climbing frame in the playground, and were almost ready to strike.

His attention was elsewhere. He had a new novel coming out in

England. On the cover was a black-and-white picture of the Empire State Building with a small black cloud directly above it, glowing at the edges. It was a book about fury, and yet its author had no idea of the fury to come.

It was his worst received novel since *Grimus*. One or two critics liked the novel and wrote about it with sympathy and understanding. Many other British reviewers treated it as thinly disguised autobiography and above more than one review there appeared a picture of himself and his "hot new girlfriend." This was painful, yes, but in the end it released him into another kind of freedom. He had always cared, sometimes too much, about being well reviewed. Now he saw that this, too, was another version of the trap of wanting to be loved into which he had catastrophically fallen several years before. Whatever was being said about his new book, he remained proud of it, he knew why it was the way it was and still felt that there were good artistic reasons for his choices. So all of a sudden he became capable of shrugging off the obloquy. Like all writers, he wanted his work to be appreciated, that was still true. Like all writers, he was going on an intellectual, linguistic, formal, and emotional journey; the books were messages from that journey, and he hoped readers would enjoy traveling with him. But, he now saw, if at some point they were unable to go down the road he'd taken, that was too bad, but that was still the road he was going to take. *If you can't come with me, I'm sorry,* he silently said to his critics, *but I'm still going this way.*

In Telluride, Colorado, he had to be careful how fast he walked, how quickly he climbed stairs, how much alcohol he drank. The air was thin, and he was an asthmatic. But this was a mountain paradise. Maybe the air was thin in the other Eden, too, he thought, but he was sure there weren't as many good movies being screened in that snake-and-apple man trap situated somewhere to the west of the land of Nod.

Tom Luddy and Bill Pence, the curators of the Telluride Film Festival, each year invited a third guest curator to join them, and in 2001 it was his turn. He had selected a short roster of "personal" films to show, including Satyajit Ray's *The Golden Fortress,* about a boy who dreamed of an earlier life in a golden fortress filled with jewels; Andrei Tarkovsky's *Solaris,* about a planet that was a single mind so powerful that it could bring men's deepest desires to life; and Fritz Lang's silent-era masterwork *Metropolis,* a dark poem about tyranny and freedom, man and machine, restored and rescued at last from Giorgio Moroder's electronica sound track.

It was Labor Day weekend, his last free time before *Fury*'s American publication. He met Padma in Los Angeles and they flew to Colorado, to spend her thirty-first birthday, which fell on September 1, watching movies in the mountains and walking the informal streets of the town where Butch and Sundance had robbed their first bank, having a coffee with Werner Herzog here, a chat with Faye Dunaway there. At Telluride nobody was hustling or selling and everyone was approachable. The movie polymaths Leonard Maltin and Roger Ebert, the documentary filmmaker Ken Burns and other well-informed movie folk were on hand, imparting wisdom and cracking wise. The agreed position of everyone at Telluride was that Tom Luddy knew everyone on earth. The great Luddy, Lord of Misrule and master of ceremonies, took it all in good part. Telluride was a jokey place. To ride the ski lift up the mountain to the Chuck Jones theater you had to make a Wabbit Weservation.

They saw the hit French movie *Amélie* with its slightly-too-sweet elements of fantasy and the Croatian *No Man's Land,* directed by Danis Tanovic, which was like *Waiting for Godot* in a trench under fire, and Agnieszka Holland's workmanlike, HBO-financed *Shot in the Heart,* an adaptation of Mikal Gilmore's book about his murderer brother Gary. They saw three movies a day, fell asleep in some of them, and in between and after the screenings there were parties. They came down from the mountain on September 3 and eight days later it would be impossible not to remember that Edenic moment as a paradise from which not just they, but the whole world had been expelled.

The official U.S. publication date of *Fury* was September 11, 2001. On that date a novel intended as an ultracontemporary, satirical portrait of New York was transformed by events into a historical novel about a city that was no longer the one he had written about, whose golden age had ended in the most abruptly appalling way; a novel that, when read by those who remembered the city as it had been, inspired an emotion that was not part of its author's plan: nostalgia. In Garry Trudeau's *Doonesbury* comic strip one of the characters said, sadly, "You know, I really miss September 10th." That was what had happened to his novel, he understood. The events of September 11 had turned it into a portrait of the day before. The golden fortress full of jewels was now only a dream of an earlier, lost life.

On September 10, 2001, he was not in New York but in Houston, Texas. He had read at Barnes & Noble in Union Square on the fifth, then flown to Boston on book tour and was there on the sixth and seventh. On the morning of September 8 he flew out of Logan Airport just three days before the fatal planes, and was in Chicago for two days. Then on the night of the tenth there was a full house at the Alley Theatre, Houston—nine hundred people in the theater, two hundred turned away, he was told by Rich Levy of the reading series Inprint, his hosts for the night—and a surprise outside: a small Islamic demonstration against his presence, perhaps two hundred strong. That felt like a visitation from the past. The next morning he remembered the bearded placard carriers and wondered if they regretted identifying themselves as extremists on, of all the days they could have chosen to reveal their bigotry, that particular day.

He had only just woken up when a radio journalist called his hotel room. He had agreed to talk to the station before catching his flight to Minneapolis, but it was still too early for that. "I'm sorry," said the voice in his ear, "but we're going to have to cancel. Because of what's happened in New York we're dumping into the coverage of that." He had never acquired the American habit of turning on the TV first thing in the morning. "What's happening in New York?" he asked. There was a pause and then the voice said, "Turn on your TV now." He reached for the remote, and less than a minute later he saw the second plane.

He couldn't sit down. It didn't seem right to sit. He stood in front of the TV with the remote in his hand and the number *fifty thousand* kept repeating in his brain. Fifty thousand people worked in the Twin Towers. He couldn't imagine the numbers of the dead. He thought about his first night in New York City, his visit to the Windows on the World. He remembered Paul Auster telling him about Philippe Petit's high-wire walk between the two towers. But mostly he just stood there and watched the buildings burn and then in agonized disbelief cried out, at the same time as thousands of others around the world, "It's not there! It's not there anymore!" as the South Tower fell.

Birds were screaming in the sky.

He didn't know what to do so he set out for the airport but when they were halfway there the radio told them to turn back because of the nationwide ground stop. Back at the Four Seasons he didn't have a room anymore and the lobby was crowded with other people in the same situation. He found an armchair in a corner and started making calls. Rich Levy of Inprint came to the rescue. He spoke to the poet Ed Hirsch and his wife, Janet, who were stranded in D.C., and they offered him their house near the Menil Collection in the Museum District if he agreed to feed their dog. It was comforting that day to be in a writer's house, alone among books, in the world of the mind while mindlessness ruled the world.

Nobody he knew was dead but thousands were. Peter Carey's wife, Alison Summers, had been at the ATM at the foot of the North Tower when the first plane hit but she had lived. Caryl Phillips on Hudson Street saw it happen and so did Robert Hughes on Prince. Young Sophie Auster, on her first day at high school and alone on a subway train for the first time in her life, passed under the Twin Towers as the atrocity was happening above. September 12 was a second day of horror and sadness. *Look at our beautiful broken city,* he thought, weeping, and realized how deeply he was attached to it already. He walked down the street from the Hirsches' home to the Rothko Chapel. Even for a godless man it felt like a good place to be. There were others there; not many people, just a grave few. Nobody spoke to anyone else. There was nothing to say. Everyone was alone with his or her sorrow.

Obviously his book tour was canceled. Nobody was interested in books. The only books that sold in the following weeks were the Bible, the Qur'an, and books about al-Qaeda and the Taliban. A psychologist on the TV was saying that New Yorkers who had been away from their families on 9/11 should go and show themselves to their loved ones to prove they were okay. It wasn't enough to phone them. They would need the evidence of their own eyes. *Yes,* he thought, *I should go to London.* But it wasn't possible yet. The ground stop was lifted and airports had begun to reopen. Houston reopened, and then LAX but the New York airports remained closed and international travel, too, was at a standstill. He would have to wait a few more days.

He called Padma in Los Angeles to say he was coming to see her. She said she was doing a lingerie shoot.

Ten days after the attacks, on his last night in L.A. before he flew to London, he had dinner at the home of Eric and Tania Idle with Steve Martin, Garry Shandling, and others. At least three of the funniest men in America were around the table but comedy was hard to find. Finally Garry Shandling said, his voice and body full of bloodhound lugubriousness, "Such an awful thing. Seems like everyone lost someone, or knows someone who lost someone. . . . Actually, I knew several of the terrorists. . . ." It was the blackest of black comedy, the first 9/11 joke, and laughter released some of the grief everyone was feeling, but he somehow doubted that Shandling would be using the gag in his routine anytime soon.

Robert Hughes, *Time* magazine's art critic, told him on the phone that after he saw the planes flying over SoHo he had walked around in shock. On his way home he had stopped by a bakery and found the shelves cleaned out. Not a loaf remained, not a bagel, and the old baker standing amid the emptiness spread his arms and said, "Should happen every day."

In London, his marital problems seemed trivial now. Elizabeth briefly relented and allowed Milan to stay at Pembridge Mews. He picked his son up from school, fed him, washed his hair, put him to bed, and stood over him for an hour and watched him sleep. Milan had hugged him long and hard when he returned, and Zafar, too, had been more physically demonstrative than was his wont. The psychologist had been right. Even though they had both known, with the "knowing" part of their brains, that he hadn't even been in New York City, so he was obviously safe, they had needed the evidence of their own eyes.

In *Le Nouvel Observateur* in France and *The Guardian* in London his novel was being called prescient, even prophetic. He wasn't a prophet, he told one journalist. He had had some trouble with prophets in his time and he wasn't interested in applying for the job. But he wondered why the book had felt so urgent, why it insisted on being written *at once,* and where did they come from, those Furies hovering over New York and within his character's heart?

He was being asked to write something—the news agenda had certainly come around to him now—but he didn't do so for two weeks after the attacks. Many of the first think pieces felt redundant to him. Everyone had seen the horror and didn't need to be told how to feel about it. Then slowly his thoughts coalesced. "The fundamentalist seeks to bring down a great deal more than buildings," he wrote. "Such people are against, to offer just a brief list, freedom of speech, a multi-party political system, universal adult suffrage, accountable government, Jews, homosexuals, women's rights, pluralism, secularism, short skirts, dancing, beardlessness, evolution theory, sex. . . . The fundamentalist believes that we believe in nothing. In his worldview, he has his absolute certainties, while we are sunk in sybaritic indulgences. To prove him wrong, we must first know that he is wrong. We must agree on what matters: kissing in public places, bacon sandwiches, disagreement, cutting-edge fashion, literature, generosity, water, a more equitable distribution of the world's resources, movies, music, freedom of thought, beauty, love. These will be our weapons. Not by making war, but by the unafraid way we choose to live shall we defeat them. How to defeat terrorism? Don't be terrorized. Don't let fear rule your life. Even if you are scared."

(While he was writing this, a story about his being banned from American carriers by the U.S. Federal Aviation Administration broke in the press. British Airways and the Europeans remained calm but in America the general panic created a travel problem for him all over again. "I see," he thought, not without some bitterness, "first you let all the terrorists onto the planes, and now you want to ground the antiterrorist novelists, and that's your plan for keeping America safe." When things calmed down the FAA calmed down too and lifted their restrictions; his problems immediately eased, though two American carriers refused to carry him for a further ten years.)

He went to France for the publication of *Furie,* which in the new world that had just come into being was received far better than it had been in the English language, in the old world that had ceased to exist. When he got back to London he went to a dinner at a friend's apartment and another guest, a Mr. Proudie, launched into the already common "America asked for this/America deserved it" argument. He objected strongly, saying it was no time for this kind of British anti-Americanism, which disrespected and criminalized the innocent dead. Mr. Proudie responded, with extreme aggression, "We protected you, didn't we?" As if that proved his point. In the argument that followed they almost came to blows.

He wrote a second article, which concluded, "If terrorism is to be defeated, the world of Islam must take on board the secularist-humanist principles on which the modern is based, and without which their countries' freedom will remain a distant dream." At the time this was thought by many to be a pipe dream at best, and, at worst, a liberal's foolish refusal to accept the resilience of the Islamic worldview. A decade later the young people of the Arab world, in Tunisia, Egypt, Libya, Syria and elsewhere, tried to transform their societies according to exactly these principles. They wanted jobs and liberty, not religion. It was not clear that they would get what they wanted, but they left the world in no doubt that they wanted it.

It was a beautiful fall in New York but the city was not itself. He walked the streets and saw the same spooked look in every eye. Loud noises were harbingers of revenant doom. Every conversation was an act of mourning, every gathering felt like a wake. Then slowly the spirit returned. There was a day when the Brooklyn Bridge was closed because of a reported threat against it, and instead of being scared, people were angry about the disruption to their journeys. That was the *I'm-walking-here*

New York he loved. It was getting its groove back. The restrictions on travel below Fourteenth Street were still there, but they were lessening. The Statue of Liberty was still closed to visitors, but it would reopen. The dreadful hole in the ground, and the equally melancholy hole in the sky above, were still there, and fires still burned belowground, but even that agony could be borne. Life would vanquish death. It would not be the same as before, but it would be all right. He spent Thanksgiving that year at the home of Paul, Siri and Sophie Auster, and Peter Carey and Alison Summers were there too, and they gave thanks for the survival of Sophie and Alison, and for what was good in the world, which needed, more than ever, to be cherished.

The story of his little battle, too, was coming to an end. The prologue was past and now the world was grappling with the main event. It would have been easy, after everything that had happened to him, and after the enormity of the crime against this city, to succumb to hatred of the religion in whose name these things were done and of its adherents too. Anyone who looked even vaguely Arab experienced some of that backlash in those weeks and months of aftermath. Young men wore T-shirts reading DON'T BLAME ME, I'M HINDU. Drivers of yellow cabs, many of whom had Muslim names, decked out their taxis with flags and patriotic decals to ward off their passengers' rage. But in this matter of wrath, too, the city, on the whole, showed restraint. The many were not held guilty of the crimes of the few. And he too refused anger. Rage made you the creature of those who enraged you, it gave them too much power. Rage killed the mind, and now more than ever the mind needed to live, to find a way of rising above the mindlessness.

He chose to believe in human nature, and in the universality of its rights and ethics and freedoms, and to stand against the fallacies of relativism that were at the heart of the invective of the armies of the religious (*we hate you because we aren't like you*) and of their fellow travelers in the West, too, many of whom, disappointingly, were on the left. If the art of the novel revealed anything, it was that human nature was the great constant, in any culture, in any place, in any time, and that, as Heraclitus had said two thousand years earlier, a man's *ethos*, his way of being in the world, was his *daimon*, the guiding principle that shaped his life—or, in the pithier, more familiar formulation of the idea, that character was destiny. It was hard to hold on to that idea while the smoke of death stood in the sky over Ground Zero and the murders of thousands of men and women whose characters had not determined their fates were on everyone's mind, it hadn't mattered if they were hard workers or generous friends or loving parents or great romantics, the planes hadn't cared about their *ethos;* and yes, now terrorism could be destiny, war could be destiny, our lives were no longer wholly ours to control; but still our sovereign natures needed to be insisted on, perhaps more than ever amid the horror, it was important to speak up for individual human responsibility, to say that the murderers were morally responsible for their crimes, and neither their faith nor their rage at America was any excuse; it was important, at a time of gargantuan, inflated ideologies, not to forget the human scale, to continue to insist on our essential humanity, to go on making love, so to speak, in a combat zone.

In the pages of a novel it was clear that the human self was heterogeneous not homogeneous, not one thing but many, multiple, fractured and contradictory. The person you were for your parents was not the person you were with your children, your working self was other than your self as a lover, and depending on the time of day and your mood you might think of yourself as tall or skinny or unwell or a sports fan or conservative or fearful or hot. All writers and readers knew that human beings had broad identities, not narrow ones, and it was the breadth of human nature that allowed readers to find common ground and points of identification with Madame Bovary, Leopold Bloom, Colonel Aureliano Buendía, Raskolnikov, Gandalf the Gray, Oskar Matzerath, the Makioka Sisters, the Continental Op, the Earl of Emsworth, Miss Marple, the Baron in the Trees, and Salo the mechanical messenger from the planet Tralfamadore in Kurt Vonnegut's *The Sirens of Titan.* Readers and writers could take that knowledge of broad-based identity out into the world beyond the pages of books, and use the knowledge to find common ground with their fellow human beings. You could support different football teams but vote the same way. You could vote for different parties but agree about the best way to raise your children. You could disagree about child rearing but share a fear of the dark. You could be afraid of different things but love the same music. You could detest each other's musical taste but worship the same God. You could differ strongly on the question of religion but support the same football team.

This was what literature knew, had always known. Literature tried to *open the universe,* to increase, even if only slightly, the sum total of what it was possible for human beings to perceive, understand, and so, finally, to be. Great literature went to the edges of the known and pushed against the boundaries of language, form, and possibility, to make the world feel larger, wider, than before. Yet this was an age in which men and women were being pushed toward ever-narrower definitions of themselves, encouraged to call themselves just one thing, Serb or Croat or Israeli or Palestinian or Hindu or Muslim or Christian or Baha'i or Jew, and the narrower their identities became, the greater was the likelihood of conflict between them. Literature's view of human nature encouraged understanding, sympathy, and identification with people not like oneself, but the world was pushing everyone in the opposite direction, toward narrowness, bigotry, tribalism, cultism and war. There were plenty of people who didn't want the universe opened, who would, in fact, prefer it to be shut down quite a bit, and so when artists went to the frontier and pushed they often found powerful forces pushing back. And yet they did what they had to do, even at the price of their own ease, and, sometimes, of their lives.

The poet Ovid was exiled by Caesar Augustus to a little hellhole on the Black Sea called Tomis. He spent the rest of his days begging to be allowed to return to Rome, but permission was never granted. So Ovid's life was blighted; but the poetry of Ovid outlasted the Roman Empire. The poet Mandelstam died in one of Stalin's labor camps, but the poetry of Mandelstam outlived the Soviet Union. The poet Lorca was killed by the Falangist thugs of Spain's Generalissimo Franco, but the poetry of Lorca outlived Franco's tyrannical regime. Art was strong, artists less so. Art could, perhaps, take care of itself. Artists needed defenders. He had been defended by his fellow artists when he needed it. He would try to do the same for others in need from now on, others who pushed boundaries, transgressed, and, yes, blasphemed; all those artists who did not allow men of power or the cloth to draw lines in the sand and order them not to cross.

He delivered the Tanner Lectures at Yale. They were titled "Step Across This Line."

As to the battle over *The Satanic Verses,* it was still hard to say if it was ending in victory or defeat. The book had not been suppressed, and nor had its author, but the dead remained dead, and a climate of fear had grown up that made it harder for books like his to be published, or even, perhaps, to be written. Other religions quickly followed Islam's lead. In India, Hindu extremists attacked films and movie stars (the superstar Shah Rukh Khan was the target of violent protests merely for saying that Pakistani cricketers should have been included in a tournament in India) and works of scholarship (such as James Laine's biography of the Maratha warrior-king Shivaji, which so "offended" that monarch's contemporary admirers that they attacked the research library in Pune where Laine had done some of his research and destroyed many irreplaceable ancient documents and objects). In Britain, Sikhs attacked the Sikh author of *Behzti* (Dishonor), a play they disapproved of. And the Islamic violence continued. In Denmark, a Somali man with an ax and a knife, linked to the radical al-Shabab militia, broke into the home of the cartoonist Kurt Westergaard in Aarhus, after the publication of the so-called "Danish cartoons" that had aroused the ire of Islamic extremists. In America, Yale University Press, publishers of a book discussing the case of the "Danish cartoons," would be too cowardly to include the cartoons in that book. In Britain, the home of the publisher of a book about the Prophet Muhammad's youngest wife was letter-bombed. A much longer struggle would be necessary before the age of menaces and fears could be said to have come to an end.

As 2001 drew to a close the Royal Shakespeare Company's stage adaptation of *Midnight's Children* was on its way to America, to be staged in Ann Arbor, Michigan, and then at the Apollo Theater in Harlem; one night during the New York run he would be interviewed on stage after the performance and so achieve something beyond his craziest dreams—to play the Apollo. At the same time he was working on *Shalimar the Clown.* This in the end was who he was, a teller of tales, a creator of shapes, a maker of things that were not. It would be wise to withdraw from the world of commentary and polemic and rededicate himself to what he loved most, the art that had claimed his heart, mind and spirit ever since he was a young man, and to live again in the universe of once upon a time, of *kan ma kan,* it was so and it was not so, and to make the journey to the truth upon the waters of make-believe.

From his Dickensian, let's-tie-up-the-loose-strings seat in the future he saw the flowering of his niece Mishka's musical talent; his niece Maya contentedly moving into a life teaching little children; and the marriage of his niece Meena, his estranged sister Bunno's daughter. He saw Zafar doing good work and being happy, and Milan growing into another fine young man. And Elizabeth and he on good terms again. Bill Buford divorced, remarried more happily, and became the successful author of books about food. Nigella Lawson became a gigantically successful author of books about food and married the art collector Charles Saatchi. Frances D'Souza became a baroness and then, in 2011, the Speaker of the House of Lords. William Nygaard retired and his son Mads took over his job at Aschehoug. Marianne Wiggins taught literature at the University of Southern California. James Fenton and Darryl Pinckney left Long Leys Farm and moved to New York. Pauline Melville was assaulted by a murderous intruder at her home in Highbury Hill but managed to wriggle free and escape through a window. The intruder was caught and jailed. Human life continued. Things worked out as well as things ever did, and far better than he had been able to hope on that dark Valentine's Day in 1989.

Not everything ended well. In August 2005 Robin Cook had a heart attack on a mountain in the Scottish Highlands and died.

And what of his Illusion, his Phantom of Liberty? On March 24, 2002, he took Padma to the *Vanity Fair* dinner and party in Hollywood on the day of the Academy Awards. They arrived at Morton's and as he watched her pose and pirouette for the human wall of screaming photographers, burning with the bright flame of her youth and beauty, he looked at the expression on her face and suddenly thought, *She's having sex, sex with hundreds of men at the same time, and they don't even get to touch her, there's no way any actual man can compete with that.* And in the end he lost her, yes, but it was better to lose one's illusions and live in the knowledge that the world was real, and that no woman could make it what he wanted it to be. That was up to him.

Two days after the Oscars he flew back to London and was met off the plane by Nick Cottage, a genial Special Branch officer with an old-fashioned mustache, who told him that one of the higher-up officers, Bob Sait, himself the owner of a fine Lord Kitchener–like growth on his upper lip, wanted to come and see him the next morning. "If I were you," Nick added mysteriously, "I'd make your own arrangements for later in the day." He refused to explain what he meant but smiled an enigmatic secret policeman's smile.

He was driven to the Halcyon Hotel in Holland Park, an elegant pink edifice, where he had booked a suite. Jason Donovan had taken his Pembridge Mews house back at the end of the year's rental. Before he flew to L.A. for the Academy Awards he had found another Notting Hill house to rent, in Colville Mews, across the way from the young designer Alice Temperley's rapidly burgeoning fashion house. The new place was available in a couple of weeks, so he had put his stuff in storage and booked the Halcyon to cover the gap, initially for just two nights. Milan's Easter holidays were beginning the next day, and he had planned a week in France with both the boys. They would drive down to friends in Courtoin in Burgundy, and then visit Paris and EuroDisney on the way back.

At 10 A.M. sharp on the morning of Wednesday, March 27, 2002, Bob Sait and Nick Cottage met him at the Halcyon Hotel. "Well, Joe," said Sait, and then corrected himself, "Excuse me—Salman, as you know, we've been maintaining this protection on advice from the intelligence services, until such time as they felt it was right to lower their assessment of the threat against yourself."

"It's been a little strange, Bob," he said, "because in America I've been acting like an ordinary citizen for years, but when I've come back here you've insisted on going on. . . ."

"I hope you'll be pleased, then," Bob Sait said, "that the threat level has been reduced, quite drastically, in fact, and we would not normally offer protection to anyone assessed at the new level."

His heart had begun to pound but he tried to remain outwardly controlled. "I see," he said. "So you'll be withdrawing the protection, then."

"I just wanted to give you the opportunity," Bob Sait said, "of saying if that would be acceptable to you. It would be in line with what you've been arguing, would that be correct to say?"

"Yes," he said, "it would, and yes, it would be acceptable."

"We'd like to give a party for you at the Yard as soon as it's convenient," said Nick Cottage. "To get as many of the lads as possible who have worked with you over the years. It's been one of our very longest prots and there's a lot of pride in what's been done. And a lot of appreciation of what you endured as well, a lot of the team have said they know they couldn't have stuck it out the way you did, so it would be good to have a chance to celebrate, if you're agreeable."

"That would be lovely," he said, the blood rising in his face.

"We'd like to ask some of your close friends too," Nick said. "The ones who have helped so much over the years."

Then there was nothing more to say. "So what happens now?" he asked. "How do we go about this?" Bob and Nick stood up. "It's been a privilege, Joe, excuse me, Salman," Bob Sait said, and stuck out his hand. "Good for you, mate," said Nick. He shook their hands, and they turned, and left. That was it. More than thirteen years after the police walked into his life, they spun on their heels and walked out of it. The abruptness of it made him laugh out loud.

The Special Branch party did take place soon afterward. One of the officers who attended it was Rab Connolly, who had completed the degree course in postcolonial literature he had begun during the prot. "I've got something for you," he whispered like a stage villain, and slipped a small metal object into his palm. "What is it?" he asked Rab. "It's the bullet," Rab said, and so it was. The bullet that poor Mike Merrill had accidentally fired inside the Bishop's Avenue house while cleaning his gun. "That was a close one," Rab said. "I thought you might like it as a souvenir."

———

He was standing in the doorway of the Halcyon Hotel watching the police Jaguars pull away. Then he remembered that he ought to go to see the real estate agents in Westbourne Grove, sign the rental papers for the Colville Mews house, and take another look at the place. "All right then," he thought, "here goes." He walked out of the Halcyon Hotel onto Holland Park Avenue and stuck out an arm to hail a passing cab.

Acknowledgments

I would like to thank all those whose help and advice shaped this memoir: everyone at Emory University's MARBL archives, without whose ordering and cataloging work over the last several years my papers would have been in far too chaotic a condition to allow me even to think about this project, and thanks to whom it became possible to write it; Vanessa Manko, for her invaluable media research; my editors at Random House, Louise Dennys, Dan Franklin, Will Murphy, and Susan Kamil, for their commentary on the draft text; and the book's other early readers, Andrew Wylie, Sameen Rushdie, Elizabeth West, Aimee Mullins, Taryn Simon, Hanan al-Shaykh, Bill Buford, Ian McEwan, Pauline Melville, Reggie Nadelson, Min Katrina Lieskovsky, Francesco Clemente, Deepa Mehta and Christopher Hitchens, for their helpful responses. A few of the passages in these pages have appeared before, in somewhat different form, as essays and articles in various newspapers and magazines, notably *The New Yorker* and *The New York Times.* Thanks to Universal Studios for permission to quote from Evan Hunter's screenplay of Alfred Hitchcock's *The Birds;* to Harvill Secker for permission to quote a passage from Mikhail Bulgakov's *The Master and Margarita,* translated by Michael Glenny; to New Directions for permission to quote parts of "The Ivy Crown" by William Carlos Williams; to George Braziller for permission to quote from the anthology *For Rushdie;* and to Lisa Appignanesi and Sara Maitland, editors of *The Rushdie File,* Carmel Bedford, editor of *Fiction, Fact, and the Fatwa,* as well the many other commentators whose thoughts and opinions are quoted throughout.

Some people's names have been changed, for the most part those of the serving members of my protection teams, to all of whom, finally, I would like to express my very special thanks. If it had not been for the efforts of the officers of "A" Squad, Special Branch, Metropolitan Police, and their colleagues in the Special Intelligence Service (SIS) of the United Kingdom, I might not have been in a position to write this—or indeed any other—book.

S.R.

ABOUT THE TYPE

This book was set in Bembo, a typeface based on an old-style Roman face that was used for Cardinal Bembo's tract *De Aetna* in 1495. Bembo was cut by Francisco Griffo in the early sixteenth century. The Lanston Monotype Company of Philadelphia brought the well-proportioned letterforms of Bembo to the United States in the 1930s.